AF278334

MEDIEVAL DISABILITY SOURCEBOOK

Before you start to read this book, take this moment to think about making a donation to punctum books, an independent non-profit press,

@ https://punctumbooks.com/support/

If you're reading the e-book, you can click on the image below to go directly to our donations site. Any amount, no matter the size, is appreciated and will help us to keep our ship of fools afloat. Contributions from dedicated readers will also help us to keep our commons open and to cultivate new work that can't find a welcoming port elsewhere. Our adventure is not possible without your support.

Vive la Open Access.

Fig. 1. Hieronymus Bosch, *Ship of Fools* (1490–1500)

Medieval Disability Sourcebook: Western Europe. Copyright © 2020 by the editor and authors. This work carries a Creative Commons BY-NC-SA 4.0 International license, which means that you are free to copy and redistribute the material in any medium or format, and you may also remix, transform and build upon the material, as long as you clearly attribute the work to the authors (but not in a way that suggests the authors or punctum books endorses you and your work), you do not use this work for commercial gain in any form whatsoever, and that for any remixing and transformation, you distribute your rebuild under the same license. http://creativecommons.org/licenses/by-nc-sa/4.0/

First published in 2020 by punctum books, Earth, Milky Way.
https://punctumbooks.com

ISBN-13: 978-1-950192-73-1 (print)
ISBN-13: 978-1-950192-74-8 (ePDF)

DOI: 10.21983/P3.0276.1.00

LCCN: 2020934559
Library of Congress Cataloging Data is available from the Library of Congress

Book design: Vincent W.J. van Gerven Oei

HIC SVNT MONSTRA

Medieval Disability Sourcebook

Western Europe

Edited by Cameron Hunt McNabb

p.

Table of Contents

Acknowledgments

To tweak the old adage, many hands make quality work. The collaborative nature of this project means that many, many hands had a part in it, and I am thankful for each of them. These hands include the early visionaries of the Society for the Study of Disability in the Middle Ages (SSDMA), who saw the need for such a volume; the contributors, who worked hard to meet the project's goals and specifications; the copy editors, whose hands have shaped countless details; the publisher, who has graciously supported the volume; and all those who have contributed feedback and encouragement along the way.

The idea for a sourcebook on medieval disability was first conceived back in 2012 by the members of SSDMA. The concept was originally Moira Fitzgibbons's, and those members first involved were Jonathan Hsy, Wendy Turner, John Sexton, Joshua R. Eyler, Tory V. Pearman, Will Eggers, Julie Singer, and others. I am grateful for their vision for moving medieval disability studies forward and making it more accessible to students. I inherited not just their vision but their ideas and even sample entries when I took over as General Editor. Without these foundational documents, the project would not be what it is today.

This volume boasts forty contributors, myself excluded, and each has worked diligently to make their texts as engaging and accessible to the readers as possible. The contributors hail from numerous disciplines (as well as half a dozen countries and as many languages), and has brought different perspectives and expertise to their entries. They truly were a pleasure to work with.

I am also grateful to the copy-editing skills of Anna Yates and Emma E. Duncan, whose diligence and attention to detail is to be commended.

Many heartfelt thanks must be extended, too, to Eileen Joy and punctum books for their support of the project and open access materials in general. Also, my gratitude to the initial anonymous reader, whose feedback guided the later stages of the project.

This project was several years in the making, and some wonderful colleagues have been with me through the entire journey: a tremendous round of thanks to Frank Napolitano, Kisha Tracy, Will Eggers, John Sexton, Andrew Pfrenger, Paul T. Corrigan, and Charles J. Hulin IV. I am also grateful to Dr. William Hackett, Provost of Southeastern University, who granted me release time to devote to the volume.

Lastly, I owe more thanks than I can give to Joshua R. Eyler, who not only took a chance on me and trusted me with this project but who has stood by me every step of the way. His advice, feedback, encouragement, and support have been paramount in bringing this project to fruition.

Introduction

Cameron Hunt McNabb

Introduction

The medieval biblical play "The Cure of the Blind Man" stages the popular healing of the blind man episode from John 9. In the biblical telling, the disciples ask Jesus, "who hath sinned, this man, or his parents, that he should be born blind?" Jesus replies, "Neither hath this man sinned, nor his parents; but that the works of God should be made manifest in him." This short passage illustrates common misconceptions about disability—namely that it results from sin and needs remedy—but also upends them by calling disability a redeeming "work of God." Yet, even while seeking to redeem disability, the passage ignores the difficulties that people with some disabilities experience and ascribes the source of the impairment to God rather than to the dynamic physical, mental, and social impairments and constructs that shape what we call "disability." Neither of the passage's interpretations of the man's blindness capture the complex and nuanced category disability represents.

In contrast, "The Cure of the Blind Man" play digs deeper in unpacking disability by informing the audience that the blind man "is your owne neighbour and of your owne kind" (l. 39). Instead of emphasizing either the disciples' misconceptions or Jesus' words of redemption, the play focuses on disability as part of our humanity, part of our neighbors' and our own kind. Although how people interpret and ascribe meaning to disability changes across time and cultures, disability is a universal human experience. It is the condition of our historical neighbors. And of ourselves.

In the Book of John and in the biblical play, the blind man narrates his own story of his healing and interprets it for himself and the Pharisees who question him. But the biblical play also asks the disciples, and by extension the audience, to listen, interpret, and ultimately "remember" (l. 37) the blind man. For figures marginalized by bodily, social, and mental difference, medieval disability studies seeks to do precisely that, and this volume provides a starting point to do so.

Medieval Disability Studies

Medieval texts and Medieval Studies have garnered increased attention recently, partly motivated by medieval-adjacent popular media, like *Lord of the Rings* and *Game of Thrones*, and partly by appropriations of the field by modern movements, including white nationalism. But these representations of the period—and the assumptions they generate—drastically oversimplify the complex and varied Middle Ages. In fact, as medieval scholars often point out, using the definite article "the" to describe the Middle Ages fails to capture the period's diversity, as if we can make any definitive statements about a term that spans almost a thousand years.

Disability studies, too, is burgeoning, moving perhaps from infancy to adolescence as a field. It began as a modern social justice movement advocating for those with disabilities, but scholars have expanded its inquiries to history and literature. The term "disability" presents complexities similar to "the Middle Ages," including under its umbrella disabilities marked as physical, emotional, and mental; chronic and acute; visible and invisible. There is no singular understanding or experience of "disability," nor a definitive representation of it. This volume provides a more nuanced, but certainly not exhaustive, look.

In short, there is no single concept of "medieval disability," nor a single response to the empirical existence of disability within the period. The sources collected here serve as testaments to the complex and wide-reaching realm of disability in medieval Western Europe. Ultimately, it is up to readers to listen, interpret, and remember what they encounter.

Key Terms and Concepts

Although medieval languages have many terms for specific impairments, most work on medieval disability studies opens with an acknowledgment that the period did not have the term *disability* nor even a comparable term in Latin or the extant vernacular languages. The term *disability*, like the terms *race*, *gender*, and *sexuality*, is a modern construct that we use to talk about the texts of the past. However, the absence of a term does not mean the absence of a concept, and while we should use our modern terms conscientiously and cautiously, we can use and benefit from them nonetheless.

Medieval scholar Tory V. Pearman notes that modern discussions of medieval disability have sometimes congregated around "a monolithic view of the Middle Ages as intolerant" or "an equally monolithic view that borders on nostalgic."[1] However, as Irina Metzler demonstrates in her highly influential *Disability in Medieval Europe: Thinking about Physical Impairment during the High Middle Ages, c. 1100–1400*, disability was pervasive in the period and attitudes toward it ranged from "intolerant" and associated with sin to ameliorate and apologetic, as seen in the perspectives in "The Cure of the Blind Man." As Metzler notes, "no discussion of medieval bodies could be complete without reference to sin,"[2] and the relationship between sin and disability is crucial in the period. The

treatment of disability in medieval Europe is heavily linked to the *Christus medicus* ("Christ the Physician") tradition, which positioned all disease as a manifestation of sin, for which Christ's redemption was the cure. However, Metzler examines both Old and New Testament treatments of impairment, including the John 9 passage discussed above, and notes they are "not of a uniformed nature"[3]: "Some Old Testament references link sin and physical 'blemishes,' one very specific occupation (the priesthood) is barred to some impaired people, and some instances of impairment are mentioned without any qualifying moral overtones. In the New Testament, on the whole, the emphasis is on healing, and, with two exceptions, the spiritual condition of the healed person is not of importance. Faith of the supplicant is of far greater consequence for a successful healing than their sin."[4] Metzler's work emphasizes the spectrum of interpretations on disability found in medieval Europe.

The texts in this volume span that spectrum, with significant range and conflict often existing within a single text. For instance, the miracle accounts included in this volume rely on a framework that presents disability as something that needs to be cured (by the saint or shrine in question), but the very saint responsible for the miracles can often do so only because of his or her own disability, itself interpreted as a sign of holiness. Further, the miracles' narratives simultaneously—and perhaps inadvertently—testify to the community's aid and support for individuals with disabilities, all while attempting to solidify the Church's monopoly on cures.

The critical lens of disability studies evokes a number of helpful terms for readers to use while wrestling with these sources. At some points, the European Middle Ages are particularly conducive to the lines of inquiry already established by the field, but in other cases, these theoretical tools need to be adapted in order to accommodate this period and these cultures. I discuss some of the field's major terms and concepts below and explore ways in which they can—or cannot—be applied to the sources in this volume.

One of the earliest approaches to disability, termed the **medical model**, attempts to diagnose and cure impairments. Predicated on disability as bodily or mental difference that is considered "abnormal" and in need of "repair," such a model always presents those with disabilities as deviant and subordinate, with medicine as the "fix" needed to "correct" the impairment. Medieval scholar Edward Wheatley expands and adapts this framework to discuss how the European Middle Ages has a similar **religious model**, because "the church's control over discourse related to disability [is] in a manner analogous to the way modern medicine attempts to maintain control over it now."[5] He cites the pervasive role of the Bible and religious literature in shaping the medieval West's views on disability. By investigating the Church's control over miraculous "cures," the practice of confession, almsgiving and charity, and the Eucharist, Wheatley's model examines how the Church controlled the bodies of those with impairments and framed the culture's interpretation of disabilities. The religious orientation of numerous texts in this volume demonstrates Wheatley's theory well, while other entries provide nuance and even resistance to his claims.

Other scholars have explored disability as a social rather than medical phenomenon. The **social model** first argued for the distinction between the terms *impairment* and *disability*. Within disability studies, "impairment" is often used to describe mental or physical functions that impair the daily lives of the individuals who have them. For instance, blindness, deafness, and mobility restriction are impairments. In contrast, "disability" is often defined as a cultural or social construct that limits an individual's access due to impairment. In the cases listed above, an environment that lacks braille, close-captioning or sign language interpreters, and elevators (just to name a few accommodations) would cast those impairments as disabilities. According to the social model, as expressed by the Union of the Physically Impaired Against Segregation, "it is society which disables physically impaired people. Disability is something imposed on top of our impairments, by the way we are unnecessarily isolated and excluded from full participation in society."[6] The texts in this volume document both the impairments of medieval people as well as the ways in which those impairments became or did not become disabilities.

While the social model's terms "impairment" and "disability" are helpful in teasing out some of disability studies' distinctions and subtleties, Joshua R. Eyler notes, "the [social] model forces the binary opposition of 'impairment' and 'disability' in ways that at times seem rather misleading."[7] Eyler prefers the **cultural model**, proposed by David T. Mitchell and Sharon Snyder, which argues that "[e]nvironment and bodily variation (particularly those traits experienced as socially stigmatized differences) inevitably impinge upon each other."[8] Tom Shakespeare's **critical realist model** is similar in its emphasis on disability as "the whole interplay of different factors that make up the experience of people with impairments,"[9] including "the independent existence of bodies which sometimes hurt, regardless of what we may think or say about those bodies."[10] Shakespeare's model provides a framework for analyzing the disciples' and Jesus' interpretations of the man's blindness in John 9: the disciples stigmatize blindness by associating it with sin, while Jesus' response overlooks the blind man's physical experiences resulting from his impairment.[11]

Shakespeare complicates his own model to include a concept of *universal impairment*, noting that "impairment is a universal phenomenon, in the sense that every human has limitations and vulnerabilities, and ultimately is mortal"[12]; or, in the words of "The Cure of the Blind Man," disability is our "owne neighbour and of [our] owne kind" (l. 39). Advocating the understanding that all humans will experience impairment at one time or another is useful in demonstrating disability's ubiquity, but it also underscores the wide-ranging, varied, and difficult to define spectrum the term encompasses. I have argued elsewhere that universal impairment is crucial for the medieval West's Christian framework: if impairment is (sometimes) caused by sin, and according to the doctrine of original sin, all are sinners, then all are also impaired.[13] The concept of universal impairment, in "The Cure of the Blind Man" or in Tom Shakespeare's work, can and should be an avenue of empathy for all our neighbors.

These various disability models have in turn fostered discussion about what language is appropriate for talking about persons with disabilities. Different groups and even individuals within those groups have explored what language best captures their experiences with physical, emotional, or mental disability. Two main lines of thought—and thus language—have emerged from these discussions. The first employs *person-first language,* which refers to individuals with disabilities as people first and "with disabilities" second, such as a "person in a wheelchair" or a "person with dementia." This type of language foregrounds commonality (we are all people) and only qualifies that commonality based on disability as a secondary consideration. Person-first language has been employed throughout this entire introduction thus far, and it is the preferred, but not the only, language of the volume.

However, some people with disabilities find that their disability is integral to their identity, not secondary to it. They feel they are not a person first and a disability second but rather the disability so constitutes part of their being that the two cannot be separated. In these cases, people prefer *identity-first language,* which, as the term suggests, foregrounds a specific social, physical, or religious characteristic that a person presents as an essential component of personhood. This type of language is common in other descriptors—one usually identifies as "Muslim," "female," or "African American," rather than a "person of Islam," "person who is female," or a "person who is African American." Identity-first language is more common in some disability groups than others, and within some communities, preference is split.[14]

With either approach, the important point to note is who is wielding the language about whom. Ultimately, whatever term or identity an individual prefers is what others should use to refer to that individual. Unfortunately, in the medieval texts that follow, the voices of those with disabilities are often silenced, by the authors and recorders of the texts; by the social restrictions of the disabilities themselves; and by their distance from us in time, space, and language. In some instances in this volume, people with disabilities speak for themselves, such as in Margery's *Book* or Hoccleve's *Complaint,* but in most cases, they are spoken about by others. Readers must be critically aware of the voices that shape their stories, particularly when those voices are not their own.

Another crucial concept in disability studies is the idea of the *normate body.* Rosemarie Garland Thomson coins this term in her work *Extraordinary Bodies* to refer to the "normal" body from which all "disabled" bodies deviate: "Normate, then, is the constructed identity of those who, by way of the bodily configurations and cultural capital they assume, can step into a position of authority and wield the power it grants them."[15] Mitchell and Snyder extend this concept and argue that "[a] normal body...is a theoretical premise from which all bodies must, by definition, fall short...a body divorced of time and space."[16] The fiction of the normate becomes apparent when certain questions are raised: What height is the normate body? How much does it weigh? How well can it see and hear? In medieval Western Europe, the religious culture once again brought these questions to bear through the lens of Christianity. I have argued elsewhere that for the Christian medieval, Christ is the normate body, although it is unclear precisely what that body is like.[17] Augustine posits that each individual's resurrected body will be perfected, although he admits that he is also unclear on what that might mean. In both constructs, however, the normate body (either Christ's or the resurrected body) is defined by its lack of sin, a connection that is, as Wheatley, Metzler, and others suggest, problematic.

Disability studies' roots in activism can be seen in the concepts and approaches outlined above, but theorists have also extended its tenets to history and literature. Two central terms, coined by Mitchell and Snyder, analyze disability's role in narrative texts: *narrative prosthesis* and the *materiality of metaphor*. They argue that "disability pervades literary narrative, first, as a stock feature of characterization, and second, as an opportunistic metaphorical device."[18] Their concept of narrative prosthesis refers to this "stock feature" of characterization or plot in order to signal a conflict or difference that is ultimately cured or resolved. Thus disability serves as a prosthesis for characterization and plot and fails to be authentically represented in the narrative. Similarly, Mitchell and Snyder point out the frequency with which disability is used as an "opportunistic metaphorical device," an observation crucial to understanding Christian culture in the Middle Ages, which frequently deployed biblical metaphors about blindness, deafness, and lameness, such as in the tales of Constance and Aelfric's sermon. Mitchell and Snyder's frameworks call on us to distinguish between exploited uses of disability and authentic representations of lived experiences in the narratives we encounter.

Intersections at the Margins

If disability is part of the universal human experience, then it is not surprising that disability studies intersects with other avenues of inquiry both within the period and now. Far from being a niche field, its project of listening, interpreting, and remembering those in the margins is wide-reaching. Mitchell and Snyder recount that their interest in how "disability fit on the map of marginality and identity"[19] began when they considered how disability marks bodies as Other, just as race, gender, and sexuality do. For medieval people, disability was connected to issues of the Self and the Other, and often persons with disabilities were also members of marginalized gender, racial, or economic groups. While some medieval persons with disabilities also appear in the dominant majority, such as Hoccleve, and some do not experience marginalization but rather veneration, such as in many saints' lives, many are Othered on multiple fronts, such as the Jews in the *Croxton Play of the Sacrament* or the Wife of Bath in *The Canterbury Tales*. These figures demonstrate how disability contributes to a variety of intersectional identities in the period.

The social, cultural, and critical realist models described above also have much in common with other critical fields, making interdisciplinary intersections fruitful. In particular, drawing on Women's and Gender Studies, Pearman has developed a **gendered model** to medieval disability in Western Europe. She argues that "[w]hen biblical, medical, and literary representations of the female body merge with the Aristotelian construction of the female body as a deformed male body, a web of Otherness begins to surface, demonstrating the intricate bonds between discursive notions of embodied identity categories."[20] This "web of Otherness" pervades the texts in this volume: when the person with a disability is female, such as Chaucer's Wife of Bath or Dame Sirith, the gendered model reminds us that these figures are doubly disabled and doubly marginalized.

More fundamentally, discussions of disability in the European Middle Ages asked what it means to be human. As discussed above, rather than viewing disability as an identity marker for those with specific physical, mental, or emotional impairments, the concept of universal disability calls for disability to be seen as an aspect of everyone's identity. Texts in the period intrinsically interrogate not only what is the normate self but what is the human self. In the physical sense, some sources connect persons with disabilities to non-human entities, like changelings in *The Man of Law's Tale* and *A Miracle of Thomas Becket*, fairies in *Evadeam*, or animal images in *Bisclavret*. In a spiritual sense, saints with disabled bodies, like St. Margaret and St. Cuthbert, seem to transcend the traditional bounds of humanity and border on the divine. These associations—both positive and negative—demonstrate an uneasiness about what constitutes a human body and more importantly what it means to be human. Disability and disability studies provide spaces for texts and readers to explore with these issues.

The Medieval Disability Sourcebook: Western Europe

As far back as 2012, the Society for the Study of Disability in the Middle Ages (SSDMA) desired to create a sourcebook of medieval texts that deal with disability for use in the classroom. At that time, medieval disability studies was a relatively small field and its scholarship was mostly limited to academic conferences and university presses. The SSDMA felt it imperative the field be explored in classrooms and be accessible to students.

Such a desire for accessibility, a central tenet in disability studies itself, has guided all of the major decisions of this project. The press, punctum books, was chosen for its support for burgeoning, interdisciplinary scholarship and its open access model. Most of the texts presented here were taken from the public domain, which means that they are older editions but are free from copyright, making the sourcebook affordable for students.

The texts have been translated from or edited in their original languages in order to be accessible to a modern English-speaking audience. These considerations, though, have yielded a collection of texts that represent Western Europe, only a narrow slice of a global Middle Ages. They are bounded by a specific geography and time period and most are marked by the period's and culture's engagement with Christianity. Likewise, the disability theories used to explore them are rooted in the Western tradition. Therefore, although this volume provides a nuanced look at disability the period, it is by no means representative or exhaustive. Moreover, while these texts may provide a starting point for thinking about disability and the medieval West's global neighbors, those traditions deserve their own volumes for us to listen, interpret, and remember. We hope that this volume will be just one of many and that more diverse sourcebooks on disability will be forthcoming.

The volume's contents have been organized by genre, beginning with historical and medical documents that provide crucial insights into how physicians, politicians, judges, and citizens viewed a variety of impairments. The second section focuses on religious texts, including relevant biblical passages, commentaries, miracle accounts, and saints' lives, to explore Christianity's engagement with disability in medieval Europe. The next three sections, on poetry, prose, and drama, survey the literary texts of the period. Many of the texts included are staples of medieval British literature courses, such as selections from Bede's *Ecclesiastical History*, Chaucer's *The Canterbury Tales*, and *The Book of Margery Kempe*, but many are texts less often translated and taught in the classroom, bringing less recognized voices alongside more canonical ones. The concluding section examines visual depictions of disability in medieval Europe, opening up fields of inquiry beyond the written word. Each entry includes an introduction and bibliography, as well as textual notes and glosses, in order to highlight disability issues within the text and serve as springboards for students' or scholars' inquiry deeper into the field. All of these factors are designed to encourage as many people as possible, inside and outside the classroom, to participate in medieval disability studies.

Ultimately, I hope that this volume invites readers to listen to, interpret, and remember the voices and experiences of our historical neighbors; and I hope that participating in such a project of empathy means extending the same to our contemporary neighbors and to our own selves.

Bibliography

Connelly, Erin, and Stefanie Künzel, eds. *New Approaches to Disease, Disability and Medicine in Medieval Europe.* Archaeopress Archaeology, 2018.

Crawford, Sally, Elizabeth Ellen, and Christina Lee, eds. *Social Dimensions of Medieval Disease and Disability.* Archaeopress, 2014.

Davis, Lennard J. *The End of Normal: Identity in a Biocultural Era.* University of Michigan Press, 2013.

Eyler, Joshua, ed. *Disability in the Middle Ages: Reconsiderations and Reverberations.* Ashgate, 2010.

Garland Thomson, Rosemarie. *Extraordinary Bodies: Figuring Physical Disability in American Culture and Literature.* Columbia University Press, 1997.

———. *Staring: How We Look.* Oxford University Press, 2009.

Godden, Richard H, and Asa Simon Mittman, eds. *Monstrosity, Disability, and the Posthuman in the Medieval and Early Modern World.* Palgrave Macmillan, 2019.

Hsy, Jonathan, Tory V. Pearman, and Joshua R. Eyler, eds. *A Cultural History of Disability in the Middle Ages,* vol. 2. Bloomsbury Publishing, 2019.

Kuuliala, Jenni. *Childhood Disability and Social Integration in the Middle Ages: Constructions of Impairments in Thirteenth- and Fourteenth-Century Canonization Processes.* Brepols, 2016.

Linton, Simi. *Claiming Disability: Knowledge and Identity (Cultural Front).* New York University Press, 1998.

———. "What Is Disability Studies?" *PMLA,* vol. 120, no. 2, 2005, pp. 518–22.

Metzler, Irina. *Disability in Medieval Europe: Thinking about Physical Impairment during the High Middle Ages, c. 1100–1400.* Routledge, 2006.

———. *A Social History of Disability in the Middle Ages: Cultural Considerations of Physical Impairment.* Routledge, 2015.

———. "Intellectual Disability in the European Middle Ages." *The Oxford Handbook of Disability History,* edited by Michael A. Rembis, et al. Oxford University Press, 2018.

Mitchell, David T., and Sharon L. Snyder. *Cultural Locations of Disability.* University of Chicago Press, 2006.

———. *Narrative Prosthesis: Disability and the Dependencies of Discourse.* University of Michigan Press, 2000.

Pearman, Tory Vandeventer. *Women and Disability in Medieval Literature.* Palgrave Macmillan, 2015.

"Prosthesis in Medieval and Early Modern Culture," special issue of *Textual Practice* vol. 30, iss. 7, 2016.

Richardson, Kristina L. *Difference and Disability in the Medieval Islamic World: Blighted Bodies.* Edinburgh University Press, 2014.

Rushton, Cory, ed. *Disability and Medieval Law: History, Literature, Society.* Cambridge Scholars Publishing, 2013.

Scalenghe, Sara. "Disability in the Premodern Arab World." *The Oxford Handbook of The Oxford Handbook of Disability History,* edited by Michael A. Rembis, et al. Oxford University Press, 2018.

Scarborough, Connie L. *Viewing Disability in Medieval Spanish Texts: Disgraced or Graced.* Amsterdam University Press, 2018.

Sexton, John P., and Kisha G. Tracy, eds. *The Ashgate Research Companion to Medieval Disability Studies.* Routledge, forthcoming.

Shakespeare, Tom. *Disability Rights and Wrongs Revisited.* 2nd edn. Routledge, 2014.

———. "The Social Model of Disability." *The Disability Studies Reader,* edited by Lennard J. Davis. Routledge, 2010, pp. 266–73.

Shakespeare, Tom, and Nicholas Watson. "Defending the Social Model." *Disability and Society*, vol. 12, no. 2, 1997, pp. 293–300.

Shoham-Steiner, Ephraim. *On the Margins of a Minority: Leprosy, Madness, and Disability among the Jews of Medieval Europe*. Wayne State University Press, 2014.

Siebers, Tobin. *Disability Theory*. University of Michigan Press, 2008.

Singer, Julie. "Disability and the Social Body." *postmedieval: a journal of medieval cultural studies*, vol. 3, no. 2, 2012, pp. 135–41. doi:10.1057/pmed.2012.15.

———. "Toward a Transhuman Model of Medieval Disability." *postmedieval: a journal of medieval cultural studies*, vol. 1, no. 1–2, 2010, pp. 173–79. doi:10.1057/pmed.2009.4.

Stiker, Henri-Jacques. *A History of Disability*. University of Michigan Press, 2009.

Wendell, Susan. *The Rejected Body: Feminist Philosophical Reflections on Disability*. Taylor and Francis, 2013.

Wheatley, Edward. *Stumbling Blocks Before the Blind: Medieval Constructions of a Disability*. University of Michigan Press, 2010.

Endnotes

1   Tory Vandeventer Pearman, *Women and Disability in Medieval Literature* (Palgrave Macmillan, 2015), p. 5.

2   Irina Metzler, *Disability in Medieval Europe: Thinking about Physical Impairment during the High Middle Ages, c. 1100–1400* (Routledge, 2006), p. 38.

3   Ibid., p. 42.

4   Ibid., pp. 42–43.

5   Edward Wheatley, *Stumbling Blocks Before the Blind: Medieval Constructions of a Disability* (University of Michigan Press, 2010), p. 9

6   Quoted in Tom Shakespeare, "The Social Model of Disability," *The Disability Studies Reader*, ed. Lennard J. Davis (Routledge, 2010), pp. 214–21, at p. 215.

7   Joshua R. Eyler, ed., *Disability in the Middle Ages: Reconsiderations and Reverberations* (Ashgate, 2010), p. 5.

8   David T. Mitchell and Sharon L. Snyder, *Cultural Locations of Disability* (University of Chicago Press, 2006), p. 6.

9   Tom Shakespeare, *Disability Rights and Wrongs Revisited*, 2nd ed. (Routledge, 2014), p. 77.

10   Ibid., p. 73.

11   One reading of the passage might argue that Jesus' healing of the blind man constitutes attention to and concern for his physical experiences, even as he valorizes those experiences as the "work of God."

12   Shakespeare, *Disability Rights and Wrongs Revisited*, p. 87.

13   Cameron Hunt McNabb, "Staging Disability in Medieval Drama," forthcoming in the *Ashgate Research Companion to Medieval Disability Studies*.

14   In speaking generally of people with disabilities, the volume will use person-first language. However, when speaking of specific groups or sometimes of a medieval source's discussion of a specific group, identity-first language may be employed. Discretion was given to contributors in the case of the latter.

15   Rosemarie Garland Thomson, *Extraordinary Bodies: Figuring Physical Disability in American Culture and Literature* (Columbia University Press, 1997), p. 8.

16   Mitchell and Snyder, *Cultural Locations of Disability*, p. 7.

17   McNabb, "Staging Disability in Medieval Drama."

18   David T. Mitchell and Sharon L. Snyder, *Narrative Prosthesis: Disability and the Dependencies of Discourse* (University of Michigan Press, 2000), p. 47.

19   Mitchell and Snyder, *Cultural Locations of Disability*, p. x.

20   Pearman, *Women and Disability in Medieval Literature*, p. 5.

HISTORICAL
& MEDICAL
DOCUMENTS

York Cause Paper E.92: Redyng c. Boton[1] (1366–67)

Contributed by Alison Purnell

Introduction

The episcopal court case of *Redyng contra Boton* offers a rare opportunity to explore issues of mental disability in a low-status person. Records of the lowest social classes rarely survive, since they had little money or status to be considered worth the parchment. Unlike many higher-status people deemed mentally incompetent, William de Bridsall, a crucial witness in *Redyng c. Boton*, had no inheritance or possessions to be held in trust, and seemed to be of no profit to the crown or any other.

In July 1366, Alice Redyng of the village of Scameston appeared in the consistory court of York to claim that John Boton, a chapman of Scameston, was her husband. John denied the charge. During July 28–29, Alice submitted the reasons for her claim and produced two eyewitnesses to testify on her behalf, including a local beggar named William de Bridsall, who claimed to have overheard the marriage contract in dispute.

Redyng c. Boton took place under very specific conditions. The documents which survive must be examined in the light of their context: a marriage litigation which followed a pre-set procedure and progressed according to the rules laid down by long-distant canonists. Telling a story from this type of material is difficult, says Charles Donahue: "The litigation context distorts the story, particularly if one is trying to tell a story of what happened, as opposed to the story of *what happened in the litigation*" (*Law, Marriage, and Society*, 63; emphasis mine).

According to the canonists, a marriage could be contracted by any man and woman where there was no impediment simply by an exchange of words of consent. The words could either be of present consent (e.g., "I take you as my husband/wife") or of future consent (e.g., "I will take you as my husband/wife"). Words of future consent were not binding, unless they were followed by sexual intercourse, which was then treated as implicit present consent. There was no requirement for a formal ceremony or witnesses: the exchange of words of consent was considered to be the sacrament itself. While the Church urged that a marriage be initiated with the publication of the banns and solemnized *in facie ecclesiae* and required this solemnization for a marriage to be canonically *licit*, it admitted the *validity* of any marriage formed by words of present consent or words of future consent followed by sexual intercourse. It was common in the thirteenth, fourteenth, and into the fifteenth century for parties to contract a marriage outside the formal process the Church prescribed.

In *Redyng c. Boton*, Alice claimed that they had contracted both with words of present consent and, separately, words of future consent followed by sexual intercourse. Either one of these situations alone created a canonically valid marriage; had their contract been made in front of a large crowd—or better yet—in a church, Alice would never have had to bring her cause to court.

Unfortunately, the alleged contract between Alice and John was made informally and in private, what the Church referred to as "clandestine." Clandestine marriages could be, and were, contracted almost anywhere: Richard Helmholz notes marriages contracted "under an ash tree, in a bed,…in a blacksmith's shop, near a hedge, in a kitchen, by an oak tree, at a tavern."[2] Alice and John allegedly exchanged their vows outside the sheepfold. Although canonically valid, trouble arose when John denied they had happened. Canon law demanded a minimum of two eyewitnesses to a contract, and without them, no matter how obvious the existence of a contract, the court could not decide in favor of the plaintiff. Alice produced for the court two eyewitnesses to the alleged contract. Alice's case was extremely weak; she had only the bare minimum for proof in the ecclesiastical courts, and both of the men were only accidental witnesses to the contract, having overheard it without the knowledge of Alice or John at the time.

Any marriage litigation followed the same basic process, which might be adapted slightly to fit the particular circumstances of a given cause. A marriage cause was properly begun with the publication of the *libel*, or what the plaintiff sought of the court and why. The defendant was then offered the opportunity to submit *exceptions*, or a response to the libel. The plaintiff then submitted *articles*, specific arguments which outlined what they intended to prove, and how. After the articles were published, the defendant submitted *interrogatories*, questions they wished the Official to put to the witnesses being questioned. The goal of the interrogatories was to uncover any inconsistencies or disagreements in the witnesses' testimonies. The articles and interrogatories were put to the witnesses, who would be questioned individually by the Official of the court. The record of their testimonies, the depositions, were then published openly in the court.

The defendant, John Boton, would present as many arguments as he was able, whether or not they contradicted each other. In *Redyng c. Boton*, John's arguments why he could not be married to Alice had two focuses: he argued that Alice was of servile condition and could not contract a marriage, and that her two critical witnesses were unreliable and thus their testimony could not be trusted. Of relevance to this volume, he argued that William de Bridsall, who testified that he overheard Alice and John contract marriage,

was a notorious drunk, a beggar, and a *stultus* ("fool"), and easily corrupted into presenting false testimony. William's testimony was crucial to Alice's cause, and so a significant proportion of the proceedings came to revolve around William's capacity and reliability as a witness.

Redyng c. Boton cannot be read as a straightforward account of the dispute in question, let alone the question of William de Bridsall's mental capacity. On the question of witness reliability, it is difficult to say for sure that someone is lying. Mental capacity and impairment exist along a spectrum, such that it is possible for William de Bridsall to be mentally impaired in some way while still being perfectly competent to depose. The motivations for both parties to sway the Official are clear, particularly given that Alice had only the minimum number of eyewitnesses to make her case.

Interpreting the texts is likewise complicated by the process by which depositions were received and recorded. They are not at all comparable to modern court transcriptions. The Official recording the witnesses' testimony did not write down what was said verbatim. It was his job to pick out and record the essential information in what the witness said. Thus we have no way of determining the level of importance which the actual witness might have placed on any aspect of his own testimony.

As legal documents, depositions were recorded in Latin, but the witnesses themselves would have been speaking a local dialect of Middle English. In particular, any of the language regarding William de Bridsall's mental capacity is highly formulaic. In this edition, I have opted to leave the phrases used to describe mental impairment in Latin rather than speculating what might be equivalent phrasing in modern English because they hold procedural significance. The scribe who recorded the depositions used words and phrases that were semantically significant, as a key issue in *Redyng c. Boton* was William de Bridsall's capacity to testify.

Bibliography

Ashley, Kathleen, and Robert L.A. Clark, eds. *Medieval Conduct.* University of Minnesota Press, 2001.

Bassett, William W. "Canon Law and the Common Law." *Hastings Law Journal,* vol. 29, 1978, art. 6. https://repository.uchastings.edu/hastings_law_journal/vol29/iss6/6/.

Brooke, Christopher. *The Medieval Idea of Marriage.* Oxford University Press, 1991.

Brundage, James. *Law, Sex, and Christian Society in Medieval Europe.* University of Chicago Press, 1990.

Donahue, Charles. "Roman Canon Law in the Medieval English Church: Stubbs vs. Maitland Re-examined after 74 years in Light of Some Records from the Church Courts." *Michigan Law Review,* vol. 72, 1974, pp. 647–716.

———. *Law, Marriage, and Society in the Later Middle Ages.* Cambridge University Press, 2008.

Goldberg, P.J.P. *Women in Medieval England c. 1275–1525.* Manchester University Press, 1995.

Fenster, Thelma, and Daniel Lord Smail. *Fama: The Politics of Talk and Reputation in Medieval Europe.* Cornell University Press, 2003.

Helmholz, Richard. *Marriage Litigation in Medieval England.* Cambridge University Press, 1974.

———. *The Oxford History of the Laws of England,* vol. 1. Oxford University Press, 2004.

——— "Marriage Contracts in Medieval England." *To Have and To Hold,* edited by Philip L. Reynolds and John Witte. Cambridge University Press, 2007, pp. 260–86.

McCarthy, Conor. *Marriage in Medieval England.* Boydell Press, 2004.

McSheffrey, Shannon. "Place, Space, and Situation: Public and Private in the Making of Marriage in Late-Medieval London." *Speculum,* vol. 79, 2004, pp. 960–90.

Owen, Dorothy. "Ecclesiastical Jurisdiction England 1300–1550: The Records and Their Interpretation." *Studies in Church History,* vol. 11, 1975, pp. 199–221.

Pedersen, Frederik. *Marriage Disputes in Medieval England.* Hambledon Press, 2000.

———. "Marriage Contracts and the Church Courts of Fourteenth-Century England." *To Have and To Hold,* edited by Philip L. Reynolds and John Witte. Cambridge University Press, 2007, pp. 287–331.

Phillips, Susan E. *Transforming Talk: The Problem with Gossip in Late Medieval England.* Pennsylvania State University Press, 2007.

Poos, L.R. "Sex, Lies, and the Church Courts in Pre-Reformation England." *Journal of Interdisciplinary Studies,* vol. 25, 1995, pp. 585–607.

Sheehan, Michael M. *Marriage, Family, and Law in Medieval Europe,* edited by James K. Farge. University of Toronto Press, 1996.

Smith, D.M. *Ecclesiastical Cause Papers and York: The Court of York 1301–1399.* Borthwick Institute of Historical Research, 1988.

Membrane 15 recto
Libel
July 21, 1366

In dei nomine amen. Petit Alicia Redyng de Scameston Johannem Boton Chapman de Scameston pro eo quod iidem Johannes et Alicia matrimonium per verba mutuum consensum exprimentia de presenti ac sponsalia° per verba de future carnali copula inter eosdem postmodum subsecuta adiunctum libere contraxerunt. Quos quidem contractus matrimonialis et sponsalia ac copulam carnalem dictus Johannes in presentia dicte Alicie et aliorum fidedignorum sponte sepius et ex certa sciencia est confessus, super quibus in diocese Ebor,° ac in villa de Scameston et locis vicinis, laboravit et adhuc laborat publica vox et fama.° Per vos dominus Iudex dicta Alicia in virum suum legitimum ad eamdem Aliciam in uxorem suam legitime [[ ]] adiudicari dictum quare Johannem ad solempnizandum matrimonium in facie ecclesie° ut mores est cum eadem canonice compelli et coherceri ulterius quod sit fieri in premissis et ea contingit in omnibus quod est iustum. Hoc dicit et petit ac probare intendit dicta Alicia coniunctim et diversim [...]

Membrane 10 recto
Exceptions *contra* Alice Redyng
September 30, 1366

In deo nomine amen. Coram vobis domino officere curia Ebor vestro vel commissare generali excipiendo dicit et in iure proponit procurator Johannis Boton nomine procuratore pro eodem contra Aliciam Redyng et contra quemlibet pro eadem in iudicio libere comparentem necnon contra intentionem dicte Alicie in quadam causa quam movet contra dictem Johannem petendo eum in virum suum. Quod si dictus Johannis Boton in festo natalis domini vel matrimoniam vel sponsalia cum dicta Alicia contraxerat quod dictus procurator non fatetur sed totaliter differetur non est tum dem Johannes ad solempni-

Membrane 15 recto
Libel
July 21, 1366

In the name of God, amen. Alice Redyng of Scameston seeks John Boton, Chapman, of Scameston because the same John and Alice freely contracted marriage through expressed words of mutual present consent, and betrothal through words of future consent with carnal joining between them afterward. To which matrimonial contract and betrothal and carnal joining indeed the said John confessed, in the presence of the said Alice and other worthies, of his own will very often and from sure knowledge, upon which the public voice and fame laboured and still labours in the diocese of York and the village of Scameston and nearby places. Through you, Lord Judge, the said Alice [asks] you to adjudicate the said John as the legitimate husband to the same Alice, his legitimate wife, wherefore the said John is in addition to be compelled and coerced to licit solemnisation of their marriage, as the custom is, which should result in the premises and affect them in all things, which is just. This the said Alice says and seeks and intends to prove together and singly.

Membrane 10 recto
Exceptions *contra* Alice Redyng
September 30, 1366

In the name of God, amen. In your presence, Lord Official of the York Curia, or the commissioner general, the procurator in name of John Boton speaks to be heard, and in court puts forth, for him against Alice Redyng and against whoever appears for her freely in court and does not appear against the intention of the said Alice in the cause which she moves against the said John, seeking him as her husband. If the said John Boton at Christmas contracted marriage or betrothal with the said Alice, which the said proctor does not confess but totally disagrees, the same John, however, should not be

sponsalia *betrothal, or promise of a future marriage was common knowledge*   **in facie ecclesie** *in the face of the church, i.e. canonically licit.*   **Ebor** *Eboracum, or York*   **laborat...fama** *the matter*

zandum matrimonium cum eadem quomodolibet compellendus pro eo et ex eo quod dicta Alicia fuit a tempore natalitatis sue et adhuc est serva seu ancilla et servilis conditionis et pro tali ad presentem publice habita et reputata at ex servilis et ancillis domini de Latymer et progenitorum suorum procreata concepta et nata et educata. Idemque Johannis liber et ingenuus notorie° existens ignorans dicte Alicie conditionem servulem sibi in copula carnali adherit, nec a tempore quo de conditione sue extitit †cretioratus† nec ante nec post facto vel verbo ad habendum ipsam Aliciam in uxorem suam consensit sed dissensit et reclamavit tam tacite quam expresse, dissentit et reclamat in presenti. Que sunt publica notoria et manifesta in diocese Ebor et locis vicinis. At super hiis ibidem laboravit et laborat publica vox et fama. [...] Hic dicit, allegat, proponit, et petit ac probare indendit dictus procurator nomine quo supra coniunctim et diversim iure beneficio in omnibus sibi salvo.

compelled to solemnisation of matrimony of any sort with her, for and from the fact that the said Alice was from the time of her birth and still is a servant or maidservant and of servile condition. And from such time to the present she is publicly held and reputed to be begotten, conceived, born, and raised from a servant and maidservant of the Lord Latymer and of their forebears. And the same John, free and free-born, notoriously being ignorant of the servile condition of the said Alice, adhered to her in carnal knowledge. Not at the time in which she existed in that condition (being descended from it), nor before nor after, in deed or word, did he consent to having that Alice as his wife, but he disagreed and protested, tacitly and expressly, and he dissents and protests in the present. Whereby the notorious facts are public and manifest in the diocese of York and nearby places. On these facts again the public voice and fame laboured and still labours. [...] The said procurator named above says, alleges, proposes, and seeks and intends to prove this together and separately, always to the sound benefit of the court in all things.

Membrane 14, recto and verso
Articles *pro* Alice
July 28, 1366

In dei nomine amen. Positiones et articulos infrascriptos et contenta in eisdem facit et dat ac probare intendit coniunctim et divisim procuratore Alicie Redyng de Scameston nomine procuratore pro eadem contra Johannem Boton de Scameston Chapman in causa matrimoniale inter dictas partes in curia Ebor mote et pendente. Et si que positiones sint multiplices eas ponit divisim et sic petit easdem responderi.

In primis ponit et probare intendit dictus procuratore nomine quo supra quod dictus Johannes in die natalis domini ulterius preteriti a quocumque contractu matrimoniali seu sponsalitio cum aliqua muliere libere fuit penitus et solutus.

Item ponit et probare intendit quod post dictum diem natalis domini tractatus habe-

Membrane 14, recto and verso
Articles *pro* Alice
July 28, 1366

In the name of God, amen. The procurator named as procurator of Alice Redyng of Scameston gives and intends to prove, collectively and singly, the positions and below-written articles for her against John Boton, Chapman of Scameston, in the matrimonial cause moved and pending in the York Curia between the said parties. And although these positions are multiple, he lays them out singly, and he requests they be responded to thus.

In the first, the said procter named above sets forth and intends to prove that the said John, on Christmas last, was completely free from any matrimonial or spousal contract with another free woman.

Likewise, he puts forth and intends to prove that after the said Christmas day a

batur inter dictos Johannem et Aliciam de matrimonio inter eosdem contrahendo. Item ponit at probare intendit quod dictus Johannes promisit prefate Alicie quod ipsam in uxorem suam duceret et heret. Et quod dixit idem Johannes prefate Alicie quod ipsam habere voluit in uxorem at eam postmodum carnaliter cognovit.

Item ponit at probare intendit quod dicti Johannes et Alicia sponsalia per verba de future carnali copula inter eos postmodum subsecuta ac matrimonium per verba mutuum consensum exprimentia de presenti adiunctem libere contraxerunt.

Item ponit et probare intendit quod dictus Johannes dicit contractum sponsaliam matrimonialem ac carnalem copulam ut [premittitur] subsecutam in presentia dicte Alicie et aliorum fidedignorum sponte sepius et ex certa scientia est confessus.

Item ponit et probare intendit quod premissa sunt publica nota et manifesta in villa de Scameston diocese Ebor et locis vicinis ac super ibidem laboravit et adhuc laborat publica vox et fama.

contract concerning matrimony was had between the said John and Alice to be entered into by the same. Likewise, he puts forth and intends to prove that the said John promised the aforesaid Alice that he would take her and cling to her as his wife. And that the same John told the aforesaid Alice that he wished to have her to wife and that he knew her carnally afterwards.

Likewise, he puts forth and intends to prove that the said John and Alice freely contracted a betrothal through words of future consent with carnal joining between them afterward, and matrimony through words of mutual present consent expressing their joining.

Likewise he puts forth and intends to prove that the said John spoke of the betrothal and marriage contract and carnal joining, as said below, in the presence of the said Alice and other worthies very often of his own free will, and from this certain knowledge it was confessed.

Likewise he puts forth and intends to prove that the premises are publicly known and manifest in the village of Scameston in the diocese of York and in nearby places and upon the same the public voice and fame laboured and still labours.

Membrane 13 recto
Interrogatories *pro* John
Undated

Interrogentur testes omnes et singuli° ex parte Alicie de Redyng de Scameston contra Johannem Boton de Scameston Chapman producti et producendi de causa sua cuiuslibet dicti sui.

Item si deponant quod dictus Johannes promisit dicte Alicie quod ipsam duceret in uxorem seu quod matrimonium vel sponsaliam contraxerat cum eadem vel quod huius contractum matrimonialem seu sponsalia inter eos contractum est, confessus contractum tunc ubi, quo loco, quibus, et quos presens tibi, quo anno, quo mense, quo die, qua hora

Membrane 13 recto
Interrogatories *pro* John
Undated

Let witnesses, together and individually, for the part of Alice Redyng of Scameston against John Boton of Scameston, Chapman, produced and to be produced for her cause be interrogated, whatever their words.

If they depose that the said John promised the said Alice that he would take her to wife or that he contracted betrothal or marriage with her or that a matrimonial or bethrothal contract between them was confessed where the contract was confessed, in what place, by whom, and who was present with you, in what year, in what month, on what day,

---

testes omnes et singuli *to evaluate their truthfulness by comparing details*

diei, et an semel vel pluries et subiecti qua forma verborum huius contractus vel confessio fiebant et an animo contrahendi sponsalia vel matrimonium prolata fuerunt verba predicta.

Item interrogentur omnes et singuli testes quantum habunt in bonis et an sint communiti consanguinitate affinitate vel familiaritate dicte Alicie et quam partem mallent optinere victoriam in causa et an sint subornati informati vel instructi aut prece vel precio inducti vel corrupti ad deponendum pro parte dicte Alicie contra Johannem predictum in causa predicta.

Item interrogetur William de Bridsall cuius sit conditionis et status et an solebat et solet victuum suum mendicando querere hostiatim.°

Item interrogentur testes omnes et singuli° de causis scientie cuiuslibet dicti sui et de aliis circumstantiis ex quibus moveri poterit vel debebit animus iudicantis.

in which hour of the day, and whether once or repeated, and to them in which form of words was the contract or confession of this made, and whether in an agreeable spirit the aforesaid betrothal or matrimonial words were said.

Likewise let the witnesses, together and individually, be interrogated as to how much they have in goods and whether they are secured by consanguinity, affinity, or familiarity of the said Alice, and which party they wish to obtain victory in the cause and whether they are suborned, informed, or instructed, or influenced or corrupted by prayer or by gift to testify on the part of the said Alice against the aforesaid John in the aforesaid cause.

Likewise let William de Bridsall be interrogated as to what his condition and status may be and whether he was or is accustomed to beg for his bread by wandering house to house.

Likewise let each and all witnesses be interrogated as to the source of their said knowledge and on other circumstances from which their spirit of judgement be able or ought to be moved.

Membrane 12 recto
Depositions pro Alice
July 28–29, 1366

Walter Warner de Scameston etatis xliii annos et amplius iure extra et super articulis et interrogetur pendentibus extra dicit quod novit partes inter quas agitur per septimos annos proxima preteritis. Et dicit super primo et secundo articulis dicit quod secundum communem famam in parochia de Ryllington et Winteringham dicti articuli continent veritatem. Et dicit super tertio et quarto articulos quod a feste nativitatis domini ulterioribus preteritis videlicet a die sancti Johannis Evangeli quo die videlicet post horam nonam° ipsius diei prefati, et Alicie matrimonium prout iste iure didicit ex relato illorum

Membrane 12 recto
Depositions pro Alice
July 28–29, 1366

Walter Warner of Scameston, aged 43 years and more, a supplementary witness. Questioned about the pending articles [anno] he says that he knows the parties between whom this is conducted for the last seven years. And he says on the first and second articles that according to common fame in the parish of Rillyngton and Winteringham, the said articles contain the truth. And he says on the third and fourth articles that from Christmas last, namely on the day of St John the Evangelist, that is, after the hour of nones° of the aforesaid day, this witness learned of the marriage of Alice just as from the report of those

---

hostiatim *for ostiatim* **testes omnes et singuli** *to evaluate their truthfulness by comparing details* **nonam** *approximately 3pm* **nones** *approximately 3pm*

qui eidem interfuerunt audivit contraxerunt fama alicqualiter [...] laboravit a quo festo Pascha fuerat dictus contractus matrimonialis divulgatus ita quod ab ipso tempore. Et citra hucusque fama publica tam super ipso contractu matrimoniali habito inter dictas partes quam carnali copula subsecuta et ipsum contractum matrimonialem precedente in dicta villa de scameston laboravit, et adhuc laborat publica vox et fama sed ut dicit iste iure numquam audivit prefatum Johannem fateri matrimonialem contractum predictum sed carnalem copulam cum dicta Alicia habitam audivit cum fateri vollet. Dicit quod ipsa Alicia si iusticia haberet optineret in causa, quod habet bona fide per se ut dicit. Sic dicit quod prefatus Johannes habuit expeditum accessum ad dictam Aliciam et similiter ipsam Aliciam ad cameram ipsius Johannis et dimisit cum eadem diversa bona videlicet lanas et linteum pro paniis faciendum propterea eo quod ipse est mercator et ipsa est mulier bone industrie et bone dives dicebatur ante dictum contractum matrimonialem habitum in dicta villa de Scameston quod prefatus Johannes ipsam Aliciam debet ducere in uxorem.

William de Bridsall de Scampston aetatis treginta annorum, vel habens in bonis praeter vestimenta sua, aliquam mendicans et sic quaerens victuum suum et aliquam operator in fenis et bladis tempore estivali et autumpnali, libere condicionis ut dicit, non consanguineus, affinis, vel familiaris dicte Alicie et vellet quod optineret in causa eo quod credet quod habet iusticiam in causa pro ea, non instructus vel corruptis ut dicit iure et extra super premissis. Super primo articulo requisatus dicit quod continet veritatem pro aliquo quod iste iure unquam scivit. Super secundo tertio et quarto articulis requisatus dicit quod iste iuratus per triennium ultro preteritis hospitabatur in domo Richardi Fouler de Scamston et uxorem ipsius Richardi eius amica Johannis Boton et ideo prefatus Johannes habet communem accessum ad dictum domum et sepius misit pro Alicia ut veniret illum ad loquendi cum eo et die san-

who were present, he heard the fame that in some way they contracted marriage. [...] The fame laboured from Easter that the said matrimonial contract was divulged so from that time. And previously to this point, the public fame laboured as much on the matrimonial contract held between the said parties as on the subsequent carnal knowledge and the matrimonial contract preceding it in the said village of Scameston, and the public voice and fame labours yet, but as this witness says he never heard the aforesaid John to confess the aforesaid matrimonial contract but he heard he wished to have had carnal knowledge with the said Alice. He says that he wishes Alice prevail in the cause if she has justice, which he has good faith for himself as he says. And he says that the aforesaid John had free access to the said Alice and similarly Alice had to the room of the said John, and he distributed through her diverse goods, namely wools and linens for making cloth, and because he is a merchant and she is a woman of good inductry and wealth, the said before the said marriage contract in the said village of Scameston, that the aforesaid John ought to take Alice as wife.

William de Bridsall de Scamston, thirty years of age, having nothing in goods except his clothing, sometimes begging and thus seeking his bread and sometimes a worker in the hays and grains in summer and autumn, of free condition as he says, not consanguineus, affined, or related by close friendship with the said Alice, and he wishes that she prevail in her cause because he believes that she has justice in the cause for herself, not instructed or corrupted as a witness as he says and from the above premises. Questioned on the first article, he says that it contains the truth for anything that this witness ever knew. Questioned on the second, third, and fourth articles, he says that this witness through the last three years has been lodged at the house of Richard Fouler de Scameston, and the wife of that Richard is the friend of John Boton, and therefore the aforesaid John has common access to the said house and he often sent for

cti Johanni apostoli et evangeli proxima post diem Natalis domini ulterioribus preteritis inter hora nonam° et hora vesperam° eiusdem diei sancti Johanni predicti Johannes et Alicia stabant infra bercaria° dicti Richardi modicum infra hostium et ipsa Alicia tunc dixit prefato Johanni Johannes non dicas mihi aliquo nisi ea que velis servare quia ante hoc tempora ego fui decepta. Et si velis habere me in uxorem suam dicas mihi. Et cui ipse Johannes respondit Fideliter, sic. Volo habere te in uxorem meam et ecce fidem meam ego ducam te in uxorem meam. Tunc ipsa Alicia dixit "Johannes placet anglice I vouchesaffe quod tunc dicis. Et ego volo habere te in maritum meum." Et uterque eorumdem alteri ad hoc faciendum astrinxerunt fide sua. Dicit quod nulli fuerunt presentis nisi partes predictas dumtaxat et iste iure venit ad eos antequam sciverunt et audivint prolocutionem dictorum et verborum stans ad ostium iuxta eos. Sic dicit quod die Sancti Thome proxima tunc sequenti post horam nonam ipsius diei et ante horam vesperam sicut iste iure ivit gardino dicti Richardi invenit dictas partes stantes iuxta et prope unam cassam bladi in dicte gardino solum cum sola et audivit eos ut dicit recitare et dicere eadem verba eo modo quo dixerunt et recitarunt in bercaria supradicta. An dicte partes sciverunt quod iste iure audivit prefata verba inter eos proferri dicit quod sic in bercaria sed non in gardino et dicit quod de articulo copulam subsecutam laborat publice vox et fama super contractu predicto, laboravit fama per tres septimanias proxima preteritis et aliter super contentis in dictis articulis nescere deponere ut dicit.

Dominus Rogerus Vicarius de Rillyngton iure extra super premissis dicit quod novit partes inter quas agitur per vi annos proxima preteritis ulteris. Dicit requisatus super dictos articulos quod super eisdem nescere deponere nisi quidem super continentias in secundo, tertio, quarto, quinto, et sexte articulos in villa de Scameston dum ante pre-

Alice so that she came there to speak with him. On the day of St. John, Apostle and Martyr next after last Christmas between the hours of nones and vespers,° the aforesaid John and Alice stood before the sheepfold of the said Richard a little ways inside the door. Then Alice said to the aforesaid John: "John, do not say anything to me except that which you wish to stand by, because I have been deceived before. And if you wish to have me as you wife, you will tell me." And to this John replied: "I wish to have you as my wife and behold my faith: I will take you as my wife." Alice then said to John, "It pleases me" – in English, "I vouchessauf" – "what you say now. And I wish to have you as my husband" and each of them pledged their faith to the other to do this. He says that none were present except the aforesaid parties up to this point, and this witness came to them before they knew and heard their speaking and words while standing at the door near them. Thus he says that on the day of St Thomas following that, after the hour of nones of that day and before the hour of vespers, as this witness went into the garden of the said Richard he found the said parties standing next to and close by one bin of grain in the said garden, one man alone with one woman alone, and he heard them, as he says, recite and say the same words in that way which they said and recited them in the aforesaid sheepfold before. Whether the said parties knew that this witness heard the aforesaid words between them be put forth, he says that they did in the sheepfold, but not in the garden, and he says concerning the article on the subsequent intercourse that the public voice and fame labours on the aforesaid contract, and the fame laboured for three weeks after and otherwise on the contents in the said articles he does not know to depose as he says.

Lord Roger, the Vicar of Rillyngton, a supplementary witness to the premises, says that he knows the parties between whom the

---

nonam *approximately 3pm*   **vesperam** *approximately 6pm*   **bercaria** *a sheepfold*   **the hours of nones and vespers** *between approximately 3pm and 6pm*

sentem litem motam laboravit adhuc laborat publica vox fama.

Thomas Fouler de Scameston etate viginti habens in bonis ad valenciam quinque marcorum non consanguineus nec affinis dicte Alicie non instructus aut [[]] corruptus ut dicit iure et extra super premissis. Dicit quod novet partes inter quas agitur per †anno† proxime preteritis. [...] Super secundo, tertio, et quarto articulos requisatus dicit quod presens fuit in gardenio Richardi Fouler de Scameston proxima bercaria dicti patris sui super eadem se inclinando die sancti Johanni Evangeli proxima festem Natalis Domini ulterioribus preteritis media hora post tertie diei midoverondern vulgariter dicte quam dicti Johannes et Alicia in dicta bercaria [[]] verba matrimonialia [[ ]] sub hac forma proclamavit dicto Johanno primo dicente dicte Alicie per fidem meam ego ducam te in uxoram meam et per fidem mean ego faciam te ita bonam mulierem sicut ego sum virum. Es tu ne contenta. Cui dicte Alicie statim respondit si tu es contenta ego sum contenta. [...]

cause is moved for six years previously. He says, questioned on the said articles, that on the same he does not know to depose except indeed on the contents in the second, third, fourth, fifth, and sixth articles that in the village of Scameston before the present litigation was moved that the public voice and fame laboured and yet labours.

Thomas Fouler de Scameston, aged 20 years, having in goods to the value of 5 marks, not consanguineous nor affined to the said Alice, not instructed or corrupted as he says, a supplementary witness to the premises. He says that he knows the parties between whom this cause is argued from the previous year. [First article laregly illegible.] Questioned on the second, third, and fourth articles, he says that he was present in the garden of Richard Fouler de Scameston, his said father, next to the sheepfold, leaning himself on it, on the say of Saint John the Evangelist after Christmas last in the middle hour after the third day - commonly called "midoverondern" - when the said John and Alice, in the sheepfold, pronounced words of matrimony together in this form, John first saying to Alice, 'By my faith I will take you to my wife and by my faith I will make you as good a woman as I am a man. Are you not content?' To which the said Alice at once replied, 'If you are content, I am content." [Remainder of membrane heavily damaged. Thomas Fouler deposes that John asked him not to reveal what he heard, but in confession a friar urges him to not be silent.]

Membrane 11 recto and verso
Petition to present deponents *pro* John Boton
September 24, 1366

In deo nomine amen. Coram vobis domino officere curia Ebor vestro ve commissare generali excipiendo dicit et in iure proponit procurator Johannis Boton nomine procuratoris pro eodem contra Aliciam Redyng de Scamston et contra quemlibet pro eadem coram vobis in indicio libere comparentem ac contra Walter Warner, William de Bridsall de Scamston, Dominus Roger vicare ut dicitur

Membrane 11 recto and verso
Petition to present deponents *pro* John Boton
September 24, 1366

In the name of God, amen. In your presence, Lord Official of the York Curia, or the commissioner general, the procurator in name of John Boton speaks to be heard, and in court puts forth, for him against Alice Redyng and against whoever is for her appearing freely in your presence in court, and against Walter Warner, William de Bridsall of Scameston, Lord Roger, the vicar (as he

de Rillyngton, et Thomas Fouler quos dicta Alicia in quadam causa matrimoniale presenta inter partes predictos in curia Ebor mote et pendente produxit dicta et depositiones eorumdem quidem ipsius testibus. Nulla vel modica est pro vos fides adhibenda in causa predicta contra partem dicti Johannis Boton et precipue in ea parte ubi dicere videntur quidem super contractu matrimoniale inter dictos partes inter ut asseritur laboravit publica vox et fama ante presentem litem motere pro eo quidem signa fama fuerat de contractu matrimoniale habentur presento seu aliqualis locutio inde quomodolibet antea habebatur. Et hoc fuerat ex eo quidem eadem Alicia per se et amicos suos falso publicavit divulgavit ac publicari et devulgari fecit quidem dictus Johannes matrimonium contraxit cum eadem ac ipsa fama presenta a dicta Alicia et amicis et adherentibus sibi in causa predicta et non aliis ortum habuit. Et ab aliis quam a dicta Alicia et sibi adherentibus in hac parte in nullo tempore creditum fuerat seu quomodolibet dictum vel predicatum prefatus quod William de Bridsall fuerat et est testis in dicta causa notorie suspectus pro eo et ex eo quidem idem William omnibus temporibus receptionis depositionis et examinationis sue in dicte causa ac ante et post fuerat adeo pauper et notoria pauperitate depressus quidem hostiatim panem suum mendicando querebat. Ad omnibus dictis temporibus fuerat dictus William et adhuc est notorie mente captus° et discretionem naturalem nullatenus habebat, sed propter data et promissa sibi per dictam Aliciam et partem suam suum falsum in dicta causa corruptus et informatus dixit et protulit testimonium. Idemque William fuerat etiam omnibus dictis temporibus male fame conversationis et reputationis inhoneste ac talis qui volebat defacili denerare et falsum testimonium perhibere qui faciliter per dictam Aliciam corrumpi et informari ad falso dicendo et prederendo in dicta causa faciliter potuit prout fuerat realiter in eadem causa corruptus et informatus ut prefertur.

is called) of Rillyngton, and Thomas Fouler, who the said Alice produced in the matrimonial cause, moved and pending in the York curia, present between the aforesaid parties, against the words and depositions of the same, her witnesses. You should lend little or no credence in the aforesaid cause against the party of the said John Boton and especially in that part where she seems to speak on the matrimonial contract between the said parties, as she claims the public voice and fame laboured before she moved the present litigation for it, indeed the proof was the fame of the matrimonial contract held in the present or some sort of speech, from the time it was held previously in some way. This was from that time indeed falsely published, divulged, and made to be published and divulged by the same Alice herself and by her friends that the said John contracted marriage with her, and the present fame had its origin from the said Alice and her friends and adherents to her in the aforesaid cause and from no others. And by others as much as by the said Alice and her adherents in this party at no time was it believed or in any way said or aforesaid, because William de Bridsall is a witness notoriously suspect in the said cause, and for and from that fact, the same William at all times of his reception, deposition, and examination in the said cause, and before and after, was to this point a pauper and notoriously depressed by poverty, who sought his bread by begging door to door. And at all the said times, the said William was and to this point is notoriously *mente captus°* and in no way had natural discretion, but because of gifts and promises to him by the said Alice and her party, corrupted and informed, he gave and put forth his false testimony in the said cause. And the same William was at all the said times of bad fame and conduct, and of dishonest reputation and such a one who was willing to speak carelessly and to bear false witness, who was easily able to be corrupted and informed to false speaking by the said

mente captus *lit. "seized mind," a phrase used to denote mental impairment*

Prefatusque Thomas Fouler in dictis et depositionibus suis notorie dicit et exprimit falsitatem et precipue ut dicit et deponit quidem non fuit dicte Alicie et parti sue consanguineus vel affinis et quidem in bonis habuit et habet ad valenciam quinque marcorum cum idem Thomas fuerat omnibus dictis temporibus dicte Alicie consanguineus et in proximo gradu consanguinitatis eidem Alicie et nimia amicitia coniunctus, modicum vel nichil in bonis sed dictus Thomas est et fuit dictis temporibus pauper vilis et abiecta persona dictusque Thomas promotionem dicte Alicie consanguinee sue affectans suum in dicta causa falsum dixit et protulit testimonium ac isdem William de Bridsall et Thomas pro talibus quales supernis specificantur habitis fuerant et per dicta tempora publice reputati habentur et reputantur de presenti. Super quibus in diocese Ebor et locis vicinis laboravit et laborat publica vox et fama. Quare petit dictus procuratore nomine quo supra probatis in hoc casu de iure probandis dictis et depositionibus testum predictorum prout natura et qualitas premissorum exigit et requirit nullam seu modicam fidem adhiberi et ulterius fieri secundum naturam et qualitatem eorumdem in omnibus quod est iustum. Hec dicit, allegat, proponit, et petit ac probare intendit dictus procuratore nomine quo supra coniunctim et divisim iuris beneficio semper salvo.

Alice, and to put forth false testimony in the said cause, just as he was in reality in the same cause corrupted and informed as was put forth. And the aforesaid Thomas Fouler, in his words and depositions notoriously spoke and pronounced falsity and especially as he says and deposes that he is not consanguineous or affined to the said Alice and her party, and that he had and has in goods the value of five marks, when the same Thomas was at all the said times consanguineous in the second grade of consanguinity to the said Alice, and joined by excessive friendship, having little or nothing in goods, but the said Thomas is and was at the said times a common pauper and low person. And the said Thomas, desiring the promotion of the said consanguineous Alice, said and brought forth in the said cause his false testimony, and the same William de Bridsall and Thomas were held as such men as the above specified, and at the said times were publicly held in repute and reputed at the present. Upon these things in the diocese of York and nearby places the public voice and fame laboured and labours. Therefore the said procurator named above seeks in this cause of law, by testing the words and depositions of the aforesaid witnesses as to the nature and quality of the premises, that they be weighed and demanded to be nothing, or to be cited as little or no faith, and further, to be valued according to the nature and quality of the same in all things, which is just. Here the said proctor by name says, alleges, proposes, and intends to prove by what is above jointly and separately to the sound benefit of the law always.

Membrane 9 recto and verso
Articles *pro* John
October 13, 1366

In dei nomine Amen. Positiones et articulos infrascriptos et contenta in eisdem coniunctim et divisim facit et dat ac probare intendit procurator Johannis Boton de Scameston nomine procuratore pro eodem contra Aliciam Redyng de Scameston ac contra Walterum Warner, Williamum de Bridsall de

Membrane 9 recto and verso
Articles *pro* John
October 13, 1366

In the name of God, amen. The procurator for John Boton of Scameston produces and imparts and intends to prove the positions and articles herein written and the contents in the same, jointly and singly against Alice Redyng of Scameston and against Walter Warner, William de Bridsall of Scameston,

Scameston, dominum Rogerum qui se dicit vicarium de Rillyngton, et Thomas Fouler quos dicta Alicia in quadam causa matrimoniali presenta inter dictas partes in Curia Ebor mote et pendente in testibus produxit, dicta et depositiones eorum, et cuiuslibet eorumdem super exceptionibus dicti Johannis contra dictam Aliciam et eius testes ac contra eam et causam presentam [[]].

[...]

Item ponit et probare intendit quod dictus William de Bridsall omnibus et singulis temporibus receptionis, depositionis, et examinationis sue in dicta causa et ante et post fuerat et est adeo pauper et notorie pauperitate depressus quod hostiatim panem suum mendicando querebat ac omibus dictis temporibus fuerat dictus William et adhuc est notorie mente captus qui nullatenus discretionem habuit naturalem et quod dicte William propter data et promissa sibi predictam Aliciam et partem suam suum falsum in dicta causa corruptus et informatus dixit et pretulit testimonium.

Item ponit et probare intendit quod predictus William de Bridsall fuerat omnibus temporibus antedictis et adhuc est male fame conversationis et reputacionis inhoneste ac talis qui voluit et vult defacili deierare et falsum testimonium perhibere ac talis qui faciliter per dictam Aliciam corrumpi et informari potuit ad falso dicendum et preferendum testimonium in dicta causa prout realiter fuerat in eadem causa corruptus et ad falsum dicendum realiter informatus.

Item ponit et probare intendit quod predictus Thomas Fouler omnibus et singulis temporibus receptionis, examinationis, et depositionis sue in dicta causa fuerat et est consanguineus predicte Alicie †tertio† consanguinitate gradu attingens ac eidem Alicie nimia amicitia coniunctus modicum vel nichil habens in bonis ac pauper vilis et abiecta persona promotionem dicte Alicie consanguinitate [[]] indebite affectans ac talis qualitas supra describitur existens suum falsum

Lord Roger the Vicar of Rillyngton, as he calls himself, and Thomas Fouler who the said Alice produced as witnesses in the matrimonial cause present between the said parties, moved and pending in the York Curia, their words and depositions, and whichever of them in addition to the exceptions of the said John against the said Alice and her witnesses and against her and her present cause.

[Fame of the contract was published by Alice and her adherents.]

Likewise, he puts forth and intends to prove that William de Bridsall at each and every time of his reception, deposition, and examination in the said cause, and before and after, was and is truly a pauper and notoriously depressed by poverty, that he seeks his bread door-to-door by begging, and that at all the said times the said William is hitherto notoriously *mente captus*,° who in no way has natural discretion, and that the said William, because of gifts and promises to him by the aforesaid Alice and her party, corrupted and informed, spoke and offered his false testimony.

Likewise, he puts forth and intends to prove that the aforesaid William de Bridsall was at all the aforesaid times, and hitherto, is of poor fame, dishonest conduct and reputation, and thus one who wishes and wished to carelessly perjure and to present false testimony and thus one who could easily be corrupted and informed by the said Alice to false speaking and presenting testimony in the said cause, exactly as he really was in the same cause corrupted and really informed to false speaking.

Likewise, he puts forth and intends to prove that the aforesaid Thomas Fouler at each and every time of his reception, examination, and deposition in the said cause was and is consanguineous to the aforesaid Alice in the third degree of consanguinity and joined to the same Alice by undue friendship, having little or nothing in goods and is a common pauper and low-status person,

---

mente captus *lit. "seized mind," a phrase used to denote mental impairment*

pro predicte Alicie et contra dictum Johannem protulit testimonium in causa predicta.

Item ponit et probare intendit quod dicti William de Bridsale et Thomas Fouler pro talibus quales superius specificantur habiti fuerant per tempora predicta et adhuc sunt in diocese Eboracum et locis vicinis ac publice reputata.

[...]

Item ponit et probare intendit quod premissa sunt publica notorie et manifesta in diocese Ebor et locis vicinis et super hiis laboravit et laborat publica vox et fama.

unduly desiring the promotion of the said Alice for their consanguinity, and being of such quality described above that he brings forth his false testimony for the aforesaid Alice against the said John in the aforesaid cause.

Likewise, he puts forth and intends to prove that the said William de Bridsall and Thomas Fouler for such reasons were considered the sort of men specified above during the aforesaid times and as yet are in the diocese of York and nearby places and publicly reputed so.

[Alice is of servile condition.]

[John is free-born and was ignorant of Alice's servile status.]

Likewise he puts forth and intends to prove that the premises are notoriously public and manifest in the diocese of York and nearby places and upon these facts the public voice and fame laboured and labours.

Membrane 8 recto
Interrogatories *pro* Alice
Undated

Interrogetur testes omnes et singuli° pro partem Johannis Boton de Scameston Chapman contra Aliciam Redyng de eadem producti et producendi:

[...]

Item si incitantur deponere quod William de Bridsall fuit et est mente captus prout in secundo articulo per partem dicto Johanno traditur continentur. Et interrogetur dicitur de causa scientie, et per quod sciant deponere quod dictus William aliquid recepit seu sibi per prefatam Aliciam promissum fuerat et suum diceret testimonium in hac causa et an viderunt vel audierunt prefatam Aliciam aliquid promittere seu dare eidem William pro suo testimonio in hac parte.

Item si incitantur deponere quod Thomas Fouler sit consanguineus dicte Alicie. Et interrogetur dicti in quo gradu consanguinitatis ipsam attingit. Et semper de causa scientie dicti sui.

Membrane 8 recto
Interrogatories *pro* Alice
Undated

Let the witnesses, produced and to be produced, for the part of John Boton of Scameston, Chapman, against Alice Redyng of the same, be interrogated together and singly:

[Question them as to where they heard the fame of the contract.]

Likewise, if they were incited to depose that William de Bridsall was and is *mente captus*° just as is contained in the second article for his part by the said John. And let them be interrogated on the cause of their knowledge, and through who that they know to depose that the said William received anything or there was a promise to him for the aforesaid Alice and that he said his testimony in this cause. And whether they saw or heard the aforesaid Alice promise or give anything to the same William for his testimony for her part.

Likewise, if they were incited to depose that Thomas Fouler may be consanguineus to

---

testes omnes et singuli *to evaluate their truthfulness by comparing details*   mente captus *lit. "seized mind," a phrase used to denote mental impairment*

[...]

Membrane 7 recto
Depositions pro John Boton
October 14–15, 1366

Robert, filius Philip de Scamston libere conditionis non consanguineus nec affinis partis ipsum producentis non iuratis ut dicit [...] Et primis, super primo articulo requisatus, dicit quod die sancti thome martyris ulterioribus preteritis primo et non ante, audivit famam laborantem super contractu matrimoniale inter partes de quibus agitur. Habito quo die dictes partes fuerat apud Scardburgh in peregrinatione et ibidem erat orta dissentio inter eas sed quae causa nescere iste iure. Et ipso die quod redierint de Scardburgh apud Scameston divulgabatur contractus matrimonialis inter dictas partes in commune sed non advertebat an per amicos unius partis vel alterius. Super secundo articulo requisatus dicit quod William de Bridall testes in dicto articulo nominatus est pauper et adeo pauperitate depressus quod hostiatim et per villas vicinis ville de Scameston querit victum suum mendicando et non reputat eum valde sapientem quare non videt eum emere nequare vendere sed villatim mendicare ideo non cognoscit sensum suum. Sed an corruptus vel informatus deposuit in presenta causa nescere iste vire deponere ut dicit. Super tertio articulo requisatus dicit quod super dicto articulo nescere deponere aliter quam supra deponet hoc excepta quod dictus William est pauper. Super quarto articulo requisatus dicit quod Thomas Fouler attingit Alicie de quo agitur in tertio gradu consanguinitatis quare ave dictorum Thome et Alicie fuerunt sorores carnales et una vocabatur Alicia Redyng et alia Alicia Fouler sed utrum dictus Thomas affectabat promotionem dicte

the said Alice. And let the said witnesses be interrogated in which grade of consanguinity he has to the same. And always as to the cause of their knowledge.

[Question them regarding Alice's servile status.]

[Question them regarding their relationship to John Boton.]

Membrane 7 recto
Depositions pro John Boton
October 14–15, 1366

Robert, son of Philip of Scamston, of free condition, not consanguineus nor affined to the party that produced him nor held by oath as he says. [He wishes justice for John Boton.] And firstly, questioned on the first article, he says that on the day of St Thomas Martyr last and not before, he heard the fame labouring concerning the matrimonial contract between the parties concerning whom this cause is conducted. On that day, the said parties were at Scarborough on pilgrimage and while they were there a dispute arose between them but what the cause was this witness does not know. And on that day when they returned from Scarborough to Scameston, the matrimonial contract between the parties was divulged in public, but he did not recall whether through the friends of one party or the other. Questioned on the second article, he says that William de Bridsall, named as a witness in the said article, is a pauper and so depressed by poverty that he seeks his food by begging door to door and though the villages nearby to the village of Scameston, and he does not consider him very wise because he does not see him buy or sell but to beg village to village, and therefore he does not know his own thoughts. But whether he deposed while corrupted and informed in the present cause this witness does not know to depose as he says. Questioned on the third article he says that on the said article he does not know to depose other than he deposed above except that the said William is a pauper. Questioned on the fourth article, he says that Thomas Fouler strives

Alicie partis ignorat iste iure ut dicit. Preterea dicit predictus Thomas habet in bonis as valencia quattuor vel quinque martiarum et reputat homo fidelis sicut filius patrisfamilias de Scameston debet habere. Et aliter super premissis articulo sive quinto articulo nescere deponere ut dicit quod supra deponet. Super sexto articulo requisatus dicit quod dicta Alicia de Redyng pars in presenti negotio fuit procreata concepta nata et educata de patre servo et servile conditionis domini de Latymer sed mater sua fuit libera et libere conditionis orienda de Knapton. Dicit tum quod postmodum dicta Alicia pars fuit facta libera huius ad tres annos proximo elapsere et amplius per domini Clementem de Chamblayn qui fuit senescallus magnus dicti domini de Latymer locum tenens et attornatus generale in toto domo suo in regno Anglice cum tota sequela sua. Super septimo articulo requisatus dicit quod dictus Johannes est liber et libere conditionis reputatus et credit quod excedit dictam Aliciam partem in divitiis quare mercator est sed non reputat honorem in persona [...] et de ceteris in dicto septimo articulo nescere deponere ut dicit. Super ulteriore articulo requisatus dicit quod super premissis in forma de positionis sue laboravit et adhuc laborat in villa de Scameston et locis vicinis publica vox et fama.

Thomas son of Ydonson de Rillyngton etatis xxx annos affinis Johannis Boton quare dixit consanguineam suam in uxorem sed nescere quanto gradu, affectans ut dicit quod ipsa pars optineat victoriam in presenti causa que digna est. Iure extra et super premisses dicere requisatus. Super primo articulo requisatus dicit in iuramento suo quod fama sive locutio que habebatur et habetur de contractu matromoniale inter partes predictas pretenso habito ortum habunt et publicata ac divulgata fuit de et per Thomas Fouler et William de Bridsall qui Thomas ut dicit iste iure est consanguineus dicte Alicie partis in tertio gradu consanguinitatis qui ut credere iste iure affectat victoriam in presenti causa pro parte dicte Alicie ratione consanguinitatis huius et qui Thomas ut dicit est serviens

for Alice in that which she urges because of their consanguinity, because the grandmothers of the said Thomas and Alice were blood sisters and one was called Alice Redyng and the other Alice Fouler, but whether the said Thomas desired the promotion of the party of the said Alice this witness does not know as he says. In addition, the said Thomas has goods to the value of four or five marks and he judges him a faithful man just as the son of his father ought to be held in Scameston. And otherwise on the following article or the fifth article he does not know to despose as he says other than what he deposed above. Questioned on the sixth article, he says that the said Alice Redyng in the present business was begotten, conceived, born, and raised from a father who was a servant and of servile condition to the Lord Latymer, but her mother was a free woman and of free condition being born in Knapton. He says then that afterwards the said Alice was made free from that for the past three years and more by the Lord Clement the Chamberlain who was the head seneschal of the said Lord Latymer, holding his place and being his attorney general in his whole house in the English kingdom with all that follows. Questioned on the seventh article, he says that the said John is free and of free condition, reputed and believed that he exceeds the said Alice in wealth because he is a merchant, but he does not judge him honorable in person [...] and on the rest in the said seventh article he does not know to depose as he says. Questioned on the last article, he says that upon the premises in the form of the positions that the public voice and fame laboured and yet labours in the village of Scameston and nearby places.

Thomas son of Ydonson of Rillyngton, aged thirty years, affined to John Boton because he said he is consanguineous by his wife, but he does not know in what grade, desiring as he says that that party obtain victory in the present cause which is worthy. He is a supplementary witness to the premises. Further, the witness was questioned to speak on the premises. Questioned on the first ar-

patris sui per stipendio suo et habet in bonis ad valenciam quattuor martiarum et amplius et reputat ipsam Thomam esse bonam famam ut dicit iste iure, que iste iure novit per septimam annos festem Nativitate Sancti Johannis Baptiste ulterioribus preteritis et non ante ut dicit. Et dictis William est pauper et adeo notorie pauperitate depressus quod villatim et hostiatim querit cibum suum et querebat medicando prout iste iure sepius videt non habens aliquod receptaculum certum. Et reputatur stultus et talis fame quod vult ex magno corde ortius dicere contrarium veritatis quam ipsam veritatem et quod fama laborat in dicta villa de Scameston et locis vicinis quod prefatus William per dictam Aliciam corruptus et informatus falsum dixit et deponet in presente causa sed an aliquid recepit vel si promissum fuit pro suo testimonio ferendo in presenti causa nescere iste vire deponere ut dicit. Et quod extra communi relatu didicit quod prefatus William dixit quod deberet morari perpetuo inferno nisi ipsa Alicia pars haberet dictum Johannem in virum suum. Et predicti Thomas et William pro talibus reputantur et habentur et reputabantur et habentur quales ipse superius specificantur. [...]

William filius Johannis filii Roberti de Scameston, non consanguineus nec affinis partis ipsum producentis, affectans ut dicit victoriam Johannis Boton in iure suo et non aliter ut dicit iure et extra et super premissis. [...] Super secundo articulo requisatus dicit quod William de Bridsall notorie est pauper mendicans hostiatim et potius reputat stultus quam sapiens sed an aliquid recepit de dicta Alicia pro testimonio suo prebendis vel aliquid si promissus fuerat per eadem nescere deponere ut dicit nisi ex relatu aliorum. Et iste iure dicit quod ante diem receptionis et examinationis dicti William audivit Johannem Boton ipsum William alloqui isto modo William recolas quod tu es homo senex et non perdas animam tuam pro aliqua data vel promissa. Cui dictus William repondit "Sive anima mea vadat ad celum sive ad infernum ego tenebo illud quod promissi" sic innuendo

ticle, he says that in his judgement the fame or gossip which was and is held regarding the matrimonial contract between the aforesaid parties in the present had its origin and was published and divulged by and through Thomas Fouler and William de Bridsall, and Thomas, as this witness says, is consanguineous to the said Alice in the third degree of consanguinity, who as this witness believes desires victory in the present cause for the party of the said Alice by reason of his consanguinity, and who it is said is a servant of his father for wages and has goods to the value of four marks or more, and he judges Thomas to be of good fame as this witness says, who this witness knew for seven years at the feast of the Nativity of St John the Baptist last and not before as he says. And the said William is a pauper and so depressed by poverty that he begs his bread village to village and door to door, and sought it by begging just as this witness very often saw, not having some sure shelter. And he judges him a fool and of such fame that he would speak from great affection of the origin of the fame contrary to the truth, which truth the fame labours on in the said village of Scameston and nearby places, that the aforesaid William, corrupted and informed by the said Alice, said and deposed falsity in the present cause. But whether he received or if he was promised anything for bearing his false testimony in the present cause this witness does not know to depose as he says. And beyond the common rumour, he learned that the aforesaid William said that he ought to die in perpetual hell unless Alice had the said John for her husband. And the aforesaid Thomas and William for such reasons are reputed and held and were reputed and held the sorts of men who were specified above. [Remainder of deposition similar to that of Robert son of Phillip.]

William son of John son of Robert de Scameston, not consanguineous nor affined to the party producing him, desiring victory as he says for John Boton in his lawsuit and none other as this witness says, a supplementary witness to the premises. [He first heard

de dicta Alicia. Super tertio articulo requisatus dicit quod dictus William est ut serviens deponet pauper sed de aliqua mala fama de William vel conversatione honesta nescere deponere ut dicit aliter quam supra deponet nec utrum fuerat informatus ad deponendum ut deponet. Super quarto articulo requisatus dicit quod est notorius quod Thomas Fouler attingit dictam Aliciam in tertio gradu consanguinitate ex utraque latere eo quod Alicia Redyng ava dicte Alicie et Alicia dicta del Wald ava dicti Thome fuerant sorores carnalles sed ipsas non novit ut dicit. De Alicia Redyng processit Richardis Redyng filius suus carnalis Alicie de quam agitur, et de Alicia del Wald ex alio latere processit Richardus Fouler pater suus carnalis iure dicti Thome et Richardi, et Richardum iste iure novit et vidit ut dicit. Item dicit quod dictus Thomas est serviens patris sui habens in bonis ad valenciam quattuor martiarum quod affectans ut iste iure dicit se credere ratione consanguinitatis huius promotionem dicte Alicie indebite. Et dicit quod si idem Thomas deposuit in presenti causa quod non fuit consanguineus dicte Alicie falsum dixit et deposuit. [...]

the fame of the contract on the feast of the Translation of St. Thomas, but he does not know where it began.] Questioned on the second article he says that William de Bridsall is notoriously a pauper, wandering door to door, and he judges him more a fool than wise, but whether he received anything from the said Alice for providing his testimony or if he was promised anything by the same he does not know to depose as he says, except from the judgement of others. And this witness says that before the day of the reception and deposition of the said William, he heard John Boton speaking to William in this way: "William, remember that you are an old man and you should not lose your soul for any gift of promise." To which the said William replied: "Whether my soul goes to heaven or to hell, I will stand by that which I have promised," nodding thus to the said Alice. Questioned on the third article, he says that the said William is a pauper—as he deposed, a servant—but concerning any ill fame or honest conduct of William, he does not know to depose as he says, other than what he deposed above, nor whether he was informed to deposing as he deposed. Questioned on the fourth article, he says that it is notorious that Thomas Fouler touches the said Alice in the third degree of consanguinity and from either side because Alice Redyng, the grandmother of the said Alice, and Alice, called "de Wald," the grandmother of the said Thomas, were blood sisters but he did not know them as he says. From Alice Redyng was Richard Redyng, her blood son, from whom came the Alice who moved this cause, and from Alice de Wald on the other side came Richard Fouler, the blood father of the said Thomas and Richard, and Richard this witness knew and saw as he says. Likewise, he says that the said Thomas is a servant of his father, having goods to the value of four marks, who desires the undue promotion of the said Alice, as this witness says he believes for reason of this consanguinity. And he says that if the same Thomas deposed in the present cause that he was not consanguineous to the said Alice,

he said and deposed falsity. [The remainder of the membrane is heavily damaged. He deposes regarding Alice's servile status. There appears to be no further mention of William de Bridsall.]

Membrane 5 recto and verso
Petition to present deponents *pro* Alice
October 15 or 23, 1366

[...] Proponit procuratore Alicie Redyng de Scameston nomine procuratore pro eadem contra Johannem Boton de Scameston ac contra quemlibet pro eodem coram vobis in iudicio libere comparentem ac contra quasdam exceptiones per partem dicti Johanni contra prefatam Aliciam, Walter Warner, William de Bridsall de Scameston, Dominum Roger vicarium ecclesie de Rillyngton, et Thomas Fouler, testes pro parte dicte Alicie in causa matrimoniale inter prefatas partes in Curia Ebor mota et pendente. productis iure et examinationis dictas et depositiones eorumdem proponitas vim, formam, effectum earumdem et contra positiones et articulos ab eisdem exceptionibus ut dicitur elicitos et extractos et contenta in eisdem quod dicti testes omnes et singuli in suis dictis et depositionibus in dicta causa factis et depositis suum verum dixerunt et deposuerunt testimonium et precipue in ea parte depositionum suarum et cuiuslibet earumdem quod dixerunt et deposuerunt et eorum quilibet dixit et deposuit quod super contractum matrimonialem inter dictos Johannem et Aliciam [...]

Item quod William de Bridsall testis ac Thomas Fouler testis in dicta causa productis omnibus temporibus receptionis examinationis et depositionis eorum in causa predicta ac ante et post fuerant et adhuc sunt satis divites ac nullatenus nimia seu notorie pauperitate depressi seu eorum aliquis depressus sed sufficienter omnibus temporibus predictis habuerunt et eorum quilibet habuit et adhuc habet habuerunt et habent quilibet eorumdem in bonis ex omnibus secundum sui status detenciam honeste vivere potuerunt et possunt ac potuit et potest quilibet eorumdem ac

Membrane 5 recto and verso
Petition to present deponents *pro* Alice
October 15 or 23, 1366

[Salutation.] The proctor of Alice Redyng named above, puts forth this petition for her against John Boton and anyone for him appearing in your presence in evidence and against certain exceptions on the part of the said John Boton against the aforesaid Alice, William Warner, William de Bridsall de Scamston, lord Roger the vicar of the church of Rillyngton, and Thomas Fouler, witnesses on the part of the said Alice in the matrimonial cause between the two aforementioned parties moved and pending in the court of York. You will produce in the court the said examinations and depositions of those same witnesses, relating the strength, form, and effect of the same, and against the positions and articles, by the same exceptions elicited, extracted, and contained as it is said in the same. Indeed the said witnesses, together and singly in their words and depositions made and deposed in the said cause, said their truth and deposed their testimony and especially in that part of their depositions and of whatever of the same indeed they said and deposed...

Likewise, that William de Bridsall and Thomas Fouler, witnesses produced for Alice in the said cause, at all times of their reception, examination, and deposition in the aforesaid cause were and yet are both before and after wealthy enough and in nowise excessively or notoriously either depressed by poverty or depressed by anything else, but sufficient at all the aforesaid times, singly and together, and had and have in goods from all according to their status. They were and are, singly and together, able to be honestly and agreeably maintained. The said William de Bridsall, indeed at all the aforesaid times,

commode sustentari. Dictus quidem William de Bridall omnibus temporibus predictis fuerat et adhuc est notorie sane mentis ac discretionem naturalem et sufficientem habens, qui absque omni promissione seu dono sibi per dictam Aliciam seu partem eiusdem dato seu facto suum verum in dicta causa absque omni corruptione et informatione, seu affecione indebita. dixit et protulit testimonium. Prefati qui William et Thomas omnibus dictis temporibus bone fame et conversatione et reputatione honeste fuerunt et adhuc sunt et eorum quilibet fuerat et adhuc est. Ac tales qui pro aliquo deierare seu falsum testimonium perhibere seu ad falsum testimonium in dicta causa seu alia quacumque dicendum et proferendum nullatenus induci poterant, sed homines fideles et fidedigni in dicta villa de scameston et locis vicinis communiter habiti et publice reputati et eorum quilibet habitus fuit et publice reputatus et etiam habentur et reputantur et eorum quilibet habetur et reputatur in presenti. Super quibus in diocese Ebor et locis vicinis laboravit et adhuc laborat publica vox et fama. [...]

was and yet is notoriously of sound mind, and having sufficient natural discretion, who, free from any promise or gift given or made to him by the said Alice or her party, said and put forth his true testimony in the said cause without any corruption, information, or undue affection. The aforesaid William and Thomas, singly and together, at all the said times were and yet are of good fame and conduct and honest reputation. And they are, singly and together, such who for anything in no way perjure or present false testimony or are able to be induced to speaking or presenting false testimony in the said cause or in any whatsoever, but are commonly held and reputed faithful men and worthy in the said village of Scameston and nearby places. And, singly and together, they are held and reputed so at the present. On these facts, in the diocese of York, the public voice and fame laboured and labours. [He intends to prove these facts.]

Membrane 1 recto
Articles *pro* Alice Redyng
November 6, 1366

Item ponit et probare intendit quod dictus William de Bridsall omnibus temporibus productionis, receptionis, et examinationis sue in causa predicta fuerat et adhuc est notorie sane mentis ac discretionem naturalem et sufficientem habens, qui absque omni promissione seu dono sibi per dictam Aliciam seu partem euisdem dato seu facto suum verum in dicta causa absque omni corruptione et informacione seu affectione indebita dixit et protulit testimonium.

Item ponit et probare intendit quidem prefati William de Bridsall et Thomas, testes predicti omnibus temporibus productionis, receptionis, et examinationis eorum et cuiuslibet eorumdem in dicta causa fuerunt et adhuc sunt et eorum quilibet fuerat et adhuc est bone fame conversatione et reputatione

Membrane 1 recto
Articles *pro* Alice Redyng
November 6, 1366

Likewise, he puts forth and intends to prove that the said William de Bridsall at all times of his production, reception, and examination in the aforesaid cause was and until now is notoriously of sound mind and having sufficient natural discretion, who without promise or gift given or made to him by the said Alice said his truth and advanced his testimony in the said cause without any corruption or information or undue affection.

Likewise, he puts forth and intends to prove that the aforesaid William de Bridsall and Thomas Fouler, the aforesaid witnesses, singly and together, at all times in their production, reception, and examination, were and until now are in the said cause, and were and are, of good fame in their conduct and honest in reputation and of such kind who

honesta ac tales qui pro aliquo deierare seu falsum testimonium perhibere seu ad falsum testimonium in dicta causa seu alia quandocumque [dicendum ei proferendum] nullatenus induci poterant sed homines fideles et fidedigni in dicta villa de scameston et locis vicinis communiter habiti et publice reputati et eorum quilibet communiter habitus fuit et publice reputatus ac etiam habentur et reputantur ac habetur et reputatur eorum quilibet in presenti.

[...]

Item ponit et probare intendit quod premissa sunt publica notorie et manifesta in communitate et diocese Ebor et locinis vicinis ac super hiis ibidem laboravit et laborat publica vox et fama.

take an oath. They were able in no wise to perjure false testimony or to introduce a false testimony in the said cause, or another at any time, in speaking or bringing it forward, but they are held and publicly reputed honest and worthy men in the said village of Scamston and nearby places, both generally and whichever of them is held and publicly reputed. And they are even held and reputed so, and whichever of them is held and reputed so in the present.

[He intends to prove that Alice is and was of free condition.]

Likewise, he puts forth and intends to prove that the premises are publicly notorious and manifest in the community and diocese of York and nearby places, and upon these facts the public voice and fame laboured and labours.

Membrane 6 recto
Depositions *pro* Alice Redyng
November 9, 1366

Geoffrey Rayneson de Rillyngton libere conditionis ut dicit, etatis xl annos fere non consanguineus nec affinis partis ipsum producentis affectans quod illa pars habeat victoriam in presenti causa que [[]] ius habet in eadem ut dicit iure et extra super premissis. Super primo articulo requisatus dicit quod die Translatio sancti Thome martyris ulterioribus preteritis iste iure primo et non ante audivit famam tam de contractu inter prefatas partes habito quam de carnali copula subsecuta que fama ut dicit habuit ortum de incolis et inhabitoribus ville de Scameston. Interrogatus an fuerint amici vel adherentes dicte Alicie illi a quibus primo audivit huius famam dicit quod fuerunt omnes amici utriusque partis sed non credebatur per contractum quod contractus matrimonialis habebatur inter dictas partes ut dicit, sed a quo primo audivit dictam famam [...]. Super secundo articulo requisatus, dicit quod novit William de Bridsall per aspectum corporis et reputat eum potius stultum quam sapientem quem sepius vidit ostiatim mendicare panem in parochia de Rillyngton sed nescit si cor-

Membrane 6 recto
Depositions *pro* Alice Redyng
November 9, 1366

Geoffrey Rayneson de Rillyington, of free condition as he says, aged forty years, not consanguineous nor affined to the party producing him, desiring that that party have victory in the present cause because he believes she has justice for her as he says, a supplementary witness to the premises. Questioned on the first article, he says that on the day of the Translation of St Thomas Martyr last this witness first and not before heard the fame, as much concerning the contract between the aforementioned parties as concerning the subsequent carnal knowledge, which fame as he says had its origin with the residents and inhabitants of the village of Scameston. Questioned whether it was the friends or adherents of the said Alice who he first heard that fame, he says that it was all friends of both parties, but he did not believe by the contract alone that a matrimonial contract has had between the said parties as he says, but from he who first heard the said fame [...]. Questioned on the second article, he says that he knew William de Bridsall from the appearance of his body and judges him

45

ruptus vel informatus protulit suum testimonium in presenti causa nec aliter super dicto secundo articulo scit deponere ut dicit. Super tertio articulo requisatus dicit quod dictus William hospitibatur cum quodam amico dicte Alicie et aliter quam supra deponet nescere deponere contra eumdem William eo quod non novit eum nisi dictam festem nativitatis beati Johannis Baptiste ulterioribus preteritis. Super quarto articulo requisatus dicit quod bene dedicit per relatum aliorum quos audivit computare quantus consanguineatis inter Thomam Fouler et Aliciam de Redyng quod sunt consanguinei in tertio gradu consanguinitatis ex utroque latere. Qui Thomas est serviens patris sui qui pater est bonus paterfamilias et dives husbandus et alia de divitiis ipsius Thome seu pauperitate nescere deponere ut dicit, quod numquam audivit eum loqui verbum de presenti causa ne scit de testimonio suo falso sive vero quod perhibent in presenti causa nisi quatenus iste iure deponet super de consanguinitatis gradibus inter dictum Thomam et ipsam Aliciam quod in ea parte falsum dixit et deponet. Et hoc si necesse esset vellet iste iure probare ut dicit per centem homines sumptibus suis propriis. Et aliter super dicto quarto articulo nescere deponere ut dicit, nec super quinto articulo proximo sequenti nisi quod dictus William sepius vult inebriari et sic ebrius vult iacere in campis et fossati et hoc reputat factum insipientis. Interrogatus an vidit dictum William sic facere dicit quod non sed bene audivit a vicinis suis quod sic consuevit facere. Super sexto articulo requisatus dicit quod bene audivit dici quod dicta Alicia fuit procreata, concepta, et nata de patre servo sed dicit quod postmodum per quemdam dominum Clementem senescallum domini de Latymer fuit manumissa et iste scit et dedicit ex relatu aliorum ut dicit. Super septimo articulo requisatus dicit quod Johannes Boton est liber [[]] nec scit iste iure ut dicit deponere de divitiis suis nec divitiis prefate Alicie aut aliter super ceteris sequentibus in prefate

more foolish than wise, who he often saw begging his bread door to door in the parish of Rillyngton, but he does not know if he was corrupted or informed when he gave his testimony in the present cause, nor otherwise on the said second article does he know to depose as he says. Questioned on the third article, he says that the said William was lodged with a certain friend of the said Alice and other than he deposed above he does not know to depose against the same William because he does not know him, except that from the said feast of St John the Baptist last. Questioned on the fourth article, he says that he well knew through the judgement of others who he heard to calculate the degree of consanguinity between Thomas Fouler and Alice Redyng that they are consanguineous in the third degree of consanguinity from either side. That Thomas is a servant of his father, whose father is a good *paterfamilias*° and wealthy husbandman and otherwise concerning the wealth or poverty of that Thomas he does not know to depose as he says, because he never heard him speak a word on the present cause nor knows whether his testimony which he presented in the present cause was false or true, except to what extent this witness deposed on the grades of consanguinity between the said Thomas and Alice, because in that part he said and deposed a falsity. And this, if it should be necessary, this witness is willing to prove as he says with a hundred men at his own expense. And otherwise on the said fourth article he does not know to depose as he says, nor on the fifth article following it except that the said William often wishes to be drunk and when drunk casts himself onto fields and into ditches and he judges this done from foolishness. Asked whether he saw the said William to do so, he says not but he well heard it from his neighbours that William was accustomed to do so. Questioned on the sixth article, he says that he well heard it said that the said Alice was begotten, conceived, and born from a servant

paterfamilias *male head of household*

septimo articulo. Super ultimo articulo requisatus, dicit quod fama publica laborat in tota parochia de Rillyngton predicta quod dictus William de Bridsall est pauper homo et mendicus ut supra deponet, et quod dictus Thomas et Alicia sic attingunt in tertio gradu consanguinitatis. Interrogatus qui Alicia fuit facta libera dicit quod nunc ad octo annos elapsere prout audivit diu et aliter super dictos articulos seu interrogatores nescere deponere ut dicit.

Johannes Emmotson de Scamston etatis xxx annos libere conditionis consanguineus Johannis Boton sed nescere in quo gradu iure et extra super premissis. Super primo articulo requisatus dicit quod fama super dicto contractu die translationis sancti Thome ulterioribus preteritis primo quod iste iure sciat habuit ortum a dicta Alicia ut dicit. Iste iure interrogatus an iste iure hoc audivit dicit quod non sed bene retulit et credere quod ipso die sancti Thome ante horam vesperarum et post horam nonam homines et mulieres ad numerum viginti qui venerant cum dicta Alicia de peregrinatione sua facta apud Scardburgh sedebant in quadam domo de Scamston potando et ibi [] iste iure audivit famam de ipso contractu, et qui sic sedebant fuerant communes amici utriusque partis. Et dixerunt quod prefata Alicia ipso die in dicta villa de Scardburgh sic retulit eis et ab illo tempore cita divulgabatur dicta fama per totam viciniam. Super secundo articulo requisatus dicit quod William de Bridsall notorie est depressus pauperitate quare ostiatim querit panem suum mendicando et videtur sibi quod potius debeat dici stultus quam sapiens quare habet caput ita debile et qui bibit in aliqua quantitate notabili de servisia statim inebriatur adeo quod non potest ire ad hospitium suum nisi suffultus auxilia aliunde, tum discretionem naturalem habet ut dicit sed an fuit instructus vel corruptus per dictam Aliciam in presenti causa nescere deponere ut dicit, et dicit quod reputatur pauper fidelis ac bone fame pro aliquo quod iste iure sciat

father but he says that afterward, through a certain Lord Clement, seneschal of the Lord Latymer, she was manumitted and he knew and learned this through the relating of others as he says. Questioned on the seventh article, he says that John Boton is free and this witness does not know as he says to depose on John's wealth nor the aforesaid Alice's wealth, or otherwise on the remaining aspects of the aforementioned seventh article. Questioned on the final article, he says that the public fame labours in the whole Parish of Rillyngton that the said William de Bridsall is a poor man and a beggar, as he deposed above, and that the said Thomas and Alice thus connect in the third degree of consanguinity. Asked when Alice was made free he says that now to eight years past, as he long heard it, and otherwise on the said articles and interrogatories he does not know to depose as he says.

John Emmotson de Scameston, aged thirty years, of free condition, consanguineous to John Boton but he does not know in what grade, a supplementary witness to the premises. Questioned on the first article, he says that the fame of the said contract first had its origin that this witness knows on the day of the Translation of St Thomas, from the said Alice as he says. This witness, asked whether he heard this, says not but it well related to him and he believes that on that day of St Thomas before the hour of vespers and after the hour of nones,⁰ men and women to the number of twenty who came with the said Alice from her pilgrimage made to Scarborough sat in a certain house in Scameston, drinking and there this witness first heard the fame of that contract, and those who were seated thus were friends common to both parties. They said that the aforementioned Alice on that day in the village of Scarborough so related it to them and from that time the said fame was quickly divulged through the whole neighbourhood. Questioned on the second article, he says that William de Bridsall is no-

hour of vespers...nones *before approximately 6pm and after approximately 3pm*

nisi quod potius credere quod falsum dixit in presenti causa quam non. [...]

Johannes filius Radulphi de Pokethorpe liberi conditionis etatis xxii annos et amplius iure et extra super premissis. Super primo articulo requisatus dicit quod audivit dici quod fama que laborat super dicto contractu habuit ortum de ipsa Alicia et amicis suis et per ipsam fuit divulgata et publicata et aliter nescere super primo articulo nescere deponere ut dicit. Super secundo articulo dicit quod notorie est quod dictus William de Bridsall querit panem suum ostiatim mendicando quem iste iure novit per annum elapsere et non vidit ipsum aliquam stulticiam medio tempore facere nec audivit excepto quod fuit ita ebrius die Omnium Sanctorum ulterioribus preteritis quod amisit armilausam suam et aliter super secundo articulo nescere deponere ut dicit. Super tertio articulo requisatus dicit quod super eodem nescere deponere. [...]

toriously depressed by poverty, wherefore he seeks his bread by begging door to door and it seems to him that he ought to be called a fool rather than wise, because he has a head so feeble and he drinks of beer in such notable quantity that he is immediately drunk to the point that he cannot go to his lodging unless propped up by some aid from another person, besides which he has natural discretion as he says. But whether he was instructed or corrupted by the said Alice in the present cause he does not know to depose as he says, and he says that he judges him to be an honest pauper and of good fame from some that this witness knew, except that he would rather depose a falsity in the present cause than not. [Remainder of deposition similar to Geoffrey Rayneson.]

John son of Ralph de Pokethorpe, of free condition, aged thirty years and more, a supplementary witness to premises. Questioned on the first article, he says that he heard it said that the fame which labours on the said contract had its origin from Alice and her friends, and was divulged and published by her and he does not know to depose otherwise on the first article as he says. Questioned on the second article, he says that it is notorious that William de Bridsall seeks his bread by begging door to door which this witness knows from a year past, and he did not him do see any other foolishness in the meantime, nor hear it, except that he was so drunk on the day of All Saints last that he lost his garment. And otherwise on the second article he does not know to depose as he says. Questioned on the third article, he says that he does not know to depose on the same as he says. [Remainder of the deposition is similar to the above.]

Membrane 4(b) recto
Depositions *pro* Alice Redyng
November 9–10, 1366

Robertus Webster de Rillyngton libere conditionis etatis xxx annos. [...] Super primo articulo requisatus dicit quod bene novit persones in eodem descripte sed a quo vel a

Membrane 4(b) recto
Depositions *pro* Alice Redyng
November 9–10, 1366

Robert Webster de Rillyngton, of free condition, aged thirty years. Questioned on the first article, he says that he knows the people described in it well, but from whom

quibus fama super dictum contractum matrimonialem habuit ortum nescere iste iure ut dicit. Super secundo articulo requisatus dicit quod William de Bridsall reputatur homo fidelis et deleterius quod iste iure novit in persona eiusdem William est quod est mendicus et aliquo vult inebriari et utrum aliunde sit mente captus vel non nescere iste iure ut dicit. Super tertio articulo requisatus dicit quod dicti William et Thomas Fouler reputantur et habentur fideles homines et bone fame salvo hoc quod sic deponit de William et numquam audivit ut dicit quod in aliquam causam deierant seu deierat nec quod potuerunt corrumpi vel corrupti fuerunt in presenti causa vel aliquam alia. [...]

Richardus Peckett de Rillyngton libere conditionis non consanguineus vel affinis alius partum predictarum iure et extra super premisses. Super primo articulo requisatus dicit quod novit Walter Warner et Rogerum vicarum de Rillyngton pro bonis hominibus et William de Bridsall novit qui est pauper mendicans ostiatim novit a festum nativitatis sancti Johannis Baptiste vel preteritis et Thomas Fouler non novit et ut dicit nisi infra mensem proxima preteritis umquam audivit loqui de matrimonio contractu et carnali copula supradicta. Super secundo articulo requisatus dicit quod William de Bridsall est pro aliquo quod iste iure unquam scivit vel audivit excepto quod die Omnium Sanctorum ulterioribus preteritis vidit eum ita ebrius quod non potuit ire solus de loco in quo fuit ad hospitium suum nisi cum auxilio istius iure ac aliorum est sane mentis et sic fuit habens sufficientem discretionem naturalem reputationem istius iure ita paratam sicut iste iure habet qui ut credere iste iure absque omni promissione seu dono sibi dato vel facto per dictam Aliciam seu partem eiusdem suum in presenti causam pretulit verum testimonium. Et dicit quod dictus William reputatur fidelis, bone fame et reputationis in statu suo, qui secundum scientiam istius iure pro aliquod non poterit induci ad deierandus

the fame of the said matrimonial contract had its origin this witness does not know as he says. Questioned on the second article, he says that William de Bridsall is reputed a faithful man, and the worst that this witness knows in person of the same William is that he is a beggar and also that he likes to be drunk and whether he is in any way *mente captus*[o] or not this witness does not know as he says. Questioned on the third article, he says that the said William and Thomas are reputed and held to be faithful men and of good fame and sound mind that he deposes thus of William, and he never heard, as he says, that they perjured, and they were not able to be perverted or corrupted in the present cause or any other.

Richard Peckett de Rillyngton, of free condition, not consanguineous or affined either of the aforesaid parties, a supplementary witness to the premises. Questioned on the first aticle, he says that he knows Walter Warner and Roger, the vicar of Rillyngton, for good men, and he knows William de Bridsall is a pauper who begs door to door and he knows him from the feast of the birth of St John the Baptist last, and he does not know Thomas Fouler as he says, except within the last month when he heard him to speak on the matrimonial contract and the aforesaid carnal knowledge. Questioned on the second article, he says that William de Bridsall, for anything this witness ever knew or heard - except that on the day of All Saints last he saw him so drunk that he was not able to go by himself from the place where he was to his lodging except with the aid of this witness and others - is of sound mind and thus having sufficient natural discretion, the reputation of this witness thus provided, just as this witness holds, who as this witness believes offered his true testimony without any promise or gift given or made by the said Alice or her party in the present cause. And he says that the said William is reputed faithful, of good fame and reputation for his state, who

---

mente captus *lit. "seized mind," a phrase used to denote mental impairment*

vel testmonium perhibendus in presentem causam vel aliqua alia et dicit quod bene audivit loqui de dicto Thomas quod est serviens patris sui et fidelis homo et pro talibus dicti William et Thomas habentur et reputantur.

Johannes Dogeson de Scamston etatis lvii annos servus domini de Latymer ac servilis conditionis [...] non affectans ut dicit victoriam plus pro parte dicte Alicie quam pro parte dicte Johannes iure et extra super premissis. Super primo articulo requisatus dicit quod novit testes in eosdem descriptos pro fidelibus hominibus et bone fame et pro talibus sunt habiti et publice reputati in parochia de Rillyngton et locis vicinis. Item dicit quod Alicia de Redyng die festi sancti Johannis Apostoli et Evangeli infra octavo Nativitatis Domini ulterioribus preteritis sicut iste iure venit cum eadem de Malton usque Scamston narravit sic quod Johannes Boton et ipsam fuerant conventi ita quod debet habere eam in uxorem. [...] Item dicit quod dictam festem Purificatione Beate Virginis ulterioribus preteritis dictus Thomas Fouler narravit isti iurato quod audivit et presens fuit quod dictus Johannes affidavit dictam Aliciam et William de Bridsall prius dictam festem Purificatione hoc idem retulit isti iurato duodecies ut credere et habere quod dictus William fuit †itenus et bene mane† et dicit in iuramenta sua quod antequam dicti Thomas et William retulerunt premissa iste iurato audivit famam super hoc contractu matrimoniali inter ipsas partes habiti laboravit inter amicos et cognatos ipsius Johannis [...] Item dicit quod dictus William de Bridsall est pauper sed valde fidelis qui ut dicit iste iure non potuit induci aliqualiter ad deierandum in presenti sive absque alia causa nec ut dicit pro aliquo quod ipse iuratus unquam scivit vel audivit fuit corruptus et instructus ad deponendum in presenti causam prout deponet, et est ut dicit in statu suo homo bone fame sane mentis sufficientem habens discretionem naturalem nisi sit inebriatus se servisia et hoc contigit valde raro. Item dicit quod dictus Thomas Fouler de eadem est homo valde bone fame sufficientem habens in bonis vel ad valorum

according to the knowledge of this witness will not be induced to taking an oath or presenting testimony for anything in the present cause or any other, and he says he well heard it said that the said Thomas is the servant of his father and a faithful man, and for such the said William and Thomas are held and reputed.

John Dogeson de Scameston, fifty-seven years and servant of the Lord Latymer and of servile condition [...] not affecting as he says victory for the part of the said Alice over the part of the said John, a supplementary witness to the premises. Questioned on the first article, he says that he knew the witnesses in the same described for faithful men and of good fame, and for such they are held and publicly reputed in the parish of Rillyngton and nearby places. Likewise he says that Alice Redyng, on the day of the feast of St John the Apostle and Evangelist, within the octave of Christmas last, as this witness came with her from Malton to Scameston, told him that John Boton and herself were of the agreement so that he ought to have her as wife. [He saw John and Alice naked in bed together. Alice told him they were married, but John denied it.] Likewise he says that on the said feast of the Purification of the Blessed Virgin last the said Thomas Fouler told this witness that he heard and was present when the said John swore to the said Alice, and William de Bridsall before the said feast of the Purification told this witness the same a dozen times, as he believes and holds that the said William was going and well remaining, and he says in his judgement that before the said Thomas and William related the premises this witness heard the fame of the matrimonial contract had between the parties laboured among the friends and acquaintences of John [...] Likewise he says that the said William de Bridsall is a pauper but is very faithful, who as this witness says could not be induced in any way to perjure in the present or any other cause just as he deposed, and William is, as he says, for his status a man of good fame and of sound mind, having sufficient natural discre-

sex marciarum et amplius et pro talibus sunt dicti William et Thomas habenti et publice reputati ut dicit. [...]

Thomas Megson de Scameston servilis conditionis etatis xl annos iure et extra super premissis, dicit quod non initium advertebat ad fama laboravit super dictum contractum matrimonialem. [...] Item dicit quod William de Bridsall est pauper sed reputata fidelis homo et bone conversationis ac honeste nisi sit aliquam qui est ebrius et homo non contingit nisi magnis festis. Item dicit quod Thomas Fouler similiter est homo bone fame, fidelis ac honeste conversatione, habens in bonis usque quattuor, quinque, ut sex marciarum et pro talibus sunt dicti William et Thomas habenti et publice reputati. [...]

Dominus Robertus filius Martini cappellanus consanguineus Alicie in quarto gradu consanguinitatis affectans victoriam pro parte eiusdem qualiter habet iusticiam ut dicit. [...]

tion unless he is drunk with wine and that happens very rarely. Likewise he says that the said Thomas Fouler de Scameston is a man of very good fame, having sufficient in goods to the value of six marks or more, and for such reasons are the said William and Thomas held and publicly reputed as he says.

Thomas Megson de Scameston, of servile condition, aged forty years, a supplementary witness to the premises, says that he did not in the beginning turn his attention to the fame that laboured on the said matrimonial contract. Likewise he says that William de Bridsall is a pauper but reputed a faithful man and of good conduct and honest, except largely if he is a drunk man and it does not happen except on the great feasts. Likewise he says that Thomas Fouler is similarly a man of good fame, faithful and of honest conduct, having in goods up to four, five, or six marks, and for such reasons the said William and Thomas are held and publicly reputed.

Lord Robert, the son of Martin, chaplain, consanguineous to Alice in the fourth degree of consanguinity, desiring vistory for the part of the same because she has justice as he says. [Membrane heavily damaged, appears to say nothing regarding William de Bridsall.]

Membrane 4(b) verso
Second Deposition of William de Bridsall
Undated

Qui tempore estivali et autumpnali querit victua sua ex opera manorum suarum et aliis temporibus non.

Qui non potuit laborare propter frigiditatem mendicat ostiatim.

Membrane 3 recto
Deposition of Alice Redyng
March 22, 1367

[...]

Item an Thomas Fouler fuerat auctor, fautor, vel promotor causae pro parte dicte Alicie contra Johannem Boton. Dicit quod non.

Item an William de Bridsall hostiatim mendicet panem suum et mendicare consuevit ante et post tempus depositionis sue.

Membrane 4(b) verso
Second Deposition of William de Bridsall
Undated

He in summer and autumn seeks his bread from the work of his hands and at other times not.

He was not able to labour because of the coldness, and he begs door to door.

Membrane 3 recto
Deposition of Alice Redyng
March 22, 1367

[Alice questioned if she is of servile status. She was, but now is free.]

Likewise, whether Thomas Fouler was the author, patron, or promotor of the cause of the said Alice against John Boton. She says not.

Dicit quod aliquando operatur et aliquod mendicet.

Item an dictus William fuerat tempore depositionis sue ac ante et post levis opinionis vel male fame. Dicit quod est fame bone.

Item an idem William sit vel fuerat tempore depositionis sue mente captus vel quasi adeo quidem naturalem discretionem non habebat. Dicit quod habet et habuit discretionem sufficientem ad perhibendum testimonium veritatem.

Item an Thomas et William testes praedicti affectarant et affectant victoriam in causa contra dictum Johannem Boton. Respondeat lex Marcellus.°

Likewise, whether William de Bridsall begs his bread door-to-door and was accustomed to beg before and after the time of his deposition. She says that sometimes he works and sometimes he begs.

Likewise, whether the said William was at the time of his deposition and before and after it of light opinion or bad fame. She says that he is of good fame.

Likewise, whether the same William is or was at the time of his deposition *mente captus*° or as it were indeed truly did not have natural discretion. She says that he has and had sufficient discretion to present true testimony.

Likewise whether Thomas and William, the aforesaid witnesses, desired and desire victory in the cause against John Boton. Let the Lex Marcellus° answer.

Membrane 4, recto and verso
Deposition of John Boton
March 22, 1367

Interrogetur Johannes Boton de Scamston an unccuam carnaliter cognovit Aliciam de Redyng. Dicit quod sit.

Item interrogetur idem Johannem quo tempore prefata Alicia ultimo carnaliter cognovit. Dicit quod non cognovit circa festem Pascalem ultimis preteritis et mulier dicit non die dominica ad noctem proximam post festem purificationis ultimo preteritis fuit unus annus elapsus ultimo cognovit eam carnaliter.

Item interrogetur idem Johannem an circa festem purificationis beate Marie virginis ultimo preteritis fuit unus annus elapsus carnaliter cognovit Aliciam supradictam. Dicit quod non.

Item dicit quod pater Alicie de Redyng fuit servus domini de Latymer et moriebatur in magna pestilencia° hunc ad xvi annos vel amplius et credit quod si mater dictae Alicie non esset coniugata esset libera et nescit se dicta Alicia sit liberata vel ancilla.

Membrane 4, recto and verso
Deposition of John Boton
March 22, 1367

Let John Boton of Scameston be interrogated whether he ever knew Alice Redyng. He says he may have.

Likewise, let the same John be interrogated at what time he last carnally knew the aforesaid Alice. He says he did not know her around Easter last year. He knew the woman carnally around the Feast of the Purification last year, and he says not on the Sunday night closest to the feast of the Purification last. It has been one year passed since he knew her carnally.

Likewise, let the same John be interrogated whether around the feast of the Purification of the Blessed Virgin Mary last year it was one year passed since he knew the above-said Alice carnally. He says not.

Likewise he says that the father of Alice Redyng was a servant of the Lord Latymer and died in the great pestilence here more than sixteen years ago, and he believes that if the mother of the said Alice was not married

---

Lex Marcellus *probably a reference to Justinian's Digest*   magna pestilencia *the Black Death*   mente captus *lit. "seized mind," a phrase used to denote mental impairment*

Interrogetur an uncquam promissit ducere dictam Aliciam in uxorem. Dixit non et quod nuncquam contraxit cum ea.

Interrogetur dictus quod numcquam audivit loqui de servitute vel libertate dicte Alicie antequam fuit propositum in lecto isto dicit et quod fuerit reputata servilis conditionis apud Scameston per xiiii annos per quod tempus iste iure novit eam. Interrogatus dicit quod ipse melius credidit quod fuit servilis conditionis suis per dictos xiiii annos quam libere eo quod pater eiusdem fuit servilis conditionis.

then she was free, and he does not know if the said Alice herself is free or a maidservant.

Let him be asked whether he ever promised to take the said Alice as wife. He says not and that he never contracted marriage with her.

The said John, interrogated, says that he never heard the servitude or liberty of the said Alice spoken of before he was laid in bed, and that she was reputed to be of servile condition in Scameston for fourteen years, throughout the time this witness knew her. He says when asked that he he believed very well that she was of servile condition through the fourteen years rather than free because her father was of servile condition.

Membrane 12 verso
Second Deposition of Thomas Fouler
April 8, 1367

Thomas Fouler iuratus et repetitus ex officio tuum dixit quod cum semel audivit verba matromoniale proferri inter partes de quibus agitur et concordat de verba sicut [a??] deponet et quod sedentes erant partes tempore presentationis dictorum verborum et quod est aliqui presentes tunc quod sciat et quod William de Bridsall et homo fidelis et bone fama et pro Thomas est habitus et reputat. [...]

Membrane 12 verso
Second Deposition of Thomas Fouler
April 8, 1367

Thomas Fouler, called to witness again and demanded back by the Official said that, although he heard once the matrimonial words exchanged between the parties concerning whom this cause is moved, he agrees on the words just as he deposed, and because those seated were parties at the time of the presentation of his words and because in some way he was present then because he knows, and because William de Bridsall is a trustworthy man and of good fame, and to Thomas he was so considered and reputed. [The public fame labours on the contract.]

Membrane 6 verso
Sentence
April 9, 1367

In dei nomine amen. Auditis et intellectis meritis cause matrimoniali mote et pendente coram nobis Domini Officere Curia Ebor commissare generali inter Aliciam Redyng de Scameston primo personaliter et postmodo per Magistrum Henricum de Haxholme clericum procuratorem suum in presenti causa libere constitutam partem accretionem ex parte una, et Johannem Boton Chapman de Scameston primo personaliter et postmodum per Magistrum Johannem de Stanton cleri-

Membrane 6 verso
Sentence
April 9, 1367

In the name of God, amen. Having heard and understood the merits of the matrimonial cause moved and pending in our presence, the Lord Official of the York Curia, commissioner general, between Alice Redyng de Scameston, at first personally, and later through Master Henry de Haxholme, her clerk procurator in the present cause, freely constituted for the party gathered from one party, and John Boton de Scameston, Chapman, at first personally, and later through

53

cum procuratorem suum in dicta causa libere constitutum partem ream ex altera comparentes oblato libello eo qui sequuntur sub tenore. In dei nomine amen. [...] Nos commissare antedictus iuratis et plene discussis ipsibus cause †veritatis† invocata spiritus gratia ad summam diffinitivam procedimus in hunc modum. Quia [[]] dictam partem intentionem suam coram nobis in iudicis deductam sufficienter probavisse prefatum Johannem eidem Alicie in uxorem sive legitimum adiudicamus ipsumque Johannem ad solempnizandum matrimonium in facio ecclesie ut moris est cum dicta Alicia canonice compellendum et cohabitendum fore [[]] in hiis scriptis. Recta et lata fuit ista sententia per dominum commissare.

Master John de Stanton, his clerk procurator in the said cause, freely constituted for the guilty party from others appearing in the petition presented to him who follows under the law. [...] We the aforesaid commissioner, with these things having been sworn and clearly discussed in the cause of truth with the spirit of grace invoked, proceed to the definitive summary in this way. Because [...] the said part to have proved their intention in our presence sufficiently from the summons of the judge, we assign the aforesaid John to the same Alice for his wife or legitimate spouse and that John to the solemnization of their matrimony in the presence of the church, as is the custom, with the said Alice, for compelling him according to Church discipline and for cohabitation in the same dwelling [...] in these written documents. This sentence was proper and broad from the Lord Commissioner.

Endnotes

1   *Redyng c. Boton.* York, England. Borthwick Institute for Archives. CP E.92. It consists of fifteen membranes of varying sizes. The membranes are numbered, but are not arranged chronologically. There is no m. 3, and two membranes are marked "4". In this edition I have numbered the first m. 4 and the second m. 4(b) for clarity. The text as I have presented it here is in chronological order. I have chosen to normalize all proper names for ease of comprehension. Abbreviations are silently expanded and unreadable passages are marked with standard sigla: †...† indicates a passage where the meaning is unclear from the Latin, while [[...]] indicates a passage where the maniscript is damaged or otherwise unreadable.

2   Richard Helmholz, *Marriage Litigation in Medieval England* (Cambridge University Press, 1974), p. 29.

Mental Competency Inquisitions from Medieval England[1] (ca. late 12th c.–early 15th c.)

Contributed by Eliza Buhrer

Introduction

The records below are culled from hundreds of inquisitions involving alleged "idiots" and their land held between the thirteenth and sixteenth centuries in England. During the mid-thirteenth century, the English royal courts began to oversee inquisitions aimed at assessing the mental competency of people accused of being "idiots" (*idiota* in Latin), and "natural fools." While there was no standard set of practices for handling these cases, in most instances, an alleged *idiota*'s interactions with the law began when Chancery received a request to examine them, generally after they inherited or alienated land. These requests could be made by anyone who could pay the requisite fees, but frequently came from people who hoped to be appointed custodians of the alleged's estate. Once Chancery received a request, it sent a writ to officials in the accused's town, village, or county, asking them to assess whether the allegations were true, and report back. If the officials determined that the person in question seemed to be an *idiota* after conducting an examination or simply asking people in their community about their condition, the Crown would take their land into the king's hand, and grant their wardship—the right to manage and profit from their estates for the duration of their lives, paired with responsibility for their care—to people outside their line of hereditary succession. These practices remained largely unchanged until the Court of Wards began to handle cases involving so-called "idiots" in the early sixteenth century.

The records of these cases are significant to both the histories of disability and law because they document the earliest systematic mental competency examinations held in Europe. They also marked the first time the law distinguished between *idiota*, who lacked the capacity for self-governance from birth, and temporarily mentally incompetent people (*non compos mentis* in Latin), who lacked it because of temporary illness or injury. Thirteenth-century legal treatises like the *Prerogative Regis*, *Fleta*, and *Britton* asserted that "fools and idiots" differed from people with other mental disorders because their condition was present at birth, permanent, and uninterrupted by moments of lucidity. They then used this permanence to justify treating them differently than other categories of mentally impaired individuals. Specifically, the Crown could not profit from the lands of people suffering from temporary mental illnesses, but had the right to profit from the estates of people found to be "idiots" for the duration of their lives.

It is unclear why the royal courts began to administer inquisitions involving alleged "idiots." Ostensibly, it was to prevent their lands from "being wasted or alienated" to the disparagement of their heirs, as noted in the case of Nicholas, son of the earl of Dessemond, below. By granting such individuals' wardships to people outside their line of succession, the Crown theoretically ensured that people without the capacity to manage their own affairs would not be taken advantage of by less than scrupulous relatives.

Yet in practice, the Crown often chose their guardians for reasons other than concern for their well-being. In some instances, like those of Andrew le Merk and William Berchaud, the Crown gifted wardships to its servants to reward their loyalty. Later, it treated wardships as a saleable commodity, a practice that frequently led to protest from the accused's relatives, less than pleased to see land leave their family's control.

In light of the fact that the Crown had financial incentives to confirm allegations of "idiocy," one question we should ask when reading these cases is whether the people identified as "idiots" by the royal courts would have met our criteria for intellectual disability. It is tempting to make this assumption, since if we assume that the people identified as "idiots" were actually intellectually disabled, then the records of their inquisitions present the tantalizing possibility of accessing the lived experiences of people otherwise absent from the historical record. That said, there are reasons to be cautious about conflating legal terminology with medical reality.

History demonstrates that legal terminology frequently fails to reflect reality beyond the courtroom. Today, people who meet the clinical requirements for mental illness often fail to meet the legal requirements for the insanity defense, and of course, the women identified as witches in the courts of Early Modern Europe did not actually commune with the devil. However, like many women accused of "idiocy" in medieval England, they possessed land without male guardians and enjoyed a relatively high degree of legal and economic autonomy. Scholarship on the early modern Court of Wards has also emphasized that the Crown's ability to profit from the sale of wardships created a strong incentive for it to identify mentally competent individuals as incompetent, and there is no reason not to be similarly cynical when considering the Crown's motives in medieval "idiocy" inquisitions. Finally, the royal courts only involved themselves in matters concerning alleged "idiots" when the individuals in question possessed landed wealth, so the people subject to these inquisitions did not reflect the full set of people born with intellectual disabilities in medieval England. Instead, all we can know for certain is that they represented the set of people who possessed land and were deemed poorly suited to the task of managing it by people who felt they had something to gain by accusing them of "idiocy."

People ultimately accused others of "idiocy" for a variety of reasons. William de Aston, for instance, claimed that he had been declared an *idiota* on account of the "malicious suit of certain enemies." Similarly, Adam le Gayte, the king's watchmen, requested that the court find William Berchaud to be an *idiota* and grant him his wardship, just as William was about to inherit the estate of his uncle John Danethorp, also an *idiota*, whose wardship Adam had held prior to his death. The officials who examined William undoubtedly had an incentive to support his claim, since Adam was a favored servant of the king, who had held John's wardship by the "king's gift," and he claimed that without William's wardship, he would be unable to support himself. More broadly, the initial findings of these inquisitions were frequently overturned, and even when they were upheld there was no consistent criteria for determining whether someone was an *idiota*. For even as legal treatises held that "idiocy" was a permanent and congenital condition, many of the people accused of "idiocy" had previously been mentally competent, like Robert de Corbrigg who became an *idiota* only after going to Oxford, or Margery Anlauby, who was declared an *idiota* after the death of her husband.

Nevertheless, whether the legal "idiots" of medieval England were intellectually disabled or not, the records of their inquisitions offer insight into how mental incompetency was defined and treated before intellectual disability emerged as a medical category during the early modern period.

Bibliography

Buhrer, Eliza. "Law and Mental Competency in Late Medieval England." *Reading Medieval Studies*, vol. XL, 2014, pp. 82–100.

———. "But what is to be said of a fool? Intellectual Disability in Medieval Thought and Culture." *Mental Health, Spirituality, and Religion in the Middle Ages and Early Modern Period*, edited by Albrecht Classen, Fundamentals of Medieval and Early Modern Culture. Walter de Gruyter, 2014, pp. 314–43.

Metzler, Irina. "Non-consenting Adults: Laws and Intellectual Disability." *Fools and Idiots? Intellectual Disability in the Middle Ages.* Manchester University Press, 2016, pp. 140–83.

Neugebauer, Richard. "Mental Handicap in Medieval and Early Modern England: Criteria, Measurement, and Care." *From Idiocy to Mental Deficiency: Historical Perspectives on People with Learning Disabilities*, edited by Anne Digby and David Wright, Routledge Studies in the History of Medicine. Routledge, 1996, pp. 22–44.

Parkin, Kate. "Tales of Idiots Signifying Something: Evidence of Process in the Inquisitions *Post Mortem*." *The Fifteenth Century Inquisitions Postmortem: A Companion*, edited by Michael Hicks. Boydell and Brewer, 2013, pp. 79–97.

Roffe, David, and Christina Roffe. "Madness and Care in the Community: A Medieval Perspective." *British Medical Journal*, vol. 311, no. 7021, 1995, pp. 1708–12.

Turner, Wendy. *Care and Custody of the Mentally Ill, Incompetent, and Disabled in Medieval England*, Cursor Mundi 16. Brepols, 2013.

———. "Defining Mental Afflictions in Medieval English Administrative Records." *Disability and Medieval Law: History, Literature, and Society*, edited by Cory James Rushton. Cambridge Scholars Publishing, 2013, pp. 134–56.

———. "Town and Country: A Comparison of the Treatment of the Mentally Disabled in Late Medieval English Common Law and Chartered Boroughs." *Madness in Medieval Law and Custom*, edited by Wendy Turner. Brill, 2010, pp. 17–38.

———. "Silent Testimony: Emotional Displays and Lapses in Memory as Indicators of Mental Instability in Medieval English Investigations." *Madness in Medieval Law and Custom*, edited by Wendy Turner. Brill, 2010, pp. 81–96.

"Idiocy" in *Britton*[2] (ca. 1290)

And whereas it sometimes happens that the heir is an idiot from his birth whereby he is incapable of taking care of his inheritance, we will that such heirs, of whomsoever they hold, and whether they be male or female, remain in our custody, with all their inheritances, saving to every lord all other services° belonging to him for lands held of him, and that they so remain in our wardship as long as they continue in their idiocy. But this rule shall not hold with regard to those who become insane by any sickness.

Mental Incompetency in the *Prerogativa Regis*[3] (ca. 1324)

The King shall have custody of the lands of natural fools°[4] taking the profits of them without waste or destruction, and shall find them their necessaries from whose fee soever the lands be holden; and after the death of such idiots he should render [it] to the rightful heirs, so that such fools shall not alien,° nor their heirs be disinherited. Also, the King shall provide, when anyone who previously had memory and understanding should become of unsound mind as certain people are through lucid intervals° that their lands and tenements may be safely protected, without waste and destruction, and that they and their household may live and be reasonably sustained from the profits of the same, and the residue beyond their sustenance be preserved for their use, to be delivered to them when they regain their memory so that such lands and tenements shall in no way be aliened within the aforesaid time; The king should not take anything from the profits for his own use, and if the party should die in such a state, then the residue° should be distributed for his soul at the advice of an ordinary.

Andrew le Merk, an "Idiot of Unsound Mind" Entrusted to the King's Tailor[5] (1285)

To the justices in eyre° in co. Essex. As the king is given to understand that Andrew le Merk is an idiot and of unsound mind,[6] so that he is incapable of administering his lands and goods, the king orders the justices to cause Andrew to come before them in their eyre, and to examine him carefully, and if it appear clearly to them that he has been an idiot from his birth and is still, so that the custody of his body and lands ought to pertain to the king, they are to deliver such custody to Adynettus, the king's tailor, to be held during the king's pleasure,° so that he may cause suitable necessaries to be administered to Andrew, his wife, and his household.

William Berchaud, The Nephew of an "Idiot," Accused of "Idiocy" by the Man who Held his Uncle's Wardship[7] (1302)

2 August 1302. Westminster. Commission of enquiry to the escheator° north of the Trent to discover whether William Berchot is an idiot. By petition of council.

Writ to the escheator to enquire whether the said William is an idiot or not &c. 2 Aug. 30 Edw. I. Cumberland. Inquisition° made at Carlisle on Tuesday before St. Matthew, 30 Edw. I.

Alenburgh. The jury know nothing of the person of the said William or whether he is an idiot or not because they have never seen him for he has dwelt in Holdernesse since his birth, but they have heard say that he has been

---

services *feudal services* **natural fools** *fools from birth* **alien** *transfer property* **lucid intervals** *periods of mental competence* **residue** *remaining profits* **eyre** *a circuit court presided over by an itinerant justice* **during...pleasure** *an indefinite length of time* **escheator** *a royal official who handled transfers of property to the Crown* **Inquisition** *an inquiry*

an idiot from his birth. John de Danethorp who was an idiot from his birth, was uncle of the said William, and the said William, son of Alice his sister, and Joan, daughter of Margery another sister, who is of full age and discretion,° are his next heirs. The king committed to Adam le Wayte the wardship of the said John's lands in Alenburgh, which by his death have been taken into the king's hand, viz.—a messuage,° 145a. land, 14½ bovates let to farm to divers tenants, a toft° and 1 bovate° of land which were of John Ravene, 14½a. meadow, rents of cottars° and herbage° in a place called Alenbank, a custom called 'breumale,' a water-mill, and works, held of Sir Thomas de Lucy by cornage° and service of 5s. yearly.

York. Inquisition made at Hedone on Thursday the eve of St. Bartholomew, 30 Edw. I. Outteneuton. The said William is an idiot from his birth. He holds 12l. of land, of the inheritance of Geoffrey Berchaude his father, of the king in chief,° as of the honour of Albemarle, by knight's service, which John Berchaud holds by the king's commission for the sustenance of the said William, rendering 12 marks yearly at the king's exchequer.°

Danthorp. The said William, son of Alice one of the sisters of John de Danthorp, and Joan, daughter of Margery another sister, who is of discretion, are heirs of the said John, and by his death have in Danthorp 7 bovates and two parts of a bovate of land, a moiety of a close° containing 2a., tofts called Abbitoft and Dundraghecroft, and tofts and land held by divers tenants (named), held of

the king in chief as of the honour of Albemarle, service unspecified; also a capital messuage containing 4a., a moiety of a close called Milnecroft, 8 bovates of land, and a toft and 2a. land which William the smith holds, held of the provost of Beverley, rendering 10s. yearly; and a toft containing 3½a., held of John de Melsa rendering 10s. yearly. All the above have been in the king's hand from the day of St. Nicholas last, by the death of the said John de Danethorp.

Memorandum (from the escheator?)° that he has personally examined the said William and finds that he is manifestly an idiot, and has been so from his birth, nor does he enjoy lucid intervals,° but, as he has heard, at lunations° is worse and raves with madness. (*Undated.*)

Petition to the king from Adam le Gayt to grant him what William Berchot is heir of, for what he had of the other fool his uncle has been loyally expended in the king's service, and he cannot otherwise maintain his estate.

Margery de Anlauby, who became an "Idiot" after the Death of her Husband[9] (1279 and 1289)

Writ of certiorari° to Thomas de Normanvill, the king's steward, 9 Sept. 7 Edw. I.

York. *Inq.* The octave of St. Michael, 7 Edw. I.
Anlauby. Land (unspecified), worth 13 marks yearly, excepting 4s. held of the abbot of St. Mary's, York, by service of 2 marks

---

full...discretion *the age of legal adulthood*   **messuage** *a dwelling with outbuildings and land*   **toft** *site of a house*   **bovate** *the amount of land that could be ploughed by one ox, usually 15–20 acres*   **cottars** *tenant farmers*   **herbage** *pasture land*   **cornage** *payment on beasts at 2 pence per head*   **of...chief** *land held directly from the king*   **exchequer** *government office responsible for royal finance*   **moiety...close** *portion of land*   **escheator** *a royal official who handled transfers of property to the Crown*   **lucid intervals** *periods of sanity*   **lunations** *the period of time from one new moon to the next, referencing the contemporary belief that mental competency waxed and waned with the moon's cycles*   **Writ of certiorari** *written order to review a previous finding*

yearly as a free farmer for all services, excepting two suits at the abbot's court on reasonable summons; and the said Margery fell ill a fortnight° before the Purification last and is so infirm that she is not of sound mind; after which date came Robert de Stotevyll of Cotingham, of whom the said Margery held nothing,° and without any authority took away John her son and heir, and still unjustly detains him.

Writ of certiorari,° concerning the state of the said Margery, whose custody with that of her lands and goods the king sometime committed to William de Beverlaco, deceased, 25 May, 17 Edw. I.

York. *Inq.* Tuesday after Holy Trinity, 17 Edw. I.

The said Margery is an idiot, not from her birth, but she has been so continuously since the death of her husband nine years ago. William de Beverlaco had her wardship and that of her lands, viz.—of 10½ bovates° for eight years, and similarly for a year of 4 bovates which she had by escheat° by the death of Alan le Moyn of Hesel; she had also 25s. 3d. rent of assize,° and 5s. from cottages; out of all which she paid 2 marks yearly to the abbot of St. Mary's, York, and, by the grant of her father, 10s. to Josiana her sister, a nun in Swyn, as long as she should live. All the goods arising from the said lands beyond the sustenance of the said Margery, her four children, and household, came to the said William.

The Children of Geoffrey Berthald, All "Idiots" of "Unsound Mind"[10] (1290)

January 24, Westminster. To Thomas de Normanvill, escheator° beyond Trent. Order to deliver to John Berthald of Holdernesse the custody of the lands that belonged to Geoffrey Berthald, tenant in chief, in Out Newton in Holdernesse, as it is testified before the king that Geoffrey's children are idiots and of unsound mind, so that they are insufficient for the rule of themselves and their things and the lands of Geoffrey, which are in the king's hands by reason of his death, and the king, wishing to provide for the estate of the children lest dilapidation of the lands should be made by their ignorance and fatuity, has granted the custody of the lands to John Berthald during pleasure, so that he may maintain the children reasonably in all necessaries and shall render to the king 10 marks yearly for so long as he shall have the custody, and shall cause Juliana, Geoffrey's daughter, when she come to marriageable years, if she be fit for marriage,° to be married out of the issues of the lands, the costs whereof the king will cause to be allowed to him in payment of the ferm.°

Joan de la Chaumbre, Found to be an "Idiot" by a Corrupt Escheator[11] (1316)

October 12, 1316, York. To Master John Walewayn, escheator beyond Trent. Order to restore to Joan de la Chaumbre of Whittukkesmed her lands, and the issues of the same, which were taken into the king's hands° by John Abel, late escheator beyond Trent, who delivered them to the present escheator, pretending that they were in the king's hands by

---

fortnight *two weeks*   **held nothing** *was not his tenant*   **Writ of certiorari** *written order to review a previous finding*   **bovates** *the amount of land that could be plowed by one ox, usually 15-20 acres*   **by escheat** *property that reverted to the Crown in the absence of legal heirs*   **rent of assize** *a fixed rent*   **escheator** *a royal official who handled transfers of property to the Crown*   **fit for marriage** *legally able to marry; "Idiots" were not able to marry because they lacked the capacity to consent*   **ferm** *tax*   **taken... hands** *taken into the custody of the Crown*

reason of the madness of Joan, as it appeared by inquisition taken by John Abel that she was an idiot and mad woman, the present escheator° having returned that he had gone in person, by virtue of the king's order, to her place of residence, and that he had seen and examined her, and that he found that she was not an idiot and had not been at any time from her birth.

Writ of plenius certiorari,° the (late) escheator having returned that the lands &c. of the said Joan were in the king's hand by reason of her idiocy, 4 May, 9 Edw. II. *Endorsed by the escheator, that he cannot find any cause in her for being reputed an idiot.*

Somerset. Inquisition. Friday after SS. 9 Edward II.

The said Joan is not an idiot nor ever has been.

Whittokesmede. A messuage,° ½a. meadow, 18a. arable, and 2a. wood, descended to her after her father's death, and are held of Elias Cotel, knight, by service of ½d., and suit at his court of Camelerton.

Alexander Tothe, who Lost his Memory on Account of "Malign Spirits"[12] (1318)

October 26, York. To Master Richard de Clare, escheator beyond Trent. Order to cause John de Northgrave, son and heir of Alfred de Northgrave, tenant in chief of the late king, to have seisin° of his father's lands, as he proved his age before Master John Walewayn, late escheator beyond Trent, and the king has taken his homage.

To Robert de Sapy, escheator this side Trent. Order to deliver to John de Yucflete and Joan his wife, mother of Alexander Tothe, son and heir of James Tothe of Middelton, the lands of the said Alexander, which cannot descend to them by right of inheritance, as his nearest friends for his maintenance and profit, the escheator having taken the lands into the king's hands° because he understood that Alexander was a madman and an idiot from his birth, as the king learns by inquisition taken by the escheator that Alexander is not an idiot from birth, that he was of good memory for three years after his birth, and that he was afterwards impaired by malign spirits so that he lost his memory for two years, after which time he recovered his good state, so that he was sufficient for the rule of himself and his lands and chattels had he been of full age, and that he enjoys lucid intervals°[13] in the new moon, and that he holds lands in Middelton of divers lords by various services, and that he does not hold of the king,° and that he is aged fourteen years.

Robert, Son of Hugh, Son of Ascelin de Corbrigg, who became an "Idiot" after going to Oxford[14] (1333)

Writ to the escheator to enquire whether the said Robert is an idiot, and whether he has alienated any lands, &c., 23 May, 6 Edward III.

August 20, Stow Park, 1333.

To John de Louthre, escheator in cos. York, Northumberland, Cumberland and Westmorland.

Order not to intermeddle with two messuages, 30 acres of land and 4s. rent in Corbrigg, which he had taken into the king's hand because of the idiocy of Robert son of Hugh son of Ascelin de Corbrigg, restoring

---

escheator *a royal official who handled transfers of property to the Crown*   Writ...certiorari *order to conduct a second inquest*   messuage *a dwelling with outbuildings and land*   seisin *legal possession*   taken... hands *taken into the Crown's custody*   lucid intervals *periods of mental competence*   hold...king *hold land directly from the king. Initially, the royal courts only oversaw inquisitions involving allegations of mental incompetence that involved the Crown's tenants in chief*

the issues,° but to permit the near friends of Robert, to whom the said tenements ought not to descend or remain, to have the custody of them, so that they may answer for the issues thereof for the benefit of Robert, as the king has learned by inquisition taken by that escheator° that the said Robert is an idiot, of unsound mind, and unfit to govern himself or his lands and goods, and that he was not an idiot from his birth but only for the last 16 years, and that he enjoys no lucid intervals,° and that the said messuages, lands and rent which Hugh son of Ascelin gave to the said Robert his son and to William, Robert's brother, deceased, and the heirs of their bodies, with reversion to the said Hugh and his heirs, are held of Henry de Percy by the service of rendering 11s. 7d. to him yearly.

Writ to the escheator to enquire whether the said Robert is an idiot, and whether he has alienated° any lands, &c., 23 May, 6 Edward III.

Northumberland. Inq. 10 June, 6 Edward III.

The said Robert is an idiot, but was not so from his birth, for 17 years ago he left Corbrigg for Oxford of sound mind and memory, and when he returned 16 years ago he was an idiot, and from that time has remained so, and has not enjoyed lucid intervals, and if he alienated any lands, he did so in that state. The aforesaid Hugh son of Ascelin, father of the said Robert, gave two messuages, 30a. land, and 4s. rent in Correbrigg to the said Robert and William his brother, to hold to them and the heirs of their bodies, with reversion to himself and his heirs, which William died ten years ago: the said tenements are held of Henry de Percy by service of 11s. 7d.

William, son of Hugh de Correbrigg, and John, son of Thomas de Wytton, are next heirs in blood to the said Robert, and of full age. The said Robert was examined in person by the escheator in the presence of the jury.

Thomas heir of Griffin de Grenestede, Found to be Sane because he Could Count Money and Measure Cloth[15] (1341)

11 May, 15 Edward III. Writ to the escheator in cos. Southampton, Bedford etc. to enquire whether the said Thomas is an idiot, and whether he has alienated a great portion of his lands and tenements in Kerdyngton, co. Bedford, or not, and who is his heir etc. 11 May, 15 Edward III.

Endorsed by the escheator that he went in person to Kerdyngton and examined the said Thomas in every way he could as to his state, and that he found him of good mind and sane memory in word and deed, counting money, measuring cloth° and doing all other things.

John atte Berton, Who Lost his Memory from Terror and Grief[16] (1345)

November 17. 1345. Westminster.

To John de Mussenden. Order to restore to John atte Berton his lands, together with the issues thereof, and not to intermeddle° further therewith, as on it being found by inquisition taken by Thomas de Aspale, escheator in co. Southampton, that John was an idiot, the king caused his lands to be taken so that they should not suffer dilapidation and granted them to Thomas de Mussenden for rendering a certain thing at the exchequer and finding John's maintenance, and John afterwards beseeching the king to order those lands to be restored to him, as he is of sound mind and was so before the taking of the inquisition, the king ordered the eschea-

---

issues *profits from the estate*   escheator *royal official who handled transfers of property to the Crown*   lucid intervals *periods of mental competence*   alienated *sold or given away*   counting...cloth *customary markers of legal majority for burgesses' sons*   intermeddle *interfere*

tor° to take an inquisition upon the matter, by which it is found that John was of sound mind from his infancy to the completion of twenty-one years of age and more, having no hope of idiocy, but by the great terror and grief caused by the death of James atte Berton, his father, he has lost much of his memory and has remained almost without memory for three years, although he enjoys certain lucid intervals,° so that he was reputed an idiot at that time, but afterwards he regained his health and has preserved a good memory for more than the last five years and is at present of sound mind and not an idiot.

Nov. 18. Westminster.

To the treasurer and barons of the exchequer. Order to discharge Thomas de Mussenden of 61s. 1d., as on its being found by inquisition taken by Thomas de Aspale, escheator in co. Southampton, that John atte Berton was an idiot, the king caused his lands in Wotton and Oklee to be taken into his hands, which were worth 101s. 1d. yearly beyond the rents and services due thereon by extent made by the escheator, and on 8 March last the king committed them to Thomas de Mussenden for rendering 61s. 1d. yearly at the exchequer, wishing the remaining 40s. to be reserved for John's maintenance, and afterwards the king ordered Thomas to restore those lands to John and not to intermeddle° further therewith.

John de Heton, who had a "Fancy in his Head"[17] (1353–1354)

Writ of plenius certiorari° to William de Notton, William de Fyncheden, John de Bollyng and John de Upton to ascertain whether John de Heton is an idiot or not. 4 July, 27 Edward III.

Writ of venire facias° to the sheriff of York to summon a jury, 4 July, 27 Edward III.

Jury panel, Doncaster, Monday after the Epiphany, 28 Edward III.

York. Examination made by William de Fyncheden and John de Upton on the idiocy of John de Heton, and inquisition of the value of his lands &c. Doncaster, Monday after the Epiphany, 28 Edward III.

John de Heton appeared and was examined and found to be an idiot and incapable of ruling himself or his lands. From his birth, which was on the day of the Annunciation, A.D. 1324, until the feast of St. James, 22 Edward III, viz. until he was 24 years of age, he was in good sense and quite sane; and since then till to-day he has been continuously an idiot, insensible to his surroundings, having a fancy in his head, whereby he remains unconscious of his own personality and paying no heed to anything at all. He enjoys no lucid intervals.

The jurors being asked what lands of the said John de Heton have been occupied by others and of the value of his goods and chattels, say that those which he had on the aforesaid feast of St. James, viz. six oxen, price 8s. each, four horses, price 4s. each, and 40 sheep, price 40s., were used by Margaret his wife for the support of him, herself, two sons and one daughter who are under the age of ten years, and of Margery, daughter of Adam de Hopton, married to John, eldest son of the said John, and for the support of his household, up to the feast of St. Michael, 26 Edward III; since when the said Margaret would not dwell with her husband in the company of William de Heton, his brother, and the latter would not let his brother be away from his guardianship in that of his wife. By the mediation of friends the lands of the said John in Myrfeld,

---

escheator *royal official who handled transfers of property to the Crown*   lucid intervals *periods of mental competence*   intermeddle *interfere*   Writ...certiorari *order to conduct a second inquisition*   Writ... facias *write directing a sheriff to assemble a jury*

Hopton, Estheton and Balne, with a moiety° of his goods and chattels, were assigned for the support of himself, William his son and Joan his daughter, in the guardianship of the said William his brother; and his lands &c. in Estheton and Erdeslawe, with a moiety of his goods and chattels, were assigned to Margaret for her support and that of John, her eldest son, and Margery his wife, daughter of Adam de Hopton. Margaret has remained until now in the household of the said Adam, who intervened touching the lands, goods and chattels assigned to her. In the winter after the assignment all the sheep died of murrain° and there are no other goods or chattels except those which are appraised above. The lands, goods, and chattels hardly suffice for the support of the said John, his wife, sons and household.

The said John has by inheritance the following lands:

Estheton. A messuage,° 80a. land, 7a. meadow, 20a. pasture and 40s. yearly rent of free tenants, all held of Sir Edmund de Langele as of the soke of Wakefeld by service of 15s. 9d. yearly payable by the tenants beside their own rent.

Erdeslawe. Six marks rent payable by the free tenants, held of Robert de Nevyll by fealty only.

Myrfeld. A messuage, a water-mill, 140a. land in demesne,° 5a. meadow and 37s. rent from free tenants in Myrfeld and Hopton. All held of Sir Henry, duke of Lancaster, as of the honour of Pontefract, by homage and fealty and by suit of court every three weeks.

Westheton. A messuage, 90a. land, 4a. meadow, 12a. pasture and 25s. 6d. rent of free

tenants held of John de [Burnell] by homage and fealty only.

Polyngton in Balne. Thirteen shillings and fourpence rent from free tenants held of Sir Henry, duke of Lancaster, as of the honour of Pontefract by homage and fealty only.

The goods and chattels of the said John are in the custody of William his brother and Margaret his wife. The said William, John de Malet, who married the aunt of the said John, John de Hellay, who married the said John's sister, are the nearest relations and friends of the said John and can best have the guardianship of him.

Nicholas, Son of Maurice, Earl of Dessemond[18] (1358)

8 October 1358. Westminster. To the justiciary° of Ireland. Order to cause Nicholas, son of Maurice earl of Dessemond, to come before him and to be examined, and if he find him to be an idiot, to cause all his lands to be seized into the king's hand and extended by inquisition, and to be delivered for keeping to Ralph earl of Stafford, so that he shall answer to the king for the issues there of over and above the maintenance of Nicholas and his servants, and if necessary to make inquisition whether Nicholas has been an idiot from birth, or how long, and to send the inquisition and extent to the chancery of England° without delay, as the king is informed that Nicholas is an idiot so that he cannot suffice for the governance of himself or his lands, and it pertains to the king to provide for the good governance of the lands of idiots, that they may not be wasted or alienated. By K.

---

moiety *portion*   **murrain** *an infectious disease*   **messuage** *a dwelling with land and outbuildings*   **demesne** *land attached to a manor retained for the owner's use*   **justiciary** *administrators of justice*   **chancery of England** *office responsible for producing official documents*

William de Aston, Accused of "Idiocy" by his Enemies[19] (1402)

Inquisition ex officio.° Gloucester. 16 March 1402.

William Aston of Aston Ingham has been an idiot since 9 Jan. 1400. He holds a tenement called 'Astonescourt' in Ley by Westbury, annual value 26s.8d. He and Alice his wife have taken the profits during this time.

July 7, 1402 Westminster

To Robert de Whityngton escheator° in Gloucestershire and the march of Wales adjacent. Order to remove the king's hand and meddle no further with a messuage° and one carucate° of land at Leyghe in the parish of Wesebury in the said march called 'Astonescourte,' delivering to William de Aston any issues° thereof taken; as at the malicious suit of certain his enemies, untruly averring that he was an idiot, the premises were seized into the king's hand; but he has appeared in person in chancery, and being there duly examined is found of sound mind and discretion, wherefore by advice of the justices, serjeants at law and others of the council learned in the law it is determined that the king's hand shall be removed.

Christina Goloffre, an "Idiot" who cannot tell Good from Evil[20] (1404)

Inquisition *ex officio*. Ilchester. 7 July 1404.

Christina daughter of Thomas Goloffre, son and heir of John Goloffre and Christina his wife, sister and heir of Walter Englyssh, held in her demesne° as of fee 1 messuage and 24 a. arable and meadow in Ashington of the lady de Sturye of her manor of Ashington by knight service, annual value 10s. She is an idiot from birth, unable to distinguish good from evil and evil from good.°

Inquisition ex officio *inquisition conducted by the escheator's office without a writ*   **escheator** *royal official who handled land transfers to the Crown*   **messuage** *a dwelling with land and outbuildings*   **carucate** *amount of land a team of eight oxen could till in a season*   **issues** *profits*   **demesne** *land used by the owner of a manor*   **unable...good** *a measure of competency used in criminal trials when the defendant claimed they had committed a crime while mentally incompetent*

Endnotes

1 The records, which consist of inquisitions postmortem, letters of patent, letters of close, and a variety of other administrative documents, are held in the British National Archives, mostly in the C series. They are also catalogued in several publications of the British Government, specifically; *Calendar of Inquisitions Miscellaneous (Chancery), Henry III–Henry V,* 7 vols. HMSO, 1916–2003; *Calendar of Inquisitions Postmortem and Other Analogous Documents Preserved in the Public Record Office,* 20 vols. HMSO, 1904–70; *Calendar of Patent Rolls Preserved in the Public Record Office, 1216–1509,* 52 vols. HMSO, 1891–1901.

2 *Britton,* ed. and trans. Francis Morgan Nichols, vol. 2 (Clarendon Press, 1865), p. 349.

3 *The Statutes of the Realm,* ed. and trans. Alexander Luders and Sir Thomas Edlyne Tomlins (Record Commission, 1810–22), vol. 1, p. 226.

4 *fatuorum naturalium* in the original

5 "Close Rolls, Edward I: November 1285." *Calendar of Close Rolls, Edward I: Volume 2, 1279–1288,* ed. H.C. Maxwell Lyte (His Majesty's Stationery Office, 1902), pp. 343–44. Available at *British History Online,* 6 July 2017, http://www.british-history.ac.uk/cal-close-rolls/edw1/vol2/pp343-344.

6 *sui inmemor* in the original.

7 "Edward I: Summer 1302." *Parliament Rolls of Medieval England,* eds. Chris Given-Wilson, Paul Brand, Seymour Phillips, Mark Ormrod, Geoffrey Martin, Anne Curry, and Rosemary Horrox (Boydell, 2005). Available at *British History Online,* http://www.british-history.ac.uk/no-series/parliament-rolls-medieval/summer-1302; "Inquisitions Post Mortem, Edward I, File 106." *Calendar of Inquisitions Post Mortem: Volume 4, Edward I,* eds. J.E.E.S. Sharp and A.E. Stamp (His Majesty's Stationery Office, 1913), pp. 67–84. Available at *British History Online,* http://www.british-history.ac.uk/inquis-post-mortem/vol4/pp67-84.

8 *discreta* in the original.

9 "Inquisitions Post Mortem, Edward I, File 23." *Calendar of Inquisitions Post Mortem: Volume 2, Edward I,* eds. J.E.E.S. Sharp (His Majesty's Stationery Office, 1906), pp. 185–94 Available at *British History Online,* http://www.british-history.ac.uk/inquis-post-mortem/vol2/pp185-194; "Inquisitions Post Mortem, Edward I, File 54." *Calendar of Inquisitions Post Mortem: Volume 2, Edward I,* ed. J.E.E.S. Sharp (His Majesty's Stationery Office, 1906), pp. 441–49 *British History Online,* 7 July 2017, http://www.british-history.ac.uk/inquis-post-mortem/vol2/pp441-449.

10 "Close Rolls, Edward I: January 1290." *Calendar of Close Rolls, Edward I: Volume 3, 1288–1296,* ed. H.C. Maxwell Lyte (His Majesty's Stationery Office, 1904), pp. 61–66. *British History Online,* 13 July 2017, http://www.british-history.ac.uk/cal-close-rolls/edw1/vol3/pp61-66.

11 "Close Rolls, Edward II: October 1316." *Calendar of Close Rolls, Edward II: Volume 2, 1313–1318,* eds. H.C. Maxwell Lyte (Her Majesty's Stationery Office, 1893), pp. 367–74 Available at *British History Online,* http://www.british-history.ac.uk/cal-close-rolls/edw2/vol2/pp367-374; "Inquisitions Post Mortem, Edward II, File 46." *Calendar of Inquisitions Post Mortem: Volume 5, Edward II,* eds. J.E.E.S Sharp and A.E. Stamp (His Majesty's Stationery Office, 1908), pp. 361–72. *British History Online,* http://www.british-history.ac.uk/inquis-post-mortem/vol5/pp361-372.

12 "Close Rolls, Edward II: October 1318." *Calendar of Close Rolls, Edward II: Volume 3, 1318–1323,* ed. H.C. Maxwell Lyte (Her Majesty's Stationery Office, 1895), pp. 18–24. Available at *British History Online,* http://www.british-history.ac.uk/cal-close-rolls/edw2/vol3/pp18-24.

13 *lucidis intervallis* in the original.

14 "Close Rolls, Edward III: August 1333." *Calendar of Close Rolls, Edward III: Volume 3, 1333–1337,* ed. H.C. Maxwell Lyte (Her Majesty's Stationery Office, 1898), pp. 133–34 *British History Online,* http://www.british-history.ac.uk/cal-close-rolls/edw3/vol3/pp133-134; "Inquisitions Post Mortem, Edward III, File 34." *Calendar of Inquisitions Post Mortem: Volume 7, Edward III,* eds. J.E.E.S. Sharp and A.E. Stamp (His Majesty's Stationery Office, 1909), pp. 347–52. Available at *British History Online,* http://www.british-history.ac.uk/inquis-post-mortem/vol7/pp347-352.

15 "Inquisitions Post Mortem, Edward III, File 63." *Calendar of Inquisitions Post Mortem: Volume 8, Edward III*, eds. J.E.E.S. Sharp, E.G. Atkinson, and J.J. O'Reilly (His Majesty's Stationery Office, 1913), pp. 201–13. Available at *British History Online*, http://www.british-history.ac.uk/inquis-post-mortem/vol8/pp201-213.

16 "Close Rolls, Edward III: November 1345." *Calendar of Close Rolls, Edward III: Volume 7, 1343–1346*, ed. H.C. Maxwell Lyte (His Majesty's Stationery Office, 1904), pp. 620–27. Available at *British History Online*, http://www.british-history.ac.uk/cal-close-rolls/edw3/vol7/pp620-627.

17 "Inquisitions Post Mortem, Edward III, File 125." *Calendar of Inquisitions Post Mortem: Volume 10, Edward III*, eds. A.E. Stamp, E. Salisbury, E.G. Atkinson, and J.J. O'Reilly (His Majesty's Stationery Office, 1921), pp. 111–34. Available at *British History Online*, http://www.british-history.ac.uk/inquis-post-mortem/vol10/pp111-134.

18 "Close Rolls, Edward III: August 1358." *Calendar of Close Rolls, Edward III: Volume 10, 1354–1360*, ed. H.C. Maxwell Lyte (His Majesty's Stationery Office, 1908), pp. 461–70. Available at *British History Online*, http://www.british-history.ac.uk/cal-close-rolls/edw3/vol10/pp461-470.

19 "Inquisitions Post Mortem, Henry IV, Entries 678-740." *Calendar of Inquisitions Post Mortem: Volume 18, Henry IV*, ed. J.L. Kirby (Her Majesty's Stationery Office, 1987), pp. 227–44. Available at *British History Online*, http://www.british-history.ac.uk/inquis-post-mortem/vol18/pp227-244; "Close Rolls, Henry IV: July 1402." *Calendar of Close Rolls, Henry IV: Volume 1, 1399–1402*, ed. A.E. Stamp (His Majesty's Stationery Office, 1927), pp. 542–45. Available at *British History Online*, http://www.british-history.ac.uk/cal-close-rolls/hen4/vol1/pp542-545.

20 "Inquisitions Post Mortem, Henry IV, Entries 1000-1048." *Calendar of Inquisitions Post Mortem: Volume 18, Henry IV*, ed. J.L. Kirby (Her Majesty's Stationery Office, 1987), pp. 346–60. Available at *British History Online*, http://www.british-history.ac.uk/inquis-post-mortem/vol18/pp346-360.

Nuremberg Town Records: Select Entries Pertaining to the "Mad" and Intellectually Disabled[1] (1377–1492)

Contributed by Anne M. Koenig

Introduction

As German cities expanded in the later Middle Ages, town authorities were confronted with ever-growing issues of poverty, transience, and illness. In response to the pressures that different needy, marginal, and disruptive populations put on municipal coffers, city governments promulgated new policies and crafted new institutional responsibilities. For instance, over the course of the fourteenth and fifteenth centuries, German city councils began running municipal brothels, hired and oversaw midwives as sworn town officials, and took over the administration of city hospitals. Such actions were done in the joint interest of public health and morality. They also increasingly allowed city officials to micromanage any aspect of urban life that intersected with the expanding scope of city councils and the ruling elites.

As secular authorities played ever-greater roles in dealing with issues like poverty, civic order, and crime, the lives of the sick and those with disabilities came to fall increasingly under the purview of municipal officials. City councils rarely crafted explicit policies regarding populations affected by disability, but interactions between city officials and persons with physical or intellectual disabilities were frequent. Authorities labeled such individuals by their disability or illness and often identified them in their own bookkeeping as simply "the fool," the "blind man," or "the mad woman." It is only occasionally that a name, an occupation, or other specific identifying detail was included. This labeling suggests that a disability or illness became the most defining identity marker for a person, at least from the perspective of town authorities. It also draws attention to the fact that, with only few exceptions, the illness or disability itself was central to why and how the council intervened in the lives of these individuals.

We know of these interactions thanks to the survival of several types of documents created by the bureaucracy of city governments, namely council log books and city financial accounts. While Nuremberg's records are the focus below, in part because these records are particularly rich and in part because late medieval Nuremberg was an especially vibrant city, such documents survive from cities as widespread as Munich and Frankfurt to Hildesheim and Lübeck. These civic records are not very "narrative" sources. Their authors did not intend to tell a story; they simply recorded the mundane, day-to-day business of running a town. Council minute books or logbooks produced by city scribes, for instance, merely recorded the decisions that the city mayors made as they presided over all aspects of town management. Even less narrative are the financial books kept by the scribes. These accounting records only note the incomes and expenditures of the city over the course of the year, but in doing so give us glimpses of interactions with the sick and those with disabilities that involved a civic payout.

Yet despite their limitations, these records show us the reactions that municipal authorities had to those with illnesses and disabilities and they give us glimpses into how authorities understood madness and intellectual disability. Town leaders, and medieval people in general, understood the two conditions to be different; they were not often conflated or confused by onlookers. Nuremberg's records distinguish between the "mad" (a general category covering those they called "mad," "senseless," "out-of-their-minds," or "reasonless") and the disabled (called "fools," "natural idiots," or simply "weak-minded"). But the management of the two populations were often parallel, and sometimes specifically overlapped. For instance, some towns built rooms or small structures to house the "mad" and the intellectually impaired alike, calling such spaces "fool's huts" (in Nuremberg, *Narrenheuslin*, or in Hildesheim, *Dorenkisten*). These "huts," moreover, had both juridical and charitable functions: they incarcerated but also cared for these vulnerable populations. Indeed, the management of such spaces often fell under the care of the city hospital.

Offered below is a selection of entries involving madness or intellectual disability that were entered into Nuremberg's financial accounts between 1377 and 1492 and into their council books between 1450 and 1493. All told, the surviving books from these two bodies of records contain almost 250 entries that involve the "mad" or intellectually disabled. In a typical year, four or five cases could easily pass through the council's docket, most of them during the summer months. (For perspective: Nuremberg's population in the fifteenth century was about 20,000.) The persons labeled as "mad" or disabled in these records, moreover, were only a small subset of those who lived their lives in the city but never drew the council's attention. Most of those who experienced rational impairment were cared for by their families and friends; only when more private methods of manage-

ment failed—like when a woman with mental illness was not native to the city, when a man with a disability was accused of immodesty, or when a spouse was unwilling to accept responsibility—did public authorities step in. If we keep in mind this silent majority while analyzing the minority "problematic" individuals whose lives left traces in the records, we can begin to comprehend just how central such experiences of mental illness and disability were in the urban landscape.

The entries below reveal that persons experiencing intellectual disability or mental illness were largely at the mercy of the council, whose primary interest was to protect the order and wellbeing of the city. The council therefore responded to these individuals with a range of management techniques, from the helpful or benign to the stern or even persecutory. Expulsion and imprisonment feature prominently. Of particular note is the frequent mention of the town of Regensburg, which despite lying some sixty miles away, was the easiest place to access the Danube river. Nuremberg sent "mad" persons to Regensburg over two dozen times, sometimes as just a first stop before sending them further downriver to Passau, Vienna, and even Hungary. The council, however, also came up with more local solutions. Beatings were sometimes ordered, generally in cases where an impaired person committed a serious transgression. The claim of boisterous, unruly, or even lewd behavior was cited multiple times. Punishments even in these instances were still rare, not least because corporal punishment was forbidden by German law codes, which ruled that individuals who lacked sufficient reason could not be held fully accountable for their actions. In other rare cases, the council authorized "mad" individuals to beg. The city regulated municipal charity and public begging, and records show that at least by the 1470s multiple "mad" individuals, almost all women, were granted this right. Finally, we also find attempts made to house and care for those with mental illness within the city itself. By the end of the century Nuremberg's council had also created multiple spaces for housing the "mad" within its walls. The council also steadily enlisted the resources of the hospital in maintaining care, and they had entered into negotiations (not always pleasant) with families in attempts to get them to take responsibility for their own family members.

Bibliography

Buhrer, Eliza. "But what is to be said of a fool?" Intellectual Disability in Medieval Thought and Culture." *Mental Health, Spirituality and Religion in the Middle Ages and Early Modern Age*, edited by Albrecht Classen. De Gruyter, 2014, pp. 314–43.

Kirchhoff, Theodor. *Grundriss einer Geschichte der deutschen Irrenpflege*. Hirschwald, 1890.

Kriegk, Georg L. *Ärzte, Heilanstalten, Geisteskranke im Mittelalterlichen Frankfurt a.M.* August Osterrieth, 1863.

Mellyn, Elizabeth. *Mad Tuscans and their Families: A History of Mental Disorder in Early Modern Italy*. University of Pennsylvania Press, 2014.

Metzler, Irina. *Fools and Idiots?: Intellectual Disability in the Middle Ages*. Manchester University Press, 2016.

Midelfort, H.C. Erik. *A History of Madness in Sixteenth-Century Germany*. Stanford University Press, 1999.

Mummenhoff, Ernst. "Die öffentliche Gesundheits- und Krankenpflege im alten Nürnberg." *Festschrift zur Eröffnung des neuen Krankenhauses der Stadt Nürnberg*, Nuremberg, 1898, pp. 1–122.

Rosen, George. *Madness in Society*. University of Chicago Press, 1968.

Sander, Antje. "Dulle und Unsinnige: Irrenfürsorge in norddeutschen Städten des Spätmittelalters und der frühen Neuzeit." *Städtisches Gesundheits- und Fürsorgewesen vor 1800*, edited by Peter Jonanek. Böhlau, 2000, pp. 111–25.

———. "Die Dullen in der Kiste." *Festschrift für Peter Berghaus zum 70. Geburtstag*, edited by Thorsten Albrecht and Antje Sander. Scriptorium, 1989, pp. 147–60.

Turner, Wendy. *Care and Custody of the Mentally Ill, Incompetent, and Disabled in Medieval England*. Brepols, 2013.

———, ed. *Madness in Medieval Law and Custom*. Brill, 2010.

Vijselaar, Joost, ed. *Dolhuizen—Madhouses: Chapters from the History of Madhouses in Europe 1400–1800*. Nederlands centrum geestelijke volksgezondheid. 1995.

Selected Financial Book (*Stadtrechnungen*) Entries—German Original	Selected Financial Book (*Stadtrechnungen*) Entries—English Translation
1377 Item d[edimus] von einer Unsinigen xiii s. hl. daz man sie schikt gen Weizzenburg.[2]	1377 Item: We pay 8 silver *heller*° to drive a mad woman to Weizzenburg.
1378 Item d[edimus] xvi s. hlr. einer unsinnigen umb einen peltz und umb zwen schuh und umb einen slayer.[3]	1378 Item: We pay 16 silver *heller* to a mad woman for a fur, two shoes and a veil.[14]
1378 Item d[edimus] lx hlr. zu kost von einer unsinnigen die in dem loch gevangen lag.[4]	1378 Item: We pay 60 silver *heller* for the cost of mad woman[15] who lies imprisoned in the jail.[16]
1385 Item dedimus iii lb. und iii S. hl. von dem unsynigen Peter Kursner den man gen regensburg sant und furbaz gen Wein.[5]	1385 Item: We pay 3 pounds and 3 silver *heller* for mad Peter Kursner, who was sent to Regensburg and then further to Vienna.
1386 Item dedimus Meister Otten Wunt Artzt ix S. hl von einem Toreten[6] den er ertzneyt.[7]	1386 Item: We pay Master Otto, surgeon, 9 silver *heller* for a mad man [in the jail] whom he doctored.[17]
1386 Item dedimus dem lochmeister i lb. hlr von einem Toroten der xiii tag gevangen lag.[8]	1386 Item: We pay the prison warden 1 pound *heller* for a mad man who was in the prison for 13 days.
1386 Item dedimus dem H. Karrenman iii lb. und viii S. hl von einem Toroten zu füren gen Reg[ensburg].[9]	1386 Item: We pay H. Karrenman[18] 3 pounds and 8 silver *heller* for driving a mad man[19] to Reg[ensburg].
1421 Item de[dimus] iiii s. hllr die Cuntz Statknecht geben het einem unsinnigen pfaffen dem man die Stat verboten und von dannen geweist het.[10]	1421 Item: We pay 4 silver *heller* to Cuntz, the city servant, regarding a mad cleric who has been forbidden from the city and has been thrown out of it.
1431 Item de[dimus] i lb hl dem lochüter von einer töroten frawen die xii tag im loch lag und auch für ettlich notdurfft im loch.[10]	1431 Item: We pay 1 pound *heller* to the prison warden for a mentally impaired woman who spent 12 days in jail and for various necessities in the prison.
1435 Item de[dimus] iii lb xvi s hl das ein törot fraw gekost hat im loch und gen Regenspurg zufüren.[11]	1435 Item: We pay 3 pounds 16 silver *heller* that a rationally impaired woman cost [for her time in] the jail and to send her to Regensburg.
1439 Item de[dimus] x s atzgelts dem lochhüter von zwaien narren die man in daz loch gelegt hette.[12]	1439 Item: We give 10 silver [*heller*] as payment to the prison warder for two fools who were placed in the jail.
1458 Item xix s. dem lochuter und zuchtiger vom unsynnigen Endlein mit gerten zu hawen und von hynnen zu schicken.[13]	1458 Item: [We pay] 19 silver [*heller*] to the prison warder and the executioner° for whipping mad Endlein[20] and sending him away from here.[21]

heller *the smallest coin of note in southern Germany, worth one-half of a penny (pfennig)* **executioner** *a city employee in charge of all corporal punishments meted out by the city, who, like the prison warden, was given a modest salary but who largely earned his keep through the payments for individual jobs*

Selected Council Book (*Ratsverlässe*)
Entries—German Original

27 Mai 1449   Item den unsinnigen im loch
    ledig lassen auf urfee.[22]
6 Juli 1449   Item den torechten von Rewt
    auf ein urf[ehd] ledig lassen.[23]
9 Juli 1449   Item die unsynnigen frawen
    austreiben und bestellen, nich mer
    hereynzulassen.[24]
5 Jan. 1471   Item der unsynigen vergont zu
    beteln.[25]
19 Juli 1475   Item den Narren Im loch ligend
    der die lewt geslagen hat, Im loch mit
    gerten hawen. und gein newnkirchen
    füren.[26]
24 Mai 1477   Item den Spitalpfleger ze biten
    ein gedult ze haben mit der frawen die
    unvernufftig gewesen und wider zu ir
    selbs komen ist, etlich zeit und nem-
    lich biss die heissen tage verscheinen,
    in dem Spital zu geduld.[27]
31 Mai 1477   Item den Spiegler von den
    synnen komen ist, in ein hëwslin in
    Marstal zu bringen.[28]
20 Juni 1478   Item den Narren im loch li-
    gend auss der Stat weisen und mit
    rwten zestreichen vor der Stat der
    Statknechen ursachhalb den er ein
    frawen erschreckt hat dan ir zu einem
    kind mislungen ist.[29]
27 Aug. 1481   Item Jobsten Tetzels seligen
    gelassen witiben und Iren vormunden
    und freunden ist uff ir bete und an-
    bringen vergonnt, desselben hern Jobs
    Tetzels seligen Sun, der nit bei vernufft
    sein sol, auff einem turn bei S. Kath-
    erin In einem Kemerlein zu enthalten
    und zu verwaren doch auff Iren Costen
    und so lang es eins Rats fug ist.[30]

11 Mai 1482   Item des Toretten manshalb,
    der yetz herkomen ist und das lew-
    ten vil schaden und unzucht beweist ,

Selected Council Book (*Ratsverlässe*)
Entries—English Translation

27 May 1449   Item: We set free the madman
    in the jail, on his oath.
6 July 1449   Item: We set free the mentally
    impaired man from Rewt° on his oath.
9 July 1449   Item: We expel the mad wom-
    an and order that she never be let back
    in.
5 Jan. 1471   Item: We allow the mad wom-
    an to beg.
19 July 1475   Item: Regarding the fool lying
    in the jail who hit people, whip him in
    the jail and drive him to Neunkirchen.°
24 May 1477   Item: We ask the hospital war-
    den to have patience with the woman
    who went mad and has come back to
    herself, and to allow her to remain in
    the hospital some time. that is, until
    warm weather comes.
31 May 1477   Item: The mirror craftsman
    who has gone mad is to be put into a
    small house in the city stables.
20 June 1478   Item: We order that the fool, ly-
    ing in the jail, be beaten with whips in
    front of the city by bailiffs and thrown
    out of the city because he frightened a
    woman and she miscarried her child.
27 Aug. 1481   Item: In response to the re-
    quest and application by the surviving
    widow of Jobst Tetzel,[39] she and her
    legal guardians and friends are per-
    mitted to place Jobst Tetzel's son, who
    does not have his reason, in a room in a
    tower by St. Katherine's [where he will
    be] contained and kept safely at their
    cost so long as it is authorized by the
    Council.
11 May 1482   Item: Regarding the mad man
    who now has come here and demon-
    strated much harm and impropriety,

Rewt *either Reut, an area about 130 miles* SE *of Nuremberg, or Reutte, Austria, about 150 miles south.*
Neunkirchen *(Newnkirchen) a small town 15 miles to the east of Nuremberg*

zuerkunden von Wannen er sei damit er denselb[31] deinen freund heym geschickt werd mochte, wo aber das nie erfaren wurde den die thunaw ab ze schickt Se[bolt] Reich[32]

18 Mai 1485   Item die Selswester, die in der Ebner Selhuß von den Synnen komen ist . In der heußlein ayns bei dem Newen Spital oder im marstal ze nemen Ga. Holtschuher[33]

3 Juni 1486   Item den Törehten Nagler umb sein ungestumikeit, auß der Stat zefüren und ine bedroen, wo er wider herkome. An. Tetzel.[34]

9 Juli 1489   Item den Jungen Ratsmid[35] der seiner synne geprechlich ist, Im einen Narrenheuslin bei dem Spital zu verwaren.[36]

27 Okt. 1489   Item einen an der stat arbeit der einen unsynnigen bruder hat zu enthaltung desselben, ein kemerlein zu vergonnen uff sein Cost.[37]

30 Dez. 1492   Item die diern, die ein spieglerin gestochen hat etlich tage in einer vancknuss zu enthalten, und uff merckung ze haben ob sie bei vernufft sei oder nit. Schopfen.[38]

we are to find out where he is from so that he might be sent home to his friend, or if that is not discovered, to send him to the Danube River. [Done by:] Se[bolt] Reich[40]

18 May 1485   Item: The souls-sister[o41] from the Ebner Soulhouse[42] who has gone out of her senses is to be put in the small hut either by the New Hospital[43] or in the stables. [Done by:] Ga[briel] Holtschuher

3 June 1486   Item: We order that the mentally impaired nail-maker, because of his unruliness be driven out of the city and threatened should he come back. [Done by:] An[thony] Tetzel

9 July 1489   Item: We order that the young brass-smith, whose mind is weak, be safely kept in a fool's hut by the hospital.

27 Oct. 1489   Item: A city worker who has a mad brother is permitted a small room to confine him, at his cost.

30 Dec. 1492   Item: We order the serving girl, who stabbed a mirror craftswoman, be held some days in a prison and to observe if she is sane or not. Court ordered.

souls-sister *a kind of religious person found in southern Germany similar to Beguines*

Endnotes

1   The following entries come from the Nuremberg Financial Accounts (*Stadtrechnungen*) held in the Nuremberg State Archives (Staatsarchiv Nürnberg, hereafter StA N): StA N, Rep. 52, No. 1–22, 177, 179–181 and the Nuremberg Council books (*Ratsverlässe*) held in the Nuremberg State Archives: StA N, Rep. 60a, Ratsverlässe, Nr. 1–285 (1450–1493). All transcriptions and translations provided by Anne M. Koenig, in consultation with Irene Stahl, ed., *Die Nürnberger Ratsverlässe: Heft 1 1449–1450* (Verlag Degner, 1983) and Martin Scheiber, ed., *Die Nürnberger Ratsverlässe: Heft 2 1452–1471* (Verlag Degner, 1995). Nuremberg's records used a variety of terms to denote different kinds of impairment; when it is unclear whether the individual in question was "mad" or intellectually disabled, the English is merely rendered as "mentally impaired."

2   StA N, Rep. 52, No. 1, p. 83 (Books 1 and 2 of the *Stadtrechnungen* have been paginated).

3   StA N, Rep. 52, No. 2, p. 150.

4   StA N, Rep. 52, No. 2, p. 152.

5   StA N, Rep. 52, No. 177, f. 151r.

6   This term is particularly problematic. In different contexts it could refer to a person with an intellectual disability, with mental illness, or who was deaf. (Non-speaking deaf people were often falsely seen as being rationally impaired.) Variants of *torot* and *torecht* appear throughout Nuremberg's records and in the 1430s the Nuremberg city scribe used this term almost exclusively.

7   StA N, Rep. 52, No. 177, f. 178v–179r.

8   StA N, Rep. 52, No. 177, f. 199v.

9   StA N, Rep. 52, No. 177, f. 200r.

10 StA N, Rep. 52, No. 6 f. 32r and copied in No. 179, f. 112r.

11 StA N, Rep. 52, No. 180, f.165v.

12 StA N, Rep. 52, No. 180, f. 339r.

13 StA N, Rep. 52, No. 13, f. 84r.

14 This entry is authorizing payment for those items to be given to the woman, not buying them from her.

15 Likely the same woman from the previous entry.

16 "Jail" is perhaps too pleasant a term. The city lock-up was a subterranean prison known as the "the loch" or "the hole" that lay directly under the city council building.

17 The entry before this one makes it clear that the man in question was in the jail.

18 H. Karrenman appears in several records. His last name, literally "Cart-man" designates him by trade to be a wagoner or driver.

19 Given the proximity in the accounts of this entry to the one regarding the man imprisoned for 13 days, it is likely the same man.

20 A last name.

21 Beating the those considered "mad" was exceptionally rare. Generally speaking, German law codes forbade the corporal punishment of those who lacked sufficient reason to be held fully accountable for their actions. We have no way of knowing why, in this case, the council chose to ignore the law.

22 Stahl, ed., *Die Nürnberger Ratsverlässe: Heft 1*, 119.

23 Ibid, 166.

24 Ibid, 174.

25 Scheiber, ed., *Die Nürnberger Ratsverlässe: Heft 2*, 52.

26 StAN Rep. 60a, No. 52. f.13r.

27 StAN Rep. 60a, No. 77. f. 12v.

28 StAN Rep. 60a, No. 77. f. 17r.

29 StAN Rep. 60a, No. 92. f. 2r.

30 StAN Rep. 60a, No. 134. f. 5v.

31 This correction was made by the scribe as he was recording the decision.

32 StAN Rep. 60a, No. 144, f. 3r.

33 StAN Rep. 60a, No. 184, f. 5r.

34 StAN Rep. 60a, No. 198, f. 3v.

35 *ratsmid* = *Rotschmied* (or red smith), which was a term used for the many workers of Nuremberg's famed brass crafts industry.

36 StAN Rep. 60a, No. 239, f. 9v.

37 StAN Rep. 60a, No. 243, f. 2r.

38 StAN Rep. 60a, No. 285, f. 6v.

39 Jobst Tetzel had been a member of one of the old, ruling families of Nuremberg and had himself been a member of the town council.

40 Many later decisions record the councilman or city official who was in some way responsible for the directed action.

41   Unmarried women, generally from poorer
classes, who followed this vocation took on the
duty of praying for the souls of the departed.

42   The Ebner Soulhouse was a modest house
for up to 10 souls-sisters, founded in 1280 by the
Ebners, one of the oldest ruling patrician families
in Nuremberg.

43   The New Hospital (more formally, the
Hospital of the Holy Ghost) was a large hospital
in the center of town that had been founded in
1330 by a wealthy patrician. By 1400 the care and
administration of the hospital were overseen by
the city council.

Tax Relief Requests from Medieval Dijon[1]
(1389–1449)

Contributed by Anne Galanaud and Pierre Galanaud[2]

Introduction

In the city of Dijon, numerous tax relief requests were submitted to the tax authorities between the end of the fourteenth century and the mid-fifteenth century. These individual applications represent an invaluable source to decipher the problems of the Middle Age population, including health problems, problems caused by warfare, recurring epidemics, economic crisis, increase of taxes and more general problems. The disability of the head of household and/or a member of their family was frequently presented in order to request a tax reduction. Convincing the tax authorities to grant the request usually required the applicant to be specific about their disability, the function of the person with the disability within the household and the impact of the disability on the finances and the daily life of the family.

These documents also shed light on the view of the tax collector about disability because they indicate the result of the requests, which petitioned to the city authorities for a relief of taxes. The taxes were levied for various reasons by the municipality (such as taxes for the defense of the city) or by the duke (such as the *fouages* taxes[3]) and the heads of household from Dijon had to pay them virtually every year in this time of warfare.[4] In a number of cases, the fate of the person or family requesting relief can be traced, from recurrent requests submitted year after year or from other sources such as the annual *marcs* tax registers.[5] As the *marcs* tax level was based on the value of one's assets in the city, its changes from year to year reflect that of a given head of household's wealth.

Age-associated blindness (possibly due to macular degeneration or cataracts) was common and had a major impact on the ability to work among the adult members of the household and on their income. The unwillingness of the tax authorities to take it into account often forced the taxpayer to mortgage or sell their entire estate, eventually becoming a pauper. This is the case of the blind winegrower Vincent de Couchey. In 1422, the year of his tax relief request submission, Vincent was rather wealthy: he paid 25 *sols* for the *marcs* tax, an amount that rates him among the top 10% of taxpayers. Two years later the *marcs* tax collector acknowledged his blindness and exempted him in view of his poverty, indicating that the disability resulted in his ruin. The unwillingness of the authorities to take visual disability into account may have other counterproductive outcomes, as exemplified by the case of Jehan Cuer de Roy's father[6] who, in spite of his blindness, was commandeered as a watchman on the city walls because of ongoing war.

The progression of age-associated physical weakness is illustrated by the successive requests submitted by Gautherin d'Isier and by Jaquot Le Roy and their wives. The authorities' response was limited to decreases in the tax level, preceding by several years the acknowledgment of their dependency by the tax collector. Gautherin, a humble winegrower, became a pauper, whereas Jaquot, a wealthy haberdasher, preserved his assets.

The rich cloth manufacturer, Maistre Estienne de Sens, represents another example of worsening health. One year after the submission of a request based on his advanced age, a new document, probably produced by his children, indicated that he was struck with hemiplegia associated with aphasia. He died two years later. Other examples of neurological diseases were documented, such as the continuous tremor that prevented the blacksmith Estienne Beaujeu from working and the epilepsy of Regnault Le Puet's daughter.

The requests indicate various kinds of support for the disabled persons. They can be entirely dependent on their neighbor's help and eager to be led to a hospital, such as the blind cobbler Jehan d'Aignay; supported by strangers they can afford to hire, such as Jaquot Leroy; or benefit from costly home caregivers, such as Michelot de Bar sur Aube's paralyzed mother.

Mobility issues were frequent, and could be the result of mutilating surgery as in the case of Jehannot Mignotet and of Jehan Le Massenet's wife. The response of the authorities to mobility issues and to chronic diseases was variable, probably insufficient in the case of the leg fistula of winegrower Oudot le Carnoisot and of the work accident of carpenter Perrenot Lomme, more efficient in the case of Estienne Beaujeu and Estienne Le Barbier who were fully exempted from their tax.

Mental illness, possibly not considered as a disability by the petitioners, is not present in the requests. The single case of mental disorder appearing in these fiscal documents is written in the tax collector's hand, referring to his inability to levy a tax from Jaquote de Fouvent who left her home and might have been eaten by wolves.[7]

In the same line, it should be pointed out that tax relief requests and fiscal documents, although they represent invaluable sources for the late Middle Ages population, leave aside the numerous underprivileged not included in fiscal households,[8] as well as those taxpayers who were unable to afford the public letter writer usually required for writing the request.

Bibliography

Galanaud, Anne. "Démographie et société à Dijon à la fin du moyen-âge (1357–447) à partir d'une analyse informatique des régistres des comptes de l'impôt des marcs." PhD thesis in History, Franche-Comté University, 2009. https://tel.archives-ouvertes.fr/tel-01166860.

Galanaud, Pierre, Anne Galanaud, and Patrick Giraudoux. "Historical Epidemics Cartography Generated by Spatial Analysis: Mapping the Heterogeneity of Three Medieval "Plagues" in Dijon." *PLoS ONE*, vol. 10, iss. 12: e0143866, 2015. doi: 10.1371/journal.pone.0143866.

Garnier, Joseph. *Correspondance de la mairie de Dijon: Extraite des archives de cette ville.* Rabutot, 1868.

Geremek, Bronislaw, and Agneszka Kolakowska. *Poverty: A History.* Wiley-Blackwell, 1997.

Metzler, Irina. *A Social History of Disability in the Middle Ages: Cultural Considerations of Physical Impairment.* Routledge, 2013.

Vaughan, Richard. *Philip the Bold: the Formation of the Burgundian State.* Longmans, 1962.

———. *John the Fearless: Growth of the Burgundian Power.* Longmans, 1973.

———. *Philip the Good: The Apogee of the Burgundy.* Longmans, 1970.

The blind winegrower Vincent de Couchey[9]

[1422] To the lords, tax collectors and aldermen of the city of Dijon,

(From the)[10] very humbly imploring Vincent de Couchey dit de Tallemer a poor and ancient man (who) cannot see a thing.

(He) henceforth is and will be unable to earn the poor and small living for himself and his wife. Because of his extreme destitution and need, during the present year he had to sell the best vineyard he had...

Nevertheless you taxed him for the first payment of his *fouages* tax in the amount of 2 francs which is a much too high and excessive tax in view of and considering his poor and small condition in which he can no more earn his living...

He will henceforth have to sell the minimal assets and inheritance that he acquired in the past.

However Jehan Bisot, tax collector for the aforementioned *fouages* tax for the Saint Philibert parish imposed several tax liens on his assets so that he would have to sell...

My dear lords would you please for God's sake and as charity consider that the aforementioned petitioner is presently blind and cannot earn a living (and) reduce the aforementioned tax from 2 *francs* to 20 *sols*.[11] This is even more than he can pay, while asking to the aforementioned Jehan Bisot to expunge him from his tax liens.

And he will pray for you.

[June 12, 1422] (The tax authority orders) Jehan Bisot to decrease the aforementioned petitioner's first payment of the present *fouages* tax by 6 *gros*.[12] Written at the city chamber...[13]

Jehan d'Aignay's[14] lost visual clarity

[1430] To the lords, tax collectors and aldermen of the city and commune of Dijon,

(We) very humbly beg you to take pity on Jehan d'Aignay (cobbler), a poor man who is visually challenged.[15] He has neither house nor inheritance nor rent nor any income and he cannot work anymore and will never work in view of his lost visual clarity...

He decided to sell his few possessions... So he owns nothing in the world except the meager bed, which he sleeps upon and the small amount of charity his neighbours give him each day.

If he is sent to a hospital for his final days (he would be willing to go because) he won't be able to take care of himself or direct his affairs.

Nevertheless you have levied the *fouages* tax and the defence of the city tax to the sum of 2 and half *francs,* which sum he cannot ever pay because, in truth he has nothing other than the above mentioned bed.

If you please, reduce the tax for this poor petitioner to 1 *franc* instead of 2 and half *francs* as you already did for the other *fouage* taxes that Jehan Bisot and Nicolas Saint Jon levied, you will do good and be charitable and he will pray to God for all of you.

[February 23, 1430] (The tax authority orders to) expunge the petitioner's debt by 18 *gros* on both taxes.[16] Written on the...[17]

Jehan Cuer de Roy's father

[August 26, 1414] From the duchesse,

Jehan Cuer De Roy informed us that, although his father is blind and disabled, the mayor of Dijon commands him to watch on the walls. And thus, upon Jehan's petition we ask you, if this is the case, to speak about it to the mayor and do as much as you can in order to exempt him from watching on the walls.

Gautherin d'Isier[18] and his wife

[July 1422] To the lords mayors and aldermen of the city of Dijon,

Very humbly implores Gautherin d'Isier (winegrower) living in Dijon in Crais street that as the aforementioned implorer for his great and ancient age and also for the great weakness of his body cannot spend long time working and plowing in order to earn his life and that of his wife who is also very poor, weak and ancient woman...However the aforementioned poor implorer was taxed to 18 *gros* which amount is very in excess.

[July 17, 1422] Jehan Bisot expunges the implorer's debt by 4 gros on his tax for the last payment of the present *fouages* tax.

[October 1422] To the lords mayors and aldermen of the city of Dijon,

Very humbly implores Gautherin d'Isier living in Dijon in Crais street...as the aforementioned implorer and his wife are very ancient people...

The aforementioned Gautherin implorer is in such a condition that he will soon be led to a hospital and he cannot earn a single *denier*[19] because, due to his weakness and old age, he cannot move unless he has a crutch or a cane in hand...Nevertheless he is taxed to 14 *gros*.

[October 25, 1422] The implorer's debt is expunged to 8 *gros*.

[June 1423] To the lords, tax collectors and aldermen of the city of Dijon,

Very humbly implores Gautherin d'Isier living in Dijon in Crais street within the Saint Jehan parish that as the aforementioned petitioner and his wife are very poor, weak and ancient people, so much that, because of their ancient age and body weakness they cannot anymore work nor plow...They are so poor that a part of their vineyard is presently hired...The aforementioned petitioner has to pay 10 *gros* for the tax presently levied for the defense of the city.

[June 15, 1423] (The tax authority orders to) expunge the petitioner's debt by 4 *gros*. Written by Jehan Bolier on June...

[September 1423] To the lords, tax collectors and aldermen of the city of Dijon,

Very humbly implores Gautherin d'Isier a poor winegrower living in Dijon that as he and his wife are ancient in age, each of them of 80 years and more...[20] Because of his ancient age and great weakness of his body, he cannot spend enough time to work and plow, to earn his living and that of his wife who is also very poor, weak and ancient. He and his

wife have nothing for their living except the milk of a single cow.

Nevertheless, Nicolas Saint Jon collector for this tax requires 10 more *gros* for the second payment. Thus the petitioner implores to expunge the second payment by the same amount as the first one and he and his wife will sell some of their furniture to pay it.

[September 17, 1423] (The tax authority orders to) expunge the petitioner's debt[21] by 4 *gros*.

Jaquot Le Roy and his wife Jaquobte[22]

[1417] Jaquot Le Roy haberdasher is taxed at 12 *francs* for the *fouages*, an amount that he cannot pay...As he possesses no house where he can live, he has to pay every year a 32 *francs* rent for housing.

[December 18, 1417] (The tax authority orders to) decrease the petitioner's debt from 7 *francs* to 5 *francs* 10 *gros*.

[June 1423 & September 1423] Jaquot Le Roy haberdasher is presently old, weak, ancient and suffering from the gout. He cannot go to fairs and markets[23] with his goods as he used to do when he was young and strong. He has no children who could help him and has to rely on strangers to the family who remove his belongings. The rich people in the city who own and sell high value merchandise and who can rely on efficient help in their houses are not taxed as much as the implorer...[24]

[June 16, 1423] (The tax authority orders to) decrease the petitioner's debt by 2 *francs*...

[September 17, 1423] (The tax authority orders to) decrease the petitioner's debt by 2 *francs*...

[1430] Jaquot Le Roy haberdasher and his wife Jaquobte are both of them weak and ancient persons, and are together in a bed. They are so sick that they cannot get up and move around, so that strangers have to bring them beverage and food like two small children, and that is a pity. Jaquot has lost his visual clarity and has to be led by the hands without seeing.

[February 26, 1430] (The tax authority orders to) expunge the (12 *francs*) petitioner's debt by 1 *franc*...[25]

Maistre Estienne de Sens[26]

[1422] Estienne de Sens, old and ancient man, who cannot earn a thing...

[1423] Maistre Estienne de Sens, lost half of his body as well as the power of speech... and his children entirely support him. Nevertheless you taxed him to 18 *francs*, that is 7 *francs* for the tax for the defense of the city and 11 *francs* for the *fouages* tax.

[November 19, 1423] (The tax authority orders to) expunge the petitioner's debt by 1 franc on the tax for the defense of the city and 2 *francs* for the *fouages* tax.[27]

Michelot de Bar sur Aube's mother[28]

[1433] The aforementioned petitioner is in charge of a wife and 4 small children and of his mother who is a very weak and old woman suffering from paralysis. Everyday she needs night and day care provided by two women. This is a heavy financial burden for the petitioner.[29]

Estienne Beaujeu[30]

[1424] (Request from) Estienne Beaujeu blacksmith living in Dijon, as the tax collector Jehan Bisot compels the aforementioned petitioner to pay for each *fouage* tax the amount of 2 *gros*, an amount that he could not pay because he is shaking all over and cannot perform his work. He must care for himself, his wife and children and he will become so poor that he will be reduced to begging.

[November 20, 1424] (The tax authority orders to) expunge 4 *gros*[31] from the implorer's debt for God and alms.

Regnault Le Puet's daughter[32]

[1449] (The petitioner) must care for a pregnant wife and of 8 small children. Among them is a daughter aged sixteen. She suffers from diseases of Saint Jean and Saint Loup[33] and half of her body is disabled.[34]

Oudot le Carnoisot[35]

[1433 & 1434] Oudot le Carnoisot winegrower poor and sick man (who) has only a poor and small and ruined house (and has) no vineyard, nor inheritance. He is also very sick because of a fistula in his leg that prevents him from working since Saint Michel's day and he earns nothing.[36]

Estienne Le Barbier[37]

[1433] Estienne Le Barbier who lives in Dijon and for 6 years has suffered from stones so awful that everyday he expels by his penis a stone the size of a hemp grain. When the stone goes down into his bladder, he brays and moans like a woman in labor. He thus earns nothing...but most of the time lives from the charity of the lords. In addition, because of the war progress, his sister moved into his place with 4 young children and there is nothing to feed them.

[November 23, 1433] In view of the poverty and disease (of the implorer, the tax authority orders to) totally expunge his tax.[38]

Jehannot Mignotet[39]

[1446] Jehannot Mignotet cares for a pregnant wife and of 3 small children...

[1448] Jehannot son of Jehan Mignotet has had a bad leg for the past 5 years and so much and so seriously (impaired) that he is on the verge of being disabled and that it has to be cut. He cannot earn a living for himself, for his wife, his 4 poor children and his mother who is an old woman aged sixty and more.[40]

Jehan Le Massenet's wife[41]

[1434] Jehan Le Massenet, cobbler living in Dijon, caring for his wife who has been sick for one year. She is so sick that she was led to the Pont de Norges (hospital) where it is agreed to cut the ends of her feet...[42]

Perrenot Lomme[43]

[1417] To the lords and aldermen of the city and commune of Dijon,

(From the) very humbly imploring Perrenot Lomme, carpenter living in Dijon in front of Andrieu Estienne's house. He cares for a pregnant wife with 5 other children, and has neither vineyard nor house nor inheritance. He has been sick for a long time and is bedridden because a piece of wood nearly killed him. He was taxed of 13 *gros* for the present *fouages* tax, an amount that he will not be able to pay unless he sells his poor beds where lie his poor wife on the verge of giving birth and his 5 children who cannot earn a single *denier*. And he has much difficulty (finding) bread for eating.

[December 19, 1417] We decrease the petitioner's tax by 1 and half *gros* on one of the taxes.[44]

[1430] Perrenot Lomme, carpenter poor and sick man...is so sick from his arms that he cannot work anymore...

You have levied the *fouages* tax and the defence of the city tax to the sum of 2 *francs*, which sum he cannot ever pay. If you would please to reduce the aforementioned tax from 10 *sols*...

[March 1, 1430] (The tax authority orders to) decrease the petitioner's debt by 4 *gros* on both taxes.[45]

Jaquote de Fouvent

[1376] (She) became mad and nobody knows where she lives but one says that the wolves ate her.

Endnotes

1 Dijon Tax Relief Requests are unpublished handwritten archive individual documents preserved at the Archives Municipales de Dijon (AMD) with the following references: L 638 (1389–1422, 43 folios), L 639 (1423–1426, 522 folios), L 640 (1430–1432, 436 folios), L 641 (1433–1439) 458 folios), L 642 (1441–1443, 609 folios), L 643 (1444, 439 folios), L 645 (1446–1449, 506 folios). These documents contain more than 3,400 individual requests, 2,679 of which were included by Anne Galanaud in a personal database linked to the Annual Marcs Tax Registers database (see below). The database was used to describe the families, health problems, or security problems in Anne Galanaud, "Démographie et société à Dijon à la fin du moyen-âge (1357–447) à partir d'une analyse informatique des régistres des comptes de l'impôt des marcs," PhD thesis in History, Franche-Comté University, 2009.

2 The selection, translation and comments of the requests included in the present Sourcebook were realized by Anne Galanaud, PhD, no present affiliation and Pierre Galanaud, MD, UMR996, Inflammation, Chemokines and Immunopathology, Inserm, Univ Paris-Sud, Université Paris-Saclay, 92140, Clamart, France (contributors' address: pierre.galanaud@u-psud.fr). Tod W. Estroff, MD is acknowledged for advice in the translation from medieval French into modern English.

3 The *fouages* tax registers are unpublished handwritten archive documents preserved at the Archives Départementales de la Côte d'Or (ADCO).

4 Information on the historical context in Burgundy can be found in Richard Vaughan, *Philip the Bold: the Formation of the Burgundian State* (Longmans, 1962); *John the Fearless: Growth of the Burgundian Power* (Longmans, 1973); and *Philip the Good: The Apogee of the Burgundy* (Longmans, 1970).

5 Dijon Annual Marcs Tax Registers are unpublished handwritten archive annual documents preserved at the Archives Départementales de la Côte d'Or (ADCO) with the following references: (B 11483–B 11502). Fifty annual registers dated between 1376 and 1447, were included by Anne Galanaud in a personal database of more than 100,000 annual entries, which identified more than 13,000 individual heads of household. This database, initially designed for Anne Galanaud's PhD dissertation, was used in the present Sourcebook in order to trace the fate of the heads of household who submitted tax relief requests. Henri Labesse (Paris 4–Sorbonne University) is acknowledged for designing the original application used for the database and for his continuous support and help.

6 Jehan, a member of Dijon financial elite, directly submitted his request to the duchesse who wrote in his favor to the bailiff [Letter of the duchesse, in Joseph Garnier, *Correspondance de la mairie de Dijon: Extraite des archives de cette ville* (Rabutot, 1868), pp. 20–21].

7 The *fouages* tax collector had to justify that he was unable to tax Jaquote (ADCO, B 11574, 1376, f° 6v).

8 Bronislaw Geremek and Agneszka Kolakowska, *Poverty: A History* (Wiley-Blackwell, 1997).

9 AMD, L 638, 1422.

10 The bracketed text corresponds to additions designed to introduce modern syntax into the fifteenth century text or to provide additional information.

11 20 *sols* are worth 1 *franc* and Vincent begs for a 50% decrease.

12 6 *gros* are worth half a *franc* and he obtained a 25% decrease.

13 Two years later, Vincent is acknowledged as blind and ruined ["he became blind and lives upon charity" (ADCO, B 11492, 1424, f° 25v)].

14 AMD, L 640, 1430.

15 Although Jehan's "lost visual clarity" might be the consequence of far-sightedness, he could not work efficiently as a cobbler.

16 Jehan's total tax amount is reduced from 2 and half *francs* to 1 and half *franc*.

17 Five years later Jehan's marcs tax was decreased from 5 *sols* to the lower limit of 1 *sol*, a level that was maintained until his death in 1438 (ADCO, B 11493, 1429, f° 73r, B 11494, 1434, f° 79v,

B 11496, 1438, f° 72r), which indicates that he lost the major part of his assets.

18 AMD, L 638, July & October1422. AMD, L 639, June & September 1423.

19 1 *denier* is the 240th part of 1 *franc*.

20 Gautherin was indeed an ancient head of household, mentioned for the first time in 1382 in the *marcs* tax registers (ADCO, B 11487, 1382, f° 59r).

21 Five years later the *marcs* tax collector acknowledged the disability of Gautherin and his wife and he exempted them for poverty ["Gautherin and his wife are bedridden since one year and are so poor that they cannot pay" (ADCO, B 11493, 1428, f° 46r)] and three years later they were no more registered in the *marcs* tax registers, implying that they were probably dead or led to a hospital.

22 AMD, L 638, 1417; L 639, June 1423 & September 1423; L 639, 1424; L 640, 1430.

23 This haberdasher had to give up presenting his goods in fairs and markets because of gout, and from 1423, his successive tax relief requests were based on this disease and on his weakness, whereas his 1417 request was based on (real or alleged) financial problems.

24 Jaquot had to pay 8 *francs* in June and 8 *francs* in September.

25 When Jaquot died in 1439 his financial situation was not impaired, in view of his unchanged high level (50 sols) taxation for the *marcs* tax (ADCO, B 11496, 1439, f° 42r), and his wife Jaqobte survived for at least 8 years, with a preserved financial status (ADCO, B 11497, 1447, f° 42r).

26 AMD, L 638, 1422; L 639, 1423.

27 Maistre Estienne died two years later (ADCO, B 11492, 1425, f° 19v).

28 AMD, L 641, 1433.

29 Michelot's tax was reduced from 30 *francs* to 25 *francs* [December 4, 1433].

30 AMD, L 639, 1424.

31 Estienne's tax was thus totally expunged, and five years later, when he died, the level of his *marcs* tax had decreased by 50%, to 2 *sols* (ADCO, B 11493, 1429, f° 01v), which suggests that, despite his *fouage* tax exemption, the value of his assets was affected by his disability.

32 AMD, L 646, 1449.

33 The disease of Saint Loup corresponds to epilepsy.

34 "ydeote de la moitié de son corps."

35 AMD, L 641, 1433 & L 641, 1434.

36 Although Oudot obtained a 4 *gros* decrease of his 2 *francs* 1433 tax [November 25, 1433] and a 2 *gros* decrease of his 8 *gros* 1434 tax [July 16, 1434], six years later, he was registered as pauper...and deceased by the *marcs* tax collector (ADCO, B 11496, f° 49r).

37 AMD, L 641, 1433.

38 Estienne was also exempted from the *marcs* tax as pauper (ADCO, B 11494, 1434, f° 49r).

39 AMD, L 645, 1446 & 1448.

40 From 1447 Jehannot's mother paid his *marcs* tax in addition to her own (she was taxed as the widow of Jehannot's father) while Jehannot was no more registered as a head of household in the marcs tax registers, indicating that Jehannot was considered as fully dependent on his mother by the tax authorities (ADCO, B 11497, 1447, f° 58r & f° 54r).

41 AMD, L 641, 1434.

42 Jehan obtained a 6 *gros* decrease of his 1 *franc* tax.

43 AMD, L 638, 1417 & L 640, 1430.

44 The tax initial amount was 7 *gros*.

45 Perrenot died in 1444 (ADCO, B 11497, 1444, f° 62v).

Examining for Leprosy in the Fifteenth Century[1] (ca. 1430–1500)

Contributed by Lucy Barnhouse

Introduction

The following are letters to and from the council of Frankfurt, and in some cases, from the examining doctors themselves, concerning the late medieval inspection for leprosy, a process known as a *Lepraschau*, literally "a looking for leprosy." Those who availed themselves of the inspection hailed from a radius of over 100 kilometers. While leper hospitals are known to have existed in Europe from the twelfth century onwards, the *Lepraschau* came into existence much later. As cities gained economic and political power, they took over the responsibility for such examinations from hospital communities and members of the clergy. Studies of late medieval medicine have sometimes represented medical professionalization and the practice of medicine as a charitable work as models of thought in competition with each other. These fifteenth-century letters, however, present a view of medicine as simultaneously professional and charitable. In translating the letters, I have kept much of the formal and often involved phrasing used by petitioners, using multiple complimentary adjectives to address the officials by whom their health would be evaluated and certified. Departures from this formality can depend on both the petitioners' relationship to the council and doctors of Frankfurt, and on their responses to the ways in which they experience leprosy as a social disability. I have also attempted to stay very close to the original in describing leprosy itself. Multiple terms are used for the disease, and for how it affected those diagnosed with it; they might be "burdened" (*beladen, be-lummt*) or, more literally, "spotted" (*befleckt*) with it.

The letters reveal a standardized medical procedure, and a variety of communal responses to the disease. The standard examination for leprosy involved an inspection of every inch of the patient's skin, not only for distinctive visual signs of disease, but for sensitivity to pain, since nerve damage was a known consequence of leprosy. The doctors would also evaluate their petitioners' breath and voice, for a smell of corruption and a hoarseness associated with leprosy, respectively. Several of the letters refer to other processes of examination, by local officials or by certified medical professionals, like barbers. In such cases, Frankfurt's doctors were appealed to for their greater medical expertise; as one letter from the doctors demonstrates, this included access to a considerable medical library. Most of the surviving records are petitions, meaning that the outcome of diagnosis is almost always unknown. The doctors might diagnose petitioners as "clean" from leprosy, "unclean" with leprosy, or "half clean," a diagnosis meaning that the petitioner would be obliged to return for a follow-up examination to see whether their symptoms had improved or deteriorated. The medically cautious diagnosis of "half clean" might be a source of distress to the examinees.

Two letters were sent to the committee by secular lords, and one by a religious community. Of the rest, a dozen come from private individuals, and eleven from civic authorities. Six of the private letters came from one disgruntled individual, Henne Maderus. Living just up the Rhine from Frankfurt, he went for a second opinion to the still more renowned examination board in Cologne, which had one of medieval Germany's oldest and most prosperous leper hospitals. Civic-issued letters typically emphasize the seriousness of the undertaking, and the respect in which the physicians are held. Several such letters specify that the putative lepers have been suspected of having the disease for a long time, or by many; some explicitly request instructions on what steps should be taken if the person in question is leprous. A letter from Aschaffenburg indicates that lepers who were not prosperous might be treated in similar ways to other sick and poor people. The town officials of Weilburg demonstrate concern for the potential threat to public health posed by a woman's putative leprosy, and also for her well-being. Three letters from the committee to their petitioners do survive, alongside one form letter for such responses, and one list of instructions for the diagnosed leper. The latter reflects the medical view that fire could help to purify air, and prescribes foods believed to be beneficial for both the symptoms and causes of the disease.

Responses to a diagnosis of leprosy were dependent on numerous social variables, including but not limited to the concerned individual's social status. Following a medical diagnosis of leprosy, the men or women so diagnosed had multiple options open to them, determined by the severity of their symptoms, by their citizenship, and by the resources of their community. While there was a widespread expectation that a diagnosis of leprosy would have social ramifications, those seeking such diagnosis appear to have depended on the doctors for individualized recommendations for how best to manage the disease and accommodate those affected by it. The standardized list of dos and don'ts for diagnosed lepers, presumably sent from the commissioned doctors to the council, contains a definition of "specially set apart" that includes the injunction "not to frequent

public kitchens or bathhouses." This calls into question assumptions about the social meanings of separation for medieval lepers.

Hospital rules and business agreements from the region make clear that lepers might beg in the fields, live together in informal communities, or enter into hospitals. All those entering hospital life gave up their legal rights over property on doing so, as did all others undertaking life in religious institutions. Hospital residence also, however, offered the privileges of community, stability, and support. For those lepers who lived outside hospitals, the question of whether they were met with avoidance or accommodation appears to have been determined more by their existing social relationships than by their disease. Many petitioners to the council and doctors of Frankfurt include requests for instructions on how to help or accommodate those diagnosed with leprosy. The petitions show that men and women believing themselves to have leprosy might suffer significant distress; whether this was a consequence of their medical symptoms, or of fear of the social consequences of diagnosis, is rarely explicit. Petitions to Frankfurt's committee, as well as the reports and advice of the physicians, show that while diagnosis had significant effects on the ways in which lepers interacted with their communities, it did not put an end to such interaction.

Bibliography

Auge, Oliver. "'Ne pauperes et debiles in... domo degentes divinis careant.' Sakral-religiöse Aspekte der mittelalterlichen Hospitalgeschichte." *Sozialgeschichte mittelalterlicher Hospitäler*, edited by Neithard Bulst and Karl-Heinz Spiess. Jan Thorbecke Verlag, 2007, pp. 77–125.

Bergman, Fred. "Hoping against Hope? A Marital Dispute about the Medical Treatment of Leprosy in the Fifteenth-Century Hanseatic Town of Kampen." *The Task of Healing: Medicine, Religion, and Gender in England and the Netherlands, 1450–1800*, edited by Hilary Marland and Margaret Pelling. Erasmus, 1996, pp. 23–48.

Brenner, Elma. *Leprosy and Charity in Medieval Rouen.* Boydell and Brewer, 2015.

Demaitre, Luke. *Leprosy in Pre-modern Medicine: A Malady of the Whole Body.* Johns Hopkins University Press, 2007.

Dross, Fritz, and Annemarie Kinzelbach. "'Nit mehr alls sein burger, sonder alls ein frembder.' Fremdheit und Aussatz in frühneuzeitlichen Reichsstädten." *Medizinhistorisches Journal*, vol. 46, 2011, pp. 1–23.

Felten, Sebastian. "Mittendrin statt außen vor? Ein neuer Ort für Melaten bei Köln und der Paradigmenwechsel in der Leprageschichtsschreibung." *Geschichte in Köln. Zeitschrift für Stadt- und Regionalgeschichte*, vol. 57, 2010, pp. 11–37.

Jankrift, Kay Peter. "Vieillir parmi les morts vivants. La léproserie, hospice pour habitants non lépreux?" *Lépreux et sociabilité du Moyen Age aux temps modernes*, edited by Bruno Tabuteau. Publications de l'Université de Rouen, 2000, pp. 31–37.

Kinzelbach, Annemarie. "Infection, Contagion, and Public Health in Late Medieval German Imperial Towns." *Journal of the History of Medicine and Allied Sciences*, vol. 61, 2006, pp. 369–89.

Mortimer, Richard. "The Prior of Butley and the Lepers of West Somerton." *Bulletin of the Institute of Historical Research*, vol. 53, 1980, pp. 99–103.

Rawcliffe, Carole. *Leprosy in Medieval England.* Boydell & Brewer, 2006.

Sudhoff, Karl. "Dokumente zur Ausübung der Lepraschau in Frankfurt am Main im XV. Jahrhundert." *Lepra: Bibliotheca Internationalis*, vol. 13, 1913, pp. 141–70.

Medicinalia Nr. 1[2]

Ich Conradus Sassenhusen Medicine Doctor Bekennen mich uffenlich mit diesen Brief das mir furbracht und geäußert worden ist N. der mit Krankheid der ußsetzikeit belummd und behafft sin sulde. ~~Des so~~ Also han ich den selben N. uff hude disen dag dar diß Brief darum besehen und besucht in wies und forma als man solche lude pliget ~~und gewohnt~~ zu besuchen und han yn von den selben Krankheit der ußsetzikeit uff diese Zijt rein und unschuldig erfonden Des zu urkund und Bekenntnis han ich myn Ingesiegel

Medicinalia Nr. 167

Unser willige fruntliche dinste zuvor fursichtigen Ersamen und wysen lieben herren als ir uns eynen brieff habt lassen horen den uwerer Ersamket Maderus Henne von Ursel uns antreffende geschrieben hat clagende wie wir yn der ußsetzekeit geschuldiget sullen han / Deshalb er dorch die uwern gedrongen sy Das er sich zu Colne habe lassen beshen da er davon ledig gesaget zy // als sin brieff mit mee worten inhielt han wir verhort und lassen uwere fursichtikeit wissen das wir den vorgenanten henchin vor unse besehunge nichtis geschuldigt han Dan nach dem wir von uwerer Gesamkeit dartzugeordent und gesast sin soliche personen zu besehen und henneckin vorgenannt als der under syme angesicht fast ungestalt mit der krangheit belumut und von den luden gemyden wart / Ist er eigener bewegunge zu uns kommen uns oitmuderlich und dinstlich gebeden yn uff das nehste zu besehen und zu ersuchen / Also angesehen sin innige bete han wir yn vor uns gennomen yne besehen und versucht nach unser gewonheit und als sich geburet und han yn befunden das er die zijt mit der ußsetzekeit angefangen und etlicher masse damyde beflecket was das wir gesaget han nach unßn besten synnen und verstentenis und als wir darzu gelobt und gesworn han und han yn sonst davor von uns selbs nichtis geschuldiget / noch / nach yme gesant dan so vil wir umb siner bede willen getan han und wissen im auch nichtis deßhalb schuldig oder

Medicinalia Nr. 1

I, Conrad Sachsenhausen, doctor of medicine, acknowledge openly with this letter that it has been brought to my attention that N. is burdened with leprosy, or rumored to be so. ~~Therefore~~ So I have examined the same N. on this day today that this letter was made, examined in the manner and form that is customary ~~and usual~~ for such people, and have found him at this time to be clean and innocent [of leprosy.] And in testimony and acknowledgment of this I have placed my seal.

Medicinalia Nr. 167

Our willing and friendly service to the cautious, honorable, and wise men of the council. As you have let us hear a letter that Henne Maderus of Ursel wrote you regarding us, complaining and claiming that we falsely accused him of having leprosy, wherefore he was oppressed by you, and that he had himself examined in Cologne, where he was pronounced free of leprosy. We have heard his letter—that contained still more words—and let your honors know that we accused the above-named Henne of nothing before our examination. For we were set and ordered by you, collectively, to examine such persons, and the above-named Henne was almost disfigured with the symptoms of disease, and was avoided by people. So he came to us of his own accord, and humbly and earnestly begged us to most closely examine and test him. Therefore, in view of his earnest request, we took him before us, examined and tested him according to our custom, in a fitting manner. And we found in him: that he is at this time in the beginning stages of leprosy, and is to a certain degree marked with it. This we said, according to our best understanding, and according to our professional oath, and have accused him of nothing else on our own account—nor did we send for him! What we have done, we did according to his request and will, and are aware of no obligation or guilt in his regard. If, however, the above-named Henne thinks that we

plichtig zu sin / Duchte aber hennechin vor-genant das wir yme deßhalb nichtes plichtig weren / So wonen wir hie by des heiligen Rijchs gerichte sunder geleide So wollen wir ime oder syme machtbotten von sinen wegen rechtes gehorsam sin oder obe er begert vor uwerer Ersamkeit dem Rade und biden uwer Ersamkeit diese unse antwort laß zum steen dann wir geschrieben konnen uns auch daruff zum antworten by glyche und rechte zu be-halden und zustedingen das wallen wir mit willen alletzijt gerne verdienen Geben under myn hennen ulm ingesigel des wir andern uns myd Henen gebruchen uff mitwochen nach dionisii anno domini lviii [edge of paper is torn/damaged]

Heinricus lose licenciatus in medicinis henne ulm gnt Augspurg und hans harpe

Medicinalia Nr. 169[3]

Den Ersamen Wysen Burgermeystern und Radt der Stadt Ffranckfurt meynen guten frunden

Madrus Henne bey Ursel und darauff der Rad nit wulde antworten[4]

Ersamen wysen lieben herren Ich enbieten uch mynen dynst zu for / So als ich von den uwern wegen geschrieben han / also hant yr mir widder geschrieben und eyn abeschriefft eyns brieffs in uwer schr. ieft geschicket dar Inn die uwern meldent / wie das sie mich von yr besehunge nit geschuldiget haben / und nach dem sie von uwer ersamkeyt wegen geordent und gesatzt sint etlich personen zu besehen und ich under mynen angesicht fast ungestalt und mit der ußsetzigkeit belumet und von den luden gemeden sii ich in eyncher bewegunge zu yen komen sie oitmudiglichen und dynstlichen gebeden mich uff das nehist zubesehen und zuversuchen angesehen myn mudige bede und mich vergenomen besehen und versucht nach yr gewonheit und sich geburt und haben mich befunden das ich die zijt der ußsetzigkeit beflecket sij gewest und meynt mir deßhalben vor uch zurecht zustene wie dann dieselbe schrieft mit etwe viel me worten inhelt / Han ich verstanden und die mynen guten frunde laßen horen er-

owe him something on this account: we live here, by the imperial court, without entou-rage, and we are ready to abide by the law in anything that he or his proxy may request of us or your honors of the council. And we ask your honors to let this our answer stand, that we have written as testimony that we will abide by the law and uphold equity. This is our earnest, obedient desire at all times. Given under my (Henne Ulm's) seal, that we others use with him, on the Wednesday after the feast of St. Dionysius, in the Year of Our Lord [14]58.

Heinricus Lose, licensed doctor of medi-cine

Henne Ulm, known as Augsburg

Hans Harpe

Medicinalia Nr. 169

To the honorable and wise mayor and council of the city of Frankfurt, my good friends

Henne Maderus, of Ursel—and the coun-cil decided not to answer it

Honorable and wise good lords, I offer you my service. As I wrote to you concern-ing your [doctors,] you wrote back to me and sent to me a copy of a letter in your writing in which your [doctors] say that they have not blamed me in their examination, and how they are ordered and set by your honors to examine many persons. [They said] I was al-most disfigured in my face, and spotted with leprosy, and avoided by people: that I came to them in considerable agitation, and humbly begged them to closely examine me, and that in view of my earnest prayer, they heard me and examined me as is customary and seemly. They said that I was found to be spotted with leprosy at that time, and that they sent me to stand openly before you.... and their let-ter had many more words in it. I understood this, and let my close friends hear it as well. Honorable good friends, your [doctors] may write what they like about their conduct with me. I don't doubt that you received and have well understood my letter that I got concern-

samen guden frunde die uwern mogent von mir schryben was yen fuget aber nach dem sie mit mir umbgangen sint / So zwyfelt mir doch nit yr habent myn schriefft der uß-setzigkeit halber die ich zu Coelen erlanget han und an dem ende do sich eyn iglicher ußsetziger uff dem Rynestromen geburt zu besehen wole verstanden / das mir die uwern villicht durch haß ungutlichen gethan und nit mit warheit mit mir umbgangen sint / des ich dan tzu großen sweren kosten komen bin und teglichen komen / Und dar umb so finden mich nit in rade myner guten frunde vor uch zu rechten oder thedigen und getru-wen uwer Ersamkeyt wole / yr sollent myn geboit und ußdrag uff myns gnedigen herren des Pfaltzgraven Amptluden uffnemen und der nit verslagen In maßen ich uch in myner ersten schrieff geboiten uch und den uwern bekommen moge / Geben under des festen Jungher Anthis Kuchen Ingesiegel uff ffrytag nach sant Lucas tag des heyligen ewangelis-ten /Anno MCCCC LVIII

ing leprosy from Cologne, where they are ac-customed to examine lepers from the entire length of the Rhine. So perhaps your [doc-tors] did unjustly by me because of hatred, and did not treat me truthfully, so that I have received great damage thereby, and still do so daily. And for this reason, I do not find myself disposed to justify or defend myself before you, my friends, and I trust your hon-ors to take up my command and order to the officials of my gracious lord the Pfaltzgrave, and not to decline it. May it be to you and your [doctors] as I directed in in my first let-ter. Given under the firm seal of the knight Anthis Kuchen, on the Friday after the feast of St. Luke the Evangelist, 1458.

Medicinalia Nr. 170

Den ersamen und wisen burgermeister und rat der stadt frankfurt mynen guden frunden

Mynen fruntlichen dinst zuvor irsamen lieben Herrn also als ich uwer Irsamkeit vormals me geschrieben han als von meyster Henrick den stede arzt und Henchin Augs-purger und Meyster Hans Scherer under den portin wegen als dan uwer Irsamkeit wolle verstanden hat was myner forderung an sye ist Irsamen lieben herren uff den uwern Ir-samkeit ye versten moge den ich sehr gerne thun wolde was uch und den uwern lieb were also wil ich eins thun den der obgenannten person zwene uz dem rade Losin und ich zwene was uns dy in fruntlichkeit entschei-din nach ergangen sachen sal myn wolle und wie thun und uns dar comin gutlichen dag beschidet und biden uch in dar yn gutliche beschedich Antwort zugeben mich dannach wyse zu richten und wolt mer soliche uwer antworte schicken gein punckten in anyus [sic; Anthis] es laßhent hat geben und In-

Medicinalia Nr. 170

To the honorable and wise mayor and council of the city of Frankfurt, my good friends.

My friendly service to the wise and be-loved men [of the council]. When I wrote to Your Honors previously, that is to Mas-ter Heinrich, the city doctor, and Hennekin Augsburger, and Master Hans Scherer under the gateway, Your Honors well understood what my demand of you was. My dear good lords: I wish that your honors may under-stand that I am very willing to do what is desired by you and your [experts], and un-dertake to do the following. Let the above-named persons choose two persons from the council, and I will choose two, who may then represent us and decide equitably between us, concerning what has passed between us. This is my desire, and shall be my conduct. I want a definite answer on a day of judgment, and pray you to give a favorable and decisive answer, and that you may send me an answer with specific points, as Anthis has given his

gesigel jaht da wart daz ich mich gebrauchen zu diser zijt dar in hier uff domini nativitatis mitwachen

Maderus Hen von ursel

favor to, and confirmed with his seal that I am using at this time, here on the Wednesday within Christmastide.

Henne Maderus of Ursel

Medicinalia Nr. 171

Den ersamen und wisen burgermeister und Rad der Stadt zu Francford unser liben herrn

Maderus Henne ab clage us die bescheid der ussetzigkeit Ist Im gesagt ebo das er Reyne besch sy daz er sich dan mache dar under und sy sie nit ryne sy

Unseren schuldigen dinst zu vor Ersamen wisen lieben Hern Also Maderus Hen von Ursel . Mynet Eyn forderunge an uns zu han von des beseches wegen . also wir in besehen han uff die maledie und begert eynen fruntlichen dag mit uns zu halden uff unser siten tzwene uß den rade tzu nehmen und uff syner siten wil he auch tzwene den tzu gebben uns zu entscheiden nach ußwysunge synes sende brieff hy inne beslossen Also thun wir uch demudeclichen zu wissen was uwer vorsichtige ersamekeit heyßen wil und begert von uns zu thunde das uns und henchin recht gescheen moge na ansprache und antworte da wollen wir willich in syn den also na zu geende und wollen us blyben an uch oder an allen den und iglichen in dem rechten dy ir dar tzu gebben wollet Datum quarto diem lyeo die martiri post pasca under Her Henrichs loser stedeartzt ingesigel das wir uff dis maele uns gebruchen

Heinrich Loser ingesigel
Oped fratrum physici
Johan Augsburg
Johan Harp uwer undersaher

Medicinalia Nr. 171

To the honorable and wise mayor and council of the city of Frankfurt, our dear lords.

Maderus, Henne: with a complaint arising from the fact that a decision of leprosy was declared to him, but that he now appears to be clean, and asks what he ought to do under this judgment, if he be not clean.

Our obligation and service to the honorable, wise, and beloved councilmen. As Henne Maderus, of Ursel, has sent a request to us regarding examination, as we have examined him for leprosy. And he desires to have us hold a day of arbitration, where two from the council may come on our side, and he wants to send two representatives as well, to make a decision in light of the display of his letter of diagnosis, herein enclosed. So, we humbly ask that we may know from you, what your honors may advisedly command, and what you wish us to do, that right may be done by Henchin [Madern] and by us, after request and answer. And we are perfectly willing to approach him again, and will abide by your decision in all points and in every detail. Given the fourth day after Easter, the feast of Leo the martyr [April 11], under the seal of Herr Heinrich Loser, civic physician, which we're using for our business this time.

Heinrich Loser seal
Oped, the physician's brother
Johan Augsburg
Johan Harp, your apprentice inspector

Medicinalia Nr. 154[5]

Unser freuntlichen dinst und waz wir liebes vermogen zuvor ersamen wysen besindere guten frunde wir laßen uch wissen wie das dieser gegen wurtige henna Kaufmann bii uns in Nerstein verkommt ist / wie das er mit der krankheit der ußseßigkeit beflecket sy. / Und han wir virstan den / die daz ire

Medicinalia Nr. 154

Our friendly service, and all that which our love may do, to our honorable and wise and very good friends. We hereby let you know that this present Henne Kaufmann came to us in Nierstein, as he might be spotted with the sickness of leprosy. And we have understood that you have masters by you in

meistere in uch in Franckefurd haben / die sich des virstene und die selben siechen auch wole versuchen und besehen können / Davon so bieten wir euch dinstlichen frundlichen und ernslichen nach den selben meistern zu schicken vor uch zu kommen und Yen mit ernste zu sagen und sie zu heißen den bob-genannte Henne Kauffman wole zuunter-suchen wie sich daz dann geburt ob er solch Krankheit an ime habe oder nit und wol-lent uwer Ratffrunde auch daz by schicken solches helfen zuversorgen / Und wie iß dar umb gelegen ist daz wollent uns mit Heyme offen versiegelten Briefe by diesen unseren bitten wissen lassen uns dar nach zu richten und wollent uns dieß bede nit virsagen und uch gunstlich und fruntlichen her inne bew-ysen das wollen wir in Metern machen um uch und die uwern verdienen wo wir morgen geben under unseres Dorfes und Gerichts In-gesiegel uff Sonntag vor unser lieben frauwen dag Naivität anno iv xxxiiij

Schultheiß und Scheffener des Gerichts zu Nerstein

Unser fr dinst zuvor lieben besunderen freunde als se uns Geschrieben hat wie daz Henne Kauffman bij euch zu Niesten verlu-ment sy daz er mit der Krankheit der uß-setzikeit befleckt sy und unsere Meinung ist nach dem unser zuschenken und in zusagen und sie zuheissen den og. Hennen Kauffman wole zuversuchen wie sich daz gelobt ob er solch Krankheit an Ime habe od. nit. und wie es darum gelegen sy daz wir uch daz sullen in unserem wissen lassen darnach zurichten des lassen wir euch wissen daz wir umb uw-ern willen de unsere de solche lude by uns pflegen zu besehen und zuversuchen vir uns virbede han und in die sache befohlen nach den sie dan darum gelobt und gesehen han. Die wieder vur uns kommen sy und han in solcher maße gesagt und erkannt daz sie in also besehen und versucht haben / und er-finden in zudiß zijt der sache halber reyne Krankheiten [ohne] alle Arglist und gevere fra. Tertia. aux Datum Nativitatem bte. Ma-rie vg. glose. Anno xiiii xxxiiii

Frankfurt, who are knowledgeable in such matters, and can well inspect and examine such sick persons. Therefore we pray you, humbly, warmly, and earnestly, to send for the said masters, that they may come before you. And we pray that you may seriously charge them to well examine the said Henne Kaufmann, as it is fitting, to say whether or not he has this sickness, and to send some of your council-members to assist as well. And however it may be, we pray you to send us word with a public letter, under seal, via this our messenger. We pray that you may not deny this plea, and show yourselves favorable and friendly to us in this matter, and pledge to repay you and your [experts.] We have giv-en this in the morning under the seal of our village and court, on the Sunday before the Nativity of Our Lady, 1434.

The sheriff and lay judges of the court in Nierstein

Our friendly service to our very dear friends, as they have written to us how Henne Kaufmann, with you in Nierstein, was reput-ed to be spotted with the sickness of leprosy, and wished us to send for our [experts] and to tell and command them that they should thoroughly and well [examine] the above Henne Kaufmann, according to their oaths, and to say whether he has that sickness or not, and what his condition is. And this we should let you know, so that you might re-spond accordingly. So, we hereby inform you that, in accordance with your request, we have given commands regarding this mat-ter to those who are accustomed to perform such examinations, and they have taken their oaths and looked [at him] accordingly. And they in turn came to us and reported in the following manner: that they have examined and inspected him, and find that regarding the matter at this present time, he is half free of sickness, without any deception or malice.

Given on the third day after the Nativity of the Blessed Virgin Mary 1434.

Medicinalia Nr. 155⁶

Wir der Rad zu Frankfurt verrichten und tun kund uffentlich mit diesem brief das Gudrus und Peter Scherer unser Burger vor uns kommen sij und mit In yner der sich genant hat Contze Lantgrave von hoenlagen in Hessen gelegen und erzalten de ob.Gudrus und Peter wie das izunt kurzlichen zu In kommen sy der og. Contze Landgrave in habe erzalt und verbracht habe daz er virlument sy von der uzsetzigkeit und feltsuchte wegen, das er darwyde beladen und befleckt nit Reyn sy sulle Des han de og. Gudrus und Peter vor uns besagit und gesprochen uff ire Eide de sie uns daruber gelobt und gesprochen han daz sie den og. Contzen besehen versucht und dazu getan haben als sich gehort und habn in zudiß zijt so der sache halb Ryne erfunden uzgeschieden alle Arglist und gewehrte Und han wir des zubekentniß der og. unser stede Ingesiegel an diesen brief tun drucken Datum anno domini M CCCC tricesimo quarto feria Quarta ante diem sancti Michahelis archangelis

Medicinalia Nr. 156

Unser fruntliche willige dynst Ewer weyßheit mit allem vermögen zuvor an bereit / fürsichtigen Ersamen und weisen besondern lieben Herren und guten fründe / Wir senden uch zeiger dis brifs samt synem eelichen gemahlen / die von uns und der ganzen gemeyn mit der Krankheit der ußsetzikeyt berüchtigt ist derhalber Sie hiebevor auch hie by den Jhenen so von Ewer weysheit solch krank lude zu besuchtigen verordnet gewest und zu disser zeit widder bescheyden und volenden danach an Ewer weißheit unser freundlich bit ir wollt uch um unserem Willem solch bemühen und an den verordneten verschaffen das sie fleyß ankeren und die Wahrheit ganzlich erfahren // Damit so sie befleckt wer kein weyther unradt daruß komme Dann wir mochten Ir wohl vergunden das sie ryn erfündig würde uch herrin gutwillig ertzeigen

Medicinalia Nr. 155

We the council of Frankfurt make known publicly by this letter that Gudrus and Peter Scherer, our citizens, came before us together with one identifying himself as Contze, Landgrave of Hohenlagen in Hessen, and the aforesaid Gudrus and Peter explained how, a short time before this, the aforesaid Landgrave Contze came to them and told them that there were rumors about him regarding leprosy, that he was supposedly unclean burdened and spotted with it. Regarding this, the aforesaid Gudrus and Peter testified before us, and swore on their oath—that they had taken in our presence—that they examined Contze and behaved as is seemly in such matters, and have at this time, in this case, [Contze] is found half-clean, without any malice or deceit. And in acknowledgment of this aforesaid matter, we have had our city seal pressed onto this letter. Given in the Year of Our Lord 1434, four days before the feast of St. Michael the Archangel.

Medicinalia Nr. 156

Our friendly and willing service to your honors, ready to do anything within our power for you from now on. Careful, honorable, and wise men [of the council], dear and good friends: we send to you the bearer of this letter, together with his wedded wife, who is thought—by us and by the whole community—to have the sickness of leprosy. So she has been examined here already by those who are commissioned to examine such sick persons, as are your honors. And at this time, we send our friendly request to your honors, that you might make a decisive and final judgment in this matter. Please, for our sakes, undertake this and make it clear to the appointed doctors that they should apply themselves diligently to this and find out the whole truth, so that, if she is so spotted, no further misfortune should come of it. For we

das wollen wir in dem oder in eyn merern gegen ewer Weisheit widerumb verdynen Datum under unser stadt gemeyn Ingesigel uff Montag nach dem heiligen Ostertag anno M/ xxviii

Bürgermeister Rat und gantz gemeyn zu Wylburg

wish, indeed, that you may report that she is found clean, and would show yourselves favorable [to us] in this matter, and we would deserve this from your honors in this or in other matters. Given under the shared seal of our city, on Monday after the holy day of Easter, [14]28.

The mayor, council, and entire community of Weilburg [an der Lahn]

Medicinalia Nr. 157

Unsern freundlichen dinst euer Ersamen lieben wissen und besonderen guden frunde wir bidden uch wissen daz iser bewißer dißes brieffes genat Henne Baddebender unser midde burger beruchtiget ist, und wir selber besorget, daz er beladen sy mit der maletzen sucht. Des han wir vernommen wij das by euch etliche lude syn solden die sich verstehen soll uff dy obegenanten maleczkeit und dy lude besehen konne und probennen und des bidden wir uch umb unseres lieben gnedigen herren von Menzen und uns disen ebengenannten Henne tzu wissen und bringen an dy jenen dy en besehen und proben konnen von der ognt. maletzheit und das ir uns des egenlich eyn beschrieben Antwort geben wollent wy eß um den ogn. menschen gelegen sy und uch dy jenen bescheiden dy solichs besehen dut her yn daz beste uff das uns und uns ern nachgeburen nicht forter schade ca von entstehen möge daz woln wir allezyt gut verdienen under unseren Secret Datum anno domini M CCCC xxxix in die blasii episcopi

Burgermeister und Rad czu Dhuneburg

Medicinalia Nr. 157

Our friendly service to your honors, dear, wise, and very good friends. We pray you know that the bearer of this letter, Henne Baddebender, our fellow-citizen, is rumored to be burdened the sickness of leprosy, and we ourselves are concerned about this. Regarding this, we've heard that there are supposedly a number of people by you who have understanding of the aforesaid sickness, who can examine and test people for it. And we pray you, for the sake of our gracious lord [the archbishop] of Mainz and our own, to acknowledge this said Henne and bring him to those who can examine and test concerning the aforesaid leprosy and that you can indeed give us a written answer concerning how it is with the above-named man and also that those chosen to examine such persons may do their best, in order that no more harm may come of this, to us and our neighbors. And we will always endeavor to deserve this of you. Given under our seal, in the Year of Our Lord 1439 on the day of St. Blaise the bishop.

The mayor and council of Duneburg.

Medicinalia Nr. 158

Wir Otto Probste, Katherina Eptissin, Katherina priorissin, und die samenunge gemeynlichen des Closters zu Blangkenauwe empbyden unsirs inges gebede / dem Erbern Rad zu Frangkffort unseren besondern guden freunden . und biden uwer Erberkeit wissen, und klagen uch das wir ein ingeseyte Jungffrauen unsir kuchemeide eine itzunt lange ziit undir uns gweste ist und die ist swache / das wir besorget sine das sie nicht reine sye

Medicinalia Nr. 158

We, Otto the provost, Katherina the abbess, Katherina the prioress, and the entire assembly of the convent of Blankenau offer our most earnest prayers to the honorable council of Frankfurt, our very good friends. We pray that Your Honors may know—and lament to you!—that one of the virgins of our community, our kitchen maid, who has been among us for a long time now, is so weak that we are worried that she might be un-

/ das uns danne gar eyn swere sache were under uns zu wonen / des sint wir underricht worden / und sine des selben Jungfrauwen here geschigket hane / daz sie moge besehen werde Biden wir uwer Errsamkeit flelichen, daz ir umme godis willen, und umme einer ganzen sammenunge willen disen geinwertigen unsern Bruder mit Namen hans genant beholfen wollt sine den wir indruwen und glauben usgeschigket hane / das hier mit der Jungfrauen zu den Meistern kume, das sie besehen werde, und eure Ehrsamkeit mögen genissen, das uns ware werde zugesayt, und ir auch gnädig sei abir icht gebore dem Meister zu geben was sie arme ist und ir freunde Elende und keine zuleigung von nymans haid So ist unser Closter seer notdürftig und hane manniche elende arme Jungfrauen under uns ist die keine zuleigunge haben, was alleine der gemeyne almose der sy siche gebruchen hir umb bidden wir uwer Ersamkeit und tugent das ir allis euer bestes zu disen sache wollet thune als wir uch geinzlichen gedruwen und glauben / das wollen wir mit einer ganzen samenunge geine gode mit unserem gebode flisslichen umb euer Ehrsamkeit verdienen zu tage und zu nacht Gegeben undir unsir probestes Ingesigel / des wir uns Gemeynlichen gebruchen zu disen sachen.

clean. And thus, it might be a difficult thing for her to live among us; we have been informed of this. And so we have sent the said young woman there, that she may be examined. And we earnestly pray Your Honors—for God's sake and for the sake of our whole community—that you may use the help of our Brother Hans, whom we have sent out in good faith to accompany the young woman to the masters for inspection. Your honors may truly judge that we are honest, and beg you to be merciful, and pay what is owed to the masters. For she is poor, and her friends are poorer, and she has no help from anyone. Our cloister, too, is impoverished, and has several poor young women who do not have any other means of support; our common alms are used exclusively by the sick. Therefore we beg your honors, that you will do all of your best in this matter, since we place our entire faith and trust in you. And we will repay this with the earnest prayers of our whole community for you, day and night. Given under our provost's seal, which we collectively use in these [business] matters.

Medicinalia Nr. 164[7]

Wir Heinricus Loße Stedearzt hen harp Johan Augspurg thun kunt ynen iglichen menschen daß wir von befelenis wegen der ersamen wisen unseren liben herren der rade von Frankfurd han besehen uff die maledye / die vornonfftige konne Hans Fransberger ~ widdewe des harnesmethir na gelaßen und han erkannt und bekennen daß dißße vorgenannte widdewe hait an der nasen und an den lippen ires mundes eyn gestockelte maledie dy man nennet die kanker von eynen floß de heuptis na dem also Avicenna sprichet in den verdenbuche von der ußsetzzekeit / Et cum cancer qui est lepra unius membri und hait dißer kanker eyn eygenschafft mit der rechten gemeyn maledie / und dißße widdewe haet nit dye maledie dy da usprunglich

Medicinalia Nr. 164

We, Heinricus Loße, civic doctor, Henne Harp, and Johann Augsburg inform anyone reading this that we, as commanded by the honorable and wise council members of Frankfurt, our dear lords, have undertaken an inspection for leprosy. We admitted the prudent relative of Hans Fransberger, widow of the harness-maker, and have seen and testify that this above-named widow has on her nose and on the lips of her mouth the putrid sickness that is known as "the canker," from a flow from the head, of which also Avicenna speaks in the book of causes of leprosy: *And concerning the cancer that is a leprosy of the whole body...and this cancer has shared characteristics with the true, common leprosy. This widow does not have the

95

kommet von swachtigkeit oder lebbir dy man nennet in sich selbis maledunge oder lepra universalis oder dy gemeyn maledie dy da dey gantzen lip beflecken mag / da dorch die lude vilth zu scheiden sint / und also dan disße widdewe dy disße vorbenannte gestorkelte maledie hait an der nasen by den munde mit alsolicher schigkungen zu dem ußfallen also daß davon den atham entzuntlich und scheddelich wirt machen da von schadden kommen mag dar umb sint wir mit redelichen sachen und bedechtelich beweget vilth disße vorg. widdewe von dy lude zu scheiden mit wisßen laube und orlaup unseren liben vorgenannten herren und mag sich gebruchen der fryheit und der almusen alsolicher apgescheiden luden / und daß in alsolicher maße han gethan wante disße sache hait in swere und eyn sunderliche ußrichtunge Datum anno domini MCCCCLVII die veneris quarta martii sub sigilli mei Henrici superscripti opidi Frankfurd phsici jurati ad instanciam et petitionem doctorum hen harp Johan Augspurg huic carte imp(ressum)

leprosy that comes originally from weakness or from the liver, that is called "malady" or "universal leprosy" or "common leprosy" that can mark the whole body, through which many people are to be separated [from others]. Since this widow has this above-named sickness on the nose and near the mouth, so that the diseased skin has the tendency to fall off, and so that the breath becomes damaging and contagious from it, so that harm might come of it, therefore we are—after mature consideration—seriously inclined to direct that this widow should be separated from the healthy, with the wise permission of our dear lords, above-named, and she may have such freedoms and such alms as are customary for such people. And we have behaved in this matter as was seemly in the situation, and have given a weighty and special judgment. *Given in the Year of Our Lord 1457, on the fourth Friday in March, under the seal of me, Heinrich the above-signed, sworn physician of Frankfurt, at the request and insistence of the doctors Henne Harp and Johan Augsburg. Thus was this page made.*

Medicinalia Nr. 165

Unser willige dinste zuvor / unde was wir gudes vermogen Ersamen wisen guten frundde disse geynwertigen dietze Koch unde Gelichen eeliche lute unser midde Burger hand uns gebeten uch zuschreiben Nach dem die itzundgenante Gelichen beruchtiget ist biz here etliche Jare das sie beladen sye mid der krangkheide der ußsetzekeyde abe von daz also sye oder nicht / wollen wir eyn wißen han / weren no yemands bie uch in uwer Stadt der da von eyn wißen hette und daruber gesatzt were Begeren wir von uch und bidten uch rechte frundlichen das ir uns ztuwillen den selben vorgnt damidde furderlichen sin wullet und bestellen das en solichs gedien möge das die vorgnt Gele probert werde wie es umb sie gelegen sye und uns des schyn und warheid brenge wie wir uns dar inne halden sullen wullet uch hie inne als gudwillig bewisen als wir uch des unde alles guten besinde gentzlich gluiben und zugetruwen wollen wir

Medicinalia Nr. 165

Our willing service and all that we may do of good to our honorable and wise good friends. These present, Dietze and Geliche Koch, a married couple, our fellow-citizens, have entreated us to write to you, because the above-named Geliche has been rumored for many years now to be burdened with the sickness of leprosy. So, we would like to know whether she is or not, if now there are those by you in your city who have knowledge about such things and are appointed to judge concerning it. We desire of you, and ask you most warmly that you may further the above-named woman's cause in this, and give orders that, as it is seemly, the above-named Gele may be tested to see how it is with her, and bring us the truth, and the writing about how we should behave accordingly. Please show yourselves favorable in this matter, as we are favorable to you in all things, and trust and believe you entirely, and will diligently

und fliße gerne verdienen uwer beschrieben antworte geben und unser der Staidt Giessen Ingeß des Fritags neste vor dem Sontage vocem Jocunditatis anno domini lviii

Burgermeyster Scheffen
und Rath zum Gießen

Medicinalia Nr. 175

Denn Ersamen fursiechtigenn und wysenn Burgermeistere Scheffene und Raidt zu frankfurt mynenn liebenn Herren

Heinrich Wixhuser von siner besehunge

Myennen undertenigen und willigen dinst Zuvor Ersamen und wysen lieben herren . Hans Offsteyner myne Swager hat als der ihene der mir gewant ist und glymppiger dann andere den das Ampts halber gevore zuwegenn bringen konne / durch befelhe meyner Herren der Bürgermeistere von uwer wysheit wegen fruntlich und swegerlich anbraicht \ wie wer wyßheit der Raidt gemeynlichen uberkommen sy mich die gesworne besehen und examinieren zulaissen / dan des Rades fründe und andere den by mir zusitzen gevore und zuhandeln schuwens und nausien haben / In maissen als obe ich mir der krangheit der maledy beladen und verlümont sülle syn ich / Uff solichs myns Swagers anbrengen Ich yne und Arnolt Swarzinberger mynen lyden wieder zu uwer wyßheit gefertiget / Sie an myn herren des Rades fründe werben damit gutlichen virten lassen hain ire werbunge furter an uwer wyßheit den Raidt zubringen das auch zugutem von mir zuverstehen und offtzunemen / das mich nit wenig befremde / derwyle und ich itzt viel jare und tzijt by uch gesessen der und derglichen verlumung von uwer wyßheit / ingemeynde oder Insünderheit nye affter uzunt / so ich leyder von gottes des herren zuschickunge / mit mancherley anderer zufelligen libes krangheit und bekommernisse myne selbst und auch myner lieben husfrauwen Georgen myns swagers Ires Bruders halber angefochten werden und beladen byn vernomen hin / also stumppff und slingen ersucht worden sülte syn / Byn des getruwens das ich und myner Hausfrauen altern sonder-

study to deserve well of you. Please give your written answer. Under our seal of the city of Gießen, on the Friday before Jocunditatis Sunday, in the Year of Our Lord [14]58.

The major, sheriff, and council of Giessen.

Medicinalia Nr. 175

To the honorable, perceptive, and wise Mayor, officials, and council of Frankfurt, my dear lords.

Heinrich Wixhuser concerning his examination

My humble and willing service to the honorable and wise men, my good lords. Hans Offsteyner, my brother-in-law, has—as someone who is related to me—brought my case before you, "in a friendly and brotherly manner," more earnestly than for the sake of office, through command of the mayor on your behalf. Now, the wise and unanimous decision of the council was to have me seen and examined by the sworn [doctors,] since my friends on the council, and others who often sit with me and do business with me have experienced nausea and disgust as if I were burdened with the sickness of leprosy, or rumored to be so. And with this presentation of my brother-in-law, I and Arnold Swarzinberger, against him, have prepared another account of my suffering for your honors, and entreat that you bring it to my lords and friends of the council, and weigh it worthily. I pray also that your wisdom will take this into account in my favor, and accept it. I am not a little astonished—as I have sat among you for such a long time for so many years—that this and similar rumors have been given credence by your honors, whether some of you or all of you, now or at any time. So, with whatever sickness or sicknesses I may be, alas, afflicted by the will of God, and for the sake of which I and my dear wife have been attacked and accused by my brother-in-law (her brother) Georg, let me be tested for it, and examined concerning the numbness [of skin] and the sound [of my voice.] You know the trust that I and my wife (setting

lichen myner lieber Sweher seliger dem got gnade solichs umb och verdienet sulden hain // Daruff uwer wysheit meynunge ist mit mir eyn echt tage zuversuchen und zubeyden obe ich dabynnen wieder zu crefften komen moge seliche examinatio zuerlyten / daruber sy esß uweren wyßheit umb anderer lute sage willen entlegen ubel lenger zu dolden Nu ist mercklichen zuversteen das eyn krancke persone als ich byn in aicht tagen wenig besserunge oder stercke erlangen moge / des ich got dem herren ergeben / So ist myne gütliche bete an uch derwyle und iß nit anders syn wil oder mag ir wüllent in sünderheit und gemeynde auch under rychen geweldigen armen und an allen andern enden was wesens oder stadts die syn / thun suchen und erforschen / den selben mir dem maß messen damit das den Rychen geweldigen und den armen mit glichem masse gemessen und daz soliche ümont nit alleyn an mir und mynen fründen ußfündig gerechtfertigt und gesmehet werden / So das Geschieht welchs tages dan uwer wysheit der examinatio an mir zuthun nit entraden wil / so byn ich bereit umb gottes willen zulyden und zuthun wes mir geboret so serre das den rychen geschee als dem armen eynem als dem andern als billich ist / Und wülle uwer wyßheit diesze myne schryben von mir gütlich versteen und zu keynem unwillen uffnemen als ich mich des und alles güten gentzlichen zu uch vermüden gebürt mir zubedencken / dan ich mich der kortzen an fertigünge ersuchunge und sinehunge geyn mir und den mynen der meynunge in diessen mynen alten tagen / Auch myn und myn er lieben husfrauwen grossen libes krangheit und anfechtunge uns itzt In viel wyse zufallen mit nichts in keyne weyse versehen hette wiederfaren sulte syn billicher langest fur oder hernach gescheen were Geben under myn ingesiegel uff Dornstag nehst nach dem Sontag Oculi Anno xiiii lxx nono ~

aside [the testimony of] my dear, deceased brother-in-law, to whom God be gracious!) have deserved of you of old. Regarding this, it is your wisdom's intention to examine me in a week's time, and to wait and see if I have recovered enough strength to undergo such an examination. And in this matter you say it is your wish to do so because, on the advice of others, you do not think this evil should be suffered any longer. Now, it's obvious that a sick person like myself can expect only slight improvement or strengthening in a week's time—but I have entrusted this matter to God! So my earnest request to you—made now, and it will be unchanging—is that you may examine me in the same way that you do all others, specially and generally, among the rich and powerful and among the poor, of whatever place or city they be, searching and examining most earnestly, and treating all—rich, powerful, or poor—with the same measure. So let it be, that such a rumor may not damage me and my friends; let your findings be thoroughly justified. So, let it be on whatever day that your honors will undertake my examination, and not deprive me of it, so I am ready to endure anything in accordance with God's will, and to do as is seemly for me, as the consequences of this are the same for rich and for poor, as is most fitting. May your honors favorably understand this writing from me, and take no offense at it, as I desire all good towards you in this and all matters, and I only am concerned because of the short time of preparation for this inspection and examination in order to reach a judgment concerning me and my family in my old age. And my dear wife and I are both much afflicted with sickness, though we have neglected nothing that ought to be done in such matters. We hope that all hereafter may fall out favorably. Given under my seal on Thursday after the Sunday "Oculi" [18 March], 1479.

Medicinalia Nr. 177

Den Ersamen vursichtigen und wyßenn Burgemeistere Scheffen und Rathe zu Franckfurt myne lleben herren

Nicolaus Wynneck Glockener ab Gemanet

Ersamen vursichtigen unnd wisenn besundern lieben Herren uwer wißheit sy myn inniges gebet mit bereitem willenn zuvor Ersamen herren uwer wißheit wol weiß durch anbrengung der burgemeister und auch schrifft halber wie ich armer hab begert mich abermals lassen besehen und myr daz verzogen ist worden beiß post Martini So bitten uwer wißheit ich lutterlich umb gottes willen so oitmudigs ich mag uwer wißheit wulle den selben uwern doctoribus den Erctzten beshen iren hohen uns in dem besehen anzukeren und mich abermals besehen und weß sie an mir befynden uwer wißheit und mich furter wissen lassen want wo ich unbeflecket were und gemeynschafft der menschen entsatzt syn solle mag weniglich versteen waß ich daran haben mag Erfindet sich aber daz ich mit der feltsiechen krangheit beladen byn und so ich des ungezwiffelt berichtiget werde So byn ich mich des gemudes mich Inne gedulte zu setzen und williglichen gottes gabe zu lyden in hoffnunge daz hymeleich dar durch zuerwerben und uwer wißheit wulle sich gegen mir armen gonstlich bewisenn und die wercke der barmhertzekeyt erzeygen gepurt mir inne myn gebeth und byn schuldig solichs umb uch Zu aller zijt gegen got zuu dienen und weßher inne uwer wille syn wirdet wullet mich durch des hoffes furmundere uwer Rat frund wissen lassen mich darnach mogen Richten Datum uff Mitwochen vor Nicolae Anno Miv lxxxprimo

Nicolaus wynneck ettwan gluckener
zu Pharre uwer williger

Medicinalia Nr. 178[8]

Denn Ersamenn und wissen
der Stat zu Franckfurt uns
guten

Medicinalia Nr. 177

To the honorable, cautious, and wise [men] the mayor, sheriff, and council of Frankfurt, my dear lords.

Nicolaus Wynneck, bell-ringer, as advised

Honorable, cautious, wise, and especially beloved lords: May your wisdoms receive my earnest prayer with a ready will before your honors. Your wisdoms know well, through the representation of the mayor and also through writing, how I, a poor man, have requested to undergo examination again, and that that was delayed for me until after the Feast of St. Martin [November 11.] So I pray your wisdoms clearly, as humbly as I can, for God's sake, that your wisdoms may see to it that the same learned men your medical doctors have turned to us in the inspection, and further let me know if I am unspotted, or if I must be put aside from the fellowship of others, and that I may at least know what I do have. And if it's discovered that I do have the sickness of leprosy, and if I am informed unambiguously of this, so I am of the disposition to take this patiently, and to willingly suffer the gift of God, in hopes of thereby winning Heaven. I hope that your wisdoms will show yourselves favorable to me, show me the works of mercy, in a manner befitting my prayer. I will be eternally obliged to you, to pray to God for you. I pray that you will let me know whatever your will is concerning me by the court representative, the friend of your council, and I shall dispose myself in accordance with it. Given on Wednesday before the Feast of St. Nicholas [December 6], 1481.

Nicolaus Wynneck, former bell-ringer of Pharre, your willing [servant]

Medicinalia Nr. 178

To the honorable and wise [. .] of the city of Frankfurt, our good [...] Mayor of Aschaffenburg requests that they may inspect a poor [man without any money] who is suspected of having leprosy.

...germeister zu Aschaffenburg bitten eynen armen...mogen mit der ußetzikeit verdacht umb gottes...zu besichtigen laißen

Unser Fruntlich dinst zuvor Besondern gutenn frunden unser mitburger Peter Spengeler zeyger diesis brieffs ist by uns belumet wie er mit dem ußsatz beladen sy Bitten wir uch mit besunderm vlys he wollet die ihenen by uch die sich der dinge zu besehen verstene vermogen den zu probiren umb gots willen abe er mit der kranckheit beladen sy oder nicht Ist er damit beladen wollet uns das schrifftlich zu wissen thun wollen wir den understene zuversehen Ist er aber nit da mit beladen wollet uns auch zu wissen thun wollen wir ime auch helffen mit unserem almüsen als anderen armen luten dann dieser gegenwertig ein zietlangk by uns Gewonet hait sich erlich und fromlich gehalten und ist gantz arme wollet wir in den sachen behilfflich unde geraten sin uch auch gutwillig bewysen als wir zu uch vertreuwens haben das sin wir tZu sampt der billichkeit in der glichen und mererm zuverdienen willig Datum mitwochen nach visitationis beate marie virginis Anno miv lxxxxmo

Vonn uns den Burger meistern zu Aschaffenburg

Medicinalia Nr. 183[9]

Den Ersamen unsern besondern gutenn frunden dem Raite zu Frangfurt.... hant Rein erfunden

Wilhelm vonn gottes gnadenn Lantgraeve zu Hessen Grave von Katzenelenbogen zu Dietz Zu Igregenhorn und zu Nidde

Unser gunstig gesinnung zuvor Ersamen besondern guten frunde Geinwertiger unser Kelner Jorge ist in gerucht das er mit der ussetzikeit beladen sij darum haben wir im zu uch gefertigt gutlich bettende ir wullet im durch uwer ertzte und dar zu verordnete nach nettneste [sic] probiren und besichtigen laissen und was sich an ime erfindet uns schrifftlich zuerkennen geben darnach wie uns rechten mogen und dar im gutwillig sin das wullin wir in besonderen gnaden gegen uch erkennen Dadtum Alffelt mitwoch nach

Our friendly service to our good friends. Our fellow-citizen Peter Spengeler, bearer of this letter, is reputed among us to have leprosy. And so we most diligently beseech you that those among you who understand examination of such things may investigate him, for God's sake, [to find out] whether he be burdened with the disease or not. If he is so burdened, please let us know in writing, so that we may be prepared to take care of him. If, however, he is not burdened with leprosy, please likewise let us know. We desire to help him with our alms as we do other poor people, since he has lived with us for some time, has behaved honorably and piously, and is very poor. We wish to act advisedly and helpfully in this matter, and pray that you show yourselves favorable in this matter. You have our trust in this: we have unanimously so agreed, and declare ourselves ready to deserve this at your hands as is most fitting. Given on the Wednesday after the Visitation of the Blessed Virgin Mary, 1490.

From us, the mayor of Aschaffenburg.

Medicinalia Nr. 183

To the honorable members of the council of Frankfurt, our good friends...have found clean. [parchment damaged; the note on the verdict was made after the original superscript]

Wilhelm, by God's grace Landgrave of Hessen, Count of Katzenellenbogen, of Dietz, of Igregenhorn and of Nidde

Our good favor to our honorable and dear friends. Our cellarer, Jorge, here present, is rumored to be burdened with leprosy, and therefore we have sent him to you, warmly requesting that you would have him most closely examined and tested through your doctors and those commissioned to do so. Please then give us a written report on what his condition is, so that we may act accordingly and be favorable to him in this matter.

dem sontag Misericordia domini anno miv xcvii

This is our wish, sent with testimony of our special grace towards you. Given at Alfeld, on Wednesday after Misericordia Sunday, in the Year of Our Lord 1497.

Medicinalia 179[10]

Mit frundlich dinst

Item Wer solich kranckheit hat soll sunderlich von den luden abgesetzend sin nit zu kuchen oder zu batstuben gehen

Item der zumkommen sol man mir[11] enten essig und nuß essen

Item der ir warte sollen nit nochtern zu In gen / Ire die stuben mag man sere warmen und eyn fenster auf tun

Item das sicherste ist eyn lucifer fore sich genomen davon vur oder funff wachs herher angebrennt und fur sich gehalte

Item sich zu huten fur gebrannt vein

Item sich zu huten fur faulem obst

Item wer eyn Camyn inn irem Camern vore vurter eyn fure zundenen

Item de appoteker sollen freizien alle matczaley

Medicinalia 179

With friendly service

Item: Who has this illness should be specially set apart from people, not going to public kitchens or bathhouses.

Item: in the future, they should eat more duck, vinegar, and nuts.

Item: those who attend them should not be shy to come into their presence. Their rooms can be kept quite warm, and a window can be opened.

Item: the safest is to take a little candle, and with it to kindle four or five wax tapers in front of oneself.

Item: they should avoid brandy.

Item: they should avoid rotten fruit.

Item: who has a chimney in their chamber should furthermore light a fire in it.

Item: the apothecaries should be free of all leprosy.

Endnotes

1   All transcriptions and translations have been made using the holdings of the Institut für Stadtgeschichte Frankfurt, Sanitätsamt: Akten des Rats (Medicinalia). Individual record numbers are indicated within the text. When possible, I have compared my own transcriptions with those in Karl Sudhoff, "Dokumente zur Ausübung der Lepraschau in Frankfurt am Main im XV. Jahrhundert," *Lepra: Bibliotheca Internationalis*, vol. 13, 1913, pp. 141–70.

2   This first surviving record of Frankfurt's commission appears to have been created at its inception, as a template for the examining physicians to follow. Conrad Sachsenhausen (d. 1450) was active in the second quarter of the fifteenth century.

3   Henne appears to be distressed particularly by the visible symptoms on his face. The letter sent to him by the committee, containing "very many more words" than the contents he summarizes here, is sadly not extant. This letter was presumably a response to the preceding record, Medicinalia Nr. 168, yet another complaint from Henne.

4   In a different hand than the original superscription, presumably an addition by the committee scribe.

5   The letter to the Frankfurt commission is neatly written out with little abbreviation; the one created following the leprosy examination is heavily abbreviated with several interlinear corrections. The letters show a remarkably rapid turnaround time—less than a week!

6   This letter testifies to the considerable social power vested in the hands of the committee. A member of the nobility personally seeks out medical judgment concerning the question of whether or not he is leprous. The surname "Scherer" indicates that Gudrus and Peter were professionally certified barbers, possessing medical knowledge.

7   This letter is somewhat unusual in its reliance on the authority of academic medicine; Avicenna, or Ibn Sina (987–1037), was one of the most influential Islamic scholars of the Middle Ages. The fact that the physicians leave a phrase defining canker in Latin suggests that they are citing a text directly. I have not found this description of leprosy in Latin translations of Avicenna's *Canon of Medicine* directly, but frequently as a summing-up of his conclusions in late medieval medical miscellanies, and in the academic medical texts written by Guglielmo da Saliceto (1210–77) and the influential French surgeon Henri de Mondeville (c. 1260–1316.) Frankfurt's physicians may have wanted to demonstrate their learned expertise to fend off possible criticisms of their severe judgement. The physicians advise that the woman should enter a leper hospital ("be separated from healthy people"), noting that such formal separation is both unusual and less than absolute.

8   The verso is damaged, but conveys that the mayor of Aschaffenburg asks the committee to receive a poor man suspected of having leprosy, and to examine him "for the sake of God," that is, without charge.

9   One of the counts of Hessen, whose seat lay on the Rhine, approximately 50 miles from Frankfurt. The condition of his cellarer would have been particularly a matter of concern because of the man's role in supervising the count's foodstuffs.

10 Vinegar was thought to react with leprous blood, and is now known to function as a mycobacterial disinfectant. Nuts can also kill certain types of bacteria.

11 Sic, for "mehr."

.

Arzneibuch, "On Madness"[1] (ca. 1300)

Ortolf of Baierland
Contributed by Anne M. Koenig

Introduction

Composed sometime around 1300, the *Arzneibuch* (Book of Medicine) penned by Ortolf of Baierland (Bavaria) was one of the first German-language medical texts. A small textbook of medicine, it would be copied by hand for decades, finding its way into the libraries of physicians, as well as those of monasteries and wealthy layfolk. It would even be printed at least six times in the 1470–80s, making it one of the most popular medical texts in German-speaking areas by the end of fifteenth century. And yet, little is known of its medieval author and even the dating of the text is uncertain. Manuscript versions of the *Arzneibuch* give some clues: that Ortolf was from Bavaria and that he was "a doctor of Würzburg" and a "master," both appellations suggesting that he was university-trained. He may have been a physician, though it is perhaps even more likely that he was surgeon, given both the text's interest in surgery and archival evidence of a "Master Ortolf" who was a surgeon in Wurzbürg in 1339.

Whoever he was and wherever he learned his medical knowledge, Ortolf was a gifted medical compiler taking part in a broad trend of medical dissemination taking place in the later Middle Ages. He took a large body of sophisticated university-level medical theory and practice and synthesized it, creating a vernacular handbook of medicine that covered every major area of medieval medicine and healing. The list of the Latin authors he knew (though some only in derivative sources) includes the most famous names of medieval medicine: Hippocrates, Galen, Avicenna, Constantinus Africanus,

Macer, Isaac and Aegidus, and Gilbertus Anglicus. Ortolf himself offered little content that was truly new to medical theory or practice. His textbook was reductive and simplified, not cutting-edge. But it was not merely a German copy of a Latin textbook. Ortolf chose what to include and what to omit, he decided how to explain complex etiologies in simplified language, and he selected which therapies to offer his audience.

Ortolf began his *Arzneibuch* with chapters that briefly explained the theoretical foundations of medicine: the elements, the qualities of heat/cold and wet/dry inherent in every natural thing, the basic temperaments, the primary organs of the body, and the fundamentals of health and disease from diet and bloodletting to pregnancy and pilltaking. He then included tracts on the pulse and on urine (the two classic diagnostic tools of the medieval physician), and a section on the most famous Hippocratic aphorisms, the "sound-bites" of ancient Greek medical theory and prognosis that were a part of any medical student's first-year studies. The bulk of the book, however, was Ortolf's rendition of a typical head-to-foot textbook of diseases. It is here that we find Ortolf's most sustained treatment of madness.

By the end of the thirteenth century, drawing from the Greek, Roman, and Arabic medical traditions, European medicine had developed a sophisticated approach to explaining and treating madness. While medical theory was largely silent on intellectual disability (finding states of "natural folly" to fall outside their purview), sudden irrationality was perceived, at least by doctors, as a medical problem. Medieval doctors understood various forms of madness as illnesses that were located in the brain. The most common illnesses known to produce irrational behaviors were frenzy, mania, melancholy, and the more catatonic states of lethargy and stupor. All of these illnesses were caused by humoral imbalances or by corrupted humors and vapors that rose up into the brain and disrupted sensory and cognitive functions. (Before the modern age, Western medicine understood the body to be governed by four primary fluids, or humors: blood, phlegm, back bile, and yellow bile.) The specific descriptions, causes, and even treatments of madness were exceptionally wide-ranging and often overlapping. Symptomatic behaviors included excessive speech or laughter, debilitating emotional states, superhuman strength, delusions, and a failure to recognize well-known people and things. Causes ranged from head injuries, bad food, and dog bites to shock, childbirth, unrequited love, and even prior demonic possession. Most medical explanations of madness, however, honed in on one or more of the *non-naturals,* factors external to the body that affected the body's health: air and environment, food and drink, bodily excretion, sleeping and waking, rest and exercise, and passions of the soul or emotions. Any imbalance in one of these areas could disrupt the health of the whole body, including the workings of the mind. Based on this principle, medieval medicine promulgated an equally wide range of remedies generally related to diet, medication, and environmental therapies both benign (e.g., sweet smells) and extreme (e.g., prescribed confinement or chaining up). Treatment often involved topical applications and ingestible concoctions made from the animal, vegetable, and mineral ingredients that comprised medieval pharmacopeia. Perhaps most striking for modern audiences is the absence of any attempt to talk to those suffering from mental illness. Indeed, there was no such thing as a medieval "psychiatric"

approach to mental illness, for the problem was perceived as fundamentally physical. Isolation, protection, and the provision of basic foods and remedies, not talk therapy, was the rule of the day.

We find very little of the complicated Latin specifications of various mental illnesses in Ortolf's text. Faced with the need to simplify medical theory as well as to determine or invent the best German words for terms that had really only existed in a Latin setting, Ortolf chose not to render the concrete, diagnostic Latin terms for different types of mental illnesses into different German terms. Instead, he called them all unsinnigkeit, or madness. Ortolf also drastically cut the complicated explanations of internal and humoral causations of each kind of madness that the Latin tradition contained, offering instead a synthetic look at the many ways madness could arise and the various symptoms displayed.

Despite his simplifications (and conflations), Ortolf was clearly very interested in madness and his textbook influenced generations of doctors and interested lay readers. Brief discussions of madness are scattered throughout the *Arzneibuch* and Ortolf explains it at length twice in his head-to-foot discussion of various diseases. These are the chapters presented below. The first section offers a description of mad states that in the Latin tradition fell under the rubric of "frenzy," but Ortolf rather intriguingly also tacks on therapies for lethargy (the sleeping sickness) at the end of his discussion. The second section, as he states himself, addresses the condition known in Latin as *mania*, but it also includes discussions and therapies related to melancholy in more sophisticated texts. By taking all of these specific diagnoses and relabeling them all as "madness," Ortolf was perhaps showing a sensitivity to the practical fact that much of his audience would not likely parse out distinctions between different mental illnesses. But he was also laying the foundation for a general category of mental illness in German culture. *Unsinnigkeit* was now claimed as a generic medical term for madness, and its prominent use in Southern Germany in legal and civic records in the fifteenth century suggests that Ortolf's text had a linguistic impact, and perhaps a medicalizing influence, on cultural conceptions of madness in Southern Germany in the later Middle Ages.

It is also important to note that Ortolf was particularly interested in therapy. His chapters on how to treat the "mad" are far longer than his chapters describing what madness actually is, and his treatments run the gamut: from complex compound medications to simple therapies. This focus on therapy emphasizes again the practical nature of Ortolf's text. One need only know a few key diagnostic markers of madness in order to understand the condition enough to try out appropriate treatments. Some of those treatments, moreover, are particularly easy to enact. Ortolf's emphasis on treatment thus serves to draw attention to the treatability and curability of irrational states. In fact, one might argue that the great takeaway from Ortolf's text is that madness is a physical malady that can be cured by physical therapies. Madness would remain a troubling and anxiety-producing phenomenon in late medieval Germany, but Ortolf's text suggests that it was not perhaps as mysterious or as irreversible a condition as modern observers might assume.

Bibliography

Doob, Penelope. *Nebuchadnezzar's Children.* Yale University Press, 1974.

Gross, Angelika. *"La Folie": Wahnsinn und Narrheit im spätmittelalterlichen text und Bild.* Carl Winter Universitätsverlag, 1990.

Katajala-Peltomaa, Sari, and Susanna Niiranen, eds. *Mental (Dis)Order in Later Medieval Europe.* Brill, 2014.

Kemp, Simon. *Medieval Psychology.* Greenwood Press, 1990.

Metzler, Irina. *Fools and Idiots? Intellectual Disability in the Middle Ages.* Manchester University Press, 2016.

Neaman, Judith. *Suggestion of the Devil: The Origins of Madness.* Doubleday, 1975.

Riha, Otrun. *Mittelalterliche Heilkunst. Das Arzneibuch Ortolfsvon Baierland (um 1300): Eingeleitet, übersetzt und mit einem drogenkundlichen Anhang versehen.* Deutscher Wissenschaftsverlag, 2014.

Turner, Wendy. *Care and Custody of the Mentally Ill, Incompetent, and Disabled in Medieval England.* Brepols, 2013.

Ortolf of Baierland, *Arzneibuch*, Chapters 82–83, 90–91

Ob der mensch von seinen sÿnnen kompt.

Und wirt der mensch unsÿnnig in einer sucht oder nach der bekerung des geschicht ettwenn von einem geswer in dem haubt. ettwenn von unbriger hitze und von dem pradem der in im pliben ist. Ist es von einem geswer das soltu also erkennen. so ist sein harnn plaich und dunne und hat zu aller zeit starcke hitze und sihet mit den augen greulichen umb und ist albeg unsÿnnig. Ist aber es von dern unraÿnen pradem. so ist der harnn nicht als weis und nicht als dunne und hat nicht als gros hitze und als gros unsÿnne.

dem hilff also, du solt den sichen in ein vinsternus legen und das man wenig mit im reden. das er icht unsÿnniger werde. darnach nÿm essig und saltz und reib im hende und fusse an den solen damitten. Darnoch ob er in dem leibe herte sei. so leret Gilbertus in seinem puch das man im sol machen das Clister. Nÿm pappeln und ebische wurtzel. linsamen. fenugrecum und ein wenig saltzes. seud es in vier pfunden wassers und seih es durch ein tuch und tu ein wenig hönig und paumöls dartzu und gewss es bei einem pfund mit einem Clistere unden in dem leib. Oder nuym das ist als gut. einen loffel vol hönigs und als vil saltzes und seud es mit einander untz das honig swartz werde so thu es herab und las es ein wenig kalten und mach da von zephelein also lang ein vinger seÿ. und schewb im eins nÿden in den leib oder zwaÿ so wirt er waich in dem leib. Man sol auch nemen ein hun und sol es auffreissenn auff dem ruchen und lege ims auff das haubt und an die stirne es sennftet sere.[2] Nim mahensamen und weissen pilsensamen Stos es klain und misch es mit einem weÿssen eins aÿs und mit frawen milch und bestreich im das haubt damit und an die

If a man goes mad

If a man goes mad during an illness or after a bettering of the condition, it is sometimes from a tumor in the head, other times from excess heat and vapor that remains inside him. If it is from a tumor, then you should find that his urine is pale and thin, and the patient continually has a strong heat, and he has an appearance with frightful eyes and is totally mad. If, however, it is from unclean vapor, then his urine is not as white and not as thin and he does not have so great a heat nor such great madness.

You help him thus: You should place the sick man in darkness and others should speak little to him so that he does not become even more mad. Then take vinegar and salt and rub his hands and the soles of his feet with it. Then, if he is constipated, Gilbert in his book teaches that one should make him this clyster: Take mallow and marshmallow root, linseed, fenugreek, and a little salt. Simmer them in four pounds of water and strain it through a cloth and add a little honey to it and olive oil and administer to the patient one pound at a time up into the body with an enema. Or take this, which is just as good: a spoonful of honey and just as much salt and simmer it together until the honey turns black. Then take it off the heat and let it cool a bit and make a suppository from it as long as a finger and position one or two in the body. Then his body will soften. One should also take a hen and cut open from the back and place it on the head and forehead and it is very calming.[4] [This is also a noble remedy:][5] Take poppy seeds and white henbane seeds° grind them small and mix them with an eggwhite and breast milk[6] and spread

---

henbane seeds *also "Pilsenkraut" (lat. Jusquianus), a plant commonly used in therapies for madness, but also often warned against as causing madness*

stiren und in die oren und in die naßlöcher und an dem schlaffe. Oder nÿm pilsensamen zwaÿ lot und stos es mit gutem wein und strich es damn an die stirne und in die oren und in die naßlocher. Es schleffet zuhant. Du solt auch mercken. Gewinnet der mensch ein sucht das haisset die schlaffenden sucht das ist gut. Wirt aber der mensch unsinnig in einer schlaffenden sucht. So stirbet es. Ist aber der mensch wol beileibe so las im die ader schlahen vornen an der stirnen. Du magst im auch mandelmilch geben zutrincken oder gerstenwasser du solt auch an die stat legen das es küle seÿ und mit roten weiden bestreichen oder mit rosen. es hilft wol.

Von der unsinne

Mania ist ein siechtumb der haisset unsinnikait und wirt etwen von pössen essen oder trincken. oder von übrigem tranck starckes weins oder von haisser kost als von knoblauch oder zu sere gefefferter kost oder von einem unsinnigen thÿre. das ein menschen gepÿssen hat oder vonn angesundem lufte oder von zorne oder von übriger trunckenheit. etwen von übriger feuchtigkeit. oder von dem plut sind sie alle fröleich und singent und lachent oft von gantzem hertzen oder das plut in dem hertten leib verprinnet. so sein sie understunden frölich und understunden zornig. kompt es aber von hitze oder von dürre so zornent sie gern und schreient und schlahent ander lewt. kompt es aber von kelten und von dürren so trawren sie albeg unnd fürchten das sie nicht fürchten süllen und waÿnent und pergent sich in die vinster. oder sie wenent das sie got sind und das man in das himelreich genomen hab. und etlich wenen das sie vi gutes haben in der hant und enkam in die nÿmant aufgewinnen. etwen so kreent sie als sie hannen sindt. etwen so wöllen sie pellen als die hunt und wenen das sie hunt sein oder sie wenen das sie nicht haubt haben.

it on his head and forehead and ears and in his nostrils and on his temples. Or take two lots[o] of henbane seeds and grind them with good wine and then spread it on the forehead and in the ears and nostrils. He will immediately sleep. One should also note that if a person prevails against the sleeping sickness,[7] that is good. If, however, he is mad after the sleeping sickness, he will die. If, however the person is physically well, then bleed him in the middle of his forehead. You can give him almond milk and barley water[8] to drink. You should also lay him in a place that is cool and strewn with red willow or with roses. This helps.

On the mad

Mania is an illness that is called madness and develops sometimes from bad food or drink. Or from the excessive drinking of strong wine. Or from hot[9] food like from garlic or overly peppered food. Or from a mad animal that has bitten a person. Or from unhealthy air. Or from anger or excessive drunkenness.[10] Sometimes the illness comes from excessive heat or moisture, or from [too much] blood. [In these cases] the mad are always happy and singing and laugh often from the whole heart. If it comes, however, from blood burned in the body, then they are sometimes happy and sometimes angry. If it comes from heat and from dryness, then they are angry and cry out and hit [themselves and][11] others. If it comes from cold and dryness, then they are always sad and fear what they should not fear and hide in the dark and cry or they imagine they are God and that Heaven has been taken from them. Some think that they have lots of goods in their hands and no one can open their hands. Some crow as though they are roosters. Others bark and believe they are dogs, or they believe that they do not have heads.

lots *a lot is unit of weight typically 1/32 of a pound*

Man sol in also helffen sind sie von grosser kranckheit und von trübnüs unsinnig worden. so sol man sie frölich machen und sol in geloben vil gutes dinges die kost sol ring sein als zigenflisch oder iunge hüner und newe gelegte aÿr und schön prot und geit man in weine den sol man in mischen mit wasser. Man sol in paden und sol in frawen geloben wan das benÿmpt in den zorn und die unsinnigkeit. du solt im lassen die adern bei der minsten zehen auf den fuesse es wart nÿe so guttes nicht. Ditz ist die aller edelste ertzneÿ für alle unsinnigkeit. Nÿm mirabolani citrini kebuli indi sandali violarum iglichs .iii. quintein cinamomi gariofoli lignum aloes spicis kasie lignee petre semis maratri elleboris nigri iglichs als vie ein quintein. radicis feniculi apii scarioli iglichs .v. quintein capilli veneris semen lactuce iglichs .ii. quintein. stos es alles miteinander sewd es mit .ii. pfunten wassers untz das drittaÿl eingesotten seÿ und solt es drücken durch ein tuch und thu zu dem wasser .iii. pfunt zuchers und sewd es mit dem zucker anderwait untz das wasser wol eingeseid und gib sein dem siechen .iiii. quintein mit warmen wein und enhilffet dem das nicht und der sieche vil pluttes hab. so las im die ader mitten an der stiren. kompt es aber von übriger hitze so gib im gerstenwasser da lacaricie und wegwart in gesotten seÿ und gib im die lectuarien die da haisset diaporiginatum dÿ reiniget das plut gar sere man so im auch kein[3] pflaster auf das haubt legen ee man im den leib reiniget. Man so im auch das haubt twahen mit einer lawgen da gamillen und uerbene in gesotten seÿ. ist aber ein grosse hitz an dem haubte so bestreich es im mit hauswurtz und mit rosen und mit frawen milich miteinander getemperirt.

One should help him thus: If a person[12] has become mad from great illness[13] and sorrow, then one should make him happy and promise him many good things. His food should be light, like goat meat or young hens and newly laid eggs and fine bread. And if he is given wine, it should be mixed with water. One should bathe him and promise him women, if that takes away anger and madness from him. One should bleed him from his smallest toe, there is none better. This is the finest remedy for all madness: Take yellow, black and kebule myrobalan,° sandalwood, violet, three-quarters° each; cinnamon, balsam, clove, aloe-wood, lavender, cinnamon bark, parsley seed, fennel, black hellebore, each a measure; fennel root, wild celery, prickly lettuce, each five measures; venus hair,° lettuce seeds, each two measures. Grind it all together and simmer it with two pounds of water until a third boils off and strain it through a cloth. And add to the water three pounds of sugar and simmer it with the sugar another time until the water boils off. Give four measures of it to the sick man with warm wine. And if that does not help and the person has a lot of blood, bleed him at the middle of the forehead. If, however, [the madness] comes from too-much heat, then give him barley water in which licorice and chicory were simmered and give him the electuary which is called *dyaboraginatum*° and which cleans the blood. One should not lay a plaster on his head before cleaning his body. One could also wash his head with brine in which chamomile and verbena have been simmered. However, if there is a great heat in the head, then smear it with a tempered mixture of houseleek and rosewater and breast milk."

---

myrobalan *trees bearing nut-like fruits, indigenous to southern Asia, that became common in medieval herbals after the influx of Arab medicine. There are five kinds: citrinus, kebulus, indus, bellericus, and emblicus.* **three-quarters** *medieval measurements varied considerably, but this likely meant three-quarters of a lot* **venus hair** *a fern with a number of medicinal uses going back to Greek medicine* **dyaborginatum** *a remedy made out of borage, a cultivated flowering plant popularly used in medieval German food and medicine*

Endnotes

1   The text below has been compiled by Anne M. Koenig based largely on the 1477 edition printed by Koberg in Nuremberg, but in consultation with three earlier manuscripts, Munich, Bayerische Staatsbibliothek (BSB) Cgm 430 and Cgm 723 and Würzburg, Universitätsbibliothek, Ms. M. ch. f. 79. A copy of the 1477 printing is held in the Bavarian State Library: Bayerische Staatsbibliothek, 2 Inc.c.a. 642, cited passages on f. 17v–18r and 20r–21r. The edition's spellings and punctuation have been retained but abbreviations have been expanded. Chapter numbers are those given by modern scholars to the text, most recently Ortrun Riha in her 2014 modern German edition of the text (see bibliography). The English translation of the text, as well as the glosses and endnotes, have also been provided by Anne M. Koenig.

2   Noticing the shifts in topic, the 1477 printed edition breaks up the rest of this paragraph and adds two new titles, the first one here: *Ob ein mensch nit geschlaggen mag.* A few lines later, after *Es schleffet zuhant,* the printer inserts the title: *Von der schlaffende sucht.* I have omitted both, since they do not belong to the earlier manuscript tradition.

3   The 1477 text prints *clein* ("small") here, however the manuscript tradition clearly indicates that word is meant to be *kein* ("no").

4   The therapy of splitting chickens (or puppies!) and placing the spatchcocked carcass on the head is a surprisingly consistent cure offered across medical and popular texts alike.

5   While not present in the 1477 printed text, the manuscript tradition introduces the next recipe with this endorsement.

6   Breast milk is a common ingredient in medicines, going back to ancient times. Pliny the Elder offers a long chapter on the therapeutic uses of "women's milk" and includes madness among the list of illnesses that it can cure (Pliny the Elder, *Naturalis historia*, Bk 28.21). Breast milk (like semen) was understood as a substance made from refining blood, and appears frequently in treatments for certain ailments, particularly those of the ears and eyes. Ortolf himself cites it

several times, each time for application to a part of the head.

7   This was another disease of the head, and one that Ortolf treats in the chapter following this one. It could cover any range of conditions, from coma and catalepsy to lethargy and excessive sleepiness. Ortolf notes that it particularly affects the aged.

8   Barley water has long been considered a healthy, restorative beverage, from ancient Greece to modern times. It was generally made by boiling barley grains in water and then, if desired, the strained liquid was sweetened or infused with herbs, fruit, or honey. Because barley water was believed to cool and moisten the body, it was a perfect therapy for "hot" maladies.

9   "Hot" here refers to the quality inherent in a thing, not the temperature at which a food is consumed. Some foods, like garlic, were considered to have "hot" properties, while others, like melon, for instance, were considered to have cold properties. Everything that a person ate thus could disrupt, maintain, or restore the body's own internal balance between hot and cold (and moist and dry).

10   The Nuremberg edition (as well as other print version from the 1470s) substitutes "drunkenness" here. Earlier manuscripts more correctly identify excessive *sadness* as a cause for madness. Anger and sadness had long been understood by doctors to be dangerous emotions (or what they called "accidents of the soul") that had clear somatic effects, from constricting the heart to affecting the brain and its psychological faculties.

11   Nuremberg 1477 omits the reference self-harm, but it is an important part of the manuscript versions of the text, so I have reinserted it in this translation.

12   There is some inconsistency in the pronouns in the first few lines, going from *ihn* to *sie* back to *ihn*. I have rendered it all as a masculine singular, in keeping with the rest of the text.

13   The manuscript tradition has "sadness" or "grief" (*trawrichait*) not "illness" here. The 1477 printed edition thus twice effaces sadness as a cause of madness (see note 11 above).

RELIGIOUS TEXTS

Selected Episodes on Healing and Disability from the Vulgate Bible—Matthew, Mark, Luke, and John[1] (ca. 382)

Translated by St. Jerome
Contributed by Will Eggers

Introduction

The Vulgate Bible was translated in the fourth century largely by St. Jerome at the request of Pope Damascus I. The translation quickly became the most influential version from its initial composition through the Early Modern period, finally becoming canon at the Council of Trent. The dating of the original texts of the four Gospels—Matthew, Mark, Luke, and John—is debated, but consensus is that the first written versions of these texts appear in the latter half of the first century CE. The first three Gospels of Matthew, Mark, and Luke—called the Synoptic Gospels—show a close relationship, with many repeated episodes and word-for-word parallels. Modern scholarly consensus—contested—is that Mark was composed first and that Matthew and Luke expanded upon it, including elements of second source text (the Q-text), of which no examples currently exist. In addition, Matthew and Luke are thought to include materials unique to the communities of Matthew (M-text) and Luke (L-text). Most medieval scholars, however, accepted Augustine's chronology that Matthew was composed first, followed by Mark and, later, Luke. The Book of John shows substantial textual differences from the other three Gospels and, due to references within the text, most modern scholars consider it the last composed. Each of the Gospels has a slightly different emphasis on often similar materials. Mark, once thought to be a summary of

Matthew, is now generally thought to target a gentile audience with an emphasis on action and miracles. Matthew, with its emphasis on placing Jesus in the Jewish tradition, seems to be composed within a community in conflict with the broader Jewish community. Luke targets an educated Greek-speaking audience and places an emphasis on social justice. The Book of John shows more independence from Judaism than the other three gospels, and it places more emphasis on the divine nature of Jesus, as well as a greater attention to the relationship of the individual to the church. John includes fewer examples of healing, suggesting that many episodes have been omitted, as "there are also many other things which Jesus did which, if they were written every one, the world itself, I think, would not be able to contain the books that should be written" (John 21:25).

With thirty-one individual instances of healing in the New Testament, it comes as no surprise that episodes mentioning impairment appear with regularity. Most of the episodes are short, focusing on the miraculous nature of the healing and offering few extended representations of the social impact of impairment on those before and after they are healed. The primary emphasis of each is on highlighting the power of Jesus, but healing is sometimes followed by the admonition to "sin no more," implying a correlation between previous sin and current impairment

(John 5:14). At other times, the key element to healing is the belief of those requesting help. When two blind men ask for help, Jesus queries them about their faith. "Do you believe, that I can do this unto you?' They say to him, 'Yea, Lord.' Then he touched their eyes, saying, 'According to your faith, be it done unto you'" (Matthew 9:28–29). But the Gospels sometimes disconnect disability from sin and belief and cast its healing as a way to glorify God, such as in the John 9 episode on the healing of a blind man. Finally, some examples of healing become metaphors for spiritual rebirth. As noted by the venerable Bede, the episode of the man born blind shows him healing in stages to parallel his spiritual growth (Mark 8:22—25). Aiding those in need of help offers people a chance to act upon their generosity and, in so doing, grow spiritually. "When thou makest a feast, call the poor, the maimed, the lame, and the blind; And thou shalt be blessed, because they have not wherewith to make thee recompense" (John 14:13–14). In this example, the maimed, the lame, and the blind are linked to the poor in their inability to repay hosts, which suggests the economic limitations of these groups rather than any immorality. The attitudes toward impairment seen here in the Gospels stand in dialogue with both Greco-Roman and ancient Jewish attitudes.[2] Greek thinkers, including Hipporates, Plato, and Aristotle, espoused infanticide for those with impairments, and the Romans' Twelve Tables codified this attitude into law. Ancient Jewish texts presented a more nuanced view. Despite the position that those with impairments should be excluded from leadership positions (Leviticus 21:16–25), the Torah distinguishes between impairments at birth, which are not to be judged, and impairments gained later in life, which indicate divine disfavor. Jesus, in John 9:2–3, follows within this Jewish tradition.

Within the Gospels, impairment is consistently portrayed as something in need of healing and therefore resembles in some ways the "medical model" of disability, though what medieval scholars might identify as medicine might be thought of as religious. Edward Wheatley's work proposes just such a medieval model of disability, arguing that religious discourses of disability controlled how those with impairments were perceived as much as medicinal discourses do today.[3] Irina Metzler does an excellent job of identifying how medieval theologians looked to healing in the Gospels when discussing the issue of impairment and argues that applying a social model of disability to medieval reception of these texts, highlighting societal stigma and limitations in contrast with impairment, does not accurately reflect the attitudes in medieval Europe.[4] Her work, in addition, challenges the notion that impairment was invariably associated with sin.[5]

The following selection of Gospel episodes is an attempt to provide a range of examples that includes some of the most popular healing stories. When possible, several versions of the same narrative are included to offer the chance for comparison. The episode of Jairus' daughter, thought to be dead but actually sleeping, for instance, provides a compelling contrast to the healing of dead Lazarus (John 11:44), who the chief priests then want to kill (John 12:9–11). Passing references to healing, such as the off-handed references to the healing of Mary Magdalene, "out of whom seven devils were cast forth," (Luke 8:2; also appears in Mark 16:5), are not included. Comparing the vocabulary of impairment in the Latin and in the Early Modern English offers opportunities to explore etymological and cultural connections. Many episodes focus on infirmities as a result of being unclean (immundus), the cure for which is cleanliness (munditiae). Physical infirmities (note the Latin root) can often be linked directly to paralysis or leprosy, but many mental conditions (e.g. self-harming, ferocity, epilepsy) are lumped together under the umbrella of possession by demons, a source of suffering and sin that can be expelled and that is not therefore essential to the person.

Bibliography

Abrams, Judith Z., and William C. Gaventa. *Jewish Perspectives on Theology and the Human Experience of Disability.* Routledge, 2007.

Brock, Brian, and John Swinton. *Disability and the Christian Tradition.* Eerdmans, 2012.

Eyler, Joshua R., ed. *Disability in the Middle Ages.* Ashgate, 2010, pp. 1–10.

Metzler, Irina. *Disability in Medieval Europe: Thinking about Physical Impairment during the High Middle Ages, c. 1100–c. 1400.* Routledge, 2006.

Mitchell, David, and Sharon Snyder. "Narrative Prosthesis." *The Disability Studies Reader.* University of Illinois at Chicago, 1997, pp. 274–87.

Moss, Candida R., and Jeremy Schipper. *Disability Studies and Biblical Literature.* Palgrave Macmillan, 2011.

Olyan, Saul. *Disability in the Hebrew Bible: Interpreting Mental and Physical Differences.* Cambridge University Press, 2008.

Schipper, Jeremy. *Disability and Isaiah's Suffering Servant.* Oxford University Press, 2011.

Shakespeare, Tom. "Social Model of Disability." *The Disability Studies Reader.* University of Illinois at Chicago, 1997, pp. 266–273.

Wheatley, Edward. "Blindness, Discipline, and Reward: Louis IX and the Foundation of the Hospice des Quinze-Vingts." *Disability Studies Quarterly,* vol. 22, 2002.

———. *Stumbling Blocks Before the Blind: Medieval Constructions of a Disability.* University of Michigan Press, 2014.

List of Selected Episodes

Healing while on First Preaching Tour in Galilee (Matthew 4:23–24, Mark 3:9–12, Luke 5:15)

A Leper (Mark 1:40–45, Luke 5:12–15)

Roman Centurion on Behalf of His Servant with Paralysis, at Capernaum (Matthew 8:5–10, Luke 7:2–10)

Demoniac(s) at at Tomb (Matthew 8:28–34, Mark 5:1–15, Luke 8:26–39)

Man with Paralysis at Capernaum (Matthew 9:1–8, Mark 2:3–13, Luke 5:17–25)

The Blind near Jericho (Bartimeus in the Book of Mark) (Matthew 9:27–30, Mark 10:46–52, Luke 18:35–43)

Man with a Withered Hand (Matthew 12:10–15, Mark 3:1–5, Luke 6:6–10)

Son with Epilepsy Near the Towns of Caesarea Philippi (Matthew 17:14–20, Luke 9:38–43)

Deaf Man with Speech Impediment in the Region of Decapolis (Mark 7:31–37)

Jairus' Daughter at Capernaum & Woman with Issue of Blood at Capernaum (Matthew 9:18–25, Mark 5:22–43, Luke 8:41–56)

Infirm Man at the Pool of Bethsaida (John 5:2–15)

Man Born Blind (John 9:1–41)

Lazarus Raised from the Dead (John 11:11–44)

Including the Those with Impairments at One's Table (Luke 14:12–14)

Healing while on First Preaching Tour in Galilee

Matthew 4:23–24

[23] Et circuibat Jesus totam Galilaeam, docens in synagogis eorum, et praedicans Evangelium regni : et sanans omnem languorem, et omnem infirmitatem in populo. [24] Et abiit opinio ejus in totam Syriam, et obtulerunt ei omnes male habentes, variis languoribus, et tormentis comprehensos, et qui daemonia habebant, et lunaticos, et paralyticos, et curavit eos.

Matthew 4:23–24

[23] And Jesus went about all Galilee, teaching in their synagogues, and preaching the gospel of the kingdom: and healing all manner of sickness and every infirmity, among the people. [24] And his fame went throughout all Syria, and they presented to him all sick people that were taken with divers diseases and torments, and such as were possessed by devils, and lunatics, and those that had palsy, and he cured them.

Mark 3:9–12

[9] Et dicit discipulis suis ut navicula sibi deserviret propter turbam, ne comprimerent eum : [10] multos enim sanabat, ita ut irruerent in eum ut illum tangerent, quotquot habebant plagas.

[11] Et spiritus immundi, cum illum videbant, procidebant ei : et clamabant, dicentes : [12] Tu es Filius Dei. Et vehementer comminabatur eis ne manifestarent illum.

Mark 3:9–12

[9] And he spoke to his disciples that a small ship should wait on him because of the multitude, lest they should throng him. [10] For he healed many, so that they pressed upon him for to touch him, as many as had evils.

[11] And the unclean spirits, when they saw him, fell down before him: and they cried, saying: [12] Thou art the Son of God. And he strictly charged them that they should not make him known.

Luke 5:15

[15] Perambulabat autem magis sermo de illo : et conveniebant turbae multae ut audirent, et curarentur ab infirmitatibus suis.

Luke 5:15

[15] But the fame of him went abroad the more, and great multitudes came together to hear, and to be healed by him of their infirmities.

A Leper

Matthew 8:1–4

[1] Cum autem descendisset de monte, secutae sunt eum turbae multae : [2] et ecce leprosus veniens, adorabat eum, dicens : Domine, si vis, potes me mundare. [3] Et extendens Jesus manum, tetigit eum, dicens : Volo. Mundare. Et confestim mundata est lepra ejus. [4] Et ait illi Jesus : Vide, nemini dixeris : sed vade, ostende te sacerdoti, et of-

Matthew 8:1–4

[1] And when he was come down from the mountain, great multitudes followed him: [2] And behold a leper came and adored him, saying: Lord, if thou wilt, thou canst make me clean. [3] And Jesus stretching forth his hand, touched him, saying: I will, be thou made clean. And forthwith his leprosy was cleansed. [4] And Jesus saith to him: See thou tell no man: but go, shew thyself to the priest,

fer munus, quod praecepit Moyses, in testimonium illis.

and offer the gift which Moses commanded for a testimony unto them.

Mark 1:40–45

[40] Et venit ad eum leprosus deprecans eum : et genu flexo dixit ei : Si vis, potes me mundare.

[41] Jesus autem misertus ejus, extendit manum suam : et tangens eum, ait illi : Volo : mundare. [42] Et cum dixisset, statim discessit ab eo lepra, et mundatus est. [43] Et comminatus est ei, statimque ejecit illum, [44] et dicit ei : Vide nemini dixeris : sed vade, ostende te principi sacerdotum, et offer pro emundatione tua, quae praecepit Moyses in testimonium illis. [45] At ille egressus coepit praedicare, et diffamare sermonem, ita ut jam non posset manifeste introire in civitatem, sed foris in desertis locis esset, et conveniebant ad eum undique.

Mark 1:40–45

[40] And there came a leper to him, beseeching him, and kneeling down said to him: If thou wilt, thou canst make me clean.

[41] And Jesus having compassion on him, stretched forth his hand; and touching him, saith to him: I will. Be thou made clean. [42] And when he had spoken, immediately the leprosy departed from him, and he was made clean. [43] And he strictly charged him, and forthwith sent him away. [44] And he saith to him: See thou tell no one; but go, shew thyself to the high priest, and offer for thy cleansing the things that Moses commanded, for a testimony to them. [45] But he being gone out, began to publish and to blaze abroad the word: so that he could not openly go into the city, but was without in desert places: and they flocked to him from all sides.

Luke 5:12–15

[12] Et factum est, cum esset in una civitatum, et ecce vir plenus lepra, et videns Jesum, et procidens in faciem, rogavit eum, dicens : Domine, si vis, potes me mundare. [13] Et extendens manum, tetigit eum dicens : Volo : mundare. Et confestim lepra discessit ab illo. [14] Et ipse praecepit illi ut nemini diceret : sed, Vade, ostende te sacerdoti, et offer pro emundatione tua, sicut praecepit Moyses, in testimonium illis. [15] Perambulabat autem magis sermo de illo : et conveniebant turbae multae ut audirent, et curarentur ab infirmitatibus suis.

Luke 5:12–15

[12] And it came to pass, when he was in a certain city, behold a man full of leprosy, who seeing Jesus, and falling on his face, besought him, saying: Lord, if thou wilt, thou canst make me clean. [13] And stretching forth his hand, he touched him, saying: I will. Be thou cleansed. And immediately the leprosy departed from him. [14] And he charged him that he should tell no man, but, Go, shew thyself to the priest, and offer for thy cleansing according as Moses commanded, for a testimony to them. [15] But the fame of him went abroad the more, and great multitudes came together to hear, and to be healed by him of their infirmities.

Roman Centurion on Behalf of His Servant with Paralysis, at Capernaum

Matthew 8:5–10

[5] Cum autem introisset Capharnaum, accessit ad eum centurio, rogans eum, [6] et

Matthew 8:5–10

[5] And when he had entered into Capharnaum, there came to him a centurion, be-

117

dicens : Domine, puer meus jacet in domo paralyticus, et male torquetur. [7] Et ait illi Jesus : Ego veniam, et curabo eum. [8] Et respondens centurio, ait : Domine, non sum dignus ut intres sub tectum meum : sed tantum dic verbo, et sanabitur puer meus. [9] Nam et ego homo sum sub potestate constitutus, habens sub me milites, et dico huic : Vade, et vadit : et alii : Veni, et venit : et servo meo : Fac hoc, et facit. [10] Audiens autem Jesus miratus est, et sequentibus se dixit : Amen dico vobis, non inveni tantam fidem in Israel.

seeching him, [6] And saying, Lord, my servant lieth at home sick of the palsy, and is grieviously tormented. [7] And Jesus saith to him: I will come and heal him. [8] And the centurion making answer, said: Lord, I am not worthy that thou shouldst enter under my roof: but only say the word, and my servant shall be healed. [9] For I also am a man subject to authority, having under me soldiers; and I say to this, Go, and he goeth, and to another, Come, and he cometh, and to my servant, Do this, and he doeth it. [10] And Jesus hearing this, marvelled; and said to them that followed him: Amen I say to you, I have not found so great faith in Israel.

Luke 7:2–10

[2] Centurionis autem cujusdam servus male habens, erat moriturus : qui illi erat pretiosus. [3] Et cum audisset de Jesu, misit ad eum seniores Judaeorum, rogans eum ut veniret et salvaret servum ejus. [4] At illi cum venissent ad Jesum, rogabant eum sollicite, dicentes ei : Quia dignus est ut hoc illi praestes : [5] diligit enim gentem nostram, et synagogam ipse aedificavit nobis.

[6] Jesus autem ibat cum illis. Et cum jam non longe esset a domo, misit ad eum centurio amicos, dicens : Domine, noli vexari : non enim sum dignus ut sub tectum meum intres : [7] propter quod et meipsum non sum dignum arbitratus ut venirem ad te : sed dic verbo, et sanabitur puer meus. [8] Nam et ego homo sum sub potestate constitutus, habens sub me milites : et dico huic, Vade, et vadit : et alii, Veni, et venit : et servo meo, Fac hoc, et facit. [9] Quo audito Jesus miratus est : et conversus sequentibus se turbis, dixit : Amen dico vobis, nec in Israel tantam fidem inveni. [10] Et reversi, qui missi fuerant, domum, invenerunt servum, qui languerat, sanum.

Luke 7:2–10

[2] And the servant of a certain centurion, who was dear to him, being sick, was ready to die. [3] And when he had heard of Jesus, he sent unto him the ancients of the Jews, desiring him to come and heal his servant. [4] And when they came to Jesus, they besought him earnestly, saying to him: He is worthy that thou shouldest do this for him. [5] For he loveth our nation; and he hath built us a synagogue.

[6] And Jesus went with them. And when he was now not far from the house, the centurion sent his friends to him, saying: Lord, trouble not thyself; for I am not worthy that thou shouldest enter under my roof. [7] For which cause neither did I think myself worthy to come to thee; but say the word, and my servant shall be healed. [8] For I also am a man subject to authority, having under me soldiers: and I say to one, Go, and he goeth; and to another, Come, and he cometh; and to my servant, Do this, and he doth it. [9] Which Jesus hearing, marvelled: and turning about to the multitude that followed him, he said: Amen I say to you, I have not found so great faith, not even in Israel. [10] And they who were sent, being returned to the house, found the servant whole who had been sick.

Demonaic(s) at at Tomb

Matthew 8:28–34

[28] Et cum venisset trans fretum in regionem Gerasenorum, occurrerunt ei duo habentes daemonia, de monumentis exeuntes, saevi nimis, ita ut nemo posset transire per viam illam. [29] Et ecce clamaverunt, dicentes : Quid nobis et tibi, Jesu fili Dei? Venisti huc ante tempus torquere nos? [30] Erat autem non longe ab illis grex multorum porcorum pascens.

[31] Daemones autem rogabant eum, dicentes: Si ejicis nos hinc, mitte nos in gregem porcorum. [32] Et ait illis : Ite. At illi exeuntes abierunt in porcos, et ecce impetu abiit totus grex per praeceps in mare : et mortui sunt in aquis. [33] Pastores autem fugerunt : et venientes in civitatem, nuntiaverunt omnia, et de eis qui daemonia habuerant. [34] Et ecce tota civitas exiit obviam Jesu : et viso eo, rogabant ut transiret a finibus eorum.

Matthew 8:28–34

[28] And when he was come on the other side of the water, into the country of the Gerasens, there met him two that were possessed with devils, coming out of the sepulchres, exceeding fierce, so that none could pass by that way. [29] And behold they cried out, saying: What have we to do with thee, Jesus Son of God? art thou come hither to torment us before the time? [30] And there was, not far from them, an herd of many swine feeding.

[31] And the devils besought him, saying: If thou cast us out hence, send us into the herd of swine. [32] And he said to them: Go. But they going out went into the swine, and behold the whole herd ran violently down a steep place into the sea: and they perished in the waters. [33] And they that kept them fled: and coming into the city, told every thing, and concerning them that had been possessed by the devils. [34] And behold the whole city went out to meet Jesus, and when they saw him, they besought him that he would depart from their coasts.

Mark 5:1–15

[1] Et venerunt trans fretum maris in regionem Gerasenorum. [2] Et exeunti ei de navi, statim occurrit de monumentis homo in spiritu immundo, [3] qui domicilium habebat in monumentis, et neque catenis jam quisquam poterat eum ligare : [4] quoniam saepe compedibus et catenis vinctus, dirupisset catenas, et compedes comminuisset, et nemo poterat eum domare : [5] et semper die ac nocte in monumentis, et in montibus erat, clamans, et concidens se lapidibus.

[6] Videns autem Jesum a longe, cucurrit, et adoravit eum : [7] et clamans voce magna dixit : Quid mihi et tibi, Jesu Fili Dei altissimi? adjuro te per Deum, ne me torqueas. [8] Dicebat enim illi : Exi spiritus immunde ab homine. [9] Et interrogabat eum : Quod tibi nomen est? Et dicit ei : Legio mihi nomen est, quia multi sumus. [10] Et deprecabatur eum multum, ne se expelleret extra regionem.

Mark 5:1–15

[1] And they came over the strait of the sea into the country of the Gerasens. [2] And as he went out of the ship, immediately there met him out of the monuments a man with an unclean spirit, [3] Who had his dwelling in the tombs, and no man now could bind him, not even with chains. [4] For having been often bound with fetters and chains, he had burst the chains, and broken the fetters in pieces, and no one could tame him. [5] And he was always day and night in the monuments and in the mountains, crying and cutting himself with stones.

[6] And seeing Jesus afar off, he ran and adored him. [7] And crying with a loud voice, he said: What have I to do with thee, Jesus the Son of the most high God? I adjure thee by God that thou torment me not. [8] For he said unto him: Go out of the man, thou unclean spirit. [9] And he asked him: What

[11] Erat autem ibi circa montem grex porcorum magnus, pascens. [12] Et deprecabantur eum spiritus, dicentes : Mitte nos in porcos ut in eos introeamus. [13] Et concessit eis statim Jesus. Et exeuntes spiritus immundi introierunt in porcos : et magno impetu grex praecipitatus est in mare ad duo millia, et suffocati sunt in mari. [14] Qui autem pascebant eos, fugerunt, et nuntiaverunt in civitatem et in agros. Et egressi sunt videre quid esset factum : [15] et veniunt ad Jesum : et vident illum qui a daemonio vexabatur, sedentem, vestitum, et sanae mentis, et timuerunt.

is thy name? And he saith to him: My name is Legion, for we are many. [10] And he besought him much, that he would not drive him away out of the country.

[11] And there was there near the mountain a great herd of swine, feeding. [12] And the spirits besought him, saying: Send us into the swine, that we may enter into them. [13] And Jesus immediately gave them leave. And the unclean spirits going out, entered into the swine: and the herd with great violence was carried headlong into the sea, being about two thousand, and were stifled in the sea. [14] And they that fed them fled, and told it in the city and in the fields. And they went out to see what was done: [15] And they came to Jesus, and they see him that was troubled with the devil, sitting, clothed, and well in his wits, and they were afraid.

Luke 8:26–39

[26] Et navigaverunt ad regionem Gerasenorum, quae est contra Galilaeam. [27] Et cum egressus esset ad terram, occurrit illi vir quidam, qui habebat daemonium jam temporibus multis, et vestimento non induebatur, neque in domo manebat, sed in monumentis. [28] Is, ut vidit Jesum, procidit ante illum : et exclamans voce magna, dixit : Quid mihi et tibi est, Jesu Fili Dei Altissimi? obsecro te, ne me torqueas. [29] Praecipiebat enim spiritui immundo ut exiret ab homine. Multis enim temporibus arripiebat illum, et vinciebatur catenis, et compedibus custoditus. Et ruptis vinculis agebatur a daemonio in deserta. [30] Interrogavit autem illum Jesus, dicens : Quod tibi nomen est? At ille dixit : Legio : quia intraverant daemonia multa in eum.

[31] Et rogabant illum ne imperaret illis ut in abyssum irent. [32] Erat autem ibi grex porcorum multorum pascentium in monte : et rogabant eum, ut permitteret eis in illos ingredi. Et permisit illis. [33] Exierunt ergo daemonia ab homine, et intraverunt in porcos : et impetu abiit grex per praeceps in stagnum, et suffocatus est. [34] Quod ut viderunt factum qui pascebant, fugerunt, et nuntiaverunt in civitatem et in villas. [35] Exierunt

Luke 8:26–39

[26] And they sailed to the country of the Gerasens, which is over against Galilee. [27] And when he was come forth to the land, there met him a certain man who had a devil now a very long time, and he wore no clothes, neither did he abide in a house, but in the sepulchres. [28] And when he saw Jesus, he fell down before him; and crying out with a loud voice, he said: What have I to do with thee, Jesus, Son of the most high God? I beseech thee, do not torment me. [29] For he commanded the unclean spirit to go out of the man. For many times it seized him, and he was bound with chains, and kept in fetters; and breaking the bonds, he was driven by the devil into the deserts. [30] And Jesus asked him, saying: What is thy name? But he said: Legion; because many devils were entered into him.

[31] And they besought him that he would not command them to go into the abyss. [32] And there was there a herd of many swine feeding on the mountain; and they besought him that he would suffer them to enter into them. And he suffered them. [33] The devils therefore went out of the man, and entered into the swine; and the herd ran violently

autem videre quod factum est, et venerunt ad Jesum, et invenerunt hominem sedentem, a quo daemonia exierant, vestitum ac sana mente, ad pedes ejus, et timuerunt.

[36] Nuntiaverunt autem illis et qui viderant, quomodo sanus factus esset a legione : [37] et rogaverunt illum omnis multitudo regionis Gerasenorum ut discederet ab ipsis : quia magno timore tenebantur. Ipse autem ascendens navim, reversus est. [38] Et rogabat illum vir, a quo daemonia exierant, ut cum eo esset. Dimisit autem eum Jesus, dicens : [39] Redi in domum tuam, et narra quanta tibi fecit Deus. Et abiit per universam civitatem, praedicans quanta illi fecisset Jesus.

down a steep place into the lake, and were stifled. [34] Which when they that fed them saw done, they fled away, and told it in the city and in the villages. [35] And they went out to see what was done; and they came to Jesus, and found the man, out of whom the devils were departed, sitting at his feet, clothed, and in his right mind; and they were afraid.

[36] And they also that had seen, told them how he had been healed from the legion. [37] And all the multitude of the country of the Gerasens besought him to depart from them; for they were taken with great fear. And he, going up into the ship, returned back again. [38] Now the man, out of whom the devils were departed, besought him that he might be with him. But Jesus sent him away, saying: [39] Return to thy house, and tell how great things God hath done to thee. And he went through the whole city, publishing how great things Jesus had done to him.

Man with Paralysis at Capernaum

Matthew 9:1–8

[1] Et ascendens in naviculam, transfretavit, et venit in civitatem suam. [2] Et ecce offerebant ei paralyticum jacentem in lecto. Et videns Jesus fidem illorum, dixit paralytico : Confide fili, remittuntur tibi peccata tua. [3] Et ecce quidam de scribis dixerunt intra se : Hic blasphemat. [4] Et cum vidisset Jesus cogitationes eorum, dixit : Ut quid cogitatis mala in cordibus vestris? [5] Quid est facilius dicere : Dimittuntur tibi peccata tua : an dicere : Surge, et ambula?

[6] Ut autem sciatis, quia Filius hominis habet potestatem in terra dimittendi peccata, tunc ait paralytico : Surge, tolle lectum tuum, et vade in domum tuam. [7] Et surrexit, et abiit in domum suam. [8] Videntes autem turbae timuerunt, et glorificaverunt Deum, qui dedit potestatem talem hominibus.

Matthew 9:1–8

[1] And entering into a boat, he passed over the water and came into his own city. [2] And behold they brought to him one sick of the palsy lying in a bed. And Jesus, seeing their faith, said to the man sick of the palsy: Be of good heart, son, thy sins are forgiven thee. [3] And behold some of the scribes said within themselves: He blasphemeth. [4] And Jesus seeing their thoughts, said: Why do you think evil in your hearts? [5] Whether is easier, to say, Thy sins are forgiven thee: or to say, Arise, and walk?

[6] But that you may know that the Son of man hath power on earth to forgive sins, (then said he to the man sick of palsy,) Arise, take up thy bed, and go into thy house. [7] And he arose, and went into his house. [8] And the multitude seeing it, feared, and glorified God that gave such power to men.

Mark 2:3–13

[3] Et venerunt ad eum ferentes paralyticum, qui a quatuor portabatur. [4] Et cum non possent offerre eum illi prae turba, nudaverunt tectum ubi erat : et patefacientes submiserunt grabatum in quo paralyticus jacebat. [5] Cum autem vidisset Jesus fidem illorum, ait paralytico : Fili, dimittuntur tibi peccata tua.

[6] Erant autem illic quidam de scribis sedentes, et cogitantes in cordibus suis : [7] Quid hic sic loquitur? blasphemat. Quis potest dimittere peccata, nisi solus Deus? [8] Quo statim cognito Jesus spiritu suo, quia sic cogitarent intra se, dicit illis : Quid ista cogitatis in cordibus vestris? [9] Quid est facilius dicere paralytico : Dimittuntur tibi peccata tua : an dicere : Surge, tolle grabatum tuum, et ambula? [10] Ut autem sciatis quia Filius hominis habet potestatem in terra dimittendi peccata (ait paralytico),

[11] tibi dico : Surge, tolle grabatum tuum, et vade in domum tuam. [12] Et statim surrexit ille : et, sublato grabato, abiit coram omnibus, ita ut mirarentur omnes, et honorificent Deum, dicentes : Quia numquam sic vidimus. [13] Et egressus est rursus ad mare, omnisque turba veniebat ad eum, et docebat eos.

Luke 5:17–25

[17] Et factum est in una dierum, et ipse sedebat docens. Et erant pharisaei sedentes, et legis doctores, qui venerunt ex omni castello Galilaeae, et Judaeae, et Jerusalem : et virtus Domini erat ad sanandum eos. [18] Et ecce viri portantes in lecto hominem, qui erat paralyticus : et quaerebant eum inferre, et ponere ante eum. [19] Et non invenientes qua parte illum inferrent prae turba, ascenderunt supra tectum, et per tegulas summiserunt eum cum lecto in medium ante Jesum. [20] Quorum fidem ut vidit, dixit : Homo, remittuntur tibi peccata tua.

[21] Et coeperunt cogitare scribae et pharisaei, dicentes : Quis est hic, qui loquitur blas-

Mark 2:3–13

[3] And they came to him, bringing one sick of the palsy, who was carried by four. [4] And when they could not offer him unto him for the multitude, they uncovered the roof where he was; and opening it, they let down the bed wherein the man sick of the palsy lay. [5] And when Jesus had seen their faith, he saith to the sick of the palsy: Son, thy sins are forgiven thee.

[6] And there were some of the scribes sitting there, and thinking in their hearts: [7] Why doth this man speak thus? he blasphemeth. Who can forgive sins, but God only? [8] Which Jesus presently knowing in his spirit, that they so thought within themselves, saith to them: Why think you these things in your hearts? [9] Which is easier, to say to the sick of the palsy: Thy sins are forgiven thee; or to say: Arise, take up thy bed, and walk? [10] But that you may know that the Son of man hath power on earth to forgive sins, (he saith to the sick of the palsy,)

[11] I say to thee: Arise, take up thy bed, and go into thy house. [12] And immediately he arose; and taking up his bed, went his way in the sight of all; so that all wondered and glorified God, saying: We never saw the like. [13] And he went forth again to the sea side; and all the multitude came to him, and he taught them.

Luke 5:17–25

[17] And it came to pass on a certain day, as he sat teaching, that there were also Pharisees and doctors of the law sitting by, that were come out of every town of Galilee, and Judea and Jerusalem: and the power of the Lord was to heal them. [18] And behold, men brought in a bed a man, who had the palsy: and they sought means to bring him in, and to lay him before him. [19] And when they could not find by what way they might bring him in, because of the multitude, they went up upon the roof, and let him down through the tiles with his bed into the midst before Jesus. [20] Whose faith when he saw, he said: Man, thy sins are forgiven thee.

phemias? quis potest dimittere peccata, nisi solus Deus? [22] Ut cognovit autem Jesus cogitationes eorum, respondens, dixit ad illos: Quid cogitatis in cordibus vestris? [23] Quid est facilius dicere: Dimittuntur tibi peccata: an dicere: Surge, et ambula? [24] Ut autem sciatis quia Filius hominis habet potestatem in terra dimittendi peccata, (ait paralytico) tibi dico, surge, tolle lectum tuum, et vade in domum tuam. [25] Et confestim consurgens coram illis, tulit lectum in quo jacebat: et abiit in domum suam, magnificans Deum.

[21] And the scribes and Pharisees began to think, saying: Who is this who speaketh blasphemies? Who can forgive sins, but God alone? [22] And when Jesus knew their thoughts, answering, he said to them: What is it you think in your hearts? [23] Which is easier to say, Thy sins are forgiven thee; or to say, Arise and walk? [24] But that you may know that the Son of man hath power on earth to forgive sins, (he saith to the sick of the palsy,) I say to thee, Arise, take up thy bed, and go into thy house. [25] And immediately rising up before them, he took up the bed on which he lay; and he went away to his own house, glorifying God.

The Blind near Jericho (Bartimeus in the Book of Mark)[6]

Matthew 9:27–30

[27] Et transeunte inde Jesu, secuti sunt eum duo caeci, clamantes, et dicentes: Miserere nostri, fili David. [28] Cum autem venisset domum, accesserunt ad eum caeci. Et dicit eis Jesus: Creditis quia hoc possum facere vobis? Dicunt ei: Utique, Domine. [29] Tunc tetigit oculos eorum, dicens: Secundum fidem vestram, fiat vobis. [30] Et aperti sunt oculi eorum: et comminatus est illis Jesus, dicens: Videte ne quis sciat.

Matthew 9:27–30

[27] And as Jesus passed from thence, there followed him two blind men crying out and saying, Have mercy on us, O Son of David. [28] And when he was come to the house, the blind men came to him. And Jesus saith to them, Do you believe, that I can do this unto you? They say to him, Yea, Lord. [29] Then he touched their eyes, saying, According to your faith, be it done unto you. [30] And their eyes were opened, and Jesus strictly charged them, saying, See that no man know this.

Mark 10:46–52

[46] Et veniunt Jericho: et proficiscente eo de Jericho, et discipulis ejus, et plurima multitudine, filius Timae Bartimaeus caecus, sedebat juxta viam mendicans. [47] Qui cum audisset quia Jesus Nazarenus est, coepit clamare, et dicere: Jesu fili David, miserere mei. [48] Et comminabantur ei multi ut taceret. At ille multo magis clamabat: Fili David, miserere mei. [49] Et stans Jesus praecepit illum vocari. Et vocant caecum, dicentes ei: Animaequior esto: surge, vocat te. [50] Qui projecto vestimento suo exiliens, venit ad eum. [51] Et respondens Jesus dixit illi: Quid tibi vis faciam? Caecus autem dixit

Mark 10:46–52

[46] And they came to Jericho: and as he went out of Jericho, with his disciples, and a very great multitude, Bartimeus the blind man, the son of Timeus, sat by the way side begging. [47] Who when he had heard, that it was Jesus of Nazareth, began to cry out, and to say: Jesus son of David, have mercy on me. [48] And many rebuked him, that he might hold his peace; but he cried a great deal the more: Son of David, have mercy on me. [49] And Jesus, standing still, commanded him to be called. And they call the blind man, saying to him: Be of better comfort: arise, he calleth

ei : Rabboni, ut videam. [52] Jesus autem ait illi : Vade, fides tua te salvum fecit. Et confestim vidit, et sequebatur eum in via.

thee. [50] Who casting off his garment leaped up, and came to him.

[51] And Jesus answering, said to him: What wilt thou that I should do to thee? And the blind man said to him: Rabboni, that I may see. [52] And Jesus saith to him: Go thy way, thy faith hath made thee whole. And immediately he saw, and followed him in the way.

Luke 18:35–43

[35] Factum est autem, cum appropinquaret Jericho, caecus quidam sedebat secus viam, mendicans.

[36] Et cum audiret turbam praetereuntem, interrogabat quid hoc esset. [37] Dixerunt autem ei quod Jesus Nazarenus transiret. [38] Et clamavit, dicens : Jesu, fili David, miserere mei. [39] Et qui praeibant, increpabant eum ut taceret. Ipse vero multo magis clamabat : Fili David, miserere mei. [40] Stans autem Jesus jussit illum adduci ad se. Et cum appropinquasset, interrogavit illum,

[41] dicens : Quid tibi vis faciam? At ille dixit : Domine, ut videam. [42] Et Jesus dixit illi : Respice, fides tua te salvum fecit. [43] Et confestim vidit, et sequebatur illum magnificans Deum. Et omnis plebs ut vidit, dedit laudem Deo.

Luke 18:35–43

[35] Now it came to pass, when he drew nigh to Jericho, that a certain blind man sat by the way side, begging.

[36] And when he heard the multitude passing by, he asked what this meant. [37] And they told him, that Jesus of Nazareth was passing by. [38] And he cried out, saying: Jesus, son of David, have mercy on me. [39] And they that went before, rebuked him, that he should hold his peace: but he cried out much more: Son of David, have mercy on me. [40] And Jesus standing, commanded him to be brought unto him. And when he was come near, he asked him,

[41] Saying: What wilt thou that I do to thee? But he said: Lord, that I may see. [42] And Jesus said to him: Receive thy sight: thy faith hath made thee whole.

Man with a Withered Hand

Matthew 12:10–15

[10] Et ecce homo manum habens aridam et interrogabant eum, dicentes : Si licet sabbatis curare? ut accusarent eum.

[11] Ipse autem dixit illis : Quis erit ex vobis homo, qui habeat ovem unam, et si ceciderit haec sabbatis in foveam, nonne tenebit et levabit eam? [12] Quanto magis melior est homo ove? itaque licet sabbatis benefacere. [13] Tunc ait homini : Extende manum tuam. Et extendit, et restituta est sanitati sicut altera. [14] Exeuntes autem pharisaei, consilium faciebant adversus eum, quomodo perderent

Matthew 12:10–15

[10] And behold there was a man who had a withered hand, and they asked him, saying: Is it lawful to heal on the sabbath days? that they might accuse him.

[11] But he said to them: What man shall there be among you, that hath one sheep: and if the same fall into a pit on the sabbath day, will he not take hold on it and lift it up? [12] How much better is a man than a sheep? Therefore it is lawful to do a good deed on the sabbath days. [13] Then he saith to the man: Stretch forth thy hand; and he stretched it forth, and it was restored to health even as

eum. [15] Jesus autem sciens recessit inde : et secuti sunt eum multi, et curavit eos omnes.

the other. [14] And the Pharisees going out made a consultation against him, how they might destroy him. [15] But Jesus knowing it, retired from thence: and many followed him, and he healed them all.

Mark 3:1–5

[1] Et introivit iterum in synagogam : et erat ibi homo habens manum aridam. [2] Et observabant eum, si sabbatis curaret, ut accusarent illum. [3] Et ait homini habenti manum aridam : Surge in medium. [4] Et dicit eis : Licet sabbatis benefacere, an male? animam salvam facere, an perdere? At illi tacebant. [5] Et circumspiciens eos cum ira, contristatus super caecitate cordis eorum, dicit homini : Extende manum tuam. Et extendit, et restituta est manus illi.

Mark 3:1–5

[1] And he entered again into the synagogue, and there was a man there who had a withered hand. [2] And they watched him whether he would heal on the sabbath days; that they might accuse him. [3] And he said to the man who had the withered hand: Stand up in the midst. [4] And he saith to them: Is it lawful to do good on the sabbath days, or to do evil? to save life, or to destroy? But they held their peace. [5] And looking round about on them with anger, being grieved for the blindness of their hearts, he saith to the man: Stretch forth thy hand. And he stretched it forth: and his hand was restored unto him.

Luke 6:6–10

[6] Factum est autem in alio sabbato, ut intraret in synagogam, et doceret. Et erat ibi homo, et manus ejus dextra erat arida. [7] Observabant autem scribae et pharisaei si in sabbato curaret, ut invenirent unde accusarent eum. [8] Ipse vero sciebat cogitationes eorum : et ait homini qui habebat manum aridam : Surge, et sta in medium. Et surgens stetit. [9] Ait autem ad illos Jesus : Interrogo vos si licet sabbatis benefacere, an male : animam salvam facere, an perdere? [10] Et circumspectis omnibus dixit homini : Extende manum tuam. Et extendit : et restituta est manus ejus.

Luke 6:6–10

[6] And it came to pass also on another sabbath, that he entered into the synagogue, and taught. And there was a man, whose right hand was withered. [7] And the scribes and Pharisees watched if he would heal on the sabbath; that they might find an accusation against him. [8] But he knew their thoughts; and said to the man who had the withered hand: Arise, and stand forth in the midst. And rising he stood forth. [9] Then Jesus said to them: I ask you, if it be lawful on the sabbath days to do good, or to do evil; to save life, or to destroy? [10] And looking round about on them all, he said to the man: Stretch forth thy hand. And he stretched it forth: and his hand was restored.

Son with Epilepsy near the Towns of Caesarea Philippi

Matthew 17:14–20

[14] Et cum venisset ad turbam, accessit ad eum homo genibus provolutus ante eum, dicens : Domine, miserere filio meo, quia luna-

Matthew 17:14–20

[14] And when he was come to the multitude, there came to him a man falling down on his knees before him, saying: Lord, have

ticus est, et male patitur : nam saepe cadit in ignem, et crebro in aquam. [15] Et obtuli eum discipulis tuis, et non potuerunt curare eum.

[16] Respondens autem Jesus, ait : O generatio incredula, et perversa, quousque ero vobiscum? usquequo patiar vos? Afferte huc illum ad me. [17] Et increpavit illum Jesus, et exiit ab eo daemonium, et curatus est puer ex illa hora. [18] Tunc accesserunt discipuli ad Jesum secreto, et dixerunt : Quare nos non potuimus ejicere illum? [19] Dixit illis Jesus : Propter incredulitatem vestram. Amen quippe dico vobis, si habueritis fidem sicut granum sinapis, dicetis monti huic : Transi hinc illuc, et transibit, et nihil impossibile erit vobis. [20] Hoc autem genus non ejicitur nisi per orationem et jejunium.

pity on my son, for he is a lunatic, and suffereth much: for he falleth often into the fire, and often into the water. [15] And I brought him to thy disciples, and they could not cure him.

[16] Then Jesus answered and said: O unbelieving and perverse generation, how long shall I be with you? How long shall I suffer you? bring him hither to me. [17] And Jesus rebuked him, and the devil went out of him, and the child was cured from that hour. [18] Then came the disciples to Jesus secretly, and said: Why could not we cast him out? [19] Jesus said to them: Because of your unbelief. For, amen I say to you, if you have faith as a grain of mustard seed, you shall say to this mountain, Remove from hence hither, and it shall remove; and nothing shall be impossible to you. [20] But this kind is not cast out but by prayer and fasting.

Luke 9:38–43

[38] Et ecce vir de turba exclamavit, dicens : Magister, obsecro te, respice in filium meum quia unicus est mihi : [39] et ecce spiritus apprehendit eum, et subito clamat, et elidit, et dissipat eum cum spuma, et vix discedit dilanians eum : [40] et rogavi discipulos tuos ut ejicerent illum, et non potuerunt.

[41] Respondens autem Jesus, dixit : O generatio infidelis, et perversa, usquequo ero apud vos, et patiar vos? adduc huc filium tuum. [42] Et cum accederet, elisit illum daemonium, et dissipavit. [43] Et increpavit Jesus spiritum immundum, et sanavit puerum, et reddidit illum patri ejus.

Luke 9:38–43

[38] And behold a man among the crowd cried out, saying: Master, I beseech thee, look upon my son, because he is my only one. [39] And lo, a spirit seizeth him, and he suddenly crieth out, and he throweth him down and teareth him, so that he foameth; and bruising him, he hardly departeth from him. [40] And I desired thy disciples to cast him out, and they could not.

[41] And Jesus answering, said: O faithless and perverse generation, how long shall I be with you, and suffer you? Bring hither thy son. [42] And as he was coming to him, the devil threw him down, and tore him. [43] And Jesus rebuked the unclean spirit, and cured the boy, and restored him to his father.

Deaf Man with Speech Impediment in the Region of Decapolis

Mark 7:31–37

[31] Et iterum exiens de finibus Tyri, venit per Sidonem ad mare Galilaeae inter medios fines Decapoleos. [32] Et adducunt ei surdum, et mutum, et deprecabantur eum, ut imponat

Mark 7:31–37

[31] And again going out of the coasts of Tyre, he came by Sidon to the sea of Galilee, through the midst of the coasts of Decapolis. [32] And they bring to him one deaf and

illi manum. [33] Et apprehendens eum de turba seorsum, misit digitos suos in auriculas ejus : et exspuens, tetigit linguam ejus : [34] et suscipiens in caelum, ingemuit, et ait illi : Ephphetha, quod est, Adaperire. [35] Et statim apertae sunt aures ejus, et solutum est vinculum linguae ejus, et loquebatur recte.

[36] Et praecepit illis ne cui dicerent. Quanto autem eis praecipiebat, tanto magis plus praedicabant : [37] et eo amplius admirabantur, dicentes : Bene omnia fecit : et surdos fecit audire, et mutos loqui.

dumb; and they besought him that he would lay his hand upon him. [33] And taking him from the multitude apart, he put his fingers into his ears, and spitting, he touched his tongue: [34] And looking up to heaven, he groaned, and said to him: Ephpheta, which is, Be thou opened. [35] And immediately his ears were opened, and the string of his tongue was loosed, and he spoke right.

[36] And he charged them that they should tell no man. But the more he charged them, so much the more a great deal did they publish it. [37] And so much the more did they wonder, saying: He hath done all things well; he hath made both the deaf to hear, and the dumb to speak.

Blind man at Bethesda

Mark 8:22–25

[22] Et veniunt Bethsaidam, et adducunt ei caecum, et rogabant eum ut illum tangeret. [23] Et apprehensa manu caeci, eduxit eum extra vicum : et exspuens in oculos ejus impositis manibus suis, interrogavit eum si quid videret. [24] Et aspiciens, ait : Video homines velut arbores ambulantes. [25] Deinde iterum imposuit manus super oculos ejus : et coepit videre : et restitutus est ita ut clare videret omnia.

Mark 8:22–25

[22] And they came to Bethsaida; and they bring to him a blind man, and they besought him that he would touch him. [23] And taking the blind man by the hand, he led him out of the town; and spitting upon his eyes, laying his hands on him, he asked him if he saw any thing. [24] And looking up, he said: I see men as it were trees, walking. [25] After that again he laid his hands upon his eyes, and he began to see, and was restored, so that he saw all things clearly.

Jairus' Daughter at Capernaum & Woman with Issue of Blood at Capernaum

Matthew 9:18–25

[18] Haec illo loquente ad eos, ecce princeps unus accessit, et adorabat eum, dicens : Domine, filia mea modo defuncta est : sed veni, impone manum tuam super eam, et vivet. [19] Et surgens Jesus, sequebatur eum, et discipuli ejus. [20] Et ecce mulier, quae sanguinis fluxum patiebatur duodecim annis, accessit retro, et tetigit fimbriam vestimenti ejus.

Matthew 9:18–25

[18] As he was speaking these things unto them, behold a certain ruler came up, and adored him, saying: Lord, my daughter is even now dead; but come, lay thy hand upon her, and she shall live. [19] And Jesus rising up followed him, with his disciples. [20] And behold a woman who was troubled with an issue of blood twelve years, came behind him, and touched the hem of his garment.

[21] Dicebat enim intra se : Si tetigero tantum vestimentum ejus, salva ero. [22] At Jesus conversus, et videns eam, dixit : Confide, filia, fides tua te salvam fecit. Et salva facta est mulier ex illa hora. [23] Et cum venisset Jesus in domum principis, et vidisset tibicines et turbam tumultuantem, dicebat : [24] Recedite : non est enim mortua puella, sed dormit. Et deridebant eum. [25] Et cum ejecta esset turba, intravit : et tenuit manum ejus, et surrexit puella.

Mark 5:22–43

[22] Et venit quidam de archisynagogis nomine Jairus, et videns eum procidit ad pedes ejus, [23] et deprecabatur eum multum, dicens : Quoniam filia mea in extremis est, veni, impone manum super eam, ut salva sit, et vivat. [24] Et abiit cum illo, et sequebatur eum turba multa, et comprimebant eum. [25] Et mulier, quae erat in profluvio sanguinis annis duodecim,

[26] et fuerat multa perpessa a compluribus medicis : et erogaverat omnia sua, nec quidquam profecerat, sed magis deterius habebat : [27] cum audisset de Jesu, venit in turba retro, et tetigit vestimentum ejus : [28] dicebat enim : Quia si vel vestimentum ejus tetigero, salva ero. [29] Et confestim siccatus est fons sanguinis ejus : et sensit corpore quia sanata esset a plaga. [30] Et statim Jesus in semetipso cognoscens virtutem quae exierat de illo, conversus ad turbam, aiebat : Quis tetigit vestimenta mea?

[31] Et dicebant ei discipuli sui : Vides turbam comprimentem te, et dicis : Quis me tetigit? [32] Et circumspiciebat videre eam, quae hoc fecerat. [33] Mulier vero timens et tremens, sciens quod factum esset in se, venit et procidit ante eum, et dixit ei omnem veritatem. [34] Ille autem dixit ei : Filia, fides tua te salvam fecit : vade in pace, et esto sana a plaga tua. [35] Adhuc eo loquente, veniunt ab archisynagago, dicentes : Quia filia tua mortua est : quid ultra vexas magistrum?

[21] For she said within herself: If I shall touch only his garment, I shall be healed. [22] But Jesus turning and seeing her, said: Be of good heart, daughter, thy faith hath made thee whole. And the woman was made whole from that hour. [23] And when Jesus was come into the house of the ruler, and saw the minstrels and the multitude making a rout, [24] He said: Give place, for the girl is not dead, but sleepeth. And they laughed him to scorn. [25] And when the multitude was put forth, he went in, and took her by the hand. And the maid arose.

Mark 5:22–43

[22] And there cometh one of the rulers of the synagogue named Jairus: and seeing him, falleth down at his feet. [23] And he besought him much, saying: My daughter is at the point of death, come, lay thy hand upon her, that she may be safe, and may live. [24] And he went with him, and a great multitude followed him, and they thronged him. [25] And a woman who was under an issue of blood twelve years,

[26] And had suffered many things from many physicians; and had spent all that she had, and was nothing the better, but rather worse, [27] When she had heard of Jesus, came in the crowd behind him, and touched his garment. [28] For she said: If I shall touch but his garment, I shall be whole. [29] And forthwith the fountain of her blood was dried up, and she felt in her body that she was healed of the evil. [30] And immediately Jesus knowing in himself the virtue that had proceeded from him, turning to the multitude, said: Who hath touched my garments?

[31] And his disciples said to him: Thou seest the multitude thronging thee, and sayest thou who hath touched me? [32] And he looked about to see her who had done this. [33] But the woman fearing and trembling, knowing what was done in her, came and fell down before him, and told him all the truth. [34] And he said to her: Daughter, thy faith hath made thee whole: go in peace, and be thou whole of thy disease. [35] While he was

[36] Jesus autem audito verbo quod dice-batur, ait archisynagogo : Noli timere : tantummodo crede. [37] Et non admisit quemquam se sequi nisi Petrum, et Jacobum, et Joannem fratrem Jacobi. [38] Et veniunt in domum archisynagogi, et videt tumultum, et flentes, et ejulantes multum. [39] Et ingressus, ait illis : Quid turbamini, et ploratis? puella non est mortua, sed dormit. [40] Et irridebant eum. Ipse vero ejectis omnibus assumit patrem, et matrem puellae, et qui secum erant, et ingreditur ubi puella erat jacens.

[41] Et tenens manum puellae, ait illi : Talitha cumi, quod est interpretatum : Puella (tibi dico), surge. [42] Et confestim surrexit puella, et ambulabat : erat autem annorum duodecim : et obstupuerunt stupore magno. [43] Et praecepit illis vehementer ut nemo id sciret : et dixit dari illi manducare.

yet speaking, some come from the ruler of the synagogue's house, saying: Thy daughter is dead: why dost thou trouble the master any further?

[36] But Jesus having heard the word that was spoken, saith to the ruler of the synagogue: Fear not, only believe. [37 And he admitted not any man to follow him, but Peter, and James, and John the brother of James. [38] And they come to the house of the ruler of the synagogue; and he seeth a tumult, and people weeping and wailing much. [39] And going in, he saith to them: Why make you this ado, and weep? the damsel is not dead, but sleepeth. [40] And they laughed him to scorn. But he having put them all out, taketh the father and the mother of the damsel, and them that were with him, and entereth in where the damsel was lying.

[41] And taking the damsel by the hand, he saith to her: Talitha cumi, which is, being interpreted: Damsel (I say to thee) arise. [42] And immediately the damsel rose up, and walked: and she was twelve years old: and they were astonished with a great astonishment. [43] And he charged them strictly that no man should know it: and commanded that something should be given her to eat.

Luke 8:41–56

[41] Et ecce venit vir, cui nomen Jairus, et ipse princeps synagogae erat : et cecidit ad pedes Jesu, rogans eum ut intraret in domum ejus, [42] quia unica filia erat ei fere annorum duodecim, et haec moriebatur. Et contigit, dum iret, a turba comprimebatur. [43] Et mulier quaedam erat in fluxu sanguinis ab annis duodecim, quae in medicos erogaverat omnem substantiam suam, nec ab ullo potuit curari : [44] accessit retro, et tetigit fimbriam vestimenti ejus : et confestim stetit fluxus sanguinis ejus. [45] Et ait Jesus : Quis est, qui me tetigit? Negantibus autem omnibus, dixit Petrus, et qui cum illo erant : Praeceptor, turbae te comprimunt, et affligunt, et dicis : Quis me tetigit?

[46] Et dicit Jesus : Tetigit me aliquis : nam ego novi virtutem de me exiisse. [47] Vi-

Luke 8:41–56

[41] And behold there came a man whose name was Jairus, and he was a ruler of the synagogue: and he fell down at the feet of Jesus, beseeching him that he would come into his house: [42] For he had an only daughter, almost twelve years old, and she was dying. And it happened as he went, that he was thronged by the multitudes. [43] And there was a certain woman having an issue of blood twelve years, who had bestowed all her substance on physicians, and could not be healed by any. [44] She came behind him, and touched the hem of his garment; and immediately the issue of her blood stopped. [45] And Jesus said: Who is it that touched me? And all denying, Peter and they that were with him said: Master, the multitudes throng and press thee, and dost thou say, Who touched me?

dens autem mulier, quia non latuit, tremens venit, et procidit ante pedes ejus : et ob quam causam tetigerit eum, indicavit coram omni populo : et quemadmodum confestim sanata sit. [48] At ipse dixit ei : Filia, fides tua salvam te fecit : vade in pace. [49] Adhuc illo loquente, venit quidam ad principem synagogae, dicens ei : Quia mortua est filia tua, noli vexare illum. [50] Jesus autem, audito hoc verbo, respondit patri puellae : Noli timere, crede tantum, et salva erit.

[51] Et cum venisset domum, non permisit intrare secum quemquam, nisi Petrum, et Jacobum, et Joannem, et patrem, et matrem puellae. [52] Flebant autem omnes, et plangebant illam. At ille dixit : Nolite flere : non est mortua puella, sed dormit. [53] Et deridebant eum, scientes quod mortua esset. [54] Ipse autem tenens manum ejus clamavit, dicens : Puella, surge. [55] Et reversus est spiritus ejus, et surrexit continuo. Et jussit illi dari manducare.

[56] Et stupuerunt parentes ejus, quibus praecepit ne alicui dicerent quod factum erat.

[46] And Jesus said: Somebody hath touched me; for I know that virtue is gone out from me. [47] And the woman seeing that she was not hid, came trembling, and fell down before his feet, and declared before all the people for what cause she had touched him, and how she was immediately healed. [48] But he said to her: Daughter, thy faith hath made thee whole; go thy way in peace. [49] As he was yet speaking, there cometh one to the ruler of the synagogue, saying to him: Thy daughter is dead, trouble him not. [50] And Jesus hearing this word, answered the father of the maid: Fear not; believe only, and she shall be safe.

[51] And when he was come to the house, he suffered not any man to go in with him, but Peter and James and John, and the father and mother of the maiden. [52] And all wept and mourned for her. But he said: Weep not; the maid is not dead, but sleepeth. [53] And they laughed him to scorn, knowing that she was dead. [54] But he taking her by the hand, cried out, saying: Maid, arise. [55] And her spirit returned, and she arose immediately. And he bid them give her to eat.

[56] And her parents were astonished, whom he charged to tell no man what was done.

Infirm Man at the Pool of Bethsaida

John 5:2–15

[2] Est autem Jerosolymis probatica piscina, quae cognominatur hebraice Bethsaida, quinque porticus habens. [3] In his jacebat multitudo magna languentium, caecorum, claudorum, aridorum, exspectantium aquae motum. [4] Angelus autem Domini descendebat secundum tempus in piscinam, et movebatur aqua. Et qui prior descendisset in piscinam post motionem aquae, sanus fiebat a quacumque detinebatur infirmitate. [5] Erat autem quidam homo ibi triginta et octo annos habens in infirmitate sua.

[6] Hunc autem cum vidisset Jesus jacentem, et cognovisset quia jam multum tem-

John 5:2–15

[2] Now there is at Jerusalem a pond, called Probatica, which in Hebrew is named Bethsaida, having five porches. [3] In these lay a great multitude of sick, of blind, of lame, of withered; waiting for the moving of the water. [4] And an angel of the Lord descended at certain times into the pond; and the water was moved. And he that went down first into the pond after the motion of the water, was made whole, of whatsoever infirmity he lay under. [5] And there was a certain man there, that had been eight and thirty years under his infirmity.

pus haberet, dicit ei : Vis sanus fieri? [7] Respondit ei languidus : Domine, hominem non habeo, ut, cum turbata fuerit aqua, mittat me in piscinam : dum venio enim ego, alius ante me descendit. [8] Dicit ei Jesus : Surge, tolle grabatum tuum et ambula. [9] Et statim sanus factus est homo ille : et sustulit grabatum suum, et ambulabat. Erat autem sabbatum in die illo. [10] Dicebant ergo Judaei illi qui sanatus fuerat : Sabbatum est, non licet tibi tollere grabatum tuum.

[11] Respondit eis : Qui me sanum fecit, ille mihi dixit : Tolle grabatum tuum et ambula. [12] Interrogaverunt ergo eum : Quis est ille homo qui dixit tibi : Tolle grabatum tuum et ambula? [13] Is autem qui sanus fuerat effectus, nesciebat quis esset. Jesus enim declinavit a turba constituta in loco. [14] Postea invenit eum Jesus in templo, et dixit illi : Ecce sanus factus es; jam noli peccare, ne deterius tibi aliquid contingat. [15] Abiit ille homo, et nuntiavit Judaeis quia Jesus esset, qui fecit eum sanum.

[6] Him when Jesus had seen lying, and knew that he had been now a long time, he saith to him: Wilt thou be made whole? [7] The infirm man answered him: Sir, I have no man, when the water is troubled, to put me into the pond. For whilst I am coming, another goeth down before me. [8] Jesus saith to him: Arise, take up thy bed, and walk. [9] And immediately the man was made whole: and he took up his bed, and walked. And it was the sabbath that day. [10] The Jews therefore said to him that was healed: It is the sabbath; it is not lawful for thee to take up thy bed.

[11] He answered them: He that made me whole, he said to me, Take up thy bed, and walk. [12] They asked him therefore: Who is that man who said to thee, Take up thy bed, and walk? [13] But he who was healed, knew not who it was; for Jesus went aside from the multitude standing in the place. [14] Afterwards, Jesus findeth him in the temple, and saith to him: Behold thou art made whole: sin no more, lest some worse thing happen to thee. [15] The man went his way, and told the Jews, that it was Jesus who had made him whole.

Man Born Blind

John 9:1–41

[1] Et praeteriens Jesus vidit hominem caecum a nativitate : [2] et interrogaverunt eum discipuli ejus : Rabbi, quis peccavit, hic, aut parentes ejus, ut caecus nasceretur? [3] Respondit Jesus : Neque hic peccavit, neque parentes ejus : sed ut manifestentur opera Dei in illo. [4] Me oportet operari opera ejus qui misit me, donec dies est : venit nox, quando nemo potest operari : [5] quamdiu sum in mundo, lux sum mundi.

[6] Haec cum dixisset, exspuit in terram, et fecit lutum ex sputo, et linivit lutum super oculos ejus, [7] et dixit ei : Vade, lava in natatoria Siloe (quod interpretatur Missus). Abiit ergo, et lavit, et venit videns. [8] Itaque vicini, et qui viderant eum prius quia mendi-

John 9:1–41

[1] And Jesus passing by, saw a man, who was blind from his birth: [2] And his disciples asked him: Rabbi, who hath sinned, this man, or his parents, that he should be born blind? [3] Jesus answered: Neither hath this man sinned, nor his parents; but that the works of God should be made manifest in him. [4] I must work the works of him that sent me, whilst it is day: the night cometh, when no man can work. [5] As long as I am in the world, I am the light of the world.

[6] When he had said these things, he spat on the ground, and made clay of the spittle, and spread the clay on his eyes, [7] And said to him: Go, wash in the pool of Siloe, which is interpreted, Sent. He went therefore, and

cus erat, dicebant : Nonne hic est qui sedebat, et mendicabat? Alii dicebant : Quia hic est. [9] Alii autem : Nequaquam, sed similis est ei. Ille vero dicebat : Quia ego sum. [10] Dicebant ergo ei : Quomodo aperti sunt tibi oculi?

[11] Respondit : Ille homo qui dicitur Jesus, lutum fecit : et unxit oculos meos, et dixit mihi : Vade ad natatoria Siloe, et lava. Et abii, et lavi, et video. [12] Et dixerunt ei : Ubi est ille? Ait : Nescio. [13] Adducunt eum ad pharisaeos, qui caecus fuerat. [14] Erat autem sabbatum quando lutum fecit Jesus, et aperuit oculos ejus. [15] Iterum ergo interrogabant eum pharisaei quomodo vidisset. Ille autem dixit eis : Lutum mihi posuit super oculos, et lavi, et video.

[16] Dicebant ergo ex pharisaeis quidam : Non est hic homo a Deo, qui sabbatum non custodit. Alii autem dicebant : Quomodo potest homo peccator haec signa facere? Et schisma erat inter eos. [17] Dicunt ergo caeco iterum : Tu quid dicis de illo qui aperuit oculos tuos? Ille autem dixit : Quia propheta est. [18] Non crediderunt ergo Judaei de illo, quia caecus fuisset et vidisset, donec vocaverunt parentes ejus, qui viderat : [19] et interrogaverunt eos, dicentes : Hic est filius vester, quem vos dicitis quia caecus natus est? quomodo ergo nunc videt? [20] Responderunt eis parentes ejus, et dixerunt : Scimus quia hic est filius noster, et quia caecus natus est :

[21] quomodo autem nunc videat, nescimus : aut quis ejus aperuit oculos, nos nescimus; ipsum interrogate : aetatem habet, ipse de se loquatur. [22] Haec dixerunt parentes ejus, quoniam timebant Judaeos : jam enim conspiraverunt Judaei, ut si quis eum confiteretur esse Christum, extra synagogam fieret. [23] Propterea parentes ejus dixerunt : Quia aetatem habet, ipsum interrogate. [24] Vocaverunt ergo rursum hominem qui fuerat caecus, et dixerunt ei : Da gloriam Deo : nos scimus quia hic homo peccator est. [25] Dixit ergo eis ille : si peccator est, nescio; unum scio, quia caecus cum essem, modo video.

[26] Dixerunt ergo illi : Quid fecit tibi? quomodo aperuit tibi oculos? [27] Respondit

washed, and he came seeing. [8] The neighbours therefore, and they who had seen him before that he was a beggar, said: Is not this he that sat and begged? Some said: This is he. [9] But others said: No, but he is like him. But he said: I am he. [10] They said therefore to him: How were thy eyes opened?

[11] He answered: That man that is called Jesus made clay, and anointed my eyes, and said to me: Go to the pool of Siloe, and wash. And I went, I washed, and I see. [12] And they said to him: Where is he? He saith: I know not. [13] They bring him that had been blind to the Pharisees. [14] Now it was the sabbath, when Jesus made the clay, and opened his eyes. [15] Again therefore the Pharisees asked him, how he had received his sight. But he said to them: He put clay upon my eyes, and I washed, and I see.

[16] Some therefore of the Pharisees said: This man is not of God, who keepeth not the sabbath. But others said: How can a man that is a sinner do such miracles? And there was a division among them. [17] They say therefore to the blind man again: What sayest thou of him that hath opened thy eyes? And he said: He is a prophet. [18] The Jews then did not believe concerning him, that he had been blind, and had received his sight, until they called the parents of him that had received his sight, [19] And asked them, saying: Is this your son, who you say was born blind? How then doth he now see? [20] His parents answered them, and said: We know that this is our son, and that he was born blind:

[21] But how he now seeth, we know not; or who hath opened his eyes, we know not: ask himself: he is of age, let him speak for himself. [22] These things his parents said, because they feared the Jews: for the Jews had already agreed among themselves, that if any man should confess him to be Christ, he should be put out of the synagogue. [23] Therefore did his parents say: He is of age, ask himself. [24] They therefore called the man again that had been blind, and said to him: Give glory to God. We know that this man is a sinner. [25] He said therefore to them: If

eis : Dixi vobis jam, et audistis : quod iterum vultis audire? numquid et vos vultis discipuli ejus fieri? [28] Maledixerunt ergo ei, et dixerunt : Tu discipulus illius sis : nos autem Moysi discipuli sumus. [29] Nos scimus quia Moysi locutus est Deus; hunc autem nescimus unde sit. [30] Respondit ille homo, et dixit eis : In hoc enim mirabile est quia vos nescitis unde sit, et aperuit meos oculos :

[31] scimus autem quia peccatores Deus non audit : sed si quis Dei cultor est, et voluntatem ejus facit, hunc exaudit. [32] A saeculo non est auditum quia quis aperuit oculos caeci nati. [33] Nisi esset hic a Deo, non poterat facere quidquam. [34] Responderunt, et dixerunt ei : In peccatis natus es totus, et tu doces nos? Et ejecerunt eum foras. [35] Audivit Jesus quia ejecerunt eum foras : et cum invenisset eum, dixit ei : Tu credis in Filium Dei?

[36] Respondit ille, et dixit : Quis est, Domine, ut credam in eum? [37] Et dixit ei Jesus : Et vidisti eum, et qui loquitur tecum, ipse est. [38] At ille ait : Credo, Domine. Et procidens adoravit eum. [39] Et dixit Jesus : In judicium ego in hunc mundum veni : ut qui non vident videant, et qui vident caeci fiant. [40] Et audierunt quidam ex pharisaeis qui cum ipso erant, et dixerunt ei : Numquid et nos caeci sumus?

[41] Dixit eis Jesus : Si caeci essetis, non haberetis peccatum. Nunc vero dicitis, Quia videmus : peccatum vestrum manet.

he be a sinner, I know not: one thing I know, that whereas I was blind, now I see.

[26] They said then to him: What did he to thee? How did he open thy eyes? [27] He answered them: I have told you already, and you have heard: why would you hear it again? will you also become his disciples? [28] They reviled him therefore, and said: Be thou his disciple; but we are the disciples of Moses. [29] We know that God spoke to Moses: but as to this man, we know not from whence he is. [30] The man answered, and said to them: Why, herein is a wonderful thing, that you know not from whence he is, and he hath opened my eyes.

[31] Now we know that God doth not hear sinners: but if a man be a server of God, and doth his will, him he heareth. [32] From the beginning of the world it hath not been heard, that any man hath opened the eyes of one born blind. [33] Unless this man were of God, he could not do any thing. [34] They answered, and said to him: Thou wast wholly born in sins, and dost thou teach us? And they cast him out. [35] Jesus heard that they had cast him out: and when he had found him, he said to him: Dost thou believe in the Son of God?

[36] He answered, and said Who is he, Lord, that I may believe in him? [37] And Jesus said to him: Thou hast both seen him; and it is he that talketh with thee. [38] And he said: I believe, Lord. And falling down, he adored him. [39] And Jesus said: For judgment I am come into this world; that they who see not, may see; and they who see, may become blind. [40] And some of the Pharisees, who were with him, heard: and they said unto him: Are we also blind?

[41] Jesus said to them: If you were blind, you should not have sin: but now you say: We see. Your sin remaineth.

Lazarus Raised from the Dead

John 11:11–44

[11] Haec ait, et post haec dixit eis : Lazarus amicus noster dormit : sed vado ut a somno excitem eum. [12] Dixerunt ergo discipuli ejus : Domine, si dormit, salvus erit. [13] Dixerat autem Jesus de morte ejus : illi autem putaverunt quia de dormitione somni diceret. [14] Tunc ergo Jesus dixit eis manifeste : Lazarus mortuus est : [15] et gaudeo propter vos, ut credatis, quoniam non eram ibi, sed eamus ad eum.

[16] Dixit ergo Thomas, qui dicitur Didymus, ad condiscipulos : Eamus et nos, ut moriamur cum eo. [17] Venit itaque Jesus : et invenit eum quatuor dies jam in monumento habentem. [18] (Erat autem Bethania juxta Jerosolymam quasi stadiis quindecim.)

[19] Multi autem ex Judaeis venerant ad Martham et Mariam, ut consolarentur eas de fratre suo. [20] Martha ergo ut audivit quia Jesus venit, occurrit illi : Maria autem domi sedebat.

[21] Dixit ergo Martha ad Jesum : Domine, si fuisses hic, frater meus non fuisset mortuus : [22] sed et nunc scio quia quaecumque poposceris a Deo, dabit tibi Deus. [23] Dicit illi Jesus : Resurget frater tuus. [24] Dicit ei Martha : Scio quia resurget in resurrectione in novissimo die. [25] Dixit ei Jesus : Ego sum resurrectio et vita : qui credit in me, etiam si mortuus fuerit, vivet :

[26] et omnis qui vivit et credit in me, non morietur in aeternum. Credis hoc? [27] Ait illi : Utique Domine, ego credidi quia tu es Christus, Filius Dei vivi, qui in hunc mundum venisti. [28] Et cum haec dixisset, abiit, et vocavit Mariam sororem suam silentio, dicens : Magister adest, et vocat te. [29] Illa ut audivit, surgit cito, et venit ad eum; [30] nondum enim venerat Jesus in castellum : sed erat adhuc in illo loco, ubi occurrerat ei Martha.

[31] Judaei ergo, qui erant cum ea in domo, et consolabantur eam, cum vidissent Mariam quia cito surrexit, et exiit, secuti sunt eam dicentes : Quia vadit ad monumentum, ut

John 11:11–44

[11] These things he said; and after that he said to them: Lazarus our friend sleepeth; but I go that I may awake him out of sleep. [12] His disciples therefore said: Lord, if he sleep, he shall do well. [13] But Jesus spoke of his death; and they thought that he spoke of the repose of sleep. [14] Then therefore Jesus said to them plainly: Lazarus is dead. [15] And I am glad, for your sakes, that I was not there, that you may believe: but let us go to him.

[16] Thomas therefore, who is called Didymus, said to his fellow disciples: Let us also go, that we may die with him. [17] Jesus therefore came, and found that he had been four days already in the grave. [18] (Now Bethania was near Jerusalem, about fifteen furlongs off.) [19] And many of the Jews were come to Martha and Mary, to comfort them concerning their brother. [20] Martha therefore, as soon as she heard that Jesus had come, went to meet him: but Mary sat at home.

[21] Martha therefore said to Jesus: Lord, if thou hadst been here, my brother had not died. [22] But now also I know that whatsoever thou wilt ask of God, God will give it thee. [23] Jesus saith to her: Thy brother shall rise again. [24] Martha saith to him: I know that he shall rise again, in the resurrection at the last day. [25] Jesus said to her: I am the resurrection and the life: he that believeth in me, although he be dead, shall live:

[26] And every one that liveth, and believeth in me, shall not die for ever. Believest thou this? [27] She saith to him: Yea, Lord, I have believed that thou art Christ the Son of the living God, who art come into this world. [28] And when she had said these things, she went, and called her sister Mary secretly, saying: The master is come, and calleth for thee. [29] She, as soon as she heard this, riseth quickly, and cometh to him. [30] For Jesus was not yet come into the town: but he was still in that place where Martha had met him.

[31] The Jews therefore, who were with her in the house, and comforted her, when they

ploret ibi. [32] Maria ergo, cum venisset ubi erat Jesus, videns eum, cecidit ad pedes ejus, et dicit ei : Domine, si fuisses hic, non esset mortuus frater meus. [33] Jesus ergo, ut vidit eam plorantem, et Judaeos, qui venerant cum ea, plorantes, infremuit spiritu, et turbavit seipsum, [34] et dixit : Ubi posuistis eum? Dicunt ei : Domine, veni, et vide. [35] Et lacrimatus est Jesus.

[36] Dixerunt ergo Judaei : Ecce quomodo amabat eum. [37] Quidam autem ex ipsis dixerunt : Non poterat hic, qui aperuit oculos caeci nati, facere ut hic non moreretur? [38] Jesus ergo rursum fremens in semetipso, venit ad monumentum. Erat autem spelunca, et lapis superpositus erat ei. [39] Ait Jesus : Tollite lapidem. Dicit ei Martha, soror ejus qui mortuus fuerat : Domine, jam foetet, quatriduanus est enim. [40] Dicit ei Jesus : Nonne dixi tibi quoniam si credideris, videbis gloriam Dei?

[41] Tulerunt ergo lapidem : Jesus autem, elevatis sursum oculis, dixit : Pater, gratias ago tibi quoniam audisti me. [42] Ego autem sciebam quia semper me audis, sed propter populum qui circumstat, dixi : ut credant quia tu me misisti. [43] Haec cum dixisset, voce magna clamavit : Lazare, veni foras. [44] Et statim prodiit qui fuerat mortuus, ligatus pedes, et manus institis, et facies illius sudario erat ligata. Dixit eis Jesus : Solvite eum et sinite abire.

saw Mary that she rose up speedily and went out, followed her, saying: She goeth to the grave to weep there. [32] When Mary therefore was come where Jesus was, seeing him, she fell down at his feet, and saith to him: Lord, if thou hadst been here, my brother had not died. [33] Jesus, therefore, when he saw her weeping, and the Jews that were come with her, weeping, groaned in the spirit, and troubled himself, [34] And said: Where have you laid him? They say to him: Lord, come and see. [35] And Jesus wept.

[36] The Jews therefore said Behold how he loved him. [37] But some of them said: Could not he that opened the eyes of the man born blind, have caused that this man should not die? [38] Jesus therefore again groaning in himself, cometh to the sepulchre. Now it was a cave; and a stone was laid over it. [39] Jesus saith: Take away the stone. Martha, the sister of him that was dead, saith to him: Lord, by this time he stinketh, for he is now of four days. [40] Jesus saith to her: Did not I say to thee, that if thou believe, thou shalt see the glory of God?

[41] They took therefore the stone away. And Jesus lifting up his eyes said: Father, I give thee thanks that thou hast heard me. [42] And I knew that thou hearest me always; but because of the people who stand about have I said it, that they may believe that thou hast sent me. [43] When he had said these things, he cried with a loud voice: Lazarus, come forth. [44] And presently he that had been dead came forth, bound feet and hands with winding bands; and his face was bound about with a napkin. Jesus said to them: Loose him, and let him go.

Including Those with Impairments at One's Table

Luke 14:12–14

[12] Dicebat autem et ei, qui invitaverat : Cum facis prandium, aut coenam, noli vocare amicos tuos, neque fratres tuos, neque cognatos, neque vicinos divites : ne forte te et ipsi

Luke 14:12–14

[12] And he said to him also that had invited him: When thou makest a dinner or a supper, call not thy friends, nor thy brethren, nor thy kinsmen, nor thy neighbours who are

reinvitent, et fiat tibi retributio; [13] sed cum facis convivium, voca pauperes, debiles, claudos, et caecos : [14] et beatus eris, quia non habent retribuere tibi : retribuetur enim tibi in resurrectione justorum.

rich; lest perhaps they also invite thee again, and a recompense be made to thee. [13] But when thou makest a feast, call the poor, the maimed, the lame, and the blind; [14] And thou shalt be blessed, because they have not wherewith to make thee recompense: for recompense shall be made thee at the resurrection of the just.

Endnotes

1   The text is taken from the online Douay-Rheims and Latin Vulgate Bible online at DRBO.org. The website relies upon the following versions of the texts. The Holy Bible Douay-Rheims Version with revisions and footnotes (in the text in italics) by Bishop Richard Challoner, 1749–52, taken from a hardcopy of the 1899 Edition by the John Murphy Company. IMPRIMATUR: James Cardinal Gibbons, Archbishop of Baltimore, September 1, 1899. The Latin Vulgate (Biblia Sacra Vulgata) Clementine Version. Translation from Greek and other languages into Latin by Saint Jerome, about 382 A.D. Footnotes and endnotes have been provided by Will Eggers.

2   Bonnie L. Gracer, "What the Rabbis Heard: Deafness in the Mishnah." *Jewish Perspectives on Theology and the Human Experience of Disability*, eds. Judith Z. Abrams and William C. Gaventa (Routledge, 2007), pp. 85–100.

3   Edward Wheatley, "Blindness, Discipline, and Reward: Louis IX and the Foundation of the Hospice des Quinze-Vingts," *Disability Studies Quarterly*, vol. 22 (2002), pp. 196–97. For a more in-depth exploration of his ideas, see Wheatley's *Stumbling Blocks Before the Blind: Medieval Constructions of a Disability* (University of Michigan Press, 2014).

4   Irina Metzler, *Disability in Medieval Europe: Thinking about Physical Impairment during the High Middle Ages, c. 1100–c. 1400* (Routledge, 2006), p. 190.

5   Ibid., p. 13.

6   For another parallel episode, see Matthew 20: 29–34.

Miracles in Apocryphal Infancy Narratives[1] (ca. 550–13th c.)

Contributed by Brandon W. Hawk

Introduction

Like the Bible, many apocryphal narratives from early Christian and medieval literature included stories about miracles concerning disabilities. Just as the canonical gospels feature Jesus performing various miracles to heal disabilities, extrabiblical stories about Jesus also highlight such feats even in Jesus' infancy. Non-canonical apocrypha, in fact, were widely popular in the medieval world, and influenced an array of literature like sermons, world histories, and poems, as well as visual arts like manuscript illuminations, wall paintings, sculptures, and church architecture. Two of the most widespread apocrypha in the Middle Ages were the *Gospel of Pseudo-Matthew* and the *Infancy Gospel of Thomas*, both of which feature episodes in which the child Jesus was involved with healing disabilities.

Composed in Latin, likely in the early seventh century, *Pseudo-Matthew* consists of an expanded adaptation of an earlier Greek apocryphon known as the *Protevangelium of James*. Both recount the story of Mary's parents, Anna and Joachim, her birth, childhood, and betrothal to Joseph, the birth of Jesus, and the holy family's flight to Egypt. The following episode about the birth of Jesus and the withering of the doubting midwife's hand is taken from chapter 13 of *Pseudo-Matthew*. The *Infancy Gospel of Thomas* was originally composed in the second century, probably in Greek or possibly in Syriac. This apocryphal gospel recounts various episodes from Jesus' childhood, many presaging his later actions and teachings as an adult (as in the canoni-

cal gospels). During the Middle Ages, a Latin translation was undertaken and began to circulate paired with *Pseudo-Matthew* in manuscripts from the twelfth century onward (often called the *pars altera* ["second part"] because of this designation by the editor Constantine von Tischendorf). The following episode about Jesus' interaction with his rabbis (Jewish teachers) is taken from chapters 6–8 of the *Infancy Gospel of Thomas* (chapter 31 in Tischendorf's edition). The other passages are taken from episodes inspired by the *Infancy Gospel of Thomas*, from an expanded narrative including *Pseudo-Matthew*, the *Infancy Gospel of Thomas*, and other additions about Jesus' childhood in the thirteenth-century manuscript Paris, Bibliothèque nationale de France, lat. 11867.[2]

All of the episodes presented here include sensational miracles, especially the healings of physical disabilities. In her discussion of canonical Gospel miracles, Sharon V. Betcher highlights "the stock feature of disablement, which always immediately signals cure as resolution," for example, "in terms of miraculous remediation."[3] This view is similarly applicable to parallel representations in apocryphal gospels like *Pseudo-Matthew* and the *Infancy Gospel of Thomas*, as with those presented here. Most of these accounts introduce disabilities for the very purpose of demonstrating miraculous powers—in other words, disabilities exist to be healed. One example appears in the episode in which Jesus teaches the rabbis: it concludes with Jesus giving a blessing, using the type of language that is directly juxtaposed to that of a curse, calling for the reversal of infertility, blindness, lameness, poorness, death, and other states presented as adversities; in response, "immediately all were restored who had fallen under evil illness" ("continuo sunt omnes restituti qui sub malis deciderant infirmitatibus"). Jesus' miracle, then, is to do away with those infirmities portrayed as "evil illness" ("malis… infirmitatibus") —here, disabilities linked to the evil state of the world (a consequence of the biblical fall of humans into sin) that must be overcome through miracles.

The majority of these apocryphal miracles also highlight a symbolic relationship between physical disability and spiritual lack. For example, there is a clear parallel between Salome's doubt and the subsequent withering of her hand and the story of the apostle Thomas' doubt in John 20:24–29. The intertextuality between these stories highlights the use of disability as metaphor for spiritual impairment. Representations of physical health as allegories for spiritual health demonstrate the multilayered uses of disabilities found in both the Bible and throughout medieval Christian literature.[4] As seen in the previous example of Jesus' general healing of infirmities seen as "evil," bodily health, spiritual righteousness, and miraculous healings are closely aligned.

A number of episodes in the *Infancy Gospel of Thomas* also pit Jesus against the Jews, creating a cast of anti-Judaism.[5] Much of this is rooted in the theological idea of Christian supersessionism, or the belief that Christianity replaced Judaism. Such anti-Judaism is especially pronounced in the symbolism of Jesus blinding the Jews who speak against him after he curses a boy. Similarly, the idea of physical blindness is meant to symbolize spiritual immaturity, or inability to understand, in the episode with Jesus and his rabbis. Master Levi expresses his amazement at not understanding Jesus, the language of blindness is used throughout the passage, and the spiritual symbolism is further emphasized by the comment about Jesus' healing of those

afflicted with illness at the end of the episode. All of this intersects with what Edward Wheatley has discussed in relation to the trope of blindness used in medieval culture (with roots in the New Testament), especially in literature about the Jews.[6] These episodes in the *Infancy Gospel of Thomas* participate in the more general trend of using blindness as a motif to express medieval Christian anxieties about Jews.

Bibliography

Betcher, Sharon V. "Disability and the Terror of the Miracle Tradition." *Miracles Revisited: New Testament Miracle Stories and their Concepts of Reality*, edited by Stefan Alkier and Annette Weissenrieder. De Gruyter, 2013, pp. 161–82

Hawk, Brandon W. *The Gospel of Pseudo-Matthew*. Cascade, 2019.

Metzler, Irina. *Disability in Medieval Europe: Thinking about Physical Impairment in the High Middle Ages, c.1100–1400*. Routledge, 2006.

Mitchell, David T., and Sharon L. Snyder. *Narrative Prosthesis: Disability and the Dependencies of Discourse*. University of Michigan Press, 2001.

Tischendorf, Constantin von, ed. *Evangelia Apocrypha*. 2nd edn., Hermann Mendelsohn, 1853.

Wheatley, Edward. *Stumbling Blocks Before the Blind: Medieval Constructions of a Disability*. University of Michigan Press, 2010.

Jesus' Birth and the Doubting Midwife

Factum est autem post aliquantum tempus ut fieret professio ex edicto Caesaris Augusti, ut profiteretur unusquisque in patria sua. Haec professio facta est a praeside Syriae Cyrino. Necesse autem fuerat ut Ioseph cum Maria proficisceretur in Bethleem, quia exinde erat, et Maria de tribu Iuda et de domo ac patria David.

Cum ergo Ioseph et Maria irent per viam quae ducit Bethleem, dixit Maria at Ioseph: "Duos populos video ante me, unum flentem et alium gaudentem."

Cui respondit Ioseph: "Sede et tene te in iumento tuo et noli superflua verba loqui."

Tunc apparuit puer speciosus ante eos, indutus veste splendida, et dixit ad Ioseph: "Quare dixisti verba superflua esse de duobus populis de quibus locuta est Maria? Populum enim Iudaeorum flentem vidit, quia recessit a deo suo, et populum gentium gaudentem, quia accessit et prope factus est ad dominum, secundum quod promisit patribus nostris Abraham, Isaac et Iacob; tempus enim advenit ut in semine Abrahae benedictio omnibus gentibus tribuatur."

Et cum haec dixisset, iussit angelus stare iumentum, quia tempus advenerat pariendi, et praecepit descendere de animali Mariam et ingredi in speluncam subterraneam, in qua lux non fuit unquam sed semper tenebrae, quia lumen diei penitus non habebat. Ad ingressum vero Mariae coepit tota spelunca splendorem habere, et quasi sol ibi esset ita tota fulgorem lucis ostendere; et quasi esset ibi hora diei sexta, ita speluncam lux divina illustravit; nec in die nec in nocte lux ibi divina defuit quamdiu ibi Maria fuit. Et ibi peperit masculum, quem circumdederunt angeli nascentem et natum adoraverunt dicentes: "Gloria in excelsis deo et in terra pax hominibus bonae voluntatis."

Iam enim dudum Ioseph perrexerat ad quaerendas obstetrices. Qui cum reversus esset ad speluncam, Maria iam infantem genuerat. Et dixit Ioseph ad Mariam: Ego tibi Zelomi et Salomen obstetrices adduxi, quae foris ante speluncam stant et prae splendore

Jesus' Birth and the Doubting Midwife[7]

Now, it came to pass that after some time a proclamation was made by an edict of Caesar Augustus that everyone should hasten to their native land. This proclamation was first made by Cyrinus, the governor of Syria, and made it necessary that Joseph go to Bethlehem with Mary, because Joseph and Mary were from the tribe of Judah and from the house and family of David.

When, therefore, Joseph and Mary were going along the road that leads to Bethlehem, Mary said to Joseph, "I see two peoples before me, one weeping and the other rejoicing."

To which Joseph responded, saying, "Sit and hold onto your mule and do not speak unnecessary words to me."

Then a beautiful boy appeared before them dressed in gleaming clothing and said to Joseph, "Why did you say that the words you heard about the two peoples were unnecessary? For she saw the Jewish people weeping because they have withdrawn from God, and the gentile people rejoicing because they have drawn near to the Lord, which he promised to your fathers Abraham and Isaac and Jacob. For the time has come that by the seed of Abraham a blessing shall be given to all nations."

And when he had said these things, he ordered the mule to stand still, and instructed Mary to get down from the animal and go into a cave in which there was always darkness because, in its innermost parts, it did not have the light of day. But when Mary went in, the whole cave began to fill with great brightness; and as if the sun were in it, so did the whole [cave] begin to exhibit the gleaming of light; and as if it were the sixth hour of the day, so did the divine light illuminate that same cave. This light did not withdraw, neither day nor night, until Mary gave birth to a male, whom angels surrounded at birth; and when he had been born on his feet, immediately they worshiped him, saying, "Glory to God in the highest, and on earth peace to men of good will."

nimio huc introire non audent. Audiens autem haec Maria subrisit. Cui Ioseph dixit: Noli subridere, sed cauta esto, ne forte indigeas medicina. Tunc iussit unam ex eis intrare ad se. Cumque ingressa esset Zelomi, ad Mariam dixit: Dimitte me ut tangam te.

Cumque permisisset se Maria tangi, exclamavit voce magna obstetrix et dixit: Domine domine magne, miserere. Numquam hoc auditum est nec in suspicione habitum, ut mamillae plenae sint lacte et natus masculus matrem suam virginem ostendat. Nulla pollutio sanguinis facta est in nascente, nullus dolor in parturiente. Virgo concepit, virgo peperit, virgo permansit.

Audiens hanc vocem alia obstetrix nomine Salome dixit: Quod ego audio non credam nisi forte ipsa probavero. Et ingressa Salome ad Mariam dixit: Permitte me ut palpem te et probem utrum verum dixerit Zelomi.

Cumque permisisset Maria ut eam palparet, misit manum suam Salome. Et cum misisset et tangeret, statim aruit manus eius, et prae dolore coepit flere vehementissime et angustari et clamando dicere: Domine, tu nosti quia semper te timui, et omnes pauperes sine retributione acceptionis curavi, de vidua et orphano nihil accepi, et inopem vacuum a me ire numquam dimisi. Et ecce misera facta sum propter incredulitatem meam, quia ausa fui temptare virginem tuam.

Cumque haec diceret, apparuit iuxta illam iuvenis quidam valde splendidus dicens ei: Accede ad infantem et adora eum et continge de manu tua, et ipse salvabit te, quia ipse est salvator seculi et omnium sperantium in se. Quae confestim ad infantem accessit, et adorans eum tetigit fimbrias pannorum, in quibus infans erat involutus, et statim sanata est manus eius. Et exiens foras clamare coepit et dicere magnalia virtutum quae viderat et quae passa fuerat, et quemadmodum curate fuerat, ita ut ad praedicationem eius multi crederent.

And Joseph, finding Mary with the child to whom she had given birth, said to her, "I have brought Zahel, a midwife, to you; behold, she is standing right outside of the cave, but is unable to enter because of the great brightness." Hearing this, Mary smiled. Then Joseph said to her, "Do not smile, but take care that she inspect you, in case you need her medicine." And Mary commanded her to enter.

When Mary allowed herself to be scrutinized, the midwife called out in a loud voice and said, "Great Lord, have mercy! Never before has it been either heard or suspected that the breasts might be full of milk, and yet this newborn makes manifest that his mother is a virgin. No stain of blood is on the child, and no pain was evident in the birth. A virgin has given birth and after giving birth she has continued to be a virgin."

Hearing this cry, another midwife named Salome said, "Certainly I will not believe this unless indeed I verify it." And Salome went in to Mary and said to her, "Let me examine you so that I should know if the words that Zahel declared to me are true."

Now when Mary allowed her examination, as soon as Salome drew away her right hand from the inspection, the hand withered and she began to be most violently stricken by the pain and to cry out, weeping and saying, "Lord, you know that I have always feared you and have taken care of all the poor without the worry of payment. I have taken nothing from the widow and the orphan and I have never sent the destitute away from me empty-handed. And behold, I am made wretched because of my unbelief, because I have dared to test your virgin, who gave birth to the Light and after this birth remained a virgin."

And while she was saying these things, a brilliant young man appeared beside her saying, "Go to the child and worship him, and touch him with your hand, and he will heal you, because this is the Savior of all who hope in him." And quickly Salome went to him and worshipped the child and touched the hems of the cloths in which the child was swaddled, and her hand was immediately healed. Then she went out and began to cry out and to speak about the great deeds of power that she had seen, and what she had endured, and how she had been cured, so that many believed because of her proclamation.

Jesus Teaches the Rabbis

Iterum magister Zachyas legis doctor dixit ad Ioseph et Mariam: Date mihi puerum, et ego tradam illum magistro Levi, qui doceat eum litteras et erudiat.

Tunc Ioseph et Maria blandientes Iesum duxerunt in scholas, ut doceretur litteras a sene Levi. Qui cum introisset, tacebat. Et magister Levi unam litteram dicebat ei: Responde.

Iesus autem tacebat et nihil respondebat. Unde praeceptor Levi iratus apprehendens virgam storatinam percussit eum in capite.

Iesus autem dixit ad didascalum Levi: Ut quid me percutis? In veritate scias quia ipse qui percutitur magis docet percutientem se quam ab eo doceatur. Ego enim te possum docere qua a te ipso dicuntur. Sed hi omnes caeci sunt qui dicunt et audiunt, quasi aes sonans aut cimbalum tinniens, in quibus non est sensus eorum quae intelliguntur per sonum illorum.

Et subiungens Iesus dixit Zachyae: Omnis littera ab Aleph usque ad Thau dispositione discernitur. Dic ergo tu primum quid sit Thau, et ego dicam tibi quid sit Aleph. Et iterum dixit ad eos Iesus: Qui non norunt Aleph, Thau quomodo dicere possunt, hypocritae? Dicite quid sit primum Aleph, et ego tunc vobis credam cum dixeritis Beth. Et coepit Iesus singularum litterarum nomina interrogare, et dixit: Dicat magister legis, prima littera quid sit, vel quare triangulos habeat multos, gradatos, subacutos, mediatos, obductos, productos, erectos, stratos, curvistratos.

Jesus Teaches the Rabbis[8]

Again, Master Zacchaeus, a doctor of the Law, spoke to Joseph and Mary, "Give the boy to me, and I will hand him over to Master Levi, who will teach him letters and instruct him."

Then Joseph and Mary, soothing Jesus, led him to school, so that he might be taught letters by old Levi. When he had entered, he was silent. And Master Levi said one letter to Jesus, and beginning with the first letter aleph he said to him, "Repeat."

But Jesus was silent and responded with nothing. At that the instructor Levi was angry, and seizing a storax-tree branch, struck him on the head.

Now, Jesus said to the teacher Levi, "Why do you strike me? In truth you should know that the one who is struck teaches the one striking him more than he learns from him. For I am able to teach you what you are saying. But all these who speak and hear are blind, like a resounding gong or a clanging cymbal, in which there is no sense of the things that are understood in their sound."

And furthermore, Jesus said to Zacchaeus, "Every letter from aleph° up to tau,° is discerned by arrangement. Therefore, say first what tau is, and I will say to you what aleph is." And again Jesus said to them, "Whoever does not know Aleph, how are they able to say Tau? Hypocrites! Say first what is Aleph, and then I will believe you when you say Beth."° And Jesus began to ask the names of each letter and said, "Let the master of the Law say what the first letter is, or why it has

---

aleph *the first letter of the Hebrew alphabet*   **tau** *the last letter of the Hebrew alphabet*   **Beth** *the second letter of the Hebrew alphabet*

Cum autem Levi hoc audisset, obstupe-factus est ad tantam dispositionem nominum litterarum.

Tunc coepit cunctis audientibus clamare et dicere: Num debet iste super terra vivere? Imo in magna cruce dignus est appendi. Nam potest ignem extinguere et alia deludere tormenta. Ego puto quod hic ante cataclismum fuerit, ante diluvium natus. Quis enim venter illum portavit? Aut qua mater genuit illum? Aut quae ubera illum lactaverunt? Fugio ante eum; non enim valeo sustinere verbum ex ore eius, sed cor meum stupescit talia verba audire. Nullum enim hominum puto eius consequi verbum, nisi fuerit deus cum eo. Nunc ego ipse infelix tradidi me huic in derisum. Cum enim me putarem habere discipulum, inveni magistrum meum, ignorans eum. Quid dicam? Non valeo sustinere verba pueri huius: de hoc iam municipio fugiam, quia non valeo haec intelligere. Ab infante senex victus sum, quia neque initium de quibus ipse affirmat invenire non possum nec finem. Difficile enim est initium ex se ipso reperire. Certe dico vobis, non mentior, quod ante meos oculos operatio huius pueri et initia sermonis eius et intentionis exitus nihil cum hominibus commune videtur habere. Hic ergo nescio an magus aut deus sit; aute certe angelus dei loquitur in eo. Unde sit aut unde venerit aut quis futurus sit, nescio.

Tunc Iesus laeto vultu subridens de eo dixit cum imperio cunctis filiis Israel astantibus et audientibus: Fructificent infructuosi et videant caeci et claudi ambulent recte et pauperes fruantur bonis et reviviscant mortui, ut redintegrato statu unusquisque revertatur et permaneat in eo ipso qui radix est vitae et dulcedinis perpetuae.

Et cum hoc dixisset infans Iesus, continuo sunt omnes restituti qui sub malis deciderant infirmitatibus. Et amplius non audebant dicere ei aliquid aut audire ab eo.

many triangles, gradations, subacutes, mediates, obducts, products, erects, strata, curvistrates."

Now, when Levi heard this, he was astonished at such an arrangement of the names of the letters.

Then in the hearing of all he began to call out and to say, "Should this one live on the earth? Certainly he is worthy to be hanged on a great cross. For he is able to extinguish fire and mock other punishments. I think that he lived before the flood and was born before the deluge. For what womb carried him? Or what mother birthed him? Or what breasts nursed him? I flee before him; for I am not able to endure the words from his mouth; no, my heart is astonished to hear such words. Indeed I think that no man is able to follow his words unless God is with him. Now I, miserable, have given myself up to be mocked by him. For when I thought I had a student, I found my master, although I did not know him. What may I say? I am not able to endure the words of this boy; soon I will flee from this town, because I am not able to understand these things. I, an old man, am defeated by a child, because I am not able to find either beginning or end of what he asserts. For it is difficult to discover the beginning of him. Certainly I tell you—I am not lying—that before my eyes the working of this boy and the beginning of his speech and the conclusion of his intention appear to have nothing in common with humanity. Because of this, I do not know whether he is a magician or a god, nor do I certainly know if an angel of God speaks in him. Whence he exists, or whence he came, or who he will be in the future, I do not know."

Then Jesus, smiling at him with a joyful face, spoke with authority to all the children of Israel standing by and listening, "Let the unfruitful bear fruit, and let the blind see, and let the lame walk right, and let the poor enjoy the good things, and let the dead be revived, so that everyone might return to a renewed state and remain in him who is the root of life and perpetual sweetness."

When the child Jesus had said this, immediately all were restored who had fallen under evil illness. And they did not dare to say any more to him or to hear any more from him.

Jesus Climbs a Sunbeam

Una autem die temporeimale cum sol in sua uirtute clarus radiaret extendit se radius solaris attingens a fenestra in parietem in domo Ioseph, ubi cum ludent cum Iesu contribules pueri uicinorum per domum discurrentes ascendit Iesus radium solis et positis super eum uestimentis suis sedebat quasi super trabem firmissimum.

Quod cum uidissent colludentes coetanei pueri opinabant se similiterposse facere. Et ascenderunt ut sederent cum Iesu ludentes exemple illius conterimur.

Iesus autem instantibus Maria et Ioseph lesiones omnium attritorum levi flatu aspirando super locum dolentem sanabat omnes et ait: Spiritus ubi uult spirat et quos uult sanat et sani facti sunt. Haec omnia nunciauerunt patribus nostris.

Et factum est palam hoc uerbum in Ierusalem et in remotis finibus Iudee. Et multiplicata est fama Iesu per circuitum prouiciarum. Et uenerunt ut benedicerent eum et ab eo benedicerentur et dixerunt ad eum: Beatus uenter cui te portauit et ubera quae suitisti.

Ioseph et Maria Deo in omnibus gratias que audierant et uiderant persoluerunt.

Jesus Curses a Boy and Blinds the Jews

Alio tempore ambulante Iesu per villam cucurrit unus de infantibus et percussit Iesum in ulnas.

Iesus autem dixit ad eum: Sic sic perficias iter tuum. Et statim cecidit in terram et mortuus est.

Illis autem uidentibus mirabilia clamauerunt dicentes: Unde est puer iste?

Jesus Climbs a Sunbeam[9]

Now, one day in winter time, when the sun shone brightly in its strength, a sunbeam stretched itself out, spanning from the window to the wall in Joseph's home. When other boys from the neighborhood were there playing with Jesus and running around the home, Jesus climbed onto the sunbeam and, with his garments spread out over it, sat down as if on a most solid beam.

When the boys of the same age playing with him saw, they thought that they were able to do the same. They ascended so that they might sit with Jesus, playing by his example, but they were bruised.

So, Jesus, at the urging of Mary and Joseph, blew a light breath over all the hurt spots and healed all the wounds. And he said, "The Spirit breathes where he wills, and he heals and makes whole whom it wills. They have told all these things to our fathers."

It came to pass that these words were well known in Jerusalem and in the remote ends of Judea, and Jesus' fame was multiplied throughout the circuit of provinces. And they came to bless him and to be blessed by him, and they said to him, "Blessed is the womb that bore you and the breasts that have nursed you."

Joseph and Mary rendered thanks to God for all that they had heard and seen.

Jesus Curses a Boy and Blinds the Jews[10]

Another time, when Jesus was walking through the country, one of the children ran and struck Jesus on the elbow.

Now, Jesus said to him, "This is the end of your journey." Immediately he fell to the earth and was dead.

At that, those who saw the wonder called out, saying, "Where does this child come from?" They said to Joseph, "It is not proper

Et dixerunt ad Ioseph: Non opportet esse nobiscum nec habere talem puerum. Ille autem abiit et tulit eum.

Et dixerunt ei: Recede de isto loco et si te oportet esse nobiscum doce eum orare et non blasphemare filii autemnostri insensati.

Uocauit Ioseph Iesum et incepit eum docere Ut quid blasphemas et alicui male dicis, habitatores isti hodium habent super nos de loco isto.

Iesus autem dixit: Ego autem tacebo pater. Ipsi autem uideant insipientiam suam.

Et ii statim qui loquebantur aduersus Iesum ceci facti sunt. Et deambulatnes dicebant: Omnes sermones qui procedunt de ore eius exsecutum habent et effectum.

Et cum uidisset Ioseph quod faceret Iesus cum furore apprehandit eum per auriculam.

Iesus autem turbatus dixit ad Ioseph: Sufficit tibi uidere me non me tangere, tu autem nescis quis ego sum, quia si scires non me contestares et quomimum ego mod tecum sum, ante te factus sum.

Jesus Heals a Boy's Foot

Post hoc ante paucos dies euolutos puer quidam in eodem loco scindebant ligna percussitque pedem plagam horribilem faciendo, et cum uenisset turba multa ut uideret eum lamentem accurit Iesus cum ipsis et deprecati sunt eum ut leniret dolorem suum. Praesertim cum pater et mater lesi non se caperent pro dolore Iesus autem mistertus eorum ait: Credite tantum et fiet quod petistis.

Cumque inalaret magister accessit ad pedem suum Iesus et blandit ad modum medici fomentantis ait: Surge sanus; in memoria potentie De sanaris.

Ipse autem sanus omnino saltum fecit et gloriam dedit item in confessione.

Cum autem uidisset turba quae facta fuerant adorauerunt Iesum et dixerunt: Vere credimus quia Deus est tu.

for him to live with us, nor for us to have such a child."

At that, he (Joseph) went and took him, and they said to him, "Go away from this place, and if it is necessary for you to live with us, teach him to pray and not to blaspheme, for our children do not understand."

Joseph called to Jesus and took him to teach him, "Why do you blaspheme and speak evil to others? The inhabitants in this place hate us."

Now Jesus said, "Then I will be silent, father. But let them see their own folly."

Immediately those who had spoken against Jesus were made blind. Walking away, they said, "All the words that go out of his mouth are followed by weight and effect."

And when Joseph saw what Jesus had done, with anger he seized him by the ear. In an uproar, Jesus said to Joseph, "It is sufficient for you to see me, but do not touch me, for you do not know who I am; and if you knew, you might not admonish me. Although I am with you presently, I was made before you."

Jesus Heals a Boy's Foot[11]

After this (before a few days went by), in the same place, a certain child was cutting wood and struck his foot, making a terrible wound. When a great crowd came and saw him wailing, Jesus ran to him along with them, and they begged him to soothe his pain.

Especially because the father and mother of the wounded child could not handle his pain, Jesus had mercy on them and said, "Only believe and what you seek will be done."

After the master (Jesus) went to him, he breathed on his foot and caressed it, like a soothing physician, and said, "Arise whole; remember that you are healed by the power of God."

Completely healed, he began leaping and also gave glory in confession.

When the crowd saw what had happened, they worshipped Jesus and said, "Truly we believe that you are God."

Endnotes

1   Endnotes and translations for all of the passages here have been provided by Brandon W. Hawk. Bibliographic information for each passage is included in the following footnotes.

2   See Brandon W. Hawk, *The Gospel of Pseudo-Matthew* (Cascade, 2019).

3   Sharon V. Betcher, "Disability and the Terror of the Miracle Tradition," *Miracles Revisited: New Testament Miracle Stories and their Concepts of Reality*, eds. Stefan Alkier and Annette Weissenrieder (De Gruyter, 2013), p. 161.

4   See Irina Metzler, *Disability in Medieval Europe: Thinking about Physical Impairment in the High Middle Ages, c.1100–1400* (Routledge, 2006); David T. Mitchell and Sharon L. Snyder, *Narrative Prosthesis, Disability and the Dependencies of Discourse* (University of Michigan Press, 2001).

5   See Hawk, *The Gospel of Pseudo-Matthew*.

6   See Edward Wheatley, *Stumbling Blocks Before the Blind: Medieval Constructions of a Disability* (University of Michigan Press, 2010), esp. pp. 63–89.

7   This episode is found in chapter 13 of the *Gospel of Pseudo-Matthew* in Tischendorf and Hawk. The translation is based on the newer critical edition, *Libri de nativitate Mariae: Pseudo-Matthaei Evangelium, textus et commentaries,* eds. Jan Gisel, Corpus Christianorum Series Apocryphorum 9 (Brepols, 1997). The Latin text provided for comparison is from Tischendorf's edition, although the Latin differs from the English translation presented here in details.

8   This episode is found as chapter 31 (part of the so-called *pars altera*, a Latin translation of the *Infancy Gospel of Thomas*) of the *Gospel of Pseudo-Matthew* in Tischendorf and Hawk. The Latin text is from Tischendorf's edition.

9   This episode is found as chapter 58 in Hawk. For this and the two following episodes, the translation is based on Paris, Bibliothèque nationale de France, lat. 11867, which is transcribed here with some modernizations of capitalization and punctuation.

10   This episode is found in Hawk, *The Gospel of Pseudo-Matthew*, chap. 61.

11   This episode is found in ibid., chap. 63.

Catholic Homilies 1.10[1] (ca. 989–ca. 992)

Ælfric of Eynsham
Contributed by Brandon W. Hawk

Introduction

In many ways, medieval sermons are significant witnesses to attitudes toward disabilities. After all, the foundations of many sermons are in the Bible, which (as seen elsewhere in this collection) includes various narratives about people with disabilities. This is particularly true of the Gospels, in which Jesus heals a number of people from blindness, deafness, paralysis, and leprosy. Also relevant are apocryphal acts, in which Jesus' apostles perform similar miracles involving the same types of impairments. Since sermons so often draw directly on biblical and apocryphal narratives, there is natural overlap. Likewise, disabilities appear in the narratives about martyrs and saints popular for sermons composed for feast days and special occasions in the church calendar. In these lives, infirmities may be found in the people to whom the saints give attention (as imitators of Jesus), or even as part of the story of a saint's life and passion. For preachers and their audiences, disability was a common concern.

Beyond narrative content, however, sermon authors also provide rich commentaries on these stories. Indeed, sermons on biblical stories prove useful for understanding medieval views of disabilities. What is significant about sermons is that they do not relate the disabilities of medieval people, but the biblical past allows preachers to discuss disabilities in a more abstract manner. This often takes the form of commentary about spiritual health, in which biblical stories stand in for allegories about the spiritual state of the soul. For example, disabilities in the Bible are often linked to ideas about divine punishment

for sinfulness or lack of faith, such as in the healing of Bartimeus in Mark 10, but the Bible can also challenge this view, such as in the healing of another blind man in John 9. In some instances, medieval sermons can echo these connections, but they can also portray more complicated representations of disabilities, in keeping with complex and varied approaches to impairment within the period, as highlighted by Irina Metzler and others. Such notions, therefore, combine images of disabilities, questions about physical wholeness, and anxieties about religious health. As Fay Skevington suggests, "a lack of distinction between illness and disability is appropriate when discussing Anglo-Saxon culture";[2] these distinctions are further broken down in sermons that address spiritual health through metaphors of physical disability and illness. This multilayered characteristic can provide both obstacles for using sermons as sources as well as nuanced and complex medieval perspectives on disabilities for modern readers to puzzle out.

Of the large number of surviving Old English preaching texts, a few offer especially poignant commentaries on biblical narratives about disabilities. One example is the following sermon by Abbot Ælfric of Eynsham (ca .955–ca. 1010), from his series of *Catholic Homilies* (1.10), about the story of Jesus healing a blind man in Luke 18:31–43. Ælfric begins his sermon with a translation of the gospel passage into English, and then proceeds with an interpretation that hinges on an extended allegorical reading of blindness signifying humanity's original sin and healing signifying redemption through Christ. In this beginning, he also draws a connection between the physical sufferings of the blind man from his impairment and of Christ at the Crucifixion. More generally, Ælfric's comments about Christ's suffering during the Passion also create a stark parallel with human suffering through illnesses and disabilities. These notions raise issues about theodicy as well as Christology, emphasizing theological underpinnings to the problem of pain as well as the belief in Christ as both fully human and fully divine. For Ælfric, both of these theological points are linked to his use of the biblical story to discuss physical impairment as spiritual allegory.

These threads in Ælfric's sermon are characteristic of the types of patristic interpretations offered by Pope Gregory the Great, who composed the Latin homily from which Ælfric's text is translated. As Aaron J. Kleist comments, "As with Augustine, Gregory, and Bede, Ælfric associates sight with both understanding and belief."[3] The disability of blindness, then, signifies something of a spiritual lack, as the man, like all of humanity, was "ablend mid geleafleaste and gedwylde" ("blind with lack of belief and error"). In contrast, as Ælfric states at the start, Christ himself had foresight of his own suffering, amounting to the perfect belief and truth of which humans fall short. Through God's intervention, however—through Jesus' miracle—the blind man is able to regain his spiritual lack and to achieve revelatory enlightenment, just as Christians are able to achieve salvation through conversion. Through his allegorical reading, Ælfric presents a more general lesson about collective human nature, belief, and Christian redemption.

Bibliography

Kleist, Aaron J. *Striving With Grace: Views of Free Will in Anglo-Saxon England*, Toronto Anglo-Saxon Series 20. University of Toronto Press, 2008.

Lee, Chistina. "Disability." *A Handbook of Anglo-Saxon Studies*, edited by Jacqueline Stodnick and Renée R. Trilling. Wiley-Blackwell, 2012, pp. 23–38.

Metzler, Irina. *Disability in Medieval Europe: Thinking about Physical Impairment in the High Middle Ages, c.1100–1400.* Routledge, 2006.

Roberts, Jane. "Some Thoughts on the Expression of 'crippled' in Old English." *Leeds Studies in English*, vol. 37, 2006, pp. 365–78.

Skevington, Fay. "The *Unhal* and the Semantics of Anglo-Saxon Disability." *Social Dimensions of Medieval Disease and Disability*, edited by Sally Crawford and Christina Lee. Archaeopress, 2014, pp. 7–14.

Tovey, Beth. "Kingly Impairments in Anglo-Saxon Literature." *Disability in the Middle Ages: Rehabilitations Reconsiderations Reverberations,* edited by Joshua Eyler. Ashgate, 2010, pp. 135–48.

Adsumpsit Iesus XII. Discipulos suos: et reliqua.

Her is geræd on þissum godspelle, þe we nu gehyrdon of ðæs diacones muðe, þæt:

Se Hælend gename onsundron his twelf leorning-cnihtas, and cwæð to him, Efne we sceolon faran to ðære byrig Hierusalem, and þonne beoð gefyllede ealle ða ðing þe wæron be me awritene þurh witegan. Ic sceal beon belæwed ðeodum, and hi doð me to bysmore, and beswingað, and syððan ofslead, and ic arise of deaðe on þam ðriddan dæge. Þa nyston his leorning-cnihtas nan andgit þyssera worda. Ða gelamp hit þæt hi genealæhton anre byrig þe is gehaten Hiericho, and ða sæt þær sum blind man be ðam wege; and þa þa he gehyrde þæs folces fær mid þam Hælende, ða acsode he hwa þær ferde. Hi cwædon him to, þæt þæt wære ðæs Hælendes fær. Þa begann he to hrymenne, and cwæð, Hælend, Dauides Bearn, gemiltsa min. Ða men, þe beforan þam Hælende ferdon, ciddon ongean ðone blindan, þæt he suwian sceolde. He clypode þa miccle swiðor, Hælend, Dauides Bearn, gemiltsa min. Þa stod se Hælend, and het lædan þone blindan to him. Þa ða he genealæhte, þa acsode se Hælend hine, Hwæt wylt ðu þæt ic þe do? He cwæð, Drihten, þæt ic mage geseon. And se Hælend him cwæð to, Loca nu: þin geleafa hæfð ðe gehæled. And he ðærrihte geseah, and fyligde þam Hælende, and hine mærsode. Ða eal þæt folc, þe þæt wundor geseh, herede God mid micelre onbryrdnysse.

Ðyses godspelles anginn hrepode ures Hælendes þrowunge, þeah-hwæðere ne ðrowade he na on ðysne timan; ac he wolde feorran and lange ær cyðan his ðrowunge his leorning-cnihtum, þæt hi ne sceoldon beon to swiðe afyrhte þurh ða þrowunge, þonne se tima come þæt he ðrowian wolde. Heora mod wearð afyrht þurh Cristes segene, ac he hi eft gehyrte mid þam worde þe he cwæð, "Ic arise of deaðe on þam ðriddan dæge."

Then Jesus took unto him his twelve disciples: and the rest.

Here it is read in this gospel which now we have heard from the deacon's mouth, that:

The Savior took his twelve disciples aside, and said to them, "Behold, we shall go to the city of Jerusalem, and then all the things that were written about me by the prophets will be fulfilled. I shall be betrayed by the people, and they will commit mockery against me, and beat me, and afterward kill me, and I will arise from death on the third day." His disciples did not know then the meaning of these words. Then it happened that they came near to a city that is called Jericho, and there sat some blind man by the road; and when he heard the passing of the people with the Savior, then he asked who passed there. They said to him, that it was the Savior passing. Then he began to cry, and said, "Savior, Son of David, have mercy on me." The men, who went before the Savior, rebuked the blind man, so that he would be silent. Then he cried all the more, "Savior, Son of David, have mercy on me." Then the Savior stood, and he commanded them to lead the blind man to him. When he neared, then the Savior asked him, "What do you wish that I do to you?" He said, "Lord, that I may see." And the Savior said to him, "Look now: your belief has healed you." And right away he saw, and he followed the Savior, and he glorified him. Then all the people who saw that wonder praised God with great excitement.

The beginning of this gospel reading concerned the passion of our Savior, although he did not suffer at this time; but from afar and long before he would make known his passion to his disciples, so that they might not be too afraid at his passion, when the time came that he would suffer. Their minds were afraid at Christ's telling them, but he heartened them again with the words that he said, "I will arise from death on the third day."

Þa wolde he heora geleafan gestrangian and getrymman mid wundrum. And hi ða comon to ðære stowe þær se blinda man sæt be ðam wege, and Crist hine gehælde ætforan gesihðe ealles þæs werodes, to ði þæt he wolde mid þam wundre hi to geleafan gebringan. Þeah-hwæðere þa wundra þe Crist worhte, oðer ðing hi æteowdon þurh mihte, and oðre ðing hi getacnodon þurh geryno. He worhte þa wundra soðlice þurh godcunde mihte, and mid þam wundrum þæs folces geleafan getrymde; ac hwæðre þær wæs oðer ðing digle on ðam wundrum, æfter gastlicum andgite. Þes an blinda man getacnode eall mancynn, þe wearð ablend þurh Adames gylt, and asceofen of myrhðe neoxena-wanges, and gebroht to ðisum life þe is wiðmeten cwearterne. Nu sind we ute belocene fram ðam heofenlican leohte, and we ne magon on ðissum life þæs ecan leohtes brucan; ne we his na mare ne cunnon buton swa micel swa we ðurh Cristes lare on bocum rædað. Þeos worul, þeah ðe heo myrige hwiltidum geðuht sy, nis heo hwæðere ðe geliccre ðære ecan worulde, þe is sum cweartern leohtum dæge. Eal mancyn wæs, swa we ær cwædon, ablend mid geleaflæste and gedwylde; ac þurh Cristes tocyme we wurdon abrodene of urum gedwyldum, and onlihte þurh geleafan. Nu hæbbe we þæt leoht on urum mode, þæt is Cristes geleafa, and we habbað þone hiht þæs ecan lifes myrhðe, þeah ðe we gyt lichamlice on urum cwearterne wunian.

Se blinda man sæt æt þære byrig þe is gehaten Hiericho. Hiericho is gereht and gehaten "mona." Se mona deð ægðer ge wycxð ge wanað: healfum monðe he bið weaxende, healfum he bið wanigende. Nu getacnað se mona ure deadlice lif, and ateorunge ure deadlicnysse. On oðerne ende men beoð acennede, on oþerne ende hi forðfarað. Þa ða Crist com to ðære byrig Hiericho, þe ðone monan getacnað, þa underfeng se blinda man gesihðe. Þæt is, ða ða Crist com to ure deadlicnysse, and ure menniscnysse underfeng, þa wearð mancyn onliht, and gesihðe underfeng. He sæt wið ðone weig; and Crist cwæð on his godspelle, "Ic eom weig, and soðfæst-

Then he would strengthen and encourage their belief with wonders. And then they came to the place where the blind man sat by the path, and Christ healed him before the sight of all the people, so that he might bring belief to them with the wonder. However, in the wonders that Christ worked, they showed one thing through power, and they signified another thing through mystery. He worked the wonders truly through divine power, and with those wonders he encouraged the belief of the people; however, there was another thing hidden in those wonders, according to spiritual understanding. This one blind man signified all humankind, who were blind through Adam's sin, and expelled from the joy of Paradise, and brought to this life, which is compared to a prison. Now we are locked out from the heavenly light, and in this life we may not enjoy the eternal light; nor may we know it except as much as we read about it in books through Christ's teaching. This world, although it sometimes might seem to be joyful, nonetheless is no more like the eternal world than some prison is to the light of day. All humankind was, as we said before, blind with lack of belief and error; but through Christ's advent we were brought out of our errors, and enlightened through belief. Now we have that light in our minds, which is belief in Christ; and we have the hope of the joy of eternal life, although we yet dwell in our bodily prisons.

The blind man sat at the city that is called Jericho. Jericho is interpreted and called "moon." The moon does both wax and wane: for half the month it is waxing, and for half it is waning. Now the moon signifies our mortal life, and the weariness of our mortality. On the one end men are born, on the other end they depart. When Christ came to the city of Jericho, which signifies the moon, then the blind man received sight. That is, when Christ came to our mortality, and received our humanity, then humankind was enlightened. He sat by the path; and Christ said in his gospel, "I am the way, and truth, and life."[4] The man who knows nothing of the

nys, and lif." Se man þe nan ðing ne cann ðæs ecan leohtes, he is blind; ac gif he gelyfð on þone Hælend, þonne sitt he wið þone weig. Gif he nele biddan þæs ecan leohtas, he sitt ðonne blind be ðam wege unbiddende. Se ðe rihtlice gelyfð on Crist, and geornlice bitt his sawle onlihtinge, he sitt be ðam wege biddende. Swa hwa swa oncnæwð þa blindnysse his modes, clypige he mid inweardre heortan, swa swa se blinda cleopode, "Hælend, Dauides Bearn, gemiltsa min."

Seo menigu þe eode beforan ðam Hælende ciddon ðam blindan, and heton þæt he stille wære. Seo menigu getacnað ure unlustas and leahtras þe us hremað, and ure heortan ofsittað, þæt we ne magon us swa geornlice gebiddan, swa we behofedon. Hit gelimpð gelomlice, þonne se man wile yfeles geswican, and his synna gebetan, and mid eallum mode to Gode gecyrran, ðonne cumað þa ealdan leahtras þe he ær geworhte, and hi gedrefað his mod, and willað gestillan his stemne, þæt he to Gode ne clypige. Ac hwæt dyde se blinda, þa þa þæt folc hine wolde gestyllan? He hrymde ðæs ðe swiðor, oð þæt se Hælend his stemne gehyrde, and hine gehælde. Swa we sceolon eac don, gif us deofol drecce mid menigfealdum geðohtum and costnungum: we sceolon hryman swiðor and swiðor to ðam Hælende, þæt he todræfe ða yfelan costnunga fram ure heortan, and þæt he onlihte ure mod mid his gife. Gif we ðonne þurhwuniað on urum gebedum, þonne mage we gedon mid urum hreame þæt se Hælend stent, se ðe ær eode, and wile gehyran ure clypunge, and ure heortan onlihtan mid godum and mid clænum geðohtum. Ne magon ða yfelan geðohtas us derian, gif he us ne liciað; ac swa us swiðor deofol bregð mid yfelum geðohtum, swa we beteran beoð, and Gode leofran, gif we ðone deofol forseoð and ealle his costnunga, ðurh Godes fultum.

Hwæt is þæs Hælendes stede, oððe hwæt is his fær? He ferde ðurh his menniscnysse, and he stod þurh þa godcundnysse. He ferde ðurh ða menniscnysse, swa þæt he wæs acenned, and ferde fram stowe to stowe, and deað þrowade, a nd of deaðe aras, and astah

eternal light is blind; but if he believes in the Savior, then he sits by the path. If he will not pray for the eternal light, then he sits by the path not praying. He who rightly believes in Christ, and eagerly prays for the enlightening of his soul, he sits by the path praying. So whoever acknowledges the blindness of his mind, he cries out with his inner heart, just as the blind man cried, "Savior, Son of David, have mercy on me."

The many who went before the Savior rebuked the blind man, and commanded that he would be silent. The many signify our evil desires and vices that hinder us, and sit in our hearts, so that we may not pray as eagerly as we need. It happens often, when a man desires to cease evil, and to atone for his sins, and turns to God with all his mind, then the old vices that he did before will come, and they trouble his mind, and will silence his voice, so that he might not cry to God. But what did the blind man do, when the people wanted to silence him? He cried all the more, until the Savior heard his voice, and healed him. So we shall do likewise, if the devil troubles us with manifold thoughts and temptations; we should cry more and more to the Savior, so that he drives the evil temptations from our hearts, and so that he enlightens our minds with his grace. Then if we continue in our prayers, then with our cries we might cause the Savior to stand, who before passed by, and he will hear our crying, and enlighten our hearts with good and pure thoughts. Evil thoughts might not harm us, if they are not pleasing to us; but the more the devil terrifies us with evil thoughts, so we will be better, and dearer to God, if we despise the devil and all his temptations, through God's help.

What is the Savior's standing, or what is his passing? He passed through his humanity, and he stood through his divinity. He passed through humanity, so that he was born, and went from place to place, and suffered death, and arose from death, and ascended to heaven. This is his passing. He stood through divinity; because through his power he is present everywhere, and he needs not go from

to heofonum. Þis is his fær. He stent ðurh ða godcundnysse; forðon ðe he is ðurh his mihte æghwær andweard, and ne ðearf na faran fram stowe to stowe; forðon ðe he is on ælcere stowe þurh his godcundnysse. Þa ða he ferde, þa gehyrde he þæs blindan clypunge; and þa þa he stod, þa forgeaf he him gesihðe; forðan þurh ða menniscnysse he besargað ures modes blindnysse, and ðurh ða godcundnysse he forgifð us leoht, and ure blindnysse onliht. He cwæð to ðam blindan men, "Hwæt wilt ðu þæt ic ðe do?" Wenst ðu þæt he nyste hwæt se blinda wolde, se ðe hine gehælan mihte? Ac he wolde þæt se blinda bæde; forðon þe he tiht ælcne swiðe gemaglice to gebedum: ac hwæðere he cwyð on oðre stowe, "Eower heofenlica Fæder wat hwæs ge behofiað, ærðan ðe ge hine æniges ðinges biddan," þeah-hwæðere wile se goda God þæt we hine goerne biddon; forðan þurh ða gebedu bið ure heorte onbryrd and gewend to Gode.

Ða cwæð se blinda, "La leof, do þæt ic mæge geseon." Ne bæd se blinda naðor ne goldes, ne seolfres, ne nane woruldlice ðing, ac bæd his gesihðe. For nahte he tealde ænig ðing to biddenne buton gesihðe; forðan ðeah se blinda sum ðing hæbbe, he ne mæg butan leohte geseon þæt he hæfð. Uton forði geefenlæcan þisum men, þe wæs gehæled fram Criste, æhðer ge on lichaman ge on sawle: ne bidde we na lease welan, ne gewitenlice wurðmyntas; ac uton biddan leoht æt urum Drihtne: na þæt leoht ðe bið geendod, þe bið mid þære nihte todræfed, þæt ðe is gemæne us and nytenum; ac uton biddan þæs leohtes þe we magon mid englum anum geseon, þæt ðe næfre ne bið geendod. To ðam leohte soðlice ure geleafa us sceal gebringan, swa swa Crist cwæð to ðam blindan menn, "Loca nu, þin geleafa ðe gehælde."

Nu smeað sum ungeleafful man, Hu mæg ic gewilnian ðæs gastlican leohtes, þæt þæt ic geseon ne mæg? Nu cwede ic to ðam menn, þæt ða ðing þe he understynt and undergytan mæg, ne undergyt he na ða ðing þurh his lichaman, ac þurh his sawle; þeah-hwæðere ne gesihð nan man his sawle on ðisum life. Heo is ungeswenlic, ac ðeah-hwæðere heo wissað

place to place; because he is in every place through his divinity. When he passed, then he heard the crying of the blind man; and when he stood, then he gave him sight; because through his humanity he laments the blindness of our minds, and through divinity he gives us light, and enlightens our blindness. He said to the blind man, "What do you wish that I do to you?" Do you think that he did not know what the blind man wanted, he who might heal him? But he desired that the blind man might pray; because he charges everyone very urgently to prayers: nonetheless he says in another place, "Your heavenly Father knows what you need, before you pray to him for anything,"[5] although the good God desires that we eagerly pray; because through prayers our heart is inspired and turned to God.

Then the blind man said, "Oh, sir, do so that I may see." The blind man did not ask for gold, nor silver, nor any worldly thing, but asked for his sight. For he did not consider praying for anything except sight; because although the blind man might have something, he may not see what he has without light. Therefore let us imitate this man, who was healed by Christ, both in body and in soul; let us pray not for false riches, nor for temporary glories; but let us pray to our Lord for light: not that light that will be ended, which will be driven away with the night, that which is common to us and beasts; but let us pray for that light that we alone with angels may see, that which will never be ended. Truly our belief shall bring us to that light, just as Christ said to the blind man, "Look now, your belief has healed you."

Now some unbelieving man will consider, "How may I desire the spiritual light, which I may not see?" Now I say to that man, about the things that he understands and may know, he understands those things not through his body, but through his soul; nonetheless no man will see his soul in this life. It is invisible, but nonetheless it guides the visible body. The body, which is visible, has life from the soul, which is invisible. As the

þone gesewenlican lichaman. Se lichama, ðe is gesewenlic, hæfð lif of ðære sawle, þe is ungesewenlic. Gewite þæt ungesewenlice ut, þonne fylð adune þæt gesewenlice; forðan þe hit ne stod na ær ðurh hit sylf. Ðæs lichoman lif is seo sawul, and þære sawle lif is God. Gewite seo sawul ut, ne mæg se muð clypian, þeah ðe he bynige; ne eage geseon, þeah ðe hit open sy; ne nan limn ne deð nan ðing, gif se lichama bið sawulleas. Swa eac seo sawul, gif God hi forlæt for synnum, ne deð heo nan ðing to gode. Ne mæg nan man nan ðing to gode gedon, butan Godes fultume. Ne bið seo synfulle sawul na mid ealle to nahte awend, ðeah ðe heo gode adeadod sy; ac heo bið dead ælcere duguðe and gesælðe, and bið gehealden to ðam ecan deaðe, þær þær heo æfre bið on pinungum wunigende, and þeah-hwæðere næfre ne ateorað.

Hu mæg þe nu twynian þæs ecan leohtes, ðeah hit ungesewenlic sy, þonne þu hæfst lif of ungesewenlicre sawle, and þe ne twynað nan ðing þæt þu sawle hæbbe, ðeah ðu hi geseon ne mage? Se blinda, ða ða he geseon mihte, þa fyligde he ðam Hælende. Se man gesihð and fylið Gode, se ðe cann understandan God, and god weorc wyrcð. Se man gesihð and nele Gode fylian, se ðe understent God,and nele god wyrcan. Ac uton understandan God and god weorc wyrcean: uton behealdan hwider Crist gange, and him fylian; þæt is þæt we sceolon smeagan hwæt he tæce, and hwæt him licige, and þæt mid weorcum gefyllan, swa swa he sylf cwæð, "Se ðe me þenige, fylige he me"; þæt is, geefenlæce he me, and onscunige ælc yfel, and lufige ælc god, swa swa ic do. Ne teah Crist him na to on ðisum life land we welan, swa swa he be him sylfum cwæð, "Deor habbað hola, and fugelas habbað nest, hwær hi restað, and ic næbbe hwider ic ahylde min heafod." Swa micel he hæfde swa he rohte, and leofode be oðra manna æhtum, se ðe ealle ðing ah.

We rædað on Cristes bec þæt þæt folc rædde be him, þæt hi woldon hine gelæccan, and ahebban to cyninge, þæt he wære heora heafod for worulde, swa swa he wæs godcundlice. Ða þa Crist ongeat ðæs folces willan, ða fleah

invisible will go out, then the visible will fall down; because, before, it did not stand by itself. The life of the body is the soul, and the life of the soul is God. As the soul will go out, the mouth may not cry, although it will gape; nor will the eye see, although it will be open; nor will any limb do anything, if the body is soulless. So also the soul, if God forsakes it for its sins, it will do nothing good. No man may do anything good, except with the help of God. Nor will the sinful soul be turned wholly to nothing, although it will be deadened to good; but it will be dead to every virtue and happiness, and will be held in eternal death, where it will always be in eternal torments, and nonetheless it will never perish.

How may you now doubt the eternal light, although it is invisible, when you have life from the invisible soul, and you do not doubt that you have a soul, although you may not see it? The blind man, when he could see, then he followed the Savior. The man sees and follows God, who can understand God, and does good works. The man sees and will not follow God, who understands God, and does no good works. But let us understand God and do good works: let us see where Christ goes, and follow him; that is, that we should consider what he teaches, and what is pleasing to him, and fulfill that with works, just as he himself said, "He who will serve me, he will follow me",[6] that is, he imitates me, and shuns every evil, and loves every good, just as I do. Christ received for himself in this life neither land nor riches, just as he himself said, "Beasts have holes, and birds have nests, where they rest, and I have nowhere that I might lay down my head."[7] He had as much as he gave, and he lived by the possessions of other men, he who owns all things.

We read in Christ's book what the people thought about him, that they would seize him, and exalted him as a king, so that he might be their worldly ruler, just as he was divinely. When Christ knew the will of the people, then he fled alone to a mountain, and his companions went to the sea, and the Savior was up on land. Then in the night the

he anstandende to anre dune, and his geferan gewendon to sæ, and se Hælend wæs up on lande. Ða on nigt eode se Hælend up on ðam wætere mid drium fotum, oðþæt he com to his leorning-cnihtum, ðær ðær hi wæron oon rewute. He forfleah þone woruldlican wurð-mynt, þa þa he wæs to cyninge gecoren; ac he ne forfleah na þæt edwit and ðone hosp, þa þa ða Iudeiscan hine woldon on rode ahon. He nolde his heafod befon mid gyldenum cyn-ehelme, ac mid þyrnenum, swa swa hit gedon wæs on his þrowunge. He nolde on ðissum life rixian hwilwendlice, se ðe ecelice rixað on heofonum. Nis ðeos woruld na ure eðel, ac is ure wræcsið; forði ne sceole we na besettan urne hiht on þissum swicelum life, ac scee-lon efstan mid godum gearnungum to urum eðele, þær we to gesceapene wæron, þæt is to heofenan rice.

Soðlice hit is awriten, "Swa hwa swa wile beon freond þisre worulde, se bið geteald Godes feond." Crist cwæð on sumere stowe, þæt "Se weig is swiðe nearu and sticol, se ðe læt to heofonan rice; and se is swiðe rum and smeðe, se ðe læt to hellewit." Se weig, se ðe læt to heofenan rice, is forði nearu and sticol, forði þæt we sceolon mid earfoðnysse geear-nian urne eðel. Gif we hine habban willað, we sceolon lufian mildheortnysse, and clænnysse, and soðfæstnysse, and rihtwisnysse, and ead-modnysse, and habban soðe lufe to Gode and to mannum, and don ælmessan be ure mæðe, and habban gemet on urum bigleofan, and gehwilce oðere halige ðing began. Þas ðing we ne magon don butan earfoðnyssum; ac gif we hi doð, þonne mage we mid þam geswincum, ðurh Godes fultum, astigan ðone sticolan weg te us gelæt to ðam ecan life. Se weg se ðe læt to forwyrde is forði brad and smeðe, forði þe unlustas gebringað þone man to for-wyrde. Him bið swiðe softe, and nan geswing þæt he fylle his galnysse, and druncennysse, and gytsunge begange and modignysse, and ða unstrangan berype, and don swa hwæt swa hine lyst: ac ðas unðeawas and oðre swilce gelædað hine butan geswince to ecum tin-tregum, buton he ær his ende yfeles geswice and god wyrce. Dysig bið se wegferenda man

Savior went up on the water with dry feet, until he came to his disciples, where they were on a ship. He fled from worldly glory, when he was chosen as king; but he did not flee from disgrace and insult, when the Jews desired to hang him on a cross. He would not encircle his head with a golden crown, but with thorns, just as it was done at his passion. He would not rule in this life for a while, who rules eternally in heaven. This world is not our homeland, but it is our place of exile; therefore we should not set our hope in this deceitful life, but we should hasten with good rewards to our homeland, for which we were created, that is, to the heavenly kingdom.

Truly it is written, "Whoever will be a friend of this world, he will be considered an enemy of God."[8] Christ said in one place, that "The path is very narrow and steep, which leads to the heavenly kingdom; and it is very wide and smooth, which leads to hell-torments."[9] The path, which leads to the heavenly kingdom, is therefore narrow and steep, so that we should earn our homeland with difficulty. If we desire to have it, we should love mercy, and purity, and truthful-ness, and righteousness, and humility, and have true love for God and for men, and give alms by our means, and have moderation in our food, and do every other holy thing. We may not do these things without difficulties; but if we do them, then with those labors we may, through God's help, ascend the steep path that leads us to eternal life. The path that leads to destruction therefore is broad and smooth, because evil desires bring man to destruction. It is very soft for him, and no labor that he does fills his lustfulness, and drunkenness, and he performs covetousness and pride, and he robs the weak, and he does whatever he desires: but those evil practices and similar others lead him without labor to eternal torments, unless before his end he stops evil and does good. The way-faring man is foolish, who takes the smooth path that misleads him, and who forsakes the steep path that brings him to the city. So also we will be truly foolish, if we love the brief soft-

se ðe nimð þone smeðan weg þe hine mislæt, and forlæt ðone sticolan þe hine gebrincð to ðære byrig. Swa eac we beoð soðlice ungerade, gif we lufiað þa sceortan softnysse and ða hwilwendlican lustas to ðan swiðe, þæt hi us gebringan to ðam ecan pinungum. Ac uton niman þone earfoðran weg, þæt we her sume hwile swincon, to ðy þæt we ecelice beon butan geswince. Eaðe mihte Crist, gif he wolde, on þisum life wunian butan earfoðnyssum, and faran to his ecan rice butan ðrowunge, and buran deaðe; ac he nolde. Be ðam cwæð Petrus se apostol, "Crist ðrowode for us, and sealde us bysne, þæt we sceolon fyligan his fotswaðum"; þæt is, þæt we sceolon sum ðing þrowian for Cristes lufon, and for urum synnum. Wel ðrowað se man, and God gecwemlice, se ðe winð ongean leahtras, and godnysse gefremað, swa swa he fyrmest mæg. Se ðe nan ðing nele on ðissum life ðrowian, he sceal ðrowian unþances wyrsan ðrowunga on þam toweardan life.

Nu genealæcð clæne tid and halig, on þære we sceolon ure gimeleaste gebetan: cume forði gehwa cristenra manna to his scrifte, and his diglan gyltas geandette, and be his lareowes tæcunge gebete; and tithe ælc oðerne to gode mid godre gebysnunge, þæt eal folc cweðe be us, swa swa be ðam blindan gecweden wæs, ða ða his eagan wæron onlihte; þæt is, Eall folc þe þæt wundor geseah, herede God, se ðe leofað and rixað a butan ende. Amen.

ness and the temporary lusts sc greatly, that they bring us to the eternal torments. But let us take the more difficult path, so that we labor for a certain time here, so that we will be without labor eternally. Christ might have easily, if he wanted, dwelled in this life without difficulties, and go to his eternal kingdom without suffering, and without death; but he did not. About this Peter the apostle said, "Christ suffered for us, and gave us an example, so that we should follow his footsteps";[10] that is, that we should suffer something for Christ's love, and for our sins. The man suffers well, and pleasingly to God, who strives against reproach, and performs goodness, just as he may best. He who will suffer nothing in this life, he shall suffer worse displeasures of suffering in the life to come.

Now approaches a pure and holy time, in which we should amend our transgressions: therefore let every Christian man come to his confessor, and confess his hidden sins, and amend by the teaching of his teacher; and let everyone urge others to good with good example, so that all people might talk about us, just as was said about the blind man, when his eyes were enlightened; that is, All people who saw that wonder praised God, who lives and rules without end. Amen.

Endnotes

1   The text and translation are based on *The Homilies of the Anglo-Saxon Church: The First Part, Containing the Sermones Catholici or Homilies of Ælfric*, edited and translated by Benjamin Thorpe, 2 vols., The Ælfric Society, 1844–1846, vol. 1, pp. 152–65, with some modifications. Endnotes and translation have been provided by Brandon W. Hawk.

2   Fay Skevington, "The Unhal and the Semantics of Anglo-Saxon Disability," *Social Dimensions of Medieval Disease and Disability*, eds. Sally Crawford and Christina Lee (Archaeopress, 2014), p. 8.

3   Aaron J. Kleist, *Striving With Grace: Views of Free Will in Anglo-Saxon England*, Toronto Anglo-Saxon Series 20 (University of Toronto Press, 2008), p. 179.

4   John 14:6: "Ego sum via et veritas et vita" ("I am the way, and the truth, and the life").

5   Matthew 6:8: "enim Pater vester quibus opus sit vobis antequam petatis eum" ("your Father knoweth what is needful for you, before you ask him").

6   John 12:26: "Si quis mihi ministrat me sequatur" ("If any man minister to me, let him follow me").

7   Matthew 8:20: "Vulpes foveas habent et volucres caeli tabernacula Filius autem hominis non habet ubi caput reclinet" ("The foxes have holes, and the birds of the air nests; but the Son of man hath not where to lay his head")

8   James 4:4: "Ergo voluerit amicus esse saeculi huius inimicus Dei constituitur" ("Whosoever therefore will be a friend of this world becometh an enemy of God").

9   Cf. Matthew 7:13: "Intrate per angustam portam quia lata porta et spatiosa via quae ducit ad perditionem et multi sunt qui intrant per eam" ("Enter ye in at the narrow gate: for wide is the gate, and broad is the way that leadeth to destruction").

10   1 Peter 2:21: "Christus passus est pro vobis vobis relinquens exemplum ut sequamini vestigia eius" ("Christ also suffered for us, leaving you an example that you should follow his steps").

The City of God against the Pagans[1] (413–26)

Augustine of Hippo
Contributed by Leah Pope Parker

Introduction

Saint Augustine of Hippo (354–430 CE) was among the most prolific of the early Christian theological writers known as the Fathers of the Church. Born in North Africa to a non-Christian father and Christian mother, Augustine led a tumultuous early intellectual life before converting to Christianity in 386, and eventually becoming bishop of Hippo (modern-day Annaba, Algeria) in late 395 or early 396. His written work remains foundational in Christian theology to this day, and was of particular importance to the development of Christian doctrine in the Middle Ages. *The City of God against the Pagans*, a lengthy treatise completed near the end of Augustine's life, defends the superiority of Christianity over other religions despite recent defeats of Rome by heretics and non-Christians (such as the sack of Rome by Goths in 410). *The City of God* traces a Christian historical trajectory from Creation to the apocalypse, with its promise of the resurrection of the dead and everlasting life. In book 22, Augustine devotes several chapters to discussing the nature of the resurrected body in terms of gender, age, size, and (dis)ability. The passage excerpted below describes the features of the resurrected body, both what the resurrected body *will* be and what it *will not*.

Augustine opens the chapter by continuing to respond to a series of questions pertaining to the nature of the body after the resurrection. The implicit questions "about the hair and nails" are: If the body must be resurrected in order for a person to obtain the bliss of the afterlife, and no part of the body will be lost in that resurrection, then what happens to the parts of our bodies that we willingly shed or trim? Will all of the hair and fingernails we have ever grown be restored to horrific effect? Conversely, if the hair and nails that had been trimmed in life are not included in the resurrected body, then is the resurrected body truly the same person?

Augustine unfolds his answer through a series of analogies, which draw upon experiences and expectations of the disabled body to describe the promised resurrected body. He compares the matter of the human body to a clay vessel that (before firing) may be collapsed into shapelessness and then remolded to its previous form, arguing that the vessel is still the same vessel even if individual particles of clay are redistributed to different parts, such as the handle or the base. Likewise, Augustine argues that if a statue is malformed, it can be recast so that the form is perfected, but none of the material is lost. For Augustine this means that there is no need for individuals' resurrected bodies to "be such as they would not have chosen to be here," simply because there is an excess or deficiency of material, or because the material is not harmoniously arranged. While this is phrased as reassuring—because one can hope for a "better" body in the afterlife—Augustine's framework also stigmatizes bodily difference, from being "too thin or too fat" to having "rare and monstrous" deformities. By interjecting that "in any case there is no purpose to deformity but to display in this life the punitive condition of mortality," Augustine unambiguously associates "deformity," and thereby disability, with the humankind's fallen state subject to sin and death. The resurrected body, in contrast, is characterized by the erasure of what Augustine calls "defect," in favor of "what is seemly," a ranking of bodily forms embedded with assumptions about what is universally desirable in a human body.

The resurrected body thus becomes akin to what Rosemarie Garland-Thomson has called the "normate," in that it is "the veiled subject position of cultural self, the figure outlined by the array of deviant others whose marked bodies shore up the normate's boundaries."[2] Augustine clearly does not expect living bodies to conform to the harmonious form of the resurrected body, and so the normative power of the resurrection body is limited to urging Christians to *anticipate* that body in the afterlife, rather than obtain that body in the present. Nonetheless, the expectation that some features are not desirable for the eternal afterlife reflects and reinforces lived experiences of disability and bodily difference in Augustine's time. That is, Augustine's theological explanations for how the body will be resurrected as the same body, but without "defect," reflect very real anxieties about and unhappiness with the ways individuals experienced their own bodies in Augustine's time, much as they do today. Augustine's reassurance that "none...should be afraid" suggests that he is more concerned with Christians' feelings about their own bodies, rather than their judgments of others. However, the concept of the resurrection body being only "what is seemly" creates a theological justification for ableist assumptions about what the body "should" be.

And yet, Augustine complicates the notion of "what is seemly" by asserting that the scars of Christ and the martyrs are honorable, even if the same wound acquired outside the service of Christ would be counted a "defect." In the same closing movement of the chapter that frames blindness as a punishment for sin and casually jokes about

blind individuals needing sighted guides, Augustine also opens up the structure of the resurrection body to include space for variation. The general argument of the chapter, that bodies will be resurrected without any disability, thus nonetheless makes room for the possibility that bodily difference can be a positive experience, both for those with scars and those who look upon them. Though it falls substantially short of supporting a full range of bodily diversity (the saints, after all, will have their amputated limbs reattached), Augustine's articulation of the resurrected body incorporates disability into both negatively and positively coded features of Christian salvation history.

Bibliography

Brock, Brian. "Augustine's Hierarchies of Human Wholeness and Their Healing." *Disability in the Christian Tradition: A Reader,* edited by John Swinton and Brian Brock. Wm. B. Eerdmans Publishing Co., 2012, pp. 58–84.

Bynum, Caroline Walker. *The Resurrection of the Body in Western Christianity, 200–1336.* Columbia University Press, 1995.

Claes, Martin, and Anthony Dupont. "Augustine's Sermons and Disability." *Disability in Antiquity,* edited by Christian Laes. Routledge, 2017, pp. 328–41.

Garland-Thomson, Rosemarie. *Extraordinary Bodies: Figuring Physical Disability in American Culture and Literature.* Columbia University Press, 1997.

Moss, Candida R. "Heavenly Healing: Eschatological Cleansing and the Resurrection of the Dead in the Early Church." *Journal of the American Academy of Religion,* vol. 79, no. 4, 2011, pp. 991–1017. https://www.jstor.org/stable/41348747.

Stainton, Tim. "Reason, Grace and Charity: Augustine and the Impact of Church Doctrine on the Construction of Intellectual Disability." *Disability & Society,* vol. 23, no. 5, Aug. 2008, pp. 485–96. doi: 10.1080/09687590802177056.

Book XXII, chapter 19

Now how am I to reply about the hair and nails? Having first understood "not a hair will be lost from the body"[3] to mean that there will be nothing deformed[4] in the body, then this is also understood: any matter that would comprise deformity, if it were left in disorder, will be drawn into the greater form of the body, but not at all in such a way that the contour of the limbs is disfigured. It is just as when a vessel is made from clay,[5] and the clay is then regathered into an unformed mass to be sculpted anew. It is not necessary that the same portion of clay that had been the handle return to the new handle, or that the base return to itself. Despite this, the whole returns to the whole; that is, the whole of that clay becomes again the whole vessel, with nothing of itself lost in having been exchanged between the vessel's parts. Therefore if the hair of the head, which so often has been shaved, or the nails which have been clipped, would by their return comprise deformity, then they will not be restored. However, neither will anything be lost in the resurrection of each person, because the harmony of the body will be restored in the same flesh, arranged precisely in its place upon the body, though changed in substance.

Indeed, the Lord said: "No hair on your head will perish,"[6] which can be understood to mean the number of hairs plentifully affixed, not the length of the hair. This is why elsewhere he said: "The hairs of your head are numbered."[7] I have not, therefore, said that I believe anything will be lost from a body that is part of its essential nature, but that anything that had been deformed in life (and in any case there is no purpose to deformity but to display in this life the punitive condition of mortality) will be returned such that material wholeness is preserved, with the deformity passing away. For example, a human artist might for whatever reason create a disfigured statue, but then restore the work to beauty by recasting it, so that no substance is added, but still the deformity is taken away.

And if any part of that prior form had protruded indecently, interrupting the balance of its parts, no portion of the whole need be shorn off and cast away, but instead the material may be redistributed and blended in such a way that no ugliness is produced nor is the strength of the sculpture lessened. What then might we think the Almighty Artist capable of? Will he not be able to eliminate any deformities upon human bodies, not limited to those that occur commonly, but also those that are rare and monstrous? These are appropriate for this wretched life, but to the future happiness of the saints they are abhorrent. Will he not thus be able to alleviate any of those unsightly growths in the substance of the body, even if they are of natural causes, without raising the body in any way diminished?

And because of this, none who are too thin or too fat should be afraid that there they will be such as they would not have chosen to be here, had they been able to choose. For all beauty of the body is due to the harmony of its parts, along with particular pleasant complexions. But where there is no harmony of its parts, then for that reason the body is unpleasant, either because it is distorted or because it is too small or excessively large. Therefore, there will be no deformity produced by unharmonious parts, in that place where both anyone that is distorted shall be straightened, and those with little of what is seemly will be made whole from a source that the Creator knows, and moreover those with more beyond what is seemly will have that excess removed, while protecting the completeness of bodily matter. How much more sweet the complexion will be in that place where the righteous will shine just like the sun in the reign of their Father![8]

It is believed that this brightness in the body of Christ, when he rose again, was concealed from the eyes of the disciples, rather than not there at all. For the weak sight of man would not have borne it, when the disciples were required to attend him closely so that they could recognize him. For the

same reason he also exposed the scars of his
wounds to be touched, and that he also took
food and drink, not for need of nourishment,
but by means of that power which likewise
made concealing his brightness possible for
him. When something is not seen, although
it is present, by those who see other equally
present things (as I have previously said about
that brightness, that it was unseen by those
who saw other things), in Greek is it called
ἀορασία,° which our interpreters were not
able to translate into Latin, and in the book
of Genesis it was interpreted as "blindness."[9]
This is what the men of Sodom endured,
when they were seeking the door of the righteous man,° but could not find it.[10] If this had
been that blindness in which nothing can be
seen, they would not have been searching for
a door to enter, but seeking guides to lead
them away from that place.

However, for reasons unknown to me, our
deep love for the blessed martyrs leads us to
desire to see the scars of their wounds, which
they have suffered for the name of Christ,
upon their bodies in that kingdom. And perhaps we will see them. For it will not be deformity in them, but distinction, and exceedingly in their body will shine a certain beauty,
which is not of the flesh but of virtue.[11] Moreover, if limbs have at any time been severed
or torn away from the martyrs, they will not
therefore be without those limbs in the resurrection of the dead, because for them it was
said: "No hair on your head will perish." But if
in that new age it is seemly that the tokens of
their famous wounds be seen in that immor-
tal flesh. then where limbs had been detached
by being struck or carved away, there will be
visible scars, but nonetheless the same limbs
will be restored, not lost. Thus, at that time
all defects that have befallen the body will
cease to exist; however, the tokens of virtue
will not be named or considered defects.

ἀορασία *sightlessness*   **the righteous man** *Lot*

Endnotes

1 The text below was compiled and translated by Leah Pope Parker, from the Latin text available in *The City of God against the Pagans*, edited and translated George E. McCracken, Loeb Classical Library 411–17, Harvard University Press, 1957, vol. VII, pp. 288–95. Glosses and endnotes are also by Leah Pope Parker.

2 Rosemarie Garland-Thomson, *Extraordinary Bodies: Figuring Physical Disability in American Culture and Literature* (Columbia University Press, 1997), p. 8.

3 This is Augustine's paraphrase of the line he returns to below, from Luke 21:18.

4 Latin *deforme* can also be translated as "misshapen," "formless," or "ugly."

5 The Latin word *limus*, which I translate here as "clay" as part of the pottery analogy, can also mean "mud," evoking both the biblical creation of man from dust and the decay of the human body into dust between death and resurrection.

6 Luke 21:18.

7 Luke 12:7.

8 This line references Matthew 13:43.

9 The Greek ἀορασία or *aorasia* translates most literally in English to "sightlessness," whereas the Latin supplied here, *caecitatem* translates most directly to "blindness." The passage in Genesis 19 to which Augustine refers was originally written in Classical Hebrew, but early translations into Latin often depended upon the Greek translation of the Old Testament known as the Septuagint. In the late fourth century, St Jerome, a contemporary and correspondent of Augustine, was notably engaged in the monumental task of newly translating the Old and New Testaments into Latin, which became the bulk of the Latin Vulgate Bible.

10 Genesis 19:11. Augustine refers to the story of Lot and the destruction of the cities of Sodom and Gomorrah as divine retribution for their sins. Lot had welcomed two angels into his home, and when the men of Sodom sought to abuse his visitors, Lot offered up his daughters in their stead. The men of Sodom refused this offer, and the angels protected Lot's household by impairing the men's vision, so that they could not see the door to Lot's home. Lot and his family are sent out from the city and thus spared from the destruction of Sodom and Gomorrah.

11 Latin *virtutis* can be translated with moral connotations as "virtue" or "courage," but it can also carry more physical connotations as "strength."

A Miracle of Thomas Becket: *De puero syntectino* (Concerning a boy suffering from a wasting disease)[1] (1172–77)

William of Canterbury
Contributed by Rose A. Sawyer

Introduction

As England's most renowned saint, numerous miraculous cures are attributed to Thomas Becket and many of these were collected and recorded by William of Canterbury in England's longest miracle collection. Miracles have long been considered a valuable source for the study of medieval attitudes towards and ideas about disability, illness, and death. This particular miracle details the cure of the infant Augustine, who was impaired by a wasting disease before being dedicated to Thomas Becket and miraculously restored in 1172. As Rachel Koopmans observes, William takes a medicalized approach to the recording of miracles. Presumably drawing upon his own study of the substantial number of Latin medical texts available in England during this period, William utilizes precise medical terminology and an understanding of medieval medical theory in order to present a vivid description of and explanation for Augustine's condition. William diagnoses Augustine as *syntecticus* (suffering from a wasting disease) and, while he does not settle upon a definite cause, he does suggest that the condition could stem from either an ulcer in his lungs, his loud cries, or another medically defined cause. William's account of the condition is very similar to Roger Frugardi's description of *ptisys* (consumption). Roger was writing in Parma at roughly the same time as William and their language and application of humoral theory is almost identical; both understand the ulcer to be consuming the body's "essential humidity."[2] However, after suggesting some medically sound theories, William also references and dismisses an alternative theory for the boy's emaciated appearance, stating that: "no-one of sound mind credits the fabulous nonsense of the people, who believe children to be substituted or transformed."

William refers here to the child substitution motif, that is the idea that a child has been removed and another being, a changeling, substituted in its place. Clerical scholars such as Jacques de Vitry (d. 1420) and William of Auvergne (d. 1249) described changelings as demons that take the form of infants who, while being perpetually hungry, do not grow or thrive. While the characteristics of medieval changelings do vary depending upon context, William of Canterbury's comments reflect his understanding that a section of the population may respond to a child with Augustine's symptoms by arguing that it was a changeling rather than the original human child. William attributes this belief to the *vulgi* (people) and, while there is no indication in his account that Augustine's parents believed that Thomas Becket had relieved them of a changeling child, one has to wonder why William chose to reference the child substitution at this point if not prompted by a careless comment from the parents.

Jean Claude Schmitt, in his seminal monograph on the medieval child substitution motif *The Holy Greyhound*, argues that the belief in changelings had three functions: first, to explain sickness or disability; second, to allow burdensome children to be removed from the family; and third, to assuage parental guilt over the death of the child as a result of these rites, since the child had been identified not as sick but as non-human. Schmitt's study focuses upon an account of the practices in a single rural region of France, and the extent to which his model can be more broadly applied is uncertain. More recently, scholars studying medieval changelings have questioned both the prevalence of changeling belief during the Middle Ages and the extent to which it could be connected to disability.

However, it is notable that, even as William of Canterbury dismisses the idea that a changeling could have been substituted for Augustine, he is at pains to describe the ways in which the infant appeared inhuman or monstrous. William makes vivid comparisons to animal bodies and inanimate objects: Augustine's arms are "just like two small twigs from the middle of a branch" and he is "an animal portentous to see." For William, Augustine's body occupies a type of hybrid space, complicating categories of human and non-human. Thus, he also states that Augustine's "inappropriate dryness denied [that he was] human," while "his wailing and alert expression suggested something of the human." Furthermore, after the miraculous cure, William states that Augustine "having been transformed into a new human, he could acquire again the appearance of his birth and insemination." The use of the verb *transformare* echoes William's earlier description of the beliefs of the *vulgi* "who believe children to be substituted or transformed." This is not to suggest that William's protestations belied a secret belief in changelings; however, it does indicate that even the most medically knowledgeable person might use language that constructed the impaired body as other than or only semi-human.

This text also deals with the notion that having an impaired child was a shameful thing. Augustine's parents are unwed and Ralph, Augustine's father, is a priest, thus their relationship is described by William as illicit and sinful. The twelfth century saw the rise of a reform movement focusing on the imposition of clerical celibacy.[3] Jenni Kuuliala has suggested that Augustine's parents believe that their son's impairment is a result or punishment for their own sin; however, this interpretation is not clearly supported in the text. Instead, it seems more likely that William figures Augustine's withered body as the symbolic fruit of his parent's shameful coupling with the intention of contributing to the debate surrounding clerical celibacy. However, when describing Augustine's cure, William also states that "the Lord heeds not our sinfulness," thus indicating that, whatever his own feelings, the Lord is ultimately merciful. If Augustine's parents did conceal him from others, it might instead indicate a level of concern about the reaction of other people to their child as this concern is reflected in other texts about changelings.

The body of an impaired child is the focus of this source; however, in describing this infant and his miraculous restoration, William provides us with a text that is rich in more than just medieval medical theory. William's presentation of Augustine's body is rooted in cutting edge medical theory; however, by studying this source we can also see the tension between his learned approach and the way in which other medieval people instead drew upon their understanding of the supernatural to explain childhood impairment through the child substitution motif. Furthermore, it is clear that other debates, such as the one to do with clerical chastity, could also inform the way in which impaired children were conceptualized and treated.

Bibliography

Goodey, C.F., and Tim Stainton. "Intellectual Disability and the Myth of the Changeling Myth." *Journal of the History of the Behavioral Sciences*, vol. 37, no. 3, 2001, pp. 223–40. doi: 10.1002/jhbs.1032.

Koopmans, Rachel. *Wonderful to Relate: Miracle Stories and Miracle Collecting in High Medieval England.* University of Pennsylvania Press, 2011.

Kuuliala, Jenni. *Childhood Disability and Social Integration in the Middle Ages: Constructions of Impairments in Thirteenth- and Fourteenth-Century Canonization Processes.* Brepols Publishers, 2016.

———. "Sons of Demons? Children's Impairment and the Belief in Changelings in Medieval Europe (c. 1150–1400)." *The Dark Side of Childhood in Late Antiquity and the Middle Ages,* edited by Katariina Mustakallio and Christina Laes. Oxbow Books, 2011, pp. 71–93.

Lindow, John. "Changelings, Changing, Re-Exchanges: Thoughts on the Relationship between Folk-Belief and Legend." *Legends and Landscape: Articles Based on Plenary Papers Presented at the 5th Celtic-Nordic-Baltic Folklore Symposium, Reykjavík, 2005,* edited by Terry Gunnell. University of Iceland Press, 2008, pp. 215–34.

Schmitt, Jean-Claude. *The Holy Greyhound: Guinefort, Healer of Children since the Thirteenth Century.* Translated by Martin Thom. Cambridge University Press, 1983. Originally published in French as *Le saint lévrier: Guinefort, guérisseur d'enfants depuis le XIIIe sècle.* Flammarion, 1979.

De puero syntectino

Quia loqui coepi de infantibus, ne, quæso, lector, videatur onerosum si modicum adhuc subjungam quod ad honorem martyris spectat et profectum nostrum, quia ex ore infantium et lactentium perfecit Deus laudem ut destruat inimicum et ultorem.

Radulfus quidam, de villa Sumeshelde, Auglicus genere, presbyteratus sublimatus dignitate, dum maledictum legis declinat, quae steriles damnat, suscepit ex consorte thori filium Augustinum.

Qui cum dimidium annum egisset ab ortu, tanta membrorum exilitate et tenuitate demolitus est, ut miserabilem speciem praeferret, minus habens carnositatis in toto corpore quam validus aliquis in uno digitorum suorum.

Corpoream namque substantiam gravis passio consumpserat, ex ulcere pulmonis proveniens, aut ex clamore vagientis vel aliis causis quas physicus assignat; nemo enim sanae mentis vulgi fabulosa deliramenta credit, quod pueros supponi putat aut transformari.

Prominebat itaque spina, radiolos suos et spondilias patenter ostendens.

Brachia vero dependebant hinc inde, tanquam virgulae duae de medio stipite; eratque miserabilis facies, non facies sed superficies, tanquam vita sine vivente, materia sine forma, corpus sine compositione.

Consumptio substantialis humiditatis et ossea congeries ariditasque deformis hominem negabant.

E contrario vagitus et erecta facies aliquod hominis innuebant.

Hinc confusi parentes nemini videndum portentuosum animal exhibuerunt, peccato suo et pudori tenebras quserentes, qui contempto jure matrimonii genium colebant.

Veruntamen non iniquitates nostras observante Domino, gravi morbo levi medicina subventum est.

Nam simul ac martyri voto obstrictus est, colori suo redditus est; ipsaque nocte qua factum est votum, membris assiccatis vigor succrevit, mutuaque societate ossa et vis-

Concerning a boy suffering from a wasting disease

Because I have begun to speak about children, reader I beseech you, may it not seem onerous if I still say a little that concerns the honour of the martyr and our success in proper measure, because out of the mouth of infants and sucklings God perfected praise in order that he may destroy the enemy and the revenger.

A certain Ralph, from the village of Somershall, from the race of the English, having been raised to the office of priest, while he avoided the reproach of the law. which condemns them to be sterile, he procreated a son, Augustine, from the consort of his bed.

He, when half a year from his birth had passed,[4] was diminished with so much weakness and gauntness of his limbs, that he displayed a wretched sight, having less flesh in his whole body than someone strong in one of their fingers.

For in fact, a serious disease, produced by an ulcer in his lungs, or else by the noise of his wailing or from other causes which a physician[5] specifies, had consumed his bodily substance; for no-one of sound mind credits the fabulous nonsense of the people. who believe children to be substituted or transformed.

Thus, his spine was jutting out, revealing openly his ribs and vertebrae.

Truly his arms were hanging down thence from that place, just like two small twigs from the middle of a branch, and his face was wretched, not a face but a mask, as it were a life without living, a substance without shape, a body without structure

The consumption of his essential moisture and [his body like] a bone heap and his inappropriate dryness[6] denied [that he was] human.

On the other hand, his wailing and alert expression suggested something of the human.[7]

Hence, the troubled parents showed to no one the animal portentous to see, hiding in the shadows for their sin and shame, the

cera coaluerunt, ut novum transformatus in hominem sementivam natalemque reciperet speciem.

Talem ergo eum fuisse a parentibus audivimus, penitus vero restitutum oculis perspeximus.

parents who were maintaining their natural instinct, despite having disregarded the law of matrimony.[8]

Nevertheless, since the Lord heeds not our sinfulness, he rescued [him] from serious illness with swift medicine.[9]

For, as soon as he was bound by oath to the martyr, he was returned to his own colour; the very night that the vow was made, the vigour in his dried-up limbs overflowed, his bones and vitals grew together in mutual partnership, so that, having been transformed into a new human, he could acquire again the appearance of his insemination and birth.[10]

Then, we heard that he had been like that from his parents, to be sure, we thoroughly examined the restored child with our own eyes.

Endnotes

1   The Latin text below is taken from: James Craigie Robertson, ed., *Materials for the History of Thomas Becket, Archbishop of Canterbury (Canonized by Pope Alexander III, A.D. 1173)* (Longman, 1875), vol. 1, p. 204. The English text is my own translation.

2   For Roger Frugardi's description of the condition, see: Tony Hunt, ed., *Anglo-Norman Medicine* (D.S. Brewer, 1994), vol. 1, pp. 266–67. For the availability of medical texts in England, see: Monica H. Green, "Salerno on the Thames: The Genesis of Anglo-Norman Medical Literature," *Language and Culture in Medieval Britain: The French of England, c. 1100–c. 1500*, eds. Jocelyn Wogan-Brown et al. (York Medieval Press, 2009), pp. 220–31.

3   Jennifer D. Thibodeaux, *The Manly Priest: Clerical Celibacy, Masculinity, and Reform in England and Normandy, 1066–1300* (University of Pennsylvania Press, 2015).

4   By stressing that six months had passed since Augustine's birth, William of Canterbury implies that the infant's impairment developed after his birth and was not congenital. As changelings were substituted for healthy babies, thus it was more likely for a child that was born apparently healthy before developing an acquired impairment to be labelled a changeling.

5   The usage of *physicus* is very specific in the twelfth century and means an academically trained practitioner.

6   Infants were thought to have a unique humoral make-up, being full of humoral blood, they were warm and moister than at any stage of life. William's descriptions of Augustine constantly draw attention to the fact that he is inappropriately dry for an infant due to his "essential moisture" being consumed.

7   Continuous crying is cited by William of Auvergne as one of the behaviors attributed to changelings. It is therefore notable that William of Canterbury chooses to identify Augustine's pained crying as evidence for the infant's humanity.

8   William configures Augustine's impairment as a "portent" or signifier of his parent's sinful relationship.

9   By describing the miracle as medicine, William effectively overturns all of his preceding theory. To William, human medical knowledge is to no avail compared to divine medicine.

10   According to *Dictionary of Medieval Latin from British Sources*, *sementivus* is "of insemination, procreation, propagation, or growth." Human nature was passed on through semen, thus the use of *sementivus* references this understanding. William figures Augustine's cure as a return to the condition of warm moistness that he held at birth and through his conception.

Njáls Saga[1] (13th c.)

Contributed by Kolfinna Jónatansdóttir

Introduction

The oldest manuscripts that preserve the Icelandic family sagas are from the thirteenth century, but various theories have been put forward as to how old individual sagas or parts of them are. The family sagas generally focus on the period around and between two major events that shaped and changed Icelandic society, the settlement of Iceland (starting c. 870) and the conversion to Christianity (c. 1000).

Njáls saga (also known as *Njála* or *Brennu-Njáls saga*) is one of the Icelandic family sagas. It takes place between c. 960–1020 and the conversion gets a fair amount of coverage and is a turning point in the narrative. Therefore Christianity, its symbolism and interplay with pre-Christian culture, and how it affects Icelanders are overarching themes in the saga. Among other prominent themes and driving forces of the narrative are honor and masculinity and how men maintain their social status, often by killing those who have wronged them in any way or getting compensation from them, thus contributing to the feudal system. There is a vast gallery of characters in the saga, but the main focus is on the friends Gunnar and Njáll and their families, particularly their wives Hallgerðr and Bergþóra as well as Njáll's sons. Although they are not chieftains, both Gunnar and Njáll are prominent men, the former known for his athletic abilities and the latter for his wisdom and cunningness. Despite their abilities, they both get sucked into a vicious cycle of vengeance and are killed as a result.

The chapter presented here combines the concepts of feud, honor, and masculinity, as well as the newly emerged Christian religion. These concepts converge in a minor character, who enters the stage, takes the spotlight for one scene, then leaves and is never mentioned again. His name is Ámundi blindi (the blind) and "he had been born blind, but for all that he was tall and strong." Ámundi is an illegitimate son of Hǫskuldr, who himself is an illegitimate son of Njáll, but often accompanies his three legitimate brothers. As a part of blood feud, Hǫskuldr's brothers kill Þráinn Sigfússon but Njáll pays compensation on their behalf to Þráinn's brothers to end the feud and ensure peace. However, Þráinn's brother in law Lýtingr af Sámsstǫðum, who is described as being "tall of growth and a strong man, wealthy in goods and ill to deal with," feels that he has been left out of the deal and gets his two brothers to help him avenge Þráinn's death by killing Hǫskuldr. The three surviving sons of Njáll attack Lýtingr and his brothers and kill the brothers, but Lýtingr escapes and later agrees to pay a monetary compensation to Njáll and his sons to avoid being killed by them.

Ámundi, however, does not receive any of that money, presumably because he doesn't have a legal status in the matter. He therefore goes to Lýtingr at a parliamentary assembly and asks him for compensation. Lýtingr refuses since he has already paid his dues according to the rules of the society. Because of his blindness and social status, Ámundi's only option is to pray to God, who in return grants him sight just long enough for him to kill Lýtingr.

Ámundi's description is very brief, and nothing is said about his role in society, what he does for a living or where he lives, but he needs the help of others to find his way around the parliament site, and he poses no threat to Lýtingr, until he gets divine help. The nickname "blind" sounds almost neutral, but nicknames in the Icelandic sagas often describe distinctive physical features of the characters. Eyes and good eyesight are however often symbols of power and masculinity and the act of blinding someone is often used as symbolic castration. When the theme of constant feud and revenge within *Njáls saga* is kept in mind, Ámundi's blindness makes him less of a man within the society; he is perceived as harmless and incapable of doing his duty as a son and avenging his father's death.

Between the encounter of Lýtingr and the sons of Njáll and Ámundi's meeting with Lýtingr, there's a long account of the conversion of Iceland. The story of Ámundi is the first narrative of *Njáls saga* within a Christian society and therefore the miracle highlights the new religion. Ámundi laments his blindness and asks God to judge between them, and all of the sudden, he can see, and praises the Lord. Not only does God aid him, but the invocation of Ámundi suggests that it is God's will that he shall kill Lýtingr. With the help of this miracle and surprise, Ámundi, who sees for the first time in his life and has therefore presumably never handled a weapon, charges forward and kills Lýtingr with an axe. The miracle is only temporary and having carried out his revenge, Ámundi loses his sight again.

This divine intervention highlights that a new faith has emerged and that the new God sympathizes with the helplessness of a blind man, who without his eyesight and divine intervention can't fulfill his social duty. The placement of this narrative shows that a new power, which is benevolent towards the marginalized, has entered the scene of the saga. Ámundi is not healed permanently, but by asking God to judge between him and Lýtingr, he surrenders to the judgment of a higher being, who rules in his favor. And as Lars Lönnroth interprets the scene, the miracle is a theological reference to the Natural Law,

that Ámundi has a right although society has settled the score. It also shows the Christian God as a source of justice and a protector of Icelandic law, even the pre-Christian revenge system. Blindness is sometimes used as a symbol of those who reject Christianity and remain non-Christians, but the opposite seems to apply to Ámundi, since his faith in God enables him to avenge his father.

Bibliography

Lassen, Annette. *Øjet og blindheden i norrøn litteratur og mytologi*. Museum Tusculanum, 2003.

Lönnroth, Lars. *Njáls Saga: A Critical Introduction*. University of California Press, 1976.

Sexton, John. "Difference and Disability: On the Logic of Naming in the Icelandic Sagas." *Disability in the Middle Ages: Reconsiderations and Reverberations*, edited by Joshua R. Eyler. Ashgate, pp. 149–63.

Wheatley, Edward. *Stumbling Blocks Before the Blind: Medieval Constructions of a Disability*. University of Michigan Press, 2010.

Sá atburðr varð þrim vetrum síðar á Þing-skálaþingi at Ámundi inn blindi var á þingi, Hǫskuldsson, Njálssonar. Hann lét leiða sik búða í meðal. Hann kom í búð þá, er Lýtingr var inni af Sámsstǫðum; hann lætr leiða sik inn í búðina og þar fyrir, sem Lýtingr sat.

Hann mælti: "Er hér Lýtingr af Sáms-stǫðum?"

"Hvað villtú þú mér?" segir Lýtingr.

"Ek vil vita," segir Ámundi, "hverju þú vil bœta mér fǫður minn. Ek em laungetinn, ok hefi ek við engum bótum tekit."

"Bœtt hefi ek víg fǫður þíns fullum bó-tum," segir Lýtingr, "ok tók við fǫðurfaðir þinn ok fǫðurbrœðr, en brœðr mínir váru ógildir. Ok varð bæði, at ek hafða illa til gǫrt, enda kom ek hart niðr."

"Ekki spyr ek at því," segir Ámundi, "at þú hefir bœtt þeim; veit ek, at þér eruð sáttir. Ok spyr ek at því, hverju þú vill mér bœta."

"Alls engu," segir Lýtingr.

"Eigi skil ek," segir Ámundi, "at þat muni rétt fyrir guði, svá nær hjarta sem þú hefir mér hǫggvit; enda kann ek at segja þér, ef ek væra heileygr báðum augum, at hafa skylda ek annathvárt fyrir fǫður minn fébœtr eða mannhefndir, enda skipti guð með okkr!"

Eptir þat gekk hann út, en er hann kom í búðardyrrin, snýsk hann innar eptir búðinni; þá lukusk upp augu hans.

Þá mælti hann: "Lofaðr sé guð, dróttinn minn! Sér nú, hvat hann vill."

Eptir þat hleypr hann innar eptir búðinni, þar til er hann kemr fyrir Lýting, ok hǫggr øxi í hǫfuð honum, svá at hon stóð á hamri, ok kippir at sér øxinni; Lýtingr fell áfram ok var þegar dauðr. Ámundi gengr út í búðardyr-rin, ok er hann kom í þau spor in sǫmu, sem upp hǫfðu lokizk augu hans, þá lukusk aptr, ok var hann alla ævi blindr síðan.

Eptir þat lætr hann fylgja sér til Njáls ok sona hans; segir hann þeim víg Lýtings.

"Ekki má saka þik um slíkt," segir Njáll, "því at slíkt er mjǫk á kveðit, en viðvǫrunarvert,

That event happened three winters after at the Thingskala-Thing[02] that Amund the blind was at the Thing; he was the son of Hauskuld[3] Njal's son. He made men lead him about among the booths, and so he came to the booth inside which was Lyting of Samst-ede. He made them lead him into the booth till he came before Lyting.

"Is Lyting of Samstede here?" he asked.

"What dost thou want?" says Lyting.

"I want to know," says Amund, "what atonement thou wilt pay me for my father, I am base-born, and I have touched no fine."

"I have atoned for the slaying of thy fa-ther," says Lyting, "with a full price, and thy father's father and thy father's brothers took the money; but my brothers fell without a price as outlaws; and so it was that I had both done an ill-deed, and paid dear for it."

"I ask not," says Amund, "as to thy hav-ing paid an atonement to them. I know that ye two are now friends, but I ask this, what atonement thou wilt pay to me?"

"None at all," says Lyting.

"I cannot see,"[4] says Amund, "how thou canst have right before God, when thou hast stricken me so near the heart; but all I can say is, that if I were blessed with the sight of both my eyes, I would have either a money fine for my father, or revenge man for man; and so may God judge between us."

After that he went out; but when he came to the door of the booth, he turned short round towards the inside. Then his eyes were opened, and he said—

"Praised be the Lord! now I see[5] what His will is."

With that he ran straight into the booth until he comes before Lyting, and smites him with an axe on the head, so that it sunk in up to the hammer, and gives the axe a pull to-wards him. Lyting fell forwards and was dead at once. Amund goes out to the door of the booth, and when he got to the very same spot on which he had stood when his eyes were

Thingskala-Thing [Þing] *an assembly*

ef slíkir atburðir verða, at stinga eigi af stokki við þá, er svá nær standa."

Síðan bauð Njáll sætt frændum Lýtings. Hǫskuldr Hvítanessgoði átti hlut, at þeir skyldi taka bótina, ok var þá lagit málit í gerð; fellu hálfar bœtr niðr fyrir sakastaði þá, er hann þótti á eiga. Eptir þat gengu menn til tryggða, ok veittu frændr Lýtings Ámunda tryggðir.

Menn riðu heim af þingi, ok er nú kyrrt lengi.

opened, lo! they were shut again, and he was blind all his life after.

Then he made them lead him to Njal and his sons, and he told them of Lyting's slaying.

"Thou mayest not be blamed for this," says Njal, "for such things are settled by a higher power; but it is worth while to take warning from such events, lest we cut any short who have such near claims as Amund had."

After that Njal offered an atonement to Lyting's kinsmen. Hauskuld the Priest[6] of Whiteness had a share in bringing Lyting's kinsmen to take the fine, and then the matter was put to an award, and half the fines fell away for the sake of the claim which he seemed to have on Lyting.

After that men came forward with pledges of peace and good faith, and Lyting's kinsmen granted pledges to Amund. Men rode home from the Thing; and now all is quiet for a long while.

Endnotes

1   The Icelandic text is from the edition of *Brennu-Njáls saga* in Íslenzk fornrit XII, 272–74, published by Hið íslenzka fornritafélag in 1954, and is used with permission from the publisher. The English translation is by George Webbe Dasent, published in 1861 as *The Story of Burnt Njal: From the Icelandic of Njals Saga.* It is in the public domain and was released on the website of Project Gutenberg in 2006. Notes and glosses have been provided by Kolfinna Jónatansdóttir.

2   *Þing* were held regularly in Iceland, both locally and on a national scale on Þingvellir. Chieftains and farmers met at such assemblies and settled their differences and court cases were held there. *Þingskálar* is the name of the place where that particular *þing* was held.

3   Icelandic names are often translated in this manner, the endings are dropped and special characters are changed.

4   Although this looks like a pun in the English translation, the original text uses the verb *skilja*, which means understand, but does not indicate sight.

5   In the original text the verb *sjá* is used, which, like the English verb "to see," can have the double meaning of eyesight and understanding.

6   The Icelandic word *goði* is used for men who in pre-Christian times were at the same time chieftains and priests. After the conversion the word *goði* was used for chieftains and *prestr* for priests, although at times one and the same man could be both. *Hvítanes* is a place name, the whiteness.

The Life and Passion of William of Norwich[1] (1152–70)

Thomas of Monmouth
Contributed by Sarah Edwards Obenauf

Introduction

During Easter Week in the year 1144, William, a twelve-year-old skinner's apprentice, was found dead in Thorpe Wood, Norwich, a town in East Anglia. According to his biographer, Thomas of Monmouth (d. ca. 1173), the boy had been ritually tortured and crucified by local Jews. This is the first such account of ritual murder by Jews in the English Middle Ages, and that aspect of *The Life and Passion of William of Norwich* has dominated recent scholarship about William. However, William's death was not the main feature of these contemporary records, for Thomas documents 110 miracles in seven books, eighty of them concerning physical and mental impairments.

Below are ten representative examples. Most of these pilgrims with disabilities were brought to William's tomb by their friends and family (Books III.vii, V.xiii, V.xvi, VI.v, VI.viii, VII.iii, and VII.xiv), while others traveled to the shrine on their own, both with technological aid (Book VI.xi) and without (Book VII.vi). For example, Gilliva (who is blind) is guided by a cord held by her nephew in Book VI.viii, and Agnes (who is wracked with gout) is brought to the tomb in the arms of her mother in Book VII.xiv. Most of the miracles attributed to William took place at his tomb. In one instance, a woman's cancer is cured by William's intervention at her home but the cancer returns when she fails to take a votive to the tomb; upon making the offering at the shrine, she is cured a second time (Book VII.vi). These examples reveal

that people with disabilities were not on the outskirts of society in the Middle Ages, even if they wished to be cured of their conditions. To the contrary, they were loved and cared for by their families, friends, and neighbors. These rich networks of support carried people with disabilities, sometimes considerable distances, in search of a cure for a variety of ailments.

Thomas' meticulous record-keeping points to a variety of medical conditions as medieval people understood them. Of the eighty miracles dealing with physical and mental impairment in *The Life and Passion*, over twenty-five distinct conditions are discussed, all of which were putatively curable by William's intervention. These conditions include being "bent double" (the seven-year-old girl in Book V.xvi, and Matilda in Book VI.xi) and "dumb" (also the seven-year-old girl in Book V.xvi), madness and demonic possession (the son of Richard de Needham and Silverun in Book V.xiii, Robert in Book VI.v, and a clerk also named Robert in Book VII.iii), kidney and knee pain (Claricia in Book III.vii), blindness (Gilliva in Book VI.viii), "a cancer" (an unnamed woman in Book VII.vi), and gout (Agnes in Book VII.xiv). Other conditions that do not appear in the examples below include deafness, dropsy, dysentery, fever, flux, a goiter, palsy, paralysis, toothache, viper attacks, weakness of constitution, and many unidentified illnesses.

The Life and Passion lends itself to a reading through the lens of disability studies both because of Thomas' careful record-keeping and because the concept of disability is so closely tied to social context. By taking what Thomas says about these miracles at face value, readers can see the social dimension of the conditions (and their purported cures) as well as how medieval people regarded these afflictions as medical conditions. Readers can detect in these examples a difference between disability and impairment, where "disability" is the social construct and can therefore change over time and place, and "impairment" is the physical condition which does not change regardless of time and place. The social construct of disability in the Middle Ages was not necessarily the same as today: these miracles show that it was often the consensus of those present at the tomb which determined whether the cure was efficacious, thus mapping a social dimension onto the impairment (and transforming it into a disability).

Bibliography

Metzler, Irina. *A Social History of Disability in the Middle Ages: Cultural Considerations of Physical Impairment*. Routledge, 2013.

———. "Have Crutch, Will Travel: Disabled People on the Move in Medieval Europe." *Travels and Mobilities in the Middle Ages from the Atlantic to the Black Sea*, edited by Marianne O'Doherty and Felicitas Schmieder. Brepols Publishers, 2015, pp. 91–117.

Rawcliffe, Carole. "Curing Bodies and Healing Souls: Pilgrimage and the Sick in Medieval East Anglia." *Pilgrimage: The English Experience from Becket to Bunyan*, edited by Colin Morris and Peter Roberts. Cambridge University Press, 2002, pp. 108–40.

Turner, Wendy J. *Care and Custody of the Mentally Ill, Incompetent, and Disabled in Medieval England*. Brepols Publishers, 2013.

Wheatley, Edward. *Stumbling Blocks before the Blind: Medieval Constructions of a Disability*. University of Michigan Press, 2010.

Book III.vii

Concerning a certain woman cured of a long-standing sickness.

Not long after this Claricia, wife of Gaufridus de Marc° and niece of the brothers Gerold came to the sepulchre of the most blessed martyr seeking a much desired remedy for her infirmity. This lady had been suffering for some years from pain in the reins° and knees, nor could she be cured by any physicians, though she spent much upon them. But coming to this worshipful sepulchre by means of those who led her there, or rather by the leading of her faith, standing there for a little while she offered up a prayer, and then bending her knees as far as she was able she applied them all bare to the bare stone. And immediately at the touch of it the aforementioned pain in her limbs began to abate so that she felt already the long lost soundness spreading through her limbs. Thus it came to pass that she who came with her feeble body by the hands of others, when the heavenly medicine did its work, went back safe and sound needing no man's support.

Book III.ix

Concerning the boy who being nigh° unto death was cured by the merits of Saint William.

In those days the infant son of Radulfus,° Prior Elias' nephew, was sick unto death and his last hour was at hand. So his father and mother were advised that a candle of the length and breadth of the little boy should be made with utmost haste, and that when it was made they should offer it to Saint William for the restoration of their son, and that without doubt they would receive back their son safe and whole. Wherefore as was advised, straightway the candle was made, and having been brought by the father's hands it was offered as a votive offering at the sepulchre of the holy martyr. The father on his return rejoiced to find his son safe whom a little while before he had given up for dead.

Book V.xiii

Of the cure of a second madman.

I also saw another possessed man healed at St. William's tomb by the divine pity in Whitsun week.° He was the son of Richard de Needham,° and his mother was named Silverun; and one day he was seized by a devil and began to handle himself so roughly that seven men were hardly able to chain him. He remained in this state, bound, for six days, eating nothing, and sleep entirely forsook him. Thus bound he was at last brought by his parents to the oft-mentioned tomb; and as he approached it he suddenly yelled with a terrible voice and said, "What do you want with me? where are you taking me to? I won't go there! I won't go there!" But as he was being dragged thither with some violence he burst his bonds, not by his strength but by that of the evil spirit, and attacking his mother, threw her to the ground and fastened his teeth in her throat. And he would certainly have killed her, had not the people run up and rescued her. Then, gnashing his teeth, and glaring fiercely on the bystanders, he maltreated° frightfully all whom he could reach. A crowd assembled; he was savagely seized and bound, and with his hands and feet tied together, was put down willy-nilly beside the holy tomb. As soon as he touched the sacred spot, wonderful to say, neither by voice nor look did he show the least token of madness. After an hour had passed he gently and meekly asked to be loosed, and was unbound by one of the servants of the Church. Thereafter he behaved himself as quietly and tamely as if he had suffered no touch of madness. In a short time sleep came upon him, and he who for many days had not slept at all, as I said, now rested for some little space.

Gaufridus de Marc *Geoffrey of March*   **reins** *kidney*   **nigh** *close to*   **Radulfus** *Ralph*   **Whitsun week**
Pentecost   **Needham** *a village in Norfolk*   **maltreated** *abused*

On waking, though he had remained many days without food, he now said that he was exceedingly hungry. Food was brought, he ate and drank, and returned home with his parents and friends, sane and whole, in the greatest joy.

Book V.xvi

Of a girl who was bent and dumb and was healed.

On Maundy Thursday° of the same year,° which Christians call the day of absolution, while Bishop William was solemnizing the mass, there came a woman to the tomb of St. William, with a daughter of seven years old, bent double and dumb. The mother put her down by the tomb in the sight of many, and after praying with tears she sat down beside Godiva the wife of Sibald, son of Brunstan, who was also seated there. After some little time, it happened that she fell asleep. Then, an egg happening to be brought to the tomb, the girl, who had never yet been able to speak or walk, arose in the sight of the said Godiva, took the egg, turned to her mother, and said in English: "Look, mother! I've got an egg!" At the sound the mother awoke, and seeing her daughter speaking and walking, burst into tears of joy; and being now assured of her daughter, proclaimed publicly to those present how great benefits the pity of God had conferred on her by the merits of St. William. I ran up and inquired diligently into the facts, and was at once informed by Godiva and many others that they truly knew the woman, and had often seen the deformed and dumb girl.

Book VI.v

Of a second wonderfully mad man who was restored to health.

At another time also we saw a second man out of his mind who was raging fearfully before the tomb of the blessed martyr: his name was Robert, of the parish of St. Michael Conisford at Norwich.° He was subject to attacks of madness at uncertain intervals, and had in consequence come with his mother to St. William, in the hope of being cured. On arriving at the church he began at once to be violent. His mother with tears contrived to coax him into the building and presented him before the martyr's tomb. But when he had sat quietly for a short time beside his mother, who was praying in the presence of a large crowd of spectators of both sexes, he suddenly began to tremble all over as if he were breaking down altogether; and he suffered indescribably. His eyes flashed fire; he emitted frightful noises. The same mouth gave utterance to every kind of sound: forgetting his humanity he tore off his clothes and stripped himself naked; unable to control himself, he exercised enormous strength. The crowd of onlookers were panic-stricken; all were astonished, some wept, others prayed for the patient's recovery. What more? By the intervention, as we believe, of the prayers of the holy martyr, God's pity looked upon the man, drove out the madness of his raving spirit, and gave him sanity for the future. The people were filled with amazement at the miracle, and proclaimed the Divine power to be wonderful in his saint William, and returned to their homes in joy.

Maundy Thursday *The Thursday before Easter*   **year** *the year in which this occurred was 1155, which Thomas mentions in Book V.x*   **St. Michael Conisford at Norwich** *a medieval parish church that was destroyed during the Reformation*

Book VI.viii

Of a blind woman who received sight.

Near the same time, at Lynn in the parish of St. Edmund,° there was a woman called Gilliva, daughter of Burcard a carpenter. She lost her sight by an accident and suffered blindness for three years. To crown her misfortune, such pains and anguish attacked her in the eyelids that for the whole of that time her lashes were always closed, and as it were glued together, and she was never able to open them. At the end of three years she determined to fly for succour to the blessed martyr William, as to her one and only refuge; and this with the more confidence as report had told her that others similarly afflicted had been cured at his tomb. Her young nephew put a clew° of thread in her hand and went before° to guide her, and in this way she reached Norwich and St. William. Standing before the altar she began to pray, and had finished but a little of her prayer when she was interrupted by a sudden and instant attack of pain. Her head reeled, her eyes were smitten with a fiery vapour; she tore her brow and cheeks with her nails, and falling on the ground in agony rolled on the pavement like a mad thing, filling the church with loud and terrifying shrieks. Yet amidst her pain she called aloud with such ejaculations as these: "O gentle boy and martyr William, pity me! many are those on whom thou hast mercy!" A large throng rapidly assembled, who had that day come to the church in procession. All compassionated° her sharp agony; and, moved with pity, poured forth prayers and tears. Both sexes wept, prayed, and cried alike at the pitiful sight. For whose heart could have been so stony as to behold this and refrain from shedding tears? At length after this long torture, at the look of the divine mercy, by the intervention, as we truly believe, of the blessed martyr's merits, the pain began slowly to abate. Then the woman, feeling that the heavenly medicine was on its way, rose, and lifting her hands to heaven, opened those lids which had been before closed, and could not be opened even for a moment, for the pain they gave her. At once a ray, as I may call it, of blood shot from either eye, and therewith the long night of blindness melted away as if at the dawn of a new light. She that had for long not seen, and had desired the light, now saw; and with joy she said, "Now unto Thee, O God most high, creator and amender of all things, and to thee also, William, most holy martyr of God, I pay the thanks and praises I owe, for that I now receive again rest after so great pain, and sight after three years' blindness." With these words she wiped the blood from her eyes and drew near the tomb of the holy martyr. She prayed, and offered a candle that she had brought with her, and, turning to the people, proclaimed that she had received her sight. The bystanders marveled; their sorrow was turned to joy, and all united their voices in extolling the glorious and evident power of the most blessed martyr William, to the praise of God.

Book VI.xi

Of the healing of a certain woman who was wonderfully bent.

There was at that time a woman named Matildis° whom a pitiable weakness had afflicted from her earliest youth. Ever since then, in fact, she had been so weak of body, that owing to the curvature of her spine she was quite doubled up, her legs were twisted together, and her knees pressed one against the other. The consequence was, that when she wished to go from one place to another she had to support her feeble limbs with a

---

Lynn...St. Edmund *King's Lynn, Norfolk. St. Edmund was an early English king who ruled East Anglia from 855 until his death at the hands of Vikings in 869*   **clew** *cord or rope*   **before** *went ahead*   **compassionated** *felt compassion*   **Matildis** *Matilda*

stick and either succeeded in getting a little way, or, sometimes, was not able to do even this. Peter, the priest of Langham,° a vill° of the Bishop's, had long housed her by way of charity, and supplied her with food and clothing. If she ever desired to visit some shrine for the recovery of her health, he used to have her taken there laid like a sack across a horse. But she was always brought back as she had gone, and no good result followed her pains. When the fame of St. William's great virtue was spread abroad, she conceived the hope of being cured by his means, and with eagerness born of confidence took her stick and started for Norwich. Her steps were helped by the fervent emotions of her mind more than by the material assistance of her feet, and she trusted to her own strength less than to the stick that supported her. Each step was hardly a finger's length, and there was considerable delay between them, so that one watching her progress would judge her to be slower than any tortoise. The result was that, though she started on the twelfth day before Lent, she reached Norwich in the fourth week after Easter. At the moment of her entering the cathedral church, she felt the soles of her feet pricked as if by thorns: but when she stood before the tomb of the glorious martyr, and supporting her feeble limbs on her stick raised her hands in prayer, and poured out her whole soul before God, in the midst of her prayer she was interrupted by a sudden attack of pain. The anguish increased, and she rolled upon the ground, beating it with head, shoulders, feet and hands, and filled the church with cries—behaving herself altogether in a marvellous and pitiable manner. Who, I ask, would be so stony-hearted as to stand and look upon this and refrain his eyes from weeping? At last, after all this anguished writhing the violence of the pain

abated, as the raging of the troubled sea is calmed when the mad winds are stilled. So the woman after a little got up, and since she was still in a feeble condition, she made her way to the screen,° and passed along it by clinging to the shafts,° and so finally reached the desired tomb of the blessed martyr. Here, in prayer and thanksgiving, she passed a good part of the day; and then turned to the throng of onlookers and boldly testified to the great things that had been done for her by the merits of St. William. But, inasmuch as a faithless and unbelieving individual was inclined to ascribe the cure to craft° rather than miracle, she vowed that she would not leave Norwich until her aforesaid Sir Peter of Langham should come, and by bearing witness to the truth put an end to the wordy° contentions of unbelief. And this was accomplished; for she awaited the coming of Peter, and he, when he came, bore witness to the truth.

Book VII.iii
Of a mad clerk healed.

I also saw one Robert, a clerk, son of William de Crachesford, who was troubled in his wits, and mad, being brought to the tomb of the blessed martyr by a number of people. After spending the night there with his friends quietly enough, at dawn he was overcome with sleep and, waking about the third hour, felt that his madness and the pain in his limbs were alike appeased.° His friends were rejoiced and rendered thanks to the holy martyr for his recovery, and the people present also exulted at so great and sudden a miracle, for they saw him go away sane, who had come mad.

Langham *a village in Norfolk*   vill *village*   screen *wall enclosing the tomb*   shafts *columns*   craft *deceit*   wordy *gossipy*   appeased *soothed*

Book VII.vi

Of a woman twice cured of a cancer.

In the same vill° of the Bishop's was a woman whose name I have forgotten, who suffered terribly in her breast. It discharged a great deal, and was afflicted with a cancer. She was long troubled with it, and got no aid from physicians; so, despairing of man's help, she betook herself to God's. She took wax, accordingly, softened it at the fire, and in the name of the holy martyr William applied it to her breast, and let it remain there for some time, praying and making vows with tears to the aforesaid martyr. Wonderful to say, the pain abated at once, and the creeping disease ceased to irritate her, while the discharge also was stayed. But as from day to day she put off presenting the wax I have mentioned to St. William at Norwich in accordance with her vow, the disease again attacked her breast more violently than before. Hence I conjecture that the blessed martyr was minded° that her sin in breaking her vow should be expiated° by severe punishment, and that she should be reminded to pay her vow by the trouble of a second attack of her disease. She, then, recognising her fault, took the wax and once more applied it to her breast, and in a short while recovered her lost health. She was more careful for the future, and made haste to go to Norwich, where she offered the wax at the tomb of the holy martyr, paid her vow and returned home in joy.

Book VII.xiv

Of a maid cured of gout.

There was at Norwich a maid eight years old called Agnes, whose father was Bondo, surnamed Hoc, her mother's name being Gunnilda. From her birth she had suffered severely from gout in the hands and feet, being unable to raise herself or even to turn from one side to the other without assis-tance. To make matters worse, the sinews in her neck were contracted and her left cheek adhered so firmly to her left shoulder that you saw the one imbedded in the other, and the neck could not be bent in any direction whatever without bending the shoulder. All these afflictions therefore she suffered: walk she could not with her gouty feet, nor touch anything with her contracted hands, while the adherence of her head to the shoulder deprived her of the wonted° power of seeing, standing, turning, nay, eating: for when she had to take food, it was cut up on the ground or on a trencher,° and she lay down and fed like a beast, able only to eat what her tongue or teeth caught hold of. In this absolutely helpless state she was turned, raised, and moved about by others' help. This poor creature was brought in her mother's arms to the tomb of the holy martyr William at the hour of matins the second Sunday in Lent, and, in presence of the crowds who assembled in greater numbers than usual on that day, by the intercession of the merits of the saint, immediately obtained relief and healing. Hence we ought to consider how great and how merciful is the power of the saints, since it can immediately upon their arrival send back whole those who are destitute of all strength.

---

vill *village (here, Thornage, as explained in the previous chapter)*   **minded** *wished or wanted*   **expiated** *atone for her sins*   **wonted** *customary or usual*   **trencher** *wooden platter for serving food*

Endnotes

1   The text is taken from Thomas of Monmouth, *The Life and Miracles of St. William of Norwich*, ed. and trans. Augustus Jessopp and M.R. James (Cambridge University Press, 1896). The original text is in Latin, and survives in MS Additional 3037 at Cambridge University Library. Those who wish to read more of the miracles should consult Miri Rubin's excellent 2014 translation from Penguin Books.

Testimony from the Canonization Proceedings of Charles of Blois[1] (1371)

Contributed by Leigh Ann Craig

Introduction

Charles of Blois, Duke of Brittany (1319–64), was a descendant of the French royal family via his mother, Margaret of Valois, sister to King Philip IV "The Fair." Though remembered by associates for his deep Christian devotion, Charles spent the majority of his adult life defending his claim to the duchy of Brittany (with the support of the crown) in the War of the Breton Succession (1341–65). This conflict eventually claimed his life in the Battle of Auray in September of 1364. Charles was buried at the Franciscan monastery in Guingamp, where, by 1366, pilgrims had begun to appear at his tomb seeking miracles. By 1368, a canonization inquest began hearing testimony related to Charles' life and deeds, and to the claims of miraculous events at his shrine. The following is an excerpt from the Latin records of that investigation, which were themselves transcribed from the oral, vernacular legal proceedings.

The vast majority of miraculous narratives that appear in medieval European canonization proceedings and miracle collections relate the healing of an illness, injury, or disability. In these excerpts, two different Franciscan friars from Guingamp give their recollections about an anonymous woman's miraculous recovery from a condition that we would categorize as mental illness. The friars each claim this miracle to have taken place in the summer of 1368, about two years before they gave testimony before the canonization inquest. The woman, they testified, had survived a rape, which distressed her so much that she became *furiosa* (mad) or *demoniaca*

(possessed). While the testimony offered by the friars is largely similar, there are narrative differences in the way they describe the woman's recovery which are worthy of our consideration. In particular, one set of testimony would seem to recount a much more abrupt recovery, while the second offers details of incremental improvement in health status which uses the woman's reaction to contact with holy water as the measure.

The text is particularly compelling because it offers a glimpse of medieval people—including clerical observers, family members, and a person with a disability herself—as they attempted to come to grips with an invisible disability (i.e., one which does not mark the surface of the body.) The goal of canonization inquests such as the one in which this testimony was preserved was to discern the truth about a miraculous claim. Investigators sought to discount as miracle any recovery of health that could be explained by natural causes. Invisible disabilities—here, a problem of *mens* (mind) or *modum* (manner, bearing, or behavior)—posed a special kind of problem in this context. In the absence of some pre-extant externally verifiable mark upon a body, it was difficult to verify whether the purported recipients of miracles had experienced an impairment at all, much less experienced a miraculous cure. As such, both witnesses were pressed to explain how they knew that the woman was genuinely impaired. Their answers offer us insight into the contemporary social coding of *amentia* (loss of mind), but also into contemporary norms about the etiology of *amentia* and about trauma.

However, it appears, based on this testimony, that the inquest was not the only source of doubt about the anonymous woman's disability. After her recovery, the woman herself sought written documents to bring to her husband that would offer support of her claims about her former condition. This is particularly interesting in light of the fact that the woman had arrived at the shrine "without a guide." Her solitary appearance sets her apart from the majority of the "mad" or "possessed" recipients of miracles, who were typically conducted to shrines—often by force—by the same people who had consigned them to ropes, chains, or other forms of restraint. This woman, however, interpreted and publicly performed her experience of disability without participation from her family or home community. The friars' letters subsequently provided an authoritative interpretation of her invisible disability that she could use to alleviate doubt from her family.

Bibliography

Caciola, Nancy. *Discerning Spirits: Divine and Demonic Possession in the Middle Ages.* Cornell University Press, 2003.

Craig, Leigh Ann. "The Spirit of Madness: Uncertainty, Diagnosis, and the Restoration of Sanity in the Miracles of Henry VI." *The Journal of Medieval Religious Cultures*, vol. 39, no. 1, pp. 60–93.

Davis, N. Ann. "Invisible Disability." *Ethics*, vol. 116, no. 1, Oct. 2005, pp. 153–213.

Finucane, Ronald. "Authorizing the Supernatural: An Examination of Some English Miracles around 1318." *Aspects of Power and Authority in the Middle Ages*, edited by Brenda Bolton and Christine Meek, Brepols, 2007, pp. 290–302.

Katajala-Peltomaa, Sari, and Susanna Niiranen, editors. *Mental (Dis)Order in Later Medieval Europe.* Brill, 2014.

Turner, Wendy. *Care and Custody of the Mentally Ill, Incompetent, and Disabled in Medieval England.* Brepols, 2013.

Witness 120

Father Paganus de Kelen, priest of the order of Friars Minor of the convent of Guingamp, Diocese of Trecor, of the age of fifty-six years or thereabouts...

...Next, asked about other miracles of the Lord Charles, he said that once a certain mad[2] or possessed[3] woman who was bound in iron manacles, just as demoniacs are accustomed to be bound or chained, came to the church of the said Friars Minor of Guingamp in which the body of the said Lord Charles rested; that woman approached the grave of the said Lord Charles, and a certain friar minor of the said convent sprinkled holy water over her, and at once the said iron manacles or chains fell from the hands of that woman, and she, as if stunned, began to say that she had not been able to tolerate holy water for a great span of time; and accordingly it appeared to him, and it appeared to other bystanders, that she began to regain her sanity.[4]

Asked how he knew this,

He said because he saw it and heard it.

Asked in which year, day and month,

He said that he did not remember; it seemed to him, however, that this was in the year of our Lord 1368, after the feast of Pentecost of Our Lord.

Asked from what homeland the said woman was, and what she was called,

He said this, that this woman, as she began thus to recover, said to bystanders that she was from France, and that he did not recall her name.

Asked what words the said woman uttered, when she thus began to recover and was liberated from the chains,

He said that he did not recall, except in accord with the testimony above.

Asked how infirmity befell the said woman, and how the woman had come to the said church,

He said that he had heard it said, and that it was confirmed by that woman after she began to recover her sanity, that she, while married, had been raped by some man of high rank; after which she was so disturbed,[5]

and also fearful lest her husband have hate for her because of this thing, that she was made out of her mind[6] and possessed; and that seeing this same woman, some of her neighbors said that she ought to go to Lord Charles and that she would regain her sanity; which she said she did not know how to do, but that it seemed to her that she proceeded day and night by roads, fields and woodlands, and traveled without a guide, until she found her way to the aforesaid church, and she held firmly that she achieved this by the merits of the same Lord Charles.

Asked if he had seen her before this,

He said no. He said, however, that he saw her in the aforesaid church for nine continuous days after the time when she was freed from the bindings or iron manacles; and that the said woman heard Mass in the said church each day, and approached the tomb of the said Lord Charles and kissed it devoutly; and so it seemed to this witness that at the end of the said nine days the said woman was totally healed, such that this could be seen. And then this woman sought testimonial letters from the brothers of the said house to show to her husband, as to how she had been there, and how she had also been healed. Some of the brothers gave this woman the aforesaid letters, which she took, and left that place, and afterwards this witness says he has not seen her.

Asked who was present, when the said woman began to recover her health/sanity,

He said Brother Derianus Parvi of the said convent and many other brothers of the convent, and many laypeople whose names he does not remember.

Asked if the woman was truly out of her mind and mad, or possessed, or pretended to be mad or possessed,

He said that he believed by his oath that the said woman was truly and not falsely possessed or mad. He also believed that she came miraculously to the said place and was healed by the merits of the Lord Charles.

Asked why he believed that she was truly possessed or mad,

He said, because she was thusly tied up, and because of her manner[7] and her deeds, and because she was pale of face, and had her hair loose over her arms, and because of the other things to which he testified above. And because all who beheld her held her to be possessed and mad. And they reported and honored all of the above by public voice and fame in the village of Guingamp, and in neighboring areas in which it was discussed.

Witness 125

Father Derianus Parvi, Order of the Friars Minor of the convent of Guingamp in the diocese of Trecor, of the age of fifty-six years or thereabouts...

...Also he said that he saw a certain demented and mad woman; this woman was bound in iron chains, with her hair hanging down around her neck to her shoulders, and she alone, without a guide, inclined herself to come directly to the grave of the said Lord Charles, and stretched out her hands towards the said grave, and as it seemed to that witness, slept for a little while; and roused afterwards, the said woman rose up freed from the said chains; and then one of the said brothers, whose name he did not recall, sprinkled her with holy water, and the said woman said, "holy water does harm[8] to me;" and after a small interval this witness sought from her if at that time it did harm to her? To which the woman responded, "Not so great as before." Afterwards, holy water was given to her again, and she said it did no harm to her. He said also that the said woman stayed for nine days in the said village of Guingamp, visiting the shrine of the said Lord Charles each day, and by the merits of the said Lord Charles was healed, and cured, and freed from madness and infirmity.

Asked how he knew that she was mad,

He said because this woman appeared to be to him by her manner and deeds; and because she was tied up, and all who saw her judged her to be out of her mind.

Asked how the said woman fell into this infirmity,

He said that he did not know, except according to what he heard said about her, which is to say that she was raped and violently assaulted by someone of high rank.

Asked in what year, what month, what day, and who was present when she was thus healed,

He said that two years ago from the present twenty-sixth of the month of September in the year of our Lord 1371, and of the year, month, and day he does not recall anything else. Brother Paolo Quintini, Brother Alanno Guezonesii, Philippo de Vigou and someone called Colober were present for this, and many others whose names he does not recall.

Asked about the name of the said mad person,

He said he did not know her name.

Asked whether he knew her after this,

He said no, nor did he see her after this incident, except for the nine days mentioned above.

Asked for how long the said women was held in the said infirmity,

He said that he did not know, but he heard from her that it was for about three months.

Asked in what place she was born,

He said that according to what he heard her say, she was from the part of France near the diocese or facing the diocese of Le Mans.

Endnotes

1   Translated from the Latin edition, *Monuments du procès de canonization du bieneureux Charles de Blois, Duc de Bretagne, 1320–1364* (Imprimerie de Réné Prud'Homme, 1921), pp. 285–300.

2   *Furiosa*, a general, non-etiological term for loss of mind (comparable to "crazy" in modern English usage) that carries a connotation of active and aggressive behaviors.

3   *Demoniaca*, literally "devilish" or "demonic."

4   *Sanitatem*, a word meaning both soundness of mind (sanity) and soundness of body (health).

5   *Turbata fuit*, literally translating as "she was stirred up."

6   *Demens*, literally "out of one's mind," and the root of the English word "demented."

7   *Modum*, also meaning "mannerisms" or "bearing."

8   *Malum*, also meaning "evil" or "badness," a word that is nonspecific in connotation and was used across medical, magical, and religious contexts.

On a Miracle of Saint Thomas Aquinas[1] (ca. 1325)

Bernard Gui

Contributed by Leigh Ann Craig

Introduction

Thomas Aquinas (1225–74) was a philosopher, theologian, university professor, and Dominican who is widely considered to be one of the most important representatives of high medieval Scholastic theology. His grave at the Dominican monastery of Fossanova, south of Rome, drew the immediate attention of pilgrims. Indeed, the friars, fearing they would be asked to relinquish the relics of so potentially important a saint, hid his body the day after his death by moving it from a grave near the high altar of their church and reburying it in an adjoining chapel. (They returned it to the original, more honorable location several months later.) Thomas' formal canonization was approved in 1323, amid many reports of miracles. The miracle below appears in the *Life of St. Thomas* written by another important figure of the high medieval Dominican order, the French inquisitor and bishop, Bernard Gui (1261–1331). Gui wrote his *Life* just after the successful canonization of his subject. It seems likely that the events he related here took place within few months after Thomas' death, as the narrative mentions that the grave was in a different location than the main altar of the church.

This miracle is interesting, from a disability perspective, for its careful navigation of medical and theological concerns, especially as they are presented by a well-educated, scholarly man whose career was greatly concerned with the pursuit of truth in a legal setting. Gui is unusual among the author of these sorts of narratives for his use of learned medical terminology in attempting to describe the girl whose illness was healed. How-

ever, his medical observations, while learned, were also uncertain. He refers to three illnesses which appear in the medical compendia of the day: *lethargy* (a state of semiconsciousness), *phrenesy* (delirium from fever or inflammation of membranes around the brain), and *mania and melancholia* (loss of reason from excess humors). Gui suggests that it appeared as though the first of these had developed out of one of the other two conditions. His reference to *mania* is particularly unusual; while the diagnoses of *lethargy* and *phrenesy*, which have concrete external bodily symptoms, appear occasionally in miracle narratives, conditions which might be diagnosed as *mania and melancholia* are usually instead referred to by a number of more legal or pedestrian terms (such as *amens* or *demens*, "out of one's mind"). Gui also chooses not to declare any of these diagnoses as a singular, pervasive, or internal truth; instead, he uses medical terminology to convey something of the girl's external "seeming," and more confidently and colloquially names her condition upon her arrival at the monastery as "half-alive."

Gui's diagnostic caution remains continuous as he recounts the actions and conversations that took place at the grave site, and events turn more clearly theological. While the girl's illness was initially presented as seeming akin to a number of medical diagnoses, she herself eventually explains that it was demonic in origin, claiming that she was "held bound up" by a "black man." (Demons are frequently represented in hagiographic literature as being black, sometimes with explicit, racialized references to sub-Saharan African peoples.) The remainder of the miracle figures the unnamed Aquinas of this vision in a role as healer, who first is mentioned defending the girl from the black man, and then passing his hands over the body of the sufferer before declaring her cured. But even here, the nature of the girl's health crisis is not entirely clear. While the author acknowledges that the girl claimed to have had a vision, he presents those claims not as facts, but as claims made by one person ("she said," and "a vision was given to the girl"), a dispassionate approach which brings to mind the contemporary debates over discernment of spirit and the possibility of false visions. Further, Gui had already established that she seemed to be ill from *phrenesy* or *mania*, etiologies which would suggest that her perceptions might not have been reliable. As such, Gui reports the claim of a vision and also about the outward appearance of both severe sickness and sudden cure, but he never stakes a firm claim about the etiology of the sickness. This caution suggests a strong desire for accurate diagnostic categorization of the girl's experience, especially coming from an author who was familiar with both learned theology and learned medical diagnoses, and was also writing in a celebratory mode about an illustrious member of his own religious order whose canonization had recently been successful.

Bibliography

Craig, Leigh Ann. "The Spirit of Madness: Uncertainty, Diagnosis, and the Restoration of Sanity in the Miracles of Henry VI." *The Journal of Medieval Religious Cultures*, vol. 39, no. 1, pp. 60–93.

Elliott, Dyan. *Proving Woman: Female Spirituality and Inquisitional Culture in the Later Middle Ages.* Princeton University Press, 2004.

García Ballester, Luis. "Soul and Body: Disease of the Soul and Disease of the Body in Galen's Medical Thought." *Galen and Galenism: Theory and Medical Practice from Antiquity to the European Renaissance,* edited by Jon Arrizabalaga, Montserrat Cabré, Lluís Cifuentes, and Fernando Salmón. Ashgate Publishing, 2002, pp. 117–52.

Hollywood, Amy. "Acute Melancholia." *Harvard Theological Review*, vol. 99, no. 4, 2006, pp. 381–406.

Katajala-Peltomaa, Sari. "Demonic Possession as Physical and Mental Disturbance in the Later Medieval Canonization Processes." *Mental (Dis)Order in Later Medieval Europe*, edited by Sari Katajala-Peltomaa and Susanna Niiranen. Brill, 2014, pp. 108–27.

Kemp, Simon. *Medieval Psychology.* Greenwood Press, 1990.

Thiher, Allen. *Revels in Madness: Insanity in Medicine and Literature.* University of Michigan Press, 1999.

In the castle of St. Laurence of the Valley next to the Monastery of Fossanova there
lived a certain girl who was struck by some
loss of mind;[2] because of this illness, in the
time that followed, she was made immobile
like a stone, and she was neither able to eat,
nor to speak, nor to breathe normally. It
seemed as if the infirmity of lethargy[3] had
overcome her out of phrenesy[4] or manic passions.[5] As this illness could not be alleviated
by medical remedies, her father, hearing the
fame of the miracles of Saint Thomas, made a
vow and promised her to Saint Thomas, praying that through his merits that she would
either be removed from life, or healed by
the mercy of God. Therefore he carried the
girl half-alive to the monastery, and in the
church, by permission, she was carried to the
grave of St. Thomas; and he placed her on top
of the grave until the monks had returned
from the monastery's altar in the church, to
which they had gone so that they might offer
thanks. When the father therefore wished to
lift his daughter from the tomb out of proper
reverence, she said this: "Father, do not touch
me, because one great Friar Preacher stands
before me, who heals me, and defends me
from a certain black[6] man who holds me tied
up in this way." The abbot and monks gathered there, and they prayed that by the merits of Saint Thomas (having heard the prayers
of the father), the girl might be freed. Then a
vision was also given to the girl in which the
aforesaid Friar drew both of his hands from
the girl's head down to her feet, saying to her:
"Girl, get up, because you are cured." At these
words the girl got up at once, having been
made perfectly healthy.

Endnotes

1 *Acta Sanctorum*, March I, p. 722.

2 *amentia*, a general term meaning "away from" (*ab*) one's "mind," "understanding," or "reason" (*mens*).

3 *letargia*, a learned medical diagnostic category for semi-consciousness or torpor.

4 *phrenesi*, a learned medical diagnostic category for fever delirium, or inflammation of the membrane around the brain caused by excessive hot humor which caused delirium.

5 *maniaca passio*, literally "the disease of mania," referring to *melancholia et mania*, a learned medical diagnostic term for a loss of reason caused by humoral imbalance.

6 The word used here may also be translated as "evil," but demons are frequently figured as being black in color.

The Prose *Life of Cuthbert*[1] (ca. 721)

Bede
Contributed by Marit Ronen

Introduction

The prose *Life of Cuthbert* was written by Bede around 721, and was based on an earlier anonymous version written between 699 and 705 in Lindisfarne, following the translation of the saint's body. In it, scholars may find a unique intersection of a variety of attitudes towards impairment and disability common in early medieval England. Through the voices of Cuthbert, the anonymous author, and (overlaying them) Bede, often contradicting perceptions of disability are in dialogue with each other. Several chapters dealing specifically with constructions of disability are brought here, in order to showcase the wealth of interpretations employed by early English writers. Four themes run through Bede's constructions of impairment and disability in the text: causes of impairment, moral dimensions of it, caregiving, and agency of impaired people.

Cuthbert was likely himself impaired, for most if not all of his life. Suffering from an injury to the knee at a young age, its maleffects seem to have remained with him from that point on. Throughout Bede's text, there are hints that Cuthbert had a degenerative illness in his leg which caused him pain, flared up periodically, and necessitated his use of a staff for walking. Although the saint's impairment received very little attention from Bede, its influence is nonetheless evident in Cuthbert's quoted attitudes, in healing miracles performed by him, and in the way he was remembered.

Several etiologies of impairment are present in the *Life*. First are natural causes, such as weather conditions, defective diet, or pestilence. Classical theories of the four humors and of miasma (the belief that some diseases were caused by "bad air") as causing disease and impairment were known in early medieval England and were perhaps imported in the mid-seventh century by the Greek Archbishop Theodore and the African Abbot Hadrian who accompanied him, both of whom were learned men.[2] The *Life of Cuthbert* is one example of the transmission of such theories into more popular texts.

Alongside natural etiologies, the Devil was also presented as causing impairment (as in chapter XV)—a view which not only imagined a malignant agent at work, but also transferred impairment into the field of religion, and healing into the hands of religious men (and, to a lesser extent, women). A second perceived cause which had a similar effect was sin. Although not as common as sometimes believed by modern scholars (as has been pointed out by Irina Metzler), sin was nonetheless seen by early English writers, at times, to be the cause of impairment. In his book *Stumbling Blocks before the Blind: Medieval Constructions of a Disability*, Edward Wheatley puts forward the "religious model" as a more period-appropriate way to understand the role of religion in constructions of disability in the Middle Ages. Comparing the medical model with the authority of the church over the care and cure of impaired people, Wheatley portrays the church as controlling the lives of impaired people through alms-giving and confession, and utilizing their bodies for the benefit (financial and cultural) of the church. As a result, he writes, impaired bodies became "docile bodies" in the Christian community. It was through this model that impairment was most often transformed into disability in the Middle Ages.

The *Life of Cuthbert* is especially interesting on the issue of moral culpability. It both attests to such views' existence—for example in chapter II, wherein Cuthbert explains his own impairment by saying: "were I not, for my sins, held bound by this infirmity," or in chapter XXIII, which includes a reference to impaired people being denied cure due to their unworthiness—and at the same time resists it—as in chapter XV, in which Cuthbert explains: "for not only the wicked but the innocent are sometimes permitted by God to be afflicted in body."

Morals and spirituality and their relation to impairment are relatively common subjects in Bede's *Life of Cuthbert*, especially in the context of the moral character of impaired people and of purifying pain. The question of the relationship between impairment, sin, and sainthood appears in almost all chapters of the *Life* dealing with impairment, and it is difficult to draw one coherent conclusion. At times we seem to hear the voice of Cuthbert, at others those of his brethren; sometimes popular attitudes are preserved in the text, and sometimes Bede's own views are presented.

As mentioned, sin could be considered a cause of impairment, but not all impaired people were believed to have sinned. This is articulated by Cuthbert in chapter XV (see above), and can be seen throughout the *Life*, as most people miraculously healed by the saint are said to have been religious or good Christians. Further positing impairment, not only as morally neutral but even beneficial, are stories such as that of Herebert (chapter XXVIII), who in order to join Cuthbert in the rewards of the afterlife on an equal footing had to first undergo a period of impairment—not as punishment for sins, but as a kind of purifying pain, almost martyrdom.

A third issue appearing often in the text is that of caregiving. It is possible to identify a variety of caregivers—parents, servants, spouses, friends and neighbors—and the emphasis is on the community at large as the provider of care and support. In a society which did not have hospitals (or, as some have suggested, had very few),[3] care was provided amongst the community and by the community. This does not appear didactically in the *Life*, but rather as off-handed details, which suggests care by the community was an established norm. The beneficial influences of the integration of impaired people in normative life are evident in the text.

Also evident is the struggle between physicians and miracle workers: often Bede mentions a failed attempt by physicians to heal an impairment, followed by a triumph of the healing power of God and the saints. Even in such cases as in chapter XLV, when the physicians in question were part of the community at Lindisfarne (an evidence to the concentration of medical professionals and knowledge in monasteries), God was the only reliable source of healing. This was doubtless a result of the role of the *Life* in advertising Cuthbert's tomb as a pilgrimage site, in the ever-growing competition for pilgrims and donations so common in medieval hagiographies.

Finally, a fourth important point arising from the *Life* is that of the agency of people with impairments and their control over the healing process. In some cases, miracle seekers display high levels of agency, including the ability to explain their own condition, to decide on a course of action, and to command others. In other cases, the agency of individuals was curbed, and at times they are completely silent in the narrative. When considering the subject of agency, it is important to remember the conventions of the genre, which often treated all miracle seekers as objects to be acted upon; additionally, Bede's preoccupation with status and authority could have also influenced his presentation of agency in the narrative.

In order to better understand the complexity of this important issue, a short comparison of one episode from the two prose versions of the *Life of Cuthbert* will be illuminating. In the anonymous version, on which Bede had based his own, appears the story of a paralyzed youth brought to Lindisfarne for treatment. When the physicians at the monastery were unable to help him, the youth took matters into his own hands.

> When the boy saw himself deserted by human doctors, he said to his servant with lamentations and tears: 'This powerlessness and mortification first began from my feet and so spread through all my members. So I ask the abbot for the shoes which were on the feet of the holy and incorruptible martyr of God.' According to his counsel, the servant brought the shoes and he put them on his feet that night and rested.[4]

This version of events ascribes very high levels of agency to the youth. In contrast, in Bede's version (chapter XLV below) the level of the youth's agency is very different.

> Being thus given over by all worldly physicians, he had recourse to Him who is in heaven, who, when He is sought out in truth, is kind towards all our iniquities, and heals all our sicknesses. The poor man begged of his attendant to bring him something which had come from the incorruptible body of the holy man; for he believed that by means thereof he might, with the blessing of God, return to health. The attendant, having first consulted the abbot, brought the shoes which the man of God had worn in the tomb, and having stripped the poor man's feet naked, put them upon him; for it was in his feet that the palsy had first attacked him.

This version eliminates almost all signs of the youth's control over his condition, his care, and his cure. This is not to say that Bede's version of the *Life* stripped people with impairments of their agency completely and always. Rather, it shows how other factors—in this case the youth's subordination to a monastic hierarchy—could alter the narrative in ways which might distort our view.

To summarize, Bede's *Life of Cuthbert* offers a unique window into the complex nexus of perceptions of disability in early medieval England, and which could be found in even only one source. It also allows us a (filtered) view of the lived realities and experiences of people with impairments, and their thoughts and feelings as well as those of their loved ones.

Bibliography

Bayless, Martha. *Sin and Filth in Medieval Culture: The Devil in the Latrine.* Routledge, 2013.

Craig, Elizabeth, and Jo Buckberry. "Investigating Social Status Using Evidence of Biological Status: A Case Study from Raunds Furnells." *Burial in Later Anglo-Saxon England, c. 650–1100 AD,* edited by Jo Buckberry and Annia K. Cherryson. Oxbow Books, 2010, pp. 128–42.

Crawford, Sally. "Differentiation in the Later Anglo-Saxon Burial Ritual on the Basis of Mental or Physical Impairment: a Documentary Perspective." *Burial in Later Anglo-Saxon England, c. 650–1100 AD,* edited by Jo Buckberry and Annia K. Cherryson. Oxbow Books, 2010, pp. 93–102.

Gleeson, Brendan. *Geographies of Disability.* Routledge, 1999.

Lee, Christina. "Body and Soul: Disease and Impairment in Anglo-Saxon England." *The Material Culture of Daily Living in the Anglo-Saxon World,* edited by Maren Clegg Hyer and Gale R. Owen-Crocker. University of Exeter Press, 2011, pp. 293–309.

———. "Disability." *A Handbook of Anglo-Saxon Studies,* edited by Jacqueline Stodnick and Renée Trilling. Wiley-Blackwell, 2012, pp. 23–38.

Looy, Heather. "Embodied and Embedded Morality: Divinity, Identity, and Disgust." *Zygon*, vol. 39, 2004, pp. 219–35.

Metzler, Irina. *Disability in Medieval Europe: Thinking about Physical Impairment during the High Middle Ages, c. 1100–1400*. Routledge, 2006.

Reindal, Solveig Magnus. "Independence, Dependence, Interdependence: Some Reflections on the Subject and Personal Autonomy." *Disability & Society*, vol. 14, no. 3, 1999, pp. 353–67.

Tovey, Beth. "Kingly Impairments in Anglo-Saxon Literature: God's Curse and God's Blessing." *Disability in the Middle Ages: Reconsiderations and Reverberations*, edited by Joshua Eyler. Routledge, 2010, pp. 135–48.

Wheatley, Edward. *Stumbling Blocks Before the Blind: Medieval Constructions of a Disability*. University of Michigan Press, 2010.

Chapter II

How He Became Lame with a Swelling in His Knee, and Was Cured by an Angel

But because to everyone who hath shall be given, and he shall have abundance;[5] that is, to everyone who hath the determination and the love of virtue, shall be given, by Divine Providence, an abundance of these things; since Cuthbert, the child of God, carefully retained in his mind what he had received from the admonition of man, he was thought worthy also of being comforted by the company and conversation of angels. For his knee was seized with a sudden pain, and began to swell into a large tumor; the nerves of his thigh became contracted, and he was obliged to walk lamely, dragging after him his diseased leg, until at length the pain increased, and he was unable to walk at all. One day he had been carried out of doors by the attendants, and was reclining in the open air, when he suddenly saw at a distance a man on horseback approaching, clothed in white garments, and honorable to be looked upon, and the horse, too, on which he sat, was of incomparable beauty. He drew near to Cuthbert, and saluted him mildly, and asked him as in jest, whether he had no civilities to show to such a guest. "Yes," said the other, "I should be most ready to jump up and offer you all the attention in my power, were I not, for my sins, held bound by this infirmity: for I have long had this painful swelling in my knee, and no physician, with all his care, has yet been able to heal me." The man, leaping from his horse, began to look earnestly at the diseased knee. Presently he said, "Boil some wheaten flour in milk, and apply the poultice warm to the swelling, and you will be well." Having said this, he again mounted his horse and departed. Cuthbert did as he was told, and after a few days was well. He at once perceived that it was an angel who had given him the advice, and sent by Him who formerly deigned to send his archangel Raphael to restore the eyesight of Tobit. If anyone think it incredible that an angel should appear on horseback, let him read the history of the Maccabees, in which angels are said to have come on horseback to the assistance of Judas Maccabaeus, and to defend God's own temple.

Chapter VIII

How Cuthbert Was Recovered from Sickness, and Boisil, on His Death-Bed, Foretold to Him His Future Fortunes

Meanwhile, as everything in this world is frail and fluctuating, like the sea when a storm comes on, the above-named Abbot Eata, with Cuthbert and the other brethren were expelled from their residence, and the monastery given to others. But our worthy champion of Christ did not by reason of his change of place relax his zeal in carrying on the spiritual conflict which he had undertaken; but he attended, as he had ever done, to the precepts and example of the blessed Boisil.[6] About this time, according to his friend Herefrid the priest, who was formerly abbot of the monastery of Lindisfarne, he was seized with a pestilential disease, of which many inhabitants of Britain were at that time sick. The brethren of the monastery passed the whole night in prayer for his life and health; for they thought it essential to them that so pious a man should be present with them in the flesh. They did this without his knowing it; and when they told him of it in the morning, he exclaimed, "Then why am I lying here? I did not think it possible that God should have neglected your prayers: give me my stick and shoes." Accordingly, he got out of bed, and tried to walk, leaning on his stick; and finding his strength gradually return, he was speedily restored to health: but because the swelling on his thigh, though it died away to all outward appearances, struck into his inwards, he felt a little pain in his inside all his life afterwards; so that, as we find it expressed in the Apostles, "his strength was perfected in weakness."[7]

When that servant of the Lord, Boisil, saw that Cuthbert was restored, he said, "You see, my brother, how you have recovered from your disease, and I assure you it will give you no further trouble, nor are you likely to die at present. I advise you, inasmuch as death is waiting for me, to learn from me all you can whilst I am able to teach you; for I have only seven days longer to enjoy my health of body, or to exercise the powers of my tongue." Cuthbert, implicitly believing what he heard, asked him what he would advise him to begin to read, so as to be able to finish it in seven days. "John the Evangelist," said Boisil. "I have a copy containing seven quarto sheets: we can, with God's help, read one every day, and meditate thereon as far as we are able." They did so accordingly, and speedily accomplished the task; for they sought therein only that simple faith which operates by love, and did not trouble themselves with minute and subtle questions. After their seven days' study was completed, Boisil died of the above-named complaint; and after death entered into the joys of eternal life. They say that, during these seven days, he foretold to Cuthbert everything which should happen to him: for, as I have said before, he was a prophet and a man of remarkable piety. And, moreover, he had three years ago foretold to Abbot Eata, that this pestilence would come, and that he himself would die of it; but that the abbot should die of another disease, which the physicians call dysentery; and in this also he was a true prophet, as the event proved. Among others, he told Cuthbert that he should be ordained bishop. When Cuthbert became an anchorite, he would not communicate this prophecy to anyone, but with much sorrow assured the brethren who came to visit him, that if he had a humble residence on a rock, where the waves of the ocean shut him out from all the world, he should not even then consider himself safe from its snares, but should be afraid that on some occasion or other he might fall victim to the love of riches.

Chapter XV
How He Cast Out a Devil from the Prefect's Wife, Even before His Arrival

But, as we have above related how this venerable man prevailed against the false stratagems of the devil, now let us show in what way he displayed his power against his open and undisguised enmity. There was a certain prefect of King Egfrid, Hildemer by name, a man devoted with all his house to good works, and therefore especially beloved by Saint Cuthbert, and often visited by him whenever he was journeying that way. This man's wife, who was devoted to almsgiving and other fruits of virtue, was suddenly so afflicted by a devil, that she gnashed her teeth, uttered the most pitiable cries, and, throwing about her arms and limbs, caused great terror to all who saw or heard her. Whilst she was lying in this state, and expected to die, her husband mounted his horse, and, coming to the man of God, besought his help, saying, "My wife is ill, and at the point of death: I entreat you to send a priest to visit her before she dies, and minister to her the sacrament of the body and blood of Christ; and, also, that when she is dead, she may be buried in this holy place." He was ashamed to say that she was out of her senses, because the man of God had always seen her in her right mind. Whilst the holy man was going to find out a priest to send to her, he reflected in his mind that it was no ordinary infirmity, but a visitation of the devil; and so, returning to the man who had come to entreat him in his wife's behalf, he said, "I will not send any one, but I will go myself to visit her."

Whilst they were going, the man began to cry, and the tears ran down his cheeks, for he was afraid lest Cuthbert, finding her afflicted with a devil, should think that she had been a false servant of the Lord, and that her faith was not real. The man of God consoled him: "Do not weep because I am likely to find your wife otherwise than I could wish; for I know that she is vexed with a devil, though you are afraid to name it: and I know, moreover, that, before we arrive, she will be freed, and come to meet us, and will herself take the reins, as sound in mind as ever, and will invite us in and minister to us as before; for not only the wicked but the innocent are sometimes permitted by God to be afflicted in body, and are even taken captive in spirit by the devil." Whilst he thus consoled the man, they approached the house, and the evil spirit fled, not able to meet the coming of the holy man. The woman, freed from her suffering, rose up immediately, as if from sleep, and, meeting the man of God with joy, held the bridle of his horse, and, having entirely recovered her strength, both of mind and body, begged him to dismount and to bestow his blessing upon her house; and ministering sedulously to him, testified openly that, at the first touch of the rein, she had felt herself relieved from all the pain of her former suffering.

Chapter XXIII
How Elfled the Abbess and One of Her Nuns Were Cured

But though our man of God was thus secluded from mankind, yet he did not cease from working miracles and curing those who were sick. For a venerable handmaid of Christ, Elfled by name, who, amid the joys of virginity, devoted her motherly care and piety to several companies of Christ's handmaids, and added to the luster of her princely birth the brighter excellence of exalted virtue, was inspired with much love towards the holy man of God. About this time, as she afterwards told the reverend Herefrid, presbyter of the church of Lindisfarne, who related it to me, she was afflicted with a severe illness and suffered long, insomuch that she seemed almost at the gates of death. The physicians could do her no good, when, on a sudden, the Divine grace worked within her, and she by degrees was saved from death, though not fully cured. The pain in her inside left her, the strength of her limbs returned, but the power of standing and walking was still denied her; for she could not support herself on her feet, nor move from place to place, save on all fours. Her sorrow was, therefore, great; and she never expected to recover from her weakness, for she had long abandoned all hope from the physicians. One day, as she was indulging her bitter thoughts, she turned her mind to the holy and tranquil life of the

reverend father Cuthbert; and expressed a wish that she had in her possession some article that had belonged to him; "for I know, and am confident," said she, "that I should soon be well." Not long after this, there came a person who brought with him a linen girdle from Saint Cuthbert: she was overjoyed at the gift, and perceiving that Heaven had revealed to the saint her wish, she put it on, and the next morning found herself able to stand upon her feet. On the third day she was restored to perfect health.

A few days after, one of the virgins of the same monastery was taken ill with a violent pain in the head; and whilst the complaint became so much worse that she thought she should die, the venerable abbess went in to see her. Seeing her sorely afflicted, she brought the girdle of the man of God to her, and bound it round her head. The same day the pain in the head left her, and she laid up the girdle in her chest. The abbess wanted it again a few days after, but it could not be found either in the chest or anywhere else. It was at once perceived that Divine Providence had so ordered it, that the sanctity of the man of God might be established by these two miracles, and all occasion of doubting thereof be removed from the incredulous. For if the girdle had remained, all those who were sick would have gone to it, and whilst some of them would be unworthy of being cured, its efficacy to cure might have been denied, whereas their own unworthiness would have been to blame. Whereof, as I said before, Heaven so dealt forth its benevolence from on high, that when the faith of believers had been strengthened, all matter for detraction was forthwith removed from the malice of the unrighteous.

Chapter XXVIII
How He Foretold His Own Death to Herebert, the Hermit, and by Prayers to God Obtained His Attendance

Not very long afterwards, the same servant of God, Cuthbert, was summoned to the same city of [Carlisle], not only to consecrate priests, but also to bless the queen herself with his holy conversation. Now there was a venerable priest of the name of Herebert, who had long been united to the man of God, Cuthbert, in the bond of spiritual friendship, and who, leading a solitary life, in an island in the large marsh from which the Derwent rises, used to come to him every year, and receive from him admonitions in the way of eternal life. When this man heard that he was stopping in that city, he came according to his custom, desiring to be kindled up more and more by his wholesome exhortations in aspiring after heavenly things. When these two had drunk deeply of the cup of celestial wisdom, Cuthbert said, among other things, "Remember, brother Herebert, that you ask me now concerning whatever undertaking you may have in hand, and that you speak to me about it now, because, after we shall have separated, we shall see each other no more in this life. I am certain that the time of my death approaches, and the time of leaving my earthly tenement is at hand." Upon hearing these words, he threw himself at his feet with tears and lamentations, saying, "I beseech you by the Lord not to leave me, but be mindful of your companion, and pray the Almighty Goodness that, as we have served Him together on earth, we may at the same time pass to heaven to see his light. For I have always sought to live according to the command of your mouth; and what I have left undone through ignorance or frailty, I have equally taken care to correct, according to your pleasure." The bishop yielded to his prayers, and immediately learnt in spirit, that he had obtained that which he had sought from the Lord. "Arise, my brother," says he, "and do not lament, but rejoice in gladness, for his great mercy has granted us that which we asked of Him." The event confirmed his promise and the truth of the prophecy; for they never met again, but their souls departed from their bodies at one and the same moment of time, and were joined together in a heavenly vision, and translated at the same time by angels to the heavenly kingdom. But Herebert was first

afflicted with a long infirmity, perhaps by a dispensation of holy piety, in order that the continual pain of a long sickness might supply what merit he had less than the blessed Cuthbert, so that being by grace made equal to his intercessor, he might be rendered worthy to depart this life at one and the same hour with him, and to be received into one and the same seat of everlasting happiness.

Chapter XXIX
How, Through His Priest, He Cured the Wife of an Earl with Holy Water

When he was one day going round his parish to give spiritual admonitions throughout the rural districts, cottages, and villages, and to lay his hand on all the lately baptized, that they might receive the Holy Spirit, he came to the mansion of a certain earl, whose wife lay sick almost unto death. The earl himself, meeting him as he entered, thanked the Lord on his knees for his arrival, and received him with kind hospitality. When his feet and hands were washed, according to the custom of hospitality, and the bishop had sat down, the man began to tell him about the sickness of his wife, who was despaired of, and besought him to consecrate some water to sprinkle on her. "I believe," said he, "that by-and-by she will either, by the grace of God, be restored to health, or else she will pass by death to life eternal, and soon receive a recompense for so heavy and long-continued trouble." The man of God assented to his prayers, and having blessed the water which was brought to him, gave it to the priest, directing him to sprinkle it on the patient. He entered the bedroom in which she lay, as if dead, and sprinkled her and the bed, and poured some of the healing draught down her throat. Oh, wonderful and extraordinary circumstance! the holy water had scarcely touched the patient, who was wholly ignorant what was brought her, than she was so restored to health, both of mind and body, that being come to her senses she blessed the Lord and returned thanks to Him, that He thought her worthy to be visited and healed by such exalted guests. She got up without delay, and being now well, ministered to those who had been instrumental in curing her; and it was extraordinary to see her, who had escaped the bitter cup of death by the bishop's benediction, now the first of the nobleman's family to offer him refreshment, following the example of the mother-in-law of the Apostle Peter, who, being cured of a fever by the Lord, arose forthwith and ministered unto Him and his disciples.

Chapter XXX

How He Cured a Girl of a Pain in the Head and Side by Anointing Her with Oil

But the venerable Bishop Cuthbert effected a cure similar to this, of which there were many eye-witnesses, one of whom is the religious priest, Ethelwald, at that time attendant on the man of God, but now abbot of the monastery of Melrose. Whilst, according to his custom, he was travelling and teaching all, he arrived at a certain village, in which were a few holy women, who had fled from their monastery through fear of the barbarian army, and had there obtained a habitation from the man of God a short time before: one of whom, a sister of the above-mentioned priest, Ethelwald, was confined with a most grievous sickness; for during a whole year she had been troubled with an intolerable pain in the head and side, which the physicians utterly despaired of curing. But when they told the man of God about her, and entreated him to cure her, he in pity anointed the wretched woman with holy oil. From that time she began to get better, and was well in a few days.

Chapter XXXI

How He Cured an Infirm Man by Consecrated Bread

I must not here pass over a miracle which was told to me as having been worked by his holiness, though he himself was absent. We mentioned a prefect of the name of Hildemer, whose wife the man of God freed from an unclean spirit. The same prefect afterwards fell seriously ill, so that his malady daily in-creased, and he was confined to his bed, apparently near death. Many of his friends were present who had come to console him in his sickness. Whilst they were sitting by the bedside, one of them mentioned that he had with him some consecrated bread which Cuthbert had given him: "And I think," said he, "that if we were in faith to give him this to eat, nothing doubting, he would be well." All present were laymen, but at the same time very pious men, and turning to one another, they professed their faith, without doubting, that by partaking of that same consecrated bread he might be well. They therefore filled a cup with water, and putting a little of the bread into it, gave it him to drink: the water thus hallowed by the bread no sooner touched his stomach than all his inward pain left him, and the wasting of his outward members ceased. A perfect recovery speedily ensued, and both himself and the others who saw or heard the rapidity of this wonderful cure were thereby stirred up to praise the holiness of Christ's servant, and to admire the virtues of his true faith.

Chapter XXXII

How, by Prayer, He Restored to Life a Young Man Whom He Found at the Point of Death on a Journey

As this holy shepherd of Christ's flock was going round visiting his folds, he came to a mountainous and wild place, where many people had got together from all the adjoining villages, that he might lay his hands upon them. But among the mountains no fit church or place could be found to receive the bishop and his attendants. They therefore pitched tents for him in the road, and each cut branches from the trees in the neighboring wood to make for himself the best sort of covering that he was able. Two days did the man of God preach to the assembled crowds; and minister the grace of the Holy Spirit by imposition of hands upon those that were regenerate in Christ; when, on a sudden, there appeared some women bearing on a bed a young man, wasted by severe illness, and having placed him down at the outlet of the wood, sent to the bishop, requesting permission to bring him, that he might receive a blessing from the holy man. When he was brought near, the bishop perceived that his sufferings were great, and ordered all to retire to a distance. He then betook himself to his usual weapon, prayer, and bestowing his blessing, expelled the fever, which all the care and medicines of the physicians had not been able to cure. In short, he rose up the same hour, and having refreshed himself with food, and given thanks to God, walked back to the women who had brought him. And so it came to pass, that whereas they had in sorrow brought the sick man thither, he now returned home with them, safe and well, and all rejoicing, both he and they alike.

Chapter XXXIII

How, at a Time of Sickness, He Restored a Dying Boy in Health to His Mother

At the same time the plague made great ravages in those parts, so that there were scarcely any inhabitants left in villages and places which had been thickly populated, and some towns were wholly deserted. The holy father Cuthbert, therefore, went round his parish, most assiduously ministering the word of God, and comforting those few who were left. But being arrived at a certain village, and having there exhorted all whom he found there, he said to his attendant priest, "Do you think that any one remains who has need that we should visit and converse with him? Or have we now seen all here, and shall we go elsewhere?" The priest looked about, and saw a woman standing afar off, one of whose sons had died but a little time before, and she was now supporting another at the point of death, whilst the tears trickling down her cheek bore witness to her past and present affliction. He pointed her out to the man of God, who immediately went to her, and, blessing the boy, kissed him, and said to his mother, "Do not fear nor be sorrowful; for your child shall be healed and live, and no one else of your household shall die of this

pestilence." To the truth of which prophecy the mother and son, who lived a long time after that, bore witness.

Chapter XXXVII

Of the Temptations which He Underwent in His Sickness, and His Orders concerning His Burial

The solemn day of the nativity of our Lord was scarcely over, when the man of God, Cuthbert, returned to his dwelling on the island. A crowd of monks were standing by as he entered into the ship; and one of them, an old and venerable monk, strong in faith but weak in body, in consequence of a dysentery, said to him, "Tell us, my lord bishop, when we may hope for your return." To this plain question, he replied as plainly, "When you shall bring my body back here." When he had passed about two months in the enjoyment of his rest, and had as usual subdued both his body and mind with his accustomed severity, he was suddenly seized with illness, and began to prepare for the joy of everlasting happiness, through pain and temporal affliction. I will describe his death in the words of him who related it to me, namely, his attendant priest Herefrid, a most religious man, who also at that time presided over the monastery of Lindisfarne, in the capacity of abbot.

"He was brought to the point of death," said he, "after having been weakened by three weeks of continued suffering. For he was taken ill on the fourth day of the week; and again on the fourth day of the week his pains were over, and he departed to the Lord. But when I came to him on the first morning after his illness began—(for I had also arrived at the island with the brethren three days before)—in my desire to obtain his blessing and advice as usual, I gave the customary signal of my coming, and he came to the window, and replied to my salutation with a sigh. 'My lord bishop,' said I, 'what is the matter with you? Has your indisposition come upon you this last night?' 'Yes,' said he, 'indisposition has come upon me.' I thought that he was speaking of an old complaint, which vexed him almost every day, and not of a new malady; so, without making any more inquiries, I said to him, 'Give us your blessing, for it is time to put to sea and return home.' 'Do so,' replied he; 'go on board, and return home in safety. But, when the Lord shall have taken my spirit, bury me in this house, near my oratory, towards the south, over against the eastern side of the holy cross, which I have erected there. Towards the north side of that same oratory is a sarcophagus under the turf, which the venerable Abbot Cudda formerly gave me. You will place my body therein, wrapping it in linen, which you will find in it. I would not wear it whilst I was alive, but for the love of that highly favored woman, who sent it to me, the Abbess Verca, I have preserved it to wrap my corpse in.' On hearing these words, I replied, 'I beseech you, father, as you are weak, and talk of the probability of your dying, to let some of the brethren remain here to wait on you.' 'Go home now,' said he 'but return at the proper time.' So I was unable to prevail upon him, notwithstanding the urgency of my entreaties; and at last I asked him when we should return to him. 'When God so wills it,' said he, 'and when He Himself shall direct you.' We did as he commanded us; and having assembled the brethren immediately in the church, I had prayers offered up for him without intermission; 'for,' said I, 'it seems to me, from some words which he spoke, that the day is approaching on which he will depart to the Lord.'

"I was anxious about returning to him on account of his illness, but the weather prevented us for five days; and it was ordered so by God, as the event showed. For God Almighty, wishing to cleanse his servant from every stain of earthly weakness, and to show his adversaries how weak they were against the strength of his faith, kept him aloof from men, and put him to the proof by pains of the flesh, and still more violent encounters with the ancient enemy. At length there was a calm, and we went to the island, and found him away from his cell in the house where we were accustomed to reside. The brethren who came with me had some occasion to go back to the neighboring shore, so that I was left alone on the island to minister to the holy father. I warmed some water and washed his feet, which had an ulcer from a long swelling, and, from the quantity of blood that came from it, required to be attended to. I also warmed some wine which I had brought, and begged him to taste it; for I saw by his face that he was worn out with pain and want of food. When I had finished my service, he sat down quietly on the couch, and I sat down by his side.

"Seeing that he kept silence, I said, 'I see, my lord bishop, that you have suffered much from your complaint since we left you, and I marvel that you were so unwilling for us, when we departed, to send you some of our number to wait upon you.' He replied, 'It was done by the providence and the will of God, that I might be left without any society or aid of man, and suffer somewhat of affliction. For when you were gone, my languor began to increase, so that I left my cell and came hither to meet anyone who might be on his way to see me, that he might not have the trouble of going further. Now, from the moment of my coming until the present time, during a space of five days and five nights, I have sat here without moving.'—'And how have you supported life, my lord bishop?' asked I; 'have you remained so long without taking food?' Upon which, turning up the couch on which he was sitting, he showed me five onions concealed therein, saying, 'This has been my food for five days; for, whenever my mouth became dry and parched with thirst, I cooled and refreshed myself by tasting these;'—now one of the onions appeared to have been a little gnawed, but certainly not more than half of it was eaten; 'and,' continued he, 'my enemies have never persecuted me so much during my whole stay in the island, as they have done during these last five days.' I was not bold enough to ask what kinds of persecutions he had suffered: I only asked him to have someone to wait upon him. He consented, and kept some of us with him; amongst whom was the priest Bede the elder, who had always been used to familiar attendance upon him. This man was consequently a most faithful witness of everything which he gave or received, whom Cuthbert wished to keep with him, to remind him if he did not make proper compensation for any presents which he might receive, that before he died he might render to everyone his own. He kept also another of the brethren with him, who had long suffered from a violent diarrhea, and could not be cured by the physicians; but, for his religious merit, and prudent conduct, and grave demeanor, was thought worthy to hear the last words of the man of God, and to witness his departure to the Lord.

"Meanwhile I returned home, and told the brethren that the holy father wished to be buried in his own island; and I added my opinion, that it would be more proper and becoming to obtain his consent for his body to be transported from the island, and buried in the monastery with the usual honors. My words pleased them, and we went to the bishop, and asked him, saying, 'We have not dared, my lord bishop, to despise your injunction to be buried here, and yet we have thought proper to request of you permission to transport your body over to the monastery, and so have you amongst us.' To which he replied, 'It was also my wish to repose here, where I have fought my humble battles for the Lord, [where] I wish to finish my course, and whence I hope to be lifted up by a righteous Judge to obtain the crown of righteousness. But I think it better for you, also, that I should repose here on account of the fugitives and criminals who may flee to my corpse for refuge; and when they have thus obtained an asylum, inasmuch as I have enjoyed the fame, humble though I am, of being a servant of Christ, you may think it necessary to intercede for such before the secular rulers, and so you may have trouble on my account.' When, however, we urged him with many entreaties, and asserted that such labor would be agreeable and easy to us, the man of God at length, after some deliberation, spoke thus: 'Since you wish to overcome my

scruples, and to carry my body amongst you, it seems to me to be the best plan to bury it in the inmost parts of the church, that you may be able to visit my tomb yourselves, and to control the visits of all other persons.' We thanked him on our bended knees for this permission, and for his advice, and returning home, did not cease to pay him frequent visits.

Chapter XXXVIII

How, During His Illness, He Cured One of His Attendants of a Diarrhea

"His malady now began to grow upon him, and we thought that the time of his dissolution was at hand. He bade his attendants carry him to his cell and oratory. It was the third hour of the day. We therefore carried him thither, for he was too feeble to walk himself. When we reached the door, we asked him to let one of us go in with him, to wait upon him; for no one had ever entered therein but himself. He cast his eyes round on all, and, fixing them on the sick brother above mentioned, said, 'Walstod shall go in with me.' Now Walstod was the man's name. He went in accordingly, and stayed till the ninth hour: when he came out, and said to me, 'The bishop wishes you to go in unto him; but I have a most wonderful thing to tell you: from the moment of my touching the bishop, when I supported him into the oratory, I have been entirely free from my old complaint.' No doubt this was brought about by the effect of his heavenly piety, that, whereas in his time of health and strength he had healed many, he should now heal this man, when he was himself at the point of death, that so there might be a standing proof how strong the holy man was in spirit, though his body was at the lowest degree of weakness. In this cure he followed the example of the holy and reverend father and bishop, Aurelius Augustine, who, when weighed down by the illness of which he died, and lying on his couch, was entreated by a man to lay his hand on a sick person whom he had brought to him, that so he might be made well. To which Augustine replied, 'If I had such power, I should first have practiced it towards myself.' The sick man answered, 'I have been commanded to come to you: for someone said to me in a dream, Go to Bishop Augustine, and let him place his hand upon you, and you shall be well.' On hearing this, Augustine placed his hand upon him, gave him his blessing, and sent him home perfectly recovered.

Chapter XLIV

How a Sick Man Was Cured at His Tomb by Prayer

Lastly, there came from foreign parts a certain priest of the reverend and holy Willibrord Clement, bishop of the Fresons, who, whilst he was stopping at the monastery, fell into a severe illness, which lasted so long, that his life was despaired of. Overcome with pain, he seemed unable either to live or die, until, thinking on a happy plan, he said to his attendant, "Lead me, I beg of you, to-day after mass," (for it was Sunday,) "to the body of the holy man of God, to pray: I hope his intercession may save me from these torments, so that I may either return whole to this life, or die, and go to that which is everlasting." His attendant did as he had asked him, and with much trouble led him, leaning on a staff, into the church. He there bent his knees at the tomb of the holy father, and, with his head stooping towards the ground, prayed for his recovery; when, suddenly, he felt in all his limbs such an accession of strength from the incorruptible body of the saint, that he rose up from prayer without trouble, and returned to the guests' chamber without the assistance of the conductor who had led him, or the staff on which he had leaned. A few days afterwards he proceeded in perfect health upon his intended journey.

Chapter XLV

How a Paralytic Was Healed by Means of His Shoes

There was a young man in a monastery not far off, who had lost the use of all his limbs by a weakness which the Greeks call paralysis.

His abbot, knowing that there were skillful physicians in the monastery of Lindisfarne, sent him thither with a request that, if possible, he might be healed. The brethren, at the instance of their own abbot and bishop also, attended to him with the utmost care, and used all their skill in medicine, but without effect, for the malady increased daily, insomuch that, save his mouth, he could hardly move a single limb. Being thus given over by all worldly physicians, he had recourse to Him who is in heaven, who, when He is sought out in truth, is kind towards all our iniquities, and heals all our sicknesses. The poor man begged of his attendant to bring him something which had come from the incorruptible body of the holy man; for he believed that by means thereof he might, with the blessing of God, return to health. The attendant, having first consulted the abbot, brought the shoes which the man of God had worn in the tomb, and having stripped the poor man's feet naked, put them upon him; for it was in his feet that the palsy had first attacked him. This he did at the beginning of the night, when bedtime was drawing near. A deep sleep immediately came over him; and as the stillness of night advanced, the man felt a palpitation in his feet alternately, so that the attendants, who were awake and looking on, perceived that the virtue of the holy man's relics was beginning to exert its power, and that the desired restoration of health would ascend upwards from the feet. As soon as the monastery bell struck the hour of midnight prayer, the invalid himself was awakened by the sound and sat up. He found his nerves and the joints of his limbs suddenly endowed with inward strength: his pains were gone; and perceiving that he was cured, he arose, and in a standing posture spent the whole time of the midnight or matins song in thanksgiving to God. In the morning he went to the cathedral, and in the sight of all the congratulating brethren he went round all the sacred places, offering up prayers and the sacrifice of praise to his Savior. Thus it came to pass, that, by a most wonderful vicissitude of things, he, who had been carried thither weak and borne upon a cart, returned home sound in his own strength, and with all his limbs strengthened and confirmed. Wherefore it is profitable to bear in mind that this change was the work of the right hand of the Most High, whose mighty miracles never cease from the beginning of the world to show themselves forth to mankind.

Chapter XLVI
How the Hermit Felgeld Was Cured of Swelling in the Face by Means of the Covering of the Wall of the Man of God's House

Nor do I think I ought to omit the heavenly miracle which the Divine mercy showed by means of the ruins of the holy oratory, in which the venerable father went through his solitary warfare in the service of the Lord. Whether it was effected by the merits of the same blessed father Cuthbert, or his successor Ethelwald, a man equally devoted to the Lord, the Searcher of the heart knows best. There is no reason why it may not be attributed to either of the two, in conjunction with the faith of the most holy father Felgeld; through whom and in whom the miraculous cure, which I mention, was effected. He was the third person who became tenant of the same place and its spiritual warfare, and, at present more than seventy years old, is awaiting the end of this life, in expectation of the heavenly one.

When, therefore, God's servant Cuthbert had been translated to the heavenly kingdom, and Ethelwald had commenced his occupation of the same island and monastery, after many years spent in conversation with the monks, he gradually aspired to the rank of anchoritic perfection. The walls of the aforesaid oratory, being composed of planks somewhat carelessly put together, had become loose and tottering by age, and, as the planks separated from one another, an opening was afforded to the weather. The venerable man, whose aim was rather the splendor of the heavenly than of an earthly mansion, having taken hay, or clay, or whatever he could get, had filled

up the crevices, that he might not be disturbed from the earnestness of his prayers by the daily violence of the winds and storms. When Ethelwald entered and saw these contrivances, he begged the brethren who came thither to give him a calf's skin, and fastened it with nails in the corner, where himself and his predecessor used to kneel or stand when they prayed, as a protection against the storm.

Twelve years after, he also ascended to the joys of the heavenly kingdom, and Felgeld became the third inhabitant of the place. It then seemed good to the right reverend Eadfrid, bishop of the church of Lindisfarne, to restore from its foundation the time-worn oratory. This being done, many devout persons begged of Christ's holy servant Felgeld to give them a small portion of the relics of God's servant Cuthbert, or of Ethelwald his successor. He accordingly determined to cut up the above-named calf's skin to pieces, and give a portion to each. But he first experienced its influence in his own person: for his face was much deformed by a swelling and a red patch. The symptoms of this deformity had become manifest long before to the monks, whilst he was dwelling among them. But now that he was living alone, and bestowed less care on his person, whilst he practiced still greater rigidities, and, like a prisoner, rarely enjoyed the sun or air, the malady increased, and his face became one large red swelling. Fearing, therefore, lest he should be obliged to abandon the solitary life and return to the monastery; presuming in his faith, he trusted to heal himself by the aid of those holy men whose house he dwelt in, and whose holy life he sought to imitate. For he steeped a piece of the skin above mentioned in water, and washed his face therewith; whereupon the swelling was immediately healed, and the [scab] disappeared. This I was told, in the first instance, by a religious priest of the monastery of Jarrow, who said that he well knew Felgeld's face to have been in the deformed and diseased state which I have described, and that he saw it and felt it with his hand through the window after it was cured. Fel-geld afterwards told me the same thing, confirming the report of the priest, and asserting that his face was ever afterwards free from the blemish during the many years that he passed in that place. This he ascribed to the agency of the Almighty Grace, which both in this world heals many, and in the world to come will heal all the maladies of our minds and bodies, and, satisfying our desires after good things, crown us forever with its mercy and compassion, AMEN.

Endnotes

1   Bede, "Life and Miracles of St. Cuthbert," in *Ecclesiastical History of the English Nation*, ed. and trans. J.A. Giles (London and New York, 1910), pp. 286–349. This edition is in the public domain. Glosses and notes are provided by Marit Ronen.

2   J.H.G. Grattan and Charles Singer, *Anglo-Saxon Magic and Medicine: Illustrated Specially from the Semi-Pagan Text "Lacnunga"* (Oxford, 1952), pp. 41–42, 45–47; Lois Ayoub, "Wæta and the Medical Theory of the Humours," *The Journal of English and Germanic Philology*, vol. 94 (1995), p. 344; Malcolm Laurence Cameron, *Anglo-Saxon Medicine* (Cambridge, 1993), pp. 27–28.

3   See Rotha Mary Clay, *The Medieval Hospitals of England* (London, 1909), and work published on the archaeologic site at Nazeingbury [Essex], such as Peter Huggins, "Nazeingbury 20 Years on, or Where Did the Royal Ladies Go?" *London Archaeologist*, vol. 8 (1997), pp. 105–11.

4   Anonymous Monk of Lindisfarne, "The Life of St. Cuthbert by an Anonymous Author," in Bertram Colgrave (editor and translator), *Two Lives of Saint Cuthbert: A Life by an Anonymous Monk of Lindisfarne and Bede's Prose Life* (New York, 1969), pp. 137–39.

5   Matthew 25:29.

6   Boisil (d. 661) was a monk of Melrose Abbey, and Cuthbert's teacher and mentor.

7   2 Corinthians 12:9.

The Miracles of King Oswald from *Ecclesiastical History*[1] (late 9th c.[2])

Bede
Contributed by Heide Estes

Introduction

The Old English *Ecclesiastical History* contains several passages describing saintly miracles in curing illness or impairment. The miracles of Oswald depict the cures of a horse and a young woman followed by a story of a great fire, in which dust from Oswald's place of death, stored in the pocket of a cloak, keeps flames from consuming a single pillar of a house destroyed by fire. What is interesting in these narratives of saintly cures, and comes across particularly clearly here, is that the identity or any details of afflicted person or animal are unimportant. The narratives serve to demonstrate the curative powers of the individual saint. The miracles of St. Oswald provided here are not unique in the conflation of sick humans and sick animals; several other saints are demonstrated as miraculous in curing humans and animals alike. The quick succession of miracles in the passage translated below, from horse to woman to house, foregrounds the way in which the sick person serves as a prop in the narrative, indistinguishable from an animal or even an object. Mitchell and Snyder's formulation of disability as functioning metaphorically is also already visible in the miracle-narrative's elision of any differences between horse, human, and house-beam.[3] The passages narrating saintly miracles suggest that those with illness and/or impairment, whether humans, animals or objects, are interchangeable in their utilitarian purpose to demonstrate the power of saintly intervention.

Bibliography

Eyler, Joshua R., ed. and introd. *Disability in the Middle Ages: Reconsiderations and Reverberations.* Ashgate, 2010.

Singer, Julie. "Editor's Introduction: Disability and the Social Body." *postmedieval,* vol. 3, no. 2 "Disability and the Social Body," 2012, pp. 135–41. doi: 10.1057/pmed.2012.15.

Metzler, Irina. *Disability in Medieval Europe: Thinking about Physical Impairment during the High Middle Ages, c. 1100–1400.* Routledge, 2006.

Wheatley, Edward. "Monsters, Saints, and Sinners: Disability in Medieval Literature" *The Cambridge Companion to Literature and Disability,* edited by Clare Barker and Stuart Murray. Cambridge University Press, 2018, pp. 17–31.

"The Miracles of King Oswald" (Book III, from Chapters 7, 8)

Chapter 7

Oswald the most Christian king of Northumbria ruled the kingdom for nine years, counting the year of the wild faithlessness of the king of the Britons and the hateful turning away from faith in Christ of the English kings, as we said before. When the course of these years was fulfilled, Oswald was killed. A great and heavy battle was advanced by the same heathen king and the heathen people of Mercia, by whom his predecessor Eadwin had also been killed, in the places that is called Maserfield. Oswald had lived thirty-seven winters of fleshly life when he was slain on the fifth day of the month of August.

What the king's faith and the devotion of his mind to God had been were made known after his death through mighty wonders. For in the place where he fought for his land with his people and was slain by the heathens, until this present day, there are famous healings of diseased men and beasts. Then it happened that many men were taking the dirt from where his body fell and putting it in water and giving it to their diseased men and beasts to drink; and they immediately became well. And men so frequently took the dirt, little by little, until a pit had been dug so deep that a man could stand in it up to his neck. It is not a great wonder, that the place of his death gave health to the sick, since in life, he was always quick to give alms to the needy and the infirm, and was their helper in their afflictions. And it was said in days of yore that many great wonders occurred in that place as a result of that dirt, and also from the dirt that had been taken away from that place. But it will suffice us now to hear of two or three.

It happened, not much time after his death, that a man rode by that place. And then suddenly his horse began to grow weary and stand still, and laid his head on the ground, and foam came out of his mouth, and unmeasured pains grew and became bigger, until it fell on the ground. Then the rider

alighted and took off the bridle, and waited there for a while, until his horse became better or he had to leave it there, dead. Then for a long time it suffered with heavy pain and it rolled and writhed in various places, until suddenly it came to that place, where the aforementioned king had been killed. Then there was no delay, until that pain was relieved, and it stopped its unhealthy agitation of its body, and as horses usually do after exhaustion began to roll around, and throw itself onto one side and the other, and soon it got up all healthy and sound, and began greedily to eat the grass. When the man saw that, then he understood with clear wisdom that there was something wondrously holy in that place, where his horse had been so quickly healed. And there, he set a token and marked the spot, and leapt on his horse and rode thither where he had previously intended. When he came there to the men whom he had previously sought, he met there a woman who was a niece [granddaughter] of the head of household: she had for a long time been badly afflicted, lying in bed [afflicted] with infirmity. When the household began to sigh before him about the grim sickness of the woman, then he started to tell them about the place where his horse was healed. Now they immediately readied a wagon and put the woman in it and carried her to that place, and set her there. When she had been set in that place, she became weary, and slept for a little while. As soon as she woke up, she perceived that she had been healed from her bodily infirmity, and asked for water, and washed herself and fixed her hair and wrapped herself in clothing, and with the men that had led her there, turned and walked home, healthy and sound.

Chapter 8

Similarly, in that same time another man came of whom men said he was of the Britons. He was traveling past that same place where the aforementioned fight had occurred. Then he saw part of one place that was greener and fairer than the other fields. Then with wise mind, he began to think and consider, that there could be no other cause for the greenness and fairness of that place, except that there some man had been killed there, holier than anyone else in the army. He took some of the dirt from that place, wrapped in his clothing, because he thought that same dirt might be medicine and cure to sick men, and afterward he went forth on his way. Then in the evening he came to a house and went inside, where the household was all assembled to feast. He was received by the lord of that house, and they showed him a seat and he sat with them at that feast. He hung his garment with the dirt that he had carried on a pillar of the wall. There was a great fire in the middle of the house. When they had long been eating and drinking, sparks flew up on the roof of the house, and it was interwoven with twigs and covered over with thatch, and it happened that that house was all on fire and began suddenly to burn. When the guests saw that, then they fled out in fear, and there was no help that could be given to the burning house, but it burned completely down, except for the one pillar that the dirt was hanging on: that one stood sound and remained untouched by the fire. Then they wondered greatly at that, and carefully searched what that depended on. Then it was told to them that the dirt hung there, that had been taken from that place where the blood of Oswald the king had been shed. That wonder was celebrated and related far and wide, and many men since then sought that place every day, and began to take that gift of healing for themselves and their friends.

Endnotes

1   The Old English Version of Bede's *Ecclesiastical History of the English People*, edited by Thomas Miller, Early English Text Society O. S. 95, 96 (Trübner, 1890). Translated by Heide Estes.

2   This date represents the date of the Old English translation of the Latin text. The Latin manuscripts date to the eighth century.

3   David T. Mitchell and Sharon L. Snyder, *Narrative Prosthesis: Disability and the Dependencies of Discourse* (University of Michigan Press, 2000).

The *Life of St. Margaret of Antioch*[1] (11th c.)

Contributed by Leah Pope Parker

Introduction

According to Christian hagiographic tradition, Margaret of Antioch was a young Christian woman living in late third- or early fourth-century Antioch (near modern-day Antakya in Turkey). In accounts of her martyrdom, Margaret is determined to protect her chastity from the pagan prefect who wishes to marry her and is therefore tortured, imprisoned, and eventually killed. While this is a common narrative structure for hagiography about virgin martyrs, Margaret's legend is unusual in two ways. First, while imprisoned, Margaret defeats not just a devil but also a dragon; in many versions, including this one, she is swallowed by the dragon and bursts out of its belly when she makes the sign of the cross. Second, before ultimately being beheaded, Margaret prays to secure privileges and comforts for those who would venerate her, including that wherever there is kept a copy of her saint's *life*, "Let there not be born a child that is blind, nor halt [with a mobility impairment], nor dumb, nor deaf, nor vexed by an unclean spirit." Margaret's narrative thus brings virginity and childbirth into dialogue with monstrosity and disability. Because of this, Margaret is still to this day considered by many Catholics a patron saint of childbirth, though she was removed from the Roman Catholic Church's calendar of saints' feast days in 1969, due to an absence of evidence for her historical existence. Legends of St. Margaret survive from as early as the eighth century. The Old English version of the *Life of St. Margaret* translated here draws upon Latin sources, and was most likely composed at Canterbury in southern England in the middle of the eleventh century.

Margaret's prayer before her execution that invoking her name or the book of her martyrdom might prevent children from being born with various disabilities draws upon a moralization of disability that is evident throughout the narrative. Repeatedly, the idols said to be worshipped by pagans such as Margaret's father Theodosius or the prefect Olibrius are described as "dumb and deaf." The Old English uses medieval forebears of the modern words: *dumbe* and *deafe*. In religious terms, these labels frame the false gods of pagans as neither able to hear the prayers of their followers, nor able to make any reply. They are thus cast not just as blasphemous, but also as disabled.

The association between sin and disability, and conversely between salvation and health, is embedded in the vocabulary of Christian texts such as this. The trope of Christ the Physician (*Christus medicus*) highlights Christ's biblical miracles of physical healing as parallels for his metaphorical healing of the soul through salvation. In Germanic languages, this evolved into epithets such as *Hælend*, which in Old English means "Healer," but is typically translated in its metaphorical usage as "Savior."[2] In contrast to Latin *medicus*, OE *Hælend* contains within it the word for health or wholeness: *hælu*. Its opposite, *unhælu* or "unwholeness," served as a widespread descriptor of a variety of impairments in early medieval England, including physical, sensory, and cognitive impairments, violent injuries, chronic illness, and bodily forms considered monstrous, such as that of Grendel in *Beowulf*.[3] In order to emphasize the connection between Christ and healing in this text, this translation retains the OE *Hælend*, encompassing both the physical implications of "Healer" and the spiritual implications of "Savior."

The correlation between healing and salvation is crucial context for Margaret's prayer that the veneration of her cult as a saint might prevent children from being born with impairments, as well as the divine response that those who already have impairments will be healed by touching her bodily remains. The text distinguishes between the forgiveness of sins and the healing of the body, but nonetheless parallels them as desirable outcomes in a Christian moral framework; as is often the case in medieval Christian texts, people with disabilities are expected to want to be healed. If any affirming construction of disability is to be found in this model, it is in the collection of a wide range of disabilities under the realm of those that might be healed, including blindness, mobility impairment, deafness, being non-verbal, being "vexed by an unclean spirit" (likely describing many forms of mental illness), those with physical "impairment" (OE *untrumnesse*, literally, "disorder"), and those "in poor health" (i.e., with chronic illness or disease). No single word in Old English encompasses all of these experiences of the body, but their collection together here suggests that they were recognized as all having something in common. There is a nascent sense of community in this grouping, hinting at the possibility of solidarity across forms of impairment and disability that is difficult to locate elsewhere in the Middle Ages. And that community is not as isolated from the general population as we might expect. The impaired body may be stigmatized, but it is embedded in a stigma associated with all bodies, not just those with disability; as Margaret says: "We are flesh and blood, always sinning and never ceasing."

Bibliography

Bruce Wallace, Karen. "*Hælu* and *Unhælu*: The Anglo-Saxons' Concept of the Normate Individual and Its Implications for Impairment and Disease." *The Ashgate Research Companion to Medieval Disability Studies*, edited by John P. Sexton and Kisha G. Tracy. Routledge, forthcoming.

———. "Grendel and Goliath: Monstrous Superability and Disability in the Old English Corpus." *Monstrosity, Disability, and the Posthuman in the Medieval and Early Modern World*, edited by Richard H. Godden and Asa Simon Mittman. Palgrave Macmillan, 2019, pp. 107–26.

Cooper, Tracey-Anne. "Why Is Margaret's the Only Life in London, BL, Cotton MS Tiberius A.iii?" *Writing Women Saints in Anglo-Saxon England*, edited by Paul Szarmach. University of Toronto Press, 2013, pp. 55–81.

Dendle, Peter. "Pain and Saint-Making in Andreas, Bede, and the Old English Lives of St. Margaret." *Varieties of Devotion in the Middle Ages and Renaissance*, edited by Susan C. Karant-Nunn. Brepols, 2003, pp. 39–52.

Parker, Leah Pope. "Eschatology for Cannibals: A System of Aberrance in the Old English Andreas." *Monstrosity, Disability, and the Posthuman in the Medieval and Early Modern World*, edited by Richard H. Godden and Asa Simon Mittman. Palgrave Macmillan, 2019, pp. 227–48.

Skevington, Fay. "The Unhal and the Semantics of Anglo-Saxon Disability." *Social Dimensions of Medieval Disease and Disability*, edited by Sally Crawford and Christina Lee. Archaeopress, 2014, pp. 7–13.

Treharne, Elaine M. "A Note on the Sensational Old English Life of St. Margaret." *Saints and Scholars: New Perspectives on Anglo-Saxon Literature and Culture in Honour of Hugh Magennis*, edited by Stuart McWilliams. D.S. Brewer, 2012, pp. 5–13.

After the Crucifixion and the Resurrection and the glorious Ascension of our Lord, Hælend° Christ, to God the Father Almighty, a great many martyrs suffered, and through that suffering attained eternal rest with the holy Thecla and Susanna.[4] And a great many also were seduced by the devil's teaching, that they worshipped dumb and deaf[5] idols, the handiwork of men, which could provide advantages neither to themselves nor to anyone.

Now I, Theotimus, have learned through the grace of God from a certain number of books and eagerly meditated and inquired about the Christian faith, and have never found in books that any man might come to eternal rest, unless he truly believes in the Holy Trinity, that is Father and Son and the Holy Spirit, and that the Son took the form of man and suffered death for all mankind, just as is said here above. He illuminated the blind,[6] gave hearing to the deaf,[7] and awakened the dead to life,[8] and he hears all those who truly believe in him. Thereupon I, Theotimus, eagerly wished to know how the blessed Margaret fought against the devil and overpowered him and then received that eternal crown of glory from God. Hear now all and witness how the blessed Margaret suffered in the name of God and through that toil came to eternal rest with the holy Thecla and Susanna.

The blessed Margaret was Theodosius' daughter. He was a patriarch of the heathens; he worshipped idols and provided for his daughter. She was filled with the Holy Spirit and through baptism she was renewed. She was given to her foster mother to be raised, near the city of Antioch,° and after her own mother had departed from this life, her foster mother loved her much more than she had before. She was greatly loathed by her father and greatly loved by God.

And when she was fifteen years old, she rejoiced to be in her foster mother's house. She heard of the strife of the martyrs, because at that time the blood of many was poured out onto the earth for our Lord's name, Hælend Christ, and she was filled with the Holy Spirit and entrusted her virginity to God.

One day, when she was watching her foster mother's sheep with other women, who were much like her, Olibrius the prefect was traveling from Asia to the city of Antioch. When he saw the blessed Margaret sitting by the road, he immediately desired her and said to his thane: "Go hastily and seize that woman and ask her if she is free, so that I might take her to wife, and if she is a slave, I will render payment for her, and she will be as a concubine to me and there will be riches for her in my house."

Then the soldiers went and seized her. The blessed Margaret began to call to Christ and said this: "Have mercy on me, Lord, and do not let my soul be undone by dishonorable men, but permit me to rejoice and praise you eternally and never let my soul nor my body become defiled. But send to my right side and to my left angels of peace to open my heart and to respond with boldness to this dishonorable man and these unjust executioners. I am now, Lord, just as cattle in the middle of a field and just as a sparrow in a net and just as a fish on a hook. Help me, my Lord, and hold me and do not forsake me into the hands of dishonorable men."

The soldiers then came to the prefect and said, "Lord, you cannot take her, because she prays to the God who was executed by the Jews." Olibrius the prefect commanded them to lead her to him, and said to her: "Of what kin are you? Tell me, are you free or a slave?" The blessed Margaret said to him: "I am free." The prefect said to her: "Of what faith are you or what is your name?" She answered and said: "In the Lord I am called."[9] The prefect said to her: "Which god do you worship?" The holy Margaret said to him: "I pray to the

Hælend *Healer/Savior*   **Antioch** *modern-day Antakya in Turkey*

Almighty God and his Son, Hælend Christ, who holds my virginity undefiled to this present day." The prefect said to her: "Do you call upon that Christ whom my fathers executed?" The holy Margaret said to him: "Your fathers executed Christ and thus they all perished, but he endures in eternity and his reign is forever without end." The prefect was very angry and commanded the holy Margaret to be enclosed in prison until he thought of how he might destroy her virginity.

The prefect said to her: "If you do not pray to my god, my sword will become acquainted with your body and I will crush all your bones. If you listen to me and believe in my god, before all these people I say to you that I will take you as my wife and for you it will be as well as it is for me." Margaret said to him: "For this reason I give up my body to torment, that my soul might rest with righteous souls."

The prefect then commanded her hung up and with small switches violently flogged. The holy Margaret looked up to heaven and said: "In you, Lord, I trust, that I will not be harmed. Watch over me and have mercy on me from dishonorable hands and from the hands of these killers, lest my heart here be terrified. Send me wholeness[10] that I might be illuminated[11] by my torment and that my pain might come to gladden me."

And when she had prayed thus, the killers beat her pure body so that her blood flowed on the earth like water does from the cleanest wellspring. The prefect said to her: "Alas, Margaret, submit to me and it will be well for you above other women." And all the women who stood there wept bitterly for that blood and said: "Alas, Margaret, truthfully we grieve entirely with you, because we see you naked and your body being tortured. This prefect is a very rash man and he wants to defile you and blot out[12] the memory of you upon the earth. Submit to him and you will live." The holy Margaret said to them: "Alas, you evil counsellors, go you wives to your houses and you men to your work! God is an ally to me. Therefore I do not wish to hear you, nor will I

ever pray to your god, who is dumb and deaf. But believe in my God, who is mighty in power, and he immediately hears those who believe in him."

And then she said to the prefect: "Alas, you vile dog, my God is an ally to me and, though you have power over my body, Christ protects my soul from your terrible hands." The holy Margaret looked up to heaven and said: "Give me strength, Spirit of life, that my prayer might travel through heaven and that it might ascend before your sight. And send me your Holy Spirit from heaven, which comes to me as an ally, that I might hold unstained in my virginity and so that I might confront my adversary, which fights with me face-to-face, and so that this will be an exemplar and inspiration forever for all women who believe in you, because your name is blessed in all things."[13] Then the soldiers went and tortured her body, and the dishonorable prefect wrapped his face with his cloak, so that he might not look at her because of that blood and he said to the woman: "Why do you not obey my word and be merciful to yourself? Behold: your body is tortured at my terrible judgment. Consent to me and pray to my god, lest you be devastated unto death. If you do not listen to me, my sword shall have power over your body. If you do listen to me, before all these people I say to you that I will take you as my wife." The holy Margaret said to him: "Alas, you are a fool! I thus give up my body to torment, so that my soul will be triumphant in heaven."

The prefect commanded that she be enclosed in a dark prison, and when she had gone therein, she blessed all her body with the sign of Christ's cross and began to bless herself with her hands and thus said: "Look upon me and have mercy on me, Lord, because I am alone in here, and my father has forsaken me. Do not forsake me, my Lord, but have mercy on me, because I understand that you are Judge of the living and the dead. Judge now between me and this devil. Behold, I suffer in my torments. Do not be angry with me, my Lord, because you know that

I give up my soul for you. You are blessed in all things."

Then I, Theotimus, was providing her with bread and with water, and I saw through an eye-hole all her strife that she had with that dishonorable devil; and I wrote down all of her prayers.

Out of a corner of that prison there came very terrible dragon of many colors. His hair and his beard seemed golden, and his teeth were like wrought steel, and his eyes shined like precious gems, and out of his nose went great smoke, and his tongue breathed out, and a great foulness he made in that prison. And he reared up and he hissed an immense noise. Then a great light came into that dark prison from the fire that burst from the dragon's mouth. The holy woman became very afraid and bent her knees to the ground and extended her hands in prayer and said thus: "God Almighty, quench the strength of this great dragon and have mercy on me in my need and hardship and never let me perish, but shield me against this wild beast."

And when she prayed thus to Christ, the dragon set his mouth over the holy woman's head and swallowed her. But when the holy Margaret made the sign of Christ's cross inside the dragon's belly, it tore him in two, and the holy woman went out from the dragon's belly unharmed. And at the same time she saw on her left side a devil sitting like a dark man,[14] his hands bound upon his knees. And when she saw him, she prayed to Christ and said thus: "I praise and glorify you, resurrected Christ the King. You are the support of faith and the source of all wisdom and the foundation of all strength. Now I see my faith flourishing and my soul illumined[15] and this dragon fallen in mortal defeat. I thank you, holy and resurrected God. You are Hælend of all healers.[16] May your name be blessed in all things."

And when she had thus prayed, the devil rose up and took the holy woman's hand and said: "You have done enough. Depart from me, because I see you persist in continence. I sent my brother Rufus to you in the like-

ness of a dragon, so that he might devour you and your virginity, and that your beauty might perish and your memory be blotted out from this earth. You killed him with the sign of Christ's cross and now you wish to kill me. But I bid you for the sake of your virginity, do not strike at me." The holy Margaret then grabbed that devil by the hair and cast him to the ground and thrust out his right eye and she crushed all his bones and set her right foot over his neck and said to him: "Stay away from my virginity! Christ is an ally to me, because his name shines in all things."

And when she had said this, there shone a very great light in that dark room and the cross of Christ was seen from earth up to heaven, and a white dove perched on that cross, and it spoke and said: "Speak to me, Margaret, you who through virginity have yearned for the eternal kingdom, which is therefore granted for you along with Abraham and with Isaac and Jacob.[17] Blessed are you that overpowered the fiend." The holy Margaret then said: "You are glorious, Christ, you alone who make many wonders. I glorify and praise you, because you are holy and great in all things, you who deign to reveal to your handmaid that you alone are the sole hope of all who believe in you."

The dove then spoke and said: "Margaret, ask him who you have under your foot about his deeds so that he will reveal all his work, and when you have overpowered him, you will come to me." The holy Margaret then said to that devil: "What is your name, you unclean spirit?" The devil said to her: "You servant of Christ, lift your foot from my neck, so that I might rest my bones a little and I will tell you all of my deeds." The holy woman then lifted her foot from his neck. And the devil then said: "I have seized many honest men and I fought against them and they could not overpower me. But you thrust out my eye and crushed all my bones and killed my brother. Now I see Christ dwells in you and you perform all work in righteousness. I blinded them to faith and I overthrew them from the heavenly happiness, and when they were asleep, I came over them and when I might not take them from their bed, I caused them to sin in their sleep. And now by a serving woman I am overpowered. What shall I do now, when all my weapons are broken? And it troubles me most of all that your father and your mother were mine."

The holy woman said to him: "Tell me now your kind and from whence you come." The devil said to her: "Tell me, Margaret, from whence is your life and your body and from whence is your soul and your faith, or else how has Christ been dwelling in you? Tell me this, then I will tell you all of my deeds." The holy woman answered him and said: "It is not fitting for me that I say anything to you, because you are not worthy of hearing the sound of my voice. The commands of God I desire to hear and proclaim. And you, devil, be silent[18] now, because I will not listen to a word out of your mouth." And immediately the earth grimly swallowed up that bloodthirsty devil.

Then the next day, the prefect commanded that the holy woman be led to him, and when she was going out, she blessed all her body with the sign of Christ's cross. The prefect said to her: "Alas, Margaret, submit to me and pray to my god." The holy Margaret said to him: "Truly, it would be more fitting for you to pray to my God." The prefect then became very angry and commanded that she be hung up and burned with candles and it was done as he commanded. The holy Margaret then called out and said: "I will never pray to your god, who is dumb and deaf. Nor may you overpower a pure woman. Christ himself has blessed my body, and to my soul he will deliver a crown of glory."

The dishonorable prefect commanded there to be brought a great vat made of lead and commanded it be filled with water and made very hot and commanded that holy woman to be bound by the feet and hands and put therein. The executioners did as they were commanded. The blessed Margaret looked to heaven and said: "Lord, God Almighty, you who dwell in heaven, grant me that this water might be health to me and a bath of illumination[19] and baptism, that it might cleanse me for the eternal life and strip from me all my sins and heal me in your glory, because you are blessed in all things." And when this prayer was fulfilled, then there came a great earthquake, and at that same time a dove came from heaven bearing a crown in its mouth and immediately the holy woman's feet and hands were released and she went up from that water, praising and glorifying God, and she said thus: "Glory I say to you, Lord God, Hælend Christ, because you have enlightened and glorified me and you have been merciful to me, your servant. You are blessed in all things." And when she said "Amen," a voice came from heaven saying: "Come, Margaret, to heaven. You are blessed, you who have yearned for virginity. For this you are blessed in eternity." And at that moment, fifteen thousand people among the populace believed, not counting women and children.

Olibrius the prefect commanded the death of all who believed in Christ, and they were killed in the field of Lim, outside the city of Armenia. And after that he commanded the killing of the blessed Margaret and that she be slain with a sword. The soldiers then led her outside the city walls and then one of them said (who was called by the name Malchus): "Extend your neck now and yield to my sword and have mercy on me, because I see here Christ standing among his angels with you." Margaret then said: "I bid you, brother, if you see Christ here, honor me until I pray to him and entrust my spirit to him." The soldier said to her: "Pray however you wish."

The blessed Margaret then began praying and thus said: "God, you who made heaven by hand and who measure the earth in your grasp, hear my prayer that any person who writes of my suffering or hears it read, at that time let their sins be blotted out; or if anyone puts a light in my church from their labor, let whatever guilt for which they ask forgiveness not be tallied among their sins. I ask you, Lord, that if any person might meet your terrible judgment and they might recall my name and yours, deliver them, Lord, out of torment. Furthermore I ask you, Lord, that anyone who makes a book of my martyrdom or has one in their house have all their sins remitted, because we are flesh and blood, always sinning and never ceasing. And furthermore I ask you, Lord, that one who builds a church in my name and there writes my martyrdom or purchases it through their labor, send to them, Lord, the Holy Spirit. And where there is the book of my martyrdom, let there not be born a child that is blind, nor halt,° nor dumb, nor deaf, nor vexed by an unclean spirit,[20] but let peace and love and truth be there. And any who prays there for the forgiveness of their sins, respond, Lord, to their prayer.

Then a voice came from heaven accompanied by thunder, and a dove came bearing a cross and said: "Arise, Margaret, blessed was the womb[21] that bore you, because you have been mindful of all things in your prayer. Through the strength of angels I promise you that it will be as you ask, it will all be heard before the sight of God, and everything you were mindful of, that God grants you. God will set on your church three hundred angels for the purpose of receiving each of those people's prayers, those who call in your name to the Lord that their sins be blotted out. Now furthermore, I proclaim to you that angels will come to you and take your head and lead it into paradise; and your body will be venerated among mankind, that whosoever touches your relics, at that time will be healed from any impairment[22] that he has. And where your relics are or the book of your martyrdom, neither evil nor unclean spirit will draw near there. But there will be peace and love and truth and joy and gladness. And those who invoke your name with all their heart and the shedding of tears, they will be delivered from all their sins. Blessed you are and those who trust in you and in the place where you are going. Come immediately to the place that is prepared for you and sit on the right side of the blessed Thecla and Susanna. Blessed are you who maintained your virginity. Come now, lamb of God, I await you."

The holy Margaret looked at those who circled around her and said: "I ask on your behalf in the name of our Lord, Hælend Christ, that he forgive you of your sins and bring you to empowerment in the kingdom of heaven. I thank him who glorifies and honors me in the name of righteousness. I praise him and bless him who rules in all things."

And after that prayer she raised herself up and said to that soldier: "Brother, take now your sword and slay me, because I will now overcome this earth." He said: "I do not deem that just, nor will I kill a woman of holy God. God was speaking to you in front of me. I do not dare to do this." The holy Margaret said to him: "If you do not do this, you will not have your part of paradise with me." The soldier then with apprehension took his sword and struck off her head and turned and said: "Lord, do not count this as a sin for me," and impaled himself with his sword and fell on the blessed woman's right side. Thereafter a thousand angels came above the holy Margaret's body and blessed him.

Then twelve angels came and took her head to their Father, and they sang and said: "You are holy, you are holy, you are holy, Lord God, Glory-king of hosts, the heavens and earth are filled with your glory." And thus singing, they placed it in paradise. And all those who were in poor health, halt° and blind, dumb and deaf, if they would touch the holy woman's body, they were entirely healed. And the voice of angels was heard over her body, saying thus: "Blessed are you and those who believe through you, because you dwell in rest

halt *having an impairment that affects the ability to walk*

216

until the end with holy women. And be not sorrowful for your holy body, because it is granted on earth that whichever person thus touches your relics or your bones, they at that time will have their sins blotted out and their name written in the Book of Life."[o]

I, Theotimus, took the relics of that holy woman and I set them in a new shrine which I myself had previously made of stone and perfumed with sweet herbs, and I protected her in a certain good woman's house. Her name was Sincletica. I, Theotimus, had ministered to her with bread and with water, and I saw all her strife that she had against those dishonorable devils, and I wrote down her prayer and sent it to all Christian people. And the holy Margaret fulfilled her martyrdom in the month of July, on the third and twentieth day. All that hear this be happy in heart, and those who pray in Lord Christ and believe in him, and think on the holy Margaret that she with her prayers might entrust us to the sight of Hælend Christ. To him may there be glory and love and honor and majesty and power and greatness in the world of all worlds, truly eternal without any end. Amen.

their...Life *granted salvation*

Endnotes

1   The text below was compiled and translated by Leah Pope Parker, from the manuscript, London, British Library, Cotton MS Tiberius A.iii, in consultation with the Old English text available in *The Old English Lives of St. Margaret*, ed. and trans. Mary Clayton and Hugh Magennis (Cambridge University Press, 1994), pp. 112–48. Cotton Tiberius A.iii is available online at http://www.bl.uk/manuscripts/FullDisplay. aspx?ref=Cotton_MS_Tiberius_A_III. Glosses and endnotes are also by Leah Pope Parker.

2   The "Healer" epithet is also present in other Germanic languages; for example, a ninth-century account of the life of Christ in Old Saxon is known as the *Heliand*.

3   See Fay Skevington. "The Unhal and the Semantics of Anglo-Saxon Disability," *Social Dimensions of Medieval Disease and Disability*, eds. Sally Crawford and Christina Lee (Archaeopress, 2014), pp. 7–13; Karen Bruce Wallace, "Hælu and Unhælu: The Anglo-Saxons' Concept of the Normate Individual and Its Implications for Impairment and Disease," *The Ashgate Research Companion to Medieval Disability Studies*, eds. John P. Sexton and Kisha G. Tracy (Routledge, forthcoming); and "Grendel and Goliath: Monstrous Superability and Disability in the Old English Corpus," *Monstrosity, Disability, and the Posthuman in the Medieval and Early Modern World*, eds. Richard H. Godden and Asa Simon Mittman (Palgrave Macmillan, 2019), pp. 107–26.

4   Thecla and Susanna were Christian saints who in the Middle Ages were believed to have lived in the first and third centuries, respectively. Both women were ardent defenders of their virginity: Susanna became a martyr for refusing to marry a pagan, while Thecla engaged in combat and performed miracles to protect her virginity from repeated threats.

5   OE *dumbe* and *deafe*. In translating terms for impairments from the Old English, I use Present-Day English cognates where possible. Many of these terms carry stigma today—such as the more frequent use of "dumb" to mean "of low intelligence," rather than "non-verbal"—which is not necessarily the same stigma they may have

borne in the early Middle Ages. In retaining modern forms of the Old English words, even when the meaning has shifted, I aim to highlight the moral stigma associated with the language of disability in the Old English text and invite discussion of the etymological backgrounds of present uses of the language of disability.

6   E.g., John 9.

7   E.g., Mark 7:32–37.

8   E.g., Mark 5:22–43; Luke 8:41–56.

9   The manuscript omits any name for Margaret here, perhaps in error, but it may also be a play on the sense of "being called" to the faith in contrast to "being called" a name.

10   OE *hælo*, meaning both physical health and spiritual wholeness; cf. *Hælend*, meaning both "Healer" and "Savior."

11   OE *onleohte*; a form of the same word used earlier to describe Christ's giving sight to the blind.

12   OE *adiligian*, which can also mean "destroy" or "obliterate," potentially puns here on the similar OE word *adlian*, "to ail" or "to be sick."

13   OE *weorulde* literally means "world," but could refer to the temporal world, all of existence, or the eternal world of the Christian afterlife. In all instances, I translate as "all things" in order to encompass this ambiguity.

14   OE *swilcne anne sweartne man*. This could be a reference to skin color, but could also be a metaphorical reference to the devil's moral "darkness," especially given that the binding of the devil's hands evokes the criminal punishment of fettering hands and feet in early medieval England. Either or both interpretations are possible because "dark" skin tones were both known about and present in early medieval England, as was a metaphorical association between literal darkness and moral iniquity in the Old English language.

15   OE *anlyht*, cf. *onleohte*, see note 11.

16   OE *Þu eart ealra hælende Hælend*.

17   The stories of Abraham, his son Isaac, and Isaac's son Jacob are recounted in the Old Testament; see Genesis 11–35.

18   OE *adumbe*, the imperative form of *adumbian* "become unable to speak."

19   OE *lihtnesse*, related to *onleohte*; see note 11.

20 While in literal terms, to be "vexed by an
unclean spirit" evokes demonic possession,
descriptions of possession and exorcism in
other texts in Old English (and other medieval
languages) suggest that this was not an
uncommon interpretation of some symptoms of
mental illness. For example, Bede's *Prose Life of St
Cuthbert* recounts the saint casting a devil from a
woman who was afflicted such that she thrashed,
wept, and cried out.

21 OE *innoþ*, meaning "inner parts," "womb," or
"belly"; this same word is used for the belly of the
dragon from which Margaret burst.

22 OE *untrumnesse*; literally, "disorder," and
frequently used in OE saints' lives to describe
individuals who seek healing from a saint.

Life of Mary of Oegines (Oignies)[1] (ca. 15th c.)

Contributed by Kisha G. Tracy and Alicia Protze

Introduction

St. Mary (or Marie) of Oegines, a Beguine, was born in 1177 in Nivelles, which is now Belgium. Although born into wealth, she preferred the pious life, and, even after marriage, she lived a celibate life. Following a life of asceticism and active charity, she died in 1213. Her *Life* was written by James of Vitry around 1215. She was later beatified, and her feast day is June 23rd.

In her *Life*, St. Mary of Oegines is described as self-harming, especially through fasts to the point of destroying her body, cutting, and suffering of excessive weeping and mood shifts. These actions all seem to indicate mental disability and illness—indeed, a layering of mental illnesses—experiences described certainly in graphic, violent terms but also balanced against their benefits.

Mary herself perceived her conditions as a positive and a spiritual benefit. She declares in her own words, "Whan I am sieke, thanne am I stronge and mighty [When I am sick, then am I strong and mighty]" (149, l. 34). Her relationship with God is defined according to her illness: "oure lorde hadde proved his chosen childe with this infirmyte [our Lorde had proved his chosen child with this infirmity]" (149, l. 35). We also read:

> And whanne she prayed specially for any body, as with a wondirful experiens oure lorde shewyd to hir 7 answerid hire spirite. Soothly, she perceyued othere-while by elevacyone of hir spirite or depressyone whether she were herde or noon. (141, ll. 44–45; 142, ll. 1–2)

[And when she prayed specially for anybody, as with a wonderful experience our Lord showed to her and answered her spirit. Truly, she perceived meanwhile by elation of her spirit or depression whether she were heard or not.]

For Mary, it is through "elevacyone of hir spirite or depressyone" that she determines the success of her communication with God. The word used here is "depressyone," different than the "wod [mad]" used in many other hagiographies—for instance, in St. Julian, but also in the *South English Legendary Lives of St. Frideswide*, in John Mirk's sermon on Saint Katherine, and in the *Stanzaic Life of Margaret*, among others. "Wod" as a catch-all for mental illness is quite common in Middle English hagiography. The deliberate use of "depressyone" in *St. Mary* is perhaps a more definitive and specific indication of a shift in mental state. Interestingly enough, the Middle English Dictionary only references the *Life of Mary of Oegines* in the use of this word in this fashion as a "lowering of spirits, dejection." The Oxford English Dictionary cites "depression" in terms of "the condition of being depressed in spirits; dejection" as first being used in 1665 by E. Phillips in *Baker's Chronicle Kings of England.*

Unlike other saints, St. Mary is unique in the variety of mental illness indicators that she exhibits. For instance, Mary uses food to define her relationship with God: "For whether she eet or fasted, she didde alle to the worshyp of god [For whether she eat or fasted, she did all to the worship of God]" (140, ll. 35–36). While she truly believes that fasting will bring her closer to God, this could be considered anorexia and/or a sign of depression. While it was common in the Middle Ages for Christians to fast before receiving communion, Mary takes this further as she decides to fast after seeing an old enemy who says to her: "loo thou gloten, thou fillith the overe-mykelle [Look, thou glutton, thou fill thee over much]" (140, ll. 28–29). She proceeds to fast because "she hadde dissese oftentyme in etynge [she had disease often time in eatinge]" (140, l. 29). She only eats bread and drinks water. Sometimes the bread is so dry and hard that it cuts her throat while she eats. Other times her fasting includes only consuming communion:

> And certaynly, oure lorde rewardid hir bodily delites insoule, that she hadde forsaken for the love of Criste, as hit is writen: 'Man lyueth not in brede allon'. Otherewhile thurgh comforte of this mete she fastid, neith etynge ne drynkynge eyghte dayes, sumtyme ellevne. (141, ll. 3–7)

> [And certainly, our Lord rewarded her bodily delights in soul, that she had forsaken for the love of Christ, as it is written: "Man lives not on bread alone." Meanwhile through comfort of this meat she fasted, neither eating nor drinking for eight days, sometimes eleven.]

Moreover, Mary is filled with the spirit of Christ. When receiving communion and while at Mass, Mary has a sweet sensation in her mouth. However, if the host is unconsecrated, Mary vomits and cleanses her mouth. It is possible that this is another sign of her eating disorder, not wanting to consume anything and purging when doing so.

Sometimes Mary also fasts to help others; she once fasts for forty days to drive a demon out of a nun. Yet, often times, Mary fasts because she feels guilty for eating. Guilt is common when it comes to anorexia. Mary's guilt stems from not suffering like Christ, and her eating is something she can control. By controlling her intake of food, she is able to replicate a diet similar to Christ's, allowing her to consider herself closer to God:

> Ever the more that she made hir body lene with fastynges, the more freer was hir spirite and replete with praiynges; the body with abstynens was febled, 7 the soule more in oure lorde was strengthed. (141, ll. 34–36)

> [Ever the more that she made her body lean with fastings, the more free was her spirit and replete with prayers; the body with abstinence was feebled, and the soul more in our Lord was strengthened.]

By weakening her body through fasting, Mary finds spiritual strength.

Rudolph M. Bell describes anorexia as a disease in which individuals voluntarily starve themselves, often risking their lives. Mary fits this definition, and in this particular case her anorexia is deemed holy. Mary sees the Devil, who claims that she did not have faith in God. When this happens, she becomes depressed, believing that this devilry might not be cast out by fasting or prayer. However, she does fast anyway, for forty days. When she foresees her death, she stops eating, ultimately starving herself to death:

> For soth, whan hir holy body shulde be washen in her oby, she was founden so smalle and lene thurgh infirmite 7 fastynges, that the rigge-bone of hir bak was clungen to hir wombe, and as undir a thynne lynnen clothe the bones of hir bak semyd undir ththe litil skynne of bely. (183, ll. 42–46).

> [For truth, when her holy body should be washed in her funeral, she was found so small lean through infirmity and fastings that the spine of her back clung to her womb, and as under a thin linen cloth the bones of her back seemed under the little skin of her belly.]

Caroline Walker Bynum in *Holy Feast and Holy Fast* agrees with Bell in his definition of anorexia. She also describes anorexia as a form of depression, which is applicable to several medieval women including Mary of Oegines. While Mary truly believes that fasting will bring her closer to God spiritually, it alters her everyday life. She self-harms out of guilt when she eats, which is a sign of depression. In fasting, her diet is affected and her health is compromised. This aversion to food, particularly when it includes fasting for religious reasons, has often been ignored by scholars, which is, as Bynum points out, due to the fact that it occurred often in the lives of saints and medieval women.

Another indicator of mental illness is Mary's excessive weeping, a characteristic she shares with other figures, including Margery Kempe:

> But where as she enforced hir to restreyne hir wepynge, there encresed mervelously teerys moor and moor. For what she toke hede how grete he was that suffred for us so mykel dispite, hir sorowe was efte renewyd, and hir soule with new teerys was refressed by a swete compunxione. (137, ll. 39–43)

> [But whereas she enforced her to restrain her weeping, there increased marvelously more and more tears. For when she took heed how great he was that suffered for us so much despite, her sorrow was often renewed, and her soul with new tears was refreshed by a sweet compunction.]

While uncontrollable weeping can be considered a sign of depression and there has been much discussion about this possibility with Margery, it is here allied with words such as "mervelous," "refressed" (similar to the "reste" from the cutting incident that will be dis-

cussed below), and "swete compunxione." Mary's tears are actually contrasted with disease; she says that they "dissese not the heed, but feden the mynde [disease not the head, but feed the mind]" (138, ll. 33–34). She considers her weeping as a gift from God and asks of God that the priest who tries to stop her weeping be shown that it is not in her control:

> Wherfore that preste, the wihile hee sange masse that same daye, was so overcomen with abundauns of terys, that his spirite was wel nyghe strangelyd; and the more that hee bisyed hym to reffreyne his terys, the moor not oonly hee but also the buke and the auter-clothes were wette with water of wepynge: soo that hee unavisyman, he that blamer of Crystes mayden, leeryd with schame by experiens what hee schulde do that hee wolde not firste knowe by meeknesse and compassyone. (138, ll. 8–15)

> [Wherefore that priest, while he sang mass that same day, was so overcome with abundance of tears, that his spirit was well-nigh strangled; and the more that he busied him to refrain his tears, the more not only he but also the skin and the outer clothes were wet with water of weeping: so he that ill-advised, he that put blame on Christ's maiden, learned with shame by experience what he should do that he would not first know by meekness and compassion.]

The priest "leeryd with schame by experiens" what he did not at first treat with "meeknesse and compassyone."

Another potential indicator of mental illness is Mary's penchant for cutting. In a dramatic instance of this, Mary, after walking through a town which filled her mind

---

Hælend *Healer/Savior*   **Antioch** *modern-day Antakya in Turkey*

with sin, cuts herself: "askynge a knyfe of hir mayden, whan she was with-oute the toune, wolde have kitte the skynne fro hir feet [asking for a knife from her maid, when she was outside the town, would have cut the skin from her feet]" (163, ll. 21–22). After this action, she is described as having, albeit with difficulty, "reste" (163, l. 27), indicating that the act of cutting and the subsequent act of beating her feet together is a relief. It is to a certain extent an individual mimicking of Christ's wounds, and, if so, then Mary's cutting is presented as a holy act of cleansing.

The *Life of St. Mary of Oegines* is a useful example of how disability manifests in hagiography as it incorporates so many different indicators and it is clear in its discussion of the benefits of mental disability, particularly to saints. The following excerpts from the *Life* were chosen because they represent extended episodes of Mary's various disabilities.

Bibliography

Bell, Rudolph M. *Holy Anorexia*. University Chicago Press, 1997.

Bynum, Caroline Walker. *Holy Feast and Holy Fast: The Religious Significance of Food to Medieval Women*. University of California Press, 1987.

Gertsman, Elina, ed. *Crying in the Middle Ages: Tears of History*. Routledge, 2012.

Millard, Chris. *A History of Self-Harm in Britain: A Genealogy of Cutting and Overdosing*. Palgrave Macmillan, 2015.

Wogan-Browne, Jocelyn, and Glyn S. Burgess, eds. *Virgin Lives and Holy Deaths*. Everyman, 1996.

Book 1, Prologue

Worshipful James, bishop of Accone,° wrote to the bishop of Tholose° a long prologue into the life that here follows: in which prologue he writes concisely many different commendations and marvels of many devout and holy women in the diocese of Leody° and in that country.

And among his writing, as learning and rhetoric asks, he put authorities and figurative speakings that are not easy to turn into English language without more explanation; and if a man would take some of the same prologue, the meaning would not well accord: and therefore I leave all that prologue, except this overly short mention.

Here begins the chapters of the first book the life of Saint Mary of Oegines: the which life Master James, confessor and intimate of the same Mary, afterwards bishop of Accone, and after that Cardinal of the court of Rome, written in Latin, in the year of grace 1215.

Book 1, Chapter V

Of Her Compunction and Tears

Lord, you art full good to them that trust in you, you art true to them that abide by you. Your maiden has despised the sickness of the world and all the worship thereof for your love: truly, you have given her again the hundredfold in this world and ever-lasting life in that which is to come.

Then look we with how great stones of virtues, as a strong and whole vessel of gold honored with every precious stone, you have arrayed and attired your full dear friend, with how great miracles you have worshipped her, that rejected and scorned of lay people. The beginning of her conversion to you, first fruits of her life, was your cross and your passion; your glory she heard and dread, she beheld your works and was afraid.

For why upon a day when she, sanctioned and inspired by you, considered the benefits that you merciful showed in flesh to mankind, she found so much grace of compunction, so great plenty of tears, thrusted out in your passion with the pressure of your cross, that her tears copiously rained down on the church pavement showed where she went.

Wherefore a long time after this visitation of her she might not behold an image of the cross, nor speak nor hear other folk speaking of the passion, but if she fell into a swooning for high desire of heart.

And therefore meanwhile, to temper her sorrow and to withhold abundance of tears, she left the human form of Christ and held up her mind to the godhead and majesty, that she might find comfort in his invulnerability.

But whereas she enforced her to restrain her weeping, there increased marvelously more and more tears.

For when she took heed how great he was that suffered for us so much despite, her sorrow was often renewed, and her soul with new tears was refreshed by a sweet compunction.

It was upon a day before Good Friday near Christ's passion, when she had offered herself to our Lord with much water of tears, sobbings and sighings, a priest of the church as with (God's) wish blaming her, bade that she should pray softly and let be her weeping. She, truly, as she ever was shamefast and in all things simple as a young dove, did her best to obey.

Then she, knowing her weakness, went privately out of the church and hid her in a private place far from all folk: and asked our lord with tears that he would show to the same priest that it is not in man's power to withhold the strong stream of tears, when a great blast blows and the water flows. Wherefore that priest, while he sang mass that same day, was so overcome with abundance of tears, that his spirit was well-nigh strangled; and the more that he busied him to refrain

---

James...Accone *James of Vitry, author of the Life* **bishop of Tholose** *Fulk of Toulouse* **Leody** *in modern-day Liege in Belgium*

his tears, the more not only he but also the skin and the outer clothes were wet with water of weeping: so he that ill-advised, he that put blame on Christ's maiden, learned with shame by experience what he should do that he would not first know by meekness and compassion.

For after many sobbings, pronouncing many words inordinately now and now, at last with difficulty he escaped from peril; and he bore witness, that both saw and knew, and we know that his witness is true.

Truly, then a long time after mass had ended, Christ's maiden, returning again and puzzling as if she had been present told with reproach what fell unto the priest. "Now," she said, "you have learned by experience that it is not in a man to withhold the forces of the wind when the truth blows."

And while both day and night continually water left by her eyes, and not only her tears in her cheeks but also, lest they should be perceived in the pavement, she kept them in kerchiefs with which she covered her head; and such linen cloths she used full many, that which she needed often to change, that, as one wet, another might dry.

And then, certainly, when men of compassion with desire after so long fasting, after so many wakings, and after so many weepings asked her whether she felt any sore or aching, as it is want to be of a light head: "These tears," she said, "are my refreshing, these are my sustenance night and day; that disease not the head, but feed the mind; they torment with no aching, but they lighten the soul with a shining; they void not the brain, but they fill the will of the soul with a fullness, and soften it with an easy anointing, when they are not wrung out with labour and violence, but held out graciously and given of our Lord."

Book 1, Chapter VIII
Of Fasting

Christ's maiden passed and was excellent by so great grace of fasting, that those days in which she was required to have recreation of body, she went to meat as to medicine. She ate only a little in the day, in summer at evening, in winter at the first hour of the night. Wine drank she none; she used no flesh, and fish ate she never, but seldom small fishes; and she was sustained with fruits of trees, herbs, and soup. And long time she ate full black, sharp bread, that dogs with difficulty might eat of; so that for overmuch sharpness and hardness her jowls were flayed within and blood came out of the wounds. But thinking of Christ's blood made it sweet to her, and with wounds of Christ her wounds were linked, and the sharpness of bread was sweetened with softness of heavenly bread.

Upon a day, while she ate, she saw the old enemy° all pained with envy; and when he had no more that he might do, he scorned her and said: "Look, thou glutton, thou fill thee over much."

Truly, she had disease often time in eating, for much fasting and long; more over her stomach ached and wrought, as loathing meat for coldness and boiling.

But she knew the slights and wiles of the enemy, that gladly would strangle her whom he knew fearful, after she was weak with over much abstinence.

Therefore ever the more that the venomous spirit was tormented with her eating, in so much she enforced her to eat the more and scorned him.

For whether she eat or fasted, she did all to the worship of God.

Truly, she fasted three years together in bread and water, from Christmas until Passover; yet nevertheless she suffered no harm of body nor of her handy work. And when she refreshed her body with a little bread and

---

the old enemy *the Devil*

water in her cell within the church at evening or in the night, for the beginning of grace until after grace some of holy angels stood before her at that sober supper, and they come up and down as through a bright window: of whose presence she had so great comfort and so great joy of spirit, that the spiritual sweetness passed all delight of savour.

Also Saint John Evangelist, whom she loved with entire affection, came meanwhile to her board, while she ate; and in his presence her sensible appetite was so voided for devout desire, that she might with difficulty take any meat. And certainly, our Lord rewarded her bodily delights in soul, that she had forsaken for the love of Christ, as it is written: "Man lives not on bread alone."º Meanwhile through comfort of this meat she fasted, neither eating nor drinking for eight days, sometimes eleven, that is from the Ascension of our Lord until Whitsunday: and wondrously, her head ached no time, nor she left not for that labour of her hands, as strong the last day of her fasting as the first.

And if she would have eaten those days, she might not, unto the sensuality that was as slackened with the spirit, come again to herself; for as long as the soul, abundant so copiously, was so full of spiritual feeding, (it) would not suffer her receive any refreshment of bodily meat.

Also meanwhile she rested easily with our Lord thirty-five days in a sweet and blessed silence, used no bodily meat, and some days she might bring forth no word but this alone: "I will the body of our Lord Jesus Christ"; and when she had received the sacrament, she dwelled with our Lord every day in silence.

Truly, she felt in those days her spirit as departed from the body, so being in the body as if it were hidden in a vessel of clay, and her body as a cloth of clay overlaying and covering her spirit—in this manner she was removed from worldly things and transported above herself in a rapture.

And after five weeks she returned again to herself, opened her mouth and spoke and received bodily food; and they that stood about, marveled. Long time after it happened to her that she might in no manner suffer the savours of flesh or of any cooking or of wine, but when she took wine in the rinsing after the sacrament; and then she might suffer the smell without any grievance.

Also when she went by many towns to a bishop to have the sacrament of confirmation, the savours that she might not suffer before, feared her not a bit.

Book 1, Chapter IX
Of Her Prayer

Ever the more that she made her body lean with fastings, the more free was her spirit and replete with prayers; the body with abstinence was feebled, and the soul more in our Lord was strengthened.

She got of our Lord so great grace and so special of praying, that nights and days never or seldom her spirit was overcome nor released for prayer.

She prayed without stopping, except crying to God with still heart, or else with her mouth expressing the heart's desire.

So that, while she wrought with her hands and spun, she had a psalter set before her and sweetly said psalms there to our Lord, with the which as with nails she coupled her heart to God, lest it wandered in vain. And when she prayed specially for anybody, as with a wonderful experience our Lord showed to her and answered her spirit.

Truly, she perceived meanwhile by elation of her spirit or depression whether she were heard or not.

"**Man lives not on bread alone**" *Matthew 4:4*

Book 1, Chapter XIII

Of Her Bearing and Composition of Appearance and Other Members of Her Body

Composition of bearing of her outward and further parts showed the inward making of her mind, and the seemliness of her features would not let the joy of her heart be hid.

Truly, in a marvelous measure she tempered the sadness of her heart with gladness of appearance, and somewhat covered the mirth of her mind with the humility of shame of face. And for the apostle says: "Women shall prey with covered head," the white veil that hid her head, hung before her eyes.

She went meekly with a slow and easy pace, her head bowed and her face looking to the earth. In so much, truly, the grace of her soul shined in her face of the plenty of her heart, that may of those looking at her were spiritually refreshed and stirred to devotion and weeping; and reading in her appearance the unction of the holy ghost as in a book, knew that from her came virtue.

And so it fell on a day that a goodly man, intimate and friend of religious persons, Guy, sometimes chanter of the church Cameracense,° turned out of his way to visit her. Then one of his fellows, who which happily until then knew not by experience how much visitation and friendliness of good folk may do to meek minds, as in scorning the good labour of the before said devout man, said: "For God's love, sir chanter, what do you seek? Why do you leave your way?

Wherefore will you follow and take flies and flying butterflies with children?" He, truly, that was meek, mild, and suffering, left not his way that he proposed for such words, but devoutly went to Christ's maiden of whose presence another time he had not a little comfort.

And while he spoke to her, his fellow, as lay manner is, set little by such words and on another side was occupied with many and idle words. Then when he was full and tired of abiding, he came to the chanter to bid him that he should go in haste. And it happened as he looked rudely in the face of Christ's maiden, suddenly and marvelously he fell into such great weeping of tears that with difficulty he might be brought a long time after from that place and her presence.

Then the chanter, though he would for shame have held counsel, taking heed and knowing the circumstance, was glad and scorned his fellow again and said: "Go we hence, what stops us? Perhaps we will drive and chance butterflies." And he, after many sighings and tears, with difficulty at last he might be pulled hence, saying: "Forgive me, Father, for I knew not what I said before; now, truly, I have perceived by experience God's virtue in this woman."

Also upon a time, when her body might no more bear the fury of spirit, she fell into a great sickness; so much, truly, the meek father disciplined his daughter, that he loved, about what the limbs and members of her body wondrously wrought; for meanwhile her arms were writhing as a garment of sorrow, and she was constrained to beat her breast with her hands.

And when the strength of the sickness a little while slacked and rested, then she thanked our Lord with so much joy, that chastely like a child that he received, as the apostle's word is only fulfilled in her, saying thus: "When I am sick, then am I strong and mighty." Then after our Lord had proved his chosen child with this infirmity as gold in a furnace, she, pure and polished at the full, from thence forth got so great strength of God in wakings, fastings, and other labours, that with difficulty strong men might suffer the third part of her labour.

Nevertheless, meanwhile, when any of her friends were grieved with any disease or cast

---

Cameracense *city in northern France*

down with any temptation, then she was sick with the sick and was burned with the shame with a huge sorrow: and then sometime she felt somewhat the same sickness in some of her members.

Then anon in a new manner of miracle, she called her priest, that should make a cross with his finger on the sore place of sickness: and the evil fled to another place, as it feared the virtue of the holy cross.

And so again and again he made a cross: and the wavering evil and the fugitive dare no longer abide the burden of the cross, but at last went all away from the body of Christ's maiden, with a marvelous and unheard manner of worshipping the Crucifix.

Truly, she, looking the eyes of faith into the brazen serpent, and delivered from the bitings of the snake's evil, thanked God and the holy cross many times.

Book 2, Chapter IV
Of the Spirit of Knowledge

She, truly, hearing that strangers were coming, lest it happened she should slander any man, compelled her spirit with so great sorrow from her joy of contemplation and spiritually embracing of her spouse, that sometimes she vomited pure blood in great quantity as if her bowels had burst; having rather to be tormented with that martyrdom than to disturb or disease her fellow Christians, and principally peace of pilgrims.

...

Wherefore it fell on a time that, in order to visit some of her gentle friends, while she dwelled at Oegines,° she went to Willambroc,° and in her returning as she went through Nivelle,° filled to her mind sins and abominations that the people did often in that town. And she conceived and took in her heart so great offense and loathing that she began to cry for sorrow, and, asking for a knife from her maid, when she was out-

side the town, would have cut the skin from her feet for that she had passed by places in which wretched men provoked her person with so many wrongs and provoked God with so many misdeeds and sins. And since she sorrowed not only in soul, but also, what is more marvelous, felt sore in her feet with which she trod, nevertheless at last with difficult she might have rest, after she had often times beaten her feet together.

Book 2, Chapter XIII
Of her Death

For truth, when her time came near, our Lord showed to his daughter a portion of her heritage among her brethren, and she saw a place in heavenly things ordained to her from our Lord; she saw and was joyful. The height of which place, the greatness of which joy we might in some way suppose if we might hold in the heart the precious stones and virtues of pearls and gems that she wondrously described, and the names of stones that she named through showing of our Lord; but, for it is written: "Eyes have not seen, God, except that you have ordained to them that love you." We may not comprehend, but we may know how great joy she is worth that served God so devoutly, that loved Christ so fervently, and whom our Lord honored on earth with so many singular privileges. The Thursday before the day of her passing, while we were present and stood by her in the evening, she would not speak to us nor turned her eyes towards us, but she lay unmoving with her eyes ever looking into heaven—for she lay without her cell under the sky—and her appearance began to turn clear as with a brightness.

Then she for joy full long was smiling began to sing with a low voice, I know not what: for then might she not sing high. And when I moved nearer and listened intently, I might

---

Oegines *a town in Belgium*   **Willambroc and Nivelle** *cities in Belgian province of Walloon Brabant*

not understand but a little of her song and that was this: *Quam pulcher rex noster domine.*[o]

That is to say in English: Full fair king, our Lord. When she had long abided in such great joy, singing, laughing, and otherwise clapping her hands, then she returned to herself with a renewed feeling of infirmity that she had not felt before, and began a little to be grieved. And when we asked of her what she had seen: since she was not able to speak to us but a little. "Nevertheless," she said, "I would say to you if I could."

Truly, the same Saturday at evening when the day of joy and mirth was near, the day that our Lord made, the day that our Lord showed to his maiden, our Lord's day, the day of resurrection, the day of the vigil of Saint John the Baptist, in which also, as men say, Saint John Evangelist passed from this world, although his feast is held another time: then Christ's maiden, that had eaten no manner of meat for fifty-two days, began with a sweet voice to sing halleluiah, and almost all that night as bidden to a feast she was in joy and mirth.

Truly, the fiend appeared on the Sunday and vexed her greatly: for she began somewhat to fear and also to ask help of them that stood about. But then she, taking again trust of our Lord and strongly breaking the dragon's head and shielding herself with the sign of the cross. "Go back," she said, "you filth and foulness." For she called him not foul, but foulness.

Then the fiend flying away, she began to sing and thanked God of his great grace.

And then, certainly, when the evening came near, before the feast of Saint John the Baptist, about that hour that our Lord held the ghost in the cross, that is the hour of noon, she truly passed to God, never changing for any sorrow of death the gladness of features or face of enjoyment; nor I have mind that altogether she had more gladness of appearance and more likeness of life; nor, as is custom after death, did she seem dull or discolored in face, but with an angel's countenance and gentle simpleness, white and clear in face, in her dying and after her death she stirred many to devotion.

Also many were wet sweetly at her funeral with plenteous flood of tears, and they perceived themselves visited by God through her prayers, as a holy woman saw before of the holy ghost and said before that they that come together at her passing should receive much comfort of our Lord.

For truth, when her holy body should be washed in her funeral, she was found so small lean through infirmity and fastings that the spine of her back clung to her womb, and as under a thin linen cloth the bones of her back seemed under the little skin of her belly.

Quam pulcher rex noster domine *How fair a king, our Lord* [*Latin*]

Endnotes

1   The excerpts are translated by Kisha G. Tracy and Alicia Protze from the *Life of Mary of Oegines (or Oignies)* taken from the edition by Carl Horstmann: "Prosalegenden: die Legenden des MS Douce 114," *Anglia*, vol. 8 (1885), pp. 134–84. The paragraph breaks reflect the breaks marked in the edition with some edits for clarity.

POETRY

Bisclavret[1] (ca. 12th c.)

Marie de France
Contributed by Kisha G. Tracy

Introduction

Known only from what she reveals about herself in her writings, Marie de France is a twelfth-century Anglo-Norman author, perhaps the first female French author. She is known for her collection of *Lais*, twelve short poems that follow a Breton romance style.

Marie de France's *Bisclavret* can be read through the lens of disability studies, specifically in the text's depictions of shape-shifting or lycanthropy, disfigurement, and the psychological issues resulting from domestic abuse. The physical appearance of the first and second are quite clear within the text in the titular character and his wife, respectively, while the third requires more interpretation in terms of the relationship between the two.

Marie de France, as the narrator, gives the reader specific information at the beginning of the text about werewolves:

> Garualf, c[eo] est beste salvage:
> Tant cum il est en cele rage,
> Hummes devure, grant mal fait,
> Es granz forez converse e vait. (ll. 9–12)[2]

[The Were-Wolf is a fearsome beast. He lurks within the thick forest, mad and horrible to see. All the evil that he may, he does. He goeth to and fro, about the solitary place, seeking man, in order to devour him.]

We learn later that the titular character is himself one of these figures, although this description is the antithesis of Bisclavret. He is indeed, even in his werewolf form, noble and good, described in the Eugene Mason translation, which is provided in full below, as a "christened man." The narrator is setting us up, only to play with our preconceptions about werewolves.

Bisclavret's lycanthropy only becomes disabling once his wife traps him in his wolf form by having his clothes stolen; clothing is both the literal mechanism that allows his transformation and the metaphorical difference between human and beast. The impairing features of his lycanthropy are an initial separation from his previous position in society and an inability to communicate as a human, both of which are resolved by the end of the text. Indeed, in every other way, he acts the same as before, particularly in terms of his demonstration of fealty and behavior towards his king. The king and the people of the court are able to perceive in him the same characteristics that they find in Bisclavret in his human form. In Mason's translation, the king says that Bisclavret in werewolf form is "a beast who has the sense of man. He abases himself before his foe, and cries for mercy, although he cannot speak." It is these characteristics that lead them to install the wolf, thereby reinstalling Bisclavret in the court. At the end of the text, when he returns to his human form, when as Mason notes "the ravening beast may indeed return to human shape," he also regains "man's speech." His wife then is the only character who disables Bisclavret due to his condition.

When reading *Bisclavret*, the moment the wife decides to turn against her husband, after learning he is a werewolf, is often a point of confusion and discussion. Are we meant to blame the wife? Given she later finds herself disfigured and tortured for her actions, it seems like a simple question; she is punished for her betrayal of her husband. Nonetheless, as with everything medieval and everything Marie de France, the question is far more complex than it seems.

First, to address the disfigurement, the wife's nose is torn off by Bisclavret:

Le neis li esracha del vis.
Quei li peüst il faire pis? (ll. 235–36)

[Breaking from his bonds he sprang at the lady's face, and bit the nose from her visage.]

In Judith Shoaf's translation, she provides the commentary in the original text missing from the Mason translation:

He tore her nose right off her face.
Could anything be worse than this is?[3]

In the original and Shoaf's translation, it is indicated by the question that disfigurement is considered by the narrator as a tragic circumstance. The emphasis does not seem to be on the pain of the physical experience, but rather what it has done to her appearance. Given that women's beauty in romances is often a defining trait, such a reaction is understandable. Mason's translation also does not provide the further commentary about the wife's succeeding daughters; Shoaf, however, does:

Enfanz en ad asés eüz,
Puis unt esté bien cuneüz
[E] del semblant e del visage:
Plusurs [des] femmes del lignage,
C'est verité, sen nes sunt nees
E si viveient esnasees. (ll. 309–14)

[She had plenty of children; grown,
They were, all of them, quite well-known,
By their looks, their facial assembly:

More than one woman of that family
Was born without a nose to blow,
And lived denosed. It's true! It's so!]

With this statement, we find a clear use of the moral model of disability: the mother's actions are represented by the public disability of the children.

And yet the question persists: are we meant to blame the wife? If we consider romances in terms of their role as fantasy fulfillment for noble readers, we might look at the wife's actions in *Bisclavret* from another angle, not one of blame or of defense, but of the psychology of abuse. Imagine, for a moment, a woman who grew up in the nobility, a woman who was aware from an early age that she would be married to someone her family selected and approved. Fortunately for her, she married, according to Mason, "a stout knight," who is "comely." Their relationship builds to what they both believe is love, and all is well—with one exception, that he disappears periodically.

When the wife confronts him, her phrasing is that of fear:

Mes jeo creim tant vostre curuz,
Que nule rien tant ne redut. (ll. 35–36)

[Right willingly would I receive this gift, but I fear to anger you in the asking. It is better for me to have an empty hand, than to gain hard words.]

She fears his anger. We have no indication of why. This phrasing could be dismissed as courteous language between husband and wife, that she does not desire to anger him with her questioning. But what if we look at it from the perspective of a wife who knows very little about her husband although she has to this point been comforted that he does not seem to possess the qualities she feared in a husband? Could her statement indicate the lingering fear of how her husband will treat her? Has she heard stories of men who were kind to their wives until a moment when they seemed to turn against them? We certainly have examples in romances of abusive knights—for instance, Erec in Chrétien de Troyes' *Erec and Enide*, the knight-rapist in *The Wife of Bath's Tale*, and, elsewhere in Marie de France's *Lais*, the lord in *Yonec*.

When Bisclavret assures her with physical caresses that he will answer her questions, she replies:

> Par fei, fet ele, ore sui guarie!
> Sire, jeo sui en tel effrei
> Les jurs quant vus partez de mei,
> El quor en ai mut grant dolur
> E de vus perdre tel poür,
> Si jeo n'en ai hastif cunfort,
> Bien tost en puis aver la mort. (ll. 42–48)

["By my faith," said the lady, "soon shall I be whole. Husband, right long and wearisome are the days that you spend away from your home. I rise from my bed in the morning, sick at heart, I know not why. So fearful am I, lest you do aught to your loss, that I may not find any comfort. Very quickly shall I die for reason of my dread.]

This response is phrased in the language of illness. His treatment of her, his seeming tender care, makes her "whole." She talks about living in terror, about fearing to lose him. She indicates she will die from what she is experiencing, that she is "sick at heart," which is at odds with her desire to be "whole." On one hand, this certainly could be hyperbole and her attempt to push him into telling about his disappearances, even using the language of illness to elicit guilt on his part. On the other hand, if we read it in the same context as the previous statement, other implications arise. Perhaps her fears have indeed reasserted themselves, to the point that she feels desperately insecure. She has read his disappearances into her fears and cannot "recover" until she knows the truth.

What follows is back and forth between the couple, the wife pressing and Bisclavret denying to answer her questions. Often, this scene is perceived as nagging on the wife's part, an insatiable need to know, even though Bisclavret is blameless, but what if this fear of abuse is driving her? Finally, he relents and tells her about his shape-shifting. This revelation is certainly not what the wife expected, but it comes on top of a period of renewed psychological—if imagined—trauma related to her pre-marital fears of the kind of man she would wed. And then comes her reaction:

> La dame oï cele merveille,
> De poür fu tute vermeille;
> De l'aventure se esfrea.
> E[n] maint endreit se purpensa
> Cum ele s'en puïst partir;
> Ne voleit mes lez lui gisir. (ll. 97–102)

[On hearing this marvel the lady became sanguine of visage, because of her exceeding fear. She dared no longer to lie at his side, and turned over in her mind, this way and that, how best she could get her from him.]

Her fear starts to multiply. She dwells upon it.

In addition, she likely is aware of the information about werewolves Marie de France gave us at the beginning of the text, that they are subject to rage, acting like savage beasts. If this is a metaphor for evil men, it's certainly an even better one for abusers who present well until, as Mason states, "the fury is on them." Edward J. Gallagher translates this passage as, "A werewolf is a ferocious beast which, when possessed by this madness, devours men, causes great damage, and dwells in vast forests."[4] Gallagher's translation of "cele rage" as "by this madness" trades on the idea of rage and anger as a mental illness, especially a type of temporary insanity. If we follow this metaphor, the wife may not fear her husband simply as a werewolf, but her husband in a rage, which she has already stated scares her more than anything. Given this interpretation, her actions may indicate the trauma of prolonged fear.

235

In *Bisclavret*, Marie de France presents disability from a variety of angles. She explores the ramifications of a werewolf who lacks the negative qualities of his kind, thereby representing what might be a disability—in this case, lycanthropy—as disabling only to those who perceive and treat it so—here, to the character's wife, but not to his king. She then demonstrates how those who disable others are themselves disabled—the wife, who disabled her husband, is herself disfigured. At the same time, Marie does not depict the disabling character with simplistic motivations; rather, she introduces questions about fear and imagined trauma. The issues of disability in this text are complex and intertwined.

Bibliography

Bynum, Caroline Walker. *Metamorphosis and Identity*. Zone Books, 2005.

Cohen, Jeffrey Jerome. *Hybridity, Identity, and Monstrosity in Medieval Britain: On Difficult Middles*. Palgrave Macmillan, 2006.

Rose, Christine, and Elizabeth Robertson, eds. *Representing Rape in Medieval and Early Modern Literature*. Palgrave Macmillan, 2001.

Salisbury, Eve, Georgiana Donavin, and Merrall Llewelyn Price, eds. *Domestic Violence in Medieval Texts*. University Press of Florida, 2002.

Skinner, Patricia. *Living with Disfigurement in Early Medieval Europe*. Palgrave Macmillan, 2017.

Amongst the tales I tell you once again, I would not forget the Lay of the Were-Wolf. Such beasts as he are known in every land. Bisclavaret he is named in Brittany; whilst the Norman calls him Garwal.

It is a certain thing, and within the knowledge of all, that many a christened man has suffered this change, and ran wild in woods, as a Were-Wolf. The Were-Wolf is a fearsome beast. He lurks within the thick forest, mad and horrible to see. All the evil that he may, he does. He goeth to and fro, about the solitary place, seeking man, in order to devour him. Hearken, now, to the adventure of the Were-Wolf, that I have to tell.

In Brittany there dwelt a baron who was marvellously esteemed of all his fellows. He was a stout knight, and a comely, and a man of office and repute. Right private was he to the mind of his lord, and dear to the counsel of his neighbours. This baron was wedded to a very worthy dame, right fair to see, and sweet of semblance. All his love was set on her, and all her love was given again to him. One only grief had this lady. For three whole days in every week her lord was absent from her side. She knew not where he went, nor on what errand. Neither did any of his house know the business which called him forth.

On a day when this lord was come again to his house, altogether joyous and content, the lady took him to task, right sweetly, in this fashion, "Husband," said she, "and fair, sweet friend, I have a certain thing to pray of you. Right willingly would I receive this gift, but I fear to anger you in the asking. It is better for me to have an empty hand, than to gain hard words."

When the lord heard this matter, he took the lady in his arms, very tenderly, and kissed her.

"Wife," he answered, "ask what you will. What would you have, for it is yours already?"

"By my faith," said the lady, "soon shall I be whole. Husband, right long and wearisome are the days that you spend away from your home. I rise from my bed in the morning, sick at heart, I know not why. So fearful am I, lest you do aught to your loss, that I may not find any comfort. Very quickly shall I die for reason of my dread. Tell me now, where you go, and on what business! How may the knowledge of one who loves so closely, bring you to harm?"

"Wife," made answer the lord, "nothing but evil can come if I tell you this secret. For the mercy of God do not require it of me. If you but knew, you would withdraw yourself from my love, and I should be lost indeed."

When the lady heard this, she was persuaded that her baron sought to put her by with jesting words. Therefore she prayed and required him the more urgently, with tender looks and speech, till he was overborne, and told her all the story, hiding naught.

"Wife, I become Bisclavaret. I enter in the forest, and live on prey and roots, within the thickest of the wood."

After she had learned his secret, she prayed and entreated the more as to whether he ran in his raiment, or went spoiled of vesture.

"Wife," said he, "I go naked as a beast."

"Tell me, for hope of grace, what you do with your clothing?"

"Fair wife, that will I never. If I should lose my raiment, or even be marked as I quit my vesture, then a Were-Wolf I must go for all the days of my life. Never again should I become man, save in that hour my clothing were given back to me. For this reason never will I show my lair."

"Husband," replied the lady to him, "I love you better than all the world. The less cause have you for doubting my faith, or hiding any tittle from me. What savour is here of friendship? How have I made forfeit of your love; for what sin do you mistrust my honour? Open now your heart, and tell what is good to be known."

So at the end, outwearied and overborne by her importunity, he could no longer refrain, but told her all.

"Wife," said he, "within this wood, a little from the path, there is a hidden way, and at the end thereof an ancient chapel, where oftentimes I have bewailed my lot. Near by is a great hollow stone, concealed by a bush, and there is the secret place where I hide my raiment, till I would return to my own home."

On hearing this marvel the lady became sanguine of visage, because of her exceeding fear. She dared no longer to lie at his side, and turned over in her mind, this way and that, how best she could get her from him. Now there was a certain knight of those parts, who, for a great while, had sought and required this lady for her love. This knight had spent long years in her service, but little enough had he got thereby, not even fair words, or a promise. To him the dame wrote a letter, and meeting, made her purpose plain.

"Fair friend," said she, "be happy. That which you have coveted so long a time, I will grant without delay. Never again will I deny your suit. My heart, and all I have to give, are yours, so take me now as love and dame."

Right sweetly the knight thanked her for her grace, and pledged her faith and fealty. When she had confirmed him by an oath, then she told him all this business of her lord—why he went, and what he became, and of his ravening within the wood. So she showed him of the chapel, and of the hollow stone, and of how to spoil the Were-Wolf of his vesture. Thus, by the kiss of his wife, was Bisclavaret betrayed. Often enough had he ravished his prey in desolate places, but from this journey he never returned. His kinsfolk and acquaintance came together to ask of his tidings, when this absence was noised abroad. Many a man, on many a day, searched the woodland, but none might find him, nor learn where Bisclavaret was gone.

The lady was wedded to the knight who had cherished her for so long a space. More than a year had passed since Bisclavaret disappeared. Then it chanced that the King would hunt in that self-same wood where the Were-Wolf lurked. When the hounds were unleashed they ran this way and that, and swiftly came upon his scent. At the view the huntsman winded on his horn, and the whole pack were at his heels. They followed him from morn to eve, till he was torn and bleeding, and was all adread lest they should pull him down. Now the King was very close to the quarry, and when Bisclavaret looked upon his master, he ran to him for pity and for grace. He took the stirrup within his paws, and fawned upon the prince's foot. The King was very fearful at this sight, but presently he called his courtiers to his aid.

"Lords," cried he, "hasten hither, and see this marvellous thing. Here is a beast who has the sense of man. He abases himself before his foe, and cries for mercy, although he cannot speak. Beat off the hounds, and let no man do him harm. We will hunt no more today, but return to our own place, with the wonderful quarry we have taken."

The King turned him about, and rode to his hall, Bisclavaret following at his side. Very near to his master the Were-Wolf went, like any dog, and had no care to seek again the wood. When the King had brought him safely to his own castle, he rejoiced greatly, for the beast was fair and strong, no mightier had any man seen. Much pride had the King in his marvellous beast. He held him so dear, that he bade all those who wished for his love, to cross the Wolf in naught, neither to strike him with a rod, but ever to see that he was richly fed and kennelled warm. This commandment the Court observed willingly. So all the day the Wolf sported with the lords, and at night he lay within the chamber of the King. There was not a man who did not make much of the beast, so frank was he and debonair. None had reason to do him wrong, for ever was he about his master, and for his part did evil to none. Every day were these two companions together, and all perceived that the King loved him as his friend.

Hearken now to that which chanced.

The King held a high Court, and bade his great vassals and barons, and all the lords of his venery to the feast. Never was there a goodlier feast, nor one set forth with sweeter show and pomp. Amongst those who were bidden, came that same knight who had the wife of Bisclavaret for dame. He came to the castle, richly gowned, with a fair company, but little he deemed whom he would find so near. Bisclavaret marked his foe the moment he stood within the hall. He ran towards him, and seized him with his fangs, in the King's very presence, and to the view of all. Doubtless he would have done him much mischief, had not the King called and chidden him, and threatened him with a rod. Once, and twice, again, the Wolf set upon the knight in the very light of day. All men marvelled at his malice, for sweet and serviceable was the beast, and to that hour had shown hatred of none. With one consent the household deemed that this deed was done with full reason, and that the Wolf had suffered at the knight's hand some bitter wrong. Right wary of his foe was the knight until the feast had ended, and all the barons had taken farewell of their lord, and departed, each to his own house. With these, amongst the very first, went that lord whom Bisclavaret so fiercely had assailed. Small was the wonder that he was glad to go.

No long while after this adventure it came to pass that the courteous King would hunt in that forest where Bisclavaret was found. With the prince came his wolf, and a fair company. Now at nightfall the King abode within a certain lodge of that country, and this was known of that dame who before was the wife of Bisclavaret. In the morning the lady clothed her in her most dainty apparel, and hastened to the lodge, since she desired to speak with the King, and to offer him a rich present. When the lady entered in the chamber, neither man nor leash might restrain the fury of the Wolf. He became as a mad dog in his hatred and malice. Breaking from his bonds he sprang at the lady's face, and bit the nose from her visage. From every side men ran to the succour of the dame. They beat off the wolf from his prey, and for a little would have cut him in pieces with their swords. But a certain wise counsellor said to the King,

"Sire, hearken now to me. This beast is always with you, and there is not one of us

all who has not known him for long. He goes in and out amongst us, nor has molested any man, neither done wrong or felony to any, save only to this dame, one only time as we have seen. He has done evil to this lady, and to that knight, who is now the husband of the dame. Sire, she was once the wife of that lord who was so close and private to your heart, but who went, and none might find where he had gone. Now, therefore, put the dame in a sure place, and question her straitly, so that she may tell—if perchance she knows thereof—for what reason this Beast holds her in such mortal hate. For many a strange deed has chanced, as well we know, in this marvellous land of Brittany."

The King listened to these words, and deemed the counsel good. He laid hands upon the knight, and put the dame in surety in another place. He caused them to be questioned right straitly, so that their torment was very grievous. At the end, partly because of her distress, and partly by reason of her exceeding fear, the lady's lips were loosed, and she told her tale. She showed them of the betrayal of her lord, and how his raiment was stolen from the hollow stone. Since then she knew not where he went, nor what had befallen him, for he had never come again to his own land. Only, in her heart, well she deemed and was persuaded, that Bisclavaret was he.

Straightway the King demanded the vesture of his baron, whether this were to the wish of the lady, or whether it were against her wish. When the raiment was brought him, he caused it to be spread before Bisclavaret, but the Wolf made as though he had not seen. Then that cunning and crafty counsellor took the King apart, that he might give him a fresh rede.

"Sire," said he, "you do not wisely, nor well, to set this raiment before Bisclavaret, in the sight of all. In shame and much tribulation must he lay aside the beast, and again become man. Carry your wolf within your most secret chamber, and put his vestment therein. Then close the door upon him, and leave him alone for a space. So we shall see presently whether the ravening beast may indeed return to human shape."

The King carried the Wolf to his chamber, and shut the doors upon him fast. He delayed for a brief while, and taking two lords of his fellowship with him, came again to the room. Entering therein, all three, softly together, they found the knight sleeping in the King's bed, like a little child. The King ran swiftly to the bed and taking his friend in his arms, embraced and kissed him fondly, above a hundred times. When man's speech returned once more, he told him of his adventure. Then the King restored to his friend the fief that was stolen from him, and gave such rich gifts, moreover, as I cannot tell. As for the wife who had betrayed Bisclavaret, he bade her avoid his country, and chased her from the realm. So she went forth, she and her second lord together, to seek a more abiding city, and were no more seen.

The adventure that you have heard is no vain fable. Verily and indeed it chanced as I have said. The Lay of the Were-Wolf, truly, was written that it should ever be borne in mind.

Endnotes

1   The text is taken from *French Mediaeval Romances: From the Lays of Marie de France*, translated by Eugene Mason, 2011 as found in The Project Gutenberg. This text is in the public domain.

2   Original Old French text taken from *Lais*, trans. Philippe Walter (Paris: Gallimard, 2000). The translations are from the Eugene Mason translation.

3   Translations from Shoaf taken from "Bisclavret," translated by Judith Shoaf, 1996, http://users.clas.ufl.edu/jshoaf/marie/bisclavret.pdf

4   Translations from Gallagher taken from *The Lays of Marie de France*, trans. Edward J. Gallagher (Cambridge: Hackett, 2010).

The Book of Hope[1] (ca. 1429)

Alain Chartier
Contributed by Julie Singer

Introduction

Alain Chartier was a Norman, probably born in Bayeux between 1385 and 1395. He is twice mentioned as an officer in the household of Yolande d'Anjou in account books covering the period from 1409 to 1414. It is to these years that Chartier's earliest surviving lyrics date: these are mostly occasional *ballades* (fixed-form poems with a refrain), verse debates, and the *Lay de plaisance* (a longer and more complex fixed-form poem). Chartier entered the service of the dauphin, the future Charles VII, by 1418. He served primarily as a secretary, writing letters and royal acts, and accompanying ambassadors on several diplomatic missions. He first gained prominence with his courtly poetry, mostly composed from about 1414 to 1425. This period of his work culminates in 1424's *Belle Dame sans mercy* (a verse dialogue between an ardent suitor and an uninterested woman, culminating in the lover's reported death, which became a *succès de scandale*) and the literary quarrel that followed. He is also known for his long political poems, mostly composed during the 1420s, and for his Latin speeches and epistles. Chartier died in 1430, leaving his final work, the *Livre de l'Espérance* (*Book of Hope*), incomplete.[2]

The *Book of Hope* begins with an unusual portrayal of what we would now identify as mental illness. This unfinished prosimetrum consists of sixteen poems alternating with sixteen prose passages. In the prose sections, the suicidal *Acteur* (first-person author–narrator), beset by Lady Melancholy and her helpers (Defiance, Indignation, and Despair), becomes separated from his lethargic personified Entendement (Intellect). Entendement finally finds the wherewithal to open the rusted-shut door of the Acteur's memory, whence the three theological virtues (Faith, Hope, and Charity) come forth. The divided Acteur's impaired faculties, both sensory and intellectual, are then repaired by Faith and Hope (and, presumably, Charity, though the unfinished book neither provides her dialogue nor reveals the identity of a young lady who accompanies the three theological virtues). The metric sections are less straightforward, as the speaker of the verses, that is, the voice through which they are expressed, is not typically specified.[3] Whereas the prose expresses the melancholic sufferer's point of view, poetry appears to be the chosen vehicle of expression for the already healed voice, the one that, as Sylvia Huot puts it, "speaks from a point beyond that of the mental breakdown that he chronicles in prose."[4] The healing unrolls in suitably Boethian fashion—indeed, this rewriting of the *Consolation of Philosophy* is identified in several manuscripts as the *Consolation des trois vertus*.

The significance of this text for the history of literary discourses of disability lies in its merging of courtly literary traditions with medicalized notions of mental illness and an unusually frank and vivid account of suicidal ideation: Chartier uses the conventional devices of first-person narration, a frame narrative, and personification in order both to describe and to illustrate the plight of a seriously depressed melancholic. The *Book's* vision of mental illness as stemming from impediments to normal brain function is consistent with late medieval scientific writings; in the excerpt below he explicitly cites "Aristotle," referring to the pseudo-Aristotelian *Problemata* XXX.1 which contains the famous declaration that gifted artists typically have a melancholic complexion. Throughout the text, Chartier insists on the physiological origins of mental illness as a disease of the brain: the internal senses are "corporeal and organic," and the Acteur's suicidal thoughts come about as a direct result of Melancholy's disruption of one particular part of the brain, "the part that sits in the middle of the head in the region of the imaginative, which some call the fantasy." Moreover, the entire narrative appears to take place within an organic mental space, as Entendement releases the Theological Virtues by moving to the far end of the room in which the action unfolds and opening a door situated "back toward [the Acteur's] memory." While the personifications struggling over the Acteur's soul inscribe the *Book of Hope* firmly within a well-established medieval psychomachic tradition, the situation of this discourse on mental health *within a mental space* is extraordinary. The Acteur's overt identification of the personifications as "simulacra in feminine form" lends the prose sections a two-dimensional, surreal flavor, which is only enhanced by the uncertain point(s) of view expressed in disembodied metric sections. The text's prosimetric form offers a means of simultaneously illustrating the same character in states of sickness and of health, and its startling juxtaposition of allegorical personification and medicalized language situates it at the intersection of courtly, scientific, and devotional discourses. As a healing narrative, the book offers today's scholars of medieval disability an important opportunity to interrogate medical and religious models of disability.

While it is not widely read today, the *Book of Hope* enjoyed considerable success in the fifteenth century: it survives in more than thirty-five manuscripts, in numerous printed editions, and in two Middle English translations. This is the first translation of an excerpt into modern English.

Bibliography

Delogu, Daisy, Emma Cayley, and Joan E. McRae, eds. *A Companion to Alain Chartier (c.1385–1430): Father of French Eloquence.* Brill, 2015.

Gathercole, Patricia. "Illuminations on the Manuscripts of Alain Chartier." *Studi francesi,* vol. 20, 1976, pp. 504–10.

Huot, Sylvia. "Re-Fashioning Boethius: Prose and Poetry in Chartier's Livre de l'Espérance," *Medium Aevum,* vol. 76, no. 2, 2007, pp. 268–84.

Kemp, Simon. *Medieval Psychology.* Greenwood, 1990.

McVaugh, Michael. "Arnau de Vilanova and the Pathology of Cognition." *Corpo e anima, sensi interni e intelletto dai secoli XIII–XIV ai post-cartesiani e spinoziani,* edited by Graziella Federici Vescovini, Valeria Sorge, and Carlo Vinti. Brepols, 2005, pp. 119–38.

Minet-Mahy, Virginie. *Esthétique et pouvoir de l'oeuvre allégorique à l'époque de Charles VI. Imaginaires et discours.* Champion, 2005.

Mühlethaler, Jean-Claude. "Le 'Rooil de oubliance.' Écriture de l'oubli et écriture de la mémoire dans *Le Livre de l'Espérance* d'Alain Chartier." *Études de lettres,* vol. 276, no. 1–2, 2007, pp. 203–22.

Rouy, François. *L'esthétique du traité moral d'après les oeuvres d'Alain Chartier.* Droz, 1980.

Wittstock, Antje. "Die Inkubation des Textes. Krankheit, Melancholie und Schreiben bei Alain Chartier un Georg Wickram." *Melancholie—zwischen Attitüde und Diskurs. Konzepte in Mittelalter und Früher Neuzeit,* edited by Andrea Sieber and Antje Wittstock. V&R Unipress 2009, pp. 257–73.

[This excerpt follows the verse prologue, in which his reflections on the contrast between France's illustrious chivalric past and its piteous present state plunge the Acteur (first person author-narrator) into a profound melancholy.]

Prose I.

The Author/Narrator

In this doleful and sad train of thought, which always presents itself to my heart and accompanies me as I wake and as I fall asleep, which causes my nights to be long and my life disagreeable, I long overworked and crushed my little understanding; it is so overcome and surrounded by unpleasant frenzies that I cannot use it for anything that might bring me happiness or comfort. Not long ago the memory of things past, the frightfulness of present circumstances and the horror of the dangers to come had awakened all of my sad regrets, my pained fantasies and my insecure fear, and so I remained like a man lost, my face pale, my sense troubled, and my blood roiled.

And at this point there came toward me an old lady, all disarrayed and as if indifferent to her dress, skinny, dry and withered, with a pale, dull and colorless complexion, downcast gaze, an afflicted voice, and a drooping lip. Her head was capped with a dirty kerchief filthy with ashes, her body wrapped in a brown mantle. Upon her approach, without saying a word, she suddenly enveloped me in her arms and covered my face and body with that woeful mantle; but she squeezed me so tightly in her arms that I felt my heart crushed inside me as if in a press; and with her hands she held my head and my eyes covered and blocked, so that I was not at liberty to see or to hear. And thus like a faint swooning man she brought me to the infirmary, and threw me on the bed of anguish and malady. She brewed such strange and marvelous beverages prepared in madness and in ignorance, that even Understanding, the young and discerning bachelor who had followed me, sometimes from afar, sometimes up close, as God gave me his company—even this good and wise one, who had conducted me as far as the bed in my hour of need, remained next to me dazed, stunned, as if in a lethargy.

Later I found out that this old woman is named Melancholy, who troubles thoughts, dries the body, corrupts the humors, weakens the sensitive spirits, and leads man to lassitude and death. According to Aristotle's doctrine, the high intellect and elevated understanding of profound and excellent men have often been troubled and darkened by her, when they have dwelt on overly deep and varied thoughts. For the four internal senses of man, which we call the sensitive, imaginative, estimative, and memory, are corporeal and organic, and they can be damaged with excessively frequent or rough use, just as among the five bodily senses the eye is perturbed by looking at overly bright light, or by reading too often, or by fixing one's gaze on tiny, delicate, distinct things.

Poem II.

Puny human nature,
Born to travail and to pain,
Clothed in a fragile body,
You are so feeble, you are so vain,
Tender, vulnerable, uncertain,
And easily struck down!
Your thinking saps your strength,
Your foolish sense harms and kills you
And leads you to ignorance.
10 You are of such poor extraction
That if you are not sustained by the heavens,
You cannot live in good health.

Prose II.

The Author/Narrator

And then, so intensely unsound of body and mind, I was lain out on that disagreeable bed, where for many days I remained with a listless mouth and no appetite. And after great weakness, long fasting, bitter pain and shock in my brain, which Lady Melancholy tormented with her hard hands, I felt her open, shake, and remove the part that sits in the middle of the head in the region of the imaginative, which some call the fantasy. And at that time three terrible simulacra in feminine form, frightening to see, presented themselves to the forefront of my thought, toward the darker left-hand side of my bed.

[*The three "simulacra in feminine form" are Defiance, Indignation and Despair. Each, in turn, chastises the Acteur and exhorts him to take his own life. When the Acteur seems ready to succumb, Nature intervenes to save her creature, awakening Entendement (Intellect), who then admits the Theological Virtues to the bedchamber. The remainder of the book consists of Faith's and Hope's remedial speeches to the Acteur.*]

Endnotes

1   The translation is based on the Middle French text from *Le Livre de l'Espérance*, ed. François Rouy (Champion, 1989). Translation, footnotes, and endnotes have been provided by Julie Singer.

2   The most recent account of Chartier's biography: James C. Laidlaw, "Alain Chartier: A Historical and Biographical Overview," *A Companion to Alain Chartier (c.1385–1430): Father of French Eloquence*, eds. Daisy Delogu, Emma Cayley, and Joan E. McRae (Brill, 2015), pp. 15–32.

3   Certain metric sections are attributable to various characters in the prose narrative: meter 1 is composed in a voice that suggests the Acteur, though it is not explicitly attributed to him; proses 5 and 6 both suggest that meter 6 is voiced by Entendement; and meter 11 seems to be in Espérance's voice. The other meters, on the other hand, remain more troubling; if we accept Sylvia Huot's convincing argument that the poetic passages are spoken through the voice of the authorial persona, then we can see that they represent the end result of the pedagogical process that the three virtues undertake from Prose 5 onward. Sylvia Huot, "Re-Fashioning Boethius: Prose and Poetry in Chartier's *Livre de l'Espérance*," *Medium Aevum*, vol. 76, no. 2, 2007, pp. 268–84.

4   Ibid., p. 273.

The Merchant's Tale from The Canterbury Tales[1] (ca. 1387–1400)

Geoffrey Chaucer
Contributed by Moira Fitzgibbons

Introduction

The *Merchant's Tale* revolves around non-normative bodies and minds. An aging knight, Januarie, perceives his impending mortality, marries a much younger woman, doses himself with performance-enhancing spiced wine, and, shortly thereafter, finds himself blind. Meanwhile, a young squire of the household, Damian, takes to his bed in response to lovesickness and despair. The object of his desire, Januarie's wife May, soon declares herself pregnant; in this putative condition she climbs a tree, engages in adulterous sex, alters her husband's view of reality, and hops back down to the ground, all apparently within a few minutes' time.

Disability studies serves as a useful focal point for considering these forms of "embodied variance" and perceiving survivorship strategies depicted in the poem.[2]

Even as the tale's main characters disregard ethical, artistic, and religious values, they provide intriguing case studies in resiliency and flexibility.

Critical responses to the *Merchant's Tale* often refer to what Derek Pearsall has succinctly called the tale's "nastiness" (l. 165). A combination of factors create this impression, including the Merchant's extended, negative descriptions of Januarie's body and behavior, the decidedly unromantic sexual encounter between the young lovers, and the absence of any moral compass among the tale's main characters. Moreover, the tale's awkward combination of genres and echoes of other pilgrims' tales make it difficult

to connect with the Merchant himself or to revel in Chaucer's literary artistry. In fact, the tale explicitly mocks this kind of aesthetic pleasure: as seen below, no sooner has Januarie evoked the Song of Songs in a (incongruously) lyrical invitation to May than the Merchant curtly derides the "olde, lewde wordes" of the speech (l. 757).

It is precisely this rejection of idealism, however, that establishes common ground between the *Merchant's Tale* and disability studies. Many disability theorists have emphasized the potential for visions of human perfection to erase, dehumanize, or patronize individuals perceived as falling short of these standards. As Lennard Davis writes, Western culture has tended to privilege "a notion of wholeness, order, clean boundaries, as opposed to fragmentations, disordered bodies, [and] messy boundaries" (143). What we define as beautiful often relies upon strictly regulated modes of representation and choices of subject matter. Davis points out, for example, that sculptural depictions of nude bodies exclude "normal biological processes... there are no pregnant Venuses, there are no paintings of Venuses who are menstruating, micturating, defecating...there are no old Venuses" (l. 132). The *Merchant's Tale*, by contrast, graphically depicts aging, copulation, and other "unmentionable" human experiences. Equally important, these moments emerge not as monstrous aberrations, but as part and parcel of everyday life. When May reads Damian's note in the privy, the Merchant describes the site as the place where "ye woot that every wight hath nede" (l. 557). Everyone's body takes part in undignified processes, and everyone knows it. Crucially, this part of the tale highlights the possibilities inherent in the unseemly aspects of human experience. The privy provides May with a space to consider alternatives to her legally binding and repressive marriage.

We should acknowledge, of course, that May does not seem to engage in profound moral reflection as she reads Damian's note. Minds and hearts in the *Merchant's Tale* are no more reliable or transcendent than bodies. For example, the Merchant notes early on that "love is blind al day" (l. 206), an assertion that foreshadows Januarie's physical loss of eyesight later in the tale. In most contexts, this saying associates visual impairment with powerful emotions that override social conventions or rational self-interest. It is difficult, however, to attribute any kind of emotional or spiritual authenticity to Januarie's infatuation with May, or to May's relationship with Damian. Instead of expressing inner truths, these characters' decisions emerge via the interplay between internal urges and external stimuli. Far from a thunderbolt of desire, Januarie's choice of May results from a gradual ("day to day") activity of "heigh fantasye and curious bisinesse" that impresses itself upon his soul (ll. 185–87). Similarly, the Merchant makes clear that he does not know whether May's feelings for Damian result from "destinee," "aventure," or some other cause (ll. 575–84), but he does explain that her heart has "taken swiche impression" of Damian that she resolves to take action (l. 586). In both instances, the protagonists' choices reflect haphazard "impressions" rather than conscious thought or emotional connection. Their minds are as susceptible as the "warm wex" that is invoked by Januarie's expectations of a pliable wife (l. 38) and used in May's adulterous stratagem with the garden key (l. 725).

Cognitive vulnerability plays a crucial role in the tale's final scene. Although May takes advantage of her husband's blindness in order to consummate her relationship with Damian, it is Januarie's suggestible mind that determines the tale's eventual outcome. May's deception exploits not just Januarie's abrupt transition back into the sighted world, but also his anxiety about age-related cognitive impairment ("Ye maze, maze," l. 995) and his strong desire to preserve his marriage and produce an heir. Without overstating May's degree of liberty at the end of the tale, her actions should be connected to other Chaucerian speakers—male as well as female—in vulnerable situations who become extremely quick thinkers and adept fabricators.[3] Drawing from her own experiences being misrepresented and manhandled within Januarie's conjugal fantasies, May successfully manipulates her husband's thought processes.[4]

This is not to say that we should all ascend our own *pyries*—neither May nor any other character in the tale serves as a viable role model of ethical agency. But we would be equally mistaken to ignore May's striking combination of elasticity and toughness;[5] her ability to perceive the arbitrary meanings mapped onto bodies and minds; and her active reshaping of the story she has been forced to inhabit. Read through the lens of disability studies, the *Merchant's Tale*'s value resides in its privileging of intervention over inspiration.[6]

Bibliography

Crocker, Holly A. "Performative Passivity and Fantasies of Masculinity in the Merchant's Tale." *The Chaucer Review*, vol. 38, no. 2, 2003, pp. 178–98.

Davis, Lennard J. *Enforcing Normalcy: Disability, Deafness, and the Body.* Verso, 1995.

Hansen, Elaine Tuttle. "The Merchant's Tale, or Another Poor Worm." *Chaucer's Fictions of Gender.* University of California Press, 1992, pp. 245–66.

Hsy, Jonathan. "The Monk's Tale: Disability/Ability." *The Open Access Companion to the Canterbury Tales*, edited by the OACCT

Editorial Collective, 2017, http://open-canterburytales.dsl.lsu.edu.

Metzler, Irina, "Ageing." *A Social History of Disability in the Middle Ages: Cultural Considerations of Physical Impairment.* Routledge, 2013, pp. 92–153.

Pearman, Tory Vandeventer. "'O Swete Venym Queynte!': Pregnancy and the Disabled Female Body in the Merchant's Tale." *Disability in the Middle Ages: Reconsiderations and Reverberations,* edited by Joshua R. Eyler. Ashgate, 2010, pp. 25–38.

Pearsall, Derek. "The Canterbury Tales II: Comedy." *The Cambridge Companion to Chaucer,* edited by Piero Boitani and Jill Mann. Cambridge University Press, 2004, pp. 160–77.

Singer, Julie. *Blindness and Therapy in Late Medieval French and Italian Poetry.* Boydell and Brewer, 2011.

Wheatley, Edward. *Stumbling Blocks before the Blind: Medieval Constructions of a Disability.* University of Michigan Press, 2010.

[After lamenting the "sorwe" he has experienced in his own recent marriage, the Merchant introduces Januarie, a "worthy knyght" in Lombardy who has begun to contemplate wedlock after sixty years of bachelorhood. Having noted the praise of marriage found in many textual sources, the Merchant depicts a lengthy debate among Januarie and two friends about the institution's costs and benefits. Januarie eventually chooses to marry and settles on a young bride named May—not by directly courting her, but by means of an odd combination of internal reflection ("heigh fantasie") and legal manuevering. The wedding includes all the usual formalities and festivities; but Damian, a young squire in Januarie's household, is painfully overcome with desire for May. Unaware of this complication and fortified with wine and spices, Januarie prepares to consummate the union.]

426 The bryde was broght a-bedde as stille
      as stoon;
    And whan the bed was with the preest
      y-blessed,
    Out of the chambre hath every wight
      him dressed.°
    And Ianuarie hath faste in armes take
430 His fresshe May, his paradys, his make.°
    He lulleth° hir, he kisseth hir ful ofte
    With thikke bristles of his berd unsofte,
    Lyk to the skin of houndfish, sharp as
      brere,°
    For he was shave al newe in his manere.
    He rubbeth hir aboute hir tendre face,
    And seyde thus, "allas! I moot° trespace
    To yow, my spouse, and yow gretly of-
      fende,
    Er° tyme come that I wil doun de-
      scende.

But nathelees, considereth this," quod
    he,
440 This wol be doon at leyser° parfitly.°
    It is no fors° how longe that we pleye;
    In trewe wedlok wedded be we tweye;°
    And blessed be the yok that we been
      inne.°
    For in our actes we mowe° do no sinne.
    A man may do no sinne with his wyf,
    Ne hurte him-selven with his owene
      knyf;
    For we han leve to pleye us by the lawe."
    Thus laboureth he til that the day gan
      dawe;°
    And than he taketh a sop in fyn clar-
      ree,°
450 And upright in his bed than° sitteth he,
    And after that he sang ful loude and
      clere,
    And kiste his wyf, and made wantoun
      chere.°
    He was al coltish, ful of ragerye,°
    And ful of Iargon° as a flekked pye.°
    The slakke skin aboute his nekke sha-
      keth,
    Whyl that he sang; so chaunteth he and
      craketh.°
    But God wot° what that May thoughte
      in hir herte,
    Whan she him saugh up sittinge in his
      sherte,°
    In his night-cappe, and with his nekke
      lene;
460 She preyseth nat his pleying worth a
      bene.
    Than seide he thus, "my reste wol I take;
    Now day is come, I may no lenger
      wake."
    And doun he leyde his heed, and sleep
      til pryme.°

every...dressed *every person removed himself*   **make** *mate*   **lulleth** *fondles*   **brere** *briars*   **moot**
must   **Er** *before*   **leyser** *leisure*   **parfitly** *perfectly*   **is no fors** *does not matter*   **tweye** *two*   **yok...**
inne *the yoke that we are in*   **mowe** *may*   **gan dawe** *began to dawn*   **sop...clarree** *piece of bread*
[dipped] in fine claret   **than** *then*   **wantoun chere** *lustful faces*   **ragerye** *joyful energy*   **largon** *chatter*   **flekked pye** *spotted magpie*   **craketh** *boasts*   **wot** *knows*   **sherte** *shirt*   **pryme** *6 a.m.*

And afterward, whan that he saugh his
    tyme,
Up ryseth Ianuarie; but fresshe May
Holdeth° hir chambre un-to the fourthe
    day,
As usage is of wyves for the beste.
For every labour som-tyme moot han
    reste,
Or elles° longe may he nat endure;
470 This is to seyn, no lyves creature,
    Be it of fish, or brid,° or beest, or man.
Now wol I speke of woful Damian,
That languissheth for love, as ye shul
    here;
Therfore I speke to him in this manere:
I seye, "O sely° Damian, allas!
Answere to my demaunde, as in this
    cas,
How shaltow° to thy lady fresshe May
Telle thy wo? She wole alwey seye 'nay';
Eek° if thou speke, she wol thy wo
    biwreye;°
480 God be thyn help, I can no bettre seye."
    This syke° Damian in Venus fyr
So brenneth,° that he dyeth for desyr;
For which he putte his lyf in aventure,°
No lenger mighte he in this wyse
    endure;
But prively a penner° gan he borwe,°
And in a lettre wroot he al his sorwe,
In manere of a compleynt or a lay,°
Un-to his faire fresshe lady May.
And in a purs of silk, heng on his
    sherte,
490 He hath it put, and leyde it at his herte.
    The mone° that, at noon, was, thilke°
    day
That Ianuarie hath wedded fresshe May,

In two of Taur, was in-to Cancre
    gliden;°
So longe hath Maius in hir chambre
    biden,°
As custume is un-to thise nobles alle.
A bryde shal nat eten in the halle,
Til dayes foure or three dayes atte leste
Y-passed been;° than lat hir go to feste.°
The fourthe day compleet fro noon to
    noon,
500 Whan that the heighe masse was y-
    doon,
In halle sit this Ianuarie, and May
As fresh as is the brighte someres day.
And so bifel, how that this gode man
Remembred him upon this Damian,
And seyde, "Seinte Marie! how may this
    be,
That Damian entendeth° nat to me?
Is he ay° syk, or how may this bityde?"°
His squyeres, whiche that° stoden ther
    bisyde,
Excused him by-cause of his siknesse,
510 Which letted° him to doon his bisi-
    nesse;
Noon other cause mighte make him
    tarie.
"That me forthinketh,"° quod this
    Ianuarie,
"He is a gentil° squyer, by my trouthe!
If that he deyde, it were harm and
    routhe;°
He is as wys, discreet, and as secree°
As any man I woot° of his degree;
And ther-to manly and eek° servisable,°
And for to been a thrifty° man right
    able.
But after mete,° as sone as ever I may,
520 I wol my-self visyte him and eek May,

Holdeth *kept to* **elles** *otherwise* **brid** *bird* **sely** *foolish* **shaltow** *shall you* **Eek** *also* **biwreye**
betray **syke** *sick* **brenneth** *burns* **aventure** *danger* **penner** *pen-case* **gan he borwe** *he went
to borrow* **lay** *song* **mone** *moon* **thilke** *the same* **two...gliden** [*had been*] *in two of Taurus, was
[now] glided into Cancer* **biden** *lingered* **Y-passed been** *had passed* **feste** *feast* **entendeth** *attends* **ay** *still* **bityde** *happen* **whiche that** *who* **letted** *prevented* **me forthinketh** *I regret* **gentil**
noble **routhe** *a pity* **secree** *reserved* **woot** *know* **eek** *also* **servisable** *useful* **thrifty** *respect-
able* **mete** *food*

251

To doon him al the confort that I can."
And for that word him blessed every
    man,
That, of his bountee° and his gentillesse,
He wolde so conforten in siknesse
His squyer, for it was a gentil dede.
"Dame," quod this Ianuarie, "tak good
    hede,
At-after mete ye, with your wommen
    alle,
Whan ye han been in chambre out of
    this halle,
That alle ye go see this Damian;
530 Doth him disport,° he is a gentil man;
And telleth him that I wol him visyte,
Have I no-thing but rested me a lyte;°
And spede yow faste,° for I wole abyde
Til that ye slepe faste by my syde."
And with that word he gan to him to
    calle
A squyer, that was marchal° of his halle,
And tolde him certeyn thinges, what he
    wolde.
This fresshe May hath streight hir wey
    y-holde,°
With alle hir wommen, un-to Damian.
540 Doun by his beddes syde sit she than,
Confortinge him as goodly as she may.
This Damian, whan that his tyme he
    say,°
In secree wise his purs, and eek his
    bille,°
In which that he y-writen hadde his
    wille,°
Hath put in-to hir hand, with-outen
    more,°
Save that he syketh° wonder depe and
    sore,
And softely to hir right thus seyde he:
"Mercy! and that ye nat discovere° me;

For I am deed,° if that this thing be
    kid."°
550 This purs hath she inwith° hir bosom
    hid,
And wente hir wey; ye gete namore of
    me.
But un-to Ianuarie y-comen is she,
That on his beddes syde sit ful softe.
He taketh hir, and kisseth hir ful ofte,
And leyde him doun to slepe, and that
    anon.
She feyned hir as that she moste gon°
Ther-as° ye woot that every wight mot
    nede.°
And whan she of this bille hath taken
    hede,
She rente° it al to cloutes° atte laste,
560 And in the privee° softely it caste.
Who studieth° now but faire fresshe
    May?
Adoun by olde Ianuarie she lay,
That sleep, til that the coughe hath him
    awaked;
Anon he preyde hir strepen hir al
    naked;
He wolde of hir, he seyde, han som
    plesaunce,
And seyde, hir clothes dide him encom-
    braunce,
And she obeyeth, be hir lief or looth.°
But lest that precious° folk be with me
    wrooth,°
How that he wroghte,° I dar nat to yow
    telle;
570 Or whether hir thoughte it paradys or
    helle;
But here I lete hem werken in hir wyse
Til evensong° rong, and that they moste
    aryse.

bountee *kindness*   Doth him disport *amuse him*   lyte *little*   spede yow faste *hurry up*   marchal *chief steward*   y-holde *taken*   say *saw*   his...bille *his purse, and also his note*   wille *desire*   more *any other action*   syketh *sighs*   discovere *expose*   deed *dead*   kid *known*   inwith *within*   gon *go*   Ther-as *where*   mot nede *must need*   rente *ripped*   cloutes *shreds*   privee *privy*   studieth *ponders*   lief or looth *eager or unwilling*   precious *prudish*   wrooth *angry*   wroghte *proceeded*   evensong *evening prayer bell*

[Having learned of Damian's passion for her, May takes pity on Damian and lets him know by letter that, when the occasion allows, she will fulfill his desires. Damian immediately feels better and waits humbly upon Januarie. In the meantime, Januarie decides to augment his pleasures by creating a walled garden. It is so lovely that the married gods Pluto and Proserpina take their pleasure there, along with their retinue of fairies. Januarie keeps the key to the garden on his person at all times and regularly takes advantage of its privacy to have sex with May there. As the Merchant laments below, however, Fortune presents Januarie with an unexpected challenge.]

665 O sodeyn hap,° o thou fortune instable,
    Lyk to the scorpioun so deceivable,
    That flaterest with thyn heed when
       thou wolt stinge;°
    Thy tayl is deeth, thurgh thyn envenim-
       inge.°
    O brotil° Ioye! o swete venim queynte!°
670 O monstre, that so subtilly canst peynte
    Thy yiftes,° under hewe° of stedfast-
      nesse,
    That thou deceyvest bothe more and
      lesse!
    Why hastow° Ianuarie thus deceyved,
    That haddest him for thy ful frend
      receyved?
    And now thou hast biraft° him bothe
      hise yen.°
    For sorwe of which desyreth he to
      dyen.°
    Allas! this noble Ianuarie free,
    Amidde his lust and his prosperitee,
    Is woxen° blind, and that al sodeynly.

680 He wepeth and he wayleth pitously;
    And ther-with-al° the fyr of Ialousye,°
    Lest that his wyf sholde falle in som
      folye,
    So brente° his herte, that he wolde
      fayn°
    That som man bothe him and hir had
      slayn.
    For neither after his deeth, nor in his
      lyf,
    Ne wolde he that she were love ne wyf,°
    But ever live as widwe in clothes blake,
    Soul° as the turtle that lost hath hir
      make.°
    But atte laste, after a monthe or tweye,
690 His sorwe gan aswage,° sooth° to seye;
    For whan he wiste° it may noon other
      be.°
    He paciently took his adversitee;
    Save,° out of doute, he may nat for-
      goon°
    That he nas Ialous evermore in oon;°
    Which Ialousye it was so outrageous,
    That neither in halle, nin° noon other
      hous,
    Ne in noon other place, never-the-mo,
    He nolde suffre° hir for to ryde or go,
    But-if that he had hand on hir alway;
700 For which ful ofte° wepeth fresshe May,
    That loveth Damian so benignely,°
    That she mot outher dyen sodeynly,°
    Or elles she mot han° him as hir leste;°
    She wayteth whan hir herte wolde
      breste.°
    Up-on that other syde Damian
    Bicomen is° the sorwefulleste man
    That ever was; for neither night ne day
    Ne mighte he speke a word to fresshe
      May,

---

sodeyn hap *sudden chance*   **when...stinge** *when you want to sting*   **enveniminge** *poisoning*   **brotil** *uncertain*   **queynte** *deceptive*   **yiftes** *gifts*   **hewe** *demeanor*   **hastow** *have you*   **biraft** *taken away*   **yen** *eyes*   **dyen** *die*   **woxen** *grown*   **ther-with-al** *along with that*   **Ialousye** *jealousy*   **brente** *burned*   **fayn** *rather*   **were...wyf** *would be a lover or wife*   **Soul** *solitary*   **make** *mate*   **gan aswage** *began to diminish*   **sooth** *the truth*   **wiste** *knew*   **noon other be** *not be any other way*   **Save** *except*   **forgoon** *refrain*   **nas...oon** *was always jealous in one respect*   **nin** *nor*   **nolde suffre** *would not allow*   **ofte** *often*   **benignely** *graciously*   **mot...sodeynly** *must either die very soon*   **han** *have*   **as hir leste** *as she wants*   **breste** *burst*   **Bicomen is** *has become*

As to his purpos, of no swich° matere,
710 But-if that Ianuarie moste it here,°
That hadde an hand up-on hir evermo.°
But nathelees, by wryting to and fro
And privee° signes, wiste he what she
    mente;
And she knew eek the fyn° of his
    entente.
O Ianuarie, what mighte it thee availle,°
Thou mightest see as fer° as shippes
    saille?
For also° good is blind deceyved be,
As be deceyved whan a man may se.
Lo, Argus,[7] which that hadde an hon-
    dred yen,°
720 For al that ever he coude poure or
    pryen,°
Yet was he blent;° and, God wot,° so
    ben mo,°
That wenen° wisly that it be nat so.
Passe over is an ese, I sey na-more.
This fresshe May, that I spak of so yore,°
In warme wex hath emprented the
    cliket,°
That Ianuarie bar° of the smale wiket,°
By which in-to his gardin ofte he wente.
And Damian, that knew al hir entente,
The cliket countrefeted prively;
730 Ther nis na-more to seye, but hastily
Som wonder by this cliket shal bityde,°
Which ye shul heren, if ye wole abyde.°

[The Merchant briefly meditates upon trickery in love as found in Ovid and other sources.]

740 But now to purpos; er° that dayes eighte
Were passed, er the monthe of Iuil,°
    bifil°

That Ianuarie hath caught so greet a wil,
Thurgh egging° of his wyf, him for to
    pleye
In his gardin, and no wight° but they
    tweye,
That in a morwe un-to this May seith
    he:
"Rys up, my wyf, my love, my lady free;
The turtles vois° is herd, my douve°
    swete;
The winter is goon, with alle his reynes
    wete;°
Com forth now, with thyn eyen
    columbyn!°
750 How fairer been° thy brestes than is
    wyn!
The gardin is enclosed al aboute;
Com forth, my whyte spouse; out of
    doute,
Thou hast me wounded in myn herte,
    o wyf!
No spot of thee ne knew I al my lyf.
Com forth, and lat us taken our dis-
    port;°
I chees° thee for my wyf and my
    confort."[8]
Swiche olde lewed° wordes used he;
On° Damian a signe made she,
That he sholde go biforen° with his
    cliket:°
760 This Damian thanne hath opened the
    wiket,
And in he stirte,° and that in swich
    manere,
That no wight mighte it see neither
    y-here;
And stille he sit under a bush anoon.°
This Ianuarie, as blind as is a stoon,

swich *such* moste it here *must hear it* evermo *always* privee *secret* eek the fyn *also the
goal* availle *help* fer *far* also *as* yen *eyes* poure or pryen *look closely or investigate* blent
deceived wot *knows* ben mo *are many* wenen *think* so yore *before* cliket *key* bar *carried* wiket *entrance* bityde *happen* wole abyde *will stay* er *before* Iuil *July* bifil *[it] happened* egging *urging* wight *person* vois *voice* douve *dove* reynes wete *wet rains* columbyn
dove-like been *are* disport *pleasure* chees *choose* lewed *ignorant, crude* On *to* biforen
ahead cliket *key* stirte *leaped* anoon *right away*

254

With Maius in his hand, and no wight
  mo,°
In-to his fresshe gardin is ago,°
And clapte° to the wiket sodeynly
"Now, wyf," quod he, "heer nis but thou
  and I,
That art the creature that I best love.
770 For, by that lord that sit in heven above,
Lever ich hadde dyen° on a knyf,
Than thee offende, trewe dere wyf!
For goddes sake, thenk how I thee
  chees,
Noght for no coveityse, doutelees,°
But only for the love I had to thee.
And though that I be old, and may nat
  see,
Beth° to me trewe, and I shal telle yow
  why.
Three thinges, certes,° shul ye winne
  ther-by;°
First, love of Crist, and to your-self
  honour,
780 And al myn heritage,° toun and tour;°
I yeve it yow,° maketh chartres° as yow
  leste;
This shal be doon to-morwe er sonne
  reste.°
So wisly god my soule bringe in blisse,
I prey yow first, in covenant ye me
  kisse.
And thogh that I be Ialous, wyte° me
  noght.
Ye been so depe enprented in my
  thoght,
That, whan that I considere your beau-
  tee,
And ther-with-al the unlykly elde° of
  me,
I may nat, certes, thogh I sholde dye,

790 Forbere to been out of your companye
For verray love; this is with-outen
  doute.
Now kis me, wyf, and lat us rome
  aboute."
This fresshe May, whan she thise wordes
  herde,
Benignely to Ianuarie answerde,
But first and forward she bigan to wepe,
"I have," quod she, "a soule for to kepe
As wel as ye, and also myn honour,
And of my wyfhod thilke tendre flour,°
Which that I have assured in your hond,
800 Whan that the preest to yow my body
  bond;°
Wherfore° I wole answere in this
  manere
By the leve of yow, my lord so dere:
I prey to god, that never dawe° the day
That I ne sterve,° as foule as womman
  may,
If ever I do un-to my kin that shame,
Or elles I empeyre° so my name,
That I be fals; and if I do that lakke,°
Do strepe me and put me in a sakke,
And in the nexte river do me drenche.°
810 I am a gentil womman and no wenche.°
Why speke ye thus? but men ben ever
  untrewe,
And wommen have repreve of yow ay
  newe.°
Ye han non other contenance,° I leve,°
But speke to us of untrust and repreve."
And with that word she saugh wher
  Damian
Sat in the bush, and coughen she bigan,
And with hir finger signes made she,
That Damian sholde climbe up-on a
  tree,

no wight mo *no other person*　ago *gone*　clapte *pushed*　Lever...dyen *I had rather die*　doutelees *undoubtedly*　Beth *be*　certes *certainly*　ther-by *in that way*　heritage *estate*　toun and tour *town and tower* [i.e. everything]　yeve it yow *give it to you*　chartres *documents*　er sonne reste *before the sun sets*　wyte *blame*　unlykly elde *unsuitable age*　thilke tendre flour *the same tender flower*　bond *bound*　Wherfore *therefore*　dawe *dawn*　sterve *would not die*　empeyre *damage*　lakke *failing*　do me drenche *drown me*　wenche *low-class woman*　repreve...newe *blame from you always these days*　contenance *behavior*　leve *believe*

That charged was with fruit, and up he
wente;
820 For verraily° he knew al hir entente,
And every signe that she coude make
Wel bet° than Ianuarie, hir owene
make.°
For in a lettre she had told him al
Of this matere, how he werchen shal.°
And thus I lete him sitte up-on the
pyrie,°
And Ianuarie and May rominge myrie.

[The Merchant turns his attention to a far
corner of the garden, where Pluto and Proserpyna are discussing the events unfolding
among Januarie, May, and Damian. Pluto
deplores the disrespect shown to "this olde,
blynde, worthy knyght" and describes May as
a case study in women's untrustworthiness.
He vows that Januarie will regain his sight
and learn about Damian and May's treachery. Proserpyna, for her part, defends women
against Pluto's accusations and asserts that
she will provide May with a sufficient answer
once Januarie learns the truth. She notes that
she herself is a woman; if she does not speak
out, she will "swelle til myn herte breke." The
couple mutually decides to stop arguing with
one another.]

928 Now lat us turne agayn to Ianuarie,
That in the gardin with his faire May
930 Singeth, ful merier than the papeiay°
"Yow love I best, and shal, and other
noon."
So longe aboute the aleyes° is he goon,
Til he was come agaynes thilke pyrie,
Wher-as this Damian sitteth full myrie
An heigh,° among the fresshe leves
grene.

This fresshe May, that is so bright and
shene,°
Gan for to syke,° and seyde, "allas, my
syde!
Now sir," quod she, "for aught that may
bityde,°
I moste han of the peres that I see,
940 Or I mot° dye, so sore longeth me°
To eten of° the smale peres grene.
Help, for hir love that is of hevene
quene!
I telle yow wel, a womman in my plyt°
May han to fruit° so greet an appetyt
That she may dyen, but° she of it have."
"Allas!" quod he, "that I ne had heer a
knave°
That coude climbe; allas! allas!" quod he,
"That I am blind." "Ye, sir, no fors,"°
quod she:
"But wolde ye vouche-sauf,° for goddes
sake,
950 The pyrie° inwith° your armes for to
take,
(For wel I woot that ye mistruste me)
Thanne sholde I climbe wel y-nogh,"°
quod she,
"So I my foot mighte sette upon your
bak."
"Certes," quod he, "ther-on shal be no
lak,°
Mighte I yow helpen with myn herte
blood."
He stoupeth doun, and on his bak she
stood,
And caughte hir by a twiste,° and up
she gooth.
Ladies, I prey yow that ye be nat
wrooth;
I can nat glose,° I am a rude man.
960 And sodeynly anon this Damian

---

verraily *truly* bet *better* make *mate* how...shal *what he will do* pyrie *pear tree* papeiay *par-
rot* aleyes *walkways* An heigh *on high* shene *fair* Gan...syke *began to sigh* for...bityde *anything
that might happen* mot *must* sore longeth me *sorely do I long* eten of *to eat* plyt *situation [i.e.
pregnancy]* to fruit *for fruit* but *unless* knave *servant boy* no fors *no matter* vouche-sauf
consent pyrie *pear tree* inwith *within* y-nogh *enough* shal...lak *will be no limitation* by a twiste
by a branch

Gan pullen up the smok,° and in he
   throng.°
And whan that Pluto saugh this grete
   wrong,
To Ianuarie he gaf° agayn his sighte,
And made him see, as wel as ever he
   mighte.
And whan that he hadde caught his
   sighte agayn,
Ne was ther never man of thing so
   fayn.°
But on his wyf his thoght was evermo;
Up to the tree he caste his eyen two,
And saugh that Damian his wyf had
   dressed°
970 In swich manere, it may nat ben ex-
   pressed
But if I wolde speke uncurteisly:
And up he yaf° a roring and a cry
As doth the moder whan the child shal
   dye:
"Out! help! allas! harrow!" he gan to
   crye,
"O stronge lady store,° what dostow?"°
And she answerde, "sir, what eyleth°
   yow?
Have pacience, and reson in your
   minde,
I have yow holpe° on bothe your eyen
   blinde.
Up peril of my soule, I shal nat lyen,
980 As me was taught, to hele with your
   yen,°
Was no-thing bet° to make yow to see
Than strugle with a man up-on a tree.
God woot, I dide it in ful good entente."
"Strugle!" quod he, "ye, algate° in it
   wente!
God yeve yow bothe on shames deeth
   to dyen!

He swyved° thee, I saugh it with myne
   yen,
And elles be I hanged by the hals!"°
"Thanne is," quod she, "my medicyne al
   fals;
For certeinly, if that ye mighte see,
990 Ye wolde nat seyn thise wordes un-to
   me
Ye han som glimsing° and no parfit°
   sighte."
"I see," quod he, "as wel as ever I
   mighte,
Thonked be God! with bothe myne eyen
   two,
And by my trouthe, me thoughte he
   dide thee so."
"Ye maze,° maze, gode sire," quod she,
"This thank have I for I have maad yow
   see;
Allas!" quod she, "that ever I was so
   kinde!"
"Now, dame," quod he, "lat al passe out
   of minde.
Com doun, my lief,° and if I have missayd,°
1000 God help me so, as I am yvel apayd.°
But, by my fader soule, I wende han
   seyn,°
How that this Damian had by thee
   leyn,°
And that thy smok had leyn up-on his
   brest."
"Ye, sire," quod she, "ye may wene as
   yow lest;°
But, sire, a man that waketh out of his
   sleep,
He may nat sodeynly wel taken keep
Up-on a thing, ne seen it parfitly,
Right so a man, that longe hath blind
   y-be,°

---

glose *speak deceptively*   smok *undergarment*   throng *pushed*   gaf *gave*   fayn *pleased*   dressed
positioned   yaf *gave*   stronge lady store *bold, shameless woman*   dostow *are you doing*   eyleth
ails   holpe *helped*   yen *eyes*   bet *better*   algate *altogether*   swyved *had sex with*   hals *neck*   glim-
sing *glimpsing*   parfit *perfect*   maze *are bewildered*   lief *dear*   missayd *misspoken*   yvel apayd *badly
displeased*   wende han seyn *thought to have seen*   leyn *lain*   wene...lest *think as you want*

Til that he be adawed° verraily;
1010 Ne may nat sodeynly so wel y-see,
   First whan his sighte is newe come
      ageyn,
   As he that hath a day or two y-seyn.
   Til that your sighte y-satled be° a whyle,
   Ther may ful many a sighte yow bigyle.°
   Beth war,° I prey yow; for, by hevene
      king,
   Ful many a man weneth° to seen a
      thing,
   And it is al another than it semeth.
   He that misconceyveth,° he misdem-
      eth."°
   And with that word she leep doun fro
      the tree.
1020 This Ianuarie, who is glad but he?
   He kisseth hir, and clippeth° hir ful
      ofte,
   And on hir wombe he stroketh hir ful
      softe,
   And to his palays° hoom he hath hir
      lad.°
   Now, gode men, I pray yow to be glad.
   Thus endeth heer my tale of Ianuarie;
   God blesse us and his moder Seinte
      Marie!

---

y-be *been*   adawed *roused*   y-satled be *is settled for*   bigyle *trick*   Beth war *beware*   weneth *thinks*   misconceyveth *thinks wrongly*   misdemeth *judges wrongly*   clippeth *embraces*   palays *palace*   lad *led*

Endnotes

1   The text is taken from *The Canterbury Tales*, edited by Walter Skeat, *The Complete Works of Geoffrey Chaucer*, 2nd edn. (Clarendon Press, 1900). This text is in the public domain, released on July 22, 2007. I have provided the footnotes and endnotes and silently changed some instances of capitalization and punctuation where it seemed to facilitate comprehension.

2   For a definition and useful discussion of "embodied variance," see Jonathan Hsy, "The Monk's Tale: Disability/Ability," *The Open Access Companion to the Canterbury Tales*, eds. OACCT Editorial Collective, 2017, http://opencanterburytales.dsl.lsu.edu.

3   We might compare May, for example, to Chauntecleer the rooster in the *Nun's Priest's Tale*, who escapes the fox's jaws by conjuring up a triumphant speech the fox might make. Although less directly threatened, Jankin the squire in the *Summoner's Tale* shows a quickness similar to May's when he devises the clever interpretation of the lord's mighty fart.

4   While Proserpina presumably helps her at this moment, May has already demonstrated through her plotting and use of multiple forms of communication that she is resourceful and clever in her own right.

5   Januarie and Damian also demonstrate this ability, albeit to a less striking extent: Januarie learns to live with his blindness (ll. 691–92), and Damian eventually picks up a penner in an attempt to do something about his lovesickness (l. 485).

6   For a seminal critique of the connection between disability and inspiration, see Stella Young, "I'm not your inspiration, thank you very much," TEDxSydney (2014), http://www.ted.com/talks/stella_young_i_m_not_your_inspiration_thank_you_very_much)..

7   In Greek mythology, Argus is a giant with a hundred eyes.

8   These lines evoke the biblical Song of Solomon (e.g., Song of Solomon 7:11).

The Man of Law's Tale from The Canterbury Tales[1] (ca. 1387–1400)

Geoffrey Chaucer
Contributed by Paul A. Broyles

Introduction

The *Man of Law's Tale*, with its border-crossing heroine Custaunce, explores many forms of difference and their roles in creating communal identity. Custaunce, daughter of the emperor of Rome, is married to the Sultan of Syria. Exiled upon his murder, she drifts to Northumberland, participates in multiple miracles, and marries the king and gives birth to his son before being exiled yet again with her child; they eventually reunite in Rome and their son becomes emperor. While the early portion of the tale set in Syria explores cultural identity through the interplay of race and religion, its Northumbrian episode (beginning at l. 505) turns to disability to define spiritual and social boundaries.

The tale places blindness at the root of the Christian history of Northumberland—a part of England—which is pagan when Custaunce arrives. Custaunce has privately taught Christian doctrine to Hermengild, the wife of her benefactor, and the two women have been practicing their religion together in secret. But Christianity does not pass beyond this female domestic sphere until they encounter a "blynde Britoun" (l. 561) on the beach, who begs Hermengild to restore his sight. He is a member of the Briton Christian population that formerly governed the island, connecting Custaunce's religion with an insular history that predates the coming of the English. Later, a knight who tries to frame Custaunce for murder is miraculously blinded, which leads King Alla to convert to Christianity.

The tale's use of blindness follows what Edward Wheatley has termed the "religious model" of disability: both the Briton's blindness and the false knight's blinding are understood exclusively in spiritual terms. The Briton's blindness is significant to the scene's religious message, yet the tale is so uninterested in the man himself that, unlike his sources, Chaucer does not even report that his sight is restored. The blind man exists to demonstrate the sanctity of Hermengild and Custaunce and to impel public recognition of their Christianity; his blindness serves narratively only to demand a miraculous cure. He thus exemplifies what David Mitchell and Sharon Snyder call "narrative prosthesis": the tale depends upon disability to disrupt the social order only to eliminate and erase its deviance.[2]

Yet within the cultural system of the tale, his blindness carries great—and double-edged—significance. Since under the religious model disabilities, including blindness, could be understood as signs of sin, the Briton's blindness might be taken to indicate a spiritual failure on the part of the Britons, earlier inhabitants of the island who (according to Bede's *Ecclesiastical History of the English People*) failed to evangelize their Germanic conquerors.[3] Elsewhere, however, the tale reports that the purpose of miracles, even those rooted in hardship, may simply be to demonstrate God's power: "God lyste to shewe his wonderfull miracle / In hire, for we shulde seen his myghti werkys" (ll. 477–78). This language recalls John 9, in which Jesus heals a man born blind and explains that his condition exists not as a punishment for sin, "but that the works of God should be made manifest in him" (John 9:3).[4] Disability under the religious model is not limited to being a sign or metaphor for sin; people with disabilities also play a privileged role in revealing God's truths. And the Briton, despite his physical blindness, shows unique spiritual sight in recognizing Hermengild's holiness. Indeed, Chaucer goes beyond his sources in noting that blind people can access other forms of vision than the physical through the "yen [eyes] of [the] mynde" (l. 552).[5]

The power of this Christianity out of Britain's past manifests itself not just as spiritual sight, but by shaping Northumbrian jurisprudence and marking a criminal's body with the sign of his sin. A Northumbrian knight frames Custaunce for murder and swears to her guilt on "a Briton Book writen with evaungiles" (l. 666)—presumably an ancient gospel-book produced by the Britons. Although this artifact carries no religious meaning for the pagan court, the knight suffers an immediate, gory punishment: a hand strikes him on the neck so that both his eyes burst out. This punitive miracle showcases the power of the Christian God so dramatically that King Alla and his court promptly convert. Once again, the Briton past is instrumental to the conversion of the realm. By associating blindness specifically with the Britons, the tale not only shows God's power but emphasizes the role of Briton Christianity in carrying Custaunce's Roman Christianity into the English future.

Custaunce herself is a figure consistently marked by her body's deviations from the norms that surround her. Set apart by her sex, her race, her religion, she fits uneasily wherever she goes. Donegild, King Alla's mother, is dismayed that her son would marry "so straunge a creature" (l. 700), emphasizing Custaunce's foreignness; Donegild pushes this language to an almost inhuman extreme when she falsely describes Custaunce's new-

born son Maurice as "so horrible a fendlyche creature" (l. 751). In making this accusation, Donegild attacks Custaunce through her maternal body, seeking to use the idea of a non-normative or "monstrous" birth to redefine Custaunce and her son not just as culturally foreign but outside the category of the human entirely.

Medieval accounts of so-called monstrous births may in part represent a framework for thinking about children born with congenital disabilities.[6] While the *Man of Law's Tale* does not actually represent a "monstrous" child—it takes pains to stress the beauty of Custaunce's son, Maurice—Custaunce is rumored to have given birth to such a baby, a charge that sheds light on the role of women's bodies and on social attitudes toward people with disabilities. In the story of Custaunce and others like it, rumors of a non-normative birth are intended to lead to the queen's banishment or execution. Monstrous births frequently carried the suggestion of moral and especially sexual deviance: nonhuman offspring might be said to result from sex with an animal or other nonhuman creature. But in Custaunce's story, the child's supposed abnormality speaks directly to his mother's body. Custaunce, Donegild asserts, is herself inhuman: "the moder was an elfe" (l. 754). While this accusation is meant to render Custaunce inhuman and perhaps monstrous, it points to the dangerous power of women's reproductive bodies that Tory Vandeventer Pearman has analyzed in the *Merchant's Tale*. Custaunce's body and that of her son, Donegild reminds us, are linked: Maurice's body, in its supposed deviance, reflects upon Custaunce's; Custaunce's body has power over her son's. Even if accusations of monstrous births often prove false in stories like Custaunce's, they suggest that the intimate biological connection between mothers and children was dangerous to both: if mothers might be to blame for their children's deviations from bodily norms, both could be excluded from human society.

But Alla, who does not take the bait, offers an alternative model for understanding non-normative births. On hearing that his son is monstrous, the king is dismayed, weeping privately. But he explicitly instructs that both child ("al be it foule or faire," l. 764) and wife should be kept until he returns; other comments indicate that he understands accepting the child as a religious duty. His attitude falls well short of embracing his "monstrous" child, but his response shows that he understands the birth to accord with God's will, and does not believe himself empowered to reject such a child—a markedly different response than Donegild anticipates. While Alla's reaction marks the birth of a non-normative child as an occasion for grief, it also asserts a Christian duty to care for such children, and dramatizes a layered human reaction.

That the tale's two major representations of disability cluster in the English section is telling. The Syrian and Northumbrian episodes parallel each other in many ways, but Northumberland is converted while Syria is destroyed because (as Geraldine Heng has argued) Syria is imagined as irreconcilably racially and religiously different from a "normative" European Christianity, while England's pagan past is not. In Northumberland, which the tale does not imagine as racially separate from Custaunce or from Chaucer's English audiences, physical impairment becomes a key category for representing difference. Spiritually charged blindness allows the tale to showcase a long tradition of Christianity in Britain and circumscribe the new community of Northumbrian Christianity; Custaunce's maternal body shows how disability might be leveraged to exclude people from the category of humanity altogether. Where distinctions of race and religion break down, the tale turns to bodily norms and disability to create and police its boundaries.

Bibliography

Eberly, Susan Schoon. "Fairies and the Folklore of Disability: Changelings, Hybrids and the Solitary Fairy." *Folklore*, vol. 99, no. 1, 1988, pp. 58–77. Reprinted with revisions in *The Good People: New Fairylore Essays*, edited by Peter Narváez. University of Kentucky Press, 1997, pp. 227–50.

Heng, Geraldine. "Beauty and the East, a Modern Love Story: Women, Children, and Imagined Communities in *The Man of Law's Tale* and Its Others." *Empire of Magic: Medieval Romance and the Politics of Cultural Fantasy*. Columbia University Press, 2003, pp. 181–237.

Pearman, Tory Vandeventer. "'O Sweete Venym Queynte!': Pregnancy and the Disabled Female Body in the *Merchant's Tale*." *Disability in the Middle Ages: Reconsiderations and Reverberations*, edited by Joshua R. Eyler. Ashgate, 2010, pp. 25–37.

Schlauch, Margaret. *Chaucer's Constance and Accused Queens*. New York University Press, 1927.

Wheatley, Edward. "Blinding, Blindness, and Sexual Transgression." *Stumbling Blocks Before the Blind: Medieval Constructions of a Disability*. University of Michigan Press, 2010, pp. 129–54.

———. "Instructive Interventions: Miraculous Chastisement and Cure." *Stumbling Blocks Before the Blind: Medieval Constructions of a Disability*. University of Michigan Press, 2010, pp. 155–85.

[The Man of Law introduces his tale by complaining that there are hardly any tales, except those concerning incest, that Chaucer has not already told. This is followed by a prologue in which he describes the misery that is caused by poverty.]

Here bigynneth the Tale of the Man of Lawe

134 In Surrye° whilom° dwelte a companye
    Of chapmen° riche, and therto° sadde° and trewe,
    That wide-where° senten here spicerye,°
    Clothis of golde and satyns riche of hewe.
    Here° chaffare° was so thrifty° and so newe
    That every wight° hath deynte° to chaffare°
140 With hem, and eke to sellen hem hire ware.
      Now fille it that the maistres of that sorte°
    Han shapen hem° to Rome for to wende.°
    Were it for chapmanhode° or for disporte,°
    Noon other message wolde they theder sende,
    But comen hymselfe to Rome—this is th'ende.
    And in swiche place as thoughte hem avauntage,
    For hire eace,° they taken here herbergage.°
      Sojourned han these merchauntes in that toune
    A certeyn tyme, as fel to hire plesaunce,
150 And so byfel° the excelent renoun

Of th'Emperoures doughter, dame Custaunce,
    Reported was with every circumstaunce
    Unto thise Surreyn merchauntz in swiche wise°
    From day to day, as I shall yow devyse.°
      This was the commune voys of every man:
    "Oure Emperoure of Rome (God hym see)
    A doughter hath that, sith° the world bygan,
    To rekne as wele hire goodnesse as beaute,
    Nas nevere swiche another as is she.
160 I preye to god in honour hir sustene,
    And wolde she were of alle Europe the quene!"

[They see Custaunce themselves and return home to Syria.]

176   Now fille it that these merchauntz stode in grace
    Of hym that was the Sowdon of Surrye,°
    For whan they come fro any straunge° place,
    He wolde, of his benyngne curtesye,°
180 Make hem good chere, and bysily espie
    Tidynges of sundry regnes,° for to lere°
    The wondres that they myght sen or here.
      Amonges other thynges, specially,
    These merchauntz han hym tolde of dame Custaunce
    So grete noblesse,° in ernest seriously,
    That this Sowdon hath caught so grete plesaunce°

Surrye *Syria* **whilom** *once* **chapmen** *merchants* **therto** *moreover* **sadde** *steadfast* **wide-where** *far and wide* **spicerye** *goods* **Here** *their* **chaffare** *merchandise* **thrifty** *high-quality* **wight** *person* **deynte** *pleasure* **chaffare** *trade* **sorte** *company* **shapen hem** *made arrangements* **wende** *go* **chapmanhode** *business* **disporte** *pleasure* **eace** *benefit, comfort* **herbergage** *loaging* **byfel** *it happened that* **in swiche wise** *in such a manner* **devyse** *relate* **sith** *since* **Sowdon of Surrye** *Sultan of Syria* **straunge** *foreign* **benyngne curtesye** *generous hospitality* **sundry regnes** *various kingdoms* **lere** *learn about* **noblesse** *renown, noble character* **plesaunce** *desire*

To han hire figure° in hise remem-
    braunce,
And alle his luste,° and alle his besy
    cure°
Was for to love hire while his lyfe may
    dure.°

[The Sowdon assembles his privy council,
who entertain many a number of options to
satisfy his desire for Custaunce, but ultimately, they conclude that the two must marry.]

218   Thanne saugh therinne swiche dif-
    ficulte
    Be way of resoun, for to speke al playn,
220   Bycause that ther was swiche dyver-
    site°
    Bitwene hire bothe° lawes, that thay
    sayn
    They trowe that no Cristen prince
    wolde fayn°
    Wedden his childe under oure lawes
    swete,°
    That us was yeven° be Mahoun° oure
    prophete.
      And he answered, "Rather than I lese
    Custaunce, I wole be cristened,° doute-
    les.
    I moot ben hires;° I may non other
    chese.
    I pray yow, holdeth youre argumentz in
    pees.
    Saveth my lyfe, and beth nat recchelees°
230 To geten hire that hath my lyfe in cure,
    For in thys woo I may not longe en-
    dure."

[An agreement is reached that Custaunce
will marry the Sowdon, bringing with her a
dowry; in exchange, he and all his men will

be baptized. Custaunce bewails the fact that
she must leave home and family to travel to a
foreign land, but she sets sail.]

323   The moder of the Sowdan (welle of
    vices)
    Espied hath hire sones pleyn entente,
    How he wole lete° his olde sacrifices,
    And right anoon° she for hire counseile
    sente,
    And they ben come to knowe what she
    mente,
    And whan assembled was this folke in
    fere,°
    She sette hire doun and seide as ye shal
    here:
330   "Lordes," she seide, "ye knowen eve-
    rychone
    How that my sone in poynt is for to
    lete°
    The holy lawes of oure Alkaron,°
    Yeven by goddes massage° Macomete.°
    But oon avow to grete God I hete:°
    The lyfe shall rather oute of my body
    sterte°
    Than Macometes lawe oute of myn
    herte.
      What sholde us tyden of° this newe
    lawe
    But° thraldom° to oure bodies and
    penaunce°
    And aftirwarde in helle to be drawe°
340 For we reneyed° Mahoun oure
    creaunce?°
    But lordynges, wyl ye make assuraunce
    As I shall seyn, assentyng to my lore,°
    And I shal maken us sauf for evermore."

---

figure *appearance, image* **luste** *desire* **besy cure** *busy effort* **dure** *last* **dyversite** *difference* **hire bothe** *both of their* **fayn** *willingly* **swete** *excellent* **yeven** *given* **Mahoun** *Muhammad* **cristened** *baptized* **I moot ben hires** *I must be hers* **recchelees** *negligent* **lete** *abandon* **right anoon** *right away* **in fere** *together* **in poynt ... lete** *is about to abandon* **Alkaron** *Qur'an* **massage** *messenger, prophet* **Macomete** *Muhammad* **hete** *promise* **lyfe...sterte** *life will sooner leave my body...* **What... of** *what would happen to us because of* **But** *except* **thraldom** *subjection* **penaunce** *suffering* **drawe** *tortured* **reneyed** *foresook* **creaunce** *faith* **lore** *teaching*

[Her council agrees to stand with her. She explains her plan:]

351   "We shulle firste feyne° us Cristen-
       dome to take.
    Coolde water° shall nat greve° us but
       a lite!
    And I shall swiche a feste and revel
       make
    That, as I trowe, I shall the Sowdan
       quyte.°
    For thogh his wyfe be cristened never
       so white,
    She shall have nede to waisshe away the
       rede,°
    Though she a fonte-ful water° with hire
       lede!"°
      O Sawdanesse, roote of iniquite,
    Virago,° thow Semyrame° the secunde;
360 O serpent under femynynytee,
    Lyke to the serpent depe in helle y-
       bounde;
    O feyned° woman, al that may con-
       founde
    Vertue and innocence, thurgh thy
       malice
    Is bred in the, as neste of every vice!

[She approaches her son, pledges to convert to Christianity, and asks his blessing to
throw a feast for the Christians. Custaunce
and her entourage arrive with great pomp,
and all go to the feast.]

428   For shortly for to tellen at a worde,
    The Soudan and the Cristen everichon
430 Ben al tohewe° and stiked° at the
       borde,°

But if it were oonly Dame Custaunce
       allone.
This olde Soudanesse—kursed krone—
Hath with hire frendes doon this cursed
       dede,
For she hireselfe wolde al the cuntre
       lede.°
      Ne was Surrien noon that was con-
       verted,
That of the counseile of the Soudan
       woot,°
That he nas al tohewe or he asterted.°
And Custaunce han they take anoon
       foot-hoot°
And in a sheppe al stereles,° God woot,
440 They han hire sette, and biddeth hire
       lerne saile
    Oute of Surrye agaynward° to Itaille.°

....

463   Yeris and daies fleet this creature
    Thurghoute the see of Grece,° unto the
       strayte
    Of Marrok,° as it was hir aventure.°
    On many a sory mele° now may she
       baite.°
    Aftir hire deeth ful ofte may she wayte,
    Or that° the wilde wawes° wole hire
       dryve
    Unto the place ther she shalle arryve.
470   Men myghten asken why she was nat
       slayn,
    Eke° at the feste, who myght hire body
       save?
    And I answere to that demaunde agayn;
    Who saved Daniel in the horrible cave,
    Ther every wight° save he, maister or
       knave,°

---

feyne *pretend*   **Coolde water** *i.e., baptism*   **greve** *harm*   **quyte** *take revenge on*   **rede** *red (of blood)*   **fonte-ful water** *enough water to fill a baptismal font*   **lede** *bring*   **Virago** *man-like woman*   **Semyrame** *Semiramis, an Assyrian queen said to have behaved like a man*   **feyned** *false*   **tohewe** *cut to pieces*   **stiked** *stabbed*   **borde** *table*   **lede** *rule*   **woot** *knew*   **or he asterted** *before he got up*   **foot-hoot** *hastily*   **stereles** *rudderless*   **agaynward** *back*   **Itaille** *Italy*   **see of Grece** *the Mediterranean Sea*   **strayte / Of Marrok** *Strait of Gibraltar*   **aventure** *fortune*   **mele** *meal*   **baite** *feed*   **Or that** *until*   **wawes** *waves*   **Eke** *also*

Was with the leuon° frete° er he
asterte?°

No wight° but God, that he bare in his
herte.

God lyste° to shewe his wonderfull
miracle

In hire, for we shulde seen his myghti
werkys.

Criste, whiche that is to every harme
triacle,°

480 By certeyn menes ofte (as knowen
clerkys)

Dooth thynge for certeyn ende that ful
derke° is

To mannes witte, that for oure igno-
raunce

Ye kunne nat° knowe his prudent purveaunce.°

....

505   She dryveth forth into oure occian,°

Thurghoute oure wilde see, til at the
laste,

Under an holde° that nempnen I ne
kan,°

Fer in Northumberland, the wawe° hir
caste,

And in the sande hire shippe stiked so
faste

510 That thennes wolde it nat of alle a
tyde.°

The wille of Criste was that she sholde
abyde.

The Constable of the castel doun is
fare°

To sen his wrak,° and alle the shippe he
sought,

And fonde this wery woman full of
care.

He fonde also the tresour that she
brought.

In hire langage mercy she besought,

The lyfe oute of hire body to twynne,°

Hire to delyver of woo that she was
ynne.

A maner Latyn corrupt was hire
speche,

520 But algate° therby was she understonde.

This Constable, whan hym lyste° no
lenger seche,°

This wofull woman broughte he to the
londe.

She kneleth doun and thanketh goddis
sonde.°

But what she was she wolde no man
seye,

For foule ne faire,° thow° that she
sholde deye.

She saide she was so mased° in the
see

That she forgate hir mynde, by hire
trouthe.

The Constable hath of hire so grete
pitee,

And eke his wife, that they wepen for
routhe,°

530 She was so diligent, withowten
sloughthe,°

To serve and please everiche in that
place,

That alle hir loven that loken in hire
face.

This Constable and Dame Hermengild his wyf

Were paiens,° and that cuntre everywhere,

wight *person*   **knave** *servant*   **leuon** *lion*   **frete** *devoured*   **asterte** *escaped*   **wight** *being*   **lyste**
wished   **to...triacle** *remedy for every harm*   **derke** *obscure*   **kunne nat** *cannot*   **purveaunce**
providence   **occian** *ocean; here, presumably the North Sea*   **holde** *castle*   **nempnen...kan** *I can-*
not name   **wawe** *wave*   **thennes...tyde** *it would not budge for the length of a tide*   **is fare** *has*
gone   **wrak** *wreck*   **twynne** *separate (i.e., to kill her)*   **algate** *nevertheless*   **lyste** *wished*   **seche**
search about   **sonde** *providence*   **foule ne faire** *bad fortune or good (i.e., no matter what)*   **thow**
though   **mased** *distraught*   **routhe** *compassion*   **sloughthe** *laziness*   **paiens** *pagans*

But Hermengild loved hire right as hire
    lyfe,
And Custance hath so longe sojourned
    there
In orisons,° with many a bitter tere,
Til Jhesu hath converted thurgh his
    grace
Dame Hermengilde, Constablesse of
    that place.
540   In al that londe no Cristen dorste
    route.°
Alle Cristene folke ben fledde fro that
    cuntre
Thurgh° payens° that conquereden al
    aboute
The plages° of the North, by land and
    se.
To Walys° fledde the Cristianyte°
Of olde Britons dwellyng in this ile:
Ther was hire refute for the mene-while.
    But yet nere° Cristen Britons so
    exiled
That there nere somme that, in hire
    privetee,°
Honoured Criste and hethen folke
    bigiled,°
550 And neigh° the castel swiche there
    dwelten three,°
That oon of hem was blynde,[7] and
    myght nat see,
But° it were of thilke yen° of his mynde[8]
With whiche men see whan that they be
    blynde.
    Bright was the sonne as in that som-
    eris day,
For whiche the Constable, and his wife
    also,
And Custance han take the right way
Toward the see a furlong wey or two,

To pleyen and to romen too and fro.°
And in hire walke this blynde man they
    mette,
560 Croked and old, with eyen faste
    yshette.°
    "In name of Criste," cride the blynde
    Britoun,
"Dame Hermengilde, yef me my sight
    agayn!"
This lady waxe afraied° of the soun,°
Leste that hire housbonde, shortly for
    to sayn,
Wolde hire for Jhesu Cristes love han
    slayn,°
Til Custaunce made hire bolde and
    bade hire werche°
The wille of Criste, a doughter of his
    chirche.
    The Constable wexe abasshed° of
    that sight,
And seide, "What amounteth° al this
    fare?"°
570 Custaunce answered, "Sire, it is Cristes
    myght,
That helpeth folke oute of the fendes°
    snare,"
And so ferforth° she gan oure lay°
    declare
That she the Constable, er it was eve,°
Converteth, and on Crist maketh hym
    byleve.
    This Constable was nothynge lord of
    thys place
Of whiche I speke, ther° he Custaunce
    fonde,
But kepte it strongely many wyntres
    space,
Under Alla, kyng of all Northumber-
    lond,

---

orisons *prayers*   dorste route *dared to assemble or travel*   Thurgh *because of*   payens *pagans*   plages *lands*   Walys *Wales*   Cristianyte *Christian people*   nere *were not*   in hire privetee *privately*   bigiled *deceived*   neigh *near*   swich...three *there lived three such people*   But *unless*   thilke yen *those eyes*   romen...fro *wander back and forth*   faste yshette *tightly closed*   waxe afraied *grew frightened*   soun *speech*   Wolde...slayn *i.e., would have slain her for loving Jesus Christ*   werche *work*   wexe abasshed *grew perplexed*   amounteth *means*   fare *commotion*   fendes *devil's*   so ferforth *to such a degree*   lay *faith*   er...eve *before nightfall*   ther *where*

That was ful wis and worthy of his
   honde°
580 Agayn the Scottes, as men may wele
   here—
   But turne I wole agayn to my matere.

[Satan seeks to undermine Custaunce by
making a young knight lust after her.]

589   He wowith° hire, but it availleth
   noght;°
590 She wolde do no synne by no weye,°
   And for despite° he compaseth° in his
   thought
   To maken hire on shameful deth to
   deye.
   He waiteth whan° the Constable was
   aweye,
   And prively on a nyght he crepte
   In Hermengildes chambre while she
   slepte.
   Wery, forwaked° in hire orisons,°
   Slepeth Custaunce and Hermengille
   also.
   This knyght thorow° Sathans tempta-
   couns
   Al softely is to bedde y-goo,
600 And kitte° the throte of Hermengild
   atwo,°
   And leyde the blody knyfe by Dame
   Custaunce
   And wente his weye—ther God yef hym
   myschaunce!°
   Sone aftir cometh this Constable
   hoom agayn,
   And eke Alla, that kyng was of that
   londe,
   And saugh his wyfe disputously° yslayn,
   For whiche full ofte he wepe and
   wronge his honde,

And in the bedde the blody knyfe he
   fonde
By Dame Custaunce. Allas, what myght
   she seye?
For verrey woo hir witte was al awey.
610   To kynge Alla was tolde alle this
   meschaunce,
   And eke the tyme, and where, and in
   what wise°
   That in a shippe was founden this
   Custaunce,
   As here-byforn that ye han herde
   devyse.
   The kynges herte of pite gan agrise°
   Whan he sey° so benyngne a creature
   Falle in disese° and in mysaventure.°

[Everyone but Custaunce's accuser speaks to
her good character and cannot imagine that
she has done such a thing. Custaunce, frightened, prays for divine aid.]

659   This Alla kyng hath swiche compassion
660 (As gentil herte is fulfilde of pite°)
   That from his eyen ranne the water
   doun.
   "Now hastely doo fecche a book," quod
   he,
   "And if this knyght wol sweren how
   that she
   This womman slowe, yet wol we us
   avyse°
   Whom that we wole that shal be° oure
   justise.°
   A Briton Book writen with evaung-
   iles°
   Was fette,° and on this booke he swore
   anoon

---

honde *conduct*   **wowith** *woos*   **availleth noght** *does no good*   **by no weye** *in any manner*   **despite** *spite*   **compaseth** *schemes*   **waiteth whan** *waits until*   **forwaked** *exhausted*   **hire orisons** *their prayers*   **thorow** *through*   **kitte** *cut*   **atwo** *in two*   **myschaunce** *ill fortune*   **disputously** *violently*   **wise** *manner*   **agrise** *to feel compassion or dread*   **sey** *saw*   **disese** *suffering*   **mysaventure** *misfortune*   **fulfilde of pite** *filled with mercy, sympathy*   **us avyse** *consider*   **wole...be** *wish to be*   **justise** *judge*   **evaungiles** *Gospels*   **fette** *fetched*

She giltife° was. And in the mene-
    whiles,
An honde° hym smote° upon the nekke
    bon,
670 That doun he fel at ones as a stoon,
And bothe his eyen broste° oute of his
    face
In sighte of everybody in that place.
    A voys was herde in general audi-
    ence,°
And seide, "Thow haste disclaundred
    gilteles°
The doughter of Holy Chirche in heigh
    presence.°
Thus hast thow doon, and yet holde I
    my pes."
Of this mervaille agaste° was alle the
    pres;°
As mazed° folke they stonden everych-
    one
For drede of wreche,° save Custaunce
    alone.
680   Grete was the drede and eke the
    repentaunce
Of hem that hadde wronge suspeccion
Upon this sely° innocent Custaunce,
And for this miracle, in conclucion,
And by Custaunce mediacion,
The kynge, and many another in that
    place,
Converted was—thanked by° Goddes
    grace!
    This fals knyght was slayn for his
    untrouth
By juggement of Alla hastyfly,°
And yet Custaunce hadde of his deth
    grete routhe.°
690 And aftir this, Jhesus of his mercie
Made Alla wedden ful solempnely°

This holy woman that is so bright and
    shene,°
And thus hath Criste made Custaunce
    a quene.
    But who was woful, yf I shal not lye,
Of this weddynge but Donegild and
    namo?°
The kynges moder, full of tyrannye,
Hir thought hire cursed herte barste
    atwo.°
She wolde nought hire sone hadde do
    so.°
Hire thought a despite° that he sholde
    take
700 So straunge° a creature unto his make.°

. . . .

715   On hire he gate° a knave-childe°
    anoon,
And to a bisshope, and his Constable
    eke,
He toke his wife to kepe whan he is gon
To Scotland-warde his foomen° for to
    seke.
Now faire Custaunce, that is so humble
    and meke,
720 So longe is goon with childe, til that
    stille
She halte° hire chamber, abydyng Cris-
    tis wille.
    The tyme is come a knave-childe she
    beer:°
Mauricius at the fonte-stoone they hym
    calle.
This Constable doth com forth a
    messynger
And wroot° unto his kynge, that
    cleped° was Alle,

---

giltife *guilty*   **honde** *hand*   **smote** *struck*   **broste** *burst*   **in general audience** *in everyone's hear-*
ing   **disclaundred gilteles** *slandered unjustly*   **heigh presence** *the presence of a noble assembly, or of*
God   **agaste** *aghast, terrified*   **pres** *crowd*   **mazed** *frightened*   **wreche** *vengeance*   **sely** *helpless*   **by**
be   **hastyfly** *speedily*   **routhe** *sorrow, pity*   **solempnely** *reverently*   **shene** *beautiful*   **namo** *nobody*
else   **barste atwo** *burst in two*   **She wolde...so** *She wished her son had not done so.*   **despite** *in-*
sult   **straunge** *alien*   **make** *mate*   **gate** *conceived*   **knave-childe** *boy*   **foomen** *enemies*   **halte**
remained inside   **beer** *gave birth to*   **wroot** *wrote*   **cleped** *called*

How that this blysful tydyng is befalle,
And other tydynges spedfull° forto seye.
He tath° the lettre and forth he goth his
weye.

[The messenger, hoping to be rewarded for
his good news, carries these tidings to the
king's mother Donegild, who invites him to
lodge with her for the night.]

743   This messager dranke sadly° ale and
wyn,
And stolen were his lettres prively
Oute of his boxe, while he sleep as a
swyn,°
And countrefeted was full sotilly°
Another lettre, wrought full synfully,
Unto the kynge directe of this matere
Fro his Constable, as ye shulle after
here.
750   The lettre spake the quene delivered
was
Of so horrible a fendlyche° creature9
That in the Castel noon so hardy° was
That any while° durste° there endure.°
The moder was an elfe, by aventure,°10
Icomen° by charmes or by sorcerie,
And everyche hatieth° hir companye.
Woo was this kyng whan he this let-
tre hadde seyn,°
But to no wight° he tolde his sorwes
sore.
But of his owene hoond he wroot
agayn:°
760   "Welcome the sonde° of Criste for ever-
moore
To me that am now lerned in his lore.
Lorde, welcome be thy luste° and thy
plesaunce;°

My luste I putte al in thyn ordenaunce.°
Kepeth this childe, al be it foule° or
faire,
And eke° my wyfe, unto my home com-
mynge.
Criste, whan hym luste,° may sende me
an eir°
Moore agreable than this to my
lykynge."
This lettre he seleth prively, wepynge,
Whiche to the messenger was take sone,
770   And forth he gooth; ther is nomore to
done.

....

778   O Donegild, I ne have non Englyssh
digne°
Unto thy malice and thy tirannye,
780   And therfore to the fende° I the resigne;°
Lete hym enditen° of thi traitorye.°
Fy, mannyssh,° fy!—o nay, by God, I
lye—
Fy, fendelich spirit! for I dare wele telle,
Thogh thow here walke, thi spirit is in
helle!

[The messenger returns by way of Donegild's
court, where he once again gets drunk.]

792   Eft° were his lettres stolen everychone
And countrefeted lettres in this wyse:°
The kyng commaundeth his Constable
anone,
Up° peyne of hangyng on on heigh
jewyse,°11
That he ne shulde suffren in no wyse

---

spedfull *appropriate* tath *takes* sadly *deeply* swyn *swine* sotilly *skillfully* fendlyche *devil-ish* hardy *bold* any while *for any time* durste *dared* endure *remain* by aventure *as fate would have it* Icomen *arrived* hatieth *hates* seyn *seen* wight *person* wroot agayn *wrote in reply* sonde *ordinance* luste *will* plesaunce *wishes* ordenaunce *government* foule *ugly* eke *also* hym luste *it pleases him* eir *heir* digne *sufficient* fende *devil* resigne *consign* enditen *write* traitorye *treachery* mannyssh *man-like (woman)* Eft *once more* wyse *way* Up *upon* on heigh jewyse *a high cross or gallows*

Custaunce inwith° his reigne° for to
    abide°
Thre dayes and a quarter of a tyde,
    But in the same shippe as he hir
    fonde,
800 Hire and hire yonge sone and al hire
    gere°
He sholde putte, and crowde° hir fro
    the londe,
And charge hire that she never efte
    come there.
O my Custaunce, wele may thy goost°
    have fere,°
And, slepyng in thy dreem, ben in
    penaunce,°
Whan Donegild caste° all this orde-
    naunce!°

[The messenger carries the counterfeit letter
to the Constable, who laments that he must
cause pain to someone as good as Custuance.]

820 Wepen bothe yonge and olde in al
    that place
Whan that the kynge this cursed lettre
    sente,
And Custaunce, with a dedly pale face,
The ferthe° day toward hir shippe she
    wente.
But natheles she taketh° in good en-
    tente°
The wille of Criste, and knelynge on the
    stronde
She seide, "Lorde, ay° welcome be thy
    sonde!"°

[Custaunce places her trust in God, tries to
comfort her son, bids farewell to the crowd,
and departs. King Alla returns home and
asks after his wife. He uncovers his mother's
deception and executes her for treason. Custaunce drifts for more than five years, escap-
ing an attempted rape along the way through
Mary's aid, and reenters the Meditertanean.]

953 Now late us stynte of° Custaunce
    butt a throwe,°
And speke we of the Romayn Empe-
    rour,
That oute of Surrye hath by lettres
    knowe
The slaughter of Cristen folke, and
    dishonour
Doon to his doughter by a fals trai-
    tour—
I mene the cursed, wikked Soudanesse
That at the feest leet slee° both more
    and lesse,°
960 For whiche this Emperour hath sente
    anon
His Senatour with roial ordenaunce,°
And oother lordes, God woot,° many
    oon,
On Surriens to take heigh vengeaunce.
They brennen,° sleen,° and brynge hem
    to meschaunce°
Full many a day—but shortly, this is
    th'ende,
Homward to Rome they shapen hem to
    wende.°
This Senatour repaireth° with victo-
    rie,
To Roome-warde seillyng° full roially,
And mette the shippe dryvynge, as seith
    the storie,
970 In whiche Custaunce sit ful pitously.
Nothynge knewe he what she was, ne
    why

---

inwith *within* reigne *realm* abide *remain* gere *possessions* crowde *drive* goost *soul* haven fere *be afraid* penaunce *distress* caste *plans* ordenaunce *plot* regnen *live, reign* moot
must shames *shameful* ferthe *fourth* taketh *accepts* good entente *good faith* ay *ever* sonde
ordinance stynte of *stop talking about* throwe *brief while* leet slee *caused to be slain* both...
lesse *everyone, both high- and low-ranking* ordenaunce *orders* woot *knows* brennen *burn* sleen
slay meschaunce *a bad end* shapen...wende *make arrangements to go* repaireth *returns* seillyng
sailing

She was in swiche array, ne she nel° seye
Of hire estate,° though she sholde deye.

[The Senator brings Custaunce back to Rome, where she dwells as a member of his household; the Senator's wife is Custaunce's aunt, but does not recognize her. King Alla makes a pilgrimage to Rome to do penance for the slaying of his mother. The Senator joins Alla for a feast, taking Custaunce's son, Maurice, with him.]

1009   Som men wolde seyne at requeste of Custaunce
1010 This Senatour hath ladde this childe to feste;
        I may nat tellen every circumstaunce.
        Be as be may, ther was he at the leste,
        But sooth° is this, that at his moders heste
        Biforn Alla, duryng the metys space,°
        The childe stood lokyng in the kynges face.
        This Alla kyng hath of this childe grete wonder,
        And to the Senatour he seyde anoon:
        "Whos is that faire childe that stondeth yonder?"
        "I noot,"° quod he, "by God and by Seint John.
1020 A moder he hath, but fader hath he noon
        That I of woot."° But shortly in a stounde,°
        He tolde Alla how that this childe was founde.

....

1030   Now was this childe as lyke unto Custaunce

As possible is a creature to be.
This Alla hath the face in remem-
    braunce
Of Dame Custaunce, and ther-on
    mused he,
If that the childes moder were aught°
    she
That is his wife, and pryvely he sight,°
And sped hym fro the table that° he
    myght.

[Alla tries to remind himself that his wife is dead at sea (as he believes), but he returns home with the Senator and asks to see Custaunce. He recognizes her immediately, and after he convinces her that he had no part in her banishment, they are joyfully reunited. They then invite her father, the Emperor, to dinner and reveal her identity for another joyful family reunion. Their son, Maurice, later becomes emperor.]

1128   This kyng Alla, whan he his tyme°
        say,°
        With his Custaunce, his holy wyfe so
        swete,°
1130 To Engelond ben they come the right
        wey,
        Whereas° they lyve in joye and in
        quyete,°
        But litel while° it lasteth, I yow hete.°
        Joye of this world for tyme wol not
        abyde;°
        Fro day to nyght it chaungeth as the
        tyde.

....

1142   For deeth, that taketh of heigh and
        lowe his rente,

nel *will not*   estate *condition, rank*   sooth *true*   metys space *mealtime*   noot *don't know*   woot
know   stounde *brief time*   aught *possibly*   sight *sighed*   that *when*   tyme *appropriate moment*   say
saw   swete *dear*   Whereas *where*   quyete *peace*   litel while *a short time*   hete *promise*   abyde
wait

Whan passed was a yere, evene as I
   gesse,
Oute of this worlde this kyng Alla he
   hent,°
For whom Custaunce hath full greet
   hevynesse.°
Now late us pray God his soule blesse!
And Dame Custaunce (finally to seye)
Toward the toun of Rome gooth hir
   weye.
   To Rome is come this holy creature
1150 And fyndeth here frendes hole and
   sounde.°
Now is she scaped° al hir aventure.
And whan that she hir fader hath
   yfounde,
Doun on hire knees falleth she to
   grounde,
Wepynge for tendernesse° in herte
   blithe;°
She herieth° god an hundred thowsand
   sithe.°
   In vertue and holy almesdede°
They leven alle, and never asonder
   wend.°
Til dethe departed hem, this lyfe they
   lede.
And fareth now wele! My tale is at an
   ende.
1160 Now Jhesu Criste that of hys myght
   may sende
Joye aftir woo, governe us in his grace,
And kepe us alle that ben in this place!
   Amen.

Here endeth the Tale of the Man of Lawe.

hent *took* hevynesse *sorrow* sounde *healthy and strong* scaped *escaped from* tendernesse *emotion* blithe *joyful* herieth *praises* sithe *times* almesdede *charitable works* asonder wend *part company*

Endnotes

1   The text below was compiled by Paul A. Broyles from the digital facsimile of Oxford, Christ Church College, MS 152, available online at http://digital.bodleian.ox.ac.uk/inquire/p/7de321ad-3dbe-4863-b402-3037e0963f27. Errors and omissions have been corrected with reference to the digital facsimile of the Ellesmere manuscript, available online at http://hdl.huntington.org/cdm/ref/collection/p15150coll7/id/2463. Further references to manuscript variants, along with minor emendations, are taken from John M. Manly and Edith Rickert, eds., *The Text of the Canterbury Tales,* vol. 5 (University of Chicago Press, 1940). Chaucer's sources, Nicholas Trevet's Anglo-French *Cronicles* and John Gower's *Confessio Amantis,* are referenced in the notes; Gower's text is available in this volume, and Trevet's may be found with accompanying English translation in Robert M. Correale and Mary Hamel, eds., *Sources and Analogues of the Canterbury Tales,* vol. 2 (D.S. Brewer, 2009), 296–329. Footnotes and endnotes are also provided by Paul A. Broyles.

2   David T. Mitchell and Sharon L. Snyder, *Narrative Prosthesis: Disability and the Dependencies of Discourse* (University of Michigan Press, 2000); see especially ch. 2.

3   This interpretation of Chaucer's treatment of the Britons was suggested by Larry Swain in an excellent exchange in the comments of Karl Steel's blog post "Weekend Fun? Reading Alla's Britoun Book," *In the Middle,* Mar. 6, 2009, http://www.inthemedievalmiddle.com/2009/03/weekend-fun-reading-allas-britoun-book.html.

4   *The Vulgate Bible: Douay-Rheims Translation,* vol. 6, *The New Testament,* ed. Angela M. Kinney (Harvard University Press, 2013).

5   The eyes of the mind were a commonplace in classical and medieval thought. St. Augustine distinguishes three categories of vision: corporeal, spiritual (memory, imagination; experienced by blind people when they see images while asleep or recall dreams), and intellectual (inerrant and concerned with divine truth); see St. Augustine, *The Literal Meaning of Genesis,* trans. John Hammond Taylor, Ancient Christian Writers 42, vol. 2 (Newman Press, 1982), book 12. It is difficult to be certain what level of insight Chaucer associates with the "eyes of the mind," but in any case, the phrase specifically assigns to blind people a capacity for vision beyond the physical.

6   Susan Schoon Eberly has shown how many traditional descriptions of changelings and other fairy creatures resemble specific identifiable medical conditions, even suggesting that such figures could lie behind stories like *Beowulf.* See also Keagan Brewer, "Wonder, Fear, Orality and Community," *Wonder and Skepticism in the Middle Ages* (Routledge, 2016), pp. 46–78: "Genetic diversity and consequent physical 'deformity', a natural and inevitable part of human and animal evolution alike, was understood through the cultural construct of the monstrous birth" (53).

7   New Haven, Beinecke Library, Takamiya MS 32 (formerly the Delamere MS) tells us that "some were" blind, making the blindness a widespread condition of the Britons rather than a characteristic of a particular Briton, perhaps suggesting that their blindness is understood as spiritual. In the previous line, the number of Britons living near the castle is not specified. The manuscript continues to pluralize the Britons' blindness until the appeal to Hermingild, which is still in the singular.

8   Some manuscripts read "thick" eyes—an obvious copying error, but one that changes the meaning significantly. By the time of Shakespeare, "thick-eyed" or "thick-sighted" meant "having obscure vision" (see *OED,* s.v. *thick,* adj. and n.), and that seems the most likely interpretation here; the reading suggests that the "eyes of the mind" are a poor substitute for physical sight. Yet another manuscript replaces the phrase "thilke yen" with "thynkynge," removing the idea that blind people might have a different way of seeing and ascribing the Briton's insight strictly to thought alone.

9   A few manuscripts describe the child as "foulle" or "fouly" instead of "fendlyche," emphasizing physical and behavioral hideousness over diabolical associations. While in this case the description is false, a non-normative birth does actually occur in another work closely connected

with the Constance stories, the fourteenth-century Middle English romance known as *The King of Tars*. In that work, a Christian princess marries the Sultan of Damascus and feigns conversion to Islam. She subsequently gives birth to a shapeless lump of flesh, which acquires human form only after the child is baptized. The Sultan subsequently converts, and his skin color changes from black to white. Geraldine Heng has shown how *The King of Tars* helps to expose the underlying racial logic of the Man of Law's Tale and its sources. It is striking that here the allegation of monstrous birth appears in the Northumbrian section, attempting to isolate Custaunce and her son from the Northumbrians, from whom they are not racially distinguished.

10 In Trevet, Custaunce is described as a "malveis espirit" (evil spirit); for Gower, she is "of faierie" (l. 370). Elves, like fairies (the terms were virtually interchangeable, and Chaucer uses them as such in *Sir Thopas*), were supernatural creatures who among other things might mate with humans or harm or abduct their babies. Chaucer's choice of "elfe" indexes Donegild's accusation against a series of other uses in the *Canterbury Tales*. In the Wife of Bath's Tale and *Sir Thopas*, elves are part of a romance landscape which, in the Wife of Bath's Tale, belongs to an idealized British past. Moreover, in the prologue to *Sir Thopas*, the Host describes Chaucer himself as seeming "elvyssh by his contenaunce"—an adjective used to mean "strange" in the Canon's Yeoman's Tale. Donegild is claiming that Custaunce is a dangerous, otherworldly creature (and one manuscript emphasizes that point by branding her an elf by "nature").

11 Some authoritative manuscripts, including Ellesmere, read "and on heigh juyse"—that is, "on pain of hanging and on high judgment." Here, *jewyse* must instead be the instrument of hanging; it can refer in Middle English to a cross, but the gallows, offered as a gloss in Henry Cockeram's 1623 dictionary, seems equally likely. See *OED*, s.v. *juise*.

The *Wife of Bath's Portrait, Prologue,* and *Tale* from *The Canterbury Tales*[1] (ca. 1387–1400)

Geoffrey Chaucer
Contributed by Tory V. Pearman

Introduction

Though the General Prologue of *The Canterbury Tales* mentions a handful of atypical physical features on the pilgrims such as the Friar's lisp, the Miller's wart, the Summoner's scarred face, and the Cook's ulcer, only Alisoun of Bath's partial deafness appears beyond the Prologue, where its cause, a strike from her fifth husband Jankyn, becomes an integral plot point in her *Prologue.* Introduced in the second line of her portrait, Alisoun's deafness becomes a primary physical marker of her identity, one in a line of physical anomalies that include her aging (and perhaps infertile), yet sexually voracious body, wide hips, gap-teeth, and visible birthmarks. The narrator deems her deafness "scathe," which the *MED* explains could indicate both "a matter of regret, a pity" and "harm resulting from war" or "punishment." And, as we see in the *Wife of Bath's Prologue,* Jankyn's blow is obviously punitive, done in retaliation after Alisoun damages his *Book of Wicked Wives,* a compilation of biblical, patristic, and medical texts outlining the defiant and disobedient nature of womankind and rooting stereotypical feminine attributes to the supposed physical deficiency of the female body itself. Alisoun's violent ripping out of three of the book's leaves foreshadows the violent injury that Jankyn will soon dole out. Her deafness is thus the punishment for her sexual voracity, a condition with its own disabling qualities, as her *Prologue* effectively demonstrates. Tellingly, in her *Tale,* Alisoun aligns herself not only with the "loathly lady" and Midas' prattling wife, but also Midas himself, whose ears have been transformed into those of an ass as penance for his own insubordination.

The condition of deafness carried many meanings in the late Middle Ages. Medical authorities distinguished between congenital and acquired deafness, noting the incurability of the condition in most cases despite the existence of some medical treatments. Though not generally doled out as a punishment, deafness was in some cases viewed as a divine punishment for sinfulness, whether committed by a deaf child's parents or committed by an individual acquiring deafness later in life. Because the ears and eyes were considered bodily portals to the soul, medieval interpretations of deafness were similar to those of blindness. As a result, deafness, like blindness, could be viewed as evidence of a limited ability to fully comprehend Christian religious truths. Upon first glance, the defiance Alisoun exhibits in response to male-authored religious and medical texts throughout her *Prologue* seems to demonstrate what David Mitchell and Sharon Snyder call the materiality of metaphor, or the metaphorical uses of disability in written texts to give tangibility to abstract concepts such as a ignorance or sinfulness; however, it becomes clear that Alisoun's deliberate and skillful manipulation of such misogynist texts to support her permissive stance on multiple marriages reveals a deep understanding of the "auctoritee" that she purports to oppose. Scholars remain divided on whether Alisoun's use of male authority allows her to break free from it or merely reiterate it, but it is clear that she exposes the sexism, ageism, and ableism institutionalized by such discourse.

A question central to understanding the literary function(s) of deafness in Alisoun's *Portrait* and *Prologue* is whether the condition truly disables her. Although it is clearly a punishment for her subversive behavior, her deafness does not seem to impede her life in any substantial ways. She remains a successful cloth-maker and manages to establish herself as a seasoned pilgrim. In fact, her impairment gives her a reason to take part in pilgrimage, as pilgrims often journeyed to shrines like Saint Thomas Beckett's in search of miraculous cure for physical ailments. Moreover, the fight that causes her deafness ends in what could be interpreted as a "victory" for Alisoun: the destruction of the book and dominion over Jankyn and his estate (ll. 813–22). Her admitted deference to him, however, calls her newfound power into question. Her Tale presents a similar dilemma. In it, an old hag, who is most certainly Alisoun's fantastical counterpart, transforms into a beautiful woman who remains deferential to her new husband, a convicted rapist. Both the *Prologue* and *Tale* thus feature women with imperfect bodies whose contested power is consistently undercut by male authority.

Bibliography

Deloney, Mikee. "Alisoun's Aging, Hearing-Impaired Female Body: Gazing at the Wife of Bath in Chaucer's Canterbury Tales." *The Treatment of Disabled Persons in Medieval Europe: Examining Disability in the Historical, Legal, Literary, Medical, and Religious Discourses of the Middle Ages*, edited by Wendy Turner and Tory Vandeventer Pearman. Edwin Mellen Press, 2011, pp. 313–45.

Pearman, Tory Vandeventer. "Disruptive Dames: Disability and the Loathly Lady in the *Tale of Florent*, the *Wife of Bath's Tale*, and the *Weddynge of Sir Gawain and Dame Ragnelle*." *The Treatment of Disabled Persons in Medieval Europe: Examining Disability in the Historical, Legal, Literary, Medical, and Religious Discourses of the Middle Ages*, edited by Wendy Turner and Tory Vandeventer Pearman. Edwin Mellen Press, 2011, pp. 291–312.

———. "Physical Education: Excessive Wives and Bodily Punishment in *The Book of the Knight* and The 'Wife of Bath's Prologue.'" *Women and Disability in Medieval Literature*. Palgrave, 2010, pp. 45–71.

Sayers, Edna Edith. "Experience, Authority, and the Mediation of Deafness: Chaucer's Wife of Bath." *Disability in the Middle Ages: Reconsiderations and Reverberations*, edited by Joshua Eyler, Ashgate, 2010, pp. 81–92.

Storm, Melvin. "Alisoun's Ear." *Modern Language Quarterly*, vol. 2., no. 3, 1981, pp. 219–26.

The Portrait of the Wife of Bath[2]

A good Wyf was ther of bisyde Bathe,
But she was som-del° deef, and that was
    scathe.°[3]
Of clooth-making she hadde swiche an
    haunt,°
She passed hem of Ypres and of Gaunt.°
In al the parisshe wyf ne was ther noon
That to the offring° bifore hir sholde
    goon;
And if ther dide, certeyn, so wrooth
    was she,
That she was out of alle charitee.
Hir coverchiefs° ful fyne were of
    ground;
10 I dorste swere they weyeden ten pound
That on a Sonday were upon hir heed.
Hir hosen weren of fyn scarlet reed,
Ful streite y-teyd, and shoos ful moiste°
    and newe.
Bold was hir face, and fair, and reed of
    hewe.
She was a worthy womman al hir lyve,
Housbondes at chirche-dore she hadde
    fyve,
Withouten other companye in youthe;
But therof nedeth nat to speke as
    nouthe.°
And thryes hadde she been at Ierusa-
    lem;°
20 She hadde passed many a straunge
    streem;
At Rome she hadde been, and at Bo-
    loigne,
In Galice at seint Iame,° and at Co-
    loigne.
She coude° muche of wandring by the
    weye.
Gat-tothed° was she, soothly for to seye.

Up-on an amblere° esily she sat,
Y-wimpled wel, and on hir heed an hat
As brood as is a bokeler° or a targe;°
A foot-mantel° aboute hir hipes large,
And on hir feet a paire of spores sharpe.
30 In felawschip wel coude she laughe and
    carpe.°
Of remedyes of love she knew per-
    chaunce,
For she coude of that art the olde
    daunce.

The Wife of Bath's Prologue[4]

Experience, though noon auctoritee°
Were in this world, were right y-nough
    to me
To speke of wo that is in mariage;
For, lordinges, sith I twelf yeer was of
    age,
Thonked be god that is eterne on lyve,°
Housbondes at chirche-dore I have had
    fyve;
For I so ofte have y-wedded be;
And alle were worthy men in hir
    degree.
But me was told certeyn, nat longe agon
    is,
10 That sith° that Crist ne wente never but
    onis
To wedding in the Cane° of Galilee,
That by the same ensample taughte he
    me
That I ne sholde wedded be but ones.
Herke eek, lo! which a sharp word for
    the nones°
Besyde a welle Iesus, god and man,
Spak in repreve of the Samaritan:°
"Thou hast y-had fyve housbondes,"
    quod he,

---

som-del *partially*   **scathe** *a pity, a penalty*   **haunt** *skill*   **Ypres…Gaunt** *centers of cloth-making*   **of-fring** *offering at Mass*   **coverchiefs** *head-coverings*   **moiste** *supple*   **nouthe** *now*   **Ierusalem et. al.** *popular pilgrimage destinations*   **seint Iame** *St. James of Compostella*   **coude** *knew*   **Gat-tothed** *gap-toothed*   **amblere** *horse*   **bokeler** *small shield*   **targe** *small shield*   **foot-mantel** *overskirt*   **carpe** *talk*   **auctoritee** *written authority*   **eterne on lyve** *lives eternally*   **sith** *since*   **Cane** *Cana*   **for the nones** *for the time*   **Samaritan** *to the Samaritan woman in John 4*

"And thilke° man, the which that hath
    now thee,
Is noght thyn housbond;" thus seyde he
    certeyn;
20 What that he mente ther-by, I can nat
    seyn;
But that I axe, why that the fifthe man
Was noon housbond to the Samaritan?
How manye mighte she have in mar-
    iage?
Yet herde I never tellen in myn ag
Upon this nombre diffinicioun;°
Men may devyne° and glosen° up and
    doun.
But wel I woot expres, with-oute lye,
God bad us for to wexe and multiplye;
That gentil text can I wel understonde.
30 Eek wel I woot he seyde, myn hous-
    bonde
Sholde lete fader and moder, and take
    me;
But of no nombre mencioun made he,
Of bigamye or of octogamye;
Why sholde men speke of it vileinye?°

[Alisoun provides examples of bigamists]

59 Whan saugh ye ever, in any maner age,
60 That hye god defended° mariage
By expres word? I pray you, telleth me;
Or wher comanded he virginitee?
I woot as wel as ye, it is no drede,°
Thapostel,° whan he speketh of
    maydenhede;°
He seyde, that precept ther-of hadde he
    noon.
Men may conseille a womman to been
    oon,°
But conseilling is no comandement;
He putte it in our owene Iugement.
For hadde god comanded maydenhede,

70 Thanne hadde he dampned° wedding
    with the dede;
And certes, if ther were no seed y-
    sowe,°
Virginitee, wher-of than sholde it
    growe?

[Alisoun discusses virginity]

105 Virginitee is greet perfeccicun,
And continence eek with devocioun.
But Crist, that of perfeccioun is welle,°
Bad nat every wight he shold go selle
All that he hadde, and give it to the
    pore,
110 And in swich wyse folwe hime and his
    fore.°
He spak to hem that wolde live parfitly;
And lordinges, by your leve, that am
    nat I.
I wol bistowe the flour of al myn age
In the actes and in fruit of mariage.
Telle me also, to what conclusioun°
Were membres maad of generacioun,
And for what profit was a wight y-
    wroght?
Trusteth right wel, they wer nat maad
    for noght.
Glose° who-so wole, and seye bothe up
    and doun,
120 That they were maked for purgacioun
Of urine, and our bothe thinges smale
Were eek to knowe a femele from a
    male,
And for noone other cause: sey ye no?
The experience woot wel it is noght so;
So that the clerkes° be nat with me
    wrothe,
I sey this, that they maked been for
    bothe,
This is to seye, for office, and for ese°

---

thilke *that*   **diffinicioun** *a definitive statement*   **devyne** *interpret*   **glosen** *comment on, gloss*   **vileinye**
reproachfully   **defended** *prohibited*   **drede** *doubt*   **Thapostel** *The Apostle (Paul)*   **maydenhede** *virginity*   **oon** *a virgin*   **dampned** *condemned*   **y-sowe** *sown*   **welle** *source*   **fore** *doctrine*   **conclusioun**
purpose   **Glose** *gloss, interpret*   **clerkes** *scholars*   **for...ese** *for duty and for pleasure*

Of engendrure,° ther we nat god dis-
plese.
Why sholde men elles in hir bokes sette,
130 That man shal yelde to his wyf hir
dette?°
Now wher-with sholde he make his
payement,
If he ne used his sely instrument?
Than were they maad up-on a creature,
To purge uryne, and eek for engendrure.
But I seye noght that every wight is
holde,°
That hath swich harneys° as I to yow
tolde,
To goon and usen hem in engendrure;
Than sholde men take of chastitee no
cure.°
Crist was a mayde, and shapen as a
man,
140 And many a seint, sith that the world
bigan,
Yet lived they ever in parfit chastitee.
I nil envye° no virginitee;
Lat hem be breed of pured° whete-seed,
And lat us wyves hoten barly-breed;
And yet with barly-breed, Mark° telle
can,
Our lord Iesu refresshed many a man.
In swich estaat as god hath cleped us°
I wol persevere, I nam nat precious.°
In wyfhode I wol use myn instrument
150 As frely as my maker hath it sent.
If I be daungerous,° god yeve me sorwe!
Myn housbond shal it have bothe eve
and morwe,
Whan that him list com forth and paye
his dette.
An housbonde I wol have, I nil nat
lette,°
Which shal be bothe my dettour and
my thral,°

And have his tribulacioun with-al
Up-on his flessh, whyl that I am his wyf.
I have the power duringe al my lyf
Up-on his propre body, and noght he.
160 Right thus the apostel tolde it un-to
me;
And bad our housbondes for to love us
weel.
Al this sentence me lyketh every-
deel'—°

[The Pardoner interrupts]

193 Now sires, now wol I telle forth my
tale.—
As ever mote I drinken wyn or ale,
I shal seye sooth, tho housbondes that
I hadde,
As three of hem were gode and two
were badde.
The three men were gode, and riche,
and olde;
Unnethe° mighte they the statut° holde
In which that they were bounden un-to
me.
200 Ye woot wel what I mene of this, par-
dee!°
As help me god, I laughe when I thinke
How pitously a-night I made hem
swinke;°
And by my fey,° I tolde of it no stoor.°

[Alisoun speaks about her first three hus-
bands]

452 Now wol I speken of my fourthe hous-
bonde.
My fourthe housbonde was a revelour,
This is to seyn, he hadde a paramour;
And I was yong and ful of ragerye,°
Stiborn and strong, and Ioly as a pye.°

---

engendrure *procreation*   **dette** *conjugal debt*   **holde** *obligated*   **harneys** *equipment*   **cure** *care*   **en-
vye** *contend*   **pured** *purified*   **Mark** *Mark 6:41*   **cleped us** *called us to*   **precious** *pretentious*   **daungerous** *stingy*   **nat lette** *not give up*   **thral** *slave*   **deel** *bit*   **Unnethe** *Hardly*   **statut** *conjugal
debt*   **pardee** *by God*   **swinke** *work*   **fey** *faith*   **I...stoor** *it didn't matter to me*   **ragerye** *lustfulness*   **Ioly as a pye** *jolly as a magpie*

Wel coude I daunce to an harpe smale,
And singe, y-wis,° as any nightingale,
When I had dronke a draughte of swete
 wyn.
460 Metellius,° the foule cherl, the swyn,
That with a staf birafte his wyf hir lyf,
For she drank wyn, thogh I hadde been
 his wyf,
He sholde nat han daunted me fro
 drinke;
And, after wyn, on Venus moste I
 thinke:
For al so siker as cold engendreth hayl,
A likerous mouth° moste han a likerous
 tayl.°
In womman vinolent° is no defence,
This knowen lechours by experience.
But, lord Crist! whan that it remem-
 breth me
470 Up-on my yowthe, and on my Iolitee,°
It tikleth me aboute myn herte rote.°
Unto this day it dooth myn herte bote°
That I have had my world as in my
 tyme.
But age, allas! that al wol envenyme,°
Hath me biraft my beautee and my
 pith;°
Lat go, fare-wel, the devel go therwith!
The flour is goon, ther is na-more to
 telle,
The bren, as I best can, now moste I
 selle;
But yet to be right mery wol I fonde.°
480 Now wol I tellen of my fourthe hous-
 bonde.
I seye, I hadde in herte greet despyt
That he of any other had delyt.
But he was quit, by god and by seint
 Ioce!°
I made him of the same wode a croce;

Nat of my body in no foul manere,
But certeinly, I made folk swich chere,
That in his owene grece I made him frye
For angre, and for verray Ialousye.
By god, in erthe I was his purgatorie,
490 For which I hope his soule be in glorie.
For god it woot, he sat ful ofte and song
Whan that his shoo ful bitterly him
 wrong.°
Ther was no wight, save god and he,
 that wiste,°
In many wyse, how sore I him twiste.
He deyde whan I cam fro Ierusalem,
And lyth y-grave under the rode-beem,°
Al is his tombe noght so curious
As was the sepulcre of him. Darius,°
Which that Appelles° wroghte subtilly;
500 It nis but wast to burie him preciously.
Lat him fare-wel, god yeve his soule
 reste,
He is now in the grave and in his cheste.
Now of my fifthe housbond wol I telle.
God lete his soule never come in helle!
And yet was he to me the moste
 shrewe;°
That fele I on my ribbes al by rewe,°
And ever shal, un-to myn ending-day.
But in our bed he was so fresh and gay,
And ther-with-al so wel coude he me
 glose,°
510 Whan that he wolde han my bele chose,
That thogh he hadde me bet on every
 boon,°
He coude winne agayn my love anoon.
I trowe I loved him beste, for that he
Was of his love daungerous° to me.
We wommen han, if that I shal nat lye,
In this matere a queynte fantasye;
Wayte what thing we may nat lightly
 have,

---

y-wis *certainly* **Metellius** *Egnatious Metellius* **likerous mouth** *gluttonous* **likerous tayl** *lech-
erous* **vinolent** *drunkenness* **Iolitee** *jollity* **herte rote** *bottom of my heart* **bote** *good* **envenyme** *poison, embitter* **pith** *vigour* **fonde** *try* **seint Ioce** *St. Judocus* **wrong** *pinched* **wiste**
knew **rode-beem** *beam of the cross* **Darius** *King of Persia* **Appelles** *raftsman of Darius* **shrewe**
cruel **by rewe** *in a row* **glose** *flatter* **bet on every boon** *beaten every bone* **daungerous** *hard to get*

Ther-after wol we crye al-day and crave.
Forbede us thing, and that desyren we;
520 Prees on us faste, and thanne wol we
    flee.
With daunger oute we al our chaffare;°
Greet prees at market maketh dere
    ware,
And to greet cheep is holde at litel prys;
This knoweth every womman that is
    wys.
My fifthe housbonde, god his soule
    blesse!
Which that I took for love and no
    richesse,
He som-tyme was a clerk of Oxenford, °
And had left scole, and wente at hoom
    to bord
With my gossib, dwellinge in oure toun,
530 God have hir soule! hir name was Ali-
    soun.
She knew myn herte and eek my priv-
    etee°
Bet° than our parisshe-preest, so moot
    I thee!

[While her fourth husband is out of town,
Alisoun, her gossip, and Jankin go on walk]

563 Now wol I tellen forth what happed me.
I seye, that in the feeldes walked we,
Til trewely we hadde swich daliance,
This clerk and I, that of my purveyance°
I spak to him, and seyde him, how that
    he,
If I were widwe, sholde wedde me.

[Alisoun describes a dream]

586 A! ha! by god, I have my tale ageyn.
Whan that my fourthe housbond was
    on bere,
I weep algate,° and made sory chere,

As wyves moten, for it is usage,
590 And with my coverchief covered my
    visage;
But for that I was purveyed of a make,
I weep but smal, and that I undertake.°
To chirche was myn housbond born
    a-morwe
With neighebores, that for him maden
    sorwe;
And Iankin oure clerk was oon of tho.
As help me god, whan that I saugh him
    go
After the bere, me thoughte he hadde
    a paire
Of legges and of feet so clene and faire,
That al myn herte I yaf un-to his hold.°
600 He was, I trowe,° a twenty winter old,
And I was fourty, if I shal seye sooth;
But yet I hadde alwey a coltes tooth.
Gat-tothed I was, and that bicam me
    weel;
I hadde the prente of seynt Venus seel.°
As help me god, I was a lusty oon,
And faire and riche, and yong, and wel
    bigoon;
And trewely, as myne housbondes tolde
    me,
I had the beste quoniam° mighte be.
For certes, I am al Venerien°
610 In felinge, and myn herte is Marcien.°
Venus me yaf my lust, my likerousnesse,
And Mars yaf me my sturdy hardinesse.
Myn ascendent was Taur,° and Mars
    ther-inne.
Allas! allas! that ever love was sinne!
I folwed ay myn inclinacioun
By vertu of my constellacioun;
That made me I coude noght withdrawe
My chambre of Venus from a good
    felawe.
Yet have I Martes mark° up-on my face,
620 And also in another privee place.

chaffare *difficulty; merchandise*   clerk of Oxenford *a scholar of Oxford*   privetee *secrets*   Bet
better   purveyance *foresight*   algate *continuously*   undertake *promise*   hold *keeping*   trowe *I*
believe   seynt Venus seel *Venus' mark, a birthmark*   quoniam *vagina*   Venerien *under Venus' influ-*
ence   Marcien *under Mars' influence*   Taur *Taurus*   Martes mark *Mars' mark, a red birthmark*

For, god so wis° be my savacioun,
I ne loved never by no discrecioun,
But ever folwede myn appetyt,
Al were° he short or long, or blak or
  whyt;
I took no kepe, so that he lyked me,
How pore he was, ne eek of what
  degree.
What sholde I seye, but, at the monthes
  ende,
This Ioly clerk Iankin, that was so
  hende,°
Hath wedded me with greet solemp-
  nitee,
630 And to him yaf I al the lond and fee
That ever was me yeven ther-bifore;
But afterward repented me ful sore.
He nolde suffre nothing of my list.°
By god, he smoot me ones on the list,°⁵
For that I rente out of his book a leef,
That of the strook myn ere wex al deef.⁶
Stiborn I was as is a leonesse,
And of my tonge a verray Iangleresse,°
And walke I wolde, as I had doon
  biforn,
640 From hous to hous, al-though he had it
  sworn.
For which he often tymes wolde preche,
And me of olde Romayn gestes° teche,
How he, Simplicius Gallus,° lefte his
  wyf,
And hir forsook for terme of al his lyf,
Noght but for open-heeded° he hir say°
Lokinge out at his dore upon a day.
Another Romayn tolde he me by name,
That, for his wyf was at a someres game
With-oute his witing, he forsook hir
  eke.
650 And than wolde he up-on his Bible seke
That ilke proverbe of Ecclesiaste,

Wher he comandeth and forbedeth
  faste,
Man shal nat suffre his wyf go roule
  aboute;
Than wolde he seye right thus, with-
  outen doute,
"Who-so that buildeth his hous al of
  salwes,°
And priketh his blinde hors over the
  falwes,°
And suffreth his wyf to go seken hal-
  wes,°
Is worthy to been hanged on the gal-
  wes!"
But al for noght, I sette noght an hawe°
660 Of his proverbes nof his olde sawe,
Ne I wolde nat of him corrected be.
I hate him that my vices telleth me,
And so do mo, god woot! of us than I.
This made him with me wood al out-
  rely;
I nolde noght forbere° him in no cas.
Now wol I seye yow sooth, by seint
  Thomas,
Why that I rente out of his book a leef,
For which he smoot me so that I was
  deef.
He hadde a book that gladly, night and
  day,
670 For his desport he wolde rede alway.
He cleped it Valerie and Theofraste,°
At whiche book he lough alwey ful
  faste.
And eek ther was som-tyme a clerk at
  Rome,
A cardinal, that highte Seint Ierome,
That made a book agayn Iovinian;°
In whiche book eek ther was Tertulan,°
Crisippus, Trotula, and Helowys,
That was abbesse nat fer fro Parys;
And eek the Parables of Salomon,

---

wis *certainly* Al were *Whether* hende *courteous* list *pleasure* list *ear* Iangleresse *blabber-mouth* gestes *stories* Simplicius Gallus *his story is told by Valerius* open-heeded *bare-headed* say *saw* salwes *willows* falwes *open fields* seken halwes *go on pilgrimages* sette...hawe *cared nothing for* forbere *endure* Valerie and Theofraste *authors of anti-marriage tracts* a...Iovinian *anti-marriage text* Tertulan et al. *misogynistic texts*

680 Ovydes Art, and bokes many on,
　And alle thise wer bounden in o°
　　volume.
　And every night and day was his cus-
　　tume,
　Whan he had leyser and vacacioun
　From other worldly occupacioun,
　To reden on this book of wikked wyves.
　He knew of hem mo legendes and lyves
　Than been of gode wyves in the Bible.
　For trusteth wel, it is an impossible
　That any clerk wol speke good of wyves,
690 But-if it be of holy seintes lyves,
　Ne of noon other womman never the
　　mo.
　Who peyntede the leoun, tel me who?
　By god, if wommen hadde writen
　　stories,
　As clerkes han with-inne hir oratories,
　They wolde han writen of men more
　　wikkednesse
　Than all the mark of Adam° may
　　redresse.
　The children of Mercurie and of Venus°
　Been in hir wirking ful contrarious;
　Mercurie loveth wisdom and science,
700 And Venus loveth ryot and dispence.°
　And, for hir diverse disposicioun,
　Ech falleth in otheres exaltacioun;°
　And thus, god woot! Mercurie is desolat
　In Pisces, wher Venus is exaltat;
　And Venus falleth ther Mercurie is
　　reysed;
　Therfore no womman of no clerk is
　　preysed.
　The clerk, whan he is old, and may
　　noght do
　Of Venus werkes worth his olde sho,
　Than sit he doun, and writ in his dotage
710 That wommen can nat kepe hir mar-
　　iage!
　But now to purpos, why I tolde thee
　That I was beten for a book, pardee.

Up-on a night Iankin, that was our
　syre,°
Redde on his book, as he sat by the fyre,
Of Eva° first, that, for hir wikkednesse,
Was al mankinde broght to wrecched-
　nesse,
For which that Iesu Crist him-self was
　slayn,
That boghte us with his herte-blood
　agayn.
Lo, here expres of womman may ye
　finde,
720 That womman was the los of al man-
　kinde.

[Jankin reads about women who have betrayed or murdered their husbands]

772 He spak more harm than herte may
　bithinke.
And ther-with-al, he knew of mo
　proverbes
Than in this world ther growen gras or
　herbes.
"Bet is," quod he, "thyn habitacioun
Be with a leoun or a foul dragoun,
Than with a womman usinge for to
　chyde.
Bet is," quod he, "hye in the roof abyde
Than with an angry wyf doun in the
　hous;
780 They been so wikked and contrarious;
They haten that hir housbondes loveth
　ay."
He seyde, "a womman cast hir shame
　away,
Whan she cast of hir smok;" and
　forther-mo,
"A fair womman, but she be chaast also,
Is lyk a gold ring in a sowes nose."
Who wolde wenen,° or who wolde sup-
　pose

---

o *one*　all...Adam *all men*　children...Venus *scholars and lovers, respectively*　dispence *extrava-*
gance　exaltacioun *when planet is at its most powerful in the zodiac*　syre *master of the house*　Eva
Eve　wenen *think*

The wo that in myn herte was, and
    pyne?
And whan I saugh he wolde never fyne°
To reden on this cursed book al night,
790 Al sodeynly three leves have I plight°
    Out of his book, right as he radde, and
    eke,
I with my fist so took him on the cheke,
That in our fyr he fil bakward adoun.
And he up-stirte as dooth a wood
    leoun,°
And with his fist he smoot me on the
    heed,
That in the floor I lay as I were deed.
And when he saugh how stille that I lay,
He was agast, and wolde han fled his
    way,
Til atte laste out of my swogh I breyde:°
800 "O! hastow slayn me, false theef?" I
    seyde,
"And for my land thus hastow mordred
    me?
Er I be deed, yet wol I kisse thee."
And neer he cam, and kneled faire
    adoun,
And seyde, "dere suster Alisoun,
As help me god, I shal thee never smyte;
That I have doon, it is thy-self to wyte.°
Foryeve it me, and that I thee biseke"—°
And yet eft-sones° I hitte him on the
    cheke,
And seyde, "theef, thus muchel am I
    wreke;°
810 Now wol I dye, I may no lenger speke."
But atte laste, with muchel care and wo,
We fille acorded, by us selven two.
He yaf me al the brydel in myn hond
To han the governance of hous and
    lond,
And of his tonge and of his hond also,
And made him brenne his book anon
    right tho.°

And whan that I hadde geten un-to me,
By maistrie,° al the soveraynetee,
And that he seyde, "myn owene trewe
    wyf,
820 Do as thee lust° the terme of al thy lyf,
    Keep thyn honour, and keep eek myn
    estaat"—
After that day we hadden never debaat.
God help me so, I was to him as kinde
As any wyf from Denmark un-to Inde,°
And also trewe, and so was he to me.
I prey to god that sit in magestee,
So blesse his soule, for his mercy dere!
Now wol I seye my tale, if ye wol here.'

[The Friar and Summoner converse]

The Wife of Bath's Tale

857 In tholde dayes of the king Arthour,
    Of which that Britons speken greet
    honour,
All was this land fulfild of fayerye.°
860 The elf-queen, with hir Ioly companye,
    Daunced ful ofte in many a grene mede;
This was the olde opinion, as I rede,
I speke of manye hundred yeres ago;
But now can no man see none elves mo.
For now the grete charitee and prayeres
Of limitours° and othere holy freres,
That serchen every lond and every
    streem,
As thikke as motes in the sonne-beem,
Blessinge halles, chambres, kichenes,
    boures,
870 Citees, burghes, castels, hye toures,
    Thropes,° bernes, shipnes,° dayeryes,°
This maketh that ther been no fayeryes.
For ther° as wont to walken was an elf,
Ther walketh now the limitour him-self
In undermeles° and in morweninges,°

---

fyne *finish* **plight** *plucked* **wood leoun** *mad lion* **breyde** *woke* **wyte** *blame* **biseke** *beseech* **eft-sones** *quickly* **wreke** *avenged* **tho** *then* **maistrie** *mastery* **as thee lust** *as you please* **Inde** *India* **fayerye** *fairies* **limitours** *begging friars* **Thropes** *villages* **shipnes** *cattle's sheds* **dayeryes** *stables* **ther** *where* **undermeles** *evenings* **morweninges** *mornings*

And seyth his matins and his holy
    thinges
As he goth in his limitacioun.°
Wommen may go saufly up and doun,
In every bush, or under every tree;
880 Ther is noon other incubus° but he,
    And he ne wol doon hem but dishon-
      our.
    And so bifel it, that this king Arthour
    Hadde in his hous a lusty bacheler,
    That on a day cam rydinge fro river;
    And happed that, allone as she was
      born,
    He saugh a mayde walkinge him biforn,
    Of whiche mayde anon, maugree hir
      heed,°
    By verray force he rafte° hir mayden-
      heed;
    For which oppressioun was swich
      clamour
890 And swich pursute un-to the king
      Arthour,
    That dampned° was this knight for to
      be deed
    By cours of lawe, and sholde han lost
      his heed
    Paraventure,° swich was the statut tho;
    But that the quene and othere ladies mo
    So longe preyeden the king of grace,
    Til he his lyf him graunted in the place,
    And yaf him to the quene al at hir wille,
    To chese, whether she wolde him save
      or spille.°
    The quene thanketh the king with al hir
      might,
900 And after this thus spak she to the
      knight,
    Whan that she saugh hir tyme, up-on
      a day:
    'Thou standest yet,' quod she, 'in swich
      array,°
    That of thy lyf yet hastow no suretee.

I grante thee lyf, if thou canst tellen me
What thing is it that wommen most
    desyren?
Be war, and keep thy nekke-boon from
    yren.°
And if thou canst nat tellen it anon,
Yet wol I yeve thee leve for to gon
A twelf-month and a day, to seche and
    lere°
910 An answere suffisant in this matere.

[The knight searches for answers]

951 Witnesse on Myda;° wol ye here the
    tale?
    Ovyde, amonges othere thinges smale,
    Seyde, Myda hadde, under his longe
      heres,
    Growinge up-on his heed two asses eres,
    The which vyce he hidde, as he best
      mighte,
    Ful subtilly from every mannes sighte,
    That, save his wyf, ther wiste of it na-
      mo.
    He loved hir most, and trusted hir also;
    He preyede hir, that to no creature
960 She sholde tellen of his disfigure.
    She swoor him 'nay, for al this world to
      winne,
    She nolde do that vileinye or sinne,
    To make hir housbond han so foul a
      name;
    She nolde nat telle it for hir owene
      shame.'
    But nathelees, hir thoughte that she
      dyde,
    That she so longe sholde a conseil hyde;
    Hir thoughte it swal so sore aboute hir
      herte,
    That nedely som word hir moste asterte;
    And sith she dorste telle it to no man,
970 Doun to a mareys° faste by she ran;

---

limitacioun *begging district* incubus *evil spirit* maugree hir heed *against her will* rafte
took dampned *condemned* Paraventure *Perhaps* spille *destroy* array *a position* yren *execution-*
er's axe lere *learn* Myda *King Midas* mareys *marsh*

Til she came there, hir herte was a-fyre,
And, as a bitore bombleth° in the myre,
She leyde hir mouth un-to the water doun:
Biwreye° me nat, thou water, with thy soun,'
Quod she, 'to thee I telle it, and namo;
Myn housbond hath longe asses eres two!
Now is myn herte all hool, now is it oute;
I mighte no lenger kepe it, out of doute,'
Heer may ye se, thogh we a tyme abyde,
980 Yet out it moot, we can no conseil hyde;
The remenant of the tale if ye wol here,
Redeth Ovyde, and ther ye may it lere.°
This knight, of which my tale is specially,
Whan that he saugh he mighte nat come therby,
This is to seye, what wommen loven moost,
With-inne his brest ful sorweful was the goost;
But hoom he gooth, he mighte nat soiourne.
The day was come, that hoomward moste he tourne,
And in his wey it happed him to ryde,
990 In al this care, under a forest-syde,
Wher-as he saugh up-on a daunce go
Of ladies foure and twenty, and yet mo;
Toward the whiche daunce he drow ful yerne,°
In hope that som wisdom sholde he lerne.
But certeinly, er he came fully there,
Vanisshed was this daunce, he niste where.
No creature saugh he that bar lyf,
Save on the grene he saugh sittinge a wyf;

A fouler wight ther may no man devyse.°
1000 Agayn° the knight this olde wyf gan ryse,
And seyde, 'sir knight, heer-forth° ne lyth no wey.
Tel me, what that ye seken, by your fey?°
Paraventure it may the bettre be;
Thise olde folk can muchel thing,' quod she.
'My leve mooder,' quod this knight certeyn,
I nam but deed, but-if that I can seyn
What thing it is that wommen most desyre;
Coude ye me wisse,° I wolde wel quyte° your hyre.'
'Plighte me thy trouthe, heer in myn hand,' quod she,
1010 'The nexte thing that I requere thee,
Thou shalt it do, if it lye in thy might;
And I wol telle it yow er it be night.'
'Have heer my trouthe,' quod the knight, 'I grante.'
'Thanne,' quod she, 'I dar me wel avante,°
Thy lyf is sauf, for I wol stonde therby,
Up-on my lyf, the queen wol seye as I.
Lat see which is the proudeste of hem alle,
That wereth on a coverchief or a calle,°
That dar seye nay, of that I shal thee teche;
1020 Lat us go forth with-outen lenger speche.'
Tho rouned she a pistel° in his ere,
And bad him to be glad, and have no fere.
Whan they be comen to the court, this knight
Seyde, 'he had holde his day, as he hadde hight,°

---

bombleth *makes a humming noise*   **Biwreye** *Betray*   **lere** *teach, learn*   **yerne** *eagerly*   **devyse** *imagine, tell*   **Agayn** *To meet*   **heer-forth** *from here*   **fey** *faith*   **wisse** *instruct*   **quyte** *reward you*   **wel avante** *boast, affirm*   **calle** *hairnet*   **Tho...pistel** *she whispered a secret*   **hight** *promised*

And redy was his answere,' as he sayde.
Ful many a noble wyf, and many a
   mayde,
And many a widwe, for that they ben
   wyse,
The quene hir-self sittinge as a Iustyse,°
Assembled been, his answere for to
   here;
1030 And afterward this knight was bode
   appere.
To every wight comanded was silence,
And that the knight sholde telle in
   audience,
What thing that worldly wommen
   loven best.
This knight ne stood nat stille as doth
   a best,
But to his questioun anon answerde
With manly voys, that al the court it
   herde:
'My lige lady, generally,' quod he,
'Wommen desyren to have sovereyntee
As wel over hir housbond as hir love,
1040 And for to been in maistrie him above;
This is your moste desyr, thogh ye me
   kille,
Doth as yow list, I am heer at your
   wille.'
In al the court ne was ther wyf ne
   mayde,
Ne widwe, that contraried that he
   sayde,
But seyden, 'he was worthy han his lyf.'
And with that word up stirte the olde
   wyf,
Which that the knight saugh sittinge in
   the grene:
'Mercy,' quod she, 'my sovereyn lady
   quene!
Er that your court departe, do me right.
1050 I taughte this answere un-to the knight;
For which he plighte me his trouthe
   there,
The firste thing I wolde of him requere,

He wolde it do, if it lay in his might.
Bifore the court than preye I thee, sir
   knight,'
Quod she, 'that thou me take un-to thy
   wyf;
For wel thou wost that I have kept° thy
   lyf.
If I sey fals, sey nay, up-on thy fey!'°
This knight answerde, 'allas! and
   weylawey!
I woot right wel that swich was my
   biheste.°
1060 For goddes love, as chees a newe re-
   queste;
Tak al my good, and lat my body go.'
'Nay than,' quod she, 'I shrewe us bothe
   two!
For thogh that I be foul, and old, and
   pore,
I nolde° for al the metal, ne for ore,
That under erthe is grave, or lyth above,
But-if thy wyf I were, and eek thy love.'
'My love?' quod he; 'nay, my dampna-
   cioun!
Allas! that any of my nacioun°
Sholde ever so foule disparaged be!'

[The knight agrees to marry her]

1080 For prively he wedded hir on a morwe,
And al day after hidde him as an oule;°
So wo was him, his wyf looked so foule.
Greet was the wo the knight hadde in
   his thoght,
Whan he was with his wyf a-bedde
   y-broght;
He walweth, and he turneth to and fro.
His olde wyf lay smylinge evermo,
And seyde, 'o dere housbond, benedic-
   ite!
Fareth every knight thus with his wyf
   as ye?
Is this the lawe of king Arthures hous?
1090 Is every knight of his so dangerous?'°

Iustyse *justice* **kept** *saved* **fey** *faith* **biheste** *promise* **nolde** *would not* **nacioun** *family* **oule** *owl* **dangerous** *fastidious, miserly*

I am your owene love and eek your wyf;
I am she, which that saved hath your
    lyf;
And certes, yet dide I yow never un-
    right;
Why fare ye thus with me this firste
    night?
Ye faren lyk a man had lost his wit;
What is my gilt? for goddes love, tel
    me it,
And it shal been amended, if I may.'
'Amended?' quod this knight, 'allas! nay,
    nay!
It wol nat been amended never mo!
1100 Thou art so loothly, and so old also,
And ther-to comen of so lowe a kinde,°
That litel wonder is, thogh I walwe and
    winde.
So wolde god myn herte wolde breste!°
'Is this,' quod she, 'the cause of your
    unreste?'
'Ye, certainly,' quod he, 'no wonder is.'
'Now, sire,' quod she, 'I coude amende
    al this,
If that me liste, er it were dayes three,
So wel ye mighte here yow un-to me.°
But for ye speken of swich gentillesse°
1110 As is descended out of old richesse,
That therfore sholden ye be gentil men,
Swich arrogance is nat worth an hen.

[The lady provides commentary on genti-
lesse]

1207 Now, sire, of elde° ye repreve me;
And certes, sire, thogh noon auctoritee°
Were in no book, ye gentils of honour
1210 Seyn that men sholde an old wight
    doon favour,
And clepe him fader, for your gen-
    tillesse;
And auctours shal I finden, as I gesse.

Now ther ye seye, that I am foul and
    old,
Than drede you noght to been a
    cokewold;°
For filthe and elde, al-so moot I thee,°
Been grete wardeyns up-on chastitee.
But nathelees, sin I knowe your delyt,
I shal fulfille your worldly appetyt.
Chese now,' quod she, 'oon of thise
    thinges tweye,
1220 To han me foul and old til that I deye,
And be to yow a trewe humble wyf,
And never yow displese in al my lyf,
Or elles ye wol han me yong and fair,
And take your aventure of the repair
That shal be to your hous, by-cause of
    me,
Or in som other place, may wel be.
Now chese your-selven, whether that
    yow lyketh.'
This knight avyseth° him and sore
    syketh,
But atte laste he seyde in this manere,
1230 'My lady and my love, and wyf so dere,
I put me in your wyse governance;
Cheseth your-self, which may be most
    plesance,
And most honour to yow and me also.
I do no fors° the whether of the two;
For as yow lyketh, it suffiseth me.°'
'Thanne have I gete of yow maistrye,'
    quod she,
'Sin I may chese, and governe as me
    lest?'
'Ye, certes, wyf,' quod he, 'I holde it
    best.'
'Kis me,' quod she, 'we be no lenger
    wrothe;°
1240 For, by my trouthe, I wol be to yow
    bothe,
This is to seyn, ye, bothe fair and good.
I prey to god that I mot sterven wood,°
But I to yow be al-so good and trewe

---

lowe a kinde *low-born ancestry*   **breste** *burst*   **yow un-to me** *behave towards me*   **gentillesse** *nobili-ty*   **elde** *age*   **auctoritee** *written authority*   **cokewold** *cuckold*   **thee** *thrive*   **avyseth** *considered*   **do no fors** *care not*   **suffiseth me** *is sufficient for me*   **wrothe** *in disagreement*   **sterven wood** *die mad*

As ever was wyf, sin that the world was
    newe.
And, but I be to-morn as fair to sene
As any lady, emperyce, or quene,
That is bitwixe the est and eke the west,
Doth with my lyf and deeth right as
    yow lest.
Cast up the curtin, loke how that it is.'
1250 And whan the knight saugh verraily al
    this,
That she so fair was, and so yong ther-
    to,
For Ioye he hente° hir in his armes two,
His herte bathed in a bath of blisse;
A thousand tyme a-rewe° he gan° hir
    kisse.
And she obeyed him in every thing
That mighte doon him plesance or
    lyking.
And thus they live, un-to hir lyves ende,
In parfit Ioye; and Iesu Crist us sende
Housbondes meke, yonge, and fresshe
    a-bedde,
1260 And grace toverbyde° hem that we
    wedde.
And eek I preye Iesu shorte hir lyves
That wol nat be governed by hir wyves;
And olde and angry nigardes° of dis-
    pence,
God sende hem sone verray pestilence.

---

hente *took*   **a-rewe** *in succession*   **gan** *began to*   **toverbyde** *to survive*   **nigardes** *misers*

Endnotes

1 The text is from *The Canterbury Tales*, edited by Walter Skeat, *The Complete Works of Geoffrey Chaucer*, 2nd edn. (Clarendon Press, 1900). This text is in the public domain, released on July 22, 2007. Glosses and endnotes provided by Tory V. Pearman.

2 The portrait of the Wife of Bath appears in lines 445–476 in The General Prologue. The text below is taken from *The Canterbury Tales*, edited by Skeat, *The Complete Works of Geoffrey Chaucer*. This text is in the public domain, released on July 22, 2007. Footnotes and endnotes have been provided by Tory V. Pearman.

3 The Wife of Bath's disability is first described here, as "som-del deef" and "scathe," with "but" serving to contrast these with her description as "good" in the line above. The manuscript variants for The General Prologue show one variant for this line. The Trinity College (Cambridge) R.3.15 reads "and" instead of "but," suggesting a correlation between her goodness and her disability rather than a contrast.

4 The text below is taken from *The Canterbury Tales*, edited by Walter Skeat, *The Complete Works of Geoffrey Chaucer*, 2nd edn. (Clarendon Press, 1900). This text is in the public domain, released on July 22, 2007. Footnotes and endnotes have been provided by Tory V. Pearman.

5 In this line, the Alisoun describes how Jankyn hit her on her ear, presumably causing her partial deafness. The manuscript variants show an important variant on this line. Cambridge University Dd.4.24, Cambridge University Gg.4.27, Harley 7334, and Helmingham read "with his fist" instead of "on the lyst," emphasizing his role in the attack rather than her consequences.

6 Alisoun explicitly mentions her own disability here, observing that one of her ears is deaf because of Jankyn's blow. The manuscript variants show an important variant on this line. Corpus Christi 198, Lansdowne 851, and Petworth read "eren wexen" instead of "ere wex," indicating both ears went deaf instead of one.

Dame Sirith[1] (ca. 1272–82)

Contributed by Danielle Allor

Introduction

The late thirteenth-century Middle English poem *Dame Sirith* is the first *fabliau* written in English.[2] While the plot begins ordinarily enough for its genre, with the young man Wilekin desperate to sleep with the married woman Margery, the signature trickery of this *fabliau* circulates around narratives of disability and animality through the figure of a crying dog. Dame Sirith's fictional explanation of the weeping dog is the clearest portrayal of the promises, threats, and strange joys of disability that characterize *Dame Sirith*, but each of the human characters experiences mental or physical difference. The titular character, the go-between Dame Sirith, complains that she is "old and sek [sick] and lame" (l. 199). Wilekin's love-sickness makes him "wod [mad]" and causes him to contemplate suicide, and his inability to win Margery for himself results in his use of Dame Sirith's services (l. 182). Margery, as a woman, is disabled according to the medical models of the Middle Ages, which characterize women's bodies as defective versions of men's. The final character, the dog, is forced eat mustard and pepper to make her weep. When Dame Sirith tells Margery that the dog is actually her own daughter, transformed into canine shape due to her refusal to sleep with a cleric, the animal becomes the centerpiece of Dame Sirith's scheme to persuade Margery to sleep with Wilekin. To convince Margery of the horror of this permanent transformation, Dame Sirith argues for the proximity of her own disabled body to that of her dog-turned-fictional-kin.

Dame Sirith (the text) and Dame Sirith (the character) emphasize the social aspects of disability. As Tory Vandeventer Pearman argues, Dame Sirith's actual physical status is indeterminate. Her disabilities are entirely self-described, first to Wilekin and then to Margery, and she understands her role as a disabled woman in the spiritual life of her ecclesiastical community. As a poor, disabled woman who receives alms from "gode [good] men" (l. 207), Dame Sirith serves as many aged, disabled, and poor people did in medieval communities: as recipients of acts of charity that furthered the spiritual welfare of the givers. But Dame Sirith's representation of her own disabled body also invokes the specter of the malingerer who pretends to be disabled in order to receive goods and services—a figure created from cultural anxieties that question the efficacy of this material and spiritual exchange. Dame Sirith then extends her manipulation of the tropes of medieval disability to harness animal transformation as a kind of impairment with which to threaten Margery into compliance with Wilekin's desires. To Margery, the weeping dog is a disabled human woman, deprived of her humanity and her ability to speak. This transformation represents not only a physical change, but also a potentially damning spiritual mutation: animals, as beings without rational souls, could not be saved. Margery's concession to Wilekin's desires becomes a way to save both her body and her soul.

As such, disability in *Dame Sirith* is not only embodied in the characters but also circulates as a narrative Dame Sirith gleefully deploys for her own ends. Dame Sirith emphasizes her infirmities to Wilekin to establish her innocence from the services he solicits her for, and in turn to prevent involvement with the ecclesiastical courts. Dame Sirith also emphasizes her disability, age, and poverty to Margery. These categories build upon one another so that Dame Sirith can unleash her carefully calibrated narrative about her daughter-turned-dog: Margery, faced with the aged woman she will definitely one day become, is also forced to contemplate Dame Sirith's disability and poverty before her attention is directed to the weeping dog. When Margery worries that Wilekin "wolle me forsape [will deform me]" (l. 369), she does so within the framework that Dame Sirith has constructed for her: age, disability, and poverty are unavoidable. Now so too is Margery's transformation into a dog rendered inevitable through Dame Sirith's narrative. The trick at the center of this *fabliau* depends on Dame Sirith framing animal existence as a disability. But while Dame Sirith draws lines of affinity between her own body, Margery's body, and the crying dog's, these affinities are limited both by Dame Sirith's trick—the threat of dog transformation is, of course, fictional—and by their different levels of immediacy. In Dame Sirith's narrative, the suffering dog represents an instantaneous deformation that Margery rejects in horror, ultimately preferring adultery to animal existence. While Margery avoids becoming a dog, rejecting an animal transformation and the disabilities that come with it, she cannot similarly refuse the disabilities that come with aging. When the tale concludes with the successful completion of Dame Sirith's plot, any thought of Margery's aging body is deferred, relegated beyond the borders of the *fabliau*.

Bibliography

Metzler, Irina. *A Social History of Disability in the Middle Ages: Cultural Considerations of Physical Impairment.* Routledge, 2013. See especially Chapter 3, "Ageing," pp. 92–153, and Chapter 4, "Charity," pp. 154–98.

Pearman, Tory Vandeventer. *Women and Disability in Medieval Literature.* Palgrave Macmillan, 2010. See especially Chapter 1, "(Dis)Pleasure and (Dis)Ability: The Topos of Reproduction in *Dame Sirith* and the 'Merchant's Tale,'" pp. 19–44.

Shahar, Shulamith. *Growing Old in the Middle Ages: "Winter Clothes Us in Shadow and Pain."* Translated by Yael Lotan. Routledge, 1997.

Wack, Mary Frances. *Lovesickness in the Middle Ages: The Viaticum and its Commentaries.* University of Pennsylvania Press, 1990.

Ci comence le fablel et la cointise de dame siriz°

1   As I com bi an waie,°
    Hof on° Ich° herde saie
    Ful modi° mon and proud;
    Wis he wes of lore,°
    And gouthlich under gore,°
    And clothed in fair sroud.°
        To lovien° he bigon°
        On° wedded wimmon –
        Therof he hevede wrong;°
10   His herte hire wes alon,°
    That reste nevede° he non,
    The love wes so strong.
    Wel yerne° he him bethoute°
    Hou° he hire gete moute,°
    In ani cunnes wise.°
    That befel on an day
    The louerd° wend away
    Hon° his marchaundise.°
        He wente him to then inne°
20   Ther hoe wonede° inne,
        That wes riche won;°
    And com in to then halle,
    There hoe° wes srud with palle,°
    And thus he bigon:
    [WILEKIN] "God almightten be
       herinne!"
    [MARGERY] "Welcome, so Ich ever
       bide winne!"°
    Quod this wif.
    "His hit thi wille,° com and site,°
    And what is thi wille let me wite,°

30   Mi leve lif.°
    Bi houre Louerd,° hevene King,
    If I mai don ani thing
    That thee is lef,°
    Thou mightt finden me ful fre;°
    Fol bletheli° will I don° for thee,
    Withhouten gref."
    [WILEKIN] "Dame, God thee foryelde!°
    Bote° on that thou me nout bimelde,°
    Ne make thee wroth,
40   Min hernde° will I to thee bede;°
    Bote wratthen° thee for ani dede°
    Were me loth."°
        [MARGERY] "Nai, iwis,° Wilekin!
        For nothing that ever is min,
        Thau° thou hit yirne,°
        Houncurteis° ne will I be;
        Ne con° I nout on vilte,°
        Ne nout I nelle lerne.°
    Thou mait saien al thine wille
50   And I shal herknen° and sitten stille,
    That thou have told.
    And if that thou me tellest skil,°
    I shal don after thi wil—
    That be thou bold.°
        And thau thou saie me ani same,°
        Ne shal I thee nouight blame
        For thi sawe."°
        [WILEKIN] "Nou Ich° have wonne
       leve,°
        Yif° that I thee shulde greve,
60   Hit were hounlawe.°

Ci...siriz *Here begins the fabliau and the trick of Dame Sirith* **waie** *way* **Hof on** *Of one* **Ich** *I* **Ful modi** *Very bold* **Wis...lore** *Wise he was in learning* **gouthlich under gore** *beautiful in clothing* **sroud** *attire* **lovien** *love* **bigon** *began* **On** *A* **hevede wrong** *was in the wrong* **hire wes alon** *was hers alone* **nevede** *had not* **yerne** *eagerly* **he him bethoute** *he thought to himself* **Hou** *How* **hire gete moute** *might get her* **ani cunnes wise** *any kind of way* **louerd** *lord [husband]* **Hon** *On* **marchaundise** *commerce* **inne** *dwelling* **Ther hoe wonede** *Where she dwelt* **won** *dwelling* **hoe** *she* **srud with palle** *clothed with rich cloth* **so...winne** *as sure as I have ever prayed for happiness* **His...wille** *If it is your will* **site** *sit* **wite** *know* **leve lif** *dear beloved* **Bi houre Louerd** *By our Lord* **lef** *desirable* **fre** *agreeable* **Fol bletheli** *Very gladly* **don** *do* **foryelde** *repay* **Bote** *But* **bimelde** *denounce* **hernde** *errand* **bede** *reveal* **wratthen** *anger* **for ani dede** *for any reason* **me loth** *disagreeable to me* **Nai, iwis** *No, indeed* **Thau** *Although* **yirne** *desire* **Houncurteis** *Discourteous* **con** *know* **nout on vilte** *nothing of spitefulness* **Ne...lerne** *Nor anything will I learn* **herknen** *listen* **skil** *is reasonable* **That...bold** *You be certain of that* **same** *shame* **sawe** *speech* **Nou Ich** *Now I* **wonne leve** *gained permission* **Yif** *If* **hounlawe** *unlawful*

Certes,° dame, thou seist as hende,°
And I shal setten spel° on ende,
And tellen thee al –
Wat Ich wolde,° and wi° Ich com;
Ne con Ich saien non falsdom,°
Ne non I ne shal.°
    Ich habbe iloved° thee moni yer,
    Thau Ich nabbe nout ben her°
    Mi love to schowe.°
70   Wile thi louerd° is in toune,
    Ne mai no mon with thee holden roune°
    With no thewe.°
Yurstendai° Ich herde saie,
As Ich wende° bi the waie,
Of oure sire;°
Me° tolde me that he was gon
To the feire of Botolfston°
In Lincolneschire.
    And for Ich weste° that he wes houte°
80   Tharfore Ich am igon aboute
    To speken with thee.
    Him burth° to liken wel his lif,
    That mightte welde secc a wif°
    In privite.°
Dame, if hit is thi wille,
Both dernelike and stille°
Ich wille thee love."
[MARGERY] "That wold I don for non thing
Bi houre Louerd,° hevene King,
90   That ous is bove!°

Ich habe mi louerd° that is mi spouse,
That maiden° broute me to house
Mid menske inou;°
He loveth me and Ich him wel,
Oure love is also trewe as stel,
Withhouten wou.°
Thau° he be from hom on his hernde,°
Ich were ounseli,° if Ich lernede
To ben on hore.°
100   That ne shal nevere be,
That I shal don selk falsete,°
On bedde ne on flore;°
    Never more his lifwile,°
    Thau he were on hondred mile
    Biyende° Rome,
    For no thing ne shuld I take
    Mon on erthe to ben mi make,°
    Ar° his hom-come."°
[WILEKIN] "Dame, dame, torn thi mod;°
110   Thi curteisi° was ever god,°
And yet shal be;
For the Louerd that ous° haveth wrout,°
Amend thi mod,° and torn thi thout,°
And rew on me."°
[MARGERY] "We,° we! Oldest thou me a fol?°
    So Ich ever mote biden Yol,°
    Thou art ounwis.°
    Mi thout ne shalt thou never wende;°

Certes *Certainly*   **seist as hende** *speak as a courteous person*   **spel** *talk*   **Wat Ich wolde** *What I would [do]*   **wi** *why*   **non falsdom** *no falsehood*   **Ne...shal** *Nor shall I [say] any*   **Ich habbe iloved** *I have loved*   **Thau...her** *Though I have not been [able] here*   **schowe** *show*   **louerd** *lord [husband]*   **holden roune** *have secret conversation*   **thewe** *proper conduct*   **Yurstendai** *Yesterday*   **wende** *went*   **oure sire** *your husband*   **Me** *Someone*   **Botolfston** *Boston*   **weste** *knew*   **houte** *out*   **Him burth** *He is obligated*   **welde...wif** *possess such a wife*   **In privite** *Privately*   **dernelike and stille** *secretly and covertly*   **Bi houre Louerd** *By our Lord*   **ous is bove** *is above us*   **louerd** *lord [husband]*   **maiden** *[as a] virgin*   **Mid menske inou** *With sufficient honor*   **wou** *grief*   **Thau** *Though*   **hernde** *errand*   **ounseli** *wicked*   **ben on hore** *be a whore*   **selk falsete** *such falseness*   **flore** *floor*   **lifwile** *lifetime*   **Biyende** *Beyond*   **make** *mate*   **Ar** *Before*   **hom-come** *homecoming*   **torn thi mod** *change your mind*   **curteisi** *courtesy*   **god** *good*   **ous** *us*   **wrout** *made*   **Amend thi mod** *Change your mind*   **torn thi thout** *turn your thought*   **rew on me** *take pity on me*   **We** *alas*   **Oldest...fol?** *Do you take me for a fool?*   **So...Yol** *So as I ever must wait for Christmas*   **ounwis** *unwise*   **Mi...wende** *You will never change my mind*

Mi louerd is curteis mon° and
hende,°
120   And mon of pris;°
And Ich am wif bothe god and trewe;
Trewer womon ne mai no mon cnowe°
Then Ich am.
Thilke° time ne shal never bitide°
That mon, for wouing° ne thoru prude,°
Shal do me scham."
[WILEKIN] "Swete leumon,° merci°!
Same ne vilani°
Ne bede I thee non;°
130   Bote derne love I thee bede,°
As mon that wolde of love spede,°
And finde won."°
[MARGERY] "So bide Ich evere mete
other drinke,°
Her° thou lesest° al thi swinke.°
Thou might gon hom,° leve° brother,
For ne wille Ich° thee love, ne non other
Bote mi wedde houssebonde;
To tellen hit thee ne wille Ich wonde."°
[WILEKIN] "Certes,° dame, that me
forthinketh;°
140   And wo is the mon that muchel
swinketh°
And at the laste leseth his sped!°
To maken menis his him ned;°
Bi me I saie ful iwis,°
That love the love that I shal mis.°
And, dame, have now godnedai!"°

And thilke Louerd° that al welde°
mai
Leve° that thi thout so tourne°
That Ich for thee no leng ne
mourne."°
Drerimod° he wente awai,
150   And thoute bothe night and dai
Hire al for to wende.°
A frend him radde° for to fare –
And leven° al his muchele kare° –
To Dame Sirith the hende.°
Thider he wente him anon,°
So suithe so° he mightte gon,
No mon he ni mette.°
Ful he wes of tene° and treie;°
Mid° wordes milde and eke sleie°
160   Faire° he hire grette.
[WILEKIN] "God thee iblessi,° Dame
Sirith!
Ich am icom° to speken thee with,
For muchele° nede;
And° Ich mai have help of thee,
Thou shalt have, that thou shalt se,
Ful riche mede."°
[SIRITH] "Welcomen art thou, leve°
sone;
And if Ich mai other cone°
In eni wise for thee do,
170   I shal strengthen me therto;°
Forthi,° leve° sone, tel thou me
What thou woldest I dude° for thee."

curteis mon *courteous man*   hende *noble*   mon of pris *man of good reputation*   cnowe *know*   Thilke *That*   bitide *come*   wouing *wooing*   thoru prude *through pride*   leumon *beloved*   merci *mercy*   Same ne vilani *Shame nor abuse*   Ne...non *I offer you none*   Bote...bede *But I offer you secret love*   spede *succeed*   won *joy*   So...drinke *So as I hope for food or drink*   Her *Here*   lesest *lose*   swinke *work*   gon hom *go home*   leve *dear*   ne wille Ich *I will not*   wonde *hesitate*   Certes *Certainly*   that me forthinketh *I am sorry for that*   muchel swinketh *works too much*   at...sped *in the end loses his progress*   To...ned *It is necessary for him to get a go-between*   iwis *truly*   That love...mis *Who loves the love that I will miss*   godnedai *a good day*   thilke Louerd *the same Lord*   welde *rule*   Leve *Grant*   thi...tourne *your thought so changes*   no...mourne *no longer mourn for you*   Drerimod *Sad at heart*   wende *change [her mind]*   him radde *advised him*   leven *leave*   muchele kare *great sorrow*   hende *clever*   anon *immediately*   So suithe so *As quickly as*   No...mette *He did not meet anyone*   tene *vexation*   treie *grief*   Mid *with*   eke sleie *also sly*   Faire *Pleasantly*   iblessi *bless*   icom *come*   muchele *great*   And *If*   Ful riche mede *Very rich reward*   leve *dear*   mai other cone *may or can*   me thereto *myself for it*   Forthi *Therefore*   leve *dear*   dude *did*

[WILEKIN] "Bote,° leve nelde,° ful
     evele° I fare;
I lede mi lif with tene° and care;
     With muchel hounsele° Ich lede mi
          lif,
     And that is for on suete° wif
     That heightte° Margeri.
     Ich have iloved° hire moni dai,°
     And of hire love hoe seiz me nai;°
180 Hider° Ich com forthi.°
Bote-if hoe wende hire mod,°
For serewe° mon° Ich wakese wod,°
Other miselve quelle.°
Ich hevede ithout° miself to slo;°
Forthen radde° a frend me go
To thee, mi sereue telle.°
     He saide me, withhouten faille°
     That thou me couthest helpe and
          vaile,°
     And bringen me of wo,°
190 Thoru thine crafftes and thine dedes;
     And Ich wile geve thee riche medes,°
     With that° hit be so."
[SIRITH] "Benedicite be herinne!°
Her° havest thou, sone, mikel sinne.°
Louerd,° for his suete° name,
Lete thee therfore haven no shame!
Thou servest affter Godes grame,°
Wen° thou seist on me silk° blame;
For Ich am old and sek° and lame;

200 Seknesse° haveth maked me ful tame.°
     Blesse thee, blesse thee, leve knave,°
     Leste thou mesaventer° have
     For this lesing° that is founded
     Oppon° me, that am harde ibounden!°
     Ich am on holi wimon,°
     On wicchecrafft nout I ne con,°
     Bote with° gode mens almesdede°
     Ilke dai mi lif I fede,°
     And bidde° mi Pater Noster and mi
          Crede,
210 That Goed hem° helpe at hore° need
     That° helpen me mi lif to lede,
     And leve° that hem mote wel spede.°
     His lif and his soule worthe ishend°
     That° thee to me this hernde° haveth
          send;
     And leve me to ben iwreken°
     On him this shome° me haveth
          speken."°
     [WILEKIN] "Leve nelde,° bilef° al
          this;
     Me thinketh that thou art onwis.°
     The mon that° me to thee taute,°
220 He weste° that thou hous couthest
          saute.°
     Help, Dame Sirith, if thou maut,°
     To make me with the sueting saut,°
     And Ich wille geve thee gift ful
          stark:°

Bote *Help*   leve nelde *dear grandmother*   ful evele *very badly*   tene *sorrow*   muchel hounsele *much misfortune*   suete *sweet*   That heightte *Who is named*   iloved *loved*   moni dai *for many days*   hoe…nai *she tells me nay*   Hider *Hither*   forthi *therefore*   Bote-if…mod *Unless she changes her mind*   serewe *sorrow*   mon *must*   wakese wod *go crazy*   Other miselve quelle *Or kill myself*   hevede ithout *have thought*   slo *slay*   Forthen radde *Therefore advised*   mi sereue telle *to tell my sorrow*   withhouten faille *without a doubt*   vaile *assist*   of wo *out of woe*   medes *rewards*   With that *Provided that*   Benedicite be herinne *Bless me!*   Her *Here*   mikel sinne *great sin*   Louerd *Lord*   suete *sweet*   servest…grame *deserve God's anger*   Wen *when*   silk *such*   sek *sick*   Seknesse *sickness*   tame *subdued*   leve knave *dear boy*   mesaventer *misadventure*   lesing *lie*   Oppon *Upon*   that…ibounden *who is bitterly oppressed*   on holi wimon *a holy woman*   nout I ne con *I know nothing*   Bote with *Only through*   almesdede *almsdeeds*   Ilke…fede *I support my life each day*   bidde *pray*   hem *them*   hore *their*   That *Who*   leve *trust*   hem…spede *they will prosper well*   His…ishend *[May] his life and his soul be disgraced*   That *Who*   hernde *errand*   iwreken *avenged*   shome *shame*   speken *spoken*   Leve nelde *Dear grandmother*   bilef *leave*   onwis *mistaken*   mon that *man who*   taute *directed*   weste *thought*   hous couthest saute *could reconcile us* [i.e., Wilekin and Margery]   maut *can*   sueting saut *reconcile with the sweetheart*   stark *great*

Moni° a pound and moni a marke,°
Warme pilche° and warme shon,°
With that min hernde° be wel don.
Of muchel godlec° might thou
yelpe,°
If hit be so that thou me helpe."
[SIRITH] "Ligh me nout,° Wilekin, bi
thi leute.°
230 Is hit thin hernest° thou tekest° me?
Lovest thou wel Dame Margeri?"
[WILEKIN] "Ye, nelde, witerli,°
Ich hire love! Hit mot me spille°
Bote° Ich gete hire to mi wille."
[SIRITH] "Wat, god° Wilekin, me
reweth thi scathe;°
Houre Louerd° sende thee help rathe!"°
Weste hic hit mightte ben forholen,°
Me wolde thunche wel solen°
Thi wille for to fullen.°
240 Make me siker° with word on
honde°
That thou wolt helen,° and I wile
fonde°
If Ich mai hire tellen.
For al the world ne wold I nout°
That Ich were to chapitre ibrout°
For none selke° werkes.
Mi jugement were sone igiven –
To ben with shome somer-driven°
With° prestes and with clarkes.°
[WILEKIN] "Iwis, nelde,° ne wold I

250 That thou hevedest vilani°
Ne shame, for mi goed.°
Her° I thee mi trouthe plightte,°
Ich shal helen bi mi mightte,°
Bi the holi roed!"°
[SIRITH] "Welcome, Wilekin, hider-
ward!°
Her° havest I maked a foreward°
That thee mai ful wel like.
Thou maight blesse thilke sith,°
For thou maight make thee ful blith;°
260 Dar thou namore sike.°
To goderhele° ever come thou hider,°
For sone will I gange thider,°
And maken hire hounderstonde.°
I shal kenne hire sulke a lore°
That hoe° shal lovien thee mikel°
more
Then ani mon in londe."
[WILEKIN] "Al so hav I Godes
grith,°
Wel havest thou said, Dame Sirith,
And goderhele° shal ben thin.
270 Have her° twenti shiling:°
This Ich geve thee to meding,°
To buggen° thee sep° and swin."°
[SIRITH] "So Ich evere brouke hous
other flet,°
Neren never penes beter biset°
Then thes shulen° ben.
For I shal don a juperti,°

Moni *Many* marke *mark* pilche *fur garments* shon *shoes* min hernde *my errand* godlec *benefit* yelpe *boast* Ligh me nout *Don't lie to me* leute *fairness* hernest *serious intention* tekest *tell* Ye, nelde, witerli *yes, grandmother, certainly* Hit...spille *It will destroy me* Bote *Unless* god *good* me...scathe *I pity your misfortune* Houre Louerd *Our Lord* rathe *quickly* Weste...for-holen *[If] I knew it might be concealed* thunche wel solen *think it very proper* fullen *fulfill* siker *certain* word on honde *a pledge* helen *conceal [it]* fonde *try* ne...nout *I would not* to chapitre ibrout *brought to chapter [ecclesiastical court]* selke *such* shome somer-driven *shame driven on a mule* With *By* with clarkes *by clerks* Iwis, nelde *Indeed, grandmother* hevedest vilani *are vexed with abuse* for mi goed *for my sake* Her *here* trouthe plightte *oath pledge* helen...mightte *conceal [it] according to my power* Bi...roed *By the holy rood [cross]* hiderward *here* Her *Here* fore-ward *agreement* thilke sith *this opportunity* blith *happy* Dar...sike *You will sigh no more* go-derhele *better fortune* hider *closer* gange thider *go there* hounderstonde *understand* kenne...lore *teach her such a lesson* hoe *she* mikel *much* Godes grith *God's peace* goderhele *better fortune* her *here* shiling *shillings* to meding *as a reward* buggen *buy* sep *sheep* swin *swine* So...flet *As I ever enjoy a house or a floor* Neren...biset *Never have pence been better used* thes shulen *these will* don a juperti *carry out a cunning plan* ferli maistri *wondrous trick*

And a ferli maistri;°
That thou shalt ful wel sen. –
[*To her dog*] Pepir nou° shalt thou eten,°
280 This mustart° shal ben thi mete,°
And gar thin eien to renne;°
I shal make a lesing°
Of thin heie-renning,°
Ich wot wel wer and wenne."°
[WILEKIN] "Wat! Nou const thou no god?°
Me thinketh that thou art wod.°
Gevest thou the welpe° mustard?"
[SIRITH] "Be stille, boinard!°
I shal mit° this ilke gin°
290 Gar° hire love to ben al thin.
Ne shal Ich never have reste ne ro°
Til Ich have told hou thou shalt do.
Abid° me her til min hom-come."
   [WILEKIN] "Yus, bi the somer blome,°
   Hethen null I ben binomen,°
   Til thou be agein comen."
Dame Sirith bigon to go
As a wrecche that is wo,
That hoe° come hire to then inne°
300 Ther° this gode wif wes inne.
Tho hoe° to the dore com,
Swithe reuliche hoe° bigon:
[SIRITH] "Louerd,"° hoe° seith, "wo is holde° wives,
   That in poverte ledeth ay lives;°
   Not no mon° so muchel of pine°
   As poure wif that falleth in ansine;°

That mai ilke° mon bi me wite,°
For mai I nouther gange ne site;°
Ded wold I ben ful fain."
310 Hounger and thurst me haveth nei° slain;
Ich ne mai mine limes onwold,°
For mikel° hounger and thurst and cold.
Warto° liveth selke° a wrecche?
Wi nul Goed° mi soule fecche?"
[MARGERY] "Seli° wif, God thee hounbinde!°
To dai wille I thee mete° finde,
For love of Goed.
Ich have reuthe° of thi woe.
For evele iclothed° I se thee go,
320 And evele ishoed;°
   Com herin, Ich wile thee fede."
   [SIRITH] "Goed almighten do thee mede,°
   And the Louerd° that wes on rode idon,°
   And faste fourti daus to non,°
   And hevene and erthe haveth to welde,°
   As thilke Louerd thee foryelde."°
[MARGERY] "Have her fles° and eke° bred,
And make thee glad, hit is mi red;°
And have her° the coppe° with the drinke;
330 Goed do thee mede° for th. swinke."°
   Thenne spac° that holde° wif –

Crist awarie° hire lif! –

[SIRITH] "Alas! Alas! That ever I live!
Al the sunne° Ich wolde forgive
The mon that smite of min heved!°
Ich wolde mi lif me were bireved!"°

[MARGERY] "Seli° wif, what eilleth°
thee?"

[SIRITH] "Bote ethe° mai I sori be:
Ich hevede a douter feir° and fre,°

340 Feiror° ne mightte no mon se.
Hoe° hevede a curteis hossebonde,
Freour° mon mightte no mon fonde.°
Mi douter° lovede him al to wel;
Forthi mak I sori del.°
Oppon a dai he was out wend,°
And tharthoru° wes mi douter shend.°
He hede on erdne° out of toune;
And com a modi clarc° with croune,°
To mi douter his love beed,°

350 And hoe nolde nout° folewe his red.°
He ne mightte his wille have,
For no thing he mightte crave;°
Thenne bigon the clerc to wiche,°
And shop° mi douter til a biche.°
This is mi douter° that Ich of speke;
For del° of hire min herte breketh.
Loke hou hire heien greten,°
On hire cheken° the teres meten.°
Forthi,° dame, were hit no wonder,

360 Thau° min herte burste assunder.

And wose ever° is yong houssewif,
Ha° loveth ful luitel° hire lif,
And eni clerc° of love hire bede,°
Bote hoe° grante, and lete him spede."°

[MARGERY] "A, Louerd° Crist! Wat
mai I thenne do?
This enderdai° com a clarc° me to,
And bed° me love on his manere,°
And Ich him nolde nout ihere.°
Ich trouue° he wolle me forsape.°

370 Hou troustu, nelde,° Ich moue ascape?"°

[SIRITH] "God almightten be thin help
That thou ne be nouther bicche ne
welp!°
Leve° dame, if eni clerc°
Bedeth° thee that love-werc,°
Ich rede° that thou grante his bone,°
And bicom his lefmon sone.°
And if that thou so ne dost,
A worse red° thou ounderfost."°

[MARGERY] "Louerd° Crist, that me
is wo,°

380 That the clarc° me hede fro°
Ar° he me hevede biwonne!°
Me were levere then ani fe°
That he hevede enes leien° bi me,
And efftsones bigunne.°
Evermore, nelde,° Ich wille be thin,
With° that thou feche° me Willekin,

Crist awarie *Christ curse* **sunne** *sin* **smite...heved** *struck off my head* **me were bireved** *taken from me* **Seli** *Good* **eilleth** *ails* **Bote ethe** *But easily* **douter feir** *daughter beautiful* **fre** *noble* **Feiror** *More beautiful* **Hoe** *She* **Freour** *Nobler* **fonde** *find* **douter** *daughter* **Forthi...del** *For this reason I make a great lament* **out wend** *gone out* **tharthoru** *thereby* **shend** *harmed* **erdne** *errand* **modi clarc** *proud clerk* **croune** *tonsure* **beed** *offered* **hoe nolde nout** *she would not* **red** *bidding* **crave** *beg* **wiche** *use magic* **shop** *transformed* **biche** *bitch* **douter** *daughter* **del** *sorrow* **heien greten** *her eyes cry* **cheken** *cheeks* **teres meten** *tears meet* **Forthi** *Therefore* **Thau** *That* **wose ever** *whoever* **Ha** *She* **luitel** *little* **And eni clerc** *If any clerk* **bede** *asks* **Bote hoe** *Unless she* **spede** *succeed* **Louerd** *Lord* **enderdai** *other day* **clarc** *clerk* **bed** *offered* **on his manere** *in his manner* **him...ihere** *would not hear him* **trouue** *believe* **forsape** *deform* **Hou troustu, nelde** *How do you think, grandmother* **moue ascape** *may escape* **nouther...welp** *neither bitch nor whelp* **Leve** *Dear* **eni clerc** *any clerk* **Bedeth** *Offers* **love-werc** *love-work* **rede** *advise* **bone** *request* **lefmon sone** *lover soon* **red** *misfortune* **ounderfost** *receive* **Louerd** *Lord* **that...wo** *woe is me* **clarc clerk** **hede fro** *went from* **Ar** *Before* **me hevede biwonne** *won me* **Me...fe** *It would be better to me than any payment* **hevede enes leien** *had once lain* **efftsones bigunne** *immediately begun* **nelde** *grandmother* **With** *If* **feche** *fetch*

The clarc° of wam° I telle;
Giftes will I geve thee
That thou maight ever the betere be,
390 Bi Godes houne belle!"°
   [SIRITH] "Sothliche,° mi swete dame,
     And if I mai withhoute blame,
     Fain° Ich wille ffonde;°
     And if Ich mai with him mete
     Bi eni wei other bi strete,°
     Nout ne will I wonde.°
   Have goddai, dame! Forth will I go."
   [MARGERY] "Allegate loke° that thou
     do so
   As Ich thee bad;°
400 Bote that° thou me Wilekin bringe,
   Ne mai I never lawe° ne singe,
   Ne be glad."
   [SIRITH] "Iwis,° dame, if I mai,
     Ich wille bringen him yet to-dai,
     Bi mine mightte."
   Hoe° wente hire to hire inne,°
   Her hoe° founde Wilekinne,
   Bi houre Drightte!°
   [SIRITH] "Swete Wilekin, be thou nout
     dred,°
410 For of thin hernde° Ich have wel sped.°
   Swithe° come forth thider with me,
   For hoe° haveth send after thee;
   Iwis° nou maight thou ben above,°
   For thou havest grantise° of hire love."
   [WILEKIN] "God thee foryelde,° leve
     nelde,°

That hevene and erthe haveth to
   welde!"°
This modi mon° bigon to gon
With Sirith to his levemon°
In thilke stounde.°
420   Dame Sirith bigon to telle,
   And swor° bi Godes ouene belle,°
   Hoe hevede him founde.°
   [SIRITH] "Dame, so have Ich Wilekin
     sout,°
     For nou° have Ich him ibrout."°
   [MARGERY] "Welcome, Wilekin, swete
     thing,
   Thou art welcomore° then the king.
     Wilekin the swete,
     Mi love I thee bihete,°
     To don al thine wille.
430   Turnd° Ich have mi thout,°
     For I ne wolde nout°
     That thou thee shuldest spille."°
   [WILEKIN] "Dame, so Ich evere bide
     noen,°
   And Ich am redi and iboen,°
   To don al that thou saie.
   Nelde, par ma fai!°
   Thou most gange awai,°
   Wile Ich and hoe shulen plaie."°
   [SIRITH] "Goddot° so I wille:
440   And loke that thou hire tille,°
     And strek out hir thes.°
   God geve thee muchel kare,°
   Yeif° that thou hire spare,°
   The wile° thou mid here bes.°

---

clarc *clerk* wam *whom* Bi...belle *By God's own bell* Sothliche *Certainly* Fain *Gladly* ffonde *try* Bi...strete *By any road or street* Nout...wonde *I will not hesitate at all* Allegate loke *By all means see* bad *asked* Bote that *Unless* lawe *laugh* Iwis *Indeed* Hoe *She* inne *dwelling* Her hoe *There she* Bi houre Drightte *By our Lord* be...dred *don't be afraid* hernde *errand* wel sped *well succeeded* Swithe *Quickly* hoe *she* Iwis *Indeed* ben above *be victorious* grantise *permission* foryelde *reward* leve nelde *dear grandmother* welde *rule* modi mon *proud man* levemon *lover* thilke stounde *that very moment* swor *swore* bi...belle *by God's own bell* Hoe...founde *She had found him* sout *sought* nou *now* ibrout *brought* welcomore *more welcome* bihete *promise* Turnd *Changed* thout *thought* ne wolde nout *would not want* thou...spille *you would kill yourself* bide noen *await 3 o'clock* iboen *prepared* Nelde...fai *Grandmother, by my faith* most gange awai *must go away* hoe shulen plaie *she will play* Goddot *God knows* tille *plow* strek...thes *stretch out her thighs* muchel kare *much sorrow* Yeif *If* hire spare *spare her* The wile *While* mid here bes *are with her*

And wose° is onwis,°
And for non pris°
Ne con geten his levemon,°
I shal, for mi mede,°
Garen° him to spede,°
450 For ful wel I con."°

---

wose *whoever*   onwis *unwise*   non pris *no prize*   Ne...levemon *Can get his lover*   mede *reward*   Garen *Cause*   spede *succeed*   con *can*

Endnotes

1   This edition is based on *A Literary Middle English Reader*, ed. Albert Stanburrough Cook (Ginn and Company, 1915) and *Middle English Humorous Tales in Verse*, ed. George H. McKnight (D.C. Heath & Co., 1913), both in the public domain. Footnotes and endnotes have been provided by Danielle Allor.

2   A *fabliau* is a short, humorous (typically bawdy) tale in verse. The genre thrived in France in the middle of the twelfth century and became popular in England during the fourteenth.

Tale of Constance[1] (1380–90)

John Gower
Contributed by Will Rogers

Introduction

John Gower's *Confessio Amantis* has long been a subject for scholars interested in impairment, disability, and age. A long poem, framed by the relationship between confessor and penitent, *Confessio Amantis* deals ultimately with cure and sickness, spiritual and physical. Amans, the old lover, is given *exemplum* after *exemplum* which are meant to guide him toward healing. *The Tale of Constance*, from Book II, fits this frame very well: a dramatization of the traffic in woman, the tale narrates the journey of Roman princess Constance from Rome to *Barbarie* (somewhere in the Middle East) to Northumberland and back to Rome, a trip that highlights the duplicity of figures she encounters on her forced journey. Book II concentrates on envy and its dangers, and Constance's voyages make clear that envy, at least for Gower's poem, concentrates on sight, and how others see Constance. While she remains constant, the sight of her causes fear, suspicion, and hatred. And tellingly, Chaucer's own version of this tale—*The Man of Law's Tale*—again foregrounds Constance as a constant in his narrative, one which remains immovable in the face of geographic and religious adversity.

For Gower (and perhaps Chaucer as well), the tale, then, is ultimately about sight and perception. The tale dramatizes the complex interplay between the senses, highlighting the slipperiness between truth and falsity. In fact, Gower describes eyes numerous times, using verbs depicting sight numerable times, and there is a simultaneous emphasis on hearing—yet one is never consistently associated with truth or its absence. Throughout

the tale, listening and reading, hearing and seeing convey how difficult it can be to discern the truth, a lesson which fits nicely into the tale's moralizations about envy. Here, one might examine the letters which Constance's mother-in-law deliberately overwrites, creating a false message about Constance and her son, Moris. Even with the ability to see, it is possible to be blind to the truth. Because envy is based on sight—seeing and wanting what others have—Gower's poem suggests that sight is an ability that is possibly always impaired. In fact, no one truly sees Constance, besides those who attempt to destroy her, those who are physically blind, or those who die or are separated from her as a result of her friendship and love.

By tying envy to sight and blindness, Gower's tale frequently evokes sight, eyes, and perception. These repeated descriptions of sightedness and blindness are most important for readers interested in impairment and disability. The tale, of course, uses these metaphors of sight and blindness conventionally: to be physically blind is to be spiritually so, a kind of link between the condition of the body and soul. This kind of blindness literally is a condition cured in the beginning of the tale by Constance and her faith, and the Knight who defames her is literally blinded by divine agency when he attempts to pin Hermengild's murder on her. Yet, even as the treatment of blindness here is rather conventional, it also tellingly is deployed beyond the expected. The blind man cured of his blindness can, nevertheless, see Constance and her faith initially for what they are: a woman with true faith which has alluded others, who are sighted, in the poem. To be clear, the tale does not seem to view blindness, however, as a condition that does not require intervention. Whether as spiritual or physical, it exists as a condition to be cured or a punishment for immoral behavior, and thus this treatment of blindness appears close to a modern medicalization of impairment and cure, reflecting the religious model of blindness, which Edward Wheatley traces in his book, *Stumbling Blocks before the Blind: Medieval Constructions of a Disability*.

Finally, because the tale emphasizes diverse locations and laws, it is a tale that speaks to the nearly impossible task of fixing norms, in terms of faith, law, and bodies. While Constance is a constant in the poem, she seems to be the only one: she is seen and rarely sees: the poem is mainly interested in reporting how the world sees her. But these diverse, and largely negative, reactions to Constance imply that perhaps, in terms of bodies and laws, there may only be diversity, even in other diverse treatments of Constance's constancy. For Gower's text, as for Chaucer's, the fiction of the normal body is just that.

Bibliography

Barrington, Candice. "The Trentham Manuscript as Broken Prosthesis: Wholeness and Disability in Lancastrian England." *Accessus: A Journal of Premodern Literature and New Media*, vol. 1, 2013, https://scholarworks.wmich.edu/accessus/.

Hsy, Jonathan. "Blind Advocacy: Blind Readers, Disability Theory, and Accessing John Gower." *Accessus: A Journal of Premodern Literature and New Media*, vol. 1, 2013, https://scholarworks.wmich.edu/accessus/vol1/iss1/2/.

———. "Close Listening: Talking Books, Blind Readers and Medieval Worldbuilding." *Postmedieval: A Journal of Medieval Cultural Studies*, vol. 7, no. 2, 2016, pp. 181–92.

———. "Disability." *The Cambridge Companion to the Body in Literature*. Edited by David Hillman and Ulrika Maude. Cambridge University Press, 2015, pp. 24–40.

Pearman, Tory Vandeventer. "Blindness, Confession, and Re-Membering in Gower's Confessio." *Accessus: A Journal of Premodern Literature and New Media*, vol. 1, 2013, https://scholarworks.wmich.edu/accessus/vol1/iss1/3/.

Schutz, Andrea. "Absent and Present Images: Mirrors and Mirroring in John Gower's *Confessio Amantis*." *The Chaucer Review*, vol. 34, no. 1, 1999, pp. 107–24.

Wheatley, Edward. *Stumbling Blocks before the Blind: Medieval Constructions of a Disability*. University of Michigan Press, 2010, pp. 155–85.

1   A worthi kniht in Cristes lawe°
Of grete rome, as is the sawe,°
The Sceptre hadde forto rihte;°
Tiberie° Constantin he hihte,°
Whos wif was cleped Ytalie;
Bot thei togedre of progenie
No children hadde bot a Maide;
And sche the god so wel apaide
That al the wide worldes fame

10   Spak worschipe of hire goode name.
Constance, as the Cronique° seith,
Sche hihte, and was so ful of feith,
That the greteste of Barbarie,
Of hem whiche usen marchandie,
Sche hath converted, as thei come
To hire upon a time in Rome,
To schewen such a thing as thei
    broghte;
Whiche worthili of hem sche boghte,
And over that in such a wise

20   Sche hath hem with hire wordes wise
Of Cristes feith so full enformed,°
That thei therto ben all conformed,
So that baptesme° thei receiven
And alle here false goddes weyven.°
Whan thei ben of the feith certein,
Thei gon to Barbarie° ayein,
And ther the Souldan° for hem sente
And axeth hem to what entente
Thei have here ferste° feith forsake.

[The Sultan hears reports of Constance's beauty from the converts and plans to marry her]

40   And furthermor with good corage°
He seith, be so he mai hire have,
That Crist, which cam this world to
    save,
He woll believe: and this recorded,

Thei ben on either side acorded,
And therupon to make an ende
The Souldan hise hostages sende
To Rome, of Princes Sones tuelve:
Wherof the fader in himselve
Was glad, and with the Pope avied

50   Tuo Cardinals he hath assissed°
With othre lordes many mo,
That with his doghter scholden go,
To se the Souldan be converted.
Bot that which nevere was wel herted,
Envie, tho began travaile
In destourbance of this spousaile°
So prively that non was war.
The Moder which this Souldan bar
Was thanne alyve, and thoghte this

60   Unto hirself: 'If it so is
Mi Sone him wedde in this manere,
Than have I lost my joies hiere,
For myn astat° schal so be lassed.'°
Thenkende thus sche hath compassed
Be sleihte° how that sche may beguile
Hire Sone; and fell withinne a while,
Betwen hem two whan that thei were,
Sche feigneth wordes in his Ere,
And in this wise gan to seie:

70   'Mi Sone, I am be double weie°
With al myn herte glad and blithe,
For that miself have ofte sithe
Desired thou wolt, as men seith,
Receive and take a newe feith,
Which schal be forthringe of thi lif:
And ek so worschipful a wif,
The doughter of an Emperour,
To wedde it schal be gret honour.
Forthi, mi Sone, I you beseche

80   That I mai thanne in special,
So as me thenkth it is honeste,
Be thilke° which the ferste feste
Schal make unto hire welcominge.'

Cristes lawe *Christendom*   sawe *familiar saying, proverb*   rihte *law*   Tiberie *Tiberius*   hihte *named*   Cronique *historical chronicle*   enformed *trained*   baptesme *baptism*   weyven *fail*   Barbarie *non-Christian lands, the Middle East*   Souldan *Sultan*   ferste *first*   corage *desire*   assissed *ordered*   spousaile *marriage, marriage negotiations*   astat *estate, condition*   lassed *diminshed*   sleihte *cunning, trickery*   double weie *of two minds, conflicted*   thilke *that*

The Souldan granteth hire axinge,
And sche was glad ynowh:°
For under that anon she drowh°
With false wordes that sche spak
Covine° of deth behind his bak.

[The Sultan's mother secretly plans the murder of all who attend the wedding, including her son, who is slain. Only Constance
remains.]

107 This worthi Maiden which was there
     Stood thanne, as who seith, ded for
        feere,
     To se the feste how that it stod,
110 Which al was torned into blod:
     The Dissh forthwith the Coppe and al
     Bebled° thei weren overal;
     Sche sih hem deie on every side;
     No wonder thogh sche wept and cride
     Makende many a wofull mone.
     When al was slain bot sche al one,
     This olde fend, this Sarazine,°
     Let take anon this Constantine
     With al the good and hire in fiere,
120 Vitailed° full for yeres fyve,
     Wher that the wynd it wolde dryve,
     Sche putte upon the wawes wilde.
     Bot he which alle thing maai schilde,
     Thre yer, til that sche cam to londe,
     Hire Schip to stiere hath take in honde,
     And in Northumberlond aryveth;
     And happeth than that sche dryveth
     Under a Castel with the flod,
     Which upon Humber banke stod
130 And was the kynges oghne also,
     The which Allee was cleped° tho,
     A Saxon and a worthi knyght,
     Bot he believeth noght ariht.
     Of this Castell was Chastellein°
     Elda the kinges Chamberlein,°
     A knyhtly man after his lawe;

And whan he sih° upon the wawe°
The Schip drivende al one so,
He bad anon men scholden go
140 To se what it betoken mai.
     This was upon a Somer dai,
     The Schip was loked and sche founde;
     Elda withinne a litel stounde°
     It wiste,° and with his wif anon
     Toward this yonge ladi gon,
     Wher that thei founden gret richesse;
     Bot sche hire wolde noght confesse,
     Whan thei hire axen what sche was.

[Constance is welcomed in Northumberland
and meets Hermyngheld, the wife of Elda.]

160 Constance loveth; and fell so
     Spekende alday betwen hem two,
     Thurgh grace of goddes pourveance°
     This maiden tawhte the creance°
     Unto this wif so parfitly,
     Upon a dai that faste by
     In the presence of hire housbonde,
     Wher thei go walkende on the Stronde,
     A blind man, which cam there lad,
     Unto this wif criende he bad,
170 To hire, and in this wise he seide:
     'O Hermyngeld, which Cristes feith,
     Enformed as Constance seith,
     Received hast, yif me my sihte.'
     Upon his word hire herte afflihte
     Thenkende what was best to done,
     Bot natheles sche herde his bone°
     And seide, 'In trust of Cristes lawe,
     Which don was on the crois and slawe,°
     Thou bysne man, behold and se.'
180 With that to god upon his kne
     Thonkende he tok his sihte anon,
     Wherof thei merveile° everychon,
     Bot Elda wondreth most of alle:
     The open thing which is befalle
     Concludeth him be such a weie,

---

ynowh *sufficiently*   **drowh** *drew*   **covine** *pledge*   **bebled** *stained*   **Sarazine** *Saracen, Muslim*   **Vi-
tailed** *stocked with provisions*   **cleped** *named*   **Chastellein** *governor of a castle*   **Chamberlein**
king's attendant   **sih** *saw*   **wawe** *water, wave*   **withinne...stounde** *shortly*   **wiste** *opened, discovered*   **pourveance** *foreknowledge*   **creance** *belief*   **bone** *request*   **slawe** *slew*   **merveile** *marvel*

That he the feith mot nede obeie.
Now lest what fell upon this thing.
This Elda forth unto the king
A morwe tok his weie and rod,
190 And Hermyngeld at home abod
Forth with Constance wel at ese.
Elda, which thoghte his king to plese,
As he that thanne unwedded was,
Of Constance al the pleine cas°
Als goodliche as he cowthe° tolde.
The king was glad and seide he wolde
Come thider upon such a wise
That he him mihte of hire avise,
The time apointed forth withal.
200 This Elda triste° in special
Upon a knyght, whom fro childhode
He hadde updrawe° into manhode:
To him tolde al that he thoghte,
Wherof that after hi forthoghte;
And natheles at thilke tide
Unto his wif he had him ride
To make redi alle thing
And seith that he himself tofore
Thenkth forto come, and bad therfore
210 That he him kepe, and told him
        whanne.
This knyht rod forth his weie thanne;
And soth was that of time passed
He hadde al in his wit compassed°
How he Constance myhte winne;
Bot he sih tho no sped therinne,
Wherof his lust began tabate,°
And that was love is thanne hate;
Of hire honour he hadde Envie,
So that upon his tricherie°
220 A lesinge° in his herte he caste.
Til he cam home he hieth faste,
And doth his ladi understonde
The Message of hire husbonde:
And therupon the longe dai
Thei setten thinges in arrai,°
That al was as it scholde be

Of every thing in his degree;°
And whan it cam into the nyht,
This wif hire hath to bedde dyht,°
230 Wher that this Maiden with hire lay.
This false knyht upon delay
Hath taried til thei were aslepe,
As he that wolde his time kepe
His dedly werkes to fulfille;
And to the bed he stalketh stille,
Wher that he wiste was the wif,
And in his hond a rasour knif
He bar, with which hire throte he cutte,
And prively° the knif he putte
240 Under that other beddes side,
Wher that Constance lai beside.
And stille with a prive lyht,
As he that wolde noght awake
His wif, he hath thus weie take
Into the chambre, and ther liggende°
He fond his dede wif bledende,°
Wher that Constance faste by
Was falle aslepe; and sodeinly
He cride alowd, and sche awok,
250 And forth withal sche caste a lok
And sih this ladi blede there,
Wherof swounende° ded for fere
Sche was, and stille as eny Ston
She lay, and Elda therupon
Into the Castell cleped° oute,
And up sterte every man aboute,
Into the chambre and forth thei wente.
Bot he, which alle untrouthe mente,
This false knyht, among hem alle
260 Upon this thing which is befalle
Seith that Constance hath don this
        dede;
And to the bed with that he yede°
After the falshed° of his speche,
And made him there forto seche,
And fond the knif, wher he it leide,
And thanne he cride and thanne he
        seide,

---

cas *situation, circumstances* **cowthe** *could* **triste** *trusted* **updrawe** *raised* **compassed** *devised* **tabate** *to lessen* **tricherie** *treachery* **lesinge** *falsehood* **arrai** *condition* **degree** *condition, state* **dyht** *prepared* **prively** *secretly* **liggende** *laying* **bledende** *bleeding* **swounende** *swooning* **cleped** *cried* **yede** *walked* **falshed** *falsity*

'Lo, seth the knif al blody hiere!
What nedeth more in this matiere°
To axe?' And thus her innocence
270 He sclaundreth° there in audience
With false wordes whiche he feigneth.
Bot yit for al that evere he pleigneth,
Elda no full credence tok:
And happeth that ther lay a bok,
Upon which, whan he it sih,
This knyht hath swore and seid on hih,
That alle men it mihte wite,°
'Now be this bok, which hier is write,
Constance is gultif,° wel I wot.'
280 With that the hond of hevene him smot
In tokne° of that he was forswore.
That he hath bothe hise yhen° lore,
Out of his hed the same stounde
Thei sterte, and so their weren founde.
A vois was herd, when that they felle,
Which seide, 'O dampned man to helle,
Lo, thus hath god the sclaundre° wroke°
That thou ayein Constance hast spoke:
Beknow the sothe er that thou dye.'
290 And he told out his felonie,°
And starf° forth with his tale anon.
Into the ground, wher alle gon,
This dede lady was begrave:°
Elda, which thoghte his honour save,
Al that he mai restreigneth sorwe.
For the second day a morwe°
The king cam, as thei were acorded;

[The King, seeing her virtue and beauty, marries Constance and she becomes pregnant.]

340 Wherof that sche was joiefull,
Sche was delivered sauf° and sone.
The bisshop, as it was to done,
Yaf him baptesme and Moris calleth;
And therupon, as it befalleth,
With lettres writen of record

Thei sende unto here liege lord,
That kepers weren of the qweene:
And he that scholde go betwene,
The Messager, to Knaresburgh,
350 Which toun he scholde passe thurgh,
Ridende cam the ferste day.
The kinges Moder there lay,
Whos rihte name was Domilde,
Which after al the cause spilde:°
For he, which thonk deserve wolde,
Unto this ladi goth and tolde
Of his Message al how it ferde.°
And sche with feigned joie it herde
And yaf him yiftes° largely,
360 Bot in the nyht al prively
Sche tok the lettres whiche he hadde,
Fro point to point and overradde,°
As sche that was thurghout untrewe,°
And let do wryten othre newe
In stede of hem, and thus thei spieke:
'Oure liege lord, we thee beseke
That thou with ous ne be noght wroth,
Though we such thing as is thee loth°
Upon oure trowthe certefie.
370 Thi wif, which is of faierie,°
Of such a child delivered is
Fro kinde° which stant all amis:
Bot for it scholde noght be seie,
We have it kept out of the weie
For drede of pure worldes schame,
A povere child and in the name
Of thilke which is so misbore
We toke, and therto we be swore,
That non bot only thou and we
380 Schal knowen of this privete:
Moris it hatte, and thus men wene
That it was boren of the qweene
And of thin oghne bodi gete.
Bot this thing mai noght be foryete,°
That thou ne sende ous word anon
What is thi wille therupon.'

matiere *situation*   sclaundreth *slandered*   wite *know*   gultif *guilty*   In tokne *as a sign*   yhen *eyes*   sclaundre *slanderer*   wroke *wrecked*   felonie *crime*   starf *died*   begrave *buried*   a morwe *in the morning*   sauf *safe*   spilde *suffered*   ferde *fared*   yiftes *gifts*   overradde *overwrote*   untrewe *false, a liar*   loth *unpleasant*   faierie *Faerie, a fairy*   fro kinde *unnatural*   mai...foryete *may not be forgotten*

This lettre, as thou hast herd devise,
Was contrefet° in such a wise
That noman scholde it aperceive:
390 And sche, which thoghte to deceive,
It leith wher sche that other tok.
This Messager, whan he awok,
And wiste nothing how it was,
Aros and rod the grete pas
And tok this lettre to the king.
And whan he sih this wonder thing.
He makth the Messager no chiere,
Bot natheles in wys manere
He wrote ayein, and yaf hem charge
400 That thei ne soffre noght at large
His wif to go, bot kepe hire stille,
Til thei have herd mor of his wille.
This Messager was yifteles,°
Bot with this lettre natheles,
Or be him lief or be him loth,
In alle haste ayein he goth
Be Knaresburgh, and as he wente
Unto the Moder his entente
Of that he fond toward the king
410 He tolde; and sche upon this thing
Seith that he scholde abide at nyht
And made him feste and chiere ariht,
Feignende as thogh sche cowthe him
    thonk.
Bot he with strong wyn which he dronk
Forth with the travail of the day
Was drunke, aslepe and while he lay,
Sche hath hise lettres overseie
And formed in an other weie.°
Ther was a newe lettre write,
420 Which seith: 'I do you forto wite
That thurgh the conseil of you tuo
I stonde in point to ben undo,
As he which is a king deposed.
For every man it hath supposed,
How that my wif Constance is faie;°
And if that I, thei sein, delaie
To put hire out of compaignie,
The worschipe of my Regalie°
Is lore;° and over this thei telle,

430 Hire child schal noght among hem
    duelle,
To cleymen° eny heritage.
So can I se non avantage,
Bot al is lost, if sche abide:
Forthi to loke on every side
Toward the meschief as it is,
I charge you and bidde this,
That ye the same Schip vitaile,
In which that sche tok arivaile,
Therinne and putteth bothe tuo,
440 Hireself forthwith hire child also,
And so forth broght unto the depe
Betaketh hire the See to kepe.
Of foure daies time I sette,
That ye this thing no longer lette,
So that your lif be noght forsfet.'°
And thus the lettre contrefet
The Messager, which was unwar,
Upon the kinges halve bar,°
And where he scholde it hath betaken.
460 Bot whan that thei have hiede take,
And rad that writen is withinne,
So gret a sorwe thei beginne.
As thei here oghne Moder sihen
Brent in a fyr before hire yhen:
Ther was wepinge and ther was wo,
Bot finaly the thing is do.

[Because of the treachery of Allee's mother, Constance and her child are set out to sea, in an echo of her escape from the Sultan's mother. She manages to sail back to Rome. In the meantime, Allee discovers his mother's treason and executes her. In order to gain absolution, Allee too travels to Rome where he is reunited with his wife and son Moris.]

741 Whan al is do that was to done,
The king himself cam after sone.
This Senatour, whan that he com,
To Couste and to his wif at hom
Hath told how such a king Allee
Of gret array to the Citee

---

contrefet *fake*   yifteles *giftless*   weie *manner*   faie *fairy*   Regalie *rulership, kingship*   lore *lost*   cleymen *claim*   forsfet *forfeit*   kinges halve bar *on the King's behalf*

Was come, and Couste upon his tale
With herte clos and colour pale
Aswoune fell,° and he merveileth
750 So sodeinly what thing hire eyleth,°
And cawhte hire up, and whan sche
    wok,
Sche syketh with a pitous lok
And feigneth seknesse of the See;
Bot it was for the king Allee,
For joie which fell in hire thoghte
That god him hath to toune broght.
This king hath spoke with the Pope
And told al that he cowthe agrope,°
What grieveth in his conscience;
760 And thanne he thoghte in reverence
Of his astat, er that he wente,
To make a feste, and thus he sente
Unto the Senatour to come
Upon the morwe and othre some,
To sitte with him at the mete.°
This tale hath Couste noghte foryete,
Bot to Moris hire Sone tolde
That he upon the morwe scholde
In al that evere he cowthe° and mihte
770 Be present in the kinges sihte,
So that the king him ofte sihe.
Moris tofore the kinges yhe°
Upon the morwe, wher he sat,
Fulofte stod, and upon that
The king his chiere upon him caste,
And in his face him thoghte als faste
He sih his oghne° wif Constance;

[After more than a decade apart, King Allee
is reunited with both his son and wife, and
Constance with the Emperor. Constance and
Allee return to England, where Allee dies,
and Constance returns to her father and
Rome, where her son Moris eventually becomes emperor.]

Aswoune fell *fainted*   **eyleth** *bothered*   **agrope** *discover*   **mete** *meal*   **cowthe** *could*   **yhe** *eye*   **oghne** *own*

Endnotes

1   The text below is taken from *Confessio Amantis*, ed. G.C. Macaulay, *The Complete Works of John Gower* (Clarendon Press, 1899). *The Tale of Constance* appears in lines 587–1613 of *The Series.* This text is in the public domain. Footnotes and endnotes have been provided by Will Rogers.

Complaint[1] (1419–21)

Thomas Hoccleve
Contributed by Will Rogers

Introduction

Thomas Hoccleve's *Series* is a text that is difficult to define. It is a collection of poems, ranging from a complaint about Hoccleve's mental illness, to a dialogue with a friend, and finally, a copy of *Lerne to Die* and translations from the *Gesta Romanorum*. The selections from the latter include *Jereslaus' Wife*—an analogue of the Constance story, similar to *The Man of Law's Tale* and Gower's *Tale of Constance*—and the *Tale of Jonathas*, which echoes *The Squire's Tale* and focuses on a son who squanders three magical gifts. These various works, discrete in nature, nevertheless form a larger, unified whole, as each text suggests something of Hoccleve's life to which he often alludes. Indeed, often nakedly autobiographical, the *Series* nevertheless blurs the line between fact and fiction, as Hoccleve's fictional moralizations are introduced by his own struggles with a mental illness, which, according to Hoccleve, have been all too real. In his beginning exposition of his illness and subsequent dialogue with a nameless "Friend," Hoccleve makes clear the severity of his mental break and the resulting alienation from London society. The dialogue with the friend which follows makes clear that Hoccleve's recovery is presumably not complete, and he needs help and encouragement—even prodding—to continue writing. The dialogue then turns to matters of patronage, and the Duke of Gloucester, before returning to harm and pain.

One of the focal points of this pain is the damage done to Hoccleve's own reputation through rumor and gossip about his extended mental illness, and these rumors introduce that Hoccleve, like his former friends, has allowed rumor and reputation to harm those who don't deserve it, namely, women. Indeed, as Hoccleve is aware and as the dialogue with the friend suggests, Hoccleve acknowledges that his writings have hurt women, by voicing false narratives like the ones he hears about his own recovery from mental illness. This writing, centered on women, becomes a reflection of the gossip, which centers on him, and spreads the story of his mental breakdown. Then by taking his own alienation into account, Hoccleve seems to internalize his own malady as reason to repent and make amends. Indeed, this malady or sickness is inseparable from the work's larger focus on the instability of the world, and the need to act moral and with virtue in spite of inhospitable circumstances, themes which the tales from the *Gesta Romanorum* and *Lerne to Die* make manifest. In a world where mental stability and health is no more secure than the seasons which change regularly, it is important to live as though each day is one's last.

But we should keep in mind that Hoccleve's poem gestures to a complex view of impairment and disability in fifteenth-century England. The difference between impairments and disability is a topic handled well by the *Series*. Impairment might simply signal some kind of bodily or mental difference from an imagined norm, as his own self-reported illness certainly does (at least in his telling). But his dialogue with his friend and complaint about the instability of social ties and friendship highlight that disabilities are often those impairments which elicit a social response or hinder some kind of communal relationship. Like a modern disability, Hoccleve's mental illness affects his employment and the quality of his life. Part of Hoccleve's *Complaint* is that, long after his illness has ended, gossip about the illness remains, and this cloud of suspicion makes recovery practically impossible. The expectation, Hoccleve tells us, is that he would relapse, due to his age and health. Here is a place we might see how impairment becomes disability, as the mental illness affects Hoccleve's employment and his status in London. His dialogue with his friend makes clear just how an impairment—according to Hoccleve, a mental breakdown caused by a variety of factors—might become disability once it affects one's social status or access to employment. Indeed, the opening *Complaint*—printed in full here—voices the fears Hoccleve's contemporaries have for his possible relapse. But the poems actually suggest that the disability is not the issue, but the quality of relationships and brokenness of the world, which make any deviation from the temporary fiction of the able body and mind fatal to one's standing in the personal and professional world of fifteenth-century London. According to Hoccleve, the fiction of the able body is a temporary one. Given enough time or age, one will encounter deviations from a bodily or mental norm (however fictional that norm may be). So, Hoccleve's words—that nothing stops change and can protect one from illness—reflect something similar: wealth, youth, all fail in the face of outside circumstances.

Finally, Hoccleve's *Series* is a wonderful example of the developing role of medical figures and late medieval attempts to reconcile science and medicine with religion, as Hoccleve ends the *Complaint* with a revaluation of bodily and mental pain. These corporeal trials become a way to rid oneself of spiritual malady tying the brokenness of Hoccleve's mind and body to the healing of his spirit, a connection suggested by the image of Christ as surgeon. The *Complaint*, therefore, in particular, offers a rich vocabulary for the medicalization of impairments, speaking of Hoccleve's *disseas, maladye*, or *wylde infirmite*. Healing, of course, comes, but through less than scientific or strictly medical means. Hoccleve finds a book with a dialogue featuring an allegorical Reason and internalizes the words as medicine. The *Complaint* ends, and the *Dialogue* begins, appropriately with Hoccleve viewing Christ as the physician, a connection made in other works of the period, as the growing power of medical figures became a symbol of God's grace.

Bibliography

Doob, Penelope B.R. *Nebuchadnezzar's Children: Conventions of Madness in Middle English Literature*. Yale University Press, 1974.

Goldie, Matthew Boyd. "Psychosomatic Illness and Identity in London, 1416–1421: Hoccleve's *Complaint* and *Dialogue with a Friend*." *Exemplaria: A Journal of Theory in Medieval and Renaissance Studies*, vol. 11, no. 2, 1999, pp. 23–52.

Hasler, Antony J. "Hoccleve's Unregimented Body." *Paragraph: A Journal of Modern Critical Theory*, vol. 13, no. 2, 1990, pp. 164–83.

Katajala-Peltomaa, Sari, and Susanna Niiranen. *Mental (Dis)Order in Later Medieval Europe*. Brill, 2014.

Scott, Anne M. "Speaking Up for the Aged: Thomas Hoccleve and The Regiment of Princes." *Sociability and Its Discontents: Civil Society, Social Capital, and Their Alternatives in Late Medieval and Early Modern Europe*, edited by Nicholas Eckstein and Nicholas Terpstra. Brepols, 2009, pp. 87–105.

Turner, Marion. "Illness Narratives in the Later Middle Ages: Arderne, Chaucer, and Hoccleve." *Journal of Medieval and Early Modern Studies*, vol. 46, no. 1, 2016, pp. 61–87.

Turner, Wendy. *Care and Custody of the Mentally Ill, Incompetent, and Disabled in Medieval England*. Brepols, 2013

1 After that hervest Inned° has his
    sheves,°
And that the broune season of Myhelm-
    esse°
was come, and gan the trees robbe of
    ther leves,
That grene had bene and in lusty fressh-
    nesse
and them in-to colowre of yelownesse
had dyen and doune throwne under
    foote,
that chaunge sank into myne herte
    roote.°
For freshely browght it to my remem-
    braunce,°
that stablenes° in this world there is
    none.
10 There is no thinge but chaunge and
    variaunce:
how welthye a man be or well be-gone,
endure it shall not he shall it for-gon.°
deathe under fote shall hym thrist
    adowne:°
that is every wites° conclusyon.
Whiche for to weyve is in no mannes
    myght,
how riche he be stronge, lusty, freshe,
    and gay.
and in the end of Novembar, upon a
    nyght,
syghenge° sore as I in my bed lay,
for this and othar thowghts whiche
    many a day
20 before I toke sleape cam none in myne
    eye,
so vexyd me the thowghtfull maladye.°
I see well, sythen I with sycknes last
was scourged, clowdy° hath bene the
    favoure

that shone me. Full bright in tymes
    past,
the sonne abatid, and the derke showre
hildyd° downe right on me, and in
    langour
he made swyme so that my wite
to lyve no lust hadd, ne delyte.
The grefe abowte my herte so swal°
30 and bolned° evar to and to so sore,
that nedes oute I must there with all.
I thowght I nolde° it kepe cloos no
    more,
ne lett it in me, for to olde and hore,°
and for to preve I cam of a woman,
I brast° oute on the morowe and thus
    began.
Allmyghty god, as lykethe his goodnes,
visytethe folks alday, as men may se,
with lose of good and bodily sikenese,
and among othar, he forgat nat me.
40 Witnes uppon the wyld infirmytie,°
which that I had, as many a man well
    knewe,
and whiche me owt of my selfe cast and
    threw.
It was so knowen to the people and
    kouthe°
that cownsell was it none ne none be
    myght;°
how it with me stode was in every mans
    mowthe,
and that full sore my fryndes affright.
They for myne helthe pilgrimages hight
and sowght them, some on hors and
    some on foote,
God yelde it them—to get me bote.°
50 But althowghe the substaunce of my
    memory
went to pley, as for a certayne space,

Inned gathered   **sheves** *bundle of grains*   **Myhelmesse** *Michaelmass, Sept. 29*   **roote** *center of the heart*   **remembraunce** *memory*   **stablenes** *stability*   **for-gon** *avoid*   **thrist adowne** *thrown down*   **wites** *wiseman*   **syghenge** *sighing*   **thowghtfull maladye** *mental illness*   **clowdy** *dim*   **hildyd** *poured*   **swal** *dark, shady*   **bolned** *swelled*   **nolde** *would not*   **hore** *grey, old*   **brast** *break*   **infirmytie** *sickness*   **kouthe** *known*   **ne...myght** *none which might have power*   **bote** *remedy*

yet the lord of vertew,° the kynge of
    glory,
of his highe myght and benynge grace,
made it to returne in-to the place
whence it cam, whiche at all hallwe
    messe,°
was five yeere neyther more ne lesse.
And evere sythen—thanked be God our
    Lord,
of his good reconsiliacion—
my wyt and I have been of suche ac-
    corde
60 as we were or the alteracion°
of it was, but by my savacion,
that tyme have I be sore sett on fire
and lyved in great torment and mar-
    tire.°
For thowgh that my wit were home
    came agayne,
men wolde it not so understond or take
with me to deale, hadden they dys-
    dayne.
A ryotows° person I was and forsake,
myn olde frindshipe was overshake,°
no wyte° withe me lyst° make daliance,
70 the worlde me made a straunge con-
    tinuance,°
whiche that myne herte sore gan tor-
    ment.
For ofte whan I, in Westmynster Hall,
and eke in London, among the prese°
    went,
I se the chere abaten and apalle°
of them that weren wonte me for to
    calle
to companye; her° heed they caste
    a-wry,
when I them mette as they not me sye.
As seide is in the sauter° might I say,
they that me sye fledden awey fro me,
80 forgeten I was all owte of mynde away,

as he that dede was from hertes cherte;°
to a loste vessell lickened myght I be;
for many a wyght abowte me dwellynge,
herd I me blame and putte in dispreis-
    inge.°
Thus spake many one and seyde by me:
'Allthowghe from hym his siknesse
    savage
withdrawne and passyd, as for a tyme
    be,
resorte it wole, namely in suche age
as he is of, and thanne my visage
90 bygan to glowe for the woo° and fere
Tho wordis, them unwar,° cam to myn
    ere:
'Whane passinge hete is,' quod they,
    'trustyth this,
assaile° hym wole agayne that maladie.'
And yet, parde,° they token them amise:
none effect at all toke there prophecie.
Manie someres ben past sithen remedye
of that, god of his grace me purveide:°
Thanked be God—it shope° nought as
    they seide!
What fall shall what men so deme° or
    gesse,
100 to hym that wott° every mans secre
reservyd is. It is a lewdnesse°
men wyser them pretende then they be,
and no wight° knoweth be it he or she,
whom, how ne whan God wole hym
    visete.
It happethe ofte whan men wene° it
    lite.
Some tyme I wend as lite as any man,
for to have fall into that wildenesse
but God, whan hym list may, wole and
    can,
helthe withdrawe and send a wyght
    sycknesse.

---

vertew *virtue*   **hallwe messe** *November 1st*   **alteracion** *change*   **martire** *martyred*   **ryotows** *aggressive*   **overshake** *discarded*   **wyte** *wise man*   **lyst** *desired*   **continuance** *countenance*   **prese** *crowd*   **apalle** *grow pale*   **her** *their*   **sauter** *Psalter*   **cherte** *esteem*   **dispreisinge** *disapproval*   **woo** *woe*   **unwar** *imprudent*   **parde** *By God*   **assaile** *attack*   **purveide** *prepared*   **shope** *was destined*   **deme** *judge*   **wott** *know*   **lewdnesse** *foolishness*   **wight** *man*   **wene** *believe*

110 Thowghe man be well this day, no
    sykernesse
  to hym bihight° is that it shall endure:
  God hurte now can and nowe hele and
    cure.
  He suffrith longe at the laste he smit;
  whane that a man is in prosperite,
  To drede a fall comynge it is a wit.
  Who so that takethe hede ofte may se
  This worldis change and mutabilite°
  in sondry wyse, howe nedeth not
    expresse:
  To my mater streight wole I me dresse
120 Men seyden I loked as a wilde steer,
  and so my loke abowt I gan to throwe;
  myne heed to hie° another side I beer,°
  ful bukkyshe° is his brayne, well may I
    trowe,
  and seyde the thirde and apt is in the
    rowe
  to site of them that a resounles° reed°
  Can geve no sadnesse is in his heed.
  Chaungid had I my pas some seiden
    eke,
  for here and there forthe stirte I as a
    Roo°—
  none abode, none arrest, but all brain-
    seke.
130 Another spake and of me seide also,
  my feete weren aye wavynge to and fro
  whane that I stonde shulde and withe
    men talke
  and that myne eyne sowghten every
    halke.°
  I leide an ere aye to as I by wente,
  and herde all, and thus in myne herte
    I cast:
  of longe abydynge here I may repent;
  leste, of hastinesse I at the last
  answere amyse best is hens° hye fast.
  For yf I in this preace amysse me gye,

140 to harme will it me turne and to folly.
  And this I demyd well and knew well
    eke,°
  whatsoevar I shuld answere or sey,
  they wold not have holde it worthe a
    leke.°
  For why, as I hadd lost my tonges key,
  kepte I me cloos, and trussyd° me my
    wey,
  drowpynge° and hevye° and all woo
    bystad:
  small cawse had I, me thowght, to be
    glade.
  My spirits laboryd bysyly
  to peinte countinaunce chere and loke,
150 for that men spake of me so wonder-
    ingly,
  and for the very shame and fere I
    qwoke,°
  thowghe myne herte had been dypped
    in the broke.
  It wete and moyste I now was of my
    swot,°
  whiche was nowe frostye colde and now
    firy hoot.
  And in my chamber at home when I
    was
  my selfe alone, I in this wyse wrowght.°
  I streit unto my myrrowr° and my glas,
  to loke how that me of my chere thow-
    ght
  yf any were it than it owght,
160 for fayne wolde I, yf it had not be right,
  amendyd it to my kunynge° and
    myght.°
  Many a sawte° made I to this myrrowre,
  thinkynge, 'Yf that I loke in this manere
  amonge folke as I now do, none errowr
  of suspecte loke may in my face appere,
  this continuance, I am surem and this
    chere,

---

bihight *promised*   **mutabilite** *variance*   **bukkyshe** *haughty*   **hie** *quickly*   **beer** *raise*   **resounles** *witless*   **reed** *counsel*   **Roo** *roe deer*   **halke** *recess or nook*   **hens** *hence*   **eke** *also*   **leke** *leek, i.e. worthless*   **trussyd** *departed*   **drowpynge** *physically weak, sad*   **hevye** *grievous*   **qwoke** *shudder*   **swot** *sweat*   **wrowght** *acted*   **myrrowr** *looking glass*   **kunynge** *cunning*   **myght** *physical ability*   **sawte** *saunter, trip*

If I forthe use is no thinge reprevable
to them that have conseytes° resonable.'
And therewithall I thowght thus anon:
170 'Men in theyr owne case bene blynd
alday,
as I haue hard say many a day agon,
and in that plyght° I stonde may.
How shall I doo, which is the best way,
my trowbled spirit, for to bringe ar
rest?
Yf I wist howe, fayne° wolde I do the
best.'
Sythen I recoveryd was have I full ofte
cawse had of angre and ympacience,°
where I borne have it esely and softe,
sufferynge wronge be done to me, and
offence,
180 and nowght answeryd ageyn, but kept
sylence,
lest that men of me deme would, and
seyne,
'Se how this man is fallen in agayne!'
As that I ones° fro Westmynster cam,
vexid full grevously withe thowghtfull
hete,
thus thowght I: 'a great fole I am,
this pavyment a dayes thus to bete,
and in and out, labour fast and swete,
wonderinge and hevynes to purchace,
sythen I stand out of all favor and
grace.'
190 And then thowght I on that othar syde:
'If that I not be sene amonge the prees,°
men deme wele that I myne heade hyde,
and am werse than I am—it is no lees.'
O lorde, so my spirite was restles,
I sowght reste and I not it found,
but aye was trouble, redy at myn hond.
I may not lett a man to ymagine
ferre above the mone° yf that hym lyst:
thereby the sowthe he may not deter-
myn.

200 But by the prefe° bene things knowne
and wiste,
many a dome° is wrappyd in the myst;
man by his dedes, and not by his lokes,
shall knowne be, as it is writen in bokes.
By taste of frewte,° men may well wete
and knowe
what that it is—othar prefe is there
none;
every man wott wel that, as that I
trowe,
right so they that demen my witt is
gone,
as yet this day there demythe many a
one
I am not well: may, as I by them goo,
210 taste and assay yf it be so or noo.
Upon a looke is harde, men them to
grownde
what a man is, thereby the sothe is hid;
whither his wittes seke bene or sounde,
by cowntynaunce it is not wist ne kyd.°
Thowgh a man harde have ones bene
bityde,
God shilde° it shuld on hym contynue
alway:
by comunynge is the best assay.
I mean to comon of things mene,
for I am but right lewde dowtles°
220 and ygnoraunte, my cunnynge is full
lene,
yet homly reason know I nevartheles;
not hope I founden be so resonles
as men demen—Marie, Christ forbede!
I can no more preve may the dede.
If a man ones fall in dronkenesse,
shall he contynewe therein evar mo?
Nay, thowghe a man doo in drinkynge
excesse
so ferforthe° that not speake he ne can,
ne goo,
and his wittes welny° ben refte° hym
froo,

---

conseytes *mental faculties*   **plyght** *trouble*   **fayne** *happily*   **ympacience** *impatience*   **ones** *once*   **prees** *crowd*   **mone** *moon*   **prefe** *proof*   **dome** *judgment*   **frewte** *fruit*   **wist ne kyd** *known*   **shilde** *shield*   **dowtles** *doubtless*   **ferforthe** *far*

230 and buryed in the Cuppe,° he aftarward
     comythe to hym selfe agayne, ellis were
       it hard.
     Right so, thowghe my witt were a
       pilgrime,
     and went fer fro home, he cam agayne.
     God me voydyd° of this grevous venyme
     that had enfectyd and wildyd° my
       brayne.
     Se how the curtese leche° most sov-
       ereyne,
     unot the sycke, gevythe medisyne
     in nede and hym relevythe of his peyne.
     Now let this passe, God wott, many a
       man
240 semythe full wyse by cowntenaunce and
       chere,
     whiche, and he tastyd were what he can,
     men myghten licken hym to a fooles
       pere.
     And some man lokethe in foltyshe°
       maner,
     as to the outward dome and Iudgement,
     that as the prese descrete is and pru-
       dent.
     But algates,° howe so be my coun-
       tynaunce,
     debate is now none bytwyxt and my
       wit,
     allthowghe there were a dysseveraunce,°
     as for a tyme, betwyxt me and it.
250 The greatar harme is myne, that never
       yet
     was I well lettered, prudent and dis-
       crete;
     there nevar stode yet wyse man on my
       fete.
     The sothe is this: suche conceit as I had,
     and undarstondynge, all were it but
       small,
     byfore that my wytts wearen unsad—

     thanked be Owr Lord Ihesu Crist of
       all!—
     suche have I now, but blowe is ny ovar
       all°
     the reverse, where thorwghe is the
       mornynge
     whiche cawsethe me thus syghe in com-
       playnynge.
260 Sythen my good fortune hathe changed
       his chere,
     hye time is me to crepe into my grace,
     to lyve Ioyles,° what do I here?
     I, in my herte, can no gladnes have;
     I may but small sey, but yf men deme I
       rave,
     sythen othar thinge the woo may I none
       grype,
     unto my sepulture° ame I nowe ripe.
     My well, adwe farwell, my good for-
       tune!
     Out of yowr tables, me playned have ye;
     sythen well ny eny wight for to comune
270 with me lothe is, farwell prosperitie!
     I am no lengar of your lyverye!°
     Ye have me put out of yowr remem-
       braunce;
     adewe° my good adventure and good
       chaunce!
     And as swithe after thus bythowght I
       me:
     yf that I in this wyse me despeyre,
     it is purchase of more advarsytye.
     What nedethe it, my feble wit appeire;
     sythe god hathe made myne helthe
       home repayre°
     blessed be he, and what men deme or
       speke
280 suffre it—thinke I and me not on me
       wreke.°
     But some dele had I reioysynge°
       amonge,
     and gladnese also in my spirite,

welny *nearly*   **refte** *robbed*   **Cuppe** *drinking cup, mug*   **voydyd** *emptied*   **wildyd** *disordered*   **leche** *physician*   **foltyshe** *ignorant*   **algates** *entirely*   **dysseveraunce** *divorce*   **blowe...all** *is known nearly everywhere*   **Ioyles** *joyless*   **sepultre** *tomb*   **lyverye** *livery*   **adewe** *endow*   **repayre** *return*   **wreke** *take vengeance*   **reioysynge** *rejoicing*

that thowghe the people toke them mis
   and wronge
me demynge of my sycknesse not quite,
yet for they compleyned the hevy plite
that they had sene me in with tendernesse
of hertes cherte, my grefe was the lesse.
In them put I no defawlte but one:
that I was hole,° they not ne deme
   kowlde,
290 and day and day, they se me by them
   gon
in heate and colde, and neythar still nor
   lowde,
knew they me do suspectly a dirke
   clowde
theyr syght obscuryd within and without,
and for all that were they in suche a
   dowt.
Axid have they full ofte sythe, and
   freined
of my fellaws of the prive seale°
and preyed them to tell them with hert
   unfeynyd,
how it stode wyth me, whither yll or
   well.
And they the sothe told them every
   dell,
300 but they helden ther words not but les:
they myghten as well have holden ther
   pes.
This troubly lyfe hathe all to longe
   enduryd,
not have I wyst how in my skynne to
   turne.
But now my selfe to my selfe have
   ensured,
for no suche wondrynge aftar this to
   morne:
as longe as my lyfe shall in me soiorne,°
of suche ymaginynge, I not ne reche.°

Lat them drem as them lyst and speke
   and dreche.°
This othar day, a lamentacion
310 of a wofull man in a bok I sye,
to whome words of consolation
Reason gave, spekynge effectually,
and well easyd my herte was therby.
For when I had a while, in the bok red,
with the speche of Reason was I well
   fed.
This hevy man, wofull and angwyssh-
   iows°
compleyned in this wyse and seyd he:
'my lyfe is unto me full encomberows;°
for whithar or unto what place I flye,
320 my wyckednesses evar followe me,
as men may se the shadow of a body
   swe,°
and in no maner I may them eschwe.°
Vexation of spirite and torment
lake I right none I have them plente.
Wondarly byttar is my taast and sent;°
wo be the tyme of my natyvyte,
unhappy man that evar shuld it be!
O deathe, they strooke, a salve is of
   swetnes
to them that lyven in suche wrechednes.
330 Gretar plesaunce were it to dye,
by many folde, than for to lyve soo.
Sorows so many in me multiplye,
that my lyfe is to me a wery foo;
comfortyd may I not be of my woo;
of my distrese se none end I can,
no force how sone I stinte° to be a man.
Than spake Reason: 'What menythe all
   this fare?
Thowghe welthe be not frindly to the
   yet,
out of thyn herte voyde wo and care!'
340 'By what skyll how, and by what rede
   and wit,'
seyd this wofull man, 'myght I done it?'

---

hole *whole, healthy*   **prive seale** *Office of the Privy Seal*   **soiorne** *travel*   **reche** *recount*   **dreche**
torment   **angwysshiows** *distressed, tormented*   **encomberows** *troublesome*   **swe** *sway*   **eschwe**
avoid   **sent** *scent*   **stinte** *cease*

320

'Wrastle,' qwode Reason, 'agayne hevy-
    nesses
of the worlde, troubles, suffring and
    duresses.
Behold how many a man suffrethe des-
    seas°
as great as thow and all a way greatar;
and thowghe it them pinche, sharply
    and ses,
yet, paciently, they it suffar and bere:
thynke here on and the lesse it shall the
    dere,
suche sufferaunce is of mans gylt°
    clensynge,
350 and them inablethe° to Ioye evar-
    lastinge.
Woo, hevynes and tribulation
comon are to men all and profitable.
Thowghe grevows° be manns tempta-
    cion,
it sleythe man not. To them that ben
    sufferable,
and to whom gods stroke is acceptable,
purveyed Ioye is, for God woundythe
    tho
that he ordeyned hathe to blysse to goo.
Gold purgyd is, thou seyst, in the
    furneis,
for the fyner and clenner it shall be;
360 of thy disease, the weyght and the peis°
bere lyghtly, for God to preve the,
scorgyd the hathe with sharp adversitie;
not gruche° and sey, "Why susteyn I
    this?"
for yf thow do, thow the takest amis.
But thus thow shuldest thinke in thyn
    herte,
and sey, "to the, Lord God, I have agylte
so sore: I moot for myn offensis smerte
as I am worthy. O Lorde, I am split,
but thow to me, thy mercy graunt wilt.
370 I am full swre,° thow maist it not denye:

Lord, I me repent and I the mercy crye.'
Lenger I thowght red haue in this boke
bot so it shope that I ne myght nowght.
He that it owght agayne it to hym toke,
me of his haste unware, yet have I
    cawght
sume of the doctryne° by Reason
    tawght
to the man as above have I sayde.
whereof I hold me full well apayde.
For evar sythen° set haue I the lesse
380 by the peoples ymagination,
talkynge this and that of my sycknesse,
whiche came of gods visytacion.
Myght I have be found in probation,
not grutchynge° but have take it in sof-
    fraunce,
holsome and wyse had be my gov-
    ernaunce.
Farwell my sorow—I caste it to the
    cok.°
With pacience, I hens forthe thinke
    unpike°
of suche thowghtfull dissease and woo,
    the lok,°
and let them out that have me made to
    sike.
390 Hereaftar Owr Lord God may, yf hym
    lyke,
make all myne olde affection resorte,
and in the hope of that woll I me com-
    forte.
Thrwghe gods iust dome and his iudge-
    ment,
and for my best, now I take and deme,
gave that Good Lorde me my punishe-
    ment:
in welthe I toke of Hym none hede or
    yeme,°
Hym for to please and Hym honoure
    and queme,°
and He me gave a bone on for to knaw,

---

desseas *disease* gylt *guilt* inablethe *enable* grevows *grievous* peis *weight* gruche *com-plain* swre *certain* doctryne *instruction, training* sythen *since then* grutchynge *complaining* caste it to the cok *neglect, throw away* unpike *unlock* lok *lock* yeme *care, attention* queme *pleasure*

me to correcte and of Hym to have awe.
400 He gave me wit and He toke it away
when that He se that I it mys dyspent,
and gave agayne when it was to His pay,
He grauntyd me my giltes to repent,
and hens forwarde to set myne entent,
unto His deitie, to do plesaunce,
and to amend my synfull governaunce.
Lawde and honore and thanke unto The
    be,
Lord God, that salve art to all hevynes!
Thanke of my welthe and myne adver-
    syte,
410 thanke of myne elde and of my seknese,
and thanke be to Thyne infinite
    goodnese
for Thy gyftes and benefices all,
and unto They mercye and grace I call.

Endnotes

1   The text below is taken from *The Series*, ed. Frederick Furnivall, *Hoccleve's Works: The Minor Poems* (Kegan Paul, Trench, Trübner, and Co., 1892). The *Complaint* appears in lines 1–413 of *The Series*. This text is in the public domain. Footnotes and endnotes have been provided by Will Rogers.

PROSE

The *Book of Margery Kempe*[1] (ca. 1450–1500)

Contributed by M.W. Bychowski

Introduction

Chapter seventy-four of the *Book of Margery Kempe* contains a scene in which God reframes her vision of disability and the Imago Dei. Beginning in prayer, Margery begs God to allow her, a creature of diverse eccentric traits and madness, into the center of His presence. God answers her prayer in an unexpected way. The *Book* says that Christ "drew His creature unto His love, and to mind of His Passion, so that she could not endure to behold a leper or other sick man, especially if he had any wounds appearing on him. So she cried, and so she wept, as if she had seen Our Lord Jesus Christ with His wounds bleeding." This is not the Imago Dei Margery would have anticipated. But when she asks to see the Image of God, she is shown the infirmed and disabled. It is the "love" of Christ that brings Margery into His "mind" and inspires a new understanding and ministry for the disabled, especially those lepers who not only will suffer in body but also emotionally from social exclusion. As a result, the Lazar House transforms in Margery's world from a place of brokenness into the place of the very presence of God.

After the transmission of Aristotle's texts during the twelfth century, there was renewed interest in Europe for classical philosophy. Evident in the work of scholastic theologians, such as Thomas Aquinas, Faith had to make room, as Reason became the measure of all things; including what it meant to be made in the image of God. These philosophical changes occur at the same time that Middle English is developing as a language, affecting how certain words would be weighted and understood. By the writing of the *Book* in the fifteenth century, the word "mad" had evolved to contain two distinct meanings. "Mad" could mean "made," a created thing, and a condition highlighted throughout the *Book* by referring to Margery almost exclusively as "the creature." "Mad" could also mean "mad" or "insane," a person with a non-normative form of cognition, "uncontrolled by reason" or "filled with enthusiasm or desire."[2] Suggesting multiple meanings, whether as a pun or poetic device, the use of the word "mad" would unlock the potential for statements to read with multiple different significances. For instance, madness could signify that a creature is both made an Imago Dei in God's Creation and also a mad person who is isolated from human society, set apart.

The doubled vision of Margery and the doubled significance of the word "mad" used throughout the *Book* in both senses creates a tension between the way that God might see disability and the way that society might see disability. In the medieval Church, where bodily signs of difference and disease could be read as moral differences and diseases, disability and especially leprosy were time and again condemned as a sign of punishment in the world that prefigures the punishments in Hell. Thus, the self-conscious work of madness in the *Book* not only challenges the rationality of the world but the cosmological order. The implication that the "mad" were Imago Dei, made in the image of God, and that to go to a Lazar House was to enter into the presence of Christ turns the value system of rational society inside out. Subsequently, Margery breaks open madness as being "mad," i.e., both "made" and "unreasonable," in the Imago Dei through the making of a spiritual treatise and comforting the poor and marginalized by entering into community, constituting an early form of liberation theology.

If the Imago Dei makes and makes without reason, it is most reflected by co-creative "madness" and not self-governing reason. The *Book* acts as such a self-conscious Imago Dei, opening and closing with descriptions of its making, proudly proclaiming, "this book was mad."[3] This recursion deepens in the only two instants in the *Book* where "madness" explicitly means unreason. The *Book* quotes the *Pryke of Life*'s author confessing to being "overcome by desire, begin to madden, for love governeth me, and not reason...they say—'Lo! yon madman crieth in the streets,' but how much is the desire of my heart they perceive not." This language is echoed in the *Book*'s other use of the word "mad" to describe Margery. In this second case, the *Book* frames her "crying and roaring" for God as a sign that she is a "mad woman."[4] The meaning of "madness" here is evidently suggestive of insanity, "uncontrolled by reason" or "filled with enthusiasm or desire." Yet in the *Book*'s use of the word, this madness is made by God, inspired by the Imago Dei and the love Christ places in the heart of the mad creature.

Turning again to Margery's prayer for God's presence, readers stand witness to how the Imago Dei in the "mad" bodies of the Lazar House inspires acts of liberation. Receiving her revelation, Margery "went to a place where sick women dwelt who were right full of the sickness, and fell down to her knees before them." Margery challenges the exclusionary logic of the Lazar House by crossing its threshold with a gesture of community. Seeing madness from the inside, Margery offers no rational answer to the woman's ills, but remains with her, "to comfort her."

The encounter with the madness of the Imago Dei breaks a barrier for Margery that prevented her, like the walls of the Lazar House, from finding comfort. "In those years of worldly prosperity," Margery regarded "nothing more loathsome or more abominable...than to see or behold a leper." The *Book* uses "abominable," like the *Book of Leviticus,* to mark things excluded from the community. It aligns the logic of exclusion with "worldly prosperity," suggesting that the Imago Dei could not be present until she accepts her own madness. Only then could she find and give comfort.

Margery finds herself most drawn to a woman "laboured with many foul and horrible thoughts." Subject to visions of her own, the woman Margery ministers to mirrors herself, "a mad woman, crying and roaring." Entering the Lazar House, Margery not only finds comfort for the leper, but for herself. The drive to comfort does not excuse the violence and isolation governing madness but seeks co-creation and co-liberation by a communal sharing of strength (physical, social, spiritual). As things are formed as disabled, they get pushed to the margins, but the Imago Dei of the *Book of Margery Kempe* gives a call to seek each other and make a co-creative community. Instead of being mad in isolation, we become mad for each other.

Bibliography

Jefferies, Diana, and Debbie Horsfall. "Forged by Fire: Margery Kempe's Account of Postnatal Psychosis." *Literature and Medicine*, vol. 32, no. 2, 2014, pp. 348–64.

McAvoy, Liz Herbert. "Bathing in Blood: The Medicinal Cures of Anchoritic Devotion." *Medicine, Religion and Gender in Medieval Culture*, edited by Naoë Kukita Yoshikawa. Boydell and Brewer, 2015, pp. 85–102.

———. "Medievalism and the Medical Humanities." *postmedieval*, vol. 8, no. 2, 2017, pp. 254–65.

Orlemanski, Julie. "How to Kiss a Leper." *postmedieval*, vol. 3, no. 2 "Disability and the Social Body," 2012, pp. 142–57.

Pearman, Tory Vandeventer. "Embodied Transcendence: Disability and the Procreative Body in the Book of Margery Kempe." *Women and Disability in Medieval Literature*, Palgrave Macmillan, pp. 113–49.

Vuille, Juliette. "'Maybe I'm Crazy?' Diagnosis and Contextualisation of Medieval Female Mystics." *Medicine, Religion and Gender in Medieval Culture*, edited by Naoë Kukita Yoshikawa, Boydell and Brewer, 2015, pp. 103–20.

Watt, Diane. "Mary the Physician: Women, Religion and Medicine in the Middle Ages." *Medicine, Religion and Gender in Medieval Culture*, edited by Naoë Kukita Yoshikawa, Boydell and Brewer, 2015, pp. 27–44.

The Proem[5]

Here beginneth a short treatise and a comfortable for sinful wretches, wherein they may have a great solace and comfort to themselves and understand the high and unspeakable mercy of our Sovereign Saviour Christ Jesus, Whose Name be worshipped and magnified without end. Who now in our days to us unworthy, deigneth to exercise His nobility and goodness. All the works of Our Saviour be for our example and instruction, and what grace that He worketh in any creature is our profit, if lack of charity be not our hindrance.

And therefore, by the leave of our merciful Lord Christ Jesus, to the magnifying of His holy Name, Jesus Christ, this little treatise shall treat somewhat in part of His wonderful works, how mercifully, how benignly and how charitably He moved and stirred a sinful caitiff unto His love, which sinful caitiff many years was in will and purpose, through stirring of the Holy Ghost, to follow the Saviour, making great promises of fasting with many other deeds of penance. And ever she was turned aback in time of temptation, like unto the reed-spear which boweth with every wind, and never is stable unless no wind bloweth, unto the time that our merciful Lord Christ Jesus, having pity and compassion on His handiwork and His creature, turned health into sickness, prosperity into adversity, worship into reproof, and love into hatred.

Thus everything turning upside down, this creature who for many years had gone astray and ever been unstable, was perfectly drawn and stirred to enter the way of high perfection, which perfect way Christ Our Saviour, in His proper Person, exampled. Earnestly He trod it and duly He went it aforetime.

Then this creature, of whom this treatise through the mercy of Jesus shall shew in part the life, was touched by the hand of Our Lord with great bodily sickness, wherethrough she lost reason and her wits a long time, till Our Lord by grace restored her again, as it shall more openly be shewn afterwards. Her worldly goods which were plenteous and abundant at that date, a little while afterwards were full barren and bare. Then was pomp and pride cast down and laid aside. They that before had worshipped her, afterwards full sharply reproved her, her kindred and they that had been friends were now most her enemies. Then she, considering this wonderful changing, seeking succour under the wings of her Ghostly Mother Holy Church, went and offered obedience to her ghostly father, accusing herself of her misdeeds, and afterwards did great bodily penance, and in a short time Our Merciful Lord visited this creature with plenteous tears of contrition day by day, insomuch that some said she might weep when she would, and slandered the work of God.

She was so used to being slandered and reproved, to being chidden and rebuked by the world for grace and virtue with which she was endued through the strength of the Holy Ghost, that it was to her, in a manner, solace and comfort when she suffered any disease for the love of God and for the grace that God wrought in her. For ever the more slander and reproof that she suffered, the more she increased in grace, and in devotion of holy meditation, of high contemplation, and of wonderful speeches and dalliance which Our Lord spake and conveyed to her soul, teaching her how she should be despised for His love, how she should have patience, setting all her trust, all her love and all her affection in Him only.

She knew and understood many secret and privy things which should befall afterwards, by inspiration of the Holy Ghost. And oftentimes while she kept by such holy speeches and dalliance, she would so weep and sob that many men were greatly awonder, for they little knew how homely Our Lord was in her soul. She herself could never tell the grace that she felt. It was so heavenly, so high above her reason and her bodily wits, and her body so feeble in time of the presence of grace that she might never express it with her word as she felt it in her soul.

Then had this creature much dread, because of illusions and deceits of her ghostly enemies. Then went she, by the bidding of the Holy Ghost, to many worshipful clerks, both archbishops and bishops, doctors of divinity and bachelors also. She spoke also with many anchorites and showed them her manner of living and such grace as the Holy Ghost, of His goodness, wrought in her mind and in her soul, as her wit would serve her to express it. And all those that she shewed her secrets unto, said she was much bound to love Our Lord for the grace that He shewed unto her, and counselled her to follow her movings and her stirrings and trustingly believe they were of the Holy Ghost, and of no evil spirit.

Some of these worthy and worshipful clerks averred, at the peril of their souls and as they would answer to God, that this creature was inspired with the Holy Ghost, and bade her that she should have them written down and make a book of her feelings and revelations. Some proffered to write her feelings with their own hands, and she would not consent in any way, for she was commanded in her soul that she should not write so soon. And so it was twenty years and more from the time this creature had her first feelings and revelations, ere she did any writing. Afterwards, when it pleased Our Lord, He commanded her and charged her that she should get written her feelings and revelations and the form of her living, that His goodness might be known to all the world.

Chapter I
Her marriage and illness after child-birth. She recovers.

When this creature was twenty years of age, or some deal more, she was married to a worshipful burgess° (of Lynne) and was with child within a short time, as nature would. And after she had conceived, she was bela-boured with great accesses till the child was born and then, what with the labour she had in childing, and the sickness going before, she despaired of her life, weening she might not live. And then she sent for her ghostly father, for she had a thing on her conscience which she had never shewn before that time in all her life. For she was ever hindered by her enemy, the devil, evermore saying to her that whilst she was in good health she needed no confession, but to do penance by herself alone and all should be forgiven, for God is merciful enough. And therefore this creature oftentimes did great penance in fasting on bread and water, and other deeds of alms with devout prayers, save she would not shew that in confession.

And when she was at any time sick or diseased, the devil said in her mind that she should be damned because she was not shriven of that default. Wherefore after her child was born, she, not trusting to live, sent for her ghostly father, as is said before, in full will to be shriven of all her lifetime, as near as she could. And when she came to the point for to say that thing which she had so long concealed, her confessor was a little too hasty and began sharply to reprove her, before she had fully said her intent, and so she would no more say for aught he might do. Anon, for the dread she had of damnation on the one side, and his sharp reproving of her on the other side, this creature went out of her mind and was wondrously vexed and laboured with spirits for half a year, eight weeks and odd days.

And in this time, she saw, as she thought, devils opening their mouths all inflamed with burning waves of fire, as if they would have swallowed her in, sometimes ramping at her, sometimes threatening her, pulling her and hauling her, night and day during the aforesaid time. Also the devils cried upon her with great threatenings, and bade her that

burgess *citizen*

she should forsake Christendom, her faith, and deny her God, His Mother and all the Saints in Heaven, her good works, and all good virtues, her father, her mother and all her friends. And so she did. She slandered her husband, her friends and her own self. She said many a wicked word, and many a cruel word, she knew no virtue nor goodness, she desired all wickedness, like as the spirits tempted her to say and do, so she said and did. She would have destroyed herself many a time at their stirrings and have been damned with them in Hell, and in witness thereof, she bit her own hand so violently, that the mark was seen all her life after.

And also she rived the skin on her body against her heart with her nails spitefully, for she had no other instruments, and worse she would have done, but that she was bound and kept with strength day and night so that she might not have her will. And when she had long been laboured in these and many other temptations, so that men weened she should never have escaped or lived, then on a time as she lay alone and her keepers were from her, Our Merciful Lord Jesus Christ, ever to be trusted, worshipped be His Name, never forsaking His servant in time of need, appeared to His creature who had forsaken Him, in the likeness of a man, most seemly, most beauteous and most amiable that ever might be seen with man's eye, clad in a mantle of purple silk, sitting upon her bedside, looking upon her with so blessed a face that she was strengthened in all her spirit, and said to her these words—

'Daughter, why hast thou forsaken Me, and I forsook never thee?'

And anon, as He said these words, she saw verily how the air opened as bright as any lightning. And He rose up into the air, not right hastily and quickly, but fair and easily, so that she might well behold Him in the air till it was closed again.

And anon this creature became calmed in her wits and reason, as well as ever she was before, and prayed her husband as soon as he came to her, that she might have the keys of the buttery to take her meat and drink as she had done before Her maidens and her keepers counselled him that he should deliver her no keys, as they said she would but give away such goods as there were, for she knew not what she said, as they weened.

Nevertheless, her husband ever having tenderness and compassion for her, commanded that they should deliver to her the keys, and she took her meat and drink as her bodily strength would serve her, and knew her friends and her household and all others that came to see how Our Lord Jesus Christ had wrought His grace in her, so blessed may He be, Who ever is near in tribulation. When men think He is far from them, He is full near by His grace. Afterwards, this creature did all other occupations as fell to her to do, wisely and soberly enough, save she knew not verily the call of Our Lord.

Chapter 30

She visits the Jordan, Mount Quarentyne, Bethania and Rafnys. Starts for Rome, and at Venice meets Richard, the broken-backed man, and goes on in his company.

Another time, this creature's fellowship would go to the Flood of Jordan and would not let her go with them. Then this creature prayed Our Lord that she might go with them, and He bade that she should go with them whether they would or not. Then she went forth by the grace of God and asked no leave of them.

When she came to the Flood of Jordan, the weather was so hot that she thought her feet would have burnt for the heat that she felt.

Afterwards she went with her fellowship to Mount Quarentyne. There Our Lord fasted forty days, and there she prayed her fellowship to help her up on to the Mount. And they said, 'Nay,' for they could not well help themselves. Then had she great sorrow, because she might not come on to the hill. And anon, happed a Saracen, a well-favoured man, to come by her, and she put a groat into his hand, making him a sign to bring her on to the Mount. And quickly the Saracen took her under his arm and led her up on to the high Mount, where Our Lord fasted forty days.

Then was she sore athirst, and had no comfort in her fellowship. Then God of His great goodness, moved the Grey Friars with compassion, and they comforted her, when her countrymen would not know her.

And so she was ever more strengthened in the love of Our Lord and the more bold to suffer shame and reproof for His sake in every place where she came, for the grace that God wrought in her of weeping, sobbing, and crying, which grace she might not withstand when God would send it. And ever she proved her feelings true, and those promises that God had made her while she was in England and other places also. They befell her in effect just as she had felt before, and therefore she durst the better receive such speeches and dalliance, and the more boldly work thereafter.

Afterwards, when this creature came down from the Mount, as God willed, she went forth to the place where Saint John the Baptist was born. And later she went to Bethania, where Mary and Martha dwelt, and to the grave where Lazarus was buried and raised from death into life. And she prayed in the chapel where Our Blessed Lord appeared to His blissful Mother on Easter Day at morn, first of all others. And she stood in the same place where Mary Magdalene stood when Christ said to her—

'Mary, why weepest thou?'

And so she was in many more places than be written, for she was three weeks in Jerusalem and the country thereabout, and she had ever great devotion as long as she was in that country.

The friars of the Temple made her great cheer and gave her many great relics, desiring that she should have dwelt still amongst them if she would, for the faith they had in her. Also the Saracens made much of her, and conveyed her, and led her about the country wherever she would go, and she found all people good to her and gentle, save only her own countrymen.

And as she came from Jerusalem unto Rafnys, then would she have turned again to Jerusalem for the great grace and ghostly comfort that she felt when she was there, and to purchase herself more pardon.

Then Our Lord commanded her to go to Rome and, so, forth home into England, and said to her—

'Daughter, as oftentimes as thou sayest or thinkest "Worshipped be those Holy Places in Jerusalem that Christ suffered bitter pain and Passion in," thou shalt have the same pardon as if thou wert there with thy bodily presence, both to thyself and to all that thou wilt give it to.'

And as she went forth to Venice, many of her fellowship were right sick, and Our Lord said to her—

'Dread thee not, daughter, no man shall die in the ship that thou art in.'

And she found her feelings right true. When Our Lord had brought them again to Venice in safety, her countrymen forsook her and went away from her, leaving her alone. And some of them said that they would not go with her for a hundred pound.

When they had gone away from her, then Our Lord Jesus Christ, Who ever helpeth at need, and never forsaketh His servants who truly trust in His mercy, said to this creature—

'Dread thee not, daughter, for I will provide for thee right well, and bring thee in safety to Rome and home again into England without any villainy to thy body, if thou wilt be clad in white clothes, and wear them as I said to thee whilst thou wert in England.'

Then this creature, being in great grief and distress, answered Him in her mind—

'If Thou be the spirit of God that speaketh in my soul, and I may prove Thee for a true spirit with the counsel of the Church, I shall obey Thy will, and if Thou bringest me to Rome in safety, I shall wear white clothes, though all the world should wonder at me, for Thy love.'

'Go forth, daughter, in the Name of Jesus, for I am the spirit of God, which shall help thee in all thy need, go with thee, and support thee in every place, and therefore mistrust Me not. Thou foundest Me never deceivable, and I bid thee nothing do, but that which is worship to God, and profit to thy soul. If thou will do thereafter, then I shall flow on thee great plenty of grace.'

Then anon, as she looked on one side, she saw a poor man sitting, who had a great hump on his back. His clothes were all clouted and he seemed a man of fifty winters' age. Then she went to him and said—

'Good man, what aileth your back?'

He said—'Damsel, it was broken in a sickness.'

She asked, what was his name, and what countryman he was. He said his name was Richard, and he was of Ireland. Then thought she of her confessor's words, who was a holy anchorite, as is written before, who spoke to her whilst she was in England in this manner—

'Daughter, when your fellowship hath forsaken you, God will provide a broken-backed man to lead you forth, wherever you will go.'

Then she, with a glad spirit, said to him—

'Good Richard, lead me to Rome, and you shall be rewarded for your labour.'

'Nay, damsel,' said he, 'I wot well thy countrymen have forsaken thee, and therefore it were hard on me to lead thee. Thy countrymen have both bows and arrows with which they might defend both thee and themselves, and I have no weapon save a cloak full of clouts, and yet I dread me that mine enemies will rob me, and peradventure take thee away from me and defile thy body, and therefore I dare not lead thee, for I would not, for a hundred pounds, that thou hadst a villainy in my company.'

And she said again—

'Richard, dread you not, God shall keep us both right well and I shall give you two nobles for your labour.'

Then he consented and went forth with her. Soon after, there came two Grey Friars and a woman that came with them from Jerusalem, and she had with her an ass, which bore a chest and an image therein, made after Our Lord.

Then said Richard to the aforesaid creature—

'Thou shalt go forth with these two men and the woman and I will meet thee morning and evening, for I must get on with my job and beg my living.'

So she did after his counsel and went forth with the two friars and the woman. And none of them could understand her language, and yet they provided for her every day, meat, drink, and harbourage as well as they did for themselves and rather better, so that she was ever bounden to pray for them.

Every evening and morning, Richard with the broken back came and comforted her as he had promised.

The woman who had the image in the chest, when they came into good cities, took the image out of her chest, and set it in worshipful wives' laps, and they would put shirts thereon, and kiss it as if it had been God Himself.

When the creature saw the worship and reverence that they gave to the image, she was taken with sweet devotion and sweet meditations, so that she wept with great sobbing and loud crying, and she was moved so much the more, because while she was in England, she had high meditations on the birth and the childhood of Christ, and she thanked God forasmuch, as she saw these creatures having as great faith in what she saw with her bodily eye, as she had had before with her ghostly eye.

When these good women saw this creature weeping, sobbing and crying so wonderfully and mightily that she was nearly overcome therewith, then they arranged a good soft bed and laid her thereon, and comforted her as much as they could for Our Lord's sake, blessed may He be.

Chapter 62

The preaching friar preaches against her,
without naming her. She loses many friends in
consequence, but others come to her help.

Afterwards, on Saint James' Day, the good
friar preached in Saint James' Chapel-yard at
Lynne—he was at that time neither bachelor
nor doctor of divinity—where were many
people and a great audience, for he had a
holy name and great favour with the people,
insomuch that some men, if they thought he
would preach in the country, they would go
with him or else follow him from town to
town, such great delight had they to hear
him, and so, blessed may God be, he preached
fully holily and full devoutly.

Nevertheless, on this day he preached
much against the said creature, not expressing her name but so exploiting his conceits
that men understood well that he meant her.

Then there was much discussion amongst
the people, for many men and many women
trusted her, and loved her right well, and
were right grieved and sorrowful because he
spoke as much against her as he did, desiring
that they had not heard him that day.

When he heard the murmur and grutch-
ing of the people, supposing to be gainsaid
another day by them that were her friends,
he, smiting his hand on the pulpit, said—'If I
hear these matters repeated any more, I shall
so smite the nail on the head,' he said, 'that it
shall shame all her maintainers.'

And then many of them that pretended
friendship to her, turned aback, for a little
vain dread that they had of his words, and
durst not well speak with her. Of whom the
same priest was one, that afterwards wrote
this book, and who was in purpose never to
have believed in her feelings afterwards.

And yet Our Lord drew him back in a
short time, blessed may He be, so that he
loved her more and trusted more to her
weeping and her crying than ever he did

before. For afterwards he read of a woman
called Maria de Oegines, and of her manner
of living, of the wonderful compassion that
she had in thinking of His Passion, and of the
plenteous tears that she wept, which made
her so feeble and so weak that she could not
endure to behold the Cross, or hear Our
Lord's Passion rehearsed, without being dis-
solved in tears of pity and compassion.

Of the plenteous grace of her tears, he
treateth specially in the book before written, the 18th Chapter that begins, *'Bonus est*
domine, sperantibus in te,' and also in the 19th
Chapter where he telleth how she, at the request of a priest that he should not be troubled or distraught in his Mass with her weeping and her sobbing, went out of the church
door, with a loud voice crying that she could
not restrain herself therefrom.

And Our Lord also visited the priest,
when at Mass, with such grace and such devotion when he would read the Holy Gospel,
that he wept wonderfully, so that he wetted
his vestment and the ornaments of the altar,
and might not measure his weeping and his
sobbing, it was so abundant, nor might he restrain it, or well stand therewith at the Altar.

Then he believed well that the good woman, whom he before had little affection for,
could not restrain her weeping, her sobbing
or her crying, and who felt more plenty of
grace than ever did he, without any comparison. Then he knew well that God gave His
grace to whom He would.

Then the priest who wrote this treatise,
through stirring of a worshipful clerk, a bachelor of divinity, had seen and read the matter
before written much more seriously and expressly than it is written in this treatise, for
here is but a little of the effect thereof, for he
had not right clear mind of the said matter
when he wrote this treatise, and therefore he
wrote the less thereof.

Bonus est...te *"Good is the one, Lord, whose hope is in you"* [Latin]

Then he drew toward and inclined more seriously to the said creature, whom he had fled and eschewed through the friar's preaching, as is before written.

Also the same priest read afterwards in a treatise that is called the 'Prick of Love,' the 2nd Chapter, that Bonaventure wrote of himself, these words following—

'Ah, Lord, why shall I more call and cry! Thou delayest, and Thou comest not, and I, weary and overcome by desire, begin to madden, for love governeth me, and not reason. I run with hasty course whereever Thou wilt. I submit, Lord. They that see me, trouble and rue not, knowing me drunken with Thy love Lord, they say—"Lo! yon madman crieth in the streets," but how much is the desire of my heart they perceive not.'

He read also of Richard Hampol, hermit, in Incendio Amoris, like matter that moved him to give credence to the said creature.

Also Elizabeth of Hungary cried with a loud voice, as is written in her treatise.

And many others, who had forsaken her through the friar's preaching, repented and turned again to her in process of time, notwithstanding that the friar kept his opinion, and would always in his sermon, have a part against her, whether she were there or not, and caused many people to deem full evil of her, many a day and long.

For some said that she had a devil within her, and some said to her own mouth that the friar should have driven those devils out of her. Thus was she slandered, eaten and gnawed by the people, for the grace that God wrought in her, of contrition, devotion, and compassion, through the gift of which graces she wept, sobbed and cried full sore against her will. She might not choose, for she would rather have wept softly and privily, than openly, if it had been in her power.

Chapter 74

Her desire for death. Her desire to kiss the lepers. Visits to sick women, and consolation of one in temptation.

The said creature one day, hearing her Mass and revolving in her mind the time of her death, sore sighing and sorrowing because it was so long delayed, said in this manner—

'Alas ' Lord, how long shall I thus weep and mourn for Thy love, and for desire of Thy presence?'

Our Lord answered in her soul and said—

'All these fifteen years.'

Then said she—

'Ah! Lord, I shall think it many thousand years.'

Our Lord answered to her—

'Daughter, thou must bethink thyself of My blessed Mother, who lived after Me on earth fifteen years, also Saint John the Evangelist, and Mary Magdalene, who loved Me right highly.'

'Ah Blissful Lord,' said she, 'I would I were as worthy to be secure of Thy love, as Mary Magdalene was.'

Then said Our Lord—'Truly, daughter, I love thee as well, and the same peace that I gave to her, the same peace I give to thee. For, daughter, there is no saint in Heaven displeased, though I love a creature on earth as much as I do them. Therefore they will not otherwise than I will.'

Thus Our Merciful Lord Christ Jesus drew His creature unto His love, and to mind of His Passion, so that she could not endure to behold a leper or other sick man, especially if he had any wounds appearing on him.

So she cried, and so she wept, as if she had seen Our Lord Jesus Christ with His wounds bleeding. And so she did, in the sight of her soul, for, through the beholding of the sick man, her mind was all taken over to Our Lord Jesus Christ.

Then had she great mourning and sorrowing because she might not kiss the lepers when she saw them, or met with them, in the streets, for the love of Jesus.

Now began she to love what she had most hated beforetime, for there was nothing more loathsome or more abominable to her, while she was in those years of worldly prosperity, than to see or behold a leper, whom now, through Our Lord's mercy, she desired to embrace and kiss for the love of Jesus, when she had time and place convenient.

Then she told her confessor what great desire she had to kiss lepers, and he warned her that she should kiss no men, but if she would anyhow kiss, she should kiss women. Then was she glad, because she had leave to kiss the sick women, and went to a place where sick women dwelt who were right full of the sickness, and fell down to her knees before them, praying them that she might kiss their mouths for the love of Jesus. So she kissed there two sick women with many a holy thought and many a devout tear, and when she had kissed them, she told them full many good words and stirred them to meekness and patience, so that they would not grutch at their sickness, but highly thank God therefor, and they should have great bliss in Heaven through the mercy of Our Lord Jesus Christ.

Then one woman had so many temptations that she knew not how she might best be governed. She was so laboured with her ghostly enemy that she durst not bless herself, or do any worship to God, for dread that the devil should slay her, and she was laboured with many foul and horrible thoughts, many more than she could tell. And, as she said, she was a maid.

Therefore the said creature went to her many times to comfort her, and prayed for her also full specially, that God should strengthen her against her enemy. And it is to be believed that He did so, blessed may He be.

Chapter 75

The man whose wife experiences mental illness[6] after child-birth. Margery visits her and she recovers[7] with her but still experiences mental illness with others. She recovers.

As the said creature was in a church of Saint Margaret to say her devotions, there came a man kneeling at her back, wringing his hands and shewing tokens of great grief. She, perceiving his grief, asked him what ailed him. He said it stood right hard with him, for his wife was newly delivered of a child, and she was out of her mind.

'And, dame,' he said, 'she knoweth not me or any of her neighbours. She roareth and crieth so that she maketh folk evil afeared. She will both smite and bite, and therefore is she manacled on her wrists.'

Then asked she the man if he would that she went with him and saw her, and he said—

'Yea, dame, for God's love.'

So she went forth with him to see the woman, and when she came into the house, as soon as the sick woman, who was alienated from her wits, saw her, she spake to her soberly and kindly and said she was right welcome to her, and she was right glad of her coming, and greatly comforted by her presence, 'For ye are,' she said, 'a right good woman, and I behold many fair angels about you, and therefore, I pray you, go not from me, for I am greatly comforted by you.'

And when other folk came to her, she cried and gaped as if she would have eaten them, and said that she saw many devils about them. She would not suffer them to touch her, by her own good will. She roared and cried so, both night and day, for the most part, that men would not suffer her to dwell amongst them, she was so tedious to them.

Then was she taken to the furthest end of the town, into a chamber, so that the people should not hear her crying, and there was she bound, hand and foot, with chains of iron, so that she should smite nobody. And the said creature went to her each day, once or twice at least, and whilst she was with her, she was meek enough, and heard her speak and chat with good will, without any roaring or crying.

And the said creature prayed for this woman every day, that God should, if it were His will, restore her to her wits again, and Our Lord answered in her soul and said she should fare right well.

Then she was more bold to pray for her curing than she was before, and each day, weeping and sorrowing, prayed for her recovery, till God gave her her wits and her mind again. And then was she brought to church and purified as other women are, blessed may God be.

It was, as they thought that knew it, a right great miracle, for he that wrote this book had never, before that time, seen man or woman, as he thought, so far out of herself as this woman was, nor so evil to rule or to manage.

And later, he saw her sad and sober enough, worship and praise be to Our Lord without end, for His high mercy and His goodness, Who ever helpeth at need.

Chapter 76

Her husband's death.

It happened, on a time, that the husband of the said creature, a man in great age, passing three score years, as he would have come down from his chamber bare-foot and bare-legged, he slithered, or else failed of his footing, and fell down to the ground from the stairs, his head under him grievously broken and bruised, insomuch that he had in his head five linen plugs for many days, whilst his head was healing.

And, as God willed, it was known to some of his neighbours how he had fallen down from the stairs, peradventure through the din and the rush of his fall. So they came to him and found him lying with his head under him, half alive, all streaked with blood, and never likely to have spoken with priest or clerk, but through high grace and a miracle.

Then the said creature, his wife, was sent for and so she came to him. Then was he taken up and his head sewn, and he was

sick a long time after, so that men thought he should have been dead.

Then the people said, if he died, his wife was worthy to be hanged for his death, forasmuch as she might have kept him and did not. They dwelt not together nor lay together, for, as is written before, they both with one assent and with the free will of each, had vowed to live chaste. Therefore, to avoid all perils, they dwelt and sojourned in diverse places where no suspicion could be had of their incontinence. For, at first, they dwelt together after they had made their vow, and then people slandered them, and said they used their lust and their pleasure, as they did before making their vow. And when they went out on pilgrimage, or to see and speak with other ghostly creatures, many evil folk, whose tongues were then own, failing the dread and love of Our Lord Jesus Christ, deemed and said they went rather to woods, groves, and valleys, to use the lust of their bodies, so that people would not espy it or know it.

Having knowledge how prone people were to deem ill of them, and desiring to avoid all occasion for it as much as they rightly might, they, of their own free will and common consent, parted asunder, as touching their board and their chambers, and went to board in divers places. And this was the cause that she was not with him, and also that she should not be hindered from her contemplation. And therefore when he had fallen, and grievously was hurt, as is said before, the people said, if he died, it was worthy that she should answer for his death. Then she prayed to Our Lord that her husband might live a year, and she be delivered out of slander, if it were His pleasure.

Our Lord said to her mind—

'Daughter, thou shalt have thy boon, for he shall live, and I have wrought a great miracle for thee in that he was not dead, and I bid thee take him home and keep him for My love.'

She said—

'Nay, good Lord, for I shall then not attend to Thee as I do now.'

'Yes, daughter,' said Our Lord, 'thou shalt have as much reward for keeping him and helping him in his need at home, as if thou wert in church, making thy prayers. Thou hast said many times thou wouldst fain keep Me. I pray thee now keep him for the love of Me, for he hath some time fulfilled thy will and My will, both. And he hath made thy body free to Me, so that thou shouldst serve Me, and live chaste and clean, and I will that thou be free to help him at his need in My name.'

'Ah! Lord,' said she, 'for Thy mercy grant me grace to obey and fulfil Thy will, and let never my ghostly enemies have any power to hinder me from fulfilling Thy will.'

Then she took home her husband with her and kept him years after, as long as he lived, and had full much labour with him, for in his last days he turned childish again, and lacked reason, so that he could not do his own easement by going to a seat, or else he would not, but, as a child, voided his natural digestion in his linen clothes, where he sat by the fire or at the table, whichever it were, he would spare no place.

And therefore was her labour much the more in washing and wringing, and her costage in firing, and it hindered her full much from her contemplation, so that many times she would have loathed her labour, save she bethought herself how she, in her young age, had full many delectable thoughts, fleshly lusts, and inordinate loves to his person.

And therefore she was glad to be punished with the same person, and took it much the more easily, and served him, and helped him, as she thought, as she would have done Christ Himself.

Endnotes

1   The text below is taken from *The Book of Margery Kempe: A Modern Version* by W. Butler Bowdon (Oxford University Press, 1936). The text is in the public domain. The introduction has been provided by Gabrielle M.C. Bychowski. The bibliography, glosses, and notes have been provided by Cameron Hunt McNabb.

2   *OED Online*, s.v. "mad," adj.

3   In the original Middle English, *made* is spelled *mad*.

4   Chapter 80, not included in this volume.

5   The Proem has been excerpted to focus on issues of disability. The remainder of the proem pertains to how The *Book* was written.

6   Bowden's translation uses the words "is insane" here and "insane" in the second sentence as well. They have been replaced with the preferred term "mental illness."

7   Bowden's translation uses the words "becomes normal" here. They have been replaced with "recovers."

Menstruation, Infirmity, and Religious Observance from *Ecclesiastical History*[1] (late 9th c.[2])

Bede
Contributed by Heide Estes

Introduction

The monk of Monkwearmouth-Jarrow in Northumbria known as the Venerable Bede wrote, about 731 in Latin, an *Ecclesiastical History of the English People* providing an account of the migration of Angles and Saxons to what would become England and a narration of their conversion to Christianity. The *Ecclesiastical History* (hereafter *EH*) was translated into Old English in the late ninth century.

It is difficult enough within modern discourse to define "disability" within the context of illness and impairment, though it is clear it is defined by social constraints as much as by the nature or extent of illness or impairment: that is, whether or not a particular embodiment counts as disabling is constructed by social norms and is not something essential or inherent about the way a given body exists in the world. For the medieval period, distinguishing disabled bodies from others is even more complicated. Joshua Eyler and Julie Singer point out that contemporary social, medical, and cultural models of disability do not well account for the representations and framings of illness and impairment in medieval narratives, and this is certainly the case for the Old English *EH*, where the vocabularies of illness and impairment overlap so that the terminology is difficult to define specifically. In the first of the passages translated here, menstruation is described as either *untrymness*, defined by dictionaries of Old English as "weakness, sickness, illness, infirmity," or *monaðadle*, "a disease that occurs at intervals of a month."[3] Susan Wendell

has argued that gender itself is constructed by modern societies as a disability, because of the ways that physical constructions of the world we live in assume an average-sized healthy man's height and strength are available to everyone: lifting a suitcase into an overhead luggage rack on a train or plane, or opening a heavy door, may be problematic for small women, thus effectively disabling them by virtue of choices about how to construct human environments. Tory Vandeventer Pearman follows Wendell in investigating intersections of gender and disability in medieval literature and demonstrating that, particularly late in the medieval period, gender was considered by medical science and religious discourse alike to be disabling.

The Old English *EH* contains passages that identify illness or impairment as punishment for sin, as when St. Albans' executioner is punished with blindness (I.7) or when St. Æthelthryth tells her companions that she suffers from a tumor because she wore a gold necklace in her youth (IV.21). A selection from a passage about women and religious observance asks, can pregnant women be baptized? How long should a woman wait after childbirth to go to church? (The answers: yes, and immediately.) The selection provided here contemplates whether menstruating women should enter church. The Old English *EH* states that hunger, thirst, heat, cold, and weariness are all kinds of human "untrymness" associated with original sin, similar to menstrual flow, so that menstruating women are linked with non-gendered bodily conditions of hunger and weariness. The text states, "it is the custom of good minds and men, that they sometimes see sin, where there is none, and often something is done without sin that came of sin." Menstruation, like hunger and fever, is the result of original sin but is not sinful in itself. Yet the text's repetition that menstruation constitutes "untrymness" creates a special category of infirmity particular to women, beyond the more general states of hunger, etc. The characterization of menstruating women as "untrym" suggests that the way later medieval as well as modern societies structurally disable women is also operative in Bede's account of menstruating women.

Bibliography

Eyler, Joshua R., ed. and introd. *Disability in the Middle Ages: Reconsiderations and Reverberations.* Ashgate, 2010.

Singer, Julie. "Editor's Introduction: Disability and the Social Body." *postmedieval*, vol. 3, no. 2 "Disability and the Social Body," 2012, pp. 135–41. doi: 10.1057/pmed.2012.15.

Metzler, Irina. *Disability in Medieval Europe: Thinking about Physical Impairment during the High Middle Ages, c. 1100–1400.* Routledge, 2006.

Pearman, Tory Vandeventer. *Woman and Disability in Medieval Literature.* Palgrave. 2010.

Wendell, Susan. *The Rejected Body: Feminist Philosophical Reflections on Disability.* Routledge, 1996.

"Menstruation, Infirmity, Religious Observance" (Book I, from Chapter 27, Question 8)

...If a woman is taken with the accustomed monthly disease [*monaðaðle*], should she be allowed to go into church or receive the sacrament of holy communion?...

Well, we know and learn from Christ's books, that the woman who was suffering from the flow of blood came meekly to the Lord's back and touched the hem of his garment, and immediately her infirmity [*untrymnes*] went away and she was made whole. Therefore if the woman in the time of flowing blood might laudably touch the Lord's clothing, then why should she who suffers the bloody flow of monthly disease not be allowed to go into the Lord's church? But now you say, she needed to touch Christ's clothing because of her illness [*untrymnes*]; the women of whom we speak now are under the sway of repeated habit. But consider, dear brother, that all that we suffer in this mortal body is arranged by the authority of the Lord's judgment on account of the suffering of our kind. It followed upon the sin of the first man, for hunger, thirst, heat, cold, weariness—all that is because of the sickness [*untrymnes*] of our kind. And what else can be sought [as a remedy] against hunger except food; against thirst, drink; against heat, coolness; against cold, clothing; against fatigue, rest; and against infirmity, to seek medicine? Now, for women, the monthly infirmity of flowing blood is sickness. Therefore now if that woman presumed appropriately to touch the Lord's clothing in the period of illness, so that the sickness of one individual was forgiven, why then should all women not be forgiven, when they are made infirm by the fault of their own nature? Likewise, in those same days it shall not be forbidden to them to take the sacrament of the holy communion. Now, if out of great reverence some one does not presume to receive, he is to be praised; but if he takes it, he is not to be condemned. For it is the custom of good minds and men, that they sometimes see sin, where there is none, and often something is done without sin that came of sin, just as it is, when we are hungry, we eat without sin, and it came to pass out of the sin of the first man that we might be hungry. For as in the old law the outer works were observed, so in the new law, the external is not at all as highly esteemed as the inward thoughts are carefully observed. Though the law forbids eating many things as unclean, however in the Gospel the Lord says, not at all that which goes into the mouth of man is degrading, but that which comes out of the mouth, those are the things that defile the man. And now after that, that was explained, and he said, Evil thoughts go out of the heart. There, it is abundantly explained that deeds which are revealed by the almighty God to be unclean and defiled, are born from the origin° of polluted and unclean thoughts. About that likewise the Apostle Paul said, all is clean to those who are clear; to the polluted and the unbelievers nothing is clean. And immediately after the apostle explained the cause of this same pollution, and said, therefore they are polluted in both mind and in conscience. But if the meat is not clean for those whose mind is not clean, then why should the woman of clean mind who suffers by her nature be counted as unclean?

origin *literally "rootstock"*

Endnotes

1   *The Old English Version of Bede's Ecclesiastical History of the English People*, ed. Thomas Miller, Early English Text Society O. S. 95, 96 (Trübner, 1890). Translated by Heide Estes.

2   This date represents the date of the Old English translation of the Latin text. The Latin manuscripts date to the eighth century.

3   Joseph Bosworth, "An Anglo-Saxon Dictionary Online," ed. Thomas Northcote Toller et al., comp. Sean Christ and Ondřej Tichý, Faculty of Arts, Charles University in Prague, 21 Mar. 2010, s.vv. *monaðadl, untrymness.* J.R. Clark Hall, *A Concise Anglo-Saxon Dictionary*, similarly has "weakness, sickliness, infirmity, illness." The *Dictionary of Old English* has so far published only letters A through H. *Dictionary of Old English: A to H online*, eds. Angus Cameron, Ashley Crandell Amos, Antonette diPaolo, Healey et al. (Dictionary of Old English Project, 2016).

Physical Disability, Muteness, Pregnancy, Possession, and Alcoholism from *Ecclesiastical History*[1] (ca. 731[2])

Bede

Contributed by Maura Bailey, Autumn Battista, Ashley Corliss, Eammcn Gosselin, Rebecca Laughlin, Sara Moller, Shayne Simahk, Taylor Specker, Alyssa Stanton, Kellyn Welch, and Kisha G. Tracy

Introduction

Bede, otherwise known as the Venerable Bede, was born ca. 672/3 in Sunderland on lands of the Monkwearmouth Benedictine monastery. He was sent to Monkwearmouth when he was seven, and then later joined the Jarrow monastery in Northumbria. Bede wrote the *Ecclesiastical History of England* (hereafter *EH*) in Latin around 721, which gained him the title "The Father of English History." He died in 735 in Jarrow. The following excerpts on disability are from the Latin text, while an Old English translation was made in the ninth century.

In the *EH*, Bede provides multiple examples of healings that collectively construct parameters about disability and healing. Each healing example provided does include a sick or injured person being cured in order to attest to the power of God. The depth of the cure and the speed of its relief are dependent upon certain factors: the person's dedication and faithfulness to God along with the care or carelessness of a person's injury. A person who is not previously faithful and dedicated to God must testify to the bishop or healer that they will become a believer. In Book I, Chapter XXI, Elafius and his countrymen must be blessed and preached to by the bishops before Elafius is able to earn help for his son. A person that is honestly devout can either have the healer miraculously appear and instantly cure them, as in the instance of Germanus in Book I, Chapter XIX, or they

can rise from kneeling while praying and be healed, such as the blind woman in Book IV, Chapter X.

The sick or injured that have become unfaithful to Christ can be healed quickly and become devoted believers. A man that is seeking guidance and declares he is possessed by the Devil needs to wait an hour to be free from the Devil's grasp and must carry a relic of King Oswald. A devout sick or injured person might wait for their cure if their injury is self-induced. A nun that let blood during an inappropriate time can wait hours before her swelling reduces, and she may never regain her former strength. Bede reveals that, although each person presented is healed, the context of each sick or injured person determines how effectively and quickly they will experience a healing miracle. The narrative then presents a correlation between an individual's sin and faith and their physical well-being. Examples in Bede include Book I, Chapter XIX, wherein a very ill man refuses medical treatment in the name of religion, yet is cured:

> Moreover, he would suffer no medicines to be applied to his infirmity; but one night he saw one clad in garments as white as snow, standing by him, who reaching out his hand, seemed to raise him up, and ordered him to stand firm upon his feet; from which time his pain ceased, and he

was so perfectly restored, that when the day came, with good courage he set forth upon his journey.

Another example is in Book V, Chapter III, wherein a young woman is cured of a serious medical malady, not by any medical means, but by faith after a lengthy suffering prolonged by religious devotion. Yet another example comes from Book IV, Chapter IX, in which a young woman suffers at death's door for days, perhaps hallucinating and speaking in an erratic manner, and all of this is attributed not to illness, but to holiness and her approaching eternal life. It seems clear, at least, that volition and awareness are essential when it comes to determining mental illness and suffering willingly for God: if the person in question willed their own suffering, or was able to recall their illness (spasms, sickness, pain, ravings, etc.) with some cognizance, then the condition was determined not to be mental illness or disability—and this is not, of course, how either mental illness or a disability are determined and diagnosed today.

In many medieval texts, there seems to be a fine line when distinguishing between "the fool"—a derogatory term in modern rhetoric—and "the holy fool," a term for an eccentric, a person with a disability, or one suffering from disease, so long as that individual is religiously inclined. In Bede's text, we see several examples of miraculous cures due to religious zeal, but a reader might ask whether there is a point at which a line can be more clearly drawn between what might now be called mental illness and what was then described as religious fervor to be emulated and admired.

The following are discussions of selected categories of disability within Bede's text.

Physical Disability

The physical disabilities in Bede's text may be variously identified as paralysis, palsy, and missing or partially missing limbs or digits. Bede's approach to documentation is sig-

nificant, as seen in the story of Germanus, wherein lameness is seen as punishment for heresy.

When the heresy was recanted, so too was the disability removed. Other examples include Book I, Chapter XIX, wherein a man's paralysis seems to have no cause, although "his [personal, spiritual] merits would be but increased by bodily affliction." This man's disability is later cured via a miracle and a vision, after the man himself is able to perform miracles for others afflicted by similar maladies. Physical disabilities have a strong presence in Bede's historical accounts and are given various causes, explanations, and remedies.

Muteness

Of the disabilities discussed in Bede, the idea of "muteness" is officially mentioned in only one story. In Book V, Chapter II, Bishop John's holiness is proven through his miraculous cure of a poor man's "dumbness." The rather unofficial diagnosis of muteness refers to any sort of speech limitation, in this case a complete inability to speak. Bishop John knew that the youth was mute because "he had never been able to speak one word." In Christ-like fashion, the bishop cures him simply by making the sign of the cross on his tongue, then directing the youth to speak. Every letter, syllable, or word the youth is bidden to speak, he is able to do so. The end of this section recalls the aforementioned "ill-favoured, miserable, and dumb" young man he had once been, but was now completely cured of his ailment. This is an example of disability as a reference to how well a person is able to function in his society. And, as is typical for those who healed any maladies, Bishop John is considered more holy and trustworthy for having cured another individual.

Pregnancy

Most of what is said in the *EH* about pregnant women is reinforced by sections in the Bible. In Book One, Chapter XXVII, a pregnant woman is allowed into the church to worship and have communion. After the birth, however, it states that a woman could not have her new born baby be baptized by the church until thirty-three days after for a male child and sixty-six for a female child, following the rules stated in Leviticus 12:1–8. Additionally Bede states that a man could not have sex with a woman following the birth of a child until the child is weaned as the woman is perceived as unclean during this period.

In response to a question about whether a woman "with child ought to be baptized," Bede presents contradictory insights around the "purpose" of childbearing. A woman's body is clearly acknowledged as the mechanism for the propagation of the human race, but every element of that reality—from menstruation to copulation to labor and delivery—is negatively presented. He acknowledges that women should not be banned from church because they cannot opt out of this natural course. At the same time, however, Bede shares that the Old Testament forbids women to enter the church, but Bede contradicts himself as he then proceeds to acknowledge that:

> Now you must know that this is to be received in a mystery; for if she enters the church the very hour that she is delivered, to return thanks, she is not guilty of any sin; because the pleasure of the flesh is a fault, and not the pain; but the pleasure is in the copulation of the flesh, whereas there is pain in bringing forth the child.

The sexism which is apparent in these writings must have been disempowering to the women who constantly were told that "in sins my mother conceived me" (Psalms 51:5),[3] and yet, it is only through copulation and childbirth that God's will is perpetuated. The irony in this chapter is heavy: we have the writer, a man who was entered into the monastic life at the age of seven, writing about the natural phenomenon of a woman's body. This belief that the only purpose of inter-course was procreation and, as Bede notes, "not to satisfy vices" suggests an abnormality—even an inherent disability—in women.

Possession

The healing powers of King Oswald's bones in Book III, Chapter XI help alleviate the fear of those possessed by the Devil. The bones of King Oswald are characterized as a gift from heaven with their healing qualities. As stated in Chapter XI, "the very earth which received that holy water, had the power of saving grace in casting out the devils from the bodies of persons possessed." One man was "suddenly seized by the Devil, and began to cry out, to gnash his teeth, to foam at the mouth, and to writhe and distort his limbs." With this man suffering from the Devil's grasp, many sought to help release his spirit and direct him to God. A priest "used exorcisms, and did all the he could to assuage the madness of the unfortunate man," but nothing worked until a woman brought in the casket containing King Oswald's bones. As the woman entered the room, the man began display changes in his behavior. After he awoke he stated, "all the evil spirits that vexed me departed and left me," indicating that he was healed by the holy bones of the king.

Alcoholism

In Book V, Chapter XIV, the topic of alcoholism is set within a monastery in which a monk drinks to excess. Bede presents alcoholism as a sin, as giving into the weakness of personal desires. When the alcoholic monk finds himself on his deathbed, he says: "There is no time for me now to change my course of life, when I have myself seen my judgement passed." The body of the monk is buried in an isolated part of the monastery cemetery because the other brothers are ashamed of the monk who died because he gave into his vices. In modern times, alcoholism is categorized as a mental illness, whereas Bede's narrative clearly casts it as a sin. In this case, however, the monk is damned, and there is a sense of bodily exile.

Bede, in the *EH*, links the social world of early England to disease and disability. The material that Bede gives the reader on how disabled and diseased individuals were treated by their communities exemplifies a social model that focuses on how such concepts were viewed both by the author and, by extension, the social sphere that the world the people he writes about inhabited. Some examples include analyzing the dependency of disabled and diseased people upon the behavior of other, healthy individuals and the ways in which disabled and diseased people were treated by the communities of which they were a part—for instance, the first few chapters of Book V, in which Bede describes healings done by the Bishop John and how his patients are treated by their communities. The first one of these is the curing of a dumb man who is brought to the Bishop by other members of his community. This contrasts with the next two entries, which record two diseased individuals, and how the Bishop attends to them, instead of receiving them. Such difference in the external circumstances of disabled and diseased individuals exists throughout the text. Particular diseases and disabilities are treated differently, depending upon type, the class of the individual, and the care available.

Bibliography

Brown, George Hardin. *A Companion to Bede.* Boydell, 2010.

Caciola, Nancy. *Discerning Spirits: Divine and Demonic Possession in the Middle Ages.* Cornell University Press, 2003.

Damico, Helen. *New Readings on Women in Old English Literature.* Indiana University Press, 1990.

Metzler, Irina. *Disability in Medieval Europe.* Routledge, 2006.

Pearman, Tory Vandeventer. *Women and Disability in Medieval Literature.* Palgrave, 2010.

Book I

Chapter XIX

How the same holy man, being detained there by sickness, by his prayers quenched a fire that had broken out among the houses, and was himself cured of his infirmity by a vision.

As they were returning thence, the treacherous enemy,° having, as it chanced, prepared a snare, caused Germanus to bruise his foot by a fall, not knowing that, as it was with the blessed Job, his merits would be but increased by bodily affliction. Whilst he was thus detained some time in the same place by his infirmity, a fire broke out in a cottage neighbouring to that in which he was; and having burned down the other houses which were thatched with reed, fanned by the wind, was carried on to the dwelling in which he lay. The people all flocked to the prelate, entreating that they might lift him in their arms, and save him from the impending danger. But he rebuked them, and in the assurance of his faith, would not suffer himself to be removed. The whole multitude, in terror and despair, ran to oppose the conflagration; but, for the greater manifestation of the Divine power, whatsoever the crowd endeavoured to save, was destroyed; and what the sick and helpless man defended, the flame avoided and passed by, though the house that sheltered the holy man lay open to it, and while the fire raged on every side, the place in which he lay appeared untouched, amid the general conflagration. The multitude rejoiced at the miracle, and was gladly vanquished by the power of God. A great crowd of people watched day and night before the humble cottage; some to have their souls healed, and some their bodies. All that Christ wrought in the person of his servant, all the wonders the sick man performed cannot be told. Moreover, he would suffer no medicines to be applied to his infirmity; but one night he saw one clad in garments as white as snow, standing by him, who reaching out his hand, seemed to raise him up, and ordered him to stand firm upon his feet; from which time his pain ceased, and he was so perfectly restored, that when the day came, with good courage he set forth upon his journey.

Chapter XXI

How, when the Pelagian heresy° began to spring up afresh, Germanus, returning to Britain with Severus, first restored bodily strength to a lame youth, then spiritual health to the people of God, having condemned or converted the Heretics.

Not long after, news was brought from the same island, that certain persons were again attempting to teach and spread abroad the Pelagian heresy, and again the holy Germanus was entreated by all the priests, that he would defend the cause of God, which he had before maintained. He speedily complied with their request; and taking with him Severus, a man of singular sanctity, who was disciple to the blessed father, Lupus, bishop of Troyes, and at that time, having been ordained bishop of the Treveri, was preaching the Word of God to the tribes of Upper Germany, put to sea, and with favouring winds and calm waters sailed to Britain.

In the meantime, the evil spirits, speeding through the whole island, were constrained against their will to foretell that Germanus was coming, insomuch, that one Elafius, a chief of that region, without tidings from any visible messenger, hastened to meet the holy men, carrying with him his son, who in the very flower of his youth laboured under a grievous infirmity; for the sinews of the knee were wasted and shrunk, so that the withered limb was denied the power to walk. All the country followed this Elafius. The bishops arrived, and were met by the ignorant mul-

---

the treacherous enemy *the Devil*   **Pelagian heresy** *theological belief in fourth to fifth centuries that promoted the choices of free will, named after British monk Pelagius*

titude, whom they blessed, and preached the Word of God to them. They found the people constant in the faith as they had left them; and learning that but few had gone astray, they sought out the authors of the evil and condemned them. Then suddenly Elafius cast himself at the feet of the bishops, presenting his son, whose distress was visible and needed no words to express it. All were grieved, but especially the bishops, who, filled with pity, invoked the mercy of God; and straightway the blessed Germanus, causing the youth to sit down, touched the bent and feeble knee and passed his healing hand over all the diseased part. At once health was restored by the power of his touch, the withered limb regained its vigour, the sinews resumed their task, and the youth was, in the presence of all the people, delivered whole to his father. The multitude was amazed at the miracle, and the Catholic faith was firmly established in the hearts of all; after which, they were, in a sermon, exhorted to amend their error. By the judgement of all, the exponents of the heresy, who had been banished from the island, were brought before the bishops, to be conveyed into the continent, that the country might be rid of them, and they corrected of their errors. So it came to pass that the faith in those parts continued long after pure and untainted. Thus when they had settled all things, the blessed prelates returned home as prosperously as they had come.

But Germanus, after this, went to Ravenna to intercede for the tranquility of the Armoricans,° where, after being very honourably received by Valentinian and his mother, Placidia, he departed hence to Christ; his body was conveyed to his own city with a splendid retinue, and mighty works attended his passage to the grave. Not long after, Valentinian was murdered by the followers of Aetius, the patrician, whom he had put to death, in the

sixth year of the reign of Marcian, and with him ended the empire of the West.

Chapter XXVII

How St. Augustine, being made a bishop, sent to acquaint Pope Gregory with what had been done in Britain, and asked and received replies, of which he stood in need.

In the meantime, Augustine, the man of God, went to Arles,° and, according to the orders received from the holy Father Gregory, was ordained archbishop of the English nation, by Aetherius, archbishop of that city. Then returning into Britain, he sent Laurentius the priest and Peter the monk to Rome, to acquaint Pope Gregory, that the English nation had received the faith of Christ, and that he was himself made their bishop. At the same time, he desired his solution of some doubts which seemed urgent to him. He soon received fitting answers to his questions, which we have also thought meet to insert in this our history:

The First Question of the blessed Augustine, Bishop of the Church of Canterbury.—Concerning bishops, what should be their manner of conversation towards their clergy? or into how many portions the offerings of the faithful at the altar are to be divided? and how the bishop is to act in the Church?

Gregory, Pope of the City of Rome, answers.—Holy Scripture, in which we doubt not you are well versed, testifies to this, and in particular the Epistles of the Blessed Paul to Timothy, wherein he endeavours to show him what should be his manner of conversation in the house of God; but it is the custom of the Apostolic see° to prescribe these rules to bishops when they are ordained: that all emoluments which accrue, are to be divided into four portions;—one for the bishop and his household, for hospitality and entertainment of guests; another for the clergy; a third for the poor; and the fourth for the repair of

---

Armoricans *a region of northwestern France*   **Arles** *a city in southern France*   **Apostolic see** *seat of authority in the Roman church*

churches. But in that you, my brother, having been instructed in monastic rules, must not live apart from your clergy in the Church of the English, which has been lately, by the will of God, converted to the faith, you must establish the manner of conversation of our fathers in the primitive Church, among whom, none said that aught of the things which they possessed was his own, but they had all things common.

But if there are any clerks not received into holy orders, who cannot live continent, they are to take wives, and receive their stipends outside of the community; because we know that it is written concerning the same fathers of whom we have spoken that a distribution was made unto every man according as he had need. Care is also to be taken of their stipends, and provision to be made, and they are to be kept under ecclesiastical rule, that they may live orderly, and attend to singing of psalms, and, by the help of God, preserve their hearts and tongues and bodies from all that is unlawful. But as for those that live in common, there is no need to say anything of assigning portions, or dispensing hospitality and showing mercy; inasmuch as all that they have over is to be spent in pious and religious works, according to the teaching of Him who is the Lord and Master of all, "Give alms of such things as ye have over, and behold all things are clean unto you."

...

Augustine's Third Question.—I beseech you, what punishment must be inflicted on one who steals anything from a church?

Gregory answers.—You may judge, my brother, by the condition of the thief, in what manner he is to be corrected. For there are some, who, having substance, commit theft; and there are others, who transgress in this matter through want. Wherefore it is requisite, that some be punished with fines, others with stripes; some with more severity, and some more mildly. And when the severity is greater, it is to proceed from charity, not from anger; because this is done for the sake of him who is corrected, that he may

not be delivered up to the fires of Hell. For it behoves us to maintain discipline among the faithful, as good parents do with their children according to the flesh, whom they punish with stripes for their faults, and yet they design to make those whom they chastise their heirs, and preserve their possessions for those whom they seem to visit in wrath. This charity is, therefore, to be kept in mind, and it dictates the measure of the punishment, so that the mind may do nothing beyond the rule prescribed by reason. You will add to this, how men are to restore those things which they have stolen from the church. But let not the Church take more than it has lost of its worldly possessions, or seek gain from vanities.

...

Augustine's Fifth Question.—To what degree may the faithful marry with their kindred? and is it lawful to marry a stepmother or a brother's wife?

Gregory answers.—A certain secular law in the Roman commonwealth allows, that the son and daughter of a brother and sister, or of two full brothers, or two sisters, may be joined in matrimony; but we have found, by experience, that the offspring of such wedlock cannot grow up; and the Divine law forbids a man to "uncover the nakedness of his kindred." Hence of necessity it must be the third or fourth generation of the faithful, that can be lawfully joined in matrimony; for the second, which we have mentioned, must altogether abstain from one another. To marry with one's stepmother is a heinous crime, because it is written in the Law, "Thou shalt not uncover the nakedness of thy father:" now the son, indeed, cannot uncover his father's nakedness; but in regard that it is written, "They twain shall be one flesh," he that presumes to uncover the nakedness of his stepmother, who was one flesh with his father, certainly uncovers the nakedness of his father. It is also prohibited to marry with a sister-in-law, because by the former union she is become the brother's flesh. For which thing also John the Baptist was beheaded, and obtained the crown of holy martyrdom. For, though he was not ordered to deny Christ, and it was not for confessing Christ that he was killed, yet inasmuch as the same Jesus Christ, our Lord, said, "I am the Truth," because John was killed for the truth, he also shed his blood for Christ.

...

Augustine's Eighth Question.—Whether a woman with child ought to be baptized? Or when she has brought forth, after what time she may come into the church? As also, after how many days the infant born may be baptized, lest he be prevented by death? Or how long after her husband may have carnal knowledge of her? Or whether it is lawful for her to come into the church when she has her courses, or to receive the Sacrament of Holy Communion? Or whether a man, under certain circumstances, may come into the church before he has washed with water? Or approach to receive the Mystery of the Holy Communion? All which things are requisite to be known by the ignorant nation of the English.

Gregory answers.—I do not doubt but that these questions have been put to you, my brother, and I think I have already answered you therein. But I believe you would wish the opinion which you yourself might give and hold to be confirmed by my reply also. Why should not a woman with child be baptized, since the fruitfulness of the flesh is no offence in the eyes of Almighty God? For when our first parents sinned in Paradise, they forfeited the immortality which they had received, by the just judgement of God. Because, therefore, Almighty God would not for their fault wholly destroy the human race, he both deprived man of immortality for his sin, and, at the same time, of his great goodness and loving-kindness, reserved to him the power of propagating his race after him. On what ground, then, can that which is preserved to human nature by the free gift of Almighty God, be excluded from the privilege of Holy Baptism? For it is very foolish to imagine that the gift can be opposed to grace

in that Mystery in which all sin is blotted out. When a woman is delivered, after how many days she may come into the church, you have learnt from the teaching of the Old Testament, to wit, that she is to abstain for a male child thirty-three days, and sixty-six for a female. Now you must know that this is to be received in a mystery; for if she enters the church the very hour that she is delivered, to return thanks, she is not guilty of any sin; because the pleasure of the flesh is a fault, and not the pain; but the pleasure is in the copulation of the flesh, whereas there is pain in bringing forth the child. Wherefore it is said to the first mother of all, "In sorrow thou shalt bring forth children." If, therefore, we forbid a woman that has brought forth, to enter the church, we make a crime of her very punishment. To baptize either a woman who has brought forth, if there be danger of death, even the very hour that she brings forth, or that which she has brought forth the very hour it is born, is in no way prohibited, because, as the grace of the Holy Mystery is to be with much discretion provided for those who are in full life and capable of understanding, so is it to be without any delay administered to the dying; lest, while a further time is sought to confer the Mystery of redemption, if a small delay intervene, the person that is to be redeemed be dead and gone.

Her husband is not to approach her, till the infant born be weaned. An evil custom is sprung up in the lives of married people, in that women disdain to suckle the children whom they bring forth, and give them to other women to suckle; which seems to have been invented on no other account but incontinency; because, as they will not be continent, they will not suckle the children whom they bear. Those women, therefore, who, from evil custom, give their children to others to bring up, must not approach their husbands till the time of purification is past. For even when there has been no child-birth, women are forbidden to do so, whilst they have their courses, insomuch that the Law condemns to death any man that shall approach unto a woman during her uncleanness. Yet the woman, nevertheless, must not be forbidden to come into the church whilst she has her courses; because the superfluity of nature cannot be imputed to her as a crime; and it is not just that she should be refused admittance into the church, for that which she suffers against her will. For we know, that the woman who had the issue of blood, humbly approaching behind our Lord's back, touched the hem of his garment, and her infirmity immediately departed from her. If, therefore, she that had an issue of blood might commendably touch the garment of our Lord, why may not she, who has her courses, lawfully enter into the church of God? But you may say, Her infirmity compelled her, whereas these we speak of are bound by custom. Consider, then, most dear brother, that all we suffer in this mortal flesh, through the infirmity of our nature, is ordained by the just judgement of God after the fall; for to hunger, to thirst, to be hot, to be cold, to be weary, is from the infirmity of our nature; and what else is it to seek food against hunger, drink against thirst, air against heat, clothes against cold, rest against weariness, than to procure a remedy against distempers? Thus to a woman her courses are a distemper. If, therefore, it was a commendable boldness in her, who in her disease touched our Lord's garment, why may not that which is allowed to one infirm person, be granted to all women, who, through the fault of their nature, are rendered infirm?

She must not, therefore, be forbidden to receive the Mystery of the Holy Communion during those days. But if any one out of profound respect does not presume to do it, she is to be commended; yet if she receives it, she is not to be judged. For it is the part of noble minds in some manner to acknowledge their faults, even when there is no fault; because very often that is done without a fault, which, nevertheless, proceeded from a fault. Thus, when we are hungry, it is no sin to eat; yet our being hungry proceeds from the sin of the first man. The courses are no

sin in women, because they happen naturally; yet, because our nature itself is so depraved, that it appears to be defiled even without the concurrence of the will, a defect arises from sin, and thereby human nature may itself know what it is become by judgement. And let man, who willfully committed the offence, bear the guilt of that offence against his will. And, therefore, let women consider with themselves, and if they do not presume, during their courses, to approach the Sacrament of the Body and Blood of our Lord, they are to be commended for their praiseworthy consideration; but when they are carried away with love of the same Mystery to receive it according to the custom of the religious life, they are not to be restrained, as we said before. For as in the Old Testament the outward works are observed, so in the New Testament, that which is outwardly done, is not so diligently regarded as that which is inwardly thought, that the punishment may be with discernment. For whereas the Law forbids the eating of many things as unclean, yet our Lord says in the Gospel, "Not that which goeth into the mouth defileth a man; but that which cometh out of the mouth, this defileth a man."[4] And afterwards he added, expounding the same, "Out of the heart proceed evil thoughts."[5] Where it is abundantly shown, that that is declared by Almighty God to be polluted in deed, which springs from the root of a polluted thought. Whence also Paul the Apostle says, "Unto the pure all things are pure, but unto them that are defiled and unbelieving, nothing is pure." And presently, declaring the cause of that defilement, he adds, "For even their mind and conscience is defiled."[6] If, therefore, meat is not unclean to him whose mind is not unclean, why shall that which a woman suffers according to nature, with a clean mind, be imputed to her as uncleanness?

A man who has approached his own wife is not to enter the church unless washed with water, nor is he to enter immediately although washed. The Law prescribed to the ancient people, that a man in such cases should be washed with water, and not enter into the church before the setting of the sun. Which, nevertheless, may be understood spiritually, because a man acts so when the mind is led by the imagination to unlawful concupiscence; for unless the fire of concupiscence be first driven from his mind, he is not to think himself worthy of the congregation of the brethren, while he sees himself burdened by the iniquity of a perverted will. For though divers nations have divers opinions concerning this affair, and seem to observe different rules, it was always the custom of the Romans, from ancient times, for such an one to seek to be cleansed by washing, and for some time reverently to forbear entering the church. Nor do we, in so saying, assign matrimony to be a fault; but forasmuch as lawful intercourse cannot be had without the pleasure of the flesh, it is proper to forbear entering the holy place, because the pleasure itself cannot be without a fault. For he was not born of adultery or fornication, but of lawful marriage, who said, "Behold I was conceived in iniquity, and in sin my mother brought me forth."[7] For he who knew himself to have been conceived in iniquity, lamented that he was born from sin, because he bears the defect, as a tree bears in its bough the sap it drew from the root. In which words, however, he does not call the union of the married couple iniquity, but the will itself. For there are many things which are lawful and permitted, and yet we are somewhat defiled in doing them. As very often by being angry we correct faults, and at the same time disturb our own peace of mind; and though that which we do is right, yet it is not to be approved that our mind should be disturbed. For he who said, "My eye was disturbed with anger,"[8] had been angry at the vices of sinners. Now, seeing that only a calm mind can rest in the light of contemplation, he grieved that his eye was disturbed with anger; because, whilst he was correcting evil actions below, he was obliged to be confused and disturbed with regard to the contemplation of the highest things. Anger against vice is,

therefore, commendable, and yet painful to a man, because he thinks that by his mind being agitated, he has incurred some guilt. Lawful commerce, therefore, must be for the sake of children, not of pleasure; and must be to procure offspring, not to satisfy vices. But if any man is led not by the desire of pleasure, but only for the sake of getting children, such a man is certainly to be left to his own judgement, either as to entering the church, or as to receiving the Mystery of the Body and Blood of our Lord, which he, who being placed in the fire cannot burn, is not to be forbidden by us to receive. But when, not the love of getting children, but of pleasure prevails, the pair have cause to lament their deed. For this the holy preaching concedes to them, and yet fills the mind with dread of the very concession. For when Paul the Apostle said, "Let him that cannot contain have his own wife;"[9] he presently took care to subjoin, "But this I say by way of permission, not of commandment."[10] For that is not granted by way of permission which is lawful, because it is just; and, therefore, that which he said he permitted, he showed to be an offence.

It is seriously to be considered, that when God was about to speak to the people on Mount Sinai, He first commanded them to abstain from women. And if purity of body was there so carefully required, where God spoke to the people by the means of a creature as His representative, that those who were to hear the words of God should abstain; how much more ought women, who receive the Body of Almighty God, to preserve themselves in purity of flesh, lest they be burdened with the very greatness of that inestimable Mystery? For this reason also, it was said to David, concerning his men, by the priest, that if they were clean in this particular, they should receive the shewbread, which they would not have received at all, had not David first declared them to be clean. Then the man, who, afterwards, has been washed with water, is also capable of receiving the Mystery of the Holy Communion, when it is lawful for him, according to what has been before declared, to enter the church.

Augustine's Ninth Question.—Whether after an illusion, such as is wont to happen in a dream, any man may receive the Body of our Lord, or if he be a priest, celebrate the Divine Mysteries?

Gregory answers.—The Testament of the Old Law, as has been said already in the article above, calls such a man polluted, and allows him not to enter into the church till the evening, after being washed with water. Which, nevertheless, a spiritual people, taking in another sense, will understand in the same manner as above; because he is imposed upon as it were in a dream, who, being tempted with uncleanness, is defiled by real representations in thought, and he is to be washed with water, that he may cleanse away the sins of thought with tears; and unless the fire of temptation depart before, may know himself to be in a manner guilty until the evening. But a distinction is very necessary in that illusion, and one must carefully consider what causes it to arise in the mind of the person sleeping; for sometimes it proceeds from excess of eating or drinking; sometimes from the superfluity or infirmity of nature, and sometimes from the thoughts. And when it happens either through superfluity or infirmity of nature, such an illusion is not to be feared at all, because it is to be lamented, that the mind of the person, who knew nothing of it, suffers the same, rather than that he occasioned it. But when the appetite of gluttony commits excess in food, and thereupon the receptacles of the humours are oppressed, the mind thence contracts some guilt; yet not so much as to hinder the receiving of the Holy Mystery, or celebrating Mass, when a holy day requires it, or necessity obliges the Mystery to be shown forth, because there is no other priest in the place; for if there be others who can perform the ministry, the illusion proceeding from over-eating ought not to exclude a man from receiving the sacred Mystery; but I am of opinion he ought humbly to abstain from offering the sacrifice of the Mystery, but not from receiving it, unless the mind of the person sleeping has been disturbed with some foul imagination. For there are some, who for the most part so suffer the illusion, that their mind, even during the sleep of the body, is not defiled with filthy thoughts. In which case, one thing is evident, that the mind is guilty, not being acquitted even in its own judgement; for though it does not remember to have seen anything whilst the body was sleeping, yet it calls to mind that, when the body was awake, it fell into gluttony. But if the illusion of the sleeper proceeds from evil thoughts when he was awake, then its guilt is manifest to the mind; for the man perceives from what root that defilement sprang, because what he had consciously thought of, that he afterwards unconsciously endured. But it is to be considered, whether that thought was no more than a suggestion, or proceeded to delight, or, what is worse, consented to sin. For all sin is committed in three ways, viz., by suggestion, by delight, and by consent. Suggestion comes from the Devil, delight from the flesh, and consent from the spirit. For the serpent suggested the first offence, and Eve, as flesh, took delight in it, but Adam, as the spirit, consented. And when the mind sits in judgement on itself, it must clearly distinguish between suggestion and delight, and between delight and consent. For when the evil spirit suggests a sin to the mind, if there ensue no delight in the sin, the sin is in no way committed; but when the flesh begins to take delight in it, then sin begins to arise. But if it deliberately consents, then the sin is known to be full-grown. The seed, therefore, of sin is in the suggestion, the nourishment of it in delight, its maturity in the consent. And it often happens that what the evil spirit sows in the thought, in that the flesh begins to find delight, and yet the soul does not consent to that delight. And whereas the flesh cannot be delighted without the mind, yet the mind struggling against the pleasures of the flesh, is after a manner unwillingly bound by the carnal delight, so that through reason it opposes it, and does not consent, yet being bound by delight, it grievously laments being so bound. Wherefore that great soldier of our Lord's host, groaned and said, "I see another law in my members warring against the law of my mind, and bringing me into captivity to the law of sin, which is in my members."[11] Now if he was a captive, he did not fight; but he did fight; wherefore he was a captive and at the same time therefore fought against the law of the mind, which the law that is in the members opposed; but if he fought, he was no captive. Thus, then, man is, as I may say, a captive and yet free. Free on account of justice, which he loves, a captive by the delight which he unwillingly bears within him.

Book III

Chapter VIII
How Earconbert, King of Kent, ordered the idols to be destroyed; and of his daughter Earcongota, and his kinswoman Ethelberg, virgins consecrated to God.

In the year of our Lord 640, Eadbald, king of Kent, departed this life, and left his kingdom to his son Earconbert, who governed it most nobly twenty-four years and some months. He was the first of the English kings that of his supreme authority commanded the idols throughout his whole kingdom to be forsaken and destroyed, and the fast of forty days to be observed; and that the same might not be lightly neglected, he appointed fitting and condign punishments for the offenders. His daughter Earcongota, as became the offspring of such a parent, was a most virtuous virgin, serving God in a monastery in the country of the Franks, built by a most noble abbess, named Fara, at a place called In Brige; for at that time but few monasteries had been built in the country of the Angles, and many were wont, for the sake of monastic life, to repair to the monasteries of the Franks or Gauls; and they also sent their daughters there to be instructed, and united to their Heavenly Bridegroom, especially in the mon-

asteries of Brige, of Cale, and Andilegum. Among whom was also Saethryth, daughter of the wife of Anna, king of the East Angles, above mentioned; and Ethelberg, the king's own daughter; both of whom, though strangers, were for their virtue made abbesses of the monastery of Brige. Sexburg, that king's elder daughter, wife to Earconbert, king of Kent, had a daughter called Earcongota, of whom we are about to speak.

Many wonderful works and miracles of this virgin, dedicated to God, are to this day related by the inhabitants of that place; but for us it shall suffice to say something briefly of her departure out of this world to the heavenly kingdom. The day of her summoning drawing near, she began to visit in the monastery the cells of the infirm handmaidens of Christ, and particularly those that were of a great age, or most noted for their virtuous life, and humbly commending herself to their prayers, she let them know that her death was at hand, as she had learnt by revelation, which she said she had received in this manner. She had seen a band of men, clothed in white, come into the monastery, and being asked by her what they wanted, and what they did there, they answered, "They had been sent thither to carry away with them the gold coin that had been brought thither from Kent." Towards the close of that same night, as morning began to dawn, leaving the darkness of this world, she departed to the light of heaven. Many of the brethren of that monastery who were in other houses, declared they had then plainly heard choirs of singing angels, and, as it were, the sound of a multitude entering the monastery. Whereupon going out immediately to see what it might be, they beheld a great light coming down from heaven, which bore that holy soul, set loose from the bonds of the flesh, to the eternal joys of the celestial country. They also tell of other miracles that were wrought that night in the same monastery by the power of God; but as we must proceed to other matters, we leave them to be related by those whose concern they are. The body of this venerable virgin and bride of Christ was buried in the church of the blessed protomartyr, Stephen. It was thought fit, three days after, to take up the stone that covered the tomb, and to raise it higher in the same place, and whilst they were doing this, so sweet a fragrance rose from below, that it seemed to all the brethren and sisters there present, as if a store of balsam had been opened.

Her aunt also, Ethelberg, of whom we have spoken, preserved the glory, acceptable to God, of perpetual virginity, in a life of great self-denial, but the extent of her virtue became more conspicuous after her death. Whilst she was abbess, she began to build in her monastery a church, in honour of all the Apostles, wherein she desired that her body should be buried; but when that work was advanced half way, she was prevented by death from finishing it, and was buried in the place in the church which she had chosen. After her death, the brothers occupied themselves with other things, and this structure was left untouched for seven years, at the expiration whereof they resolved, by reason of the greatness of the work, wholly to abandon the building of the church, and to remove the abbess's bones thence to some other church that was finished and consecrated. On opening her tomb, they found the body as untouched by decay as it had been free from the corruption of carnal concupiscence, and having washed it again and clothed it in other garments, they removed it to the church of the blessed Stephen, the Martyr. And her festival is wont to be celebrated there with much honour on the 7th of July.

Chapter XI

How a light from Heaven stood all night over his relics, and how those possessed with devils were healed by them.

Among the rest, I think we ought not to pass over in silence the miracles and signs from Heaven that were shown when King Oswald's bones were found, and translated into the church where they are now preserved. This was done by the zealous care of Osthryth, queen of the Mercians, the daughter of his brother Oswy, who reigned after him, as shall be said hereafter.

There is a famous monastery in the province of Lindsey,° called Beardaneu, which that queen and her husband Ethelred greatly loved and venerated, conferring upon it many honours. It was here that she was desirous to lay the revered bones of her uncle. When the wagon in which those bones were carried arrived towards evening at the aforesaid monastery, they that were in it were unwilling to admit them, because, though they knew him to be a holy man, yet, as he was a native of another province, and had obtained the sovereignty over them, they retained their ancient aversion to him even after his death. Thus it came to pass that the relics were left in the open air all that night, with only a large tent spread over the wagon which contained them. But it was revealed by a sign from Heaven with how much reverence they ought to be received by all the faithful; for all that night, a pillar of light, reaching from the wagon up to heaven, was visible in almost every part of the province of Lindsey. Hereupon, in the morning, the brethren of that monastery who had refused it the day before, began themselves earnestly to pray that those holy relics, beloved of God, might be laid among them. Accordingly, the bones, being washed, were put into a shrine which they had made for that purpose, and placed in the church, with due honour; and that there might be a perpetual memorial of the royal character of this holy man, they hung up over the monument his banner of gold and purple. Then they poured out the water in which they had washed the bones, in a corner of the cemetery. From that time, the very earth which received that holy water,

Lindsey *a region in northern England*

had the power of saving grace in casting out devils from the bodies of persons possessed.

Lastly, when the aforesaid queen afterwards abode some time in that monastery, there came to visit her a certain venerable abbess, who is still living, called Ethelhild, the sister of the holy men, Ethelwin and Aldwin, the first of whom was bishop in the province of Lindsey, the other abbot of the monastery of Peartaneu; not far from which was the monastery of Ethelhild. When this lady was come, in a conversation between her and the queen, the discourse, among other things, turning upon Oswald, she said, that she also had that night seen the light over his relics reaching up to heaven. The queen thereupon added, that the very dust of the pavement on which the water that washed the bones had been poured out, had already healed many sick persons. The abbess thereupon desired that some of that health-bringing dust might be given her, and, receiving it, she tied it up in a cloth, and, putting it into a casket, returned home. Some time after, when she was in her monastery, there came to it a guest, who was wont often in the night to be on a sudden grievously tormented with an unclean spirit; he being hospitably entertained, when he had gone to bed after supper, was suddenly seized by the Devil, and began to cry out, to gnash his teeth, to foam at the mouth, and to writhe and distort his limbs. None being able to hold or bind him, the servant ran, and knocking at the door, told the abbess. She, opening the monastery door, went out herself with one of the nuns to the men's apartment, and calling a priest, desired that he would go with her to the sufferer. Being come thither, and seeing many present, who had not been able, by their efforts, to hold the tormented person and restrain his convulsive movements, the priest used exorcisms, and did all that he could to assuage the madness of the unfortunate man, but, though he took much pains, he could not prevail. When no hope appeared of easing him in his ravings, the abbess bethought herself of the dust, and immediately bade her hand-maiden go and fetch her the casket in which it was. As soon as she came with it, as she had been bidden, and was entering the hall of the house, in the inner part whereof the possessed person was writhing in torment, he suddenly became silent, and laid down his head, as if he had been falling asleep, stretching out all his limbs to rest. "Silence fell upon all and intent they gazed,"[12] anxiously waiting to see the end of the matter. And after about the space of an hour the man that had been tormented sat up, and fetching a deep sigh, said, "Now I am whole, for I am restored to my senses." They earnestly inquired how that came to pass, and he answered, "As soon as that maiden drew near the hall of this house, with the casket she brought, all the evil spirits that vexed me departed and left me, and were no more to be seen." Then the abbess gave him a little of that dust, and the priest having prayed, he passed that night in great peace; nor was he, from that time forward, alarmed by night, or in any way troubled by his old enemy.

Book IV

Chapter IX
Of the signs which were shown from Heaven when the mother of that community departed this life.

Now when Ethelburg herself, the pious mother of that community devoted to God, was about to be taken out of this world, a wonderful vision appeared to one of the sisters, called Tortgyth; who, having lived many years in that monastery, always endeavoured, in all humility and sincerity, to serve God herself, and to help the mother to maintain regular discipline, by instructing and reproving the younger ones. Now, in order that her virtue might, according to the Apostle, be made perfect in weakness, she was suddenly seized with a most grievous bodily disease, under which, through the merciful providence of our Redeemer, she was sorely tried for the space of nine years; to the end, that whatever stain of evil remained amidst her virtues, either through ignorance or neglect, might all be purified in the furnace of long tribulation. This woman, going out of the chamber where she abode one night, at dusk, plainly saw as it were a human body, which was brighter than the sun, wrapped in fine linen, and lifted up on high, being taken out of the house in which the sisters used to sleep. Then looking earnestly to see what it was that drew up that appearance of the glorious body which she beheld, she perceived that it was raised on high as it were by cords brighter than gold, until, entering into the open heavens, it could no longer be seen by her. Reflecting on this vision, she made no doubt that some one of the community would soon die, and her soul be lifted up to heaven by the good works which she had wrought, as it were by golden cords. And so in truth it befell; for a few days after, the beloved of God, Ethelburg, mother of that community, was delivered out of the prison of the flesh; and her life is proved to have been such that no one who knew her ought to doubt that an entrance into the heavenly country was open to her, when she departed from this life.

There was also, in the same monastery, a certain nun, of noble origin in this world, and still nobler in the love of the world to come; who had, for many years, been so disabled in all her body, that she could not move a single limb. When she heard that the body of the venerable abbess had been carried into the church, till it should be buried, she desired to be carried thither, and to be placed bending towards it, after the manner of one praying; which being done, she spoke to her as if she had been living, and entreated her that she would obtain of the mercy of our pitiful Creator, that she might be delivered from such great and long-continued pains; nor was it long before her prayer was heard: for being delivered from the flesh twelve days after, she exchanged her temporal afflictions for an eternal reward.

For three years after the death of her Superior, the aforesaid handmaid of Christ, Tortgyth. was detained in this life and was so far spent with the sickness before mentioned, that her bones scarce held together. At last, when the time of her release was at hand, she not only lost the use of her other limbs, but also of her tongue; in which state having continued three days and as many nights, she was, on a sudden, restored by a spiritual vision, and opened her lips and eyes, and looking up to heaven, began thus to speak to the vision which she saw: "Very acceptable to me is thy coming, and thou art welcome!" Having so said, she was silent awhile, as it were, waiting for the answer of him whom she saw and to whom she spoke; then, as if somewhat displeased, she said, "I can in no wise gladly suffer this;" then pausing awhile, she said again, "If it can by no means be to-day, I beg that the delay may not be long;" and again holding her peace a short while, she concluded thus; "If it is certainly so determined, and the decree cannot be altered, I beg that it may be no longer deferred than this next night." Having so said, and being asked by those about her with whom she talked, she said, "With my most dear mother, Ethelburg;" by which they understood, that she was come to acquaint her that the time of her departure was at hand; for, as she had desired, after one day and night, she was delivered alike from the bonds of the flesh and of her infirmity and entered into the joys of eternal salvation.

Chapter X

How a blind woman, praying in the burial-place of that monastery, was restored to her sight.

Hildilid, a devout handmaid of God, succeeded Ethelburg in the office of abbess and presided over that monastery with great vigour many years, till she was of an extreme old age, in the observance of regular discipline, and carefully providing all things for the common use. The narrowness of the space where the monastery is built, led her to determine that the bones of the servants and handmaidens of Christ, who had been there buried, should be taken up, and should all be translated into the church of the Blessed Mother of God, and interred in one place. How often a brightness of heavenly light was seen there, when this was done, and a fragrancy of wonderful sweetness arose, and what other signs were revealed, whosoever reads will find in the book from which we have taken these tales.

But in truth, I think it by no means fit to pass over the miracle of healing, which the same book informs us was wrought in the cemetery of that community dedicated to God. There lived in that neighbourhood a certain thegn,° whose wife was seized with a sudden dimness in her eyes, and as the malady increased daily, it became so burdensome to her, that she could not see the least glimpse of light. Having continued some time wrapped in the night of this blindness, on a sudden she bethought herself that she might recover her lost sight, if she were carried to the monastery of the nuns, and there prayed at the relics of the saints. Nor did she lose any time in fulfilling that which she had conceived in her mind: for being conducted by her maids to the monastery, which was very near, and professing that she had perfect faith that she should be there healed, she was led into the cemetery, and having long prayed there on her knees, she did not fail to be heard, for as she rose from prayer, before she went out of the place, she received the gift of sight which she had desired; and whereas she had been led thither by the hands of her maids, she now returned home joyfully without help: as if she had lost the light of this world to no other end than that she might show by her recovery how great a light is vouchsafed to the saints of Christ in Heaven, and how great a grace of healing power.

Book V

Chapter II

How Bishop John cured a dumb man by his blessing.

In the beginning of Aldfrid's reign, Bishop Eata died, and was succeeded in the bishopric of the church of Hagustald by the holy man John, of whom those that knew him well are wont to tell many miracles, and more particularly Berthun, a man worthy of all reverence and of undoubted truthfulness, and once his deacon, now abbot of the monastery called Inderauuda, that is, "In the wood of the Deiri"°: some of which miracles we have thought fit to hand on to posterity. There is a certain remote dwelling enclosed by a mound, among scattered trees, not far from the church of Hagustald, being about a mile and a half distant and separated from it by the river Tyne, having an oratory dedicated to St. Michael the Archangel, where the man of God used frequently, as occasion offered, and specially in Lent, to abide with a few companions and in quiet give himself to prayer and study. Having come hither once at the beginning of Lent to stay, he bade his followers find out some poor man labouring under any grievous infirmity, or want, whom they might keep with them during those days, to receive alms, for so he was always used to do.

There was in a township not far off, a certain youth who was dumb, known to the bishop, for he often used to come into his presence to receive alms. He had never been able to speak one word; besides, he had so much scurf and scab on his head, that no hair could ever grow on the top of it, but only some rough hairs stood on end round about it. The bishop caused this young man to be brought, and a little hut to be made for him within the enclosure of the dwelling, in which he might abide, and receive alms from him

---

the Deiri *inhabitants in a region of northern England*   **thegn** *a man in service to a king or lord*

every day. When one week of Lent was over, the next Sunday he bade the poor man come to him, and when he had come, he bade him put his tongue out of his mouth and show it him; then taking him by the chin, he made the sign of the Holy Cross on his tongue, directing him to draw it back so signed into his mouth and to speak. "Pronounce some word," said he; "say 'gae,'" which, in the language of the English, is the word of affirming and consenting, that is, yes. The youth's tongue was immediately loosed, and he spoke as he was bidden. The bishop then added the names of the letters: "Say A." He said A. "Say B;" he said B also. When he had repeated all the letters after the bishop, the latter proceeded to put syllables and words to him, and when he had repeated them all rightly he bade him utter whole sentences, and he did it. Nor did he cease all that day and the next night, as long as he could keep awake, as those who were present relate, to say something, and to express his private thoughts and wishes to others, which he could never do before; after the manner of the man long lame, who, when he was healed by the Apostles Peter and John, leaping up, stood and walked, and entered with them into the temple, walking, and leaping, and praising the Lord, rejoicing to have the use of his feet, which he had so long lacked. The bishop, rejoicing with him at his cure, caused the physician to take in hand the healing of the sores of his head. He did as he was bidden, and with the help of the bishop's blessing and prayers, a goodly head of hair grew as the skin was healed. Thus the youth became fair of countenance, ready of speech, with hair curling in comely fashion, whereas before he had been ill-favoured, miserable, and dumb. Thus filled with joy at his recovered health, notwithstanding that the bishop offered to keep him in his own household, he chose rather to return home.

Chapter III
How he healed a sick maiden by his prayers.

The same Berthun told another miracle concerning the said bishop. When the most reverend Wilfrid, after a long banishment, was admitted to the bishopric of the church of Hagustald, and the aforesaid John, upon the death of Bosa, a man of great sanctity and humility, was, in his place, appointed bishop of York, he himself came, once upon a time, to the monastery of nuns, at the place called Wetadun, where the Abbess Heriburg then presided. "When we were come thither," said he, "and had been received with great and universal joy, the abbess told us, that one of the nuns, who was her own daughter after the flesh, laboured under a grievous sickness, for she had been lately let blood in the arm, and whilst she was under treatment, was seized with an attack of sudden pain, which speedily increased, while the wounded arm became worse, and so much swollen, that it could scarce be compassed with both hands; and she lay in bed like to die through excess of pain. Wherefore the abbess entreated the bishop that he would vouchsafe to go in and give her his blessing; for she believed that she would soon be better if he blessed her or laid his hands upon her. He asked when the maiden had been let blood, and being told that it was on the fourth day of the moon, said, 'You did very indiscreetly and unskilfully to let blood on the fourth day of the moon; for I remember that Archbishop Theodore, of blessed memory, said, that blood-letting at that time was very dangerous, when the light of the moon is waxing and the tide of the ocean is rising. And what can I do for the maiden if she is like to die?'

"But the abbess still earnestly entreated for her daughter, whom she dearly loved, and designed to make abbess in her stead, and at last prevailed with him to go in and visit the sick maiden. Wherefore he went in, taking me with him to the maid, who lay, as I said, in sore anguish, and her arm swelling so greatly that it could not be bent at all at the elbow; and he stood and said a prayer over her, and having given his blessing, went out. Afterwards, as we were sitting at table, at the usual hour, someone came in and called me out, saying, 'Quoenburg' (that was the maid's name) 'desires that you should immediately go back to her.' This I did, and entering the chamber, I found her of more cheerful countenance, and like one in good health. And while I was sitting beside her, she said, 'Shall we call for something to drink?'—'Yes,' said I, 'and right glad am I, if you can.' When the cup was brought, and we had both drunk, she said, 'As soon as the bishop had said the prayer for me and given me his blessing and had gone out, I immediately began to mend; and though I have not yet recovered my former strength, yet all the pain is quite gone both from my arm, where it was most burning, and from all my body, as if the bishop had carried it away with him; notwithstanding the swelling of the arm still seems to remain.' But when we departed thence, the cure of the pain in her limbs was followed by the assuaging of the grievous swelling; and the maiden being thus delivered from pains and death, returned praise to our Lord and Saviour, in company with His other servants who were there."

Chapter XIV

How another in like manner, being at the point of death, saw the place of punishment appointed for him in Hell.

I myself knew a brother, would to God I had not known him, whose name I could mention if it were of any avail, dwelling in a famous monastery, but himself living infamously. He was oftentimes rebuked by the brethren and elders of the place, and admonished to be converted to a more chastened life; and though he would not give ear to them, they bore with him long and patiently, on account of their need of his outward service, for he was a cunning artificer. But he was much given to drunkenness, and other pleasures of a careless life, and more used to stop in his workshop day and night, than to go to church to sing and pray and hear the Word of life with the brethren. For which reason it befell him according to the saying, that he who will not willingly humble himself and enter the gate of the church must needs be led against his will into the gate of Hell, being damned. For he falling sick, and being brought to extremity, called the brethren, and with much lamentation, like one damned, began to tell them, that he saw Hell opened, and Satan sunk in the depths thereof; and Caiaphas, with the others that slew our Lord, hard by him, delivered up to avenging flames. "In whose neighbourhood," said he, "I see a place of eternal perdition prepared for me, miserable wretch that I am." The brothers, hearing these words, began diligently to exhort him, that he should repent even then, whilst he was still in the flesh. He answered in despair, "There is no time for me now to change my course of life, when I have myself seen my judgement passed."

Whilst uttering these words, he died without having received the saving Viaticum,° and his body was buried in the farthest parts of the monastery, nor did any one dare either to say Masses or sing psalms, or even to pray for him. Oh how far asunder hath God put light from darkness! The blessed Stephen, the first martyr, being about to suffer death for the truth, saw the heavens opened, and the glory of God, and Jesus standing on the right hand of God; and where he was to be after death, there he fixed the eyes of his mind, that he might die the more joyfully. But this workman, of darkened mind and life, when death was at hand, saw Hell opened, and witnessed the damnation of the Devil and his followers; he saw also, unhappy wretch! his own prison among them, to the end that, despairing of salvation, he might himself die the more miserably, but might by his perdition afford cause of salvation to the living who should hear of it. This befell of late in the province of the Bernicians,° and being noised abroad

---

Viaticum *Eucharist for the dying*　　**Bernicians** *inhabitants in a region of northern England*

far and near, inclined many to do penance for their sins without delay. Would to God that this also might come to pass through the reading of our words!

Endnotes

1   The text is taken from Bede's *Ecclesiastical History of England*, translated by A.M. Sellar, 1907 as found in The Project Gutenberg. This text is in the public domain.

2   This date represents the earliest manuscripts of Bede's Latin version of the *EH*. A subsequent Old English translation was made in the ninth century.

3   Quotations from the Bible taken from the Douay-Rheims translation in the Unbound Bible.

4   Matthew 15:11.

5   Matthew 15:19.

6   Titus 1:15.

7   Psalm 51:5.

8   Psalm 6:7.

9   1 Corinthians 7:9.

10   1 Corinthians 7:6.

11   Romans 7:23.

12   Note from edition: "Aen. II, 1. Quotations from Vergil are frequent in Bede."

Evadeam, The Dwarf Knight from the *Lancelot-Grail Cycle*[1] (ca. 1220–30)

Contributed by Kara Larson Maloney

Introduction

Dwarfism is a medical or genetic condition that results in short physical stature, usually under the designated height of four foot ten inches. This condition does not have one singular cause, and the conditions that are most often associated with dwarfism—large head, disproportionate limb size to trunk size—are not universal affects. Though it is an acknowledged medical condition in modern times, those who manifested such traits in the Middle Ages occupied a different, liminal space in medieval European texts. Their short stature and other visible differences could be considered a physical ailment or impairment, or they could be considered part of a race of monsters and not entirely human. Celtic folk tradition, for instance, mentions dwarfs as a magical race. And while medical conditions such as achondroplasia (a genetic disorder that results in dwarfism—shortened arms and legs, reduced height, and usually a normal length torso) would have little debilitating impact on a person's function within their community, people with such conditions were still Othered and seen as being outside the norm during the medieval period.

The Middle Ages produced hundreds of texts regaling the stories of King Arthur, and peppered throughout these stories are a handful of dwarves who serve as devices to move the plot forward. David T. Mitchell and Sharon L. Snyder compare disability to the "master trope of human disqualification."[2] This human disqualification can be seen in the "accessorizing" of dwarves within the Arthurian canon, such as in the dwarf who drives Lancelot's cart in Chretien de Troyes' *La Charette*, or Gareth's dwarf in Malory's *Morte Darthur*. Some have even argued that the dwarf himself serves to enhance Gareth's masculinity and prowess as a knight, a veritable prosthesis. Mitchell and Snyder also look at disability's role in narratives to see how disability becomes coded as inferiority. Historically, dwarves in the Celtic tradition, especially that of the Welsh, are defined as a separate race, "small and handsome" who are "noted for their noble character and complete community harmony," per Vernon J. Harward.[3] Dwarves in the Arthurian tradition follow Mitchell and Snyder's idea of inferior because these dwarves are not magical fairy-folk who impart gold and wisdom, but "disfigured" people who are ridiculed and demonized. When looking at the story of Evadeam, one must consider Mitchell and Synder's question: "can one possess a physical or cognitive anomaly that does not translate into a belief in one's social inferiority?" I have chosen to focus on the story of Evadeam, the "nain chevalier," or "dwarf knight," because his disability serves as the "narrative prosthesis" that Mitchell and Snyder speak of: his condition is a "curse" that he must overcome in order to gain full membership into the Round Table. What makes his tale unique from a medieval standpoint is that Evadeam serves as the focus character of the story. The author's use of realistic detail also helps set this text apart, not quite subverting the "narrative prosthesis" trope, but at least recognizing the reality of living life with dwarfism. One other notable dwarf knight wins his lady's love in the midst of Malory's recounting of Pelleas and Etard, but no one really remarks that the lady herself chooses the dwarf of her own free will, and that the other knight goes his way, visibly disturbed, and their story ends. Evadeam, however, embodies the liminality that little people (those who manifest the physical condition of dwarfism, as they wish to be called today) could have faced in the Middle Ages.

Part of the Old French *Lestoire de Merlin* from the *Lancelot-Grail* saga, Evadeam's story tells of the knight's encounters with Gawain and others in the early days of King Arthur's court. The *Lancelot-Grail*, or *Vulgate*, Cycle is the longest Old French Arthurian romance cycle. Written sometime between 1215 and 1235, the Cycle tends to layer its adventures with heavy-handed moralizing. As such, when readers encounter Evadeam, we are quickly introduced to him as the "the most deformed and ugliest dwarf," companion of a damsel who is "the greatest beauty" and whose parallel cannot be found for four realms. The court, including Guinevere, cannot believe that such a beautiful, innocent damsel could be in love with such an ugly creature. None of them consider Evadeam, who is simply known as the dwarf knight, and what his feelings can be. They cannot see beyond his "coarse black hair," "his shoulders high and crooked," and the hump on his back. (One should note that Evadeam's shortened limbs in proportion to his torso, as well as his broad hands and soft fingers, are marks of anachondroplasia.) Even when they know his name, Evadeam, and that he is of royal birth, the main concern is whether it was the sin of his mother or father responsible for his condition. As Edward Wheatley shows in *Stumbling Blocks before the Blind: Medieval Constructions of a Disability*, the Church's attempt to dominate the field of medicine and other fields of learning in pre-modern times meant that the causes of disability were thought to be rooted in the moral and amoral deeds of his parents.[4] Impairment such as blindness, or disability such as Evadeam's dwarfism, could be seen as a spiritual test of character, which makes for an interesting choice in a narrative like the *Lancelot-Grail*. Though the narrative states that Evadeam's state "is not the fault of his father, or of his mother, or anything that [Evadeam] deserved," the question of what Evadeam or his parents had done to invoke such a "punishment" would have occurred to a medieval Western European audience in ways that modern readers might not consider.

The bulk of the *Lancelot-Grail* Cycle questions the values of chivalry. The inclusion of the dwarf knight, who despite his physical "disfigurements" and slight impairment (he must cut holes in the leather fenders of his saddle so that his spurs can actually touch the horse's flanks), makes an interesting counterpoint to the likes of Gawain, who suffers from questionable moral values, and yet is physically pleasing to the eye. Evadeam, though physically ugly by the other knights' standards, is a true gentleman and manages to fight five physically able knights to near-death, all for the sake of his love. Later in the cycle, Gawain falls victim to the same curse, disfiguring dwarfism, and must also learn a lesson in courtesy. For Evadeam, it took Gawain wishing him that God grant him joy. For Gawain, it was his very remembering to greet a lady when he met her in the forest without passing her by first. Both, in the end, regain their physical beauty, which will match their spiritual purity and courtesy as a knight. It isn't quite as satisfying as a modern ending might have been, wherein the court would have recognized Evadeam's prowess as a knight did not depend on his physical stature, but one must note Evadeam's treatment as a character. He is granted a name, a full genealogy, and a backstory, complete with conflict. He has a lady love who can see beyond his physical features to the beauty within. And that, in the end, humanizes Evadeam in ways that few other dwarfs are within the medieval Arthurian canon. He is

not a member of a fairy race, but a flesh and
blood human being.

Bibliography

Harward, Vernon J. *The Dwarfs of Arthurian Romance and Celtic Tradition.* E.J. Brill, 1958.

Huber, Emily Rebekah. "'Delyver Me My Dwarfff!': Gareth's Dwarf and Chivalric Identity." *Arthuriana*, vol. 16. no. 2, 2006, pp. 49–53.

Larrington, Carolyne. *King Arthur's Enchantresses: Morgan and Her Sisters in Arthurian Tradition.* I.B. Tauris, 2006.

Mitchell, David, and Sharon Snyder. *Narrative Prosthesis: Disability and the Dependencies of Discourse.* University of Michigan Press, 2001.

Neufeld, Christine Marie. "A Dwarf in King Arthur's Court: Perceiving Disability in Arthurian Romance." *Arthuriana*, vol. 25, no. 4, 2015, pp. 25–35.

Pearman, Tory. *Women and Disability in Medieval Literature.* Palgrave MacMillan, 2010.

Tracy, Kisha G. "Representations of Disability: The Late Medieval Literary Tradition of the Fisher King." *Disability in the Middle Ages: Reconsiderations and Reverberations*, edited by Joshua R. Eyler. Routledge, 2016, pp. 105–18.

Wheatley, Edward. *Stumbling Blocks Before the Blind: Medieval Constructions of a Disability.* University of Michigan Press, 2010.

Lestoire de Merlin: The Dwarf Knight

After Merlin had told his master all the stories of the things as they happened, one after another, he took leave of Blaise and went right to the city of Logres, where King Arthur and his wife were, and they had great joy at the sight of him. And just as Merlin got there, a maiden came to the front of the room riding a dun-colored mule, and in front of her, on the saddlebow of the mule, she carried the most deformed and ugliest dwarf that anyone had ever seen. He was snub-nosed and skinny and had red curly eyebrows, and a red beard that was so long that it fell to his feet, and his coarse and black hair an ugly combination, his shoulders high and crooked, and a big hump on his back and one in front on his breast, his fat hands and short fingers, and short legs, and a long and sharp spine. The maiden was the greatest beauty. And they all looked at one, and the other.

When she climbed down from her mule, she took her dwarf in her arms and put him down very softly and led him into the room before the king, who sat eating. And when she saw the king she greeted him genteelly, for she was full of great courtesy, and the king returned her greeting most debonairly.

The maiden said in front of them, "Sire, I have come to you from very far, because of your court's great renown throughout the world, to ask you a gift, because no maiden—as the renown witness of you—does not receive that which she asks you. And because you are the greatest gentleman in the world, I have worked to come to your court for one single request. Guard you well that you do not grant me what you do not want to do or give."

"Lady," said the king, "Ask that which you would like because you would not fail; I will give what I can by my honor and my royal authority."

"That which I would ask you," she said, "does not risk your honor."

"Lady," said the king, "Speak your wish because I will do it outright."

"Sire," said the lady, "I have come to ask that you knight this young man that I hold by the hand and who is my friend. He deserves it well by right, because he is worthy and hardy and of noble lineage. He should have been a knight before, and he could have been knighted by the hand of King Pelles of Listnois, who is a most loyal gentleman. But my friend did not want to do that, and he made an oath to only be knighted by your hand. And for this I ask that you make him a knight."

And then everyone began to laugh in the room, and Kay the Seneschal, who had a most slanderous tongue full of dangerous words, said to her while sneering, "Watch him well and keep him close to you so that the maidens of the queen will not take him. He is a great beauty, so they may try to take him from you!"

"Sire," said the damsel, "the king is such a worthy man that he would not allow anyone to do wrong against me, as it pleases God and himself."

"Certainly not, lady," said the king, "you can be completely sure and I swear it to you."

"Sire," said the lady, "I thank you. Pray do as I ask you."

"Lady," said the king, "I will do what you ask."

At these words, two squires entered the court on two strong and quick horses. One carried on his neck a shield with three leopards with crowns of blue, the field of the shield was black as mulberries, and the strap was of the gold work of a goldsmith, with an inlay of little crosses, and a sword hanging from the bow of the saddle. And the other brought a little war horse in his right hand which was of a good size, and the bridle of gold and the halter of silk. Both squires had driven out a packhorse with two very beautiful saddlebags. Then they dismounted at a pine tree and tied up their horses. Then they opened the saddlebags and drew out from one a double-mail hauberk which was as white as new snow because it was of fine silver, leg armor of the same, and one helm of silver gilding. Then they went into the room where the king and the barons were dining and they came before the lady.

When the lady saw them coming, she said to the king, "Sire, please grant my request, for it is I who have delayed too long. Here is all the apparatus that a knight needs, for I have brought the armor with which my friend will be dubbed."

"Fair, sweet friend," said the King, "I will do your bidding and your greatest wish of my free will after you come and eat."

And she said that she would not eat before her friend was made a knight.

So the lady stood in the hall before the king, and she always held her friend by the right hand, and when the king had eaten and the tablecloths were cleared, the lady drew from her purse two spurs which were wrapped in a swath of silk. Then she said to the king, "Sire, do what I ask because I have delayed too long."

Then Kay jumped in front and started to put on the right spur. And the lady seized him by the hand and she said, "What is it that you wish to do, sir knight?"

"I want to put the right spur on your friend to make him a knight at my hand."

The lady said, "With your hand is not what the Lord wants. It will only be the hand of King Arthur because he gave me a promise that he would do as I ask. Or else, he would have what the Lord wants because no hand by the hand of King Arthur because he gave me the promise that he would only do as I wish. Else he would have hurt me to the death. No one but a king will touch one as high status as my friend."

"So God help me," said the king, "Lady, you are right, and I will do that which you desire." Then the king took the spur from the lady and he put it on the right foot. And the lady put on the other. And the king put the sword on him after he had dressed in the hauberk, because the lady did not want anyone but the king to touch him. And when he was dressed in a proper way with everything a knight would need, the king took him by the neck and said that God would make him a worthy knight.

And then the lady asked if he could do anything else.

"Lady," the king said, "I have done that which you wanted."

"Sire," she said, "please ask that he will be my knight."

And the King asked him, and he said that he would do what the king wanted.

Then they left the hall and went to the pine tree. And the young lady lifted her new knight on the warhorse, which was more beautiful than any other, all covered with weapons. And then she hung his shield about his neck herself, which was as the story had said it was. Then she mounted her mule and called to the squires and sent them away to her country. Then she went the other way with her knight and they entered a great and marvelous forest.

And King Arthur had remained at his castle with her and Merlin and their company, all of whom had laughed at the lady who was in love with the dwarf.[5]

"Certainly," said Queen Guinevere, "I wonder how such a thought had come to her for I have never in my life seen such an ugly or despiteful thing.[6] And the damsel is full of such great beauty that no one can find her equal in four realms. I believe that devils or phantoms have blinded or enchanted her."

"Lady," said Merlin, "she is not blinded to anything except the great ugliness of the dwarf. In your life you have not seen as loathsome a piece of flesh as the dwarf is, and yet, he is the son of a king and queen."

"Dear sir," said the queen, "the damsel appears to come from a great line, for she is beautiful beyond all others, and her friend is so horribly ugly."

"Lady," said Merlin, "his great bounty and his bravery will get rid of a great part of the ugliness which is so very much in him, as you have seen, and you will learn about this soon."

"Noble, sweet friends," said King Arthur to Merlin, "How is the lady known to you?"

"Sire," said Merlin, "I tell you truly. I have never seen her before, but I do rightly know who she is and what her name is, but she will tell you herself in a short time, and she will be better believed than I, and you will find out who he is sooner than you think in his own words, and you will have both sorrow and joy for it."

"How will I have sorrow and joy?" said King Arthur.

[Word comes from Lucius, the emperor of Rome, and the story is not concerned with the dwarf knight.

Merlin becomes imprisoned. Arthur sends out knights to find him, and Gawain and others search, but return without success after one year. As they return to Arthur, they meet up with the damsel and the dwarf knight.]

Now continues the story, after King Arthur had knighted the dwarf at the damsel's request, that she took him away cheerfully, and they returned to their country. And they traveled that first day until just before vespers. And they left the forest and entered into a most beautiful land, which was very grand and large. And the lady saw before her an armed knight coming, riding on a black-and-white spotted charger, and she pointed the knight out to her dwarf. And he said, "Lady, don't you worry, but ride without fear, for you are safe from him."

"By God," said the lady, "he will want to take me away with him. That is the only reason for him to come this way."

And the dwarf said to the damsel, "Ride on surely."

The knight called out to them as soon as he saw her, in a voice that she could hear, "It is well that you have come, my dear lady, and now I have found that which I have loved forever."

And the dwarf who had heard him quite well, said, "Sir, do not be so hasty, for you might be discouraged before you can start so that you can take joy in her."

"I should take joy in her," the knight answered, "because I love her as if I held her as my own. And I will hold her soon enough."

And the knight kept coming closer as quickly as he was able to ride.

When the dwarf saw the knight approaching, he put his lance in its holder and hid behind his shield until only his eye could be seen. He kicked his horse with his spurs through two small openings cut through his saddle's fenders, because his legs were so short that they could not reach the stirrups of the saddle. And the horse carried him so fast that one would think he was flying. He shouted to the knight to watch himself.

The knight, who was most proud and haughty, thought it was shameful to joust with such a despicable creature. He raised his lance til it was upright and said that it was God's will that he would not joust with him. He still put his shield up against the blow. And the dwarf hit him so hard that he pierced through the shield and the knight's hauberk, and the iron tip of the lance grazed his side. And he hit the knight so hard with his body and his shield, and the horse ran so fast, that the dwarf knocked the man and the horse to the ground. As he fell, he hit his shoulder, and swooned from the pain he felt.

When the dwarf saw this, he called to the damsel and asked her to help him dismount. She took him in her arms and put him down. Then he drew his sword from its sheath and, running to the knight, cut the knight's helmet from his head. He threatened to cut the knight if he didn't acknowledge defeat. And the knight, who was very wounded, saw the sword the dwarf held about his head and was afraid of dying. He cried for mercy and said that he would trust his life to the dwarf.

The dwarf said, "Then you will go to King Arthur to be held prisoner. And tell him that the little knight that he dubbed sent you to him, and that you put yourself at his mercy."

And the knight swore it to him.

The dwarf told the knight to mount his horse, but the knight said that he didn't have the strength, because his shoulder was wounded. "So I will stay here until I can find someone to carry me. But if you mount your horse and go to the head of this valley, you will find a house of mine. It is time for you to find a place to stay. You will stay there and send some of my men to carry me back. You have nothing to fear."

And the dwarf agreed. He went back to the damsel, who held his horse. She bowed low over the neck of her palfrey, took him by the arms, and lifted him up until, with great strain, she put him in his saddle. Then they went back to the king's lodge.

Six squires who lived there ran out to greet them and help them dismount. They disarmed the dwarf and put a rich mantle on him, and the dwarf told them that their lord was wounded. They took a litter, fastened to two palfreys, and went to their lord. They put him in the litter and carried him back to the lodge. They disrobed him and then sent for the physicians, and they gave him what they could. Then the squires asked him who had done this, and he responded that it was a knight that he did not know, and he dared not say that it had been the dwarf. Then he welcomed his guests as joyfully as a wounded knight was able to do. He had them well served and made comfortable. After eating, they were given two rich beds to sleep in in a very beautiful chamber, and they slept until the next morning, when they got up and dressed. And the damsel armed the dwarf, for she loved him dearly, and only wanted to do it with her hand. And when she had armed him and readied him except for his helm, she took him by the hand and took him to where the wounded knight lay. They both said that God grant him a good day, and he returned their greeting quite meekly. They commended him to God and thanked him for the honor that he granted them.

Then they left the room, and the damsel laced his helm and helped him mount his horse, then armed him with shield and lance. Then the squires came up and brought the lady her palfrey and helped her mount. Then they left the knight's lodge and took the road toward Estrangorre.

And the knight who had been wounded started to think of fulfilling his oath, so he had a horse-drawn litter most lavishly fit out; it had a most fair and comfortable bed, and the litter was covered with expensive silk cloth. The knight was laid on the bed and the litter hitched to two sweet-natured palfreys. And they left sorrowfully, and took the road into Carduel in Wales, where King Arthur and his queen were spending time. That day, they were with many people. When they got there, King Arthur was sitting to eat his meal, so the knight had himself carried into the hall before the king.

And the knight said, "Sire, in faith and to keep my oath, I come, full of shame, to throw myself at your mercy at the order of the most despiteful creature in the world who defeated me in combat."

When he said this, he ordered his squires to carry him away, but King Arthur said to him, "What is this, sir knight? You say that you come to be my prisoner and to beg for my mercy?"

"You see, sire," said the knight, "I know well that I must tell you about my shame and my disgrace, and I will, since I have come to that. I must do your will and fulfill my oath. In truth, I fell in love with a damsel who is so beautiful and kind that she has no equal in the world. She is a noble woman, the daughter of a king, and if you desire to know her name, it is the beautiful Byanne, daughter of King Clamadon, who is very wealthy and powerful. But never by bidding, loving, or knightly service done on her behalf, could I bring her to give me her love. And I would gladly take her to be my wife, and her father would be most willing and happy about it, for I am of noble stock, son of a king and queen. But the damsel would not agree to it, because of the most despicable thing a mother ever gave birth to. The other evening, I was out riding alone through a land, all armed, when I met my damsel who had been coming back from your court and with that false dwarf knight, whose friend she is. And when I saw her coming with so little an escort, I felt great joy, and I said that God should be blessed for bringing her to that place, because I thought I could take her without a fight. But the dwarf who was with her told me that I came too soon, and it would do me no good, for things would not go as I hoped, that it was crazy for me to be carried away thus. I thought I could get what I wanted without resistance, so I told him I would certainly get what I wanted. So I let my horse gallop toward the lady, because I wanted to pick her up and carry her away on my horse's neck to my lodge that was not very far from there. But when the dwarf saw that I had started, he spurred his horse toward me and put his lance into its holder. It still seemed a shame and a disgrace to me, so I didn't want to strike him. But he struck me so hard that he dropped me to the ground and when I fell I injured my left shoulder, and I fainted in agony. He unlaced my helm and would have cut off my head if I didn't swear to make myself your prisoner at his bequest, so I am doing all of this."

"Certainly, dear friend," said the king, "the one who sent you here puts you in a good prison. Can you tell me whose son the dwarf is?"

"Sire," he answered, "he is the son of King Brandegorre of the land of Estrangorre, who is most wealthy and powerful in land and loyal subjects. He is also faithful to God."

"Certainly," said the king, "he is a true nobleman; I wonder how Our Lord could bear it that he has such offspring."

"Sir," said the knight, "Our Lord bears many things. It is not the fault of his father, or of his mother, or anything that he deserved. At one time there was no one in all the world as beautiful as he was. It was on Trinity Sunday nine years ago that it happened to him, and he will only be twenty-two years old."

And King Arthur said that he could not be only twenty-two years old, for by his looks he seems much more than sixty.

"Certainly," said the knight, "he will be just twenty-two because my father, King Evadeam, whose name he bears, has told me many times that he is no older than that."

"And how did it happen to him?" asked King Arthur.

"Sire," he said, "it was a damsel who did this to him, for he was not willing to love her. And there is a time limit to it, as I have been told many times. Now I have told you that which I was bound to say, so I make myself your prisoner and throw myself at your mercy, for I have been defeated."

"Dear friend," the king said, "you put yourself in a good prison, for I relieve you of your oath. But first tell me your name."

"Sire," he said, "What I am called is Tradelmant, and I am the godson of the king of North Wales, who by great charity gave me his name. So I will go, by your leave and to my shame."

"Go with God," said the king, "who guides you."

Then the squires took the knight and carried him out of the hall and they put him on the litter between the two palfreys, and they went back to their countries. And King Arthur and his barons spoke quite a bit about the dwarf and the maiden, and said between themselves that it would be very joyful to see the dwarf regain his beauty, and they held the damsel in great esteem that she never hated her friend for his ugliness.

[And now the story turns to Sagremor, the quest for Merlin, and how none of the knights found any word of Merlin.]

The story says that Yvain made his way, after leaving Gawain, until he and his companions rode out of a forest. And as they were riding out of the forest, they met a damsel on a mule, and she was consumed with grief. She pulled out her hair by great handfuls and cried out in a loud voice, "I am so wretched! What will become of me? I have lost the one I loved so much, and he loved me so much that he lost the great beauty that he had to win my love."

And when Yvain heard this, he felt great pity, so he went to her and asked her why she was grieving so. And she answered, "Noble knight, have mercy on me and my lover. Five knights are killing him in the valley behind that hill!"

"And who is your friend, Lady?" asked Yvain.

"Sir, he is Evadeam the dwarf, son of King Brandegorre."

"Lady, stop sorrowing now," said Yvain, "for by the faith that I give you, he will not be harmed if I can help it, if I get to him in time."

"Sir, God's mercy on you," said the damsel, "but you will have to hurry."

So Yvain set off as fast as he could get his horse to run to the place that the lady had pointed out, and his companions followed him. And the lady followed behind as best she could, because her mule went very slowly. And Yvain rode until he saw the dwarf, who was fighting hard with two knights, and Yvain also saw three others lying in the middle of the field who did not have the strength to get up, because one had been wounded by a glaive in the upper thigh, another had been hit on the shoulder, which was severed from his body, and the other was split open by a sword down to his teeth. And the other two were exhausted, and both were near death, for the dwarf kept attacking with vigor.

And when Yvain saw him behaving like this, he said to his companions that "it's a shame the dwarf is built as he is, for he is one is worthy and brave and has a great heart."

"Truly, sir," said one of the companions, "no one has ever fought with such skill with such a build. For God's sake, let us separate them so that nothing bad will happen to him, for there would be great shame if he were hurt."

"You speak the truth," said Yvain.

Then he spurred his horse to where they were, but before he could get there, the dwarf sent one of the knights to the ground and rode over him three or four times with his horse until he had nearly killed him. And when the fifth knight saw that he was all alone, he became deathly afraid for himself, and started to turn away, as if to turn in flight, for he had

deep wounds all over his body. But the dwarf, on a very expensive horse, kept on his heels, and went so fast that he would have certainly killed the knight if Yvain hadn't ridden that way at once.

So he said to the dwarf, "Dear sir, don't do that anymore. Let him go, for courtesy's sake, because we can easily see how he is, because you have fought long and hard with him."

When the dwarf heard Yvain ask that so mildly, he answered like a man more noble and courteous than any other: "Sir, is it your desire that I give up?"

"Yes," said Yvain, "with my thanks, for we can see how he is."

"Then I will do as you ask," said the dwarf, "for you seem to be a most noble gentleman."

Thus the knight whom the dwarf was fighting came to Yvain and said, "Sir, your mercy has saved me from death by coming here, and blessed be God for bringing you here." Then he surrendered his sword to the dwarf and the dwarf took it, and the others who still lived did the same. And he sent the four of them to be King Arthur's prisoners. And they went there and gave themselves over on behalf of the dwarf knight. And Yvain and his companions left the dwarf and the damsel and crossed through various countries. They quested for Merlin here and there, but they could not find him anywhere, and they were filled with great sorrow and displeasure. And then they returned to the court of King Arthur after one year, and each one told the story of their quests, and King Arthur had them written down. Thus we leave the story of King Arthur here and return to speak of Gawain.

When Sir Gawain had left his companions at the fork in the road, he made his way with ten others until they left the forest. And then, Gawain said to his companions that they should depart, and each should go on his own, for he wanted to go on alone. So they departed in this manner, and each went his own way. And Gawain rode on all alone, and he made his way over a great part of the land of Logres until one day, riding while pensive and sad, because he could not hear any news of Merlin, and while thinking on this Gawain came into a forest. And after he had ridden two Welsh leagues into it, there came a damsel riding toward him on the most beautiful palfrey in the world. Her saddle was of ivory and her stirrups of gold, and a blanket of scarlet that had bands that fell to the earth and reins of gold thread with gold studs. She wore clothing of white samite with linen fastenings, and her head was enveloped in silk. And all enveloped as she was, she passed in front of Gawain, who was deep in thought so that he did not greet her. And after she had passed him, the damsel pulled her reins and turned her palfrey and said, "Gawain, Gawain. It is not true, that which they speak of you and our renown in courts throughout the kingdom of Logres. They say, and they swear to it, that you are the best knight in the world. And they say also that you are the most courteous and the most noble in the world. But in this, your renown disagrees with the truth, for you are the rudest knight in the world that I have seen in my lifetime. You meet me in this forest all by myself, far from others, and the great crime that is in you would not allow you to show such kindness or humility so that it would stoop or dare or bear to greet me or even speak to me. So you can know well that much ill will come to you as you have done to me, and you would have to give the city of Logres and half of the realm of King Arthur to not have this."

And when Gawain heard the damsel he felt great shame and he turned his horse's head toward her and he said with heavy heart the words that you will hear:

"Lady," said Gawain, "God help me, I was thinking on a thing that I am questing for, and I ask for your mercy so that you will pardon me."

"God help me," said the damsel, "you will first pay dearly for this, and you will be very ashamed and ugly for it, so that the next time you will remember to greet young ladies when you see them, but I tell you that this will not endure the rest of your days. But

you will find that no one in the kingdom of Logres can tell you about what you are looking for. Instead in Little Brittany you will hear something about it. Now I will go about my affairs, and you will seek out that thing you wish to find. And may you look as you did the first time when you see me again."

Then Gawain left the damsel, and he had not ridden more than a Welsh league when he met the dwarf knight and the damsel, who had left Yvain the night before and sent four knights to be prisoners of King Arthur. And this happened on the day of the Trinity at the hour of noon. And as soon as Gawain saw the damsel, he thought about the damsel he met before, and he stopped thinking about it and said to the damsel, God grant you joy to her and her companion, and the damsel and the dwarf responded that God grant him good adventure. Thus they passed by, Gawain on one side and they on the other, and as they had gone a little way passed, the dwarf knight recovered his beauty as he previously was, and his right age of 22 years, and he was once again grand and well-built in the shoulder, and he had to take off the armor he was wearing, because it was no longer of use to him.

When the damsel saw her friend restored to his beauty, she had joy greater than anyone could say. So she reached up and put her arms around his neck and kissed him more than one hundred times without stopping, and then they went away, rejoicing and happy, one by the other, in great joy. So they thanked Our Lord for the honor that He had given them and wished joy and good adventure to Gawain who had said that God grant them joy, and so He had. Then they went on their way. But by right the story falls silent about these two and speaks of Gawain.

When Gawain had left the dwarf knight and the damsel, he rode through three good arrow shots before he began to feel that the sleeves of his hauberk hung over his hands and that the bottom of his hauberk hung past his two feet, for his legs had grown so short that they did not stretch below the fenders of his saddle, and he looked up and saw that his mail leggings had fallen over the top of his stirrups, and his shield hung close to the ground. He could well see that he was now a dwarf. So he said to himself that this was what the damsel had promised. So he was so angry that he almost killed himself. So he rode so full of grief and agony until he reached the edge of the forest. And there he found a cross and a block where he dismounted, and then he began to shorten his stirrups, his mail leggings, and the belt of his sword, and the straps of his shield, and the sleeves of his hauberk. And he attached straps to his shoulders and dressed the best that he could. Then filled with anger and with sorrow, he would have preferred to die rather than live.

Then he mounted his horse and went back on his way, and he cursed the day and hour that he started out on the quest, for he had been ashamed and dishonored by it. And he went on in this manner and did not pass by castle or lodge, woods or plains without seeking news of Merlin from everyone and all that he encountered. Thus he encountered those men and women who said such mocking and loathsome things to him, but he did many feats of prowess, because even though he was a dwarf, he had not lost his power to do such, nor his heart or his strength. Instead, he was hardy and enterprising and conquered many knights.

And after he had searched up and down through the realm of Logres, he knew that he would find nothing there, so it is known that he crossed the ocean and went into Little Britany, and he searched near and far, but he was not able to find Merlin. And he rode until he approached the time when he had to return. And he said to himself, "Alas, what will I do? The time has come when I must return, when I swore an oath to my lord my uncle that I would return. And I must return because otherwise I would be a liar. No, I will not, because the oath assumes I can act on my own, but I cannot act of my own will, because I am ugly and disfigured and have no power over myself. And that is why I cannot be bound to go to court. By faith, now I have misspoken.

Under no circumstances, whatever shape I have, I would not perjure myself, and because I am not locked in a prison, thus not being able to go where I want, I would only perjure myself if I didn't go to court. And for that I must go to court to not prove me faithless. And so I pray to God to grant me mercy, because the body is treated shamelessly in this age."

[Gawain rides through the forest of Broceliande and hears Merlin's voice. Merlin tells Gawain of his imprisonment and how no one from Arthur's court will ever see or hear from Merlin again. Merlin does tell Gawain that:]

"You will find the lady who did this to you in the forest where you met her previously, but do not forget to greet her, for that would be a foolish thing to do."

"Sir," said Gawain, "I will not, if it pleases God."

"Then farewell and go with God," said Merlin, "who guards King Arthur and the realm of Logres and you and all the barons who are the best men in the world."

[And Gawain rides with much to think about until he comes to the forest again.]

And when he went into the forest where he had found the damsel that he had passed without greeting her, he thought of Merlin and what he had said to not forget to greet her when he met her. And he was so full of great doubt and dread that he might pass her without greeting her that he took his helm off his head to see better. He began to look in front and behind and at all sides, everywhere, until he came to the same spot where he had encountered the lady and passed her without greeting her. Then he looked up between two areas of trees where the forest was thick and deep and he saw two knights who were still armed but for their shields and helms which they had taken off, and their horses tied to their lances. And they were holding a lady in between, and they seemed as if they were forcing her. They did not desire it, but the damsel was making them do it to try Gawain's will and heart, and she thrashed about as if they were trying to rape her in truth.

And when Gawain saw the two knights holding the damsel, one by the hands and the other by the legs as if they were going to lie with her by force, he shook with anger. And with his lance in his hand, he spurred his horse to where they were. And he said to the knights that they were as-if already dead because they were forcing a lady in the land of King Arthur. Because you know well that ladies are guaranteed their safety.

And the damsel saw him and cried, "Gawain, now I will see if you are honorable enough to save me from this shame."

"Lady," Gawain said, "God help me that you will not be dishonored if I am there to defend you. I will die if I do not save you."

And when the knights heard him it came to them as a great disdain and they sprung to their feet and tied on their helms, because they were already afraid of him. And even though the damsel had reassured them that he would not harm them, and she had enchanted them by the arts so that no one would be harmed by anyone at that time, so they felt better. And when they had laced their helms and hung their shields about their necks, they said to Gawain, "God help me, you crazy dwarf, you appear already dead. And it is a shame to us to attack an ugly thing like yourself."

And when Gawain heard that they were calling him dwarf and ugly thing, he had great grief in his heart. Then he said to them, "Ugly thing that I am, I have come here at a bad time for you, so mount your horses, for it seems to me like villainy to attack you on horseback while you are on foot."

[Gawain and the knights fight, and both fall to the ground until the damsel cries at Gawain to stop hurting her two supposed attackers.]

"Lady," he said, "is that what you wish?"

"Yes," she said.

"Then I will agree to stop at once for your love, and God grant you good adventure, to you and all the ladies of the world. You may know that if not for your plea, I would have killed him, or he would have killed me,

because they shamed and wronged you, and they dishonored me when they called me an ill-made dwarf. And they also spoke the truth, for I am the most loathsome thing in the world, and it is in this forest that it happened to me six months ago."

And the damsel and the knights began to laugh. "So then," said the damsel, "what would you give to the one who could cure you of this?"

"Certainly, lady," he said, "if I could be saved from this, I would give myself first and then as much wealth as I could gather in the whole world."

"You will not have to give me so much," said the damsel, "but swear me an oath such as I tell you."

"Lady," he said, "I will do whatever you wish. Just tell me what to do and I am ready to do it."

"You will swear to me on the oath you gave King Arthur, your uncle, that you will never fail to help any lady or damsel and that you will never meet a lady without greeting her, if you can, before she greets you."

"Lady," he said, "I swear this to you as faithful knight."

"And I accept this oath," she said, "but in the same manner if you break it you will become as you are now."

"Lady," he said, "I agree, but only if the lady's quarrel that she asks me to help in is just, for I will have nothing to do with disloyalty, even for life or death."

"I grant this to you," said the lady. And all at once the straps that he had tied on his mail leggings broke because his legs were growing out again, and soon he was back to his same likeness. And when he found himself returned to his previous state, he got to the ground and knelt before the lady and said that he would be her own knight for all her days. And the damsel thanked him and took him by the hand and it was the same lady who had sent him this mischance.

[Gawain returns to Arthur's court and tells the story of what he found, and as he's retelling the story, a familiar face comes into the court.]

As they celebrated, Evadeam came into the hall. He was twenty-two years old and so beautiful and fair that no man in two kingdoms was more beautiful. And he had the damsel by the hand and they came before the king and greeted him most courteously.

And the king greeted them, and the knight said, "Sire, you do not know who I am, and it is no marvel, because when you saw me only once before, and then I was wearing clothing that no one would have seen me in before, and no one would recognize me now who hadn't seen me as a child."

"Certainly, good friend," said King Arthur, "I don't remember having seen you before, but you are a most handsome knight."

"Sire," said Evadeam, "do you remember that a damsel brought you a dwarf for you to dub a knight?"

"Yes," said the king, "I do remember, for he had sent me five knights as prisoners whom he had conquered with his prowess."

"Sire," said Evadeam, "I am the dwarf whom you dubbed, and this is the lady who requested that you do it."

[Evadeam recounts his story to King Arthur, finishing with] "Because then I was a dwarf, ugly and hideous. For I well believe that his words and his prayers helped me so that God freed me from my shame, and for this, I thank the Lord."

And then the king asked who he was and of what family, and he told the story as I have told it to you before. And when the king and Gawain and the others heard about what happened they had much gladness and joy. And the king named him a companion with the others of the round table and the damsel stayed with the queen willingly and with much joy.

Here ends the story of Evadeam, no longer the dwarf knight.

Endnotes

1   Introduction and bibliography provided by Kara Larson Maloney and are part of the public domain. The text above was translated by Kara Larson Maloney from Oskar H. Sommer's 1909 Old French edition of *The Vulgate Version of the Arthurian Romances, vol. II: Lestoire de Merlin*, published by the Carnegie Institution of Washington. Evadeam's story is excerpted from pages 421–63 of Sommer's text, and uses N.J. Lacey's edited translation of the *Lancelot-Grail: the Old French Arthurian Vulgate and post-Vulgate in translation*, vol. I (1992). More information on the various editions can be found at the *Lancelot-Grail Project*: http://www.lancelot-project.pitt.edu/LG-web/L-G-Text-Eds.html.

2   David Mitchell and Sharon Snyder, *Narrative Prosthesis: Disability and the Dependencies of Discourse* (University of Michigan Press, 2001), p. 3.

3   Vernon J. Harward, *The Dwarfs of Arthurian Romance and Celtic Tradition* (E.J. Brill, 1958), p. 13.

4   Edward Wheatley, *Stumbling Blocks Before the Blind: Medieval Constructions of a Disability* (University of Michigan Press, 2010), pp. 9–10.

5   In Old French, *nain* or *neim* simply glosses as "dwarf." The Anglo-Norman dictionary links *neim* to *neimcel/neincel*, a pejorative that means "little dwarf, insignificant wretch." The FEW gives the etymology of *neim* as related to Latin *nanus*, meaning simply "one who is of a size smaller than normal" or "of a size very inferior to the average."

6   The word in Old French is "cose" or "chose," which the Anglo-Norman Dictionary defines as "thing (generalized term applied to all manner of objects, matters, items, business, property, goods etc.)." The second definition is "(living) thing, person," but one should note that "thing" is the more common usage. Based on Guinevere's revulsion of Evadeam and how the text treats him, I would say a gloss of "thing" is more apropos.

Morkinskinna[1] (ca. 1220)

Contributed by Ármann Jakobsson

Introduction

King Sigurðr Magnússon (1090–1130) ruled Norway from 1103, first jointly with his brothers but from 1123 on his own. Originally a popular and respected ruler, the medieval sources agree that the later years of his reign were clouded by his erratic behavior, such as foul moods, fits of anger, and inconsistency in behavior. As shown in the text below, often the episode will begin with the king becoming *fámáligr ok ókátr* (taciturn and gloomy). The text also mentions the anxiety of the courtiers, finding themselves impotent in the face of the king's condition. The subtext of many of the narratives is that the king's ailment was only the first calamity to befall Norway in the late twelfth century, followed by decades of civil wars and strife.

There is a reluctance in this narrative to refer to the king's illness in specific terms, possibly because nobody is quite sure how to characterize it, thus often it is only called *konungs mein* (the disorder of the king), as in Ch. 74 below. The sole person to refer to the king as "mad" is indeed King Sigurðr himself (in Ch. 79) when he says: *Illa eru þér at staddir, Nóregsmenn, at hafa œran konung yfir yðr* (Yours is a bad situation, men of Norway, to have a mad king). As he is the king, he is the only one allowed to mention the unmentionable, but this adds poignancy to the narrative.

The longest depiction of King Sigurðr's mental illness can be found in *Morkinskinna*, composed c. 1220. For a while regarded as an unoriginal and uncritical compendium, *Morkinskinna* is now regarded as an important kings' saga that influenced later works such as *Heimskringla*. The text, in addition to containing the longest version of the king's illness, also includes a short anecdote about Ívar Ingimundarson, a court poet who is cured of his melancholy by King Eysteinn, King Sigurðr's brother, who uses conversation as therapy with great success. King Eysteinn is also called in once to his brother when a dream has caused him melancholy. Sadly, he is dead when King Sigurðr's illness intensifies and is thus powerless to prevent it. So are the king's retainers whose anxiety when faced with an erratic king is well portrayed in *Morkinskinna*. Collectively, the saga's tales of a mentally ill king essentially concern human vulnerability and fragility as this popular and good king now causes pain and suffering around him.

Bibliography

Getz, Linn, et al. "The Royal Road to Healing: A Bit of a Saga," *BMJ* 343:d7826, 2011.

Jakobsson, Ármann. "The Madness of King Sigurðr: Narrating Insanity in an Old Norse Kings' Saga." *Studies in Early Medicine 3: Social Dimensions of Medieval Disease and Disability*, edited by Sally Crawford and Christina Lee. Oxford University Press, 2014, pp. 29–35.

———. *A Sense of Belonging: Morkinskinna and Icelandic Identity c. 1220.* The Viking Collection 22. University Press of Southern Denmark, 2014.

——— and Þórður Ingi Guðjónsson, eds. *Morkinskinna I–II.* Íslenzk fornrit 23–24. Hið íslenzka fornritafélag, 2011.

Morkinskinna: The Earliest Icelandic Chronicle of the Norwegian Kings (1030–1157). Translated by Theodore M. Andersson

and Kari Ellen Gade. Cornell University
Press, 2000.

81.

Þat er sagt at hvítsunnudag sat Sigurðr
konungr í hásæti sínu með vinum sínum ok
miklu fjǫlmenni, ok þá sá menn at konungr
var með miklu vanmegni ok þungu bragði.
Váru þá margir hræddir um hversu af myndi
reiða. Konungr leit yfir lýðinn ok arðgaði au-
gunum ok sá umhverfis sik um pallana. Þá
mælti konungr ok tók bókina þá ina dýru er
hann hafði haft í land ok ǫll var gullstǫfum
ritin, ok eigi hafði meiri gersimi komit í land
í einni bók. Dróttningin sat hjá honum. Þá
mælti konungr: „Mart kann skipask á manns
ævinni. Ek átta tvá hluti þá er mér þóttu
baztir er ek kom í land. Þat var bók sjá hé-
rna ok dróttningin, er nú þykki mér hvárr
ǫðrum verri, ok þat á ek svá í eigunni er mér
þykkir verst allra hluta. Dróttning finnr eigi
hvernug hon er, því at svá sýndisk sem gei-
tarhorn stæði ór hǫfði henni, ok því betri
sem mér þótti dróttning,“ sagði konungr, „því
ǫllu verri þykki mér hon nú.“ Þá kastaði konungr bókinni fram á eldinn er gǫrr var, en
laust dróttningu kinnhest. Hon grét konungs
mein meirr en sinn harm. Sá maðr stóð fyri
konunginum er hét Óttarr birtingr, búan-
dason ok kertisveinn, ok skyldi þá þjóna,
svartr á hárslit, lítill ok vaskligr ok kurteiss,
dǫkklitaðr ok þó vel um sik. Því var hann
kallaðr birtingr at hann var dǫkkr ok svartr.
Hann hleypr til ok tekr bókina er konungr
hafði fram kastat á eldinn ok helt á ok mælti:
„Ólíkir dagar váru þeir, herra, er þér siglduð
með prýði ok fegrð at Nóregi, ok fǫgnuðu
allir vinir þínir þér ok runnu í móti yðr, ok
játuðu allir þér at konungi með inni mestu
vegsemð. En nú eru komnir til þín á þessum
dǫgum margir vinir þínir ok megu eigi glaðir
vera fyri þínum harmi ok vanmegni. Gǫr
svá vel, inn góði konungr, hritt harminum
ok gleð vini þína. Allir vildu fegnir til þín
koma. Ok þigg þetta heilræði. Fyrst gleð þú
dróttningu, er þú hefir mikit af gǫrt, ok alla
aðra út í frá, vini þína.“ Þá svaraði konungr:
„Hvat muntu kenna mér ráð, inn versti kot-
karlsson ok innar minnstu ættar?“—hljóp
upp þegar ok brá sverði ok lét sem hann myndi hǫggva hann. Óttarr stóð réttr ok brásk

74.[2]

We are told that on Whitsunday King
Sigurðr was sitting on his throne with his
friends and a numerous company. People
observed that the king was in a sorry state
and ill disposed, and many were apprehen-
sive about what would come of it. The king
rose up and looked out over the people on
the benches around him. He took a precious
book that he had brought to Norway, all
written in gold letters. No greater treasure
of a book had come to Norway. The queen
was sitting next to him. Then the king said:
'Many things can change during a man's
lifetime. When I returned to Norway, I had
two possessions that I considered most valuable—the book that you see here and the
queen. Now one seems worse than the other
to me, and I seem possessed of the very worst
things. The queen has no idea about herself,
for it appears that goat's horns are jutting
from her head.[3] The better she used to seem
to me, the worse she now seems.' Then the
king cast the book onto a fire that had been
built and struck the queen a blow in the face.
She wept more for the king's disorder than
for her own pain. There was a man standing before the king named Óttarr birtingr,
a landowner's son and a chamberlain in his
service. He had dark hair, was small in stature but manly and courtly. He had a dark
complexion but was a fine fellow. He was
called "birtingr" because he was dark. Óttarr
ran up and seized the book that the king had
cast on the fire. Holding it, he said: 'It was a
different time, sire, when you returned and
made a fair and proud appearance in Norway, and all your friends ran to receive you
eagerly, and all approved your kingly station
and accorded you the greatest honor. This
time, many of your friends have gathered
and can manifest no joy because of your dejection and illness. Favor us, good king, put
off your moodiness and gladden your friends.
All wish to be joyful in your presence. Accept this counsel. First gladden the queen,
whom you have deeply offended, then all of
your other friends.' The king replied: 'Who

øngan veg við, en konungr brá flǫtu sverðinu er ofan kom at hǫfðinu. En fyrst reiddi hann báðum hǫndum, en sletti nú flǫtu á síðu honum. Þá þagnaði konungr ok settisk niðr í sætit, ok þǫgðu ok allir aðrir. Þá leizk konungr um, hógligar en it fyrra sinn, ok mælti síðan: „Seint má reyna mennina, hvílíkir eru. Hér sátu inir œztu vinir mínir, lendir menn ok stallarar, skutilsveinar ok allir inir beztu menn í landinu, ok varð ǫngum manni jafn vel til mín sem þessum er yðr mun þykkja lítils verðr hjá yðr. Hann unni mér nú mest, ok var þar Óttarr birtingr, af því at ek kom hér œrr inn, ok vildak spilla gǫrsimi minni. Hann bœtti með mér þat annarri hendi, en hræddisk eigi banann. Taldi síðan fagrt ørendi, stillti svá orðunum at mér yrði at virðing, en eigi taldi hann þá hlutina er minn harmr aukaðisk við. Þat felldi hann allt niðr er þó mátti at sǫnnu rœða, en svá var þó skǫruligt hans mál at øngi maðr var svá vitr hjá at snjallara myndi mæla mega. En síðan hljóp ek upp ór viti, ok létk sem ek mynda hǫggva hann, en hann var svá mikill fullhugi sem engi ótti væri um at vera. En þá er ek sá þat lét ek þetta verk fyrir farask, svá ómakligr sem hann var. Nú skulu þér, vinir mínir, vita hverju ek mun launa honum. Hann er áðr kertisveinn; nú skal hann vera lendr maðr minn, ok mun þat þó fylgja er meira er, at hann mun merkiligastr maðr vera af stundu lendra manna minna. Gakk nú í sæti hjá lendum mǫnnum ok þjóna eigi lengr." Hann gerðisk síðan virðiligr maðr af mǫrgum góðum hlutum ok dýrligum.

82.

Sigurðr konungr Jórsalafari setti stól sinn ok hǫfuðstað í Konungahellu, ok efldisk sá kaupstaðr [þá] svá mjǫk at engi var ríkari í Nóregi. Konungr lét gera þar kastala af grjóti ok torfi ok grafa um díki mikit, ok í

are you to advise me, a lowly cottager's son of no lineage?' He jumped up and drew his sword, as if he were about to cut him down. Óttarr stood erect and did not so much as wince. The king grasped his sword with both hands but turned it flat as it came down toward Óttarr's head, then let it veer off to the side. Then the king was silent, and took his seat. Everyone else was silent, too. But the king looked more amenable than before and said: 'It takes a long time to test the true nature of men. Here sat my most distinguished friends, district chieftains, marshals, court officials, and all the best men in the land. But none was so well disposed toward me as this man, who will seem of little account to you. It was Óttarr birtingr who was most devoted to me, for I entered in a rage and wished to ruin my greatest treasure. He saved me from that with one hand and did not fear death. Then he made a fair speech, and he couched his words so as to honor me, without touching on matters that would depress my spirits. He omitted those things that could indeed have been mentioned. But his words were so well chosen that no man present was so wise that he could have spoken better. Then I leapt up in anger as if I were about to strike him down, but he showed such courage as to suggest that there was no danger. When I saw that, I averted the deed, which he did not deserve. And now my friends should be informed of the reward that I will give him. Before he was my chamberlain, but now he will be a district chieftain. What is more important is that from now on he will be the most distinguished of my district chieftains. Now go and sit among the district chieftains and cease to be in my service.' Óttarr subsequently became an honorable man and outstanding in many ways.

75.

King Sigurðr Jórsalafari established his residence and capital in Konungahella. It prospered so greatly as a trade center that none was richer in Norway. The king had a fortress built there of stone and turf with a

þeim [kastala] var konungs garðr, ok þar var krossins kirkja, ok þar lét Sigurðr konungr vera krossinn helga, ok fyri altarinu var tabulum, gort af gulli ok silfri, er hann hafði haft í land. Svá bar at eitt sinn at Sigurðr konungr fór fyr land fram með liði sínu. Ok er þeir lágu í einhverri hofn fóru menn á sund af konungsskipinu. Jóan hét sá er bezt var syndr, ok hœldu margir hans fœrleik. Konungr lá í lyptingu ok var heldr skapþungt. Þeir menn váru hjá honum er annarr hét Erlendr gapamuðr, en annarr var Einarr Skúlason. Ok er þá varir minnst fleygir konungrinn út á sundit ok leggsk at honum Jóani ok fœrir hann niðr. Ok er hann kømr upp fœrir konungr hann niðr ǫðru sinni, ok eru þeir þá miklu lengr niðri. Þá kømr konungr upp, ok it þriðja sinn fœrir konungr hann niðr. Ok nú sjá þeir á konungsskipinu ok rœddu með sér at nú horfðisk til ófœru. Einarr mælti: „Þat væri nú drengiligt at hjálpa manninum ok firra konung óhappi." Erlendr svarar: „Þat er vant við konunginn, en at vísu liggr líf mannsins við." Erlendr var manna mestr ok sterkastr; hleypr af skipinu ok á sundit at konunginum ok þrífr til hans ok keyrir hann niðr ok lét hann upp ok keyrir hann niðr annat sinn ok it þriðja sinn ok lét hann upp er hann hafði lengi niðri verit, ok fóru til lands. Menn fluttu Jóan til lands, ok var hann kominn at bana, ok var þœfðr lengi, ok sátu menn yfir honum unz hann raknaði [við].

83.

Sá maðr var þá kominn til Sigurðar konungs er hét Haraldr Gillikrist ok sagðisk vera son Magnúss konungs berfœtts. Hallkell húkr hafði farit vestr um haf ok allt til Suðreyja, ok þar kom sjá maðr á fund hans, ok móðir hans fylgði honum. Haraldr var þá í for með Sigurði konungi ok ekki með miklum sóma. Hann bað Erlend forða sér, [sagði at konungr] hafði reiði á honum. Hann

---

great moat around it. In that fortress was the king's residence and the Church of the Cross as well, where King Sigurðr placed the holy cross. Before the altar was an altarpiece of gold and silver that he had brought to Norway. It happened once when King Sigurðr was sailing along the coast with his crew and was anchored in a certain harbor that men went swimming from the king's ship. The best swimmer was a man named Jón, and many praised his skill. The king was lying on deck and was not in a good mood. There were two men with him, Erlendr gapamunnr (Gaping-Mouth) and Einarr Skúlason. When they were least expecting it, the king plunged into the water. He made for Jón and ducked him. When he came to the surface again, the king ducked him a second time, and they were under water for much longer than the first time. Then the king surfaced and ducked him a third time. They saw this from the king's ship and said that things were taking a dangerous turn. Einarr said: 'It would be a brave deed to help that man and save the king from a misfortune.' Erlendr said: 'It is hard to contend with the king, but it is true that the man's life is at stake.' Erlendr was a very big and powerful man. He dove off the ship, swam to the king, grabbed him, and plunged him down, then let him up. He plunged him down a second and a third time, letting him up only when he had been down for a long time. Then they swam to shore. People got Jón to shore as well, and he was close to death. He was thumped [on the back] for a long time, and people sat by him until he came to his senses.

76.

A man had come to King Sigurðr whose name was Haraldr Gillicrist. He claimed to be the son of Magnús berfœttr (Barefoot). Hallkell húkr (Hook) had sailed west all the way to the Hebrides, and that man had joined him there with his mother. Haraldr was then in King Sigurðr's retinue but not held in much esteem. He told Erlendr to flee, saying that he was an object of the king's wrath. He

kvazk eigi mundu undan flýja en vera á landi
of nóttum. Sá maðr var á skipi næst [Haraldi
er hét Loðinn. Hann var maðr] ættsmár, ok
þó var hann áburðarmaðr mikill; lagði opt
svívirðingarorð til Haralds, kvazk ógǫrla
[vita hvat manna hann] var ok abbaðisk mjǫk
við svein hans. [Nú bar svá til á þessu sama
kveldi at Haraldr sagði sveininum at hann
skyldi rekkja í húðfati hans um nóttina, en
Haraldr gekk upp á land með Erlendi. En
er] Loðinn varð þess varr þá kvazk hann eigi
[mundu þola at knapar gengi upp á hann
ok spurði hverr honum hefði vísat at rekkja
hjá dugandi] mǫnnum. Hann kvazk þat gera
sem Haraldr bauð honum. Loðinn [rak hann
brot ór húðfatinu. Fór sveinninn ok sagði til
Haraldi. Hann reiddisk ok hljóp út á skipit,
hirði] ekki um þótt hann stigi nær fótum
Loðins. [Hann hljóp upp reiðr, kvað hann
opt vilja sér svívirðing veita. Haraldr segir
at hann hafði minni skǫmm en tilgerðir hans
váru ok hjó til] hans á ǫxlina ok á bringuna.
Þat var svǫðusár, ok [hlupu menn þá á milli.
Fór Haraldr af skipinu ok var á landi þá nótt.
Um myrgininn varp konungr af] sér klæðum
ok spyrr hvar Erlendr var gapamuðr. Einarr
[Skúlason svarar: „Eigi vitum vér þat glǫggt,
eða hversu vel mun honum fritt at koma á
yðvarn fund?"] „Engu heit ek um þat," segir
konungr. Þá kvað Einarr vísu:

Erlendr hefir undan
[allvalds gleði haldit;
gramr, skalattu, gumna,
Gapamunn um] þat kunna.
Hafa munu heiðar jǫfra
hlíðrœkjanda fríðum
– geta [verðr þess fyr gotnum—
galdrs nauðsynjar valdit].

[Konungr mælti:] „Fari eptir honum." Svá
var gǫrt. Ok er hann kom mælti konungr:
„Hversu vel þóttisk þú [leika við konung þinn
í gær?" „Herra," segir hann, „mjǫk eptir því
sem þér gerðuð] fyrir." „Svá var ok," segir konungr; „vel skal þat virða, ok sýndir þú bæði
ástsemð við mik ok karlmennsku. Þigg nú af
mér sverð ok skikkju ok heit jafnan heðan frá
betri drengr en áðr. Eða hvat hark heyrða ek
í gærkveld á skipi váru?" Honum var svarat.

said that he would not flee but would spend
the nights on shore. There was a man of small
lineage on board, closer to Haraldr than anyone. His name was Loðinn, but he was quite a
vain man. He often said cutting things about
Haraldr. He said it was unclear who he was
and was always nagging at his page. Now it
happened this same evening that Haraldr
told the boy to share Loðinn's sleeping bag
at night. But when Loðinn realized what had
happened, he said that he would not endure
pages occupying his space, and he asked who
had told him to make his bed with men of
note. He said that he was doing what Haraldr
had told him. Loðinn chased him out of
his sleeping bag. The page went to inform
Haraldr. He was angered and rushed out on
the ship, not caring whether he trampled
Loðinn's property or not. Loðinn said that
he was often in the habit of dishonoring him.
Haraldr said that he got less dishonor than he
deserved and struck a blow on his shoulder
and chest. It was a flesh wound and people
ran to separate them. Haraldr spent the night
on shore. In the morning the king threw off
his covers and asked where Erlendr gapamu-
unnr (Gaping-Mouth) was. Einarr Skúlason
replied: 'We don't know exactly, but how
good is the treatment he can expect from
you?' 'I make no promises about that,' said
the king. Then Einarr recited a stanza:

Erlendr has fled the king's good grace:
leader of men, you must not fault "gapamu-
nr" for that. Necessity must have forced the
fair tender of the chant of the kings of the
heath's slope [giants, gold, generous man]; I
shall tell people about that.

The king said: 'Bring him here.' This was
done, and when he arrived, the king said:
'How do you feel about your contest with
your king yesterday?' 'Sire,' he said, 'it was
very much in accord with your actions.' 'That
is true,' said the king, 'and I approve it. You
showed both affection for me and courage. I
make you a gift of a sword and cloak and will
always esteem you even more highly than before. But what was the racket that I heard on
our ship last night?' He was told. Then he said:

„Kalli Harald hingat ok svá Loðin,“—ok spurði hann ef þeir vildi leggja á hans vald, ok þeir játtu því. Þá mælti konungr: „Þess vættir mik at þit verðið ekki jafnmenni, en þó vil ek gøra sóma til handa Loðni, fyr því at hann hefir með mér verit. En hitt væri makligra at hann væri réttlauss ok dirfðisk eigi optarr slíkt at mæla við dugandi menn, því at berask má svá at at vér virðim þenna mann meira en einn lítinn mann fyr sér.“ Loðinn varð svá búit at hafa, en konungr skipar Haraldi í sína sveit með skutilsveinum sínum.

84.

Svá bar at eitt sinn at Sigurðr konungr sat með mǫrgum mǫnnum gǫfgum í stirðum hug. Var þat frjákveld eitt at dróttsetinn spurði hvat til matar skyldi búa. Konungr svaraði: „Hvat nema slátr?“ Svá var mikil ógn at honum at engi þorði í mót at mæla. Váru nú allir ókátir, ok bjǫggusk menn til borðanna. Kómu inn sendingar ok heitt slátr á, ok váru allir menn hljóðir ok hǫrmuðu konungs mein. En áðr matrinn væri signdr þá tók sá maðr til orða er hét Áslákr hani, hafði verit út með konungi. Ekki var hann ættstórr maðr, hvatr ok lítill vexti. Ok er hann sá at engi maðr myndi í mót mæla konunginum þá mælti hann: „Herra, hvat rýkr á diskinum fyrir þér?“ Konungr svaraði: „Hvat vildir þú, Áslákr hani, eða hvat sýnisk þér?“ „Þat sýnisk mér, sem ek vildak eigi at væri, at slátr sé.“ Konungr mælti: „En þótt svá sé, Áslákr hani?“ „Hǫrmuligt er slíkt at vita,“ segir Áslákr, „er svá mjǫk skal missýnask þeim konungi er svá mikinn sóma hefir fengit af verǫldinni af ferð sinni, ok ǫðru héztu þá er þú stétt upp ór Jórdán ok hafðir laugazk í því vatni sem Guð sjálfr, hafðir pálm í hendi en kross á bringu, at þú myndir slátr eta frjádaginn. Ok ef smæri menn gerði slíkt væri stórrefsinga fyri vert, ok eigi er svá vel skipuð sveitin sem glíkligt er, er engi verðr til nema ek, einn lítill maðr, um slíkt at ræða.“ Konungr þagnaði ok tók eigi til, ok er á leið matmálit lét hann braut bera slátrdiskana. Kom þá fram sá matr

'Summon Haraldr and Loðinn.' He asked if they wanted to leave their case to his discretion, and they agreed. Then the king said: 'I don't have the impression that you are equals, but I will give Loðinn some amends because he has been in my company, though it is more proper that he should have no rights. But do not presume again to address honorable men in this way, for it is likely that we will honor such a man more than a man of no account.' Loðinn was obliged to settle for this, but the king took Haraldr into his retinue among his court officers.

77.

It happened once that King Sigurðr was sitting with many distinguished men in a gloomy frame of mind. One Friday evening the steward asked what food should be prepared. The king replied: 'Why not meat?' People were so afraid of him that no one dared to contradict him, but everyone was downcast. The tables were set up, and the platters came in with cooked meat. Everyone was taciturn and grieved because of the king's disorder. But before the food was blessed, a man named Áslákr hani (Rooster) spoke up. He had been abroad with the king. He was not a man of great lineage, small in stature, but bold. When he saw that no one else would contradict the king, he decided to speak up: 'Sire, what is steaming on the platters before you?' The king answered: 'What would you like it to be, Áslákr hani, and what does it look like?' 'It looks to me as though I would like it not to be meat.' The king said: 'And if it is, Áslákr hani?' 'It is grievous to think,' said Áslákr, 'that a king who has earned such great honor in the world because of his expedition should have such poor judgment. This is not what you vowed when you came out of the waters of Jordan after bathing in the same water as God Himself. You had a palm sprig in your hand and a cross on your breast, and you did not undertake to eat meat on Friday. If lesser men did this, severe penalties would be in order. Your retinue is not as well manned as it should be if there is no

er honum hœfði vel, ok tók konungr heldr at kætask er á leið matmálit, ok drakk.

Menn báðu Áslák forða sér. Hann kvazk eigi mundu þat gera. „Veit ek eigi hvat þat mun tjóa, en þat sannask at nú er gott at deyja er ek hefi því fram komit er ek vilda, at firra konunginn glœp, en þat á hann heimilt at drepa mik." Ok um kveldit kallaði konungr á hann ok mælti: „Hverr eggjaði þik til, Áslákr, at mæla slíkum beryrðum við mik í slíkum mannfjǫlða?" „Herra," segir hann, „engi nema ek sjálfr." Konungr mælti: „Vita muntu nú vilja hvat þú skalt fyrir hafa dirfð þína eða hvers þú þykkisk verðr." Hann svaraði: „Viltu vel launa, herra, þá em ek því feginn, en ef ǫðruvís verðr þá er þat þitt." Konungr mælti: „Þú munt minni laun fyri taka en vert er. Ek mun gefa þrjú bú, en þann veg skipti til þó sem ólíkligra mátti þykkja, er þú firrðir mik miklu óhappi, heldr en lendir menn mínir er mér áttu mikit gott at launa." Lauk svá málinu at konungr sneri svá til sem bezt gegndi.

85.

Svá barsk at eitt jólakveld at Sigurðr konungr sat í hǫllinni ok borð váru fram sett. Þá mælti konungr: „Fái mér slátr." Þeir svǫruðu: „Eigi er þat siðr, herra, í Nóregi at eta slátr jólakveld." Konungr svaraði: „Þann sið vil ek hafa." Þeir kómu inn ok hǫfðu hnísu í sending. Konungr stangaði í knífinum ok tók eigi til. Þá mælti konungr: „Fái mér konu." Þeir kómu inn í hǫllina ok hǫfðu konu með sér. Sú hafði sítt faldit. Konungr tók hendinni til hǫfuðsins ok leit á ok mælti: „Ósællig kona ertu ok ekki svá at eigi megi sœma við slíkt." Síðan leit hann á hǫndina ok mælti: „Ófǫgr hǫnd ok illa vaxin, en þó verðr sœma við slíkt." Þá bað hann hana rétta fram fótinn, ok hann leit á ok mælti: „Ferligr fótr ok mikill

one other than an insignificant man like me to make this point.' The king was silent but did not serve himself, and when some time had passed, he had the meat platters removed and appropriate food brought in. As the meal progressed, the king began to recover his spirits and to drink. People advised Áslákr to make good his escape, but he said he would not: 'I do not know how that would help. The fact is that it is a good time to die when I have succeeded in what I wished to do, that is, to save the king from a crime. He has it in his discretion to kill me.' In the evening the king summoned him and asked: 'Who incited you, Áslákr, to speak so openly to me in public?' 'Sire,' he said, 'none other than myself.' The king said: 'You probably wish to know what you will get in return for your boldness and what it is that you think you have earned.' He answered: 'If you wish to reward me, sire, I will be happy, but if it turns out otherwise, it is up to you.' The king said: 'You will receive less of a reward than you deserve. I will give you three farms, though that may seem an unlikely outcome, because you saved me from a great misfortune, a task that should have fallen to my district chieftains, who have much to thank me for.' The episode concluded with the king's arriving at the very best resolution.

78.

It happened one evening during Christmas that King Sigurðr was sitting in the hall, where the tables were set up. The king said: 'Bring me meat.' They answered: 'It is not customary in Norway, sire, to eat meat at Christmas.' The king said: 'That is the custom I desire.' They came in with porpoise on the platters. The king stuck his knife in but did not eat. Then the king said: 'Bring me a woman.' They brought a woman into the hall. She had her face covered. The king put a hand to her head and said: 'You are an uncomely woman, but not beyond endurance.' Then he looked at her hand and said: 'Not a handsome hand and misshapen, but not intolerable.' Then he told her to stretch out

mjǫk, en ekki má þó gaum at því gefa; sœma verðr við slíkt.“ Þá bað hann þá leggja upp kyrtilinn, ok sá hann þá legginn ok mælti: „Vei verði þínum legg er bæði er blár ok digr, ok muntu vera púta ein,“—ok mælti at þeir myndi hafa hana út,—ok ekki vil ek hafa hana.“ Ofarla ævi Sigurðar konungs varð sá atburðr at hann var á veizlu at búi sínu. Ok einn morgun er hann var klæddr var hann fámálugr ok ókátr, ok hræddusk vinir hans at þá mundi enn koma at honum vanstilli. En ármaðrinn var vitr ok djarfr. Hann krafði konung máls ok spurði ef hann hefði nǫkkut tíðenda frétt er svá mikil væri at honum stœði fyr gleði, eða hvárt honum hugnaði eigi veizlan, eða nakkvarir hlutir væri þeir er menn mætti bœtr á ráða. Konungr sagði ekki þat vera er hann rœddi um;—þat heldr til at ek hugsa draum þann er fyrir mik bar í nótt.“ „Herra,“ segir ármaðrinn, „góðr draumr skyldi þat vera, en heyra vildim vér gjarna.“ Konungr svarar: „Ek þóttumk staddr hér á Jaðri ok þóttumk sjá út í haf sorta mikinn, ok var fǫr í sortanum. Ok er nálgaðisk hingat sýndisk mér sem væri tré mikit, ok óðu limarnar uppi en rœtrnar í sænum. En er tréit kom at landinu þá braut þat við landit, ok rak þat víða um strandir. Þá þóttumk ek sjá um allan Nóreg it ýtra með sæ, ok sá ek at í hverja vík var rekit af trénu brot, ok váru sum stór en sum smá.“ Þá svaraði ármaðrinn: „Herra, þat er glíkligast um þenna draum at þér munuð bezt skipa, ok vildim vér gjarna heyra at þér réðið.“ Konungr svarar: „Þat þykki mér líkligast um draum þenna at vera mun fyr kvámu manns nakkvars í landit, ok mun hann hér staðfestask, ok hans afkvæmi mun víða dreifask um land þetta ok vera mjǫk misstórt.“

En litlu síðarr urðu þau tíðendi at Hallkell húkr kom í land ok hafði með sér Harald gilla ok móður hans, sem fyrr var sagt, ok bar Haraldr fram sitt ørendi fyr konung. En Sigurðr konungr rœddi þetta við hǫfðingja, en menn lǫgðu til þessa máls [misjafnt] mjǫk ok hverr eptir sínu skaplyndi, en báðu konung fyrir ráða. En fleiri risu í móti, ok réð konungr meirr með sínu ein[ræði en vilja] liðsins. Þá lét Sigurðr konungr kalla Harald til sín ok

her foot. He looked at it and said: 'A big and monstrous foot, but let it pass.' Then he told her to lift her tunic, and he looked at her legs. 'What legs! They are both thick and black. You must be some kind of a whore.' He said that he wanted nothing to do with her and told them to take her out. Toward the end of King Sigurðr's life it happened that he was at a feast in his residence. One morning when he had risen and was dressed, he was so taciturn and gloomy that his friends were fearful that he would have another episode. But the estate steward was wise and resourceful. He addressed the king and asked whether he had learned something that was so serious that it had spoiled his mood, or whether he was dissatisfied with the feast, or whether there was something that could be remedied. The king said that it was none of these things—'but rather that I am musing on a dream I had last night.' 'Sire,' said the steward, 'perhaps it was a good dream, and we would like to hear it.' The king said: 'I dreamt I was here in Jaðarr and saw a great, rapidly moving black cloud out at sea. As it approached, it looked like an enormous tree with limbs above and roots in the sea. When it reached the coast, it was stranded and strewn about the shore. Then I seemed to see all of coastal Norway, and in each bay a piece of the tree had washed up. Some pieces were large, others small.' The steward answered: 'Sire, it is likely that you will have the best understanding of this dream, and we would like to have you interpret it.' The king said: 'The likeliest interpretation seems to be that the dream signifies the arrival of a man in Norway who will settle here, and his progeny will be spread widely but will be of greater or lesser importance.' A little later it was learned that Hallkell húkr had come to Norway bringing Haraldr gilli and his mother with him, as has already been alluded to. Haraldr told his story to the king, and King Sigurðr discussed it with his chieftains. Opinions varied greatly, each chieftain speaking for himself, but they deferred to the king. Several were opposed, but the king decided more according to his own lights than

segir honum svá at hann synjar honum eigi skírslu til faðernis, með því at hann vill [þat binda með eiði], þótt honum berisk þat faðerni sem hann segir, at hann skal eigi beiða konungdóms meðan Sigurðr konungr lifir eða Magnús konungr. Ok þessu var játat. Bjósk [Haraldr síðan til skírslu ok fastar, ok var sjá skírsla gǫr mest í Nóregi]. Ok váru glóandi sjau plógjárn lǫgð, [ok gekk Haraldr þar eptir berum fótum, ok leiddu hann byskupar tveir. Hann kallaði á inn helga] Kólumba meðan. Þar var gǫr rekkja hans hjá. [Þá mælti Magnús, sonr Sigurðar konungs: „Eigi treðr hann hugmannliga járnin.“ Konungr svaraði: „Illa] mælir þú ok grimmliga, því at hann hefir þetta mál [skǫruliga framit.“ Síðan lét Haraldr fallask í rekkjuna. Ok eptir þrjá daga síðan er] skírslan reynd þá váru fœtr hans óbrunnir. Eptir þat [tók Sigurðr konungr vel við frændsemi hans, en Magnús sonr hans óþokkaðisk mjǫk við Harald, ok margir] hǫfðingjar sneru eptir honum. Haraldi var stirt málit norrœna, [kylfði hann mjǫk til orðanna, ok hǫfðu margir menn þat mjǫk at] spotti. En Sigurðr konungr lét þat ekki við veðri komask þá er hann var við.

86.

[Þat var vandi at Haraldr fylgði Sigurði konungi til svefns á kveldum. Ok eitt sinn] gátu þeir hann eptir dvalit, ok sátu þeir [lengi ok drukku. Magnúsi hafði] sendr verit hestr einn gauzkr, gersimi mikil ok skjótr ágætliga. Rœddu [þeir um er við váru at engi myndi hestr vera jafn skjótr, ok] viku til Haralds málinu ok spurðu ef hann vissi nakkvarn jafn skjótan hest. [Haraldr svaraði, kvað ekki svá] einna ágætt at eigi mætti verða annat slíkt. Þeir kváðu hann aldregi mundu sét hafa jafn góðan hest. Hann svaraði, kvazk marga góða sét hafa ok skjóta. Þeir spurðu: „Hefir þú sét skjótari hesta?“ Hann kvazk eigi svá hafa at kveðit. „Svá sagðir þú, ok svá skaltu mælt hafa,“ sǫgðu þeir. Hann svaraði: „Með miklum ákafa takið ér þetta. Nú má vera at ek hafa

in conforming with the views of his retainers. Then King Sigurðr had Haraldr summoned to him and told him that he would not oppose an ordeal to prove his paternity, with the stipulation that he commit himself to an oath that, should his paternity be confirmed, he would not lay claim to the throne as long as King Sigurðr and King Magnús lived. That agreement was made. Haraldr then prepared for the ordeal, and people say that this was the greatest such ordeal in Norway. Seven glowing plowshares were laid out and Haraldr walked over them with bare feet and led by two bishops. As he did so, he called on Saint Columba. His bed was made by the plowshares.[4] Then King Sigurðr's son Magnús said: 'He does not tread the plowshares bravely.' The king replied: 'That is cruel and unseemly talk, because he has borne the test well.' Then Haraldr collapsed on his bed, and after three days the test was made. His feet were found to be clear of burns. After that King Sigurðr accepted his kinship, but his son Magnús took a great dislike to Haraldr, and many chieftains followed his example. Haraldr was not fluent in Norse and he stumbled over many words, so that many people ridiculed him. But King Sigurðr would allow no hint of that when he was present.

79.

It was Haraldr's custom to escort King Sigurðr to bed in the evening. One time they were able to detain him, and they sat for a long time drinking. Magnús had been sent a horse from Gautland, a great treasure and very swift. Those who were present surmised that no horse would be as swift, and they sought Haraldr's opinion, asking if he knew of any horse as swift. Haraldr answered, saying that nothing was so remarkable that it could not be matched. They doubted that he had ever seen such a good horse. He answered by saying that he had seen many good and swift horses. They asked: 'Have you seen swifter horses?' He replied that this was not what he had said. 'That's what you said, and we will hold you to it,' they insisted. He re-

sét skjótari hesta at sǫnnu, ok svá sem þér þreytið þetta þá hefi ek sét menn eigi seinni." Þeir svǫruðu: „Er eigi þat at þú munir vera eigi seinni en hestrinn?" Hann svaraði: „Eigi segi ek þat." Þá mælti Magnús konungr: „Þat sagðir þú, ok nú skulu vit reyna ok veðja um, ok legg ek við gullhring en þú annan í mót." Hann svaraði: „Eigi em ek ráðandi orðinn þess fjárins í Nóregi at vert megi vera eins gullhrings." Þá mælti Magnús konungr: „Legg við hǫfuð þitt." Hann svaraði: „Þat mun ek eigi gera." „Þat skal þó vera," segir Magnús. Þeir skilðu hjalit. Um morguninn var sagt Sigurði konungi. Hann mælti: „Þess var ván at þann veg myndi fara. Fái mér veðféit í hǫnd. Illa eru þér at staddir, Nóregsmenn, at hafa œran konung yfir yðr. En svá segir mér hugr um at þér mynduð rauðu gulli kaupa af stundu at ek væra heldr konungr en þeir Haraldr ok Magnús; annarr er grimmr en annarr óvitr." Nú ganga þeir í skíðgarð nakkvarn, ok er ætlat at þar skyli þeir reyna. Haraldr var í línbrókum nafarskeptum ok lét knéit leika laust í brókinni. Hann var í stuttri skyrtu ok hafði mǫttul á herðum ok kefli í hendi. Magnús var þá ok búinn. Sigurðr konungr var hjá staddr sjálfr ok mikit fjǫlmenni. Ok er þeir váru búnir keyrir Magnús konungr hest sinn ór sporum ok á skeið, en Haraldr var hóta mun skjótari ok fylgði fram leiðinni, ok var slíkr munr. Koma at skeiðsendanum. Þá mælti Sigurðr konungr: „Fullreynt er nú, ok er Haraldr eigi seinni." Þá mælti Magnús konungr: „Reyna skulu vit meirr." Taka annat skeið, ok er Haraldr jafn sítt fram gagntakinu. Koma af skeiðinu. Þá mælti Magnús konungr: „Hvat heldr þú í gagntak várt? Gef þik upp ef þú mátt eigi." Síðan bjoggusk þeir at þriðja skeiði, ok sá þat allir menn at hlið var á milli, ok Magnús hafði viðbragðit. En Haraldr hljóp upp ok gall við ok á skeiðit, ok varla þóttusk menn sjá at fœtrnir kvæmi við jǫrðina, ok at skeiðsendanum ok út yfir skíðgarðinn ok síðan inn á skeiðit í mót Magnúsi er hann var kominn at skeiðsendanum, ok mælti: „Heill, Magnús frændi," segir hann. Ok skilðu nú at þessu, ok fekk Sigurðr konungr Haraldi veðféit.

plied: 'You are very keen on this, and it may be that I have truly seen swifter horses. And since you make so much of it, I have seen men who are no slower.' They responded: 'Could it be that you are no slower than the horse?' 'That's not what I'm saying,' he replied. Then King Magnús said: 'That was your claim, and we will make a test and lay a wager. I will stake a gold ring, and you should stake another.' He replied: 'I have not become so rich in Norway that it amounts to a gold ring.' Then King Magnús said: 'Then bet your life on it.' 'That I will not do,' he said. 'It will come to the same thing,' said Magnús, and with that they concluded their exchange. In the morning King Sigurðr was told. 'It was bound to turn out this way,' he said. 'Give me the wagered money. You Norwegians are in a sorry state with a mad king ruling you, but I surmise that you would soon give pure gold to have me as king rather than Haraldr and Magnús. One is cruel and the other is a fool.' Now they entered an enclosure to make the test. Haraldr was in stirrup trousers that were baggy around the knees. He wore a short shirt, with a cloak about his shoulders and a stick in his hand. Magnús was also dressed for the occasion. King Sigurðr himself was present together with a great crowd. When they were ready, King Magnús spurred his horse forward and onto the track. But Haraldr was just a bit quicker and kept up the pace. That was the difference when they got to the end of the course. Then King Sigurðr spoke: 'That is a valid test, and Haraldr was not slower.' Then King Magnús said: 'Let us make another test.' They ran a second race, and Haraldr was ahead by a girth-strap at the end of the race. King Magnús asked: 'Are you holding onto my girth-strap? Concede if you are not up to the race.' Then they readied themselves for a third trial, and everyone could see that there was a space between them and that Magnús had jumped into the lead. But Haraldr leapt onto the track with a shout, and you could hardly see his feet touch the ground. At the end of the course he ran out over the enclosure, then turned back to meet Magnús when he reached the end of the course. He said: 'Greetings, kinsman.' That was the end of it, and King Sigurðr gave King Haraldr the wager.

87.

Þá er á leið ævi Sigurðar konungs gørðisk sú nýlunda um ráð hans at hann vill láta eina dróttningu en fá þeirar konu er Cecilía hét, ríks manns dóttur. Ætlar at fá at brullaupi í Bjǫrgyn. Lét búa mikla veizlu ok dýrliga. Ok er þat spyrr Magni byskup þá varð hann ókátr. Ok einn dag gengr byskup til hallarinnar ok með honum prestr hans er Sigurðr hét ok síðan var byskup í Bjǫrgyn. Kómu at hǫllinni, ok biðr byskup konung ganga út, ok hann gørði svá; gekk út með brugðit sverð. Konungr fagnaði byskupi ok býðr til drykkju með sér. Hann kvað annat ørendit,—„eða er þat satt, herra, at þú ætlar at kvángask ok láta eina dróttningu?" „Satt er þat, byskup." Konungr tók þá at þrútna ok bólgna mjǫk. Byskup mælti: „Hví sýndisk þér þat, herra, gøra þat í várri byskupsýslu, ok svívirðir Guðs rétt ok helga kirkju ok byskupdóm várn. Nú vil ek þat gera er ek em skyldr: banna þér af Guðs hálfu ok ins helga Pétrs postola ok allra heilagra þetta óráð." Ok meðan hann mælti þá stóð hann réttr ok sem hann rétti hálsinn ok væri búinn ef hann reiddi ofan sverðit. En svá hefir Sigurðr frá sagt, er síðan var byskup, at eigi þótti honum meiri himinn en kálfskinn, svá þótti honum konungrinn ógurligr. Síðan gekk konungr inn í hǫllina en byskup heim ok var svá kátr at hvert barn kvaddi hann hlæjandi ok lék við fingr sér. Þá mælti Sigurðr: „Þó eru þér nú kátir, herra. Kømr yðr ekki þat í hug at konungrinn mun leggja reiði á yðr, ok meira ráð at leita undan?" Þá mælti byskup: „Glíkligra þykki mér at þat mun hann eigi gera. En hverr væri dauðdaginn betri en deyja fyr Guðs kristni heilagri ok banna þat er eigi er sœmanda við? Nú em ek kátr er ek hefi þat gǫrt er ek átta." Síðan var þyss mikill í bœnum, ok bjoggusk nú Sigurðar konungs menn á brot með miklum kornum ok mǫltum ok hunangi. Heldr konungr síðan í Stafangr ok efnask þar til veizlu. Ok er byskup spyrr

80.

Toward the end of King Sigurðr's life his domestic situation changed, with the result that he wanted to abandon the queen and marry a woman named Cecilia, the daughter of a powerful man. He intended to celebrate the wedding in Bjǫrgvin and prepared a great and splendid feast. When Bishop Magni learned of this, he became downcast. One day the bishop went to the hall and together with him a priest named Sigurðr, who was later bishop in Bjǫrgvin. They came to the hall, and the bishop asked the king to come out. He did so, with a drawn sword. The king welcomed the bishop and invited him to drink. He said that he had other business: 'Is it true, sire, that you intend to marry and abandon the queen?' 'That is true, bishop.' The king began to swell with anger. The bishop said: 'Why have you decided to do this in our bishopric, sire, and thus disgrace God's law and Holy Church and our bishopric? Now I shall do what I am obligated to do and forbid you to commit this sin, in the name of God, Saint Peter the Apostle, and all the saints.' While he said those words he stood erect with his neck extended as if he were prepared for the king to strike him with his sword. Sigurðr, who later became bishop, related that he seemed to see no more of the heavens than a piece of parchment because the king was so monstrous in his rage. Then the king entered the hall, while the bishop went home and was in such good spirits that he greeted every child laughingly and played with his fingers. Sigurðr said: 'You are as cheerful, lord, as if it did not occur to you that the king might visit his anger on you, but it would be better to flee.' Then the bishop said: 'It seems to me unlikely that he will do that, but what death would be better than to die for God's holy Christendom and forbid what cannot be sanctioned. I am of good cheer because I have

þat, sá er þar fyrir, hittir hann konung ok spyrr ef þat væri satt at hann vill kvángask at lifandi dróttning. Konungr svaraði: „Þat er satt.“ Byskup mælti: „Ef svá er, herra, þá meguð ér sjá hvé mjǫk þat er bannat inum smærum mǫnnum. Nú er eigi ok ólíkligt at þér ætlið yðr heimilla, er meira hafið valdit, at láta yðr slíka hluti sóma, en þat er þó mjǫk í móti réttu, ok eigi veit ek hví þér vilduð þat gera í váru byskupríki at vanvirða svá Guðs boð ok helga kirkju ok várn byskupdóm. Nú munu þér vilja til leggja nǫkkur stóra hluti til þessa staðar í fjárhlutum ok bœta svá við Guð ok við oss.“ Þá mælti konungr: „Tak þar fé upp. Furðu ólíkir urðu þér Magni byskup.“ Gekk konungr í brot ok líkaði eigi við hann betr en við þann er forboðit lagði á. Síðan fekk konungr þessar konu ok unni mikit.

88.

Ok þá er Sigurðr konungr var staddr í Vík austr tekr hann sótt. Báðu þá vinir hans at hann léti konuna lausa, ok hon sjálf vildi þá í brot fara ok bað konunginn í sóttinni at hon fœri frá honum ok kvazk vildu við hann skiljask, at þat mætti honum bezt gegna ok báðum þeim. Konungr svaraði: „Eigi kom mér þat í hug at þú myndir fyrláta mik sem aðrir,“—ok snerisk frá henni ok gørði dreyrrauðan. Hon gekk í brot. En nú sœkir hann sóttin, ok í þeiri sótt fær hann bana. Ok var lík hans flutt til Ósló ok jarðat í Hallvarðskirkju. Liggr hann nú í steinveggnum útarr frá kórnum syðra [megin].

done what I ought.' Then there was a great bustle in the town, and King Sigurðr's men prepared to move great quantities of grain, malt, and honey. The king then went to Stafangr (Stavanger) and prepared his feast. When the resident bishop learned of that, he went to the king and asked if it was true that he intended to marry while the queen was still alive. The king replied: 'It is true.' The bishop went on: 'If it is true, sire, you may consider how strictly that is forbidden to lesser men. You may well think that such is permissible for you since you have greater power, but it is quite contrary to law, and I cannot imagine why, in our bishopric, you wish to dishonor God's commandments, Holy Church, and our bishopric. Perhaps you wish to endow this church with some great sum of money and thus make recompense to God and my office.' The king said: 'Assess the money, but you are very different from Bishop Magni.' Then the king departed. He was no more pleased than with the bishop who had issued an interdiction. Then the king married this woman and loved her greatly.

81.

While King Sigurðr was in residence east in Vík, he fell ill. His friends urged him to relinquish his new wife, and she herself wished to depart. As he lay ill, she asked to be released because that would serve them both best. The king said: 'It never occurred to me that you would abandon me like the others.' He turned from her and flushed red as blood. She departed, and his illness advanced until it became the cause of his death. His body was brought to Ósló and was buried in Saint Hallvarðr's Church. He now lies in the stone wall out from the south choir.

Endnotes

1   The Icelandic text below is from the Íslenzk fornrit edition, Íslenzk fornrit 23–24, eds. Ármann Jakobsson and Þórður Ingi Guðjónsson (Hið íslenzka fornritafélag, 2011), used with permission from the publisher. The translation is from *Morkinskinna: The Earliest Icelandic Chronicle of the Norwegian Kings (1030–1157)*, trans. Theodore M. Andersson and Kari Ellen Gade (Cornell University Press, 2000). It is used with permission from the translators. Names have been replicated as they are found in the source text.

2   The different chapter numbers are due to the fact that the translation is older than the Íslenzk fornrit edition and does not divide the chapters in precisely the same way.

3   The king is envisioning his wife as a demon, presumably as proof of her adultery, though in this case it is proof mainly of his insanity.

4   There are several instances in Old Norse texts of ordeals that involve treading hot iron, often to "prove" paternity as in this instance.

Ólafs saga helga from *Heimskringla*[1] (ca. 1230)

Snorri Sturluson
Contributed by Ármann Jakobsson

Introduction

"King Hrœrekr the blind" may never have existed, indeed he only appears in *Heimskringla*, a kings' saga most probably composed in the early thirteenth century, two hundred years after his supposed reign in the early eleventh century, but the dubious authenticity does not make his portrayal in this source any less compelling. Wherever he originally came from, the character portrayal of King Hrœrekr in the saga is a testament to a gifted historian, whether it was the Icelandic magnate, poet, and mythographer Snorri Sturluson (1179–1241), to whom *Heimskringla* has been attributed since the late sixteenth century, or someone else. It is also a testament to medieval Icelandic thought about disability.

In *Heimskringla*, King Ólafr the Saint (d. 1030) is credited with unifying Norway in 1015–20 by deposing various petty kings previously autonomous in their own small kingdoms. As his supposed ancestor King Haraldr Finehair (d. 930) had already accomplished this a century before, according to the legendary history of Norway presented to us by late twelfth and early thirteenth century historiographers, the need for re-unification is explained by his many sons having, after the first unification, divided the kingdom again, which makes King Ólafr and King Hrœrekr relatives according to this narrative. This blood relationship, however, detracts little from the savageness of their competition.

The narrative of King Hrœrekr begins with a planned rebellion by five petty kings, thwarted by an agent of King Ólafr. After its suppression, King Ólafr has King Hrœrekr blinded precisely since he fears him the most.

Thus, King Hrœrekr's blindness is from the outset not only meant to impede him in opposing King Ólafr but it is also, paradoxically, a sign of greatness: King Hrœrekr has become blind because he was more dangerous than his fellow petty kings. This is further exemplified by King Ólafr's treatment of his rival: he keeps him with him and treats him well.

King Hrœrekr is sullen and taciturn in public but transforms himself completely when he is awarded a guard, a young and impressionable man that he then seduces into making an attack on King Ólafr. This first attempt is foiled, but the blind and deposed king still manages to escape and assemble an army. When this second uprising is foiled as well, King Hrœrekr retains his pokerface and soon after attempts a third attack on the life of the king, this time wielding the weapon himself. This causes the king, much as he respects the spirit of his adversary, to exile him permanently, using another disabled courtier, Þórarinn Nefjólfsson, whose own disability is more or less invisible (a missing toe), to ship him to Iceland.

Notwithstanding his disability, King Hrœrekr is very active and aggressive, not to mention cunning and seductive, and though hampered in swordplay by blindness, he is very much in control of his environment, sometimes using his disability to lull his opponents into a false sense of security. It takes a powerful king such as Ólafr to repel his aggression successfully and the narrative is characterized by much respect for the blind man. Though King Hrœrekr in the end can-

not triumph over St Óláfr, he is a formidable adversary who should never be underestimated. His portrayal in *Heimskringla* is a good example of an undefeated man whose lack of sight does not render him any less dangerous.

Bibliography

Bragg, Lois. *Oedipus borealis: The Aberrant Body in Old Icelandic Myth and Saga.* Farleigh Dickinson University Press, 2004.

Jakobsson, Ármann. "Konungur og bóndi: Þrjár mannlýsingar í Heimskringlu." *Lesbók Morgunblaðsins,* 22 February 1997.

Lassen, Annette. *Øjet og blindheden i norrøn litteratur og mytologi.* Museum Tusculanum, 2003.

Lie, Hallvard. *Studier i Heimskringlas stil: Dialogene og talene,* NVAOS II, hist.-filos. kl., no. 5. Jacob Dybwad, 1937.

Sayers, William. "From Crown to Toe: Working the Wheel of Fortune in Medieval Scandinavia." *Arachne,* no. 4, 1997, pp. 123–59.

Ok er þat spurði konungr, sá er þar réð fyrir Raumaríki, þá þótti honum gerast mikit vandmæli; því at hvern dag kómu til hans margir menn, er slíkt kærðu fyrir honum, sumir ríkir, sumir úríkir. Konungrinn tók þat ráð, at hann fór upp á Heiðmörk á fund Hrœreks konungs; því at hann var þeirra konunga vitrastr, er þar váru þá. En er konungar tóku tal sín í milli, þá kom þat ásamt með þeim, at senda orð Guðröði konungi norðr í Dala ok svá á Haðaland, til þess konungs er þar var, ok biðja þá þar koma á Heiðmörk til fundar við þá Hrœrek konung. Þeir lögðust eigi ferð undir höfuð, ok hittust þeir 5 konungar á Heiðmörk, þar sem heitir á Hringisakri. Hringr var þar hinn fimti konungr, bróðir Hrœreks konungs. Þeir konungarnir ganga fyrst einir saman á tal. Tók sá fyrst til orða, er kominn var af Raumaríki, ok: sagði frá ferð Ólafs konungs digra ok þeim úfriði, er hann gerði bæði í manna aftökum ok manna meizlum; suma rak hann or landi, ok tók upp fé fyrir öllum þeim, er nökkut mæltu móti honum, en fór með her manns um landit, en ekki með því fjölmenni, er lög váru til. Hann segir ok, at fyrir þeim úfriði kvezt hann hafa þangat flýit, kvað ok marga aðra ríkismenn hafa flýit óðul sín af Raumaríki. En þó at oss sé nú þetta vandræði næst, þá mun skamt til, at þér munut fyrir slíku eiga at sitja, ok er fyrir því betra, at vér ráðim um allir saman, hvert ráð upp skal taka. Ok er hann lauk sinni rœðu, þá viku konungar þar til svara sem Hrœrekr var. Hann mælti: Nú er framkomit þat, er mik grunaði at vera mundi, þá er vér áttum stefnu á Haðalandi, ok þér várut allir ákafir, at vér skyldim hefja Ólaf upp yfir höfuð oss, at hann mundi verða oss harðr í horn at taka, þegar er hann hefði einvald yfir landit. Nú eru tveir kostir fyrir hendi, sá annarr, at vér farim á fund hans allir ok látim hann skera ok skapa alt vár í milli, ok ætla ek oss þann beztan af at taka; en sá annarr, at rísa nú í mót, meðan hann hefir eigi víðara yfir landit farit. En þótt hann hafi 300 manna eða 400, þá er oss þat ekki ofrefli liðs, ef vér verðum at einu ráði allir; en optast sigrast þeim verr, er

74.

And when the king who was ruling over Raumaríki there heard about this, then he thought there was going to be great difficulty for him, because every day many people came to him complaining about these things to him, some powerful, some humble. The king adopted this plan, that he went up into Heiðmǫrk to see King Hrœrekr, for he was the most sensible of those kings who were there then. And when the kings had their discussion, then they reached agreement that they should send word to King Guðrøðr north in Dalar and also to Haðaland to the king who was there, and ask them to come to see King Hrœrekr and him. They did not put off this journey, and these five kings met in Heiðmǫrk at a place called at Hringisakr. King Hrœrekr's brother Hringr was the fifth king there. These kings at first started making speeches one at a time. The one who was come from Raumaríki began talking first, and speaks about Óláfr digri (the Stout)'s travels and the disturbance he was causing in both killing people and maiming people, driving some out of the country and seizing property from all those who opposed him at all, and travelling around the country with a host of men, and not with the numbers that the law provided for. He also says that he declares it is because of this disturbance he has fled to this place, also declaring that many other men of rank have fled their ancestral lands in Raumaríki. 'And though these difficulties have now affected us most, yet it will not be long before you will have to face the same, and so it is better that we all discuss together what plan should be adopted.' And when he had finished his speech, then the kings turned to Hrœrekr for a response. He said: 'Now there has come to pass what I suspected would happen when we held a meeting in Haðaland and you were all eager to raise up Óláfr above our heads, that he was going to be hard to hold by the horns as soon as he had sole power over the land. Now there are two choices available, the one that we all go to see him and let him arrange and settle

fleiri eru saman jafnríkir, heldr en hinum, er einn er oddviti fyrir liðinu; ok er þat mitt ráð heldr at hætta eigi til þess at etja hamingju við Ólaf Haraldsson. En eptir þat talaði hverr þeirra konunga slíkt er sýndist; löttu sumir, en sumir fýstu, ok varð engi orskurðr ráðinn, töldu á hvárutveggja sýna andmarka. Þá tók til orða Guðröðr Dalakoaungr ok mælti svá: Undarligt þykki mér, er þér vefit svá mjök orskurði um þetta mál, ok erut þér gagnhrædir við Ólaf. Vér erum hér 5 konungar, ok er engi várr verr ættborinn heldr en Ólaf. Nú veittum vér honum styrk til at berjast við Svein jarl, ok hefir hann með várum afla eignazt land þetta. En ef hann vill nú fyrirmuna hverjum várum þess hins litla ríkis, er vér höfum áðr haft, ok veita oss pyndingar ok kúgan, þá kann ek þat frá mér at segja, at ek vil færast undan þrælkan konungs, ok kalla ek þann yðarn ekki at manna vera, er æðrast í því, at rér takim hann af lífdögum, ef hann ferr í hendr oss upp hingat á Heiðmörk; fyrir því at þat er yðr at segja, at aldregi strjúkum vér frjálst höfuð, meðan Ólafr er á lífi. En eptir eggjan þessa snúa þeir allir at því ráði. Þá mælti Hrœrekr: Svá lízt mér um rádagerð þessa, sem vér munim þurfa ramligt at gera samband várt, at engi skjöplist í einurðinni við annan. Nú. ætlit þér, þá er Ólafr kemr hingat á Heiðmörk, at veita honum atgöngu at ákveðinni stefnu, þá vil ek eigi þenna trúnað undir yðr eiga, at þér sét þá sumir norðr í Dölum, en sumir út á Heiðmörk; vil ek, ef þetta ráð skal staðfesta með oss, at vér sém ásamt dag ok nótt, þar til er þetta ráð verðr framgengt. Þessu játtu konungar, ok fara þá allir samt. Þeir láta búa veizlu fyrir sér út á Hringisakri ok drekka þar hvirfing, en gera njósn frá sér út á Raumaríki; láta þegar aðra njósnarmenn út fara, er aðrir snúa aptr, svá at þeir vitu dag í ok nótt, hvat títt er um ferðir Ólafs eða um fjölmenni hans. Ólafr konungr fór at veizlum utan um Raumaríki, ok alt með þvílíkum hætti sem fyrr var sagt. En er veizlur endust eigi fyrir fjölmennis sakir, þá lét hann þar bændr til leggja at auka veizlurnar, er honum þótti nauðsyn til bera at dveljast, en sumstaðar dvaldist hann skemr

everything between us, and I think that is the best one to take, and the other to rise now against him while he has not travelled any further through the country. And although he has three or four hundred (360-480) men, still that is not an overwhelming force for us, if we are all of one mind. But most often those that are many of equal authority are less successful than the one that is sole leader over his troop, and it is my advice instead not to risk trying to match our luck with Óláfr Haraldsson's.' And after that each of the kings spoke that which he thought fit. Some spoke against, and some spoke in favour, and there was no solution decided on, they pointed out the obvious disadvantages of both courses. Then Guðrøðr, king in Dalar, began to speak and said as follows: 'It seems amazing to me that you are getting in such a tangle about a solution to this business, and you are totally afraid of Óláfr. There are five of us kings here, and none of us is of any worse descent than Óláfr. Now we have given him support in his fight with Jarl Sveinn, and he has with us behind him gained possession of this land. But if he wants now to begrudge each of us that little power that we held before, and treat us with oppression and tyranny, then I can say this of myself, that I shall get myself out of thraldom to the king, and I declare any one of you to be no man who flinches from this, that we should deprive him of life if we get him into our power up here in Heiðmǫrk, for I can tell you this, that we shall never hold up a free head while Óláfr is alive.' And after this goading they all adopted this counsel. Then Hrœrekr spoke: 'It seems to me about this decision, that we shall need to make our alliance firm, so that no one may fail in loyalty to anyone else. Now you are planning, when Óláfr comes here to Heiðmǫrk, to make an attack on him at an arranged time. Now I do not want to have to rely on you for this, when you are some of you north in Dalar, and some out in Heiðmǫrk. I want, if this plan is going to be ratified between us, that we should stay together day and night, until this plan has been carried out.' The kings agreed

en ætlat var, ok varð hans ferð skjótari en ákveðit var upp til vatnsins. En er konungar höfðu staðfest þetta ráð sín í milli, þá senda þeir orð ok stefna til sín lendum mönnum ok ríkum bóndum or öllum þeim fylkjum; en er þeir koma þar, þá eigu konungar stefnu við þá eina saman ok gera fyrir þeim bert þetta ráð ok kveða á stefnudag, nær sjá ætlan skal framkvæmd verða; á þat kveða þeir, at hverr þeirra konunga skyldi hafa 300 manna. Senda þeir þá aptr lenda menn, til þess at þeir skyldu liði samna ok koma til móts við konunga, þar sem ákveðit var. Sjá ráðagerð líkaði flestum mönnum vel; en þó var, sem mælt er, at hverr á vin með úvinum.

Á þeirri stefnu var Ketill af Ringunesi. En er hann kom heim um kveldit, þá mataðist hann at náttverði, en síðan klæddist hann, ok húskarlar hans, ok fór ofan til vatns, ok tóku karfann, er Ketill átti, er Ólafr konungr hafði gefit honum, settu fram skipit; var þar í naustinu allr reiðinn; taka þá ok skipast til ára ok róa út eptir vatni. Ketill hafði 40 manna, alla vel vápnaða; þeir kómu um daginn snemma út til vatnsenda. Fór þá Ketill með 20 menn, en lét aðra 20 eptir at gæta skips. Ólafr konungr var þá á Eiði á ofanverðu Rau-

to this, to keep now all together. They have a feast prepared for them out at Hringisakr, and they drank with the cup passing round the whole company, but had watch kept for themselves out in Raumaríki, having one lot of watchers go out as soon as the other lot started back, so that they know day and night what is going on in Ólafr's travels and about his numbers. King Ólafr went on his visits inland round Raumaríki, and always in the same manner as was previously described. And when the provisions did not last because of the large numbers, then he made the farmers in the area give contributions to lengthen the visits, when at times he found it necessary to stay on, but in some places he stayed a shorter time than had been intended, and his travels turned out quicker up to the lake than had been arranged. And when the kings had fixed their plan between themselves, then they send word and summon to them landed men and leading farmers from all those districts. And when they gather there, then the kings hold a meeting with them on their own and reveal the plan and appoint a day when this purpose is going to be put into effect. They decide on this, that each of the kings was to have three hundred (360) men. They then send the landed men back so that they could muster troops and come to meet the kings where it had been arranged. This plan pleased most people well, but yet it was the case, as they say, that everyone has a friend among his enemies.

75.

At this meeting was Ketill of Hringunes. And when he got home in the evening, then he ate his supper, and then he and his domestic servants got dressed and went down to the water and took a carvel that Ketill owned, which King Ólafr had given him, launched the ship—all the tackle was in the boathouse—then set off and sit down to the oars and row out along the lake. Ketill had forty men, all well armed. They came early in the morning out to the end of the lake. Ketill then went with twenty men, but left the other

maríki. Ketill kom þar, þá er konungr gékk frá óttusöng; fagnaði hann Katli vel. Ketill segir, at hann vill tala við konung skjótt. Þeir ganga á tal tveir saman. Þá segir Ketill konungi, hver ráð konungarnir hafa með höndum ok alla tilætlan, þá er hann var víss orðinn. En er konungr varð þess varr, þá kallar hann menn til sín, sendir suma í bygðina, bað þá stefna til sín reiðskjótnm, suma sendi hann til vatnsins at taka róðrarskip, þau er þeir féngi, ok hafa í móti sér; en hann gékk þá til kirkju ok lét syngja sér messu; gékk síðan þegar til borða. En þá er hann hafði matazt, bjóst hann sem skyndiligast ok fór upp til vatnsins; kómu þar skip í móti honum; steig hann þá sjálfr á karfann, ok með honum menn svá margir, sem karfinn tók við; en hverr annarra tók sér þar skip sem helzt fékk. Ok um kveldit er á leið, létu þeir frá landi; logn var veðrs; þeir reru upp eptir vatninu; konungrinn hafði þá nær 400 manna. Fyrr en dagaði kom hann upp til Hringisakrs; urðu varðmenn eigi varir fyrr við, en liðit kom upp til bœjarins. Þeir Ketill vissu gerva, í hverjum herbergjum konungarnir sváfu; lét konungr taka öll þau herbergi ok gæta, at engi maðr kœmist í brott; biðu svá lýsingar. Konungarnir höfðu eigi liðskost til varnar, ok váru þeir allir höndum teknir ok leiddir fyrir konung. Hrœrekr konungr var maðr forvitri ok harðráðr; þótti Ólafi konungi hann útrúligr, þótt hann gerði nökkura sætt við hann. Hann lét blinda Hrœrek báðum augum, ok hafði hann með sér; en hann lét skera tungu or Guðröði Dalakonungi; en Hring ok aðra tvá lét han sverja sér eiða, at þeir skyldu fara í brott or Noregi ok koma aldri aptr; en lenda menn eða bœndr, þá er sannir váru at þessum svikræðum, rak hann suma or landi, sumir váru meiddir, af sumum tók hann sættir. Frá þessu segir Óttarr svarti:

twenty behind to guard the ship. King Óláfr was then at Eið in the upper part of Raumaríki. Ketill got there as the king was leaving matins. He welcomed Ketill. Ketill says that he wants to speak to the king urgently. They go and talk, the two of them together. Then Ketill tells the king what plans the kings have taken up, and what their intentions were that he had discovered. And when the king found this out, then he calls men to him, sends some into the settlement, telling them to get together mounts for him, some he sent to the lake to get what oared ships they could and bring them to meet him. And then he went to church and had Mass sung for himself, afterwards going straight to table. And when he had eaten, he got ready as quickly as he could and went up to the lake. Ships were coming there to meet him. He himself then boarded the carvel and with him as many men as the carvel would hold, and each of the others went aboard whatever ship they could. And in the evening, as it was getting late, they set out from the shore. The weather was calm. They rowed out along the lake. The king had then nearly four hundred (480) men. Before it dawned he got up to Hringisakr. The watchmen noticed nothing until the troop came up to the estate buildings. Ketill and his men knew precisely in which quarters the kings were sleeping. The king had all these quarters seized and guarded so that no one could get away, so awaited dawn. The kings had no forces for their defence, and they were all captured and led before the king. King Hrœrekr was a very intelligent man and determined. King Óláfr thought he was not to be depended on even if he made some sort of settlement with him. He had Hrœrekr blinded in both eyes and kept him with him, and he had the tongue cut out of Guðrøðr king in Dalar.[2] But Hringr and the other two he forced to swear oaths to him and leave Norway and never return. And the landed men or farmers who were guilty of this treachery, some he drove out of the country, some were maimed, some he came to terms with. Of this says Óttarr svarti (the Black):

Lýtandi hefir ljótu
landsráðundum branda
umstillingar allar
ifla folds um goldit.
Hafa léztu heiðska jöfra,
herskorðandi! forðum
mundangs laun, þá er meinum,
mætr gramr! við þik sættu.
Brant hafit, böðvar þreytir!
branda rjóðr! or landi,
meir fannsk þinn en þeirra
þrekr, döglinga rekna.
Stökk, sem þjóð um þekkir,
þér hverr konungr ferri,
heptut ér en eptir
orðreyr þess er sat norðast.
Nú ræðr þú fyrir þeirri,
þik remmir guð miklu,
fold, er forðum héldu
fimm bragningar, gagni.
Breið eru austr til Eiða
ættlönd und þér, göndlar
engr sat elda þröngvir
áðr at slíku láði.

Ólafr konungr lagði þá undir sik þat ríki,
er þessir konungar höfðu átt; tók þá gislar
af lendum mönnum ok bóndum. Hann tók
veizlugjöld norðan or Dölum ok víða um
Heiðmörk, ok sneri þá út aptr á Raumaríki
ok þá vestr á Haðaland. Þann vetr andaðist
Sigurðr sýr mágr hans. Þá sneri Ólafr konungr á Hringaríki, ok gerði Ásta móðir hans
mikla veizlu í móti honum. Bar þá Ólafr einn
konungsnafn í Noregi.

   ...

Ólafr konungr fór, er váraði, út til sævar,
ok lét búa skip sín ok stefndi til sín liði, ok
fór um várit alt út eptir Víkinni til Líðandis-
ness, ok alt fór hann norðr á Hörðaland; sendi
þá orð lendum mönnum, ok nefndi alla hina
ríkustu menn or heruðum, ok bjó þá ferð

You have handed, harmer
of hawk's land flames, to
the realm's rulers an ugly
recompense for all plotting.
You had, army-upholder,
the Heiðmork kings rewarded
fitly, who formerly,
fine king, planned wrongs against you.

Away you have driven, wager
of war, sword-reddener,
the kings out of the country—
your courage than theirs was plainer.
Each king fled, as people
are aware, far from you.
Still later you restrained
the speech-reed of the northernmost.

Now the ground you govern—
God with great victory
fortifies you—that formerly
five kings held sway over.
Broad lie, east to Eiðar,
ancestral lands beneath you.
Before, no forcer of Gondul's
fires has held such a kingdom

King Óláfr then subjected to himself the
realms that these five kings had held, then
took hostages from the landed men and
farmers. He took payments in lieu of entertainment from Dalar in the north and many
parts of Heiðmork and then turned back out
to Raumaríki and then westwards to Haðaland. That winter his stepfather Sigurðr sýr
(the Sow) died. Then King Óláfr went into
Hringaríki and his mother Ásta held a great
banquet to welcome him. Now Óláfr alone
bore the title of king in Norway.

   ...

81.

   King Óláfr went, when spring came, out to
the sea and had his ships got ready and gathered troops round him and travelled in the
spring right out along the Vík to Líðandisnes,
and he went all the way north to Hörðaland,
then sent word to landed men and summoned

sem vegligast, er hann fór í mót festarkonu sinni. Veizla sú skyldi vera um haustit austr við Elfi við landamæri. Ólafr konungr hafði með sér Hrœrek konung blinda. En er hann var gróinn sára sinna, þá fékk Ólafr honum tvá menn til þjónostu við hann, ok lét hann sitja í hásæti hjá sér, ok hélt hann at drykk ok at klæðum engum mun verr, en hann hafði áðr haldit sik sjálfr. Hrœrekr var fámálugr, ok svaraði stirt ok stutt, þá er menn ortu orða á hann. Þat var siðvenja hans, at hann lét skósvein sinn leiða sik úti um daga ok frá öðrum mönnum; þá barði hann knapann; en er hann hljóp frá honum, þá segir hann Ólafi konungi, at sá sveinn vildi honum eigi þjóna. Þá skipti Ólafr konungr við hann þjónostumönnum, ok fór alt sem áðr, at engi þjónostumaðr hélzt við með Hrœreki konungi. Þá fékk Ólafr konungr til fylgðar ok til gæzlu við Hrœrek þann mann, er Sveinn hét; ok var hann frændi Hrœreks konungs ok hafði verit hans maðr áðr. Hrœrekr hélt teknum hætti um stirðlæti ok svá um einfarar sínar. En er þeir Sveinn váru tveir saman staddir, þá var Hrœrekr kátr ok málrœtinn; hann mintist þá á marga hluti, þá er fyrr höfðu verit, ok þat er um hans daga hafði atborizt, þá er hann var konungr, ok mintist á ævi sína hina fyrri, ok svá á þat, hverr því hafði brugðit, hans ríki ok sælu, en gert hann at ölmusumanni. En hitt þykki mér þó allra þyngst, segir hann, er þú eða aðrir frændr mínir, þeir er mannvænir höfðu verit, skulu nú verða svá miklir ættlerar, at engrar svívirðingar skulu hefna, þeirrar er á ætt várri er ger. Þvílíkar harmtölur hafði hann opt uppi. Sveinn svarar ok segir, at þeir ætti við ofreflismenn mikla at skipta, en þeir áttu þá litla kosti. Hrœrekr mælti: Til hvers skulum vér lengi lifa við skömm ok meizlur? nema svá beri til, at ek mætta blindr sigrast á þeim, er mik sigraði sofanda; svá heilir drepum Ólaf digra, hann óttast nú ekki at sér; ek skal ráðit til setja, ok eigi vilda ek hendrnar til spara, ef ek mætta þær nýta, en þat má ek eigi fyrir sakir blindleiks, ok skaltu fyrir því bera vápn á hann; en þegar er Ólafr er drepinn, þá veit ek þat af forspá, at ríkit hverfr undir úvini hans. Nú kann vera, at ek verða konungr, þá skaltu

by name all the most powerful men from the districts and then set out in the finest style, when he went to meet his betrothed wife. The banquet was to be in the autumn east of the Elfr on the border between the countries. King Óláfr took with him the blind King Hrœrekr. And when he had been healed of his wounds, then King Óláfr had provided him with two men to attend him and made him sit on a throne next to himself and kept him in drink and clothes no whit worse than he had previously kept himself. Hrœrekr was untalkative and answered abruptly and curtly if people addressed words to him. It was his custom to have his servant lead him out in the daytime and away from other people. Then he began to beat the lad, and when he ran away from him, then he tells King Óláfr that the boy would not serve him. Then King Óláfr exchanged servants with him, and it all went the same as before, no servant staying with King Hrœrekr. Then King Óláfr got to be with and to look after Hrœrekr a man who was called Sveinn, and he was a kinsman of King Hrœrekr and had been one of his followers previously. Hrœrekr carried on with the behaviour he had adopted before with regard to his cussedness and also his solitariness. But when he and Sveinn were just the two of them anywhere on their own, then Hrœrekr was cheerful and talkative. He called to mind many things as they had been previously, and also what had happened in his days, when he was king, and recalled his previous life, and also who it was that had brought it to an end, his power and his happiness, and made him into a beggar. 'But that, however, seems to me hardest of all,' he says, 'that you and my other kinsmen who should have turned out the finest of men, should now have fallen so low that no disgrace is to be avenged that has been inflicted on our families.' He often expressed such lamentations. Sveinn replies and says that they had to deal with people that were much too powerful, and so they had little choice. Hrœrekr says: 'For what purpose shall we go on living in shame and mutilation except it should come about that

vera jarl minn. Svá kómu fortölur hans, at Sveinn játaði at fylgja þessu úráði. Svá var ætlat ráðit, at þá er konungr bjóst at ganga til aptansöngs, stoð Sveinn úti í svölunum, ok hafði brugðit sax undir yfirhöfninni. En er konungr gékk út or stofunni, þá bar hann skjótara at en Svein varði, ok sá hann í andlit konunginum; þá bliknaði hann ok varð föl sem nár, ok féllust honum hendr. Konungr fann á honum hræzlu ok mælti: Hvat er nú, Sveinn? viltu svíkja mik? Sveinn kastaði yfirhöfninni frá sér ok saxinn ok féll til fóta konungi ok mælti: Alt á guðs valdi ok yðru, konungr! Konungr bað menn sína taka Svein, ok var hann í járn settr. Þá lét konungr fœra sæti Hrœreks á annan pall; en hann gaf grið Sveini, ok fór hann af landi í brott. Konungr fékk þá Hrœreki annat herbergi at sofa í, en þat er hann svaf sjálfr í; svaf í því herbergi mart hirðmanna; hann fékk til tvá hirðmenn at fylgja Hrœreki dag ok nótt; þeir menn höfðu lengi verit með Ólafi konungi, ok hafði hann þá reynt at truleik við sik; eigi er þess getit, at þeir væri ættstórir menn. Hrœrekr konungr gerði ýmist, at hann þagði marga daga, svá at engi maðr fékk orð af honum; en stundum var hann svá kátr ok glaðr, at þeim þótti at hverju orði gaman, því er hann mælti; en stundum mælti hann fátt ok ilt einu; svá var ok, at stundum drakk hann hvern af stokki, ok gerði alla úfœra, er nær honum váru; en optast drakk hann lítit. Ólafr konungr fékk honum vel skotsilfr. Opt gerði hann þat, þá er hann kom til herbergis, áðr hann lagðist til svefns, at hann lét taka inn mjöð, nökkurar byttur, ok gaf at drekka öllum herbergismönnum; af því varð hann þokkasæll.

I in my blindness might overcome them who overcame me in my sleep? My goodness, let us kill Óláfr digri. He has now no fears for himself. I shall make the plans, and I would not hold back my hands if I was able to use them, but I cannot do that because of my blindness, and you must therefore make the attack on him. And when Óláfr is slain, then I can foresee that the kingdom will pass to his enemies. Now it may be that I might become king; then you shall be my jarl.' His persuasion was so successful that Sveinn agreed to follow this infamous plan. The plan was that when the king set out for evensong, Sveinn would be standing out on the balcony before he got there and have a drawn cutlass under his coat. But when the king came out of the sitting room, then he got out sooner than Sveinn expected, and he looked at the king full in the face. Then he went pale and grew as white as a corpse and his hands failed him. The king noticed his terror and said: 'What is it now, Sveinn? Are you going to betray me?' Sveinn threw down his coat and his cutlass and fell at the king's feet and said: 'Everything in God's hands and yours, Lord.' The king told his men to seize Sveinn and he was put in irons. Then the king had Hrœrekr's seat moved to the other bench, and he pardoned Sveinn, and he left the country. The king then assigned Hrœrekr different quarters to sleep in from those that he slept in himself. There was a lot of his men that slept in those quarters. He got two of his men to be with Hrœrekr day and night. These men had long been with King Óláfr, and he had tried their loyalty to him. It is not told that they were men of high lineage. King Hrœrekr was changeable, he was silent on many days, so that no one could get a word from him, but sometimes he was so cheerful and merry that they found every word he spoke amusing, but sometimes he spoke a lot, but only what was unpleasant. It also happened sometimes that he drank everyone under the table, and made all those that were near him incapable, but generally he drank little. King Óláfr gave him plenty of pocket money. Often what he did when he came into his quarters, before he lay down to sleep, was have mead brought in, several casks, and gave all the men in those quarters something to drink. As a result he was popular.

82.

Maðr er nefndr Finnr litli, upplenzkr maðr, en sumir segja, at hann væri finskr at ætt; hann var allra manna minstr ok allra manna fóthvatastr, svá at engi hestr tók hann á rás; hann kunni manna bezt við skíð ok boga; hann hafði lengi verit þjónostumaðr Hrœreks konungs, ok farit opt erenda hans, þeirra er trúnaðar þurfti við; hann kunni vega um öll Upplönd; hann var ok málkunnigr þar öllu stórmenni. En er Hrœrekr konungr var tekinn í fangelsi, þá slóst Finnr í för þeirra, ok fór hann optast í sveit með knöpum ok þjónostumönnum; en hvert sinn er hann mátti, kom hann til þjónostu við Hrœrek konung, ok opt í tal, ok vildi konungr skömmum samfast mæla við hann, ok vildi ekki gruna láta tal þeirra. En er á leið várit, ok þeir sóttu út í Víkina, þá hvarf Finnr í brott frá liðinu nökkura daga; þá kom hann enn aptr ok dvaldist um hríð. Svá fór opt fram, ok var at því engi gaumr gefinn, því at margir váru umrenningar með liðinu.

There is a man called Fiðr litli (the Small), a man from Upplǫnd, but some say that he was a Lapp by descent. He was the smallest of all men and the fastest runner of all men, so that no horse could catch him up when running. He was the most skilled of men with skis and the bow. He had long been a servant of King Hrœrekr and often gone on errands for him that needed to be confidential. He knew the routes over the whole of Upplǫnd. He also knew many important men there to speak to. And when King Hrœrekr was put under the charge of a small number of men, then Finnr joined the group, and he generally kept company with boys and servants, but whenever he could, he got into the service of King Hrœrekr and often into speech with him, and the king was willing to talk with him for just short periods at a time and wanted to avoid any suspicion about their talks. And when spring drew to a close and they made their way out into the Vík, then Fiðr disappeared from the troop for a few days. Then he came back again and stayed for a while. Thus it happened often, and no notice was taken of it, for there were many vagabonds with the troop.

83.

Ólafr konungr kom til Túnsbergs fyrir páska, ok dvaldist þar mjök lengi um várit; þar kom þá til bœjarins mart kaupskipa, bæði Saxar ok Danir ok austan or Vík ok norðan or landi; var þar allmikit fjölmenni. Þá var ár mikit ok drykkjur miklar. Þat barst at á einu kveldi, at Hrœrekr konungr var kominn til herbergis, ok heldr síðla, ok hafði mjök drukkit, ok var þá allkátr; þá kom þar Finnr litli með mjaðarbyttu, ok var þat grasaðr mjöðr ok hinn sterkasti. Þá lét konungrinn gefa at drekka öllum þeim, er inni váru, alt til þess, er

King Óláfr came to Túnsberg before Easter and stayed there for a long time in the spring. Then many ships came there to the town, both Saxons and Danes and those from Vík in the east and from the north of the country. There was a very large number of people. It was a good year and there was much drinking. It happened one evening that King Hrœrekr had come to his quarters and rather late and had drunk a lot and was now very merry. Then Finnr litli came in with a cask of mead, and it was mead with herbs in

hverr sofnaði í sínu rúmi. Finnr var þá í brott genginn; ljós brann í herberginu. Þá vakti hann upp menn þá, er vanir váru at fylgja honum, ok segir, at hann vill ganga til garðs. Þeir höfðu skriðljós með sér, en niðamyrkr var úti; mikit salerni var í garðinum ok stóð á stöfum, en rið upp at ganga til dyranna. En er þeir Hrœrekr sátu í garðinum, þá heyrðu þeir at maðr mælti: Högg þú fjándann. Þá heyrðu þeir brest ok dett, sem nökkut félli. Hrœrekr konungr mælti: Fulldrukkit munu þeir hafa, er þar eigust við; farit til skjótt ok skilit þá. Þeir bjoggust skyndiliga ok hljópu út; en er þeir kómu á riðit, þá var sá höggvinn fyrr, er síðar gékk, ok drepnir þó báðir. Þar váru komnir menn Hrœreks konungs, Sigurðr hít, er verit hafði merkismaðr hans, ok þeir 15 saman; þar var þá Finnr litli. Þeir drógu líkin upp milli húsanna, en tóku konunginn ok höfðu með sér, hljópu þá á skútu, er þeir áttu, ok reru í brott. Sigvatr skáld svaf í herbergi Ólafs konungs; hann stóð upp um nóttina, ok skósveinn hans með honum, ok géngu út til hins mikla salernis; en er þeir skyldu aptr ganga ok ofan fyrir riðit, þá skriðnaði Sigvatr ok féll á kné, ok stakk niðr höndunum, ok var þar vátt undir; hann mælti: Þat hygg ek, at nú í kveld muni konungrinn hafa mörgum oss fengit karfafótinn, ok hló at. En er þeir kómu í herbergit, þar sem ljós brann, þá spurði skósveinninn: Hefir þú skeint þik, eða hví ertu í blóði einu allr? Hann svarar: Eigi em ek skeindr, en þó mun þetta tíðindum gegna. Hann vakti þá Þórð Fólason, merkismann ok rekkjufélaga sinn, ok géngu þeir út, ok höfðu með sér skriðljós, ok fundu brátt blóðit; þá leituðu þeir, ok fundu brátt líkin ok báru á kensl; þeir sá ok, at þar lá tréstobbi mikill, ok í skýlihögg mikil, ok spurðist þat síðan, at þat hafði gert verit til úlíkinda at teygja þá út, er drepnir váru. Þeir Sigvatr mæltu sín í milli, at nauðsyn væri til, at konungr vissi þessi tíðindi sem bráðast; þeir sendu sveininn þegar til herbergis þess, er Hrœrekr konungr hafði verit; þar sváfu menn allir, en konungr var í brottu. Hann vakti þá menn, er þar váru inni, ok sagði tíðindin. Stóðu menn upp ok fóru þegar þannug í garðinn, sem líkin váru.

it and of the strongest. Then Hrœrekr had everyone that was in there given drink, going on until they all went to sleep in their seats. Finnr had then gone away. There was a light burning in the room. Then Hrœrekr woke up the men who were accustomed to attend him, saying that he wanted to go into the yard. They had a lantern with them, but it was pitch dark outside. There was a large latrine in the yard and it stood on posts, and there were steps to get up to the doorway. And while Hrœrekr and the men were sitting in the yard, then they heard a man say: 'Strike down that fiend!' Then they heard a crash and a thump, as if something had fallen. King Hrœrekr said: 'They must have drunk plenty, the ones who are fighting there. Go up quickly and separate them.' They got ready quickly and ran out, but when they got to the steps, then the one that was in the rear was struck first, though they were both killed. It was King Hrœrekr's men that had come there, Sigurðr hít (the Sack), who had been his standard-bearer, in a party of twelve. Finnr litli was now there. They dragged the bodies up between the buildings, but grabbed the king and took him with them, then leapt onto a boat that they had and rowed away. The poet Sigvatr was asleep in King Óláfr's quarters. He got up in the night and his servant with him, and they went out to the great latrine. And when they were going to go back and down the steps, then Sigvatr slipped and fell on his knee and stuck his hands down and it was wet underneath. He said: 'I think that this evening the king must have taken away the sea legs from many of us.' And he laughed about it. But when they got into their quarters, where there was a light burning, then his servant asked: 'Have you scratched yourself, or why are you all covered in nothing but blood?' He replied: 'I am not scratched, but this must mean something has happened.' He then woke up his bedfellow, the standard-bearer Þórðr Fólason, and they went out, taking a lantern with them, and soon found the blood. Then they searched and soon found the bodies and recognized them. They

En þó at nauðsyn þœtti til, at konungr vissi sem fyrst þessi tíðindi, þá þorði engi at vekja hann. Þá mælti Sigvatr til Þórðar: Hvárt viltu heldr, lagsmaðr, vekja konunginn, eða segja honum tíðindin? Þórðr svarar: Fyrir engan mun þori ek at vekja hann, en segja mun ek honum tíðindin. Þá mælti Sigvatr: Mikit er enn eptir nætrinnar, ok kann vera áðr dagr sé, at Hrœrekr hafi fengit sér þat fylskni, at hann verði síðan eigi auðfundinn, en þeir munu enn skamt brott komnir, því at líkin váru vörm; skal oss aldregi henda sú skömm, at vér látim eigi konunginn vita þessi svik; gakk þú, Þórðr, upp í herbergit, ok bíð mín þar. Þá gékk Sigvatr til kirkju ok vakti klukkarann, ok bað hann hringja fyrir sál hirðmanna konungs, ok nefndi mennina, þá er vegnir váru. Klukkarinn gerir, sem hann bað. En við hringingina vaknaði konungr ok settist upp; hann spurði, hvárt þá væri óttusöngs mál. Þórðr svarar: Verri efni eru í, tíðindi mikil eru orðin; Hrœrekr konungr er á brott horfinn, en drepnir hirðmenn yðrir tveir. Þá spurði konungr eptir atburðum, þeim er þar höfðu orðit. Þórðr segir honum slíkt, er hann vissi. Þá stóð konungr upp ok lét blása til hirðstefnu. En er liðit kom saman, þá nefndi konungr menn til at fara alla vega frá bœnum at leita Hrœreks á sæ ok landi. Þórir langi tók skútu ok fór með 30 manna, ok er lýsti, sjá þeir skútur tvær litlar fara fyrir þeim. En er þeir sást, reru hvárir sem mest máttu. Þar var Hrœrekr konungr ok hafði 30 manna. En er saman dró með þeim, þá sneru þeir Hrœrekr at landi, ok hljópu þar upp á land allir, nema konungr settist upp í lyptingina. Hann mælti, bað þá vel fara ok heila hittast. Því næst reru þeir Þórir at landi. Þá skaut Finnr litli öru, ok kom sú á Þóri miðjan, ok fékk hann hana. En þeir Sigurðr hljópu allir í skóginn. En menn Þóris tóku lík hans, ok svá Hrœrek konung, ok fluttu út til Túnsbergs. Ólafr konungr tók þá við haldi Hrœreks konungs; hann lét þá vandliga gæta hans, ok galt mikinn varhuga við svikum hans, fékk til menn nótt ok dag at gæta hans. Hrœrekr konungr var þá hinn kátasti, ok fann engi maðr á honum, at eigi líkaði honum alt sem bezt.

also saw that there was a great tree stump lying there with a great gash in it, and it was discovered later that this had been done as a trick to entice out those that were slain. Sigvatr and the others told each other that it was essential for the king to know what had happened as soon as possible. They sent the lad straightaway to the quarters where King Hrœrekr had been. There everyone was asleep, but the king was gone. He woke the men who were inside and said what had happened. Some men got up and went straight away to the place in the yard where the bodies were. But though they thought it essential for the king to know as soon as possible what had happened, no one dared to wake him. Then Sigvatr spoke to Þórðr: 'Which would you rather do, comrade, wake up the king or tell him what has happened?' Þórðr replied: 'No way do I dare to wake him, but I can tell him what has happened.' Then Sigvatr said: 'There is still much of the night to go, and it may be that before it is day, Hrœrekr will have got himself a hiding place where he will not easily be found, and they will still not have got far, for the bodies were warm. We must never fall into the disgrace of failing to let the king know of this treason. You, Þórðr, go up into the quarters and wait for me there.' Then Sigvatr went to the church and woke up the bell-ringer and told him to toll the bell for the souls of the king's men, and he gave the names of the men that had been killed. The bell-ringer did as he asked. And at the ringing the king awoke and sat up. He asked whether it was time for matins. Þórðr replied: 'The reason for it is worse than that. Something important has happened. King Hrœrekr has disappeared and two of your men are killed.' Then the king asked about these events that had taken place there. Þórðr told him as much as he knew. Then the king got up and had a horn blown to summon a meeting of his followers. And when the troop assembled, then the king named men who were to go out in all directions from the town to search for Hrœrekr by sea and land. Þórir langi took a light ship and took thir-

ty men, and when it got light they saw two small ships sailing ahead of them. And when they saw each other, each lot rowed as hard as they could. It was King Hrœrekr there and he had thirty men. And when they drew close to each other, then Hrœrekr's party turned towards the shore and all leapt up ashore there except for the king sitting up on the raised deck. He spoke, bidding them farewell and meet again in health. Next Þórir and his men rowed to land. Then Finnr litli shot an arrow, and it struck Þórir in the middle of his body, and he was killed—but Sigurðr and his men all fled into the woods—and Þórir's men took his body and also King Hrœrekr and carried them to Túnsberg. King Óláfr then took charge of King Hrœrekr. He had him guarded carefully and took great precautions against his treachery, getting men to watch him night and day. King Hrœrekr was then most cheerful, and no one could see any sign in him that he was not as pleased as could be.

84.

It happened on Ascension Day that King Óláfr was going to High Mass. Then the bishop walked in procession round the church leading the king, and when they came back into the church, then the bishop led the king to his throne on the north side of the entrance to the choir. And there next to him King Hrœrekr was sitting, as he usually did. He had his coat pulled over his face. And when King Óláfr had sat down, then King Hrœrekr felt his shoulder with his hand and squeezed. Then he said: 'You are wearing fine cloth now, kinsman,' he says. King Óláfr replies: 'Now a great festival is being kept today in memory of when Jesus Christ ascended into heaven from earth.' King Hrœrekr replies: 'I do not understand, so that it is fixed in my mind, what you say about Christ. Much of what you say seems to me rather incredible. Yet many things have happened in ancient times.' And when Mass had begun, then King Óláfr stood up and held his arms up above his head and bowed towards the altar, and his coat hung back off his shoulders. King Hrœrekr sprang

Þat barst at uppstigningardag, at Óláfr konungr gékk til hámessu; þá gékk biskup með processíu um kirkju ok leiddi konunginn, en er þeir kómu aptr í kirkju, þá leiddi biskup konung til sætis síns fyrir norðan í kórnum. En þar sat hit næsta Hrœrekr konungr, sem hann var vanr; hann hafði yfirhöfnina fyrir andliti sér. En er Óláfr konungr hafði niðr sezt, þá tók Hrœrekr konungr á öxl honum hendinni ok þrýsti; hann mælti þá: Pellsklæði hefir þú nú, frændi, segir hann. Óláfr konungr svarar: Nú er hátíð mikil haldin í minning þess, er Jesus Kristr sté til himna af jörðu. Hrœrekr konungr svarar: Ekki skil ek af, svá at mér hugfestist, þat er þér segit frá Kristi; þykki mér þat mart heldr útrúligt, er þér segit; en þó hafa mörg dœmi orðit í forneskju. En er messan var upphafin, þá stóð Óláfr konungr upp, ok hélt upp höndunum yfir höfuð sér ok laut til altaris, ok bar yfirhöfnina aptr af herðum honum. Hrœrekr konungr spratt þá upp skjótt ok hart; hann lagði þá til Óláfs konungs saxnífi þeim, er rytningr er kallaðr; lagit kom í yfirhöfnina við: herðarnar, er

hann hafði lotit undan; skárust mjök klæðin, en konungr varð eigi sárr. En er Ólafr konungr fann þetta tilræði, þá hjóp hann fram við á gólfit. Hrœrekr konungr lagði til hans annat sinni saxinn, ok misti hans, ok mælti: Flýr þú nú, Ólafr digri, fyrir mér blindum?: Konungr bað sína menn taka hann ok leiða hann út or kirkjunni, ok svá var gert. Eptir þessa atburði eggjuðu menn Ólaf konung at láta drepa Hrœrek konung, ok er þat, sögðu þeir, hin mesta gæfuraun yðr, konungr, at hafa hann með yðr, ok þyrma honum, hverigar úhæfur er hann tekr til; en hann liggr um þat nótt ok dag at veita yðr líflát. En þegar er þér sendit hann á brott frá yðr, þá sjám vér eigi mann til þess, at svá fái gætt hans, at örvænt sé, at hann komist í brott. En ef hann verðr lauss, þá mun hann þegar flokk uppi hafa ok gera mart ilt. Konungr svarar: Rétt er þat mælt, at margr hefir dauða tekit fyrir minni tilgerðir en Hrœrekr; en trauðr em ek at týna þeim sigri, er ek fékk á Upplendinga konungum, er ek tók þá 5 á einum morni, ok náða ek svá öllu ríki þeirra, at ek þurfta enskis þeirra banamaðr at verða, því at þeir váru allir frændr mínir; en þó fæ ek nú varla sét, hvárt Hrœrekr mun fá mik nauðgaðan til eða eigi at láta drepa hann. Hrœrekr hafði fyrir þá sök tekit hendinni á öxl Ólafi konungi, at hann vildi vita, hvárt hann var í brynju.

Maðr er nefndr Þórarinn Nefjólfsson; hann var íslenzkr maðr, hann var kynjaðr norðan or landi; ekki var hann ættstórr, ok allra manna vitrastr ok orðspakastr; hann var djarfmæltr við tigna menn; hann var farmaðr mikill ok var löngum utanlendis. Þórarinn var manna ljótastr, ok bar þat mest frá, hversu illa hann var limaðr; hann hafði hendr

up quickly and forcefully. He then stabbed at King Óláfr with a dagger of the kind known as rýtningr. The thrust landed on the coat by his shoulder as he bent forward away from it.[3] His clothes were much damaged, but the king was not wounded. And when King Óláfr felt this assault, then he leapt forward onto the floor. King Hrœrekr stabbed at him a second time with the dagger and missed him and said: 'You are running away now, Óláfr digri, from me, a blind man.' The king told his men to take him and lead him out of the church, and they did so. After this incident people urged King Óláfr to have Hrœrekr killed. 'And it is,' they say, 'a very great tempting of your luck, king, to keep him with you and spare him, such wickedness as he keeps committing, for he lies in wait day and night to bring about your death. But if you send him away from you, we do not know of anyone who would be able to guard him so that he had no hope of getting away. But if he goes free, then he will immediately raise a band and cause a lot of trouble.' The king replies: 'What you say is right enough, that many have suffered death for doing less than Hrœrekr, but I am reluctant to spoil the victory that I gained over the kings of the Upplendingar, when I captured five of them in one morning, and so got control of all their realms without needing to become the slayer of any one of them, for they were all kinsmen of mine. But yet I can hardly see now whether Hrœrekr will force me to it or not, to have him slain.' The reason Hrœrekr had felt King Óláfr's shoulder with his hand was that he wanted to know whether he was wearing a coat of mail.

85.

There was a man called Þórarinn Nefjólfsson. He was an Icelandic man, his family were from the north of the country. He was not of high lineage and he was the most sensible of men and most intelligent of speakers. He was bold in speech with people of rank. He was a great trader and was abroad for long periods. Þórarinn was the ugliest of men, and the

miklar ok ljótar, en fœtrnir váru þó miklu ljótari. Þórarinn var staddr í Túnsbergi, er þessi tíðindi urðu, er áðr var frásagt; hann var málkunnigr Ólafi konungi. Þórarinn bjó þá kaupskip, er hann átti, ok ætlaði til Íslands um sumarit. Ólafr konungr hafði Þórarin í boði sínu nökkura daga ok talaði mart við hann; svaf Þórarinn í konungs herbergi. Þat var einn morgin snimma, at konungrinn vakti, en aðrir menn sváfu í herberginu; þá var sól farin lítt þat, ok var ljóst mjök inni. Konungr sá, at Þórarinn hafði rétt fót annan undan klæðum; hann sá á fótinn um hríð; þá vöknuðu menn í herberginu. Konungr mælti til Þórarins: Vakat hefi ek um hríð, ok hefi ek sét þá sýn, er mér þykkir mikils um vert, en þat er mannsfótr sá, er ek hygg, at engi skal hér í kaupstaðinum ljótari vera; ok bað aðra menn hyggja at, hvárt svá sýndist. En allir er sá, þá sönnuðu, at svá væri. Þórarinn fann, hvar til var mælt, ok svarar: Fátt er svá einna hluta, at örvænt sé, at hitti annan slíkan, ok er þat líkligast, at hér sé enn svá, Konungr mælti: Heldr vil ek því at fulltingja, at eigi muni fást jafnljótr fótr, ok svá þótt ek skylda veðja um. Þá mælti Þórarinn: Búinn em ek at veðja um þat við yðr, at ek mun finna í kaupstaðinum ljótara fót. Konungr segir: Þá skal sá okkarr kjósa bœn af öðrum, er sannara hefir. Svá skal vera, segir Þórarinn. Hann brá þá undan klæðnunm öðrum fœtinum, ok var sá engum mun fegri, ok þar var af hin minsta táin. Þá mælti Þórarinn: Sé hér nú, konungr, annan fót, ok er sjá því ljótari, at hér er af ein táin; ok á ek veðféit. Konungr segir: Er hinn fótrinn því úfegri, at þar eru 5 tær ferligar á þeim, en hér eru 4, ok á ek at kjósa bœn at þér. Þórarinn segir: Dýrt er dróttins orð, eða hverja bœn viltu af mér þiggja? Hann svarar: Þá, at þú flytir Hrœrek konung til Grœnlands, ok fœrir hann Leifi Eiríkssyni. Þórarinn svarar: Eigi hefi ek komit til Grœnlands. Konungr segir: Farmaðr slíkr sem þú ert, þá er þér nú mál at fara til Grœnlands, ef þú hefir eigi fyrr komit. Þórarinn svarar fá um þetta mál fyrst. En er konungr hélt fram þessarri málaleitan, þá veikst Þórarinn eigi með öllu af hendi, ok mælti svá: Heyra skal

most extraordinary thing was how horrible his limbs were. He had large and ugly hands, but yet his feet were much uglier. Þórarinn was now located in Túnsberg when these events were taking place that have just been narrated. He and King Óláfr knew each other to speak to. Þórarinn now got a trading ship ready that he owned, and was intending to go to Iceland in the summer. King Óláfr had Þórarinn as a guest for a few days and had conversations with him. Þórarinn slept in the king's quarters. It was early one morning that the king was awake while other men in the quarters were asleep. Just then the sun had come up a little, and it was very light indoors. The king noticed that Þórarinn had stretched out one foot from under the bedclothes. He looked at the foot for a while. Then the men in the quarters began to wake up. The king said to Þórarinn: 'I have been awake for a while, and I have seen a sight that has impressed me greatly, and that is a man's foot than which I think there cannot in this market town be one uglier.' And he told other men to consider whether this did not seem to be true. And everyone who saw it agreed that it was so. Þórarinn realized what they were talking about and replied: 'There are few things so special that it cannot be expected that another such will be found, and it is very likely to be so in this case too.' The king said: 'I am still prepared to assert that another foot as ugly as this will not be found, and even if I had to lay a wager on it.' Then Þórarinn said: 'I am prepared to lay a wager with you on that, that I shall find an uglier foot in the town.' The king says: 'Then whichever of us turns out to be right shall choose a favour from the other.' 'So it shall be,' says Þórarinn. He then put his other foot out from under the bedclothes, and this was in no way more beautiful, and it lacked the big toe. Then said Þórarinn: 'See here now, king, another foot, and this is the uglier in that on this one a toe is missing, and I have won the wager.' The king says: 'The other foot is the uglier, in that there are five hideous toes on that one, but on this there are four, and it is for me

ek yðr láta, konungr, bœn þá, er ek hafða hugat at biðja, ef mér bœrist veðféit; en þat er, at ek vilda biðja yðr hirðvistar; en ef þér veitit mér þat, þá verð ek skyldari til at leggjast eigi undir höfuð, þat er þér vilit kvatt hafa. Konungr játaði þessu, ok gerðist Þórarinn hirðmaðr hans. Þá bjó Þórarinn skip sitt, ok er hann var búinn, þá tók hann við Hrœreki konungi. En er þeir skildust Ólafr konungr ok Þórarinn, þá mælti Þórarinn: Nú berr svá til, konungr, sem eigi er örvænt ok opt kann verða, at vér komim eigi fram Grœnlandsferðinni, berr oss at Íslandi eða öðrum löndum, hvernug skal ek skilja við konung þenna þess, at yðr megi líka? Konungr segir: Ef þú kemr til Íslands, þá skaltu selja hann í hendr Guðmundi Eyjólfssyni eða Skapta lögsögumanni, eða öðrum nökkurum höfðingjum, þeim er taka vilja við vináttu minni ok jartegnum. En ef þik berr at öðrum löndum, þeim er hér eru nœrr, þá haga þá svá til, at þá vitir víst, at Hrœrekr komi aldri síðan til Noregs; en ger þat því at einu, ef þú sér engi önnur föng á. En er Þórarinn var búinn ok byr gaf, þá sigldi hann alt útleið fyrir utan eyjar ok norðr frá Líðandisnesi, stefndi hann í haf út. Honum byrjaði eigi skjótt, en hann varaðist þat mest at koma við landit. Hann sigldi fyrir sunnan Ísland, ok hafði vita af, ok svá vestr um landit í Grœnlandshaf; þá fékk hann réttu stóra ok válk mikit, en er á leið sumarit, tók hann Ísland í Breiðafirði. Þorgils Arason kom þá fyrst til þeirra virðingamanna. Þórarinn segir honum orðsending ok vináttumál ok jartegnir Ólafs konungs, er fylgðu viðrtöku Hrœreks konungs. Þorgils varð við vel, ok bauð til sín Hrœreki konungi, ok var hann með Þorgilsi Arasyni um vetrinn. Hann undi þar eigi, ok beiddi, at Þorgils léti fylgja honum til Guðmundar, ok segir, at hann þóttist þat spurt hafa, at með Guðmundi var rausn mest á Íslandi, ok væri hann honum til handa sendr. Þorgils gerði sem hann beiddi, fékk menn til ok lét fylgja honum til handa Guðmundi á Möðruvöllu. Tók Guðmundr vel við Hrœreki fyrir sakir konungs orðsendingar, ok var hann með Guðmundi vetr annan; þá undi hann þar eigi lengr. Þá fékk Guðmundr ho-

to choose a favour from you.[4] Þórarinn says: 'One's lord's word outweighs others, so what favour do you wish to have from me?' He says: 'This, that you carry Hrœrekr to Greenland and take him to Leifr Eiríksson.' Þórarinn replies: 'I have not been to Greenland.' The king says: 'A voyager like you, it is time you went to Greenland if you have never been there.' Þórarinn made little response to this to begin with, but when the king persisted with this request, then Þórarinn did not entirely reject it, and said as follows: 'I shall let you hear, king, the favour that I had intended to ask if I had won the wager, and that is, that I was going to ask you if I might become one of your men. And if you will grant me that, then I shall be the more obliged not to put aside what you desire to have commissioned.' The king agreed to this, and Þórarinn became a member of his following. Then Þórarinn prepared his ship, and when he was ready, then he took charge of King Hrœrekr. And when they parted, King Ólafr and Þórarinn, then Þórarinn said: 'Now should it turn out, king, as is not unlikely and may often happen, that we are unable to complete the journey to Greenland, and we are carried to Iceland or to other countries, how shall I dispose of this king so that you may be pleased?' The king says: 'If you come to Iceland, then you shall hand him over to Guðmundr Eyjólfsson or Lawspeaker Skapti or any other leading men who are willing to accept my friendship and tokens. But if you are carried to other countries that are nearer to here, then you must arrange it in such a way that you know for certain that Hrœrekr will never come back to Norway alive, and you are only to do this if you find there is no other alternative.' Now when Þórarinn was ready and there was a favourable wind, then he sailed all along the outer route beyond the islands, and north of Líðandisnes he set his course out to sea. The winds were not very favourable, but he took care most of all to keep away from the shore. He sailed to the south of Iceland and could see signs of its closeness, and so west round the coast into the Greenland Sea. Then he

num vist á litlum bœ, er heitir á Kálfskinni, ok var þar fátt hjóna; þar var Hrœrekr hinn þriðja vetr, ok sagði hann svá, at síðan er hann lét af konungdómi, at hann hefði þar verit svá, at honum hafði bezt þótt, því at þar var hann af öllum mest metinn. Eptir um sumarit fékk Hrœrekr sótt, þá er hann leiddi til bana. Svá er sagt, at sá einn konungr hvílir á Íslandi. Þórarinn Nefjólfsson hafðist síðan lengi í förum, en var stundum með Ólafi konungi.

encountered strong currents and much tossing about, and towards the end of summer he came to land in Iceland in Breiðifjǫrðr. Þorgils Arason then came up to them first of any men of rank. Þórarinn tells him about King Ólafr's message and the friendship and tokens that would accompany his taking charge of King Hrœrekr. Þorgils responded well and invited King Hrœrekr to stay with him, and he stayed with Þorgils Arason for the winter. He was not happy there and asked Þorgils to have him taken to Guðmundr's, saying that he had heard that Guðmundr kept the highest state in Iceland, and that he had been sent into his keeping. Þorgils did as he asked, providing him with an escort and had him taken to the keeping of Guðmundr at Mǫðruvellir. Guðmundr welcomed him for the sake of the king's messages and he stayed the second winter with Guðmundr. Then he could not bear it there any longer. Then Guðmundr provided him with lodging on a small farm called at Kálfskinn, and there were few servants there. Hrœrekr stayed there the third winter, and he said this, that since he had given up his kingdom, that was the place where he had stayed, that he had been most content, because there he had been most highly respected by everyone. The following summer Hrœrekr took a sickness that brought about his death. So it is said that this is the only king who lies buried in Iceland. Þórarinn Nefjólfsson spent a long time in trading voyages, but sometimes stayed with King Ólafr.

Endnotes

1   The Icelandic text below is from Finnur Jónson's edition of *Heimskringla*, published 1893–1900 by Samfund til udgivelse af gammel nordisk litteratur and is in the public domain. The translation is from *Heimskringla* II: Óláfr Haraldsson (the Saint), translated by Alison Finlay and Anthony Faulkes, Viking Society for Northern Research, 2014 and is used with permission from the translators. Minor edits to the translation have been made, including Americanized spelling and occasional glossing.

2   In this narrative, maiming is clearly a mark of distinction, since the king's two biggest adversaries are maimed whereas the others are banished. The maiming might be symbolic: King Guðrøðr loses his tongue since he had been the most vocal of the king's opponents. King Hrœrekr is blinded because of his great wisdom, with sight and wisdom being closely connected in Old Norse culture.

3   King Hrœrekr's valiant attempt to strike King Óláfr himself, in spite of his blindness, is possibly meant as a sign of royal steadfastness and spirit, but another message of the narrative is that a blind man can also be dangerous.

4   The introduction of this secondary character, a maimed warrior who lacks a toe, to rid the king of his maimed adversary may be a pure coincidence and yet it seems significant.

The *Prose Edda*[1] (ca. 1220–40)

Snorri Sturluson
Contributed by Kolfinna Jónatansdóttir

Introduction

The Prose Edda is commonly attributed to the chieftain Snorri Sturluson and consists of four main parts: *The Prologue, Gylfaginning, Skáldskaparmál,* and *Háttatal.* A big part of the work is meant to be a handbook for poets on form and allegories, and since many of the allegories have their roots in myths, Christian poets needed to familiarize themselves with Old Norse myths in order to be able to continue the tradition. One of the narratives in *Gylfaginning* is about the death of Baldr and how Loki tricks the blind Höðr into killing him. Höðr is named as Baldr's killer in various poems as well as in Saxo Grammaticus's *History of the Danes*, but it is only in *The Prose Edda* that Höðr is explicitly said to be blind and tricked by Loki. It has to be taken into account that many of the poems just refer briefly to Baldr's death, but don't describe the situation in detail, so there is a possibility that what may have been considered common knowledge has been left out.

Höðr's blindness is important in The *Prose Edda*, and in Skáldskaparmál, which explains poetic diction, one way to refer to Höðr is to call him *hinn blindi áss* (the blind god). When he's introduced for the first time in *Gylfaginning* he is said to be blind and "of sufficient strength, but the gods would desire that no occasion should rise of naming this god, for the work of his hands shall long be held in memory among gods and men." When Loki approaches him with the fatal wand, Höðr is standing outside of the circle of gods who are having fun testing Baldr's invulnerability. Due to his blindness he can't participate in the game and is not part of the actions of the other gods, but with Loki's help he is briefly included in the game, with dire consequences. The other gods leave Höðr out of the game due to his impairment, and that isolation leads him to be willing to throw the wand Loki hands him, causing great misfortune, both to himself and ultimately the other gods, since the loss of Baldr can be seen as a retribution for not including Höðr.

Many theories have been presented to explain why Höðr is blind in *The Prose Edda's* version of the myth of Baldr's death. Scholars have wondered whether Höðr's blindness may be symbolic, have an ethical dimension, or be influenced by biblical or contemporary European narratives. Höðr isn't the only god who is impaired in the Old Norse pantheon, but his impairment is the only one that has negative connotations. Týr sacrificed one of his hands so the wolf Fenrisúlfr could be fettered and Óðinn gave one of his eyes to gain more wisdom. Those impairments do not seem to hinder those gods at all, but reflect injuries that those who fought in battle could have suffered. It has been suggested that missing body parts on gods and heroes are a sign of how their strength or abilities have been enhanced or that they may have supernatural powers, such as Óðinn's eye being an indicator of his second sight, and Týr being one handed being a symbol of his strength as a god of battle. It is unclear whether Höðr is born blind or blinded later on, and his blindness is not explained with any kind of sacrifice or special powers he could have acquired instead.

Bibliography

Bragg, Lois. "From the Mute God to the Lesser God: Disability in Medieval Celtic and Old Norse Literature." *Disability & Society*, vol. 12, no. 2, 1997, pp. 165–77. doi: 10.1080/09687599727317.

———. *Oedipus borealis: The Aberrant Body in Old Icelandic Myth and Saga.* Farleigh Dickinson University Press, 2004.

Jónatansdóttir, Kolfinna. "'Blindur er betri en brenndur sé': um norræna guði og skerðingar." *Fötlun og menning: Íslandssagan í öðru ljósi*, edited by Hanna Björg Sigurjónsdóttir, Ármann Jakobsson, and Kristín Björnsdóttir. Rannsóknarsetur í fötlunarfræðum, 2013, pp. 27–49.

Lassen, Annette. *Øjet og blindheden i norrøn litteratur og mytologi.* Museum Tusculanum, 2003.

Sexton, John. "Difference and Disability: On the Logic of Naming in the Icelandic Sagas." *Disability in the Middle Ages: Reconsiderations and Reverberations*, edited by Joshua R. Eyler. Ashgate, 2016, pp. 149–63.

Þá mælti Gangleri: "Hafa nökkur meiri tíðendi orðit með ásunum? Allmikit þrekvirki vann Þórr í þessi ferð."

Hárr svarar: "Vera mun at segja frá þeim tíðendum, er meira þótti vert ásunum. En þat er upphaf þeirar sögu, at Baldr inn góða dreymði drauma stóra ok hættliga um líf sitt. En er hann sagði ásunum draumana, þá báru þeir saman ráð sín, ok var þat gert at beiða griða Baldri fyrir allskonar háska, ok Frigg tók svardaga til þess, at eira skyldu Baldri eldr ok vatn, járn ok alls konar málmr, steinar, jörðin, viðirnir, sóttirnar, dýrin, fuglarnir, eitrit, ormarnir.

En er þetta var gert ok vitat, þá var þat skemmtun Baldrs ok ásanna, at hann skyldi standa upp á þingum, en allir aðrir skyldu sumir skjóta á hann, sumir höggva til, sumir berja grjóti, en hvat sem at var gert, sakaði hann ekki, ok þótti þetta öllum mikill frami.

En er þetta sá Loki Laufeyjarson, þá líkaði honum illa, er Baldr sakaði ekki. Hann gekk til Fensalar til Friggjar ok brá sér í konu líki. Þá spyrr Frigg, ef sú kona vissi, hvat æsir höfðust at á þinginu. Hon sagði, at allir skutu at Baldri ok þat, at hann sakaði ekki.

Þá mælti Frigg: "Eigi munu vápn eða viðir granda Baldri. Eiða hefi ek þegit af öllum þeim." Þá spyr konan: "Hafa allir hlutir eiða unnit at eira Baldri?" Þá svarar Frigg: "Vex viðarteinungr einn fyrir vestan Valhöll. Sá er mistilteinn kallaðr. Sá þótti mér ungr at krefja eiðsins." Því næst hvarf konan á braut, en Loki tók mistiltein ok sleit upp ok gekk til þings.

En Höðr stóð útarliga í mannhringnum, því at hann var blindr. Þá mælti Loki við hann: "Hví skýtr þú ekki at Baldri?" Hann svarar: "Því, at ek sé eigi, hvar Baldr er, ok þat annat, at ek em vápnlauss." Þá mælti Loki: "Gerðu þó í líking annarra manna ok

Then spake Gangleri: "Have any more matters of note befallen among the Æsir?[2] A very great deed of valor did Thor achieve on that journey."[3]

Hárr made answer: "Now shall be told of those tidings which seemed of more consequence to the Æsir. The beginning of the story is this, that Baldr[o] the Good dreamed great and perilous dreams touching his life. When he told these dreams to the Æsir, then they took counsel together: and this was their decision: to ask safety for Baldr from all kinds of dangers. And Frigg took oaths to this purport, that fire and water should spare Baldr, likewise iron and metal of all kinds, stones, earth, trees, sicknesses, beasts, birds, venom, serpents. And when that was done and made known, then it was a diversion of Baldr's and the Æsir, that he should stand up in the Thing,[o4] and all the others should some shoot at him, some hew at him, some beat him with stones; but whatsoever was done hurt him not at all, and that seemed to them all a very worshipful thing.

"But when Loki Laufeyarson saw this, it pleased him ill that Baldr took no hurt. He went to Fensalir to Frigg, and made himself into the likeness of a woman. Then Frigg asked if that woman knew what the Æsir did at the Thing. She said that all were shooting at Baldr, and moreover, that he took no hurt.

"Then said Frigg: 'Neither weapons nor trees may hurt Baldr: I have taken oaths of them all.' Then the woman asked: 'Have all things taken oaths to spare Baldr?' and Frigg answered: 'There grows a tree-sprout alone westward of Valhall: it is called Mistletoe; I thought it too young to ask the oath of.' Then straightway the woman turned away; but Loki took Mistletoe and pulled it up and went to the Thing.

Baldr *The son of Óðinn and Frigg.*   **Thing [Þing]** *An assembly.*

veit Baldri sæmð sem aðrir menn. Ek mun vísa þér til, hvar hann stendr. Skjót at honum vendi þessum."

Höðr tók mistiltein ok skaut at Baldri at tilvísun Loka. Flaug skotit í gegnum Baldr, ok féll hann dauðr til jarðar, ok hefir þat mest óhapp verit unnit með goðum ok mönnum.

Þá er Baldr var fallinn, þá féllust öllum ásum orðtök ok svá hendr at taka til hans, ok sá hverr til annars, ok váru allir með einum hug til þess, er unnit hafði verkit, en engi mátti hefna. Þar var svá mikill griðastaðr. En þá er æsirnir freistuðu at mæla, þá var hitt þó fyrr, at grátrinn kom upp, svá at engi mátti öðrum segja með orðunum frá sínum harmi. En Óðinn bar þeim mun verst þenna skaða sem hann kunni mesta skyn, hversu mikil af-taka ok missa ásunum var í fráfalli Baldrs.

"Hödr stood outside the ring of men, because he was blind. Then spake Loki to him: 'Why dost thou not shoot at Baldr?' He answered: 'Because I see not where Baldr is; and for this also, that I am weaponless.' Then said Loki: 'Do thou also after the manner of other men, and show Baldr honor as the other men do. I will direct thee where he stands; shoot at him with this wand.'

"Hödr took Mistletoe and shot at Baldr, being guided by Loki: the shaft flew through Baldr, and he fell dead to the earth; and that was the greatest mischance that has ever befallen among gods and men.

"Then, when Baldr was fallen, words failed all the Æsir, and their hands likewise to lay hold of him; each looked at the other, and all were of one mind as to him who had wrought the work, but none might take vengeance, so great a sanctuary was in that place. But when the Æsir tried to speak, then it befell first that weeping broke out, so that none might speak to the others with words concerning his grief. But Odin bore that misfortune by so much the worst, as he had most perception of how great harm and loss for the Æsir were in the death of Baldr.

Endnotes

1 The texts below are taken from Arthur Gilchrist Brodeur's 1916 edition *The Prose Edda* by Snorri Sturluson, Scandinavian Classics 5, The American-Scandinavian Foundation. Brodeur's edition was a facing text translation. The direct translation in the introduction is also taken from this edition. Notes and glosses have been provided by Kolfinna Jónatansdóttir.

2 In Old Norse myths the gods are divided into two groups, Vanir and Æsir (sg. Áss). The majority of the gods are Æsir and therefore that word is often used to refer to all the gods

3 This refers to the previous chapter where Þórr visits Útgarða-Loki.

4 Thing [Þing] were held regularly in Iceland, both locally and on a national scale on Þingvellir. Chieftains and farmers met at such assemblies and settled their differences and court cases were held.

DRAMA

The Cure of the Blind Man from the Chester Cycle[1] (ca. 1531–75)

Contributed by Kurt Schreyer

Introduction

The Cure of the Blind Man takes place during the first part of Play 13 of the *Chester Cycle*, which was performed by the Glovers' Guild and which also stages the raising of Lazarus. Declaring, *"Ego sum lux mundi* [I am the light of the world; Latin]," Jesus opens the play with a self-introduction that echoes Deus' first lines at the very beginning of the cycle: *"Ego sum alpha et oo* [I am the alpha and omega; Latin]." By declaring himself "the light of this world" (l. 1) in this way, Jesus foregrounds both the importance of being in communion with the Father and the play's use of the metaphors of light and darkness, seeing and blindness as powerful ways of understanding that relationship. Before he can "goe to Bethenye" (l. 16) and cure Lazarus, a boy enters leading a man who is "blynd and never did see" (l. 41) and whom the play identifies only as "Caecus," or "Blind Man." David Mills's suggestion that the pair would very likely have approached the pageant wagon through the crowd cannot be understated if we consider the remarkable immediacy of the play's meditation on the community's responsibility toward the blind.[2] The Blind Man is as much a contemporary citizen of Chester as he is a figure from the biblical past. Jesus thus cautions both his followers and the audience against equating physical blindness with sin: "Hit was neither for his offence, / neither the synne of his parentes, / or other fault or negligence / that hee was blynd borne" (ll. 51–54). We would do well, therefore, to follow Joshua Eyler's suggestion that—rather than imposing our own models of disability, whether re-ligious, cultural, or medical—we allow them to emerge organically from medieval texts themselves.[3] Though he is promptly healed by Jesus, Caecus must still endure the cross-examination of his fellow citizens and the Pharisees. The Glovers' play is carefully attentive to the biblical account in John 9:1–41, yet it has a poignancy which Chester audiences must have felt, as when Jesus stands side by side with the Blind Man under the scornful gaze of the Pharisees, enacting the promise that "My light to them shall well appeare / which cleeve to mee alwaye" (ll. 65–66).

Bridging familiar Nativity and Passion episodes, *The Cure of the Blind Man* and *Christ and the Leper* (discussed below) must perform the crucial task of succinctly encapsulating Jesus' public ministry. And both pageants do so brilliantly—emphasizing again and again that the Christian community must reach out to and include all people, not only those who rank high and low, but especially those who are spiritually and physically in need of "almes" and "charitie" (l. 40). Indeed, there is a very real sense in which Jesus' encounter with the Blind Man suggests that membership in the community—that is to say spiritual health—is conditioned precisely by a person's ability to treat those with disabilities as "your owne neighbour and of your owne kynd" (l. 39). As Jesus explains, his "Fathers workes" is "to heale the sicke and restore the blynd to sight" in order "that there may be one flocke and one sheppard" (ll. 23–24, 28).

If this sounds rather romantic, the Glovers' play dramatizes a community that is in fact as friable as it is fractious, quite prone to indifference if not the sneering rejection of its disadvantaged members, and we witness several characters—not only religious authorities but ordinary citizens—who willfully denigrate the Blind Man and Jesus. But they do so, the play further suggests, at the peril of alienating themselves. Most conspicuously, when Primus and Secundus Judeus (First and Second Jew) attempt to stone Jesus, they—and we, the audience—undergo a kind of blindness as he "suddenly disappears from sight" ("*et statim evanescit Jesus*," l. 284 stage direction). Whether or not this remarkable theatrical vanishing (the play itself says that it is "Quyntly" or cleverly done) serves as a warning against spiritual blindness and loss of communion with Jesus and the Father, the play rather disturbingly impels us to share the same loss of vision which the callous Primus and Secundus Judeus undergo. As a community, therefore, we are all in danger, the Glovers' play suggests, of failing to recognize the Blind Man as "your owne neighbour and of your owne kynd" (l. 39).

Bibliography

Deimling, Hermann, and G.W. Matthews, eds. *The Chester Plays*, Early English Text Society, Extra Series 62 and 115. Oxford University Press, 1892 and 1916.

Gusick, Barbara I. "Groping in Darkness: The Man Born Blind and Christ's Ministry in the York Cycle." *New Approaches to European Theater of the Middle Ages: An Ontology*, edited by Barbara I. Gusick and Edelgard E. DuBruck. Peter Lang, 2004, pp. 45–71.

Hsy, Jonathan. "Blind Advocacy: Blind Readers, Disability Theory, and Accessing John Gower." *Accessus: A Journal of Premodern Literature and New Media*, vol. 1, 2013, art. 2. https://scholarworks.wmich.edu/accessus/vol1/iss1/2/.

Lumiansky, Robert M., ed. *The Chester Mystery Cycle: Essays and Documents*. University of North Carolina Press, 1983.

————— and David Mills. *The Chester Mystery Cycle*, Early English Text Society Supplementary Series 3. Oxford University Press, 1974.

Metzler, Irina. *Disability in Medieval Europe: Thinking about Physical Impairment during the High Middle Ages, c. 1100–1400*. Routledge, 2006.

Singer, Julie. *Blindness and Therapy in Late Medieval French and Italian Poetry*. Brewer, 2011.

Wells, Scott. "The Exemplary Blindness of Francis of Assisi." *Disability in the Middle Ages: Reconsiderations and Reverberations*, edited by Joshua R. Eyler. Ashgate, 2010, pp. 67–80.

Wheatley, Edward. "'Blind' Jews and Blind Christians: Metaphorics of Marginalization in Medieval Europe." *Exemplaria: A Journal of Theory in Medieval and Renaissance Studies*, vol. 14, no. 2, 2002, pp. 351–82.

—————. *Stumbling Blocks Before the Blind: Medieval Constructions of a Disability*. University of Michigan Press, 2010.

DRAMATIS PERSONAE

Jesus
Puer°
Caecus°
Petrus°
John
Primus Vicinus°
Secundus Vicinus°
Primus Pharaseus°
Secundus Pharaseus°
Nuntius°
Mater°
Pater°
Primus Judeus°
Secundus Judeus°

JESUS *"Ego sum lux mundi. Qui sequitur
   me non ambulat in tenebris sed habebit
   lumen vitae."°*
Brethren, I am Filius Dei, the light of
   this world.
Hee that followeth me walketh not in
   dearknes
but hath the light of life; the scriptures
   so recorde;
as patriarches and prophets of me
   bearen wytnes,°
both Abraham, Isaack, and Jacob in
   there sundrye testimonies,
unto whom I was promised before the
   world beganne
to paye there° ransome and to become
   man.
Ego et Pater unum sumus:° my Father and
   I are all on,°
which hath me sent from the throne
   sempiternall°

10   to preach and declare his will unto man
because hee loveth him above his creatures all
as his treasure and dearlinge most
   principall—
man, I say agayne, which is his owne
   elect,
above all creatures peculiarlye select.
Wherfore, deare brethren, yt is my
   mynd and will
to goe to Bethenye that standeth here-
   bye,
my Fathers hestes° and command
   mentes to fulfill.
For I am the good sheppard that
   putteth his life in jeoperdye
to save his flocke, which I love so ten-
   derlye;

Puer *Boy*   **Caecus** *Blind Man*   **Petrus** *Peter*   **Primus Vicinus** *First Neighbor*   **Secundus Vicinus** *Second Neighbor*   **Primus Pharaseus** *First Pharisee*   **Secundus Pharaseus** *Second Pharisee*   **Nuntius** *Messenger*   **Mater** *Mother*   **Pater** *Father*   **Primus Judeus** *First Jew*   **Secundus Judeus** *Second Jew*   **Ego sum...vitae** *"I am the light of the world. Whoever who follows me will not walk in darkness, but will have the light of life"* [Latin; John 8:12]   **wytnes** *witness*   **there** *their*   **Ego et Pater unum sumus** *"I and the Father are one"* [Latin; John 10:30]   **on** *one*   **sempiternall** *everlasting*   **hestes** *wishes*

20   as yt is written of mee—the scripture
      beareth wytnes—
    "bonus pastor ponit animam suam pro
      [ovibus] suis."°
    Goe we therfore, brethren, while the
      day is light,
    to do my Fathers workes, as I am fully
      mynded;
    to heale the sicke and restore the blynd
      to sight,
    that the prophecye of mee may be
      fulfilled.
    For other sheepe I have which are to me
      commytted.
    They be not of this flocke, yet will I
      them regard,
    that there may be one flocke and one
      sheppard.
    But or° we goe hence, printe these say-
      inges in your mynd and harte;
30   recorde them and keepe them in memo-
      rye.
    Contynue in my worde; from yt doe not
      departe.
    Therby shall all men knowe most per-
      fectlye
    that you are my disciples and of my
      familie.
    Goe not before me, but let my word be
      your guide;
    then in your doinges you shall alwayse
      well speede.°
        "Si vos manseritis in sermone meo, veri
          discipuli mei eritis, et cognoscetis
          veritatem, et veritas liberabit vos."°
    PUER (*ducens Caecum*°) If pittie may
      move your jentyll° harte,
    remember, good people, the poore and
      the blynd,

with your charitable almes this poore
    man to comforte.
Yt is your owne neighbour and of your
    owne kynd.
40   CAECUS Your almes, good people, for
      charitie,
to me that am blynd and never did see,
your neighbour borne in this cittie;
helpe or I goe hence.
PETRUS Maister, instruct us in this
    case
why this man borne blynd was.
Is it for his owne trespas
or elles for his parentes?
JOHN Was synne the cause oryginall,
wherin we be conceived all,
50   that this blynd man was brought in
      thrall°?
JESUS Hit° was neither for his offence,
neither the synne of his parentes,
or other fault or negligence
that hee was blynd borne;
but for this cause spetiallye:°
to sett forth Goddes great glorye,
his power to shewe manifestlye,
this mans sight to reforme.°
While the daye is fayre and bright,
60   my Fathers workes I must worke right
untyll the comminge [of] the night
that light be gonne awaye.
In this world when I am heare,
I am the light that shyneth cleare.
My light to them shall well appeare
which cleeve to mee alwaye.
        Tunc Jesus super terram spuit et lu-
          tum faciat, et oculos Caeci mani-
          bus fricabit; postea dicat.°
Doe, man, as I say to thee.
Goe to the water of Siloe,
there washe thy eyes, and thou shalt see;

---

bonus pastor...suis *"A good shepherd lays down his life for his sheep"* [*Latin; John 10:11*]   **or** *before*   **well**
speede *prosper*   **Si vos manseritis...vos** *"If you remain in my word, you will truly be my disciples, and*
you will know the truth, and the truth will set you free" [*Latin; John 8:31–32*]   **ducens Caecum** *leading a*
blind man [*Latin*]   **jentyll** *gentle*   **in thrall** *slavery, bondage*   **Hit** *it*   **spetiallye** *especially*   **reforme**
restore   **Tunc Jesus...dicat** *Jesus then spits on the ground and makes clay, and rubs the eyes of the blind*
man with his hands; after which he says [*Latin*]

70 and give to God the prayse.
> *Tunc Caecus quaerit aquam et abut Jesus.*°

CAECUS Leade me, good child, right
> hastely

unto the water of Siloe.
>   *Tunc lavat, et postea dicat:*°

Praysed be God omipotent
which nowe to me my sight hath sent.
I see all thinges nowe here present.
Blessed be God alwaye.
When I had donne as God me badde,°
mye perfect sight forthwith I hadde;
wherfore my hart is now full gladde
80 that I doubt where I am.

PRIMUS VICINUS Neighbour, if I the
> trueth should saye,

this is the blynd man which yesterdaye
asked our almes as we came this waye.
Yt is the verey same.

SECUNDUS VICINUS No, no, neigh-
> bour, yt is not hee,

but yt is the likest to him that ever I
> see.

One man to another like may bee,
and so is hee to him.

CAECUS Good men, truely I am hee
90 that was blynd, and nowe I see.
I am no other verelye;
enquire of all my kynne.°

PRIMUS VICINUS Then tell the tru-
> eth, we thee praye,

how this his° happened to us saye—
thou that even yesterdaye
couldest see no yearthly thinge,
and nowe seest so perfectly.
No want of sight in thee we see.
Declare therfore to us truelye
100 withowt more reasoninge.

CAECUS The man which we call Jesus,
that worketh miracles daylye with us

and whom we finde so gratiouse,
anoynted my eyes with claye.
And to the water of Siloe
he bade me goe immediatelye
and wash my eyes, and I should see;
and thyder° I tooke my waye.
When the water on my eyes light,
110 immediately I had my sight
Was there never yearthly wight°
so joyfull in his thought.

SECUNDUS VICINUS Where is hee
> nowe, we thee praye?

CAECUS I knowe not where he is, by
> this daye.

SECUNDUS VICINUS Thou shalt with
> us come on this waye

and to the Pharasyes these wordes saye.
But yf thou would these thinges denye,
yt shall helpe thee right nought.
Looke up, lordinges and judges of right!
120 We have brought you a man that had no
> sight

and one the sabaoth day° through on
> mans might

was healed and restored forsooth.°

PRIMUS VICINUS Declare to them,
> thou wicked wight,

who did restore thee to thy sight,
that we may knowe anonright°
of this matter the trueth.

CAECUS Jesus annoynted my eyes with
> claye

and bade mee washe in Siloe,
and before I come awaye
130 my perfect sight I hadd.

PRIMUS PHARASEUS This man, the
> trueth if I should saye,

is not of God—my head I laye°—
which doth violate the sabeath daye.
I judge him to be madd.

Tunc Caecus...Jesus *The blind man then seeks the water and Jesus departs* [*Latin*]   **Tunc lavat, et postea dicat** *He washes and then says* [*Latin*]   **badde** *bade*   **kynne** *kin, family*   **his** *has*   **thyder** *thither*   **wight** *person*   **one the sabaoth day** *on the Sabbath day*   **forsooth** *truly*   **anonright** *at once*   **laye** *wager*

SECUNDUS PHARASEUS I cannot
 enter into my thought
that hee which hath thys marveyle
 wrought
should be a synner—I leeve° yt nought;
hit is not in my creede.°
Saye what is hee that did thee heale.
140 **CAECUS** A prophet hee ys, withowt
 fayle.
PRIMUS PHARASEUS Surely thou
 arte a knave of kynde°
that faynest° thyselfe for to be blynde;
wherfore nowe this is my mynde,
the trueth to trye indeede.
His father and mother, both in feere,°
shall come declare the matter heere,
and then the trueth shall soone appeare
and we put out of doubt.
Goe forth, messinger, anon in hye,°
150 and fetch his parentes by and by.°
This knave can nought but prate and
 lye;°
I would his eyes were out.
NUNTIUS Your byddinge, maister, I
 shall fulfill
and doe my dutye as is good skill,°
for this daye hither I knowe the will,
and I shall spie them out.
  Tunc circumspectat, et adloquitur eos:°
Syr and dame, both in feare,
you must afore° the Pharasies appeare.
What there° will is, there shall you
 heare.
160 Have donne and come your waye.
MATER Alas, man, what doe we heere?
Must we afore the Pharasyes appeare?
A vengeance on them farre and neare;
they never did poore men good!
PATER Dame, here is no other waye

but there commandment wee must
 obeye,
or elles they would without delaye
course° us and take our good.°
NUNTIUS Here I have brought as you
 bade me
170 these two persons that aged bee.
They be the parentes of him truely
which sayd that he was blynde.
PRIMUS PHARASEUS Come neare to
 us both too,°
and tell us truely or ere wee goe
whether this be your sonne or noe
looke noe descent° we fynde.
PATER Maysters, we knowe certaynlye
our sonne hee is—we cannot denye—
and blynd was borne, undoubtedly,
180 and that we will depose.°
But whoe restored him to his sight
we be uncertayne, by God almight.
Wherfore of him, as is right,
the trueth you must enquyre.
MATER For he hath age° his tale to
 tell,
and his mother-tonge to utter hit° well;
although hee could never bye nor sell,
lett him speake, we desyre.
PRIMUS PHARASEUS Give prayse to
 God, thou craftie knave,
190 and looke hereafter thou do not rave°
nor saye that Jesus did thee save
and restored thee to thy sight.
SECUNDUS PHARASEUS Hee is a
 sinner and that wee knowe,
disceavinge° the people to and froe.
This is most true that wee thee showe.
Beleeve us as is right.
CAECUS If he bee sinfull I doe not
 knowe,
but this is trueth that I doe showe.

---

leeve *believe*   hit is not in my creede *I cannot credit it*   knave of kynde *natural-born rogue*   faynest *feignest, pretend*   in feere *together*   anon in hye *at once*   by and by *right away*   prate and lye *babble and lie*   as...skill *as is quite right*   Tunc...eos *He then looks about and speaks to them [Latin]*   afore *before*   course *curse, excommunicate*   good *goods, belongings*   too *two*   descent *deceit*   depose *testify under oath*   hath age *is old enough*   hit *it*   rave *stray morally*   disceavinge *deceiving, misleading*

When I was blynd and in great woe,
200   hee cured me, as yee see.
    PRIMUS PHARASEUS What did hee,
      thou lither swayne°?
    CAECUS I tould you once; will you
      here hit° agayne?
Or his disciples will [you] become,
of all your sinnes to have remission°?
    SECUNDUS PHARASEUS O cursed
      caytyffe,° yll moote thow thee°!
Would thou have us his disciples to bee?
No, no! Moyses disciples binne wee,°
for God with him did speake.
But whence this is, I never knewe.
210   **CAECUS** I marvayle° of that, as I am
      trewe—
that you knowe not from whence hee
    should bee
that me cured that never did see—
knowinge this most certaynlye:
God wyll not sinners here.
But hee that honoreth God truely,
him will hee here° by and by°
and grant his askinge° gratiously,
for that man is to him deare.
And to this I dare be bould,
220   there is noe man that ever could
restore a creature to his sight
that was blynd borne and never sawe
    light.
If he of God were not, iwis,°
hee could never worke such thinges as
    this.
    PRIMUS PHARASEUS What, sinfull
      knave! Wilt thou teach us
which all the scriptures can discusse,
and of our livinge be so vertuous?
We curse° thee owt of this place.

    JESUS Beleeves thou in God Sonne
      trulye?
230   **CAECUS** Yea, gratious lord. Whoe is
      hee?
    JESUS Thou hast him seene with thy
      eyee.
Hee is the same that talketh with thee.
    CAECUS Then I here, I honour him
      with hart free,°
and ever shall serve him untill I dye.
    PRIMUS JUDEUS Saye, man that mak-
      est such maistrye,°
or thow our sowles doe anoye,°
tell us here appertly°
Christ yf that thou be.
    JESUS That I spake to you openlye
240   and workes that I doe verelye°
in my Fathers name almightie
beareth wytnes of mee.
But you beleeve not as you seene,
for of my sheepe yee ne beene;
but my flocke, withowten weene,°
here my voyce alwaye.
And I knowe them well eychon,°
for with me alwaye the gonne;°
and for them I ordayned in my owne°
250   everlasting life for aye.°
No man shall reave° my sheepe from
    me,
for my Father in majestie
ys greater then binne all yee,
or any that ever was.
    SECUNDUS JUDEUS. Thou shalt
      abye,° by my bone,°
or thou heathen passe.°
Helpe, fellowe, and gather stones
and beate him well, for cockes bones.°
He scornes us quiantlye° for the nones°

---

lither swayne *wicked slave*   here hit *hear it*   remission *forgiveness*   cursed caytyffe *miserable* *wretch*   yll moote thow thee *may evil befall the*   binne wee *are we*   marvayle *marvel*   here *hear*   by and by *soon*   askinge *request*   iwis *truly*   curse *excommunicate*   free *open*   makest such maistrye *displays such power*   or thow...anoye *before you afflict our souls*   appertly *clearly*   verelye *truly*   withowten weene *without doubt*   eychon *every single one*   the gonne *they go*   owne *house*   for aye *forever*   reave *snatch*   abye *abide*   by my bone *by my bones, upon my life*   or thou heathen passe *before you go hence*   for cockes bones *by God's bones*   quiantlye *cunningly*   for the nones *for the moment*

260 and doth us great anoye.

Tunc lapides colligunt.°

Yea, stones nowe here I have
for this rybauld° that thus can rave.
One stroke, as God me save,
he shall have soone in hye.°

JESUS Wretches, manye a good deede
I have donne, yea in great neede;
nowe quite you fowle my meede°
to stone me on° this manere.

PRIMUS JUDEUS For thy good deede
that thou hast wrought°

270 at this tyme stone we thee nought.
Both in word and thought
there thou lyes falselye.

JESUS But I doe well and truely
my Fathers biddinge by and by,°
elles may you hope well I lye
and then leeves° you me nought.
But sythen° you will not leeve me,
nor my deedes that you may see,
to them beleevinge takes yee,

280 for nothinge may be soother.°
Soe may you knowe well and verey°
in my Father that I ame aye,°
and hee in mee, sooth to saye,°
and eyther of us in other.

Tunc colligunt lapides et statim
evanescit Jesus.°

SECUNDUS JUDEUS Owt, owt, alas
where is our fonne°?
Quyntly° that hee is heathen° gonne.
I would have taken him, and that
anone,°
and fowle° him all to-frapped.°
Yea, make we never so much mone,°

290 nowe there is noe other wonne,°
for hee and his men everychone°

are from us clearly scaped.°

PRIMUS JUDEUS Nowe by the death I
shall one° dye,
may I° see him with my eye,
to syr Cayphas I shall him wrye°
and tell that° shall him deare.°
See I never none, by my faye,°
when I had stones, soe soone awaye.
But yet no force°! Another daye

300 his tabret° we shall feare.°

Tunc lapides colligunt _Then they gather stones_ [Latin]   rybauld _lewd fellow_   in hye _immediately_   nowe quite you fowle my meede _Now you repay my favor with evil_   on _in_   wrought _done, performed_   by and by _soon_   leeves _believe_   sythen _since, because_   soother _more true_   verey _truly_   aye _always_   sooth to saye _truth be told_   Tunc colligunt...Jesus _Then they gather stones as Jesus suddenly vanishes_ [Latin]   fonne _foe_   Quyntly [_How_] _cleverly_   heathen _hence_   anone _at once_   fowle _severely_   to-frapped _beaten_   make we...mone _however much we complain_   wonne _alternative_   everychone _each and every one_   scaped _escaped_   one _in_   may I _If I_   wrye _divulge_   that _what_   deare _trouble_   See...faye _I never saw anyone, truly_   no force _no matter_   tabret _tabard, garment_   feare _tear_

Endnotes

1   The text for this scene from Play 13 performed by the Chester Glovers is based on Hermann Deimling and G.W. Matthews, eds., *The Chester Plays*, Early English Text Society, Extra Series 62 and 115 (Oxford University Press, 1892 and 1916), in consultation with the work of Robert M. Lumiansky and David Mills, *The Chester Mystery Cycle*, Early English Text Society Supplementary Series 3 (Oxford University Press, 1974), vol. 1, pp. 230–42, and Robert M. Lumiansky, ed., *The Chester Mystery Cycle: Essays and Documents* (University of North Carolina Press, 1983). The author (or authors) of the Glovers' play, as well as the exact date of the play text is unknown, though it was very likely added as a supplement to the guild's older *Raising of Lazarus* play when the cycle expanded to a three-day production during Whitsun week sometime around 1531. In any case, the *terminus ad quem* is certainly the final performance of the cycle during Midsummer 1575. Footnotes and endnotes have been provided by Kurt Schreyer. Stanza breaks have been removed for ease of publication.

2   David Mills, *The Chester Mystery Cycle: A New Edition with Modernised Spelling* (Colleagues Press, 1992), p. 220.

3   Joshua R. Eyler, *Disability in the Middle Ages: Reconsiderations and Reverbations* (Ashgate, 2010), pp. 6–7.

Christ and the Leper from the Chester Cycle[1]
(ca. 1531–75)

Contributed by Kurt Schreyer

Introduction

In the 1979 film *Life of Brian*, a Monty Python satire about a mistaken messiah, the eponymous Brian meets an ex-leper who, though a skilled haggler, is not only miffed about the fact that Jesus cured him but also begrudges acts of generosity in general. The scene's punchline—"There's no pleasing some people."—goes beyond comedy to raise provocative questions about the public ministry of Jesus, above all whether those people he cured became grateful followers and what kind of lives they led following their miraculous healing.

The Chester craft guild of Cordwainers, or Shoemakers, explore these challenging issues in Play 14 as Jesus, who is on his way to Jerusalem to celebrate Passover and to undergo betrayal, torture, and crucifixion, dines at the house of Simon the Leper—or rather ex-leper whom he "healed hase / over all for to showe" who once "that fowle and mesell was" (ll. 19–20, 18). According to the *Middle English Dictionary*, "mesell" was one of the English words (besides "lazar" and "leper") commonly used from the fourteenth to the seventeenth century to describe persons "afflicted with any of various disfiguring skin diseases, such as leucoderma, psoriasis, vitiligo, etc." though of course the term carried moral implications as well, being applied to "lowly wretched" people or "sinners," or even of "diseased or infected" swine. Though potentially debilitating, medical practitioners and laypeople alike knew that incipient *lepra* or other disfiguring skin conditions might be cured, whether through the temporary remission of the disease, successful treatments, or perhaps by some miraculous means. It was by no means uncommon to know someone "that fowle and mesell was" (l. 18) but who, like Simon, was restored to society after their physical suffering and, perhaps, the public ignominy of segregation.

The Scriptures do not record the healing of Simon *per se*, and the play draws from scenes in all four Gospels whose details are vexingly interchanged but which are similar in one respect: Simon the Leper never speaks.[2] In the Chester play, however, after initially expressing his warm gratitude to Jesus for curing him, he subsequently begrudges Maria Magdalena's anointing of Jesus' head and feet. Worse, he wishes to segregate her from society as if she were a leper: "hee should...suffer her not to come him nere" (ll. 62–63). Simon confides these thoughts to a likeminded Judas, whose greed and duplicity will become apparent later in the play. Before addressing the penitent Magdalen, Jesus reprimands both men. In this way, the play works to more closely juxtapose Simon the former leper with Judas the future betrayer. The play clearly examines the intimate connections between bodily disease and moral depravity, but it does not oversimplify what would have been considered to be a complex relationship. For one thing, Simon was not merely leprous but, as he explicitly states, Jesus cured him of a great many physical and spiritual perils: "Well is me that I may see thy face / here in my house, this poore place. /

Thou comfortes me in manye a case / and that I full well knowe" (ll. 21–24).

Simon's spiritual recovery is still a work in progress, and Jesus commends his reply to the parable of the two debtors (ll. 80–112). Humble and gracious as he speaks to Jesus, he is nonetheless self-regarding and judgmental toward the unhappy woman: "Methinke that hee should lett her goe, / tis woman full of synne and woe, / for feare of worldes shame" (ll. 58–60). What Simon has forgotten (or wishes to forget) but which would have been plain to a late-medieval audience, is that leprosy, prostitution, and sexual incontinence were culturally perceived to be related and mutually sustaining. Pointing his finger at Magdalen's disreputable past, he unwittingly raises the specter of his own former life. We would be accurate in saying that the play associates Simon's leprosy with Maria's promiscuity as well as Judas' treachery, but such observations need to be carefully circumscribed, for it does not do so from any sense of moral superiority or a desire to condemn lepers. Quite the opposite is true: the Cordwainer's play seems to find more danger in being an ex-leper than in suffering from leprosy itself. Like the preceding *Cure of the Blind Man*, this play is much more interested in social wholeness and the integration of those who have been physically and morally excluded than in division and separation.

For whatever his expressed gratitude toward Jesus, Simon's lack of hospitality resembles the social ostracizing which lepers often (though not quite so often as we may think, as Carole Rawcliffe demonstrates) experienced. Keeping his distance from his guest, he treats Jesus as if he too suffered from leprosy: "Kisse syth I came thou gave non,... / With oyle thou hast not me anoynt" (ll. 105, 109). The play does not give Simon a chance to reply to Jesus' reproach, and we're left to wonder if he is cured of his spiritual pride. What we can say is that he is present to hear Maria Magdalena use the same word—"fowle" (i.e., foul)—to portray her former sinful life which Simon had used to describe his leprosy. In her final words to Jesus she says: "thou hast... from fowle life unto great lee [tranquility] / releeved me, lord, for love" (ll. 134–36). Hearing these words, Jesus immediately leaves Simon's house and enters Jerusalem to begin his Passion—"for love."

Bibliography

Deimling, Hermann, and G.W. Matthews, eds. *The Chester Plays*, Early English Text Society, Extra Series 62 and 115. Oxford University Press, 1892 and 1916.

Demaitre, Luke. *Leprosy in Premodern Medicine: A Malady of the Whole Body*. Johns Hopkins University Press, 2007.

Green, Richard Firth. "'The Vanishing Leper' and 'The Murmuring Monk': Two Medieval Urban Legends." *Truth & Tales: Cultural Mobility and Medieval Media*, edited by Fiona Somerset and Nicholas Watson. Ohio State University Press, 2015, pp. 19–37.

Higl, Andrew. "Henryson's Textual and Narrative Prosthesis onto Chaucer's Corpus: Cresseid's Leprosy and Her Schort Conclusioun." *Disability in the Middle Ages: Reconsiderations and Reverberations*, edited by Joshua R. Eyler. Ashgate, 2010, pp. 167–81.

Lumiansky, Robert M., ed. *The Chester Mystery Cycle: Essays and Documents*. University of North Carolina Press, 1983,

——— and David Mills. *The Chester Mystery Cycle*, Early English Text Society Supplementary Series 3. Oxford University Press, 1974.

Murdoch, Brian. "Innocent Blood: Redemption and the Leper." *Adam's Grace: Fall and Redemption in Medieval Literature*, Brewer, 2000, pp. 102–25.

Orlemanski, Julie. "How to Kiss a Leper." *postmedieval: A Journal of Medieval Cultural Studies*, vol. 3, no. 2, 2012, pp. 142–57.

Rawcliffe, Carole. *Leprosy in Medieval England*. The Boydell Press, 2006.

DRAMATIS PERSONAE

Jesus
Petrus°
Philippus°
Simon the Leper
Lazarus
Martha
Maria Magdalena°
Judas Iscarioth

JESUS Brethren, goe we to Bethenye
to Lazarre, Martha, and Marye;
for I love mych that companye,
thidder° now will I wend.°
Symon the lepper hath prayed° me
in his house to take charitie.°
With them nowe yt liketh mee
a while for to lend.°
PETRUS Lord, all readye shall we be
in life and death to goe with thee.   10
Great joye they may have to see
thy comminge into there° place.
PHILIPPUS Lazarre thou raysed
    through thy pittye,
and Simon also—mesell° was hee—
thou clensed,° lord, that wotten° we,
and holpe° them through thy grace.
    Tunc ibunt versus domum Simonis leprosi.°
SIMON Welcome, Jesu, full of grace,
that mee that fowle° and mesell was
all whole, lord, thou healed hase,°
over all for to showe.°   20
Well is me that I may see thy face
here in my house, this poore place.
Thou comfortes me in manye a case°
and that I full well knowe.
LAZARUS Welcome, lord, sweete Jesu.
Blessed be the tyme that I thee knewe.
From death to life through thy vertue°
thou raysed me not yore.°
Fowre dayes in yearth° when I had layne
thou grantest me life, lord, agayne.   30
Thee I honour with all my mayne°
nowe and evermore.
MARTHA Welcome, my lovely lord
    and leere;°
welcome, my deareworth° darlinge
    deare.
Fayne° may thy freindes be in feere°

Petrus *Peter*   **Philippus** *Philip*   **Maria Magdalena** *Mary Magdalen*   **Judus Iscarioth** *Judas Is-cariot*   **thidder** *thither*   **wend** *walk*   **prayed** *asked, invited*   **take charitie** *accept hospitality*   **lend** *dwell*   **there** *their*   **mesell** *a leper, a sinner*   **clensed** *healed, absolved of sin*   **wotten** *know*   **holpe** *helped*   **Tunc ibunt...leprosi** *Here they approach the house of Simon the Leper [Latin]*   **fowle** *foul*   **hase** *has*   **over all for to showe** *to appear in every way*   **manye a case** *many misfortunes*   **vertue** *power*   **not yore** *not long ago*   **yearth** *the earth*   **mayne** *will, ability*   **leere** *beautiful of face*   **deareworth** *precious*   **Fayne** *Joyful*   **in feere** *together*

to se thy freelye° face.
Syttes downe, if your will weare,°
and I shall helpe to serve you here
as I was wonte° in good manere
40   before in other place.
      Tunc Jesus sedebat, et omnes cum eo, et
      veniet Maria Magdalena cum alablas-
      tro unguenti, et lamentando dicat.°
MARIA MAGDALENA Welcome, my
  lovely lord of leale;°
welcome, my harte; welcome, my heale;°
welcome, all my worldes weale,°
my boote° and all my blys.
From thee, lord, may I not conceale
my fylth and my faultes fayle.°
Forgive mee that my flesh so frayle
to thee hath donne amysse.°
Oyntment I have here readye
50   to anoynte thy sweete bodye.
Though I be wretched and unworthye,
wayve° me not from thy wonne.°
Full of synne and sorrowe am I,
but therfore, lord, I am sorye.
Amend me through thy mercye,
that makes to thee my monne.°
      Tunc aperiet pixidem, et faciet signum
      unctionis, et rigabit pedes Jesu lach-
      rymis et tergebit capillis suis.°
SIMON A, Judas, why doth Jesus soe?
Methinke that hee should lett her goe,
this woman full of synne and woe,
60   for feare of worldes shame.°
And if hee verey prophet were,
hee should knowe hir life here
and suffer her not to come him nere,

for payringe° of his fame.°
JUDAS ISCARIOTH Naye, Simon,
  brother, sooth to saye,
hit is nothinge to my paye;°
this oyntment goeth to° fast awaye
that is so mych of pryce.
70 This ylke boyst° might have binne sould
for three hundreth penyes tould°
and dealt to poore men, whosoever
  would,
and whosoever had binne wise.
JESUS Simon, take good heed to mee.
I have an errand° to saye to thee.
SIMON Maister, what you° will maye
  bee,
save on, I you beseech.
JESUS By an example I shall thee showe
and to this companye on a rowe,°
whereby I say thou may knowe
80   to answere° to my speache.
Two detters somtyme° there were
oughten° money to a userer.°
The on° was in his dangere°
five hundreth penyes tould;°
They° other fiftie, as I saye here.
For they were poore, at there° prayer
he forgave them both in feare,°
and nought take of them he would.
Whether° of these two, read° if thou
  can,
90   was more behoulden° to that man?
SIMON Lord, as much as I can thereon
I shall saye or I passe.°
Five hundreth is more then fiftie;
therfore methinke skylfullye°

---

freelye *noble*   **if...weare** *if you wish*   **wonte** *accustomed*   **Tunc Jesus...dicat** *Jesus then sits down and the others with him. Mary Magdalen enters with a jar of ointment and, weeping mournfully, she says* [*Latin*]   **leale** *faithful people*   **heale** *health*   **worldes weale** *world's prosperity*   **boote** *redeemer*   **faultes fayle** *many faults*   **amysse** *amiss*   **wayve** *send away*   **wonne** *dwelling*   **monne** *moan*   **Tunc aperiet...suis** *Opening the box, she makes as if to anoint him, and her tears wet Jesus' feet, which she wipes dry with her hair* [*Latin*]   **worldes shame** *public disgrace*   **payringe of** *injury to*   **fame** *reputation*   **hit...paye** *it's not at all to my liking*   **to** *too*   **ylke boyst** *same jar*   **tould** *counted, reckoned*   **errand** *message*   **you** *your*   **on a rowe** *altogether*   **to answere** *how to reply*   **somtyme** *once*   **oughten** *owed*   **userer** *moneylender*   **on** *one*   **dangere** *debt*   **They** *their*   **tould** *in sum, total*   **there** *their*   **in feare** *together*   **Whether** *Which*   **read** *discern, advise, judge*   **behoulden** *indebted*   **or I passe** *before I go*   **methinke skylfullye** *it seems reasonable to me*

that hee that hee forgave° more partie,°
more houlden° to him he was.
JESUS Simon, thou deemes soothlie,°
    iwysse.°
Sees thou this woman that here is?
Sycker° shee hath not donne amysse
100 to worke on this manere.°
Into thy house here thou me geete;°
no water thou gave mee to° my feete.
Shee washed them with her teares
    weete°
and wyped them with her heare.°
Kisse syth° I came thou gave non,°
but syth shee came into this wonne°
shee hath kyssed my feete eychon;°
of weepinge shee never ceased.
With oyle thou hast not me anoynt,
110 but shee hat donne both foot and joynt.
Therfore I tell thee on° poynt,
mych synne is her released.°
        Ad Judam Iscarioth:°
And Judas, also to thee I saye:
wherto wouldest thee mispaye°
with this woman by° any waye
that eased° me this° hasse?
A good deede shee hath donne todaye,
for poore men you have with you aye,°
and me yee may not have, in faye,°
120 but a little space.°
Therfore, woman, witterlye,°
for thou hast loved so tenderly,
all thy synnes nowe forgive I;
beleeffe° hath saved thee.
And all that preach the evangelye°
through the world by and by°
of thy deed shall make memorye°
that thou hasse donne to mee.

MARIA MAGDALENA My Christ,
    my comfort and my kinge,
130 I worshippe thee in all thinge,
for nowe my hart is in likinge,°
and I at myne above.°
Seaven° devils nowe, as I well see,
thou hast dryven nowe owt of mee,
and from fowle° life unto great lee°
releeved° me, lord, for love.

---

that hee that hee forgave *that he whom he had forgiven* **more partie** *greater share* **houlden**
beholden **deemes soothlie** *judge correctly* **iwysse** *indeed* **Sycker** *certainly* **to worke...manere**
to act in this way **geete** *brought* **to** *for* **weete** *wet* **heare** *hair* **syth** *since* **non** *none* **wonne**
dwelling **eychon** *both, each one* **on** *one* **her released** *forgiven her* **Ad Judam Iscarioth** *[Jesus says]*
to Judas Iscariot [Latin] **mispaye** *be displeased* **by** *in* **eased** *comforted* **this** *thus* **aye** *always* **in**
faye *truly* **but a little space** *except for a very short time* **witterly** *truly* **beleeffe** *faith* **evangelye**
Gospel **by and by** *before long* **make memorye** *remember, commemorate* **in likinge** *content* **I at**
myne above *I am exalted* **Seaven** *Seven* **fowle** *sinful* **lee** *tranquility, peace* **releeved** *restored*

Endnotes

1   The text for this scene from Play 14 performed by the Chester Cordwainers, or Shoemakers, is based on Hermann Deimling and G.W. Matthews, eds., *The Chester Plays*, Early English Text Society, Extra Series 62 and 115 (Oxford University Press, 1892 and 1916), in consultation with the work of Robert M. Lumiansky and David Mills, *The Chester Mystery Cycle*, Early English Text Society Supplementary Series 3 (Oxford University Press, 1974), vol. 1, pp. 230–42, and Robert M. Lumiansky, ed., *The Chester Mystery Cycle: Essays and Documents* (University of North Carolina Press, 1983). While the author(s) of the Cordwainers' play and the date of its origin are not known, this particular scene at the house of Simon the Leper was probably an embellishment of an older pageant depicting Christ's entry into Jerusalem and confrontation with the moneylenders in the Temple. And while surviving records demonstrate the Cordwainers' expenditures for a similar version of the play in 1550, it is reasonable to suppose that this episode was added much earlier when the cycle expanded to a three-day production during Whitsun week sometime around 1531 and then underwent several changes and evolutions in the ensuing decades before the final performance of the cycle during Midsummer 1575. Footnotes and endnotes have been provided by Kurt Schreyer. Stanza breaks have been removed for ease of publication.

2   Yet in Luke's account of the anointing by the sinful woman, Simon the Pharisee, who has not apparently been healed by Jesus, does (see Lk 7:36–50).

The Entry into Jerusalem from the *York Cycle*[1] (ca. 1377)

Contributed by Frank M. Napolitano

Introduction

For nearly two hundred years (1377–1569), the York Plays rolled on pageant wagons throughout the city of York on the feast of Corpus Christi, depicting biblical and pseudo-biblical stories from Judeo-Christian salvation history. Celebrating their Christian faith and artisanal pride, the town's craft guilds each presented specific scenes from Jesus' life or episodes in the Hebrew Scriptures believed to refer typologically to Christ. The "Entry," produced by the Skinners (suppliers of animal skins), depicts the account, from all four Gospels,[2] of Jesus' arrival at Jerusalem and the beginning of the chain of events leading to his death. Politics and devotion co-mingle seamlessly in the play's medieval context: the crowd's welcoming of Jesus emulates the spectacle with which medieval cities greeted visiting royalty. York and Jerusalem thus become interchangeable, and the audience members become witnesses to—and participants in—the story of their own redemption.[3]

The play's treatment of disability contributes to its devotional and social significance by expanding considerably the single verse in Matthew 21:14, where Jesus heals a blind man and a lame man. The play names the figures based on their disabilities (Cecus, Latin *caecus*, "blind," and Claudus, Latin *claudus*, "lame") and assigns to them a considerable amount of dialogue, both among themselves and with Jesus. The play's extended treatment of this episode might reveal an attempt at dramatizing a familiar feature of religious narratives, in which the presence of disabilities often serves solely to provide opportunities for a religious figure to "prove his or her holiness."[4] However, this dramatic treatment of disabilities might also reveal the ways in which disabilities convey information about the human condition, in general, or about the person being healed, in particular. Richard Beadle argues that Cecus' and Claudus' "physical infirmities represent the flawed spiritual state of postlapsarian humanity."[5] The text supports, to some extent, this metaphorical interpretation of sickness. The city dignitaries, for example, refer to Jesus as humanity's "cure" (l. 495), "medecyne" (l. 499), and "balme" (l. 521).[6] The roots of this metaphorical representation of Christ the Physician can be found in Luke 5:31–32, and numerous medieval texts support the idea that physical ailments in general are the byproducts of humanity's fallen state.[7]

The medieval predilection to associate disability with personal, moral shortcomings is significant. For example, "poor blind beggars" were often associated with "stereotypes of idleness, avarice and wantonness" in thirteenth- and fourteenth-century Paris.[8] Despite this cultural association, the "Entry" provides scarce linkage between sin and literal disability. In fact, the play seems to subvert any relationship between disability and sin in a series of interactions between Jesus and three marginalized individuals. No evidence exists for the sinfulness of Cecus or Claudus, the first two characters to whom, besides his disciples, Jesus speaks. Neither character associates his disability with sin, nor does Jesus ask either one to account for any moral faults. The absence of sin in the characters with disabilities may be the result of the play's ultimate source. Associations between sin and disability are, in the Christian Scriptures at least, the exception, rather than the rule.[9] The only character in the York "Entry" presented overtly as a sinner is Zacheus, the able-bodied (albeit short) publican whose eagerness to see Jesus draws him away from the social margins and into the center of the narrative. In a display of faith, Zacheus climbs a tree to see Jesus, renounces his sinful ways, and praises him. Faith, rather than sin, remains the thread uniting these three characters, for it is not only the *sine qua non* for the healing of disabilities, but it is also the motivating factor leading characters and audience alike to their savior.

Bibliography

Beadle, Richard, ed. *The York Plays: A Critical Edition of the York Corpus Christi Play as Recorded in British Library Additional MS 35290*, 2 vols. EETS S.S. 23–24. Oxford University Press, 2009, 2013.

Crassons, Kate. *The Claims of Poverty: Literature, Culture, and Ideology in Late Medieval England.* University of Notre Dame Press, 2010.

Davidson, Clifford, ed., *The York Corpus Christi Plays.* Western Michigan University, 2011.

Farmer, Sharon. *Surviving Poverty in Medieval Paris: Gender, Ideology, and the Daily Lives of the Poor.* Cornell University Press, 2002.

Gusick, Barbara. "Christ's Healing of the Lame Man in the York Cycle's 'Entry into Jerusalem': Interpretive Challenges for the Newly Healed." *Fifteenth-Century Studies*, vol. 31, 2005, pp. 80–105.

———. "Christ's Transformation of Zaccaeus in the York Cycle's 'Entry into Jerusalem.'" *Fifteenth-Century Studies*, vol. 30, 2004, pp. 68–94.

———. "Groping in Darkness: The Man Born Blind and Christ's Ministry in the York Cycle." *New Approaches to European Theater of the Middle Ages: An Ontology*, edited by Barbara I. Gusick and Edelgard E. DuBruck. Peter Lang, 2004, pp. 45–71.

Metzler, Irina. *Disability in Medieval Europe: Thinking about Physical Impairment during the High Middle Ages, c. 1100–1400.* Routledge, 2006.

Napolitano, Frank. "Miraculous Rhetoric: The Relationship between Rhetoric and Miracles in the York 'Entry into Jerusalem.'" *Early Theatre*, vol. 12, no. 2, 2009, pp. 15–31.

O'Tool, Mark P. "Disability and the Suppression of Historical Identity: Rediscovering the Professional Backgrounds of the Blind Residents of the Hôpital des Quinze-Vingts." *Disability in the Middle Ages: Reconsiderations and Reverberations*, edited by Joshua R. Eyler. Ashgate, 2010, pp. 11–24.

Stevens, Martin. *Four Middle English Mystery Cycles: Textual, Contextual, and Critical Interpretations.* Princeton University Press, 1987.

Wheatley, Edward. *Stumbling Blocks before the Blind: Medieval Constructions of a Disability.* University of Michigan Press, 2010.

Willits, Catherine. "The Dynamics and Staging of Community in Medieval 'Entry into Jerusalem' Plays: Dramatic Resources Influencing Marlowe's Jew of Malta." *Medieval & Renaissance Drama in England*, vol. 27, 2014, pp. 78–109.

DRAMATIS PERSONAE

Jesus
Petrus
Janitor°
Philippus
Cecus (a blind man)
Zache (Zacheus the publican)
Pauper (a poor man)
Claudus (a lame man)
Octo Burgenses°

JESUS To me takis tent° and giffis gud
    hede,°
My dere discipulis that ben here,
I schalle you telle that° shalbe in dede,°
My tyme to passe hense,° it drawith
    nere,
And by this skill,°
Mannys sowle to save fro sorowes sere°
That loste was ill.°
From heven to erth whan I dyssende
Rawnsom to make I made promys,

10 The prophicie nowe drawes to ende,
My fadirs wille forsoth° it is,
That sent me hedyr.°
Petir, Phelippe, I schall you blisse,°
& go to-gedir
Un-to yone castell° that is you
    agayne,°
Gois with gud harte,° and tarie° noght,
My comaundement to do be ye bayne.°
Also I you charge loke it be
    wrought,°
That schal ye fynde

20 An asse, this feste° als ye had soght,
Ye hir un-bynde
With hir foole,° and to me hem°
    bring,
That I on hir may sitte a space;°
So the prophicy clere menyng
May be fulfilled here in this place,
'Doghtyr Syon,°
Loo! thi lorde comys rydand on an asse
The to opon.'°
Yf° any man will you gayne-saye,°

30 Say that youre lorde has nede of
    tham,°
And schall restore° thame this same
    day,
Un-to what man will tham clayme.

Janitor *porter*   **Octo Burgenses** *eight burgesses*   **takis tent** *pay attention*   **giffis gud hede** *take notice*   **that** *what*   **in dede** *indeed*   **hense** *from here*   **by this skill** *for this reason*   **sere** *great*   **ill** *sinfully*   **forsoth** *truly*   **hedyr** *here*   **blisse** *bless*   **castell** *walled town*   **agayne** *near*   **Gois...harte** *go fervently*   **tarie** *tarry*   **bayne** *obedient*   **loke...wrought** *see it be done*   **feste** *(tied) fast*   **foole** *foal*   **hem** *them*   **a space** *for a while*   **Doghtyr Syon** *Daughter of Sion*   **The to opon** *upon to you*   **Yf** *if*   **gayne-saye** *gainsay, challenge*   **tham** *them*   **restore** *return*

Do thus this thyng,
Go furthe ye both, and be ay bayne°
In my blissyng.
PETRUS Jesu, maistir, evyn at thy
    wille,°
And at thi liste° us likis to doo,
Yone° beste whilke thou desires the
    tille,
Even at thi will schall come the too,
40 Un-to thin esse.°
Sertis,° lord, we will thedyre° all
The for to plese.
PHILIPPUS Lord the to plese we are
    full bayne,°
Bothe nyght and day to do thi will.
Go we, brothere, with all oure mayne°
My lordis desire for to fulfill;
For prophycye
Us bus it do to hym by skyll°
To do dewly.°
50 PETRUS Ya! brodir Phelipp, be-halde
    grathely,°
For als he saide we shulde sone fynde,
Me-thinke° yone bestis be-fore myn eye,
Thai are the same we schulde unbynde.°
Therfore frely
Go we to hym that thame gan° bynde,
And aske mekely.
PHILIPPUS The beestis are comen,°
    wele I knawe,
Ther-fore us nedis to aske lesse leve,
And oure maistir kepis the lawe
60 We may thame take tyter,° I preve,°
For noght we lett.°
For wele I watte° oure tyme is breve,
Go we tham fett.°
JANITOR Saie, what are ye that makis
    here maistrie,°
To loose thes bestis with-oute leverie?°

Yow semes to bolde, sen noght that ye
Hase here to do, therfore rede I
such thingis to sesse,
Or ellis ye may falle in folye
70 And grette diseasse.°
PETRUS Sir, with thi leve hartely we
    praye
This beste that we myght have.
JANITOR To what in-tente, firste shall
    ye saye?
And than I graunte what ye will crave,
Be gode resoune.
PHILIPPUS Oure maistir, Sir, that all
    may save,
Aske by chesoune.°
JANITOR What man is that ye maistir
    call?
Swilke° privelege dare to hym clayme.
80 PETRUS Jesus of Jewes kyng, and ay°
    be schall,
Of Nazareth prophete the same,
This same is he,
Both God and man, with-outen blame,°
This trist° wele we.
JANITOR Sirs, of that prophette herde
    I have,
But telle me firste playnly, wher is hee?
PHILIPPUS He comes at hande, so
    God me save,
That lorde we lefte at Bephage,°
He bidis us there.
90 JANITOR Sir, take this beste, with
    herte full free,
And forthe ye fare.
And if you thynke it be to done,
I schall declare playnly his comyng
To the chiffe° of the Jewes, that thei
    may sone
Assemble same° to his metyng.

bayne *obedient*   evyn...wille *just as you wish*   at thi liste *as you please*   Yone *that*   esse *comfort*   Sertis *certainly*   thedyre *thither*   bayne *eager*   mayne *vigor*   For...skyll *For prophesy requires us to do so for this good reason*   dewly *dutifully*   be-halde grathely *behold clearly*   Me-thinke *it seems to me*   unbynde *untie*   gan *did*   comen *common (as in common property)*   tyter *readily*   preve *argue*   lett *refrain*   watte *know*   fett *fetch, get*   makis here maistrie *acts with authority*   leverie *appropriate documentation*   disease *misery*   by chesoune *for good reason*   Swilke *such*   ay *always*   blame *fault*   trist *believe*   Bephage *Bethphage*   chiffe *leaders*

What is your rede?°
PETRUS Thou sais full° wele in thy
    menyng,
Do forthe thi dede.
And sone this beste we schall the bring,
100 And it restore as resoune will.°
JANITOR This tydyngis schall have no
    laynyng,°
But to the Citezens declare it till
of this cyte,
I suppose fully that thei wolle
come mete that free.°
And sen° I will thei warned be,
Both yonge & olde, in ilke a state,°
For his comyng I will hym mete
To late tham witte,° with-oute debate.
110 Lo! wher thei stande,
That citezens cheff, withoute debate,
Of all this lande.
He that is rewler of all right,
And freely schoppe° both sande and see,
He save you, lordyngis,° gayly dight,°
And kepe you in youre semelyte°
And all honoure.
I BURGENSIS Welcome, Porter! what
    novelte°
Telle us this owre?°
120 **JANITOR** Sirs, novelte I can you tell,
And triste° thame fully as for trewe;
Her comes of kynde of Israell°
Att hande the prophete called Jesu,
Lo! this same day,
Rydand on an asse; this tydandis° newe
consayve° ye may.
II BURGENSIS And is that prophette
    Iesu nere?

Off hym I have herde grete ferlis° tolde,
He dois grete wounderes in contrees
    seere,°
130 He helys the seke, both yonge and olde,
And the blynde giffis tham ther sight.
Both dome and deffe, as hym selffe
    wolde,[10]
He cures tham right.
III BURGENSIS Ya v. thowsand° men
    with loves° fyve
He fedde, and ilkone hadde i-nowe;°
Watir to wyne he turned ryve,°
He garte corne° growe with-outen
    plogh,
Wher are° was none;
To dede men als° he gaffe liffe,
140 Lazar was one.[11]
IV BURGENSIS In oure tempill if he
    prechid
Agaynste the pepull that leved° wrong,
And also new lawes if he teched
Agaynste oure lawis we used so lang,
And saide pleynlye,
The olde schall waste,° the new schall
    gang,°
That we schall see.
V BURGENSIS Ya, Moyses lawe he
    cowed ilke dele,°
And all the prophettis on a rowe,
150 He telles tham so that ilke aman may
    fele,°
And what thei may interly° knowe
Yf thei were dyme,°
What the prophettis saide in ther sawe,°
All longis° to hym.
VI BURGENSIS Emanuell also by right

---

same *together*   **rede** *advice*   **full** *very*   **as resoune will** *as reason requires*   **schall...laynyng** *will not be concealed*   **free** *noble man*   **sen** *since*   **in...state** *in each walk of life*   **late tham witte** *let them know*   **schoppe** *created*   **lordyngis** *noblemen*   **dight** *dressed*   **semelyte** *worthiness*   **novelte** *news*   **owre** *hour*   **triste** *be confident in*   **of...Israell** *of the people of Israel*   **tydandis** *tidings*   **consayve** *understand*   **ferlis** *marvels*   **seere** *diverse*   **v. thowsand** *five thousand*   **loves** *loaves*   **ilkone hadde i-nowe** *each one had enough*   **ryve** *abundant*   **garte corne** *makes grain*   **are** *before*   **als** *also*   **leved** *lived*   **waste** *diminish*   **gang** *thrive*   **cowed ilke dele** *knew every bit*   **fele** *comprehend*   **interly** *fully*   **dyme** *difficult to understand*   **sawe** *speech*   **longis** *pertains*

Thai calle that prophette, by this skill,°
He is the same that are was hyght°
By Ysaye be-for us till,
Thus saide full clere.

160 **VII BURGENSIS** Loo! a maydýn that
    knew neverè ille°
A childe schuld bere.
David spake of him I wene,°
And lefte witnesse ye knowe ilkone,°
He saide the frute of his corse° clene
Shulde royally regne upon his
    trone,°
And therfore he
Of David kyn, and othir none,
Oure kyng schal be.

VIII BURGENSIS Sirs, me thynketh ye
    saie right wele,
170 And gud ensampelys° furth ye
    bryng,
And sen we thus this mater fele,°
Go we hym meete as oure owne kyng,
And kyng hym call.
What is youre counsaill in this thyng?
Now say ye all.

I BURGENSIS Agaynste resoune I will
    noght plete,°
For wele I wote° oure kyng he is,
Whoso agaynst his kyng liste threte,°
He is noght wise, he dose amys.°
180 Porter, come nere,
What knowlage hast thou of his co-
    myng?
Tels us all here.
And than° we will go mete that free,°
And hym honnoure as we wele awe°
Worthely tyll° oure Citee,
And for oure soverayne° lord hym
    knawe,°
In whome we triste.

JANITOR Sirs, I schall telle you all on
    rowe,°
And ye will lyste.°
190 Of his discipillis ij° this day,
Where that I stode, thei faire me grette,
And on ther maistir halfe gan praye°
Oure comon asse that thei myght gete
bot for awhile,
Wher-on ther maistir softe° myght
    sitte,
Space of a mile.
And all this mater thai me tolde
Right haly° as I saie to you,
And the asse thei have right as thei
    wolde,
200 And sone will bringe agayne, I trowe,°
So thai be-heste.°
What ye will doo avise you nowe,
Thus thinke me beste.

II BURGENSIS Trewlye as for me I say,
I rede we make us redy bowne,°
Hym to mete gudly this day,
And hym ressayve° with grete ren-
    nowne,
As worthy° is;
And therfore, sirs, in felde and towne
210 Ye fulfille this.

JANITOR Ya! and youre [childer] with
    you take,
Thoff° all in age that thei be yonge,
Ye may fare the bettir for ther sake,
Thurgh the blissing of so goode a kyng.
This is no dowte.

III BURGENSIS I kan the thanke for
    thy saying,
We will hym lowte.°
And hym to mete I am right bayne,°
On the beste maner that I canne,
220 For I desire to se hym fayne,°

by this skill *appropriately*   **are was hyght** *before was anticipated*   **ille** *sin*   **wene** *believe*   **ilkone** *each one*   **corse** *body*   **trone** *throne*   **gud ensampelys** *good examples*   **fele** *examined*   **plete** *argue*   **wote** *know*   **liste threte** *wishes to disobey*   **dose amys** *does amiss*   **than** *then*   **free** *noble man*   **awe** *ought*   **tyll** *into*   **soverayne** *all-powerful*   **knawe** *know*   **on rowe** *accordingly*   **lyste** *listen*   **of...ij** *two of his disciples*   **ther...praye** *began to ask on their master's behalf*   **softe** *comfortably*   **haly** *completely*   **trowe** *trust*   **be-heste** *request*   **redy bowne** *fully ready*   **ressayve** *receive*   **worthy** *appropriate*   **thoff** *though*   **lowte** *show honor*   **bayne** *eager*   **fayne** *gladly*

And hym honnoure as his awne° manne,
Sen° the soth° I see.
Kyng of Juuys° we call hym
  than,
Oure kyng is he.
IV BURGENSIS Oure kyng is he, that
  is no lesse,
Oure awne lawe to it cordis° well,
The prophettis all bare full witnesse,
Qwilke° full of hym secrete° gone felle;°
And thus wolde say,
230 'Emang youre selff schall come grete
  seele°
Thurgh God verray.'°
V BURGENSIS This same is he, ther is
  non othir,
Was us be-heest° full lange before,
For Moyses saide, als oure owne brothir,
A newe prophette God schulde restore.
Therfor loke ye
What ye will do, with-outen more;
Oure kyng is he.
VI BURGENSIS Of Juda come owre
  kyng so gent,°
240 Of Jesse, David, Salamon,
Also by his modir kynne° take tente,°
The Genolagye beres witnesse on;
This is right playne.
Hym to honnoure right as I canne
I am full bayne.°
VII BURGENSIS Of youre clene witte
  and youre consayte°
I am full gladde in harte and thought,
And hym to mete with-outen latt°
I am redy, and feyne° will noght,
250 Bot with you same°
To hym agayne us blisse hath brought,
With myrthe & game.
VIII BURGENSIS Youre argumentis
  thai are so clere

I can noght saie but graunte thou till,
For whanne I of that counsaille
  here,°
I coveyte hym with fervent wille
Onys° for to see,
I trowe fro thens I schall
Bettir man be.
260 **I BURGENSIS** Go we than with pro-
  cessioune
To mete that comely° as us awe,
With braunches, floures, and uny-
  soune,°
With myghtfull° songes her on a rawe,°
Our childir schall
Go synge before, that men may
  knaw
To this graunte we all.
PETRUS Jhesu! lord and maistir free,
Als thou comaunde so have we done,
270 This asse here we have brought to the,
What is thi wille thou schewe us
  sone,
And tarie° noght.
And than schall we, with-outen hune,°
Fulfill thi thought.
JESUS I thanke you brethere, mylde of
  mode,°
Do on this asse youre clothis ye laye,
And lifte me uppe with hertis gud,
That I on hir may sitte this daye,
In my blissing.
PHILIPPUS Lord thi will to do all-way
280 We graunte thing.°
JESUS Now my brethere with gud
  chere,
Gyves gode entente, for ryde I will
Un-to yone cyte ye se° so nere,
Ye shall me folowe, sam & still°
Als I are° sayde.

awne *own* Sen *since* soth *truth* Juuys *Jews* cordis *accords with* Qwilke *which* secrete *mys-tery* felle *examined* seele *happiness* verray *true* be-heest *promised* gent *noble* by...kynne *from his mother's line* take tente *take heed* bayne *eager* consayte *judgment* latt *delay* feyne *glad-ly* same *together* here *hear* Onys *once* comely *noble man* unysoune *concordant song* myght-full *loud* on a rawe *all together* tarie *tarry* hune *delay* mode *spirit* thing *this thing* Un-to... se *to the city you see* sam & still *peaceably together* are *before*

PHILIPPUS Lord! as the lyfe we graunte the till,
And halde us payde.
CECUS A lorde! that all this world has made,[12]
Bothe sonne and mone, nyght & day,
290 What noyse is this that makis me gladde?
Fro whens it schulde come I can noght saye,
Or what it mene.
Yf any man walke in this way,
Telle hym me be-dene.°
PAUPER Man! what ayles° the to crye?
Where wolde thou be? thou say me here.
CECUS A! sir, a blynde man am I,[13]
And ay has bene of tendyr yere
Sen I was borne,
300 I harde a voyce with nobill chere
Here me be-forne.
PAUPER Man, will thou oght that I can do?
CECUS Ya, sir, gladly wolde [I] witte,°
Yf thou couthe oght declare me to,
This myrthe I herde, what mene may it,
Or undirstande?
PAUPER Jesu, the prophite full of grace,
Comys here at hande,
And all the cetezens thay are bowne°
310 Gose hym to mete with melodye,
With the fayrest processioune
That evere was sene in this Jury.°
He is right nere.
CECUS Sir, helpe me to the strete hastely,
That I may here

That noyse, and also that I myght thurgh grace
My syght of hym, to crave° I wolde.
PAUPER Loo! he is here at this same place,
Crye faste° on hym, loke thou be bolde,
320 With voyce righ[t] high.
CECUS Jesu! the son of David calde.°
Thou have mercy!
Allas! I crye, he heris me noght,
He has no ruthe° of my mysfare,°
He turnes his herre,° where is his thought?
PAUPER Cry som-what lowdar, loke thou noght spare,°
So may thou spye.
CECUS Jesu, the salver of all sare,°
To me giffis gode hye.°
330 PHILIPPUS Cesse man, and crye noght soo,
The voyce of the pepill gose the by,
The ag[h]e° sette still and tente giffe° to,
Here passez the prophite of mercye.
Thou doys amys.°
CECUS A! David sone; to the I crye,
The kyng of blisse.
PETRUS Lorde! have mercy and late hym goo,
He can noght cesse of his crying,
He folows us both to and froo,
340 Graunte hym his boone° and his askyng,
And late hym wende.°
We gette no reste or that° this thing
Be broght to ende.
JESUS What wolde thou man I to the dede
In this present, telle oppynly.
CECUS Lorde my syght[14] is fro me hydde,
Thou graunte me it, I crye mercy,

Telle...be-dene *let him tell me immediately* ayles *troubles* witte *know* bowne *taking themselves* Jury *Jewry* crave *ask* faste *quickly* calde *called* ruthe *pity* mysfare *misfortune* herre *ear* spare *refrain* salver...sare *healer of all suffering* giffis gode hye *give good heed* ag[h]e *ought to* tente giffe *pay attention* doys amys *do amiss* boone *desire* wende *go* or that *unless*

This wolde I have.
JESUS Loke uppe nowe with chere
   blythely,°
350 Thi faith shall the save.
CECUS Wirschippe and honnoure ay°
   to the,
With all the service that can be done,[15]
The kyng of blisse loued mote° he be,
That thus my sight hathe sente so sone,
And by grete skill.
I was are° blynde as any stone;
I se at wille.
CLAUDUS A! wele wer tham that
   evere had liffe,
Old or yonge whedir it were,
360 Might welde ther lymmes° withouten
   striffe,
Go with this mirthe that I see here,
And contynewe,
For I am sette in sorowes sere°
That ay ar newe.°
Thou lord, that schope° both nyght and
   day,
For thy mercy have mynde on me,
And helpe me lorde, as thou wele may;[16]
I may noght gang.°
For I am lame,[17] as men may se,
370 And has ben lang.
For wele I wote,° as knowyn is ryffe,°
Bothe dome and deffe thou grauntist
   tham grace,
And also the dede that thou havyst
   geven liff,
Therfore graunte me lord, in this place,
My lymbis to welde.
JESUS My man, ryse and caste the
   cruchys° gode space°
Her in the felde.
And loke in trouthe thou stedfast be,

And folow me furth with gode me-
   nyng.°
380 CLAUDUS Lorde! lo, my crouchis
   whare thei flee,°
Als ferre° as I may late tham flenge
With bothe my hende;°[18]
That evere we have metyng
Now I defende.°
For I was halte° both lyme and
   lame,
And I suffered tene° and sorowes i-
   nowe,°
Ay lastand° lord, loved be thi name,
I am als light as birde on bowe.
Ay be thou blist,
390 Such grace hast thou schewed to
   me,
Lorde, as the list.°[19]
ZACHEUS[20] Sen first this worlde was
   made of noght,°
And all thyng sette in equite,°
Such ferly° thyng was nevere non
   wroght,°
As men this tyme may see with eye.
What it may mene?
I can noght say what it may be,
Comfort or tene.°
And cheffely of a prophete new,
400 That mekill is profite,° and that of
   latte,
Both day and nyght thai hym assewe,°
Oure pepill same thurgh strete & gatte
[new laws to lare,°][21]
Oure olde lawes as nowe thei hatte,°
And his kepis yare.°
Men fro deth to liffe he rayse,
The blynde and dome geve speche and
   sight,
Gretely therfore oure folke hym prayse,

---

with chere blithely *happily*   **ay** *ever*   **mote** *must*   **are** *before*   **welde ther lymmes** *wield their limbs*   **sere** *great*   **ay ar newe** *always have bothered* [me]   **schope** *shaped*   **gang** *move*   **wote** *know*   **ryffe** *widely*   **cruchys** *crutches*   **space** *distance*   **menyng** *intent*   **flee** *fly*   **Als ferre** *as far*   **hende** *hands*   **defende** *forbid*   **halte** *crippled*   **tene** *suffering*   **i-nowe** *great*   **Ay lastand** *everlasting*   **as the list** *as you wish*   **noght** *nothing*   **equite** *righteousness*   **ferly** *marvelous*   **was...wroght** *was never done*   **tene** *grief*   **mekill is profite** *is promoted greatly*   **assewe** *follow*   **lare** *teach*   **hatte** *hate*   **yare** *completely*

And folowis hym both day and nyght;
410 Fro towne to towne;
Thay calle hym prophite be right,
As of renowne.
And yit I mervayle of that thyng,
Of puplicans sen prince am I°
Of hym I cowthe have no knowyng;°
Yf all° I wolde° have comen hym nere,
Arly and late,
For I am lawe,° and of myne hight
Full is the gate.°
420 Bot sen° no bettir may be-falle,
I thynke what beste is for to doo,
I am schorte, ye knawe wele all,²²
Therfore yone tre I will go too,
And in it clyme;
Whedir he come or passe me fro,
I schall se hym.²³
A nobill tree thou secomoure,°
I blisse hym that the on the erthe
   brought.
Now may I see both here and thore,
430 That undir me it may be noght.°
Therfore in the°
Wille I bidde in herte & thought
Till I hym se
Un-to° the prophete come to towne
Her° will I bide what so befalle
JESUS Do Zache, do fast come downe.
ZACHEUS Lorde even at thi wille
   hastely I schall,
And tarie° noght.
To the on knes lord here I shall,
440 For sinne I wroght.°
And welcome prophete, trast° and
   trewe,
With all the pepull that to the langis.°
JESUS Zache, thi service new

Schall make the clene of all the wrong,
That thou haste done.
ZACHEUS Lorde, I lette° noght for
   this thrang°
Her to say sone,°
Me schamys with sinne, but noght to
   mende,°
I synne for-sake, therfore I will
450 Have° my gud° I have unspendid
Poure folke to geve it till;
This will I fayne.°
Whom I begylyd° to him I will
Make a-sith° agayne.
JESUS Thy clere confessionn schall the
   clense,
Thou may be sure of lastand° lyffe,
Un-to thi house, with-outen offense,
Is graunted pees withouten striffe.
Fare-wele, Zache!²⁴
460 ZACHEUS Lord, the lowte ay man and
   wiffe,°
Blist myght thou be.²⁵
JESUS My dere discipulis, beholde and
   see,
Un-to Jerusalem we schall assende,
Man sone° schall ther be-trayed be,
And gevyn in-to his enmys° hande,
With grete dispitte.°
Ther spitting on hym ther schall thei
   spende°
And smertly smyte.
Petir, take this asse me fro.
470 And lede it where thou are° it toke.
I murne,° I sigh, I wepe also,
Jerusalem on the to loke!
And so may thou,
That evere thou thi kyng for-suke,°
And was un-trewe.°

Of...I *since I am foremost of publicans* [*tax collectors*]   Of...knowyng *of him I could have no understand-*
ing   Yf all *however*   wolde *would*   lawe *short*   gate *road*   sen *since*   secomoure *sycamore*   noght
not   the *you*   un-to *until*   Her *here*   tarie *tarry*   For...wroght *for sin I committed*   trast
trusty   langis *long*   lette *delay*   thrang *throng*   sone *quickly*   Me...mende *I'm ashamed of my sin,*
but not to atone for it   Have *half*   gud *goods*   fayne *gladly*   begylyd *tricked*   a-sith *amends*   last-
and *(ever)lasting*   the...wife *may men and women praise you always*   Man sone *the Son of Man*   en-
mys *enemies'*   dispitte *malice*   spende *let loose*   are *before*   murne *mourne*   for-suke *forsook*   untrewe *disloyal*

For stone on stone schall none be lefte,
But doune to the grounde all schalbe
caste,
Thy game, thi gle,° al fro the refte,°
And all for synne that thou done hast.
480 Thou arte unkynde!
Agayne thi kyng thou hast trespast,
Have this in mynde.
PETRUS Porter, take her thyn asse
agayne,
At hande my lorde comys on his fette.
JANITOR Behalde, where all thi Bur-
geis bayne°
Comes with wirschippe hym to mete.
Therfore I will
Late hym abide her in this strete,
And lowte hym till.°
490 I BURGENSIS Hayll! prophette,
preved° withouten pere,
Hayll! prince of pees schall evere en-
dure,
Hayll! kyng comely, curteyse and clere,
Hayll! soverayne semely° to synfull
sure,°
To the all bowes.°
Hayll! lord lovely, oure cares may cure,
Ha[y]ll kyng of Jewes.
II BURGENSIS Hayll! florisshand°
floure that nevere shall fade,
Hayll! vyolett vernand° with swete
odoure,
Hayll! marke of myrthe, oure mede-
cyne° made,
500 Hayll! blossome brigh[t], hayll! oure
socoure.°
Hayll! kyng comely.
Hayll! menskfull° man, with the hon-
noure
With herte frely.

III BURGENSIS Hayll! David sone,
doughty° in dede,
Hayll! rose ruddy, hayll birrall°
clere,
Hayll! welle of welthe may make us
mede.°
Hayll! salver of oure sores sere,°
We wirschippe the.
Hayll! hendfull, with solas° sere,
510 Welcome thou be!
IV BURGENSIS Hayll! blissfull babe,
in Bedleme° borne,
Hayll! boote° of all oure bittir balis,°
Hayll! sege° that schoppe° bothe even
and morne,
Hayll! talker trystefull of trew tales.
Hayll! comely knyght,
Hayll! of mode° that most prevayles
To save the tyght.°
V BURGENSIS Hayll! dyamaunde°
with drewry dight,°
Hayll! jasper gentill° of Jewry,
520 Hayll! lylly lufsome° lemyd° with lyght,
Hayll! balme of boote,° moyste and
drye,
To all has nede.
Hayll! barne° most blist of mylde
Marie,
Hayll! all oure mede.°
VI BURGENSIS Hayll! conquerour,
hayll, most of myght,
Hayll! rawnsoner° of synfull all,
Hayll! pytefull,° hayll! lovely light,
Hayll! to us welcome be schall.
Hayll! kyng of Jues;
530 Hayll comely corse° that we the call
With mirthe that newes.°
VII BURGENSIS Hayll! sonne ay
schynand° with bright bemes,

---

gle *song*   refte *taken away*   bayne *eagerly*   lowte...till *pay homage to him*   preved *proven*   semely *honorable*   sure *reliable*   bowes *bow*   florisshand *flourishing*   vernand *blooming*   medecyne *cure*   socoure *care*   menskfull *excellent*   doughty *valiant*   birrall *beryl*   mede *reward*   sere *great*   solas *happiness*   Bedleme *Bethlehem*   boote *remedy*   balis *miseries*   sege *man*   schoppe *shaped*   mode *mind*   tyght *captive*   dyamaunde *diamond*   with drewry dight *adorned with jewels*   gentill *noble*   lufsome *lovely*   lemyd *blazing*   boote *help*   barne *child*   mede *reward*   rawnsoner *redeemer*   pytefull *merciful one*   corse *body*   newes *renews*   ay schynand *always shining*

Hayll! lampe of liff schall nevere waste,
Hayll! lykand° lanterne luffely lemes,°
Hayll! texte of trewthe the trew to taste.
Hayll! kyng & sire,
Hayll! maydens chylde that menskid°
   hir most,
We the desire.
VIII BURGENSIS Hayll! domysman°
   dredful, that all schall deme,°
540 Hayll! quyk° and dede that all schall
   lowte,°
Hayll! whom worschippe moste will
   seme,°
Hayll! whom all thyng schall drede and
   dowte.°
We welcome the.
Hayll! and welcome of all abowte,
To owre cete.°

lykand *pleasant*   luffely lemes *beloved beams of light*   menskid *honored*   domysman *judge*
(n.)   deme *judge (v.)*   quyk *living*   lowte *kneel*   whom...seme *for whom worship is most appropri-*
ate   dowte *fear*   cete *city*

Endnotes

1   The sole copy of the "Entry" is found in ff. 106v-112v of British Library Additional MS 35290, also known as the York Register (hereafter MS), compiled between 1463 and 1477 (Beadle xii). The base text for this edition is taken from "The Entry into Jerusalem upon the Ass," *York Plays: The Plays Performed by the Crafts or Mysteries of York on the Day of Corpus Christi in the 14th, 15th, and 16th Centuries*, ed. Lucy Toulmin Smith (The Clarendon Press, 1885, pp. 201–18). The text is in the public domain. I have followed Smith's lineation, though in the MS the play's short lines follow continuously from the previous ones. Instead of adhering to Smith's practice of numbering every third and seventh line, I have marked line numbers into divisions of ten. Since neither stage directions nor stanza numbers appear in the MS, I have not incorporated Smith's. I have, however, retained Smith's list of *dramatis personae*, along with her parenthetical descriptions of the characters, despite their absence from the MS. While Smith's glosses and notes are eminently useful, my glosses and end notes replace them. Smith's emendations to the MS remain [in brackets]. I have regularized the MS's use of u/v, capitalized silently the first letters of all proper names, including *God*, and substituted th for þ, and gh, y, and z for ȝ, as appropriate. In addition to Smith's and Beadle's editions, I also am indebted to the following texts: Clifford Davidson, ed., *The York Corpus Christi Plays* (Western Michigan University, 2011); and York Mystery Plays, British Library Additional MS 35290. Digitized Manuscripts, British Library, www.bl.uk/manuscripts/FullDisplay.aspx?ref=Add_MS_35290&index=0.

2   Matthew 21.1–17, Mark 11.1–11, Luke 19.28–44, and John 12.12–19.

3   Martin Stevens, *Four Middle English Mystery Cycles: Textual, Contextual, and Critical Interpretations* (Princeton University Press, 1987), p. 52.

4   Edward Wheatley, *Stumbling Blocks before the Blind: Medieval Constructions of a Disability* (University of Michigan Press, 2010), p. 11.

5   Richard Beadle, ed., *The York Plays: A Critical Edition of the York Corpus Christi Play as Recorded in British Library Additional MS 35290*. 2 vols. EETS S.S. 23–24 (Oxford University Press, 2009, 2013), p. 202.

6   Ibid., p. 208.

7   Irina Metzler, *Disability in Medieval Europe: Thinking about Physical Impairment during the High Middle Ages, c. 1100–1400* (Routledge, 2006), p. 47.

8   Mark P. O'Tool, "Disability and the Suppression of Historical Identity: Rediscovering the Professional Backgrounds of the Blind Residents of the Hôpital des Quinze-Vingts," *Disability in the Middle Ages: Reconsiderations and Reverberations*, eds. Joshua R. Eyler (Ashgate, 2010), pp. 11–24, at p. 12. See also Sharon Farmer, *Surviving Poverty in Medieval Paris: Gender, Ideology, and the Daily Lives of the Poor* (Cornell University Press, 2002), pp. 60–70; Edward Wheatley, *Stumbling Blocks before the Blind: Medieval Constructions of a Disability* (University of Michigan Press, 2010), pp. 351–82; Barbara Gusick, "Christ's Healing of the Lame Man in the York Cycle's 'Entry into Jerusalem': Interpretive Challenges for the Newly Healed," *Fifteenth-Century Studies*, vol. 31, 2005, pp. 82–83; and Barbara Gusick, "Groping in Darkness: The Man Born Blind and Christ's Ministry in the York Cycle," *New Approaches to European Theater of the Middle Ages: An Ontology*, eds. Barbara I. Gusick and Edelgard E. DuBruck (Peter Lang, 2004), p. 51.

9   Metzler, *Disability in Medieval Europe: Thinking about Physical Impairment during the High Middle Ages*, pp. 42–43.

10   M.E. *def* can refer literally to an inability to hear, or metaphorically to an unwillingness to do so (*MED def*, adj. 2b, https://quod.lib.umich.edu/cgi/m/mec/med-idx?type=id&id=MED10774). Though the literal meaning seems more likely here, the figurative one could apply to people like Zacheus (ll. 392–461).

11   The Burgess recalls Jesus' raising of Lazarus from the dead in John 12:17–18.

12   In a note to this line, Smith cites Jesus' healing of two blind men as he leaves Jericho (Matthew 20:30–34), as well as his healing of Bartimeus, son of Timeus (Mark 10:46–52).

13 The *OED* locates the first occurrence of the term "blind" in the literal sense of "destitute of the sense of sight" in the West Saxon *Gospel of Mark* (ca. 1000) 10:46: "Timeus sunu, Bartimeus, sæt blind wið þone weg wædla." (*blind* adj. 1.1.a, http://www.oed.com/view/Entry/20224?rskey=SonVJR&result=2&isAdvanced=false#eid). See *Evangelium Secundum Marcum: The Gospel of Saint Mark in West-Saxon*, ed. James Wilson Bright (D.C. Heath & Co., 1905). See Luke 19:1–10.

14 MS *syight*

15 Gusick contends that Cecus' promise of service highlights the transactional nature of his healing, for he now must use his newly restored body to contribute productively to society (Gusick, "Groping in Darkness," pp. 54–55).

16 A line is missing from the MS after 367.

17 The *OED* cites one of the earliest uses of "lame" as "disabled or impaired in any way; weak, infirm; paralyzed; unable to move," in *Bede's Ecclesiastical History* (ca. 900), 5.5: "He wæs loma & ealra his lioma þegnunga benumen" (*lame* adj. 1.a., http://www.oed.com/view/Entry/105263?rskey=3sDhvZ&result=4&isAdvanced=false#eid). See *The Old English Version of Bede's Ecclesiastical History of the English People*, 2 vols., ed. Thomas Miller, EETS (Trübner, 1890).

18 Davidson notes that this line is written on the bottom of the previous page, crossed out, and reentered to the right of 381 by John Clerke (Davidson, *The York Corpus Christi Plays*, 519). Clerke (1510–80) was the assistant to the Common Clerk of York (Beadle xxvii). Clerke erroneously entered *my* for *myn* (Davidson, *The York Corpus Christi Plays*, 519).

19 Gusick discusses how the play presents an "interpretive challenge" regarding the integration of the newly healed Claudus into the community's social structure (Gusick, "Christ's Healing of the Lame Man in the York Cycle's 'Entry into Jerusalem'," p. 87).

20 The Zacheus episode occurs in Luke 19:1–10.

21 This line is Smith's suggestion for a line missing from the MS. Beadle and Davidson use ellipses.

22 Though being short would not have been considered a disability, per se, it would have marked Zacchaeus as "marginalized"

member of the community (Gusick, "Christ's Transformation," p. 72).

23 Zacchaeus' climbing a sycamore tree in order to get a better vantage point "emphasizes how instrumental the event of seeing (and *being seen*) is to this play in particular" (Barbara Gusick, "Christ's Transformation of Zaccaeus in the York Cycle's 'Entry into Jerusalem,'" *Fifteenth-Century Studies*, vol. 30, 2004, p. 68; emphasis in original).

24 Gusick examines Zacheus' similarities with the physically disabled, and she questions whether he can become a redeemed member of the faithful community (ibid., esp. pp. 77–78).

25 Catherine Willits analyzes how spatial and narrative isolation of the disabled and poor characters reinforces the "irreducible heterogeneity" of York ("The Dynamics and Staging of Community in Medieval 'Entry into Jerusalem' Plays: Dramatic Resources Influencing Marlowe's Jew of Malta," *Medieval & Renaissance Drama in England*, vol. 27, 2014, p. 84). See also Kate Crassons, *The Claims of Poverty. Literature, Culture, and Ideology in Late Medieval England* (University of Notre Dame Press, 2010), pp. 221–74.

The *Nativity* from the *N-Town Plays*[1]
(ca. 1460–1520)

Contributed by Jeffery G. Stoyanoff

Introduction

The N-Town *Nativity* dramatizes the events leading up to and directly after the birth of Christ based on the apocryphal material found in *Pseudo-Matthew*. Perhaps unsurprisingly, the birth of Christ itself (alluded to only in a stage direction) is almost an afterthought to the action surrounding the birth. Some of the typical *fabliaux* elements of the story also appear in this version of the pageant, playing on the common cuckold trope of an older man with a younger wife, but they are not nearly as pronounced as in other biblical plays. The midwives appear in this pageant to function as witnesses to the newborn Christ and, of especial interest for this collection, to stage one of the two miracles that this pageant stages—the newborn Christ's healing of midwife Salome's hand that had withered because of her doubt only lines earlier. As Irina Metzler has demonstrated, miracles in the Middle Ages were often linked with disability, particularly because, unlike illness, disability was a static state.[2] In this pageant, then, we see two distinct impairments: Joseph's age and Salome's withered hand. Both impairments lead to staged conversions via miracle. Joseph cannot pick cherries for Mary because such labor would be difficult for a man of his age, and after the cherry tree bends down to Mary and allows her to pluck cherries from it, he is convinced that Mary indeed carries the Christ child. Similarly, the newborn Christ's healing of Salome's impairment—her withered hand—leads to her conversion.

Pageants involving Mary and Joseph across all medieval biblical plays use Joseph's age to comic effects, and Joseph's age is also presented as an impairment in the N-Town *Nativity*. At the beginning of the pageant, Mary and Joseph are traveling to Bethlehem to find a place in which Mary may give birth to her child. En route, Mary notices a cherry tree and asks Joseph to pick her some cherries from it: "For to haue therof ryght fayn I wold, / And it plesyd yow to labore se mech for me" (ll. 34–35). Mary qualifies this request as labor for Joseph, and even though this word simply could refer to work, it usually connotes difficult work. Joseph's response affirms the difficult nature of this work, and his final retort seems to fall into the cuckold vein of age jokes when he retorts "...lete hym pluk yow cheryes begatt yow with childe!" (l. 39). Despite the potential latent humor in this scene, the pageant presents Joseph's age as an impairment to fulfill his duties as Mary's spouse. His age will not allow him to retrieve cherries for Mary, and so Mary prays to God and the tree bends down to her (ll. 40–43). Joseph's response demonstrates conversion to full belief: "For now I beleve wel it may non other be / But that my spowse beryght the Kyngys Son of Blys" (ll. 46–47). The pageant uses Joseph's impairment to stage a miracle that assuages his doubt of Mary and then leads him to testify his true belief that Mary's child is indeed Christ.

The second staged impairment that leads to a miracle in the N-Town *Nativity* is Salome's withered hand that results from her doubt of the virgin birth. Unlike Joseph's age, however, Salome's hand ably functions when she enters the pageant as one of two midwives. It is only after Zelomy, the other midwife, affirms the virgin birth that Salome, incredulous, claims, "It is not trewe, it may nevyr be! / that bothe be clene I cannot beleve!" (ll. 242–43). After Mary invites Salome to examine her, Salome's hand then withers (the Latin literally translates "dries up"), which she attributes to her "grett dowth and fals beleve" (l. 255). However, her impairment is short-lived, and the second miracle of the pageant both heals Salome's hand and converts her to belief. After she touches the Christ child's clothing, she exclaims, "A, now blyssyd be this chylde eurymore! / the Sone of God, forsothe he is" (ll. 294–95). Like Joseph, Salome testifies that Mary's child is Christ; furthermore, she becomes a messenger of the good news of the coming savior. She announces, "Of this grett meracle more knowlege to make, / I xal go telle it in iche place, iwys." (ll. 308–9). In the space of slightly over sixty lines, Salome has moved from doubt into belief.

For both Joseph and Salome, physical impairment is linked to spiritual doubt, which fits Edward Wheatley's religious model of disability. For the N-Town *Nativity*, then, doubt is perhaps the impairment it hopes to cure via the miracles staged during this pageant. However, spiritual impairments and physical impairments are of two distinct natures, and one cannot help but to wonder whether this pageant exploits the real physical impairments of persons in service to its faith-driven message. Then again, perhaps if the audience also testifies true belief, such faith, so the pageant reasons, makes physical impairment inconsequential.

Bibliography

Carlson, Cindy L. "Like a Virgin: Mary and Her Doubters in the N-Town Cycle." *Constructions of Widowhood and Virginity in the Middle Ages*, edited by Cindy L. Carlson and Angela Jane Weisl. St. Martin's, 1999, pp. 199–217.

Cushman, Helen. "Handling Knowledge: Holy Bodies in the Middle English Mystery Plays." *Journal of Medieval and Early Modern Studies*, vol. 47, no. 2, 2017, pp. 279–304.

Eyler, Joshua R. "Introduction: Breaking Boundaries, Building Bridges." *Disability in the Middle Ages: Reconsiderations and Reverberations*, edited by Joshua R. Eyler. Taylor and Francis, 2010, pp. 1–8.

McNabb, Cameron Hunt. "Staging Disability in Medieval Drama." The Ashgate Research Companion to Medieval Disability Studies, edited by John P. Sexton and Kisha G. Tracy. Routledge, forthcoming.

Metzler, Irina. *A Social History of Disability in the Middle Ages: Cultural Considerations of Physical Impairment*. Routledge, 2013.

Novacich, Sarah Elliott. "Transparent Mary: Visible Interiors and the Maternal Body in the Middle Ages." *Journal of English and Germanic Philology*, vol. 116, no. 4, 2017, pp. 464–90.

Price, Merrall Llewelyn. "Re-membering the Jews: Theatrical Violence in the N-Town Marian Plays." *Comparative Drama*, vol. 41, no. 4, 2007–8, pp. 439–63.

Ryan, Denise. "Playing the Midwife's Part in the English Nativity Plays." *The Review of English Studies*, vol. 54, no. 216, 2003, pp. 435–48.

Wheatley, Edward. *Stumbling Blocks Before the Blind: Medieval Constructions of a Disability*. University of Michigan Press, 2010.

DRAMATIS PERSONAE

Joseph
Maria
Citizen
Zelomy, first midwife
Salome, second midwife
Angelus°

JOSEPH Lord, what travayl° to man is
    wrought!°
Rest in this werd° behovyth° hym non.
Octauyan, oure emperour, sadly° hath
    besought;
Oure trybute hym to bere folk must
    forth ichon;°
It is cryed in every bourgh and cety be
    name.
I that am a pore tymbre-wryth°
Born of the blood of Dauyd,
the emperorys comawndement I must
    holde with,
And° ellys I were to blame.

10   Now, my wyff, Mary, what sey ye to
    this?
For sekyr,° nedys I must forth wende°
Onto the cyté of Bedleem° fer hens,
    iwys.°
thus to labore I muste my body bende.
MARIA Myn husbond and my spowse,
    with yow wyl I wende;
A syght of that cyté fayn° wolde I se.
If I myght of myn alye° ony ther fynde,
It wold be grett joyd onto me.
JOSEPH My spowse, ye be with childe,
    I fere° yow to kary,
For mesemyth° it were werkys wylde.°

20   But yow to plese ryght fayn° wold I.
yitt women ben ethe° to greve° whan
    thei be with childe.
Now latt us forth wende as fast as we
    may,
And almyghty God spede us in oure
    jurnay.
MARIA A, my swete husbond, wolde
    ye telle to me
What tre is yon° standynge vpon yon
    hylle?
JOSEPH Forsothe, Mary, it is clepyd° a
    chery tre;

Angelus *Angel* [*Latin*]   **travayl** *toil*   **wrought** *made*   **werd** *world*   **behovyth** *behooves*   **sadly** *steadfastly*   **ichon** *each one*   **tymbre-wryth** *carpenter*   **And** *if*   **sekyr** *sure*   **wende** *go*   **Bedleem** *Bethlehem*   **iwys** *indeed*   **fayn** *gladly*   **alye** *kin*   **fere** *fear*   **mesemyth** *it seems to me*   **werkys wylde** *rash act*   **fayn** *gladly*   **ethe** *easy*   **greve** *upset*   **yon** *over there*   **clepyd** *called*

In tyme of yere° ye myght fede yow
  theron youre fylle.
Turne ageyn, husbond, and beholde yon
  tre,
How that it blomyght° now so swetly.
30 JOSEPH Cum on, Mary, that we worn
  at yon cyté,
Or ellys we may be blamyd, I telle yow
  lythly.°
MARIA Now, my spowse, I pray yow
  to behold
How the cheryes growyn vpon yon tre.
For to haue therof ryght fayn I wold,
And° it plesyd yow to labore so mech
  for me.
JOSEPH youre desyre to fulfylle I xal°
  assay, sekyrly.°
Ow!° To plucke yow of these cheries, it
  is a werk wylde!
For the tre is so hygh it wol not be
  lyghtly°—
therfore lete hym pluk yow cheryes
  begatt yow with childe!
40 Now, good Lord, I pray the, graunt me
  this boun,°
To haue of these cheries and° it be
  youre wylle.
Now I thank it God, this tre bowyth° to
  me down!
I may now gaderyn° anowe° and etyn
  my fylle.
JOSEPH Ow! I know weyl° I haue offendyd my God in Trinyté
Spekyng to my spowse these vnkynde
  wurdys.
For now I beleve wel it may non other
  be
But that my spowse beryght° the Kyngys Son of Blys;
He help us now at oure nede.

Of the kynrede° of Jesse worthely were
  ye bore,
50 Kyngys and patryarkys yow beffore.
All these wurthy of youre kynred wore,
As clerkys in story rede.
MARIA Now gramercy,° husbond, for
  youre report.
In oure weys wysely late us forth
  wende.°
the Fadyr allmyghty, he be oure comfort,
the Holy Gost gloryous, he be oure
  frende.
JOSEPH Heyl, wurchepful sere, and
  good day!
A ceteceyn° of this cyte ye seme to be.
Of herborwe° for spowse and me I yow
  pray;
60 For trewly this woman is ful weré,°
And fayn° at reste, sere, wold she be.
We wolde fulfylle the byddynge of oure
  emperour
For to pay trybute as ryght is oure.
And to kepe ourseselfe from dolowre,°
We are come to this cyté
CITIZEN Sere, ostage° in this town
  know I non
thin wyff and thu in for to slepe;
This ceté is besett° with pepyl every
  won,°
And yett thei ly withowte,° ful every
  strete.
70 Withinne no wall, man, comyst thu
  nowth°
Be thu onys° withinne the cyté gate.
Onethys° in the strete a place may be
  sowth°
theron to rest withowte debate.
JOSEPH Nay, sere, debate, that wyl I
  nowth—

---

yere *year* blomyght *blooms* lythly *gently* And *If* xal *shall* sekyrly *surely* Ow! *Oh!* lyghtly *with little effort* boun *gift* and if bowyth *bows* gaderyn *gather* anowe *enough* weyl *well* berught *bears* kynrede *family* gramercy *many thanks* wende *go* ceteceyn *citizen* herborwe *inn, lodgings* weré *weary* fayn *gladly* dolowre *suffering* ostage *lodging house* besett *full* every won *every dwelling* ly withowte *lie outside* nowth *not* onys *once* Onethys *not readily* sowth *found*

All such thyngys passyn my powere.
But yitt my care and all my thought
Is for Mary, my derlynge° dere.
A, swete wyff, what xal° we do?
Wher xal we logge° this nyght?

80 Onto the Fadyr of Heffne pray we so,
Vs to kepe from every wykkyd whyt.°
CITIZEN Good man, o° word I wyl the
sey,
If thu wylt do by the counsel of me:
Yondyr is an hous of haras° that stant
be the wey;
Amonge the bestys° herboryd° may ye
be.
MARIA Now the Fadyr of Hefne, he
mut° yow yelde.
His sone in my wombe, forsothe,° he is.
He kepe the and thi good be fryth° and
felde.°
Go we hens, husband, for now tyme it
is.

90 But herk now, good husband, a newe
relacyon,°
Which in myself I know ryght well:
Cryst, in me hath take incarnacyon,
Sone wele° be borne, the trowth I fele.
In this pore logge° my chawmere° I
take,
Here for to abyde the blyssyd byrth
Of hym that all this werd° dude° make.
Betwyn myn sydys I fele he styrth.°
JOSEPH God be thin help, spowse, it
swemyth° me sore,
thus febyly loggyd and in so pore degré.

100 Goddys sone amonge bestys° for to be
bore—
His woundyr werkys fulfyllyd must
be—

In an hous that is desolat,° withowty[n]
any wall;
Fyer nor wood non here is.
MARIA Joseph, myn husbond, abydyn°
here I xal,°
For here wyl be born the Kyngys Sone
of Blys.
JOSEPH Now, jentyll° wyff, be of good
myrth,
And if ye wyl owght° haue, telle me
what ye thynk.
I xal not spare for schep nor derth.°
Now telle me youre lust° of mete and
drynk.

110 **MARIA** For mete and drynk lust I
ryght nowth°—
Allmyghty God my fode° xal be.
Now that I am in chawmere brought,
I hope ryght well my chylde to se.
Therfore, husband, of youre honesté,
Avoyd° yow hens out of this place,
And I alone with humylité
Here xal abyde Goddys hygh grace.
JOSEPH All redy, wyff, yow for to plese
I wyl go hens out of youre way,

120 And seke sum mydwyuys° yow for to
ese
Whan that ye° trauayle of childe° this
day.
Farewell, trewe wyff and also clene
may,°
God be youre comforte in Trinyté.
MARIA To God in hevyn for yow I
pray,
He yow preserve wherso° ye be.
hic dum joseph est Absens parit Ma-
ria filium vnigenitum.°

---

derlynge *darling*   xal *shall*   logge *stay*   whyt *person*   o *one*   haras *a place where horses are*
kept   bestys *beasts*   herboryd *lodged*   mut *might*   forsothe *truly*   fryth *forest*   felde *field*   relacyon *relationship*   Sone wele *soon will*   logge *rude shelter*   chawmere *chamber*   werd *world*   dude
did   styrth *stir*   swemyth *grieves*   bestys *beasts*   desolat *ruined*   abydyn *wait*   xal *shall*   jentyll *gracious, kind*   owght *anything*   schep nor derth *abundance or scarcity*   lust *desire*   nowth
not   fode *food*   Avoyd *clear (as in "clear out")*   mydwyuys *midwives*   trauayle of childe *give*
birth   clene may *virgin*   wherso *wherever*   hic...vnigenitum *Here while Joseph is absent, Mary gives*
birth to the Begotten Son [of God] [Latin].

JOSEPH Now God, of whom comyth all releffe,
And as all grace in the is grownde,
So saue my wyff from hurt and greffe
Tyl I sum mydwyuys° for here haue fownde.
130 Travelynge° women in care be bownde
With grete throwys° whan thei do grone;
God helpe my wyff that sche not swownde.°
I am ful sory sche is alone!
It is not conuenyent° a man to be
ther women gon in travalynge.³
Wherfore sum mydwyff fayn° wold I se,
My wyff to helpe that is so yenge.°
ZELOMY Why makyst thu, man, suche mornyng?
Tell me sum dele of° youre gret mone.°
140 JOSEPH My wyf is now in gret longynge,
Trauelyng of chylde, and is alone.
For Godys loue, that sytt in trone,°
As ye mydwyuys that kan° youre good,°
Help my yonge spowse in hast anone.°
I drede me sore of that fayr food!
SALOME Be of good chere and of glad mood,
We ij° mydwyuys with the wyll go.
ther was nevyr woman in such plyght stood
But we were redy here help to do.
150 My name is Salomee, all men me knowe
For a mydwyff of wurthy fame.
Whan women travayl,° grace doth growe;
theras° I come I had nevyr shame.
ZELOMYE And I am Zelomye, men knowe my name,

We tweyn with the wyl go togedyr
And help thi wyff fro hurt and grame.°
Com forth, Joseph, go we streyth thedyr.°
JOSEPH I thank yow, damys, ye comforte my lyff.
Streyte to my spowse walke we the way.
160 In this pore logge° lyght° Mary my wyff.
Hyre° for to comforte, gode frendys, asay.°
SALOME We dare not entre this logge, in fay°—
ther is therin so gret bryghtnes!
Mone be nyght nor sunne be day
Shone nevyr so clere in ther lyghtnesse!
ZELOMYE Into this hous dare I not gon;
the woundyrifull lyght doth me affray.°
JOSEPH Than wyl myself gon in alon
And chere my wyff if that I may.
170 All heyl, maydon and wyff, I say!
How dost thu fare? Telle me thi chere.°
The for to comforte in gesyn° this day,
Tweyn gode mydwyuis I haue brought here.
The for to helpe, that art in harde bonde,°
Zelomye and Salomee be com with me.
For dowte of° drede withowte thei do stond,
And dare not come in for lyght that they se.

       Hic Maria subridendo dicat:°
MARIA The myght off the Godhede in his magesté
Wyl not be hyd now at this whyle.°
180 The chylde that is born wyl preue his modyr fre,°

---

mydwyuys *midwives* **Travelynge** *laboring* **throwys** *pains* **swownde** *faint* **conuenyent** *appropriate* **fayn** *gladly* **yenge** *young* **sum dele of** *something about* **mone** *complaint* **in trone** *enthroned* **kan** *know* **good** *profession* **in hast anone** *quickly, at once* **ij** *two* **travayl** *labor* **theras** *in which place* **grame** *grief* **thedyr** *to that place* **logge** *rude shelter* **lyght** *lies* **Hyre** *her* **asay** *examine* **fay** *faith* **affray** *frighten* **chere** *mood* **gesyn** *childbed* **in harde bonde** *in distress* **For dowte of** *for fear of* **Hic…dicat** *Here Mary, smiling, says [Latin]* **whyle** *time* **fre** *noble*

A very clene mayde,° and therfore I
   smyle.
JOSEPH Why do ye lawghe, wyff? Ye be
   to blame!
I pray yow, spowse, do no more so!
In happ° the mydwyuys° wyl take it to
   grame,°
And at youre nede helpe wele non do.°
Iff ye haue nede of mydwyuys, lo,
Perauenture° thei wyl gon hens.
therfor be sad,° and° ye may so,
And wynnyth all the mydwyuis good
   diligens.
190 MARIA Husbond, I pray yow dysplese
   yow nowth,°
thow that I lawghe and gret joye haue.
Here is the chylde this werde° hath
   wrought,°
Born now of me, that allthynge xal°
   saue.
JOSEPH I aske yow grace, for I dyde
   raue!°
O gracyous childe, I aske mercy.
As thu art Lord and I but knaue,°
Foryeue me now my gret foly.
Alas, mydwyuis, what haue I seyd?
I pray yow com to us more nere,
200 For here I fynde my wyff a mayd
And in here arme a chylde hath here—
Bothe mayd and modyr sche is in fere!°
that God wole haue may nevyrmore
   fayle.
Modyr on erth was nevyr non clere
Withowth sche had in byrth travayle.°
ZELOMY In byrth trauayle muste sche
   nedys haue,
Or ellys no chylde of here is born.
JOSEPH I pray yow dame, and° ye
   vowchsaue,°

Com se the chylde my wyff beforn.°
210 SALOME Grete God be in this place.
Swete systyr, how fare ye?
MARIA I thank the Fadyr of his hygh
   grace;
His owyn son and my chylde here ye
   may se.
ZELOMY All heyl, Mary, and ryght
   good morn.
Who was mydwyfe of this fayr chylde?
MARIA He that nothynge wyl haue
   forlorn°
Sent me this babe, and I mayd mylde.°
ZELOMYE With honde lete me now
   towch and fele
Yf ye haue nede of medycyn.
220 I xal° yow comforte and helpe ryght
   wele
As other women yf ye haue pyn.°
MARIA Of this fayr byrth that here is
   myn
Peyne nere° grevynge fele I ryght non.
I am clene mayde and pure virgyn;
Tast° with youre hand youreself alon.
     Hic palpat Zelomye Beatam
               Virginem dicens:°
ZELOMY O myghtfull God, haue
   mercy on me!
A merveyle that nevyr was herd beforn°
Here opynly I fele and se:
A fayr chylde of a maydon is born,
230 And nedyth no waschynge as other
   don:°
Ful clene and pure forsoth° is he,
Withoutyn spott or ony polucyon,
His modyr nott hurte of virgynité!
Coom nere, gode systyr Salomé.
Behobde the brestys of this clene rnayd,
Ful of fayr mylke how that thei be,

---

clene mayde *virgin* **In happ** *in case* **mydwyuys** *midwives* **grame** *grief* **wele non do** *will not
do* **Perauenture** *perchance* **sad** *sober* **and** *if* **nowth** *not* **werde** *world* **wrought** *made* **xal**
shall **raue** *behave foolishly* **knaue** *peasant* **in fere** *both together* **travayle** *labor* **and** *if* **vowchsaue** *grant* **beforn** *in front of* **forlorn** *lost* **mylde** *merciful* **xal** *shall* **pyn** *pain* **nere** *nor* **Tast**
test **Hic...dicens** *Here Zelomy touches the Blessed Virgin, saying: [Latin]* **beforn** *before* **don**
do **forsoth** *truly*

And hyre° chylde clene, as I fyrst sayd.
As other ben nowth° fowle arayd,°
But clene and pure bothe modyr and
    chylde.
240 Of this matyr° I am dysmayd,
To se them both thus vndefyled!
    SALOME It is not trewe, it may nevyr
    be!
that bothe be clene I cannot beleve!
A mayd mylke haue nevyr man dyde se,
Ne woman bere chylde withowte grett
    greve.°
I xal° nevyr trowe° it but I it preve!°
With hand towchynge but I assay,
In my conscience it may nevyr cleue°
that sche hath chylde and is a may.°
250 MARIA Yow for to putt clene out of
    dowth,
Towch with youre hand and wele asay.°
Wysely ransake° and trye the trewthe
    owth°
Whethyr I be fowlyd or a clene may.
        Hic tangit Salomee Mari[am] et
        cum arescerit manus eius vlu-
        lando et quasi flendo dicjt:°
SALOME Alas, alas, and weleawaye!°
For my grett dowth and fals beleve
Myne hand is ded and drye as claye—
My fals vntrost° hath wrought° mysch-
    eve!
Alas the tyme that I was born,
Thus to offende ayens° Goddys myght!
260 Myn handys power is now all lorn,°
Styff as a stykke, and may nowth°
    plyght.°
For I dede tempte this mayde so bryght
And helde ayens here pure clennes,
In grett myscheff now am I pyght.°

Alas, alas for my lewdnes!°
O Lord of Myght, thu knowyst be
    trowth,
that I haue evyr had dred of the.
On every power whyght° evyr I haue
    rowthe,°
And yove hem almes for loue of the.
270 Bothe wyff and wedowe that askyght,°
    for the,
And frendles chylderyn that haddyn
    grett nede,
I dude° them cure, and all for the,
And toke no rewarde of them, nor
    mede.°
Now as a wrecch for fals beleve
that I shewyd in temptynge this mayde,
My hand is ded and doth me greve.°
Alas, that evyr I here assayde!
    ANGELUS Woman, thi sorwe to haue
    delayde,
Wurchep° that childe that ther is born;
280 Towch the clothis ther he is leyde,
For he xal saue all that is lorn.°
    SALOME O gloryous chylde and Kynge
    of Blysse,
I aske yow mercy for my trespace.
I knowlege my synne, I demyd amys.°
O blyssyd babe, grawnt me sum grace!
Of yow, mayde, also here in this place
I aske mercy knelynge on kne.
Moste holy mayde, grawnt me solace,
Sum wurde of comforte sey now to me.
290 MARIA As Goddys aungel to yow dede
    telle,
My chylde is medycyn for every sor.°
Towch his clothis be my cowncelle,
yowre hand ful sone he wyl restor.

---

hyre *her*   **nowth** *not*   **fowle arayd** *unclean*   **matyr** *physical substance*   **greve** *pain*   **xal**
shall   **trowe** *have trust*   **preve** *prove*   **cleue** *firmly fixed*   **may** *virgin*   **asay** *examine*   **ransake**
examine   **owth** *oath*   **Hic...dicjt** *Here Salome touches Mary, and when her hand dries up, pitifully
weeping, she says* [*Latin*]   **weleawaye** *alas*   **vntrost** *mistrust*   **wrought** *made*   **ayens** *facing*   **lorn**
lost   **nowth** *not*   **plyght** *flex*   **pyght** *placed*   **lewdnes** *ignorance*   **power whyght** *poor person*   **rowthe** *pity*   **askyght** *asks*   **dude** *did*   **mede** *gift*   **greve** *grieve*   **Wurchep** *worship*   **xal...lorn**
shall save all that is lost   **demyd amys** *believed erroneously*   **sor** *pain*

*Hic Salomee tangit fim-
briam Christi dicens:°*

SALOME A, now blyssyd be this
   chylde euyrmore!
the Sone of God, forsothe° he is,
Hath helyd myn hand that was forlore°
Thorwe fals beleve and demynge amys!
In every place I xal telle this:
Of a clene mayde that God is born,
300 And in oure lyknes God now clad is,
Mankend to saue that was forlorn;
His modyr a mayde as sche was beforn,°
Natt fowle polutyd as other women be,
But fayr and fresch as rose on thorn,
Lely-wyte,° clene with pure virginyté.
Of this blyssyd babe my leve now do I
   take,
And also of yow, hygh Modyr of Blysse.
Of this grett meracle more knowlege to
   make,
I xal° go telle it in iche° place, iwys.°
310 MARIA Farewel, good dame, and God
   youre wey wysse.°
In all youre jurnay God be youre spede!
And of his hygh mercy that Lord so
   yow blysse
that ye nevyr offende more in word,
   thought, nore dede.
ZELOMY And I also do take my leve
   here
Of all this blyssyd good company,
Praynge youre grace bothe fere and nere
On us to spede youre endles mercy.
JOSEPH The blyssyng of that Lord that
   is most myghty
Mote sprede on yow in every place;
320 Of all youre enmyes to haue the victory,
God that best may, grawnt yow his
   grace.
AMEN

Hic...dicens *Here Salome touches the fringe of Chist['s clothes], saying:* [*Latin*] **forsothe** *truly* **forlore**
lost **beforn** *before* **Lely-wyte** *lily-white* **xal** *shall* **iche** *each* **iwys** *indeed* **wysse** *guide*

Endnotes

1   The text below was compiled by Gerard
Necastro using *Ludus Coventriae or The Plaie called
Corpus Christi, Cotton MS. Vespian D. VIII.*, ed. K.S.
Block, Early English Text Society, Extra Series,
No. CXX, 1922, pp. 135–45 and *The N-Town Plays*,
ed. Douglas Sugano, TEAMS Middle English Text
Series (Medieval Institute Publications, 2007).
Glosses and endnotes have been provided by
Jeffery G. Stoyanoff.
2   Irina Metzler, *A Social History of Disability in
the Middle Ages: Cultural Considerations of Physical
Impairment* (Routledge, 2013), p. 5.
3   Joseph exclaims here that it is inappropriate
for a man to be in the same room with a woman
as she is in labor.

Croxton *Play of the Sacrament*[1] (ca. 1461–1546)

Contributed by Cameron Hunt McNabb

Introduction[2]

The Croxton *Play of the Sacrament* stages the story of a Jewish merchant Jonathas and his companions as they purchase the Host, put it through a series of trials to test the Real Presence, and ultimately convert to Christianity. It is also a spectacle of theater, with bleeding cauldrons and exploding ovens. But an overlooked source of the play's theatricality is its representation of disability. The play explores both physical and mental disability primarily through its Jewish protagonists' grappling with doubt over the transubstantiation of the Host. Such disabling doubt manifests in two metaphors: Jonathas' dismembered hand and the Jews' descriptions of their "wode"-ness (or "madness").

In the first case, during one of the trials Jonathas and the other Jews put the Host through, the Host adheres to Jonathas' hand, and in Jonathas' attempt to nail it to a post (mimicking the Crucifixion in the Host's "new passyoun" (l. 38)), his own hand is dismembered. When the figure of Jesus appears at the play's end, he moralizes to Jonathas, "on thyn hand thow art but lame, / And ys thorow thyn own cruelnesse, / For thyn hurt thu mayest thiselfe blame" (770–72). Then Jonathas' physical healing occurs as a direct result of his repentence: "Thow wasshest thyn hart with grete contrycion. / Go to the cawdron—thi care shal be the lesse— / And towche thyn hand to thy salvacion" (ll. 775–77). The cause-and-effect relationship between doubt and disability, belief and healing in the play supports Edward Wheatley's religious model, as the Church—through the forgiveness of Jesus and the Bishop in the play—controls the means of physical and spiritual

restoration. However, Jonathas' experience of disability can also be seen as redemptive. The play aligns him, not the Christian figures, with Christ through their shared "passyoun" (l. 38), and Jonathas' doubt, symbolized by his dismembered hand, is nailed to the symbolic cross, too. The play considers Jonathas and the other Jews culpable for their doubt but also participatory in the work of their redemption.

While Jonathas' dis- and re-memberment spectacularly displays difference (to adapt David T. Mitchell and Sharon Snyder's description of disability as "the difference [that] demands display"),[3] the play's most sustained engagement with disability is actually its deployment of "wode"ness as a metaphor for doubt. Throughout the various trials of the Host, the Jewish protagonists use the word "wode" to describe their disbelief at the Host's miraculous powers. Intriguingly, though, the word "wode" is first employed to describe the Host itself, which "bledyth as yt were woode" (l. 483), drawing yet another parallel between the doubting Jewish figures and the redeeming Christ. Here, Jonathas and the Host are linguistically linked early in the play, just as they are physically linked later in his dismemberment. Moreover, Jonathas' initial description of the sacred, holy Host as "wode" before his own confession of disbelief as "woodnesse" (l. 502) highlights madness, and disability generally, as a subjective category. "Wode"ness may be in the eye of the beholder. By the play's end, though, the Jews' conversions appear to heal their madness, as the figure of Jesus instructs them to "kepe my commandementes in yowr thowght, / And unto my Godhed to take credence [belief, trust]" (ll. 729–30), and Jonathas' mental restoration parallels his the physical healing of his hand.

The play's exploration of disability demonstrates the category's complexity and ambivalence in late medieval England. The Christian merchant Aristorious initially frames the play's construct of doubt as disability and Christ as cure, much in the *Christus medicus* tradition. Two announcers open the play with the prayer that "Jhesu yow sawe from treyn [suffering] and tene [pain]" (l. 76; omitted below) and Aristorius opens the play with the line, "Now Cryst that ys our Creatour from shame He cure us" (l. 81). Moreover, the play aligns the Host specifically with healing, as the Clerk remarks that bread and wine "ys holesom, as sayeth the fesycyon" (l. 343). However, in Aristorious' selling of the Host to Jonathas, he becomes one who "from shame He [will] cure," and the play questions many of the rigid categories initially invoked. The Croxton *Play of the Sacrament* does align doubt with disability and posits orthodox faith as the only cure; however, in the process, it also evokes striking similarities between doubter and believer and casts both as essential in the work of redemption.

Bibliography

Geldenhuys, Katharine, and Margaret Mary Raftery. "Moral and Medical 'Prescriptions' in a Fifteenth-Century Sacrament Play." *Acta Academica*, vol. 35, no. 2, 2003, pp. 81–102.

Owens, Margaret E. *Stages of Dismemberment: The Fragmented Body in Late Medieval and Early Modern Drama*. University of Delaware Press, 2005.

Scherb, Victor I. "The Earthly and Divine Physicians: 'Christus Medicus' in the Croxton 'Play of the Sacrament.'" *The Body and the Text: Comparative Essays in Literature and Medicine*, vol. 22, 1990, pp. 161–71.

Sofer, Andrew. "Playing Host: the Prop as Temporal Contract on the Medieval Stage." *The Stage Life of Props*. University of Michigan Press, 2003.

Wheatley, Edward. *Stumbling Blocks Before the Blind: Medieval Constructions of a Disability*. University of Michigan Press, 2010.

The Namys and Numbere of the Players

Jhesus
Episcopus°
Aristorius, Christianus Mercator°
[Isoder], presbyter°
[Peter Paul], clericus°
Jonathas, Judeus° primus° magister°
Jason, Judeus secundus°
Jasdon, Judeus tertius°
Masphat, Judeus quartus°
Malchus, Judeus quintus°
[Brundich], magister phisicus°
Coll, servus°

Nine may play yt at ease.

[Two announcers give a summary of the play to advertise its performance]

> *Explicit.° Here after foloweth the Play of the Conversyon of Ser Jonathas the Jewe by Myracle of the Blyssed Sacrament.*

81 **ARISTORIUS** Now Cryst that ys our Creatour from shame He cure us.
He maynteyn us with myrth that meve° upon the molde,°
Unto Hys endelesse joye myghtly He restore us.
All tho that in Hys name in peas well them hold,
For of a merchante most myght therof my tale ys told:
In Eraclea ys non suche whoso wyll understond,
For of all Aragon I am most myghty of sylver and of gold,
For and yt wer a countré to by now wold I nat wond.°
Syr Arystory ys my name,
90 A merchaunte myghty of a royall araye.
Ful wyde in this worlde spryngyth my fame,
Fere kend° and knowen—the sothe° for to saye—
In all maner of londys without ony naye.

[Aristorius boasts of his riches]

125 **PRESBYTER** No man shall you tary° ne trowble thys tyde,°
But every man delygently shall do yow plesance.°
And I unto my connyng to the best shall hem guyde

Epsicopus *Bishop*   Christianus Mercator *Christian merchant*   presbyter *priest*   clericus *clerk*   Judeus *Jew*   primus *first*   magister *master*   secundus *second*   tertius *third*   quartus *fourth*   quintus *fifth*   magister phisicus *master physician*   servus *servant*   Explicit *here ends*   meve *moves*   molde *world*   wond *hesitate*   Fere kend *far spread*   sothe *truth*   tyde *time*   plesance *pleasure*

Unto Godes plesyng to serve yow to
    attrueaunce.°

For ye be worthy and notable in sub-
    stance of good—

130 Of merchauntes of Aragon ye have no
    pere—

And therof thank God that dyed on the
    Roode,°

That was your makere and hath yow
    dere!°

ARISTORIUS Forsoth, syr pryst,
    yower talkyng ys good,

And therfor after your talkyng, I wyll
    atteyn°

To wourshyppe my God that dyed on
    the Roode.

Never whyll that I lyve ageyn° that wyll
    I seyn.°

But Petyr Powle, my clark, I praye thee
    goo wele pleyn°

Thorowght all Eraclea that thow ne
    wonde°

And wytte° yf ony merchaunte be come
    to this reyn,°

140 Of Surrey or of Sabé or of Shelysdown.°

CLERICUS At your wyll for to walke, I
    wyl not say nay

Smertly° to go serche at the wateres
    syde.

Yf ony plesaunt bargyn be to your paye,

As swyftly as I can, I shall hym to yow
    guyde.

Now wyll I walke by thes pathes wyde,

And seke the haven both up and down,

To wette° yf ony onknowth shyppes
    therin do ryde,

Of Surrey or of Saby or of Shelysdown.

Now shall the merchantes man with-
    drawe hym and the Jewe Jon-
    athas shall make hys bost.

149 **JONATHAS** Now almyghty Machom-
    et,° marke in thi magesté,

150 Whose lawes tendrely I have to fulfyll

After my dethe, bryng me to thy hyh
    see°

My sowle for to save—yf yt be thy
    wyll—

For myn entent ys for to fulfyll.

As my gloryus God, thee to honer,

To do agen thy entent, yt shall grue°
    me yll,

Or agen thyn lawe for to reporte.

[Jonathas boasts of his riches]

189 Jew Jonathas ys my name.

190 Jazon and Jazdon, thei waytyn on my
    wyll;

Masfat and Malchus, they do the same.

As ye may knowe, yt ys bothe rycht and
    skyll.°

I tell yow all, bi dal and by hylle.°

In Eraclea ys noon so moche of myght,

Werfor ye owe tenderli to tende me
    tyll.°

For I am chefe merchaunte of Jewes—I
    tell yow be ryght!

But Jazon and Jazdon, a mater wollde I
    mene.

Mervelously yt ys ment in mynde:

The beleve of thes Cristen men ys false,
    as I wene.°

200 For they beleve on a cake—me thynk yt
    ys onkynd° —

And all they seye how the prest dothe
    yt bynd,°

And be° the myght of hys word make yt
    flessh and blode,

And thus be a conceyte° they wolde
    make us blynd,

---

attrueaunce *instruct*   **Roode** *Cross*   **dere** *(held) dear*   **atteyn** *aspire, achieve*   **ageyn** *against*   **seyn** *say*   **wele pleyn** *well authorized*   **wonde** *delay*   **wytte** *determine*   **reyn** *land*   **Shelysdown** *Chalcedon*   **Smertly** *briskly*   **wette** *determine*   **Machomet** *Muhammad*   **see** *throne*   **grue** *trouble*   **skyll** *reasonable*   **bi dale...hylle** *by dale and by hill (everywhere)*   **tenderli to...tyll** *pay close attention to me*   **wene** *believe*   **onkynd** *unnatural*   **bynd** *bind, join*   **be** *by*   **conceyte** *conceit, misconception*

And how that yt shuld be He that
    deyed upon the Rode.°
JASON Yea, yea, master, a strawe for
    talis.°
Tha ma not fale,° in my beleve.
But myt we yt gete onys within our
    pales,°
I trowe we shuld sone afte putt yt in a
    privye.°
JASDON Now be Machomete so
    myghty that ye doon of meve,°
210 I wold I wyste° how that we myght yt
    gete.
I swer be my grete god and ellys mote I
    nat cheve,°
But wyghtly° theron wold I be wreke.°
MASPHAT Yea, I dare sey feythfulli
    that ther feyth ys false—
That was never He that on Calvery was
    kyld
Or in bred for to be blode—yt ys on-
    trewe° als,
But yet with ther wyles° thei wold we
    were wyld.°
MALCHUS Yea, I am myghty Malchus,
    that boldly am byld.°
That brede for to bete,° byggly° am I
    bent,°
Onys out of ther handes and yt myght
    be exyled.
220 To helpe castyn° yt in care° wold I
    counsent.
JONATHAS Well, syrse, than kype
    cunsel, I cummande yow all,
And no word of all thys be wyst.°
But let us walke to see Arystories hall
And afterwarde more counsell among
    us shall caste.°

With hym to bey and to sel, I am of
    powere prest.°
A bargyn with hym to make, I wyll
    assaye.
For gold and sylver, I am nothyng
    agast,°
But that we shall get that cake to ower
    paye.°

[Jonathas purchases the Host from Aristorious for one hundred pounds; Aristorius steals
it from the Church and delivers it to him]

385 **JONATHAS** Now Jason and Jasdon, ye
    be Jewys jentyll° ,
Masfatt and Malchus, that myghty arn°
    in mynd.
Thys merchant from the Crysten temple
Hathe gett us thys bred that make us
    thus blynd.
Now Jason, as jentyll as ever was the
    lynde,°
390 Into the forsayd° parlowr prevely take
    thy pase.°
Sprede a clothe on the tabyll that ye
    shall ther fynd,
And we shall folow after to carpe° of
    thys case.
        Here the Jewys goon and lay the
        Ost on the tabyll, sayng:
JONATHAS Syres, I praye yow all
    harkyn to my sawe:°
Thes Crysten men carpyn of a
    mervelows case!
They say that this ys Jhesu that was at-
    tayntyd° in owr lawe,
And that thys ys He that crwcyfyed
    was.

Rode *Cross*   **a strawe...talis** *a straw for this tale (it's not worth a straw)*   **fale** *happen*   **pales**
walls   **privye** *test, [also] secret place*   **meve** *speak*   **wyste** *knew*   **cheve** *succeed*   **wyghtly** *quick-*
ly   **wreke** *avenged*   **ontrewe** *untrue*   **wyles** *tricks*   **wyld** *wild, mad*   **byld** *made*   **bete** *beat*   **byggly**
firmly   **bent** *determined*   **castyn** *throw*   **care** *pain, sorrow*   **wyst** *known*   **caste** *deliberate*   **prest**
pressed   **agast** *afraid*   **paye** *satisfaction*   **jentyll** *gentle, noble (pun on Gentile)*   **arn** *are*   **lynde** *linden*
tree   **forsayd** *aforesaid*   **pase** *way*   **carpe** *tell*   **sawe** *words*   **attayntyd** *condemned*

On thes wordys ther law growndyd
   hath He,
That He sayd on Shere Thursday° at
   Hys sopere:
He brake the brede and sayd, *"Accipite,"*°
400 And gave Hys dyscyplys them for to
   chere.
And more He sayd to them there,
Whyle they were all togethere and sum,
Syttyng at the table soo clere.°
"Comedite corpus meum,"°
And thys powre He gave Peter to
   proclame,
And how the same shuld be suffycyent°
   to all prechors—
The bysshoppys and curates saye the
   same—
And soo as I understond do all Hys
   progenytors.
JASON Yea, sum men in that law re-
   herse another:
410 They say of a maydyn borne was Hee,
And how Joachyms dowghter° shuld be
   Hys mothere,
And how Gabrell apperyd and sayd,
   "Ave"°
And with that worde she shuld concey-
   vyd be,°
And that in hyr shuld lyght° the Holy
   Gost.
Ageyns owr law thys ys false heresy!
And yett they saye He ys of myghtes
   most.
JASDON They saye that Jhesu to be
   owr kyng,
But I wene He bowght° that full dere.
But they make a royall aray of Hys
   uprysyng,°

420 And that in every place ys prechyd,
   farre and nere.
And how He to Hys dyscyples agayn
   dyd appere—
To Thomas and to Mary Mawdelen—
And syth° how He styed° by Hys own
   powre.
And thys ye know well ys heresy full
   playn!
MASPHAT Yea, and also they say He
   sent them wytt and wisdom
For to understond every langwage.
When the Holy Gost to them came,
They faryd° as dronk men of pymentes
   or vernage.°
And sythen how that He lykenyd Hym-
   self a Lord of Parage,°
430 On Hys Fatherys ryght hond He Hym
   sett.
They hold Hym wyser than ever was
   Syble° sage
And strenger than Alexander that all
   the worlde ded gett.
MALCHUS Yea, yet they saye as fals—I
   dare laye° my hedde—
How they that be ded shall com agayn
   to Judgement,
And owr dredfull Judge shal be thys
   same brede.
And how lyfe everlastyng them shuld
   be lent,
And thus they hold all at on consent.°
Because that Phylyppe° sayd for a lytyll
   glosse,°
To turne us from owr beleve ys ther
   entent,
440 For that he sayd, *"Judecare vivos et mortuos."*°

Shere Thursday *Shrove Thursday*   **Accipite** *"Take"* [*Latin; Matt. 26.26*]   **clere** *excellent*   **Comedite corpus meum** *"Eat, [this is] my body"* [*Latin; Matt. 26.26*]   **suffycyent** *sufficient, enough*   **Joachyms dowghter** *Joachim's daughter (Mary)*   **Ave** *"Hail"* [*Latin; Luke 1.28*]   **conceyvyd be** *conceive*   **lyght** *descend [also], pun on shine*   **bowght** *paid for*   **uprysyng** *resurrection*   **syth** *at that time*   **styed** *rose*   **faryd** *appeared, acted like*   **pymentes...vernage** *sweet wines*   **Parage** *noble rank*   **Syble** *Sybil (oracle and prophetess)*   **laye** *bet, wager*   **on consent** *one agreement*   **Phylyppe** *Philip*   **glosse** *comment*   **Judecare vivos et mortuos** *"To judge the living and the dead"* [*Latin; 1 Peter 4.5*]

JONATHAS Now serys, ye have re-
hersyd the substaunce of ther lawe,
But thys bred I wold myght be put in a
prefe:°
Whether this be He that in Bosra of us
had awe,
Ther staynyd were Hys clothys, this may
we belefe.
Thys may we know ther had He grefe.°
For owr old bookys veryfy thus,
Theron He was jugett° to be hangyd as
a thefe:
"Tinctis Bosra vestibus."°
JASON Yf that thys be He that on
Calvery was mad red,°
450 Onto my mynd I shall kenne° yow a
conceyt good.
Surely with owr daggars we shall ses on°
thys bredde,
And so with clowtes° we shall know yf
He have eny blood.
JASDON Now, by Machomyth so
myghty that mevyth in my mode,°
Thys ys masterly ment thys matter thus
to meve.°
And with owr strokys, we shall fray°
Hym as He was on the Rood.°
That He was ondon with grett repreve.°
MASPHAT Yea, I pray yow, smyte ye in
the myddys° of the cake,
And so shall we smyte theron woundys
fyve.
We wyll not spare to wyrke yt wrake,°
460 To prove in thys brede yf ther be eny
lyfe.
MALCHUS Yea, goowe to than and
take yowr space,
And looke owr daggarys be sharpe and
kene.

And when eche man a stroke smytte
hase,
In the mydyll part therof owr master
shall bene.
JONATHAS When ye have all smytyn,
my stroke shal be sene,
With this same dagger that ys so styf
and strong.
In the myddys of thys prynt, I thynke
for to prene,°
On lashe I shall Hym lende° or yt be
long.
Here shall the fowr Jewys pryk ther
daggeres in fowr quarters [...]
Here the Ost must blede.
481 Ah, owt, owt, harrow!° What devyll ys
thys?
Of thys wyrk, I am in were!°
Yt bledyth as yt were woode,° iwys,°
But yf ye helpe I shall dyspayre.
JASON A fyre! A fyre! And that in
hast,
Anoon a cawdron full of oyle.
JASDON And I shalle helpe yt were in
cast,
All the three howres for to boyle.
MASPHAT Yea here is a furneys,°
stowte and strong,
490 And a cawdron therin dothe hong.
Malcus, wher art thow so long?
To helpe thys dede were dyght.°
MALCHUS Loo, here ys fowr galouns
of oyle clere.
Have doon fast, blowe up the fere.°
Syr, bryng that ylke° cake nere,
Manly, with all yowre mygthe.
JONATHAS And I shall bryng the ylke
cak,
And throwe yt in I undertake.

---

prefe *test* **grefe** *grief* **jugett** *judged* **Tinctis Bosra vestibus** *"With dyed garments from Bozrah"*
[*Latin; Isaiah 63.1*] **mad red** *made red (killed)* **kenne** *tell* **ses on** *seize on (pun on season)* **clow-**
tes *strokes* **mevyth...mode** *moves my mind* **meve** *carry out* **fray** *attack* **Rood** *Cross* **repreve**
shame **myddys** *midst, middle* **wrake** *harm* **prene** *stab* **lende** *deliver* **afeze** *terrify* **plyght** *prom-*
ise **punche** *dagger* **augus** *an iron-working tool* **buffett** *blow* **bleyke** *make pale with fear* **harrow**
help **were** *confusion* **woode** *mad* **iwys** *indeed* **furneys** *furnace* **dyght** *arranged, done* **fere**
fire **ylke** *same*

Out, out! Yt werketh me wrake!°
500 I may not awoyd° yt owt of my hond!
I wylle goo drenche me in a lake,
And in woodnesse,° I gynne° to wake:°
I renne, I lepe over this lond!

*Her he renneth wood with
the Ost in hys hond.*

JASON Renne, felawes, renne for Cok-
kes peyn!°
Fast we had owr mayster agene.
Hold prestly on thys pleyn,
And faste bynd hyme to a poste.
JASDON Here is an hamer and naylys
three, I seye.
Lyffte up hys armys, felawe, on hey,°
510 Whyll I dryve thes nayles, I yow praye,
With strong strokys fast.
MASPHAT Now, set on, felouse, with
mayne° and myght
And pluke hys armes awey in fyght.
Wat yfe he twycche,° felouse, aryght.°
Alas, balys° breweth° ryght bade.

*Here shall thay pluke the arme
and the hond shall hang styll
with the Sacrament.*

MALCHUS Alas, alas, what devyll ys
thys?
Now hat he but oon hand, iwyse!°
For sothe,° mayster, ryght wooi me is
That ye this harme hawe° hadde.
520 JONATHAS Ther ys no more I must
enduer,
Tyll I may get me sum recuer.°
Now hastely to owr chamber, lete us
gon,
And therfor charge yow, everychoon,°
That yt be counsell that we have doon.

[An interlude with a quack doctor and his assistant follows]

653 JONATHAS Now have don, felawys,
and that anon,
For dowte of drede what after befall.
I am nere masyd,° my wytte ys gon,
Therfor of helpe I pray yow all.
And take yowre pynsonys° that ar so
sure,
And pluck owt the naylys won° and
won.
Also in a clothe, ye yt cure,°
660 And throw yt in the cawdron, and that
anon.

*Here shall Jason pluck owt the naylys and
shake the hond into the cawdron.*

JASON And I shall rape° me redely°
anon,
To plucke owt the naylys that stond so
fast.
And beare thys bred and also thys bone,
And into the cawdron I wyll yt cast.
JASDON And I shall with thys dagger
so stowte,
Putt yt down that yt myght plawe.°
And steare° the clothe rounde abowte,
That no thyng therof shal be rawe.°
MASPHAT And I shall manly, with all
my myght,
670 Make the fyre to blasé and brenne.°
And sett therunder suche a lyght
That yt shall make yt ryght thynne.°

*Here shall the cawdron byle,° ap-
peryng to be as blood.*

MALCHUS Owt and harow! What
devyll ys herein?
All thys oyle waxyth° redde as blood,
And owt of the cawdron yt begynnyth
to run.
I am so aferd, I am nere woode!°

*Here shall Jason and hys compeny
goo to Ser Jonathas, sayng:*

---

wrake *harm* awoyd *remove* woodnesse *madness* gynne *begin* wake *quake, awaken* Cok-
kes peyn *God's suffering* hey *high* mayne *strength* twycche *twitch* aryght *properly* balys
misdeeds breweth *are causing harm, brewing* iwyse *indeed* sothe *truth* hawe *have* recuer
relief everychoon *everyone* masyd *astonished, distraught* pynsonys *pincers* won *one* cure
restore rape *hasten, hurry* redely *quickly* plawe *boil* steare *stir* rawe *uncooked* brenne
burn thynne *thin* byle *boil* waxyth *grows* woode *mad*

JASON Ah, master, master! What chere
    ys° with yow?
I can nott see owr werke wyll avayle.
I beseche yow, avance° yow now,
680 Sumwhatt with yowr counsayle.
JONATHAS The best counsayle that I
    now wott,°
That I can deme, farre and nere,
Ys to make an ovyn as redd hott
As ever yt can be made with fere.
And when ye see yt soo hott appere,
Then throw yt into the ovyn fast!
Sone shall he stanche° hys bledyng
    chere.°
When ye have donne stoppe° yt, be not
    agast.

[They kindle a fire and cast the Host into a
hot oven.]

    Here the owyn must ryve asunder and
    blede owt at the cranys° and an image
    appere owt with woundys bledyng.

713 **MASPHAT** Owt, owt! Here ys a grete
    wondere!
Thys ovyn bledyth owt on every syde.
MALCHUS Yea, the ovyn on peacys
    gynnyth to ryve asundre:
Thys ys a mervelows case, thys tyde!
    Here shall the image speke to
    the Juys, sayng thus.
JESUS *O mirabiles Judei attendite et videte*
Si est dolor sicut dolor meus.°
Oh, ye merveylows Jewys!
Why ar ye to yowr Kyng onkynd?
And I, so bytterly bowt yow to my
    blysse.
720 Why fare ye thus fule° with yowre
    frende?

Why peyne yow me and straytly° me
    pynde?°
And I, yowr love so derely have bowght.
Why are ye so unstedfast in yor mynde?
Why wrath° ye me, I greve yow nowght?
Why wyll ye nott beleve that I have
    tawght?
And forsake yor fowle neclygence,
And kepe my commandementes in
    yowr thowght,
730 And unto my Godhed to take cre-
    dence?°

[The Image of Jesus continues to question
Jonathas and his companions' disobedience]

741 **JONATHAS** *"Tu es protector vite mee a*
    quo trepidabo."°
O Thu, Lord, whyche art my defendowr,
For dred of Thee I trymble and quake.
Of Thy gret mercy, lett us receyve the
    showre,
And mekely I aske mercy amendys to
    make.
    Here shall they knele down all
    on ther kneys, sayng:
JASON Ah, Lord, with sorow and care
    and grete wepyng,
All we felawys lett us saye thus:
With condolent harte and grete sorow-
    yng,
"Lacrimis nostris conscienciam nostram
    baptizemus."°
750 **JASDON** Oh Thow, blyssyd lord of
    mykyll° myght,
Of Thy gret mercy, Thow hast shewyd
    us the path.
Lord, owt of grevous slepe, and owt of
    dyrknes to lyght,

What chere ys *How are*   **avance** *assist, help*   **wott** *know*   **stanche** *staunch, stop from bleeding*   **chere**
body, appearance   **donne stoppe** *stopped*   **cranys** *crannies*   **O mirabilies Judei...dolor meus** *Oh*
marvelous Jews, attend and see if there is any sorrow that is like my sorrow [*Latin*]   **fule** *foul*   **straytly** *at*
once   **pynde** *stabbed*   **wrath** *rage against*   **credence** *belief, trust*   **Tu es protector...trepidabo** *"You*
are the protector of my life; whom will I fear?" [*Latin; Psalm 26.1*]   **Lacrimis nostris...baptizemus** *With*
our tears, let us baptize our consciences [*Latin*]   **mykyll** *much*

Ne gravis sompnus irruat.°

MASPHAT Oh Lord, I was very cursyd,
    for I wold know Thi crede

I can no mennys° make but crye to Thee
    thus:

O gracyows Lorde, forgyfe me my
    mysdede,

With lamentable hart, "*Miserere mei
    Deus.*"°

MALCHUS Lord I have offendyd Thee
    in many a sundry vyse,°

That styckyth at my hart as hard as a
    core.

760 Lord, by the water of contrycion, lett
    me aryse.

"*Asparges me Domine ysopo et mundabor.*"°

JESUS All ye that desyryn my servaunt-
    es for to be,

And to fullfyll the preceptes of my
    lawys,

The intent of my commandement
    knowe ye:

"*Ite et ostendite vos sacerdotibus meis.*"°

To all yow that desyre in eny wyse

To aske mercy, to graunt yt redy I am.

Remember and lett yowr wyttes suf-
    fyce,

"*Et tunc non avertam a vobis faciem
    meam.*"°

770 No Jonathas, on thyn hand thow art but
    lame,

And ys thorow thyn own cruelnesse,

For thyn hurt thu mayest thiselfe
    blame.

Thow woldyst preve thy powre Me to
    oppresse,

But now I consydre thy necesse,°

Thow wasshest thyn hart with grete
    contrycion.

Go to the cawdron—thi care° shal be
    the lesse—

And towche thyn hand to thy salvacion.

*Here shall Ser Jonathas put hys hand
    into the cawdron and yt shal be hole
    agayn and then say as folwyth:*

JONATHAS Oh Thow, my Lord, God,
    and Savyowr osanna!°

Thow, Kyng of Jewys and of Jerusalem!

780 O Thow, myghty strong Lyon of Juda!

Blyssyd be the tyme that Thu were in
    Bedlem.°

Oh Thu, myghty, strong, gloryows, and
    gracyows oyle streme,

Thow, myghty conquerrowr of infernall
    tene,°

I am quyt° of moche combrance°
    thorowgh Thy meane,°

That ever blyssyd mott Thou bene.

Alas, that ever I dyd agaynst Thy wyll,

In my wytt to be soo wood.°

That I so ongoodly wyrk shuld soo
    gryll,°

Agens my mysgovernaunce.° Thow
    gladdyst me with good.

790 I was soo prowde to preve Thee on the
    Roode—°

And Thou haste sent me lyghtyng° that
    late was lame—

To bete Thee and boyle Thee, I was
    myghty in moode,°

And now Thu hast put me from duresse
    and dysfame.°

But Lord, I take my leve at Thy hygh
    presens

And put me in Thy myghty mercy.

The bysshoppe wyll I goo fetche to se
    owr offens,

Ne gravis...irruat *May heavy sleep not embrace [us] [Latin]* **mennys** *petitions* **Miserere mei Deus**
"Have mercy on me, God" [Latin; Psalm 50.3] **vyse** *ways* **Asparges me...mundabor** *"Wash me, Lord,
with hissop, and I will be clean" [Latin; Psalm 50.9]* **Ite et ostendite...meis** *"Go and show yourselves
to my priests" [Latin; Luke 17.14]* **Et tunc non...meam** *And then I will not turn my face from you
[Latin]* **necesse** *need* **care** *sorrow* **osanna** *Hosanna* **Bedlem** *Bethlehem* **tene** *pain* **quyt**
relieved **combrance** *encumbrance, trouble* **meane** *mediation* **wood** *mad* **gryll** *offend, to do* **mysgovernaunce** *misgovernance, sin* **Roode** *Cross* **lyghtyng** *healing* **moode** *heart, mind* **dysfame** *ill
repute*

And onto hym shew owr lyfe how that
we be gylty.
> *Here shall the master Jew goo to the
> byshopp and hys men knele styll.*

[The Bishop blesses Jonathas and his companions. He then raises the Host.]

> *Here shall the image change
> agayn into brede.*

826 **EPISCOPUS** Oh, Thu largyfluent°
Lord, most of lyghtnesse,
Onto owr prayers Thow hast applied.°
Thu hast receyvyd them with grett
swettnesse,
For all owr dredfull dedys,° Thu hast
not us denyed.
830 Full mykyll° owte° Thy name for to be
magnyfyed,
With mansuete° myrth and gret
swettnes.
And as our gracyows God for to be
gloryfyed,
For Thu shewyst us gret gladnes.
Now wyll I take thys Holy Sacrament,
With humble hart and gret devocion,
And all we wyll gon with on consent°
And beare yt to chyrche with solempne
processyon.
Now folow me, all and summe,
And all tho that bene here, both more
and lesse.
840 Thys holy song, *O sacrum convivium,*°
Lett us syng all with grett swetnesse.

[The Bishop blesses the audience entreats
them to repent]

900 **ARISTORIUS** Holy father, I knele to
yow under benedycuté,°
I have offendyd in the syn of covytys:

I sold owr Lordys body for lucre° of
mony,
And delyveryd to the wyckyd with
cursyd advyce,
And for that presumpcion gretly I
agryse.°
That I presumed to go to the autere,
There to handyll the Holy Sacryfyce,
I were worthy to be putt in brennyng
fyre.
But gracyous lord, I can no more,
But put me to Goddys mercy and to
yowr grace.
910 My cursyd werkys for to restore,
I aske penaunce now in thys place.
EPISCOPUS Now for thys offence that
thu hast donne,
Agens the Kyng of Hevyn and Emper-
owr of Hell,
Ever whyll thu lyvest, good dedys for to
done
And nevermore for to bye nore sell.
Chastys° thy body, as I shall thee tell,
With fastyng and prayng and other
good wyrk,
To withstond the temtacyon of fendes
of Hell
And to call to God for grace, looke thu
never be irke.°

[The bishop rebukes the priest]

928 JONATHAS And I aske Crystendom,
with great devocion,
With repentant hart in all degrees,
930 I aske for us all a generall absolucion.
> *Here the Juys must knele al down.*
For that we knele all upon owr knees,
For we have grevyd° owr Lord on
ground,
And put Hym to a new paynfull passion:

---

largyfluent *bounteous* **applied** *complied* **dedys** *deeds* **mykyll** *much* **owte** *ought* **mansuete** *gentle* **on consent** *agreement* **O sacrum convivium** *O sacred feast [Latin]* **benedycuté** *blessing* **lucre**
profit **agryse** *shudder with fear* **Chastys** *chastize* **irke** *weary* **neclygens** *negligence* **pyxys** *pyxes
(containers for the Host)* **grevyd** *grieved*

With daggars styckyd Hym with grevos
　woundes
New naylyd Hym to a post, and with
　pynsonys° pluckyd Hym down.

[Jason, Jasdon, Masphat, and Malchus repent]

Here shall the bysshoppe crysten the
Jewys with gret solempnyté.

952　EPISCOPUS Now the Holy Gost at
　　thys tyme mot yow blysse,
　As ye knele all now in Hys name.
　And with the water of baptyme° I shall
　　yow blysse,
　To save yow all from the fendes blame.
　Now that fendys powre for to make
　　lame—
　In the name of the Father, the Son, and
　　the Holy Gost—
　To save yow from the devyllys flame,
　I crysten yow all, both lest and most.

[Jonathas and Aristorius express their re-
pentance again]

988　EPISCOPUS God omnypotent ever-
　　more looke ye serve,
　With devocion and prayre° whyll that
　　ye may.
990　Dowt yt not He wyll yow preserve,
　For eche good prayer that ye sey to Hys
　　pay.°
　And therfor in every dew° tyme loke ye
　　nat delay,
　For to serve the Holy Trynyté—
　And also Mary that swete may° —
　And kepe yow in perfyte love and
　　charyté.
　Crystes commandementes ten there
　　bee,
　Kepe well them doo, as I yow tell.
　Almyght God shall yow please in every
　　degré,

And so shall ye save yowr sollys° from
　Hell.
1000For there ys payn and sorow cruell,
　And in Hevyn ther ys both joy and
　　blysse,
　More then eny towng can tell.
　There angellys syng with grett swet-
　　nesse,
　To the whyche blysse He bryng us,
　Whoys name ys callyd Jhesus.
　And in wyrshyppe of thys name glory-
　　ows,
　To syng to Hys honore, *Te Deum lauda-*
　　mus.°

Finis.°

Thus endyth the Play of the Blyssyd Sacrament
whyche myracle was don in the forest of Aragon,
in the famous cité Eraclea, the yere of owr Lord
God 1461, to whom be honowr. Amen.

---

pynsonys *pincers*　baptyme *baptism*　prayre *prayer*　pay *benefit*　dew *due*　may *maid*　sollys
souls　Te Deum laudamus *To God, we give praise* [*Latin*]　Finis *the end*

469

Endnotes

1   The text below was compiled by Cameron Hunt McNabb, in consultation with the play's manuscript Trinity College MS F.4.20, the facsimile edition of the play in *Non-Cycle Plays and the Winchester Dialogues: Facsimiles of Plays and Fragments in Various Manuscripts and the Dialogues in Winchester College MS 33*, edited by Norman Davis, Medieval Drama Facsimiles 5 University of Leeds, School of English, 1979, pp. 95–131, and *The Croxton Play of the Sacrament*, ed. John Sebastian, TEAMS Middle English Texts Series (Medieval Institute Publications, 2012). Glosses and endnotes have been provided by Cameron Hunt McNabb as well.

2   My analysis here draws on McNabb, "Staging Disability in Medieval Drama," *Ashgate Research Companion to Medieval Disability Studies*, Routledge, forthcoming, where the Croxton *Play of the Sacrament* is used as a case study.

3   A letter has been canceled between "woo" and "me," leaving space that the word might have originally been "wood." Indeed "wood" makes more sense than "woo" in this context.

IMAGES

The Smithfield Decretals (ca. 1300–1340)

Contributed by Rachael Gillibrand

Introduction

The *Smithfield Decretals* is a fourteenth-century, southern French manuscript, consisting of 314 folios containing 1,971 papal letters and other documents relating to ecclesiastical law. However, despite being one of approx. 700 surviving manuscripts to contain copies of these documents, *The Smithfield Decretals* is unique in that it includes over 600 *bas-de-page* narrative scenes (i.e., any unframed images within a manuscript, often located at the bottom of the page, but not always). These images were likely commissioned by John Batayle, a canon of St. Bartholomew's at Smithfield, and added to the manuscript forty years after its initial construction. Interestingly, these marginal images do not illustrate the text, but instead pertain to biblical stories, animal fables, tales of folly and the topsy-turvy, the miracles of the Virgin, and daily life more broadly.

Each of these images comes from a long tradition of visual tropes, layered with social, cultural, and political understandings; and they are affected as much by the relationship between the patron, artist, and intended audience as they are by the subject matter itself. Consequently, marginalia should not be read as a "true" depiction of medieval life, but rather as a conduit for conveying humor, satire, and social meaning. By asking questions of marginalia (such as who commissioned/created it? What/how are the subjects depicted? And how do they compare to similar images?) the scholar can not only access the daily life of people with disabilities, but also unravel the broader response to disability by the ways in which impairment was represented.

Despite the growing corpus of scholarship on medieval disability, and the already extensive research conducted into medieval visual culture, very little work has been done to bring these two spheres of enquiry together. Manuscript marginalia allows a fascinating and multifaceted insight into medieval disability politics and should therefore be used more extensively in our attempts to access understandings impairment in the Middle Ages.

Bibliography

Bovey, Alixe. "A Pictorial Ex Libris in the Smithfield Decretals: John Batayle, Canon of St Bartholomew's, and his Illuminated Law Book." *English Manuscript Studies, 1100–1700: Decoration and Illustration in Medieval English Manuscripts*, vol. 10, edited by A.S.G. Edwards. British Library, 2002, pp. 60–82.

Brown, Michelle. *Understanding Illuminated Manuscripts: A Guide to Technical Terms.* British Library in association with the J. Paul Getty Museum, 1994.

Camille, Michael. *Image on the Edge: The Margins of Medieval Art.* Reaktion Books, 1992.

Pestilli, Livio. *Picturing the Lame in Italian Art from Antiquity to the Modern Era.* Routledge, 2017.

Taylor, Andrew. "Playing on the Margins: Bakhtin and the Smithfield Decretals." *Bakhtin and Medieval Voices*, edited by T.J. Farrell. University of Florida Press, 1996, pp. 17–37.

Below are three examples taken from *The Smithfield Decretals*. One should note that the initial titles attributed to each of these images are those that appear in the British Library catalogue. However, I have added alternative descriptions of these images in brackets, which I believe more closely align with current debates surrounding the use of language in medieval disability studies. For example, although "impairment" was not a linguistic category used to describe disability in the Middle Ages, it is currently accepted as the preferred term for discussing disability, rather than the culturally specific terms seen in medieval texts such as "cripple" or "lame."

British Library Royal 10 E IV, fol. 110
Blind Beggar and his Dog.

Depicted with closed eyes and grasping the leash of a guide dog, this illustration offers a rare medieval example of a physically impaired person using an assistance animal. Furthermore, he is depicted as alone in the outdoors with only a staff and his dog for support, discrediting the modern assumption that that disability automatically negated independence in the Middle Ages. However, the ascribed title needs to be questioned. While closed, downcast eyes are a common visual representation of blindness, the man lacks the visual signifiers associated with begging (such as an alms bowl or extended hands). His tall staff, satchel, and broad brimmed hat are images frequently associated with pilgrimage. Therefore, by deconstructing the visual symbols contained within this image, it is possible to argue that the man is a blind pilgrim, rather than a beggar.

British Library Royal 10 E IV, fol. 220

Cripples Appealing to Other Men.

Again, the title here needs to be questioned. Whilst it is true that a pair of double amputees request a young boy's attention (extending their hands in a begging motion), it appears that the 'other men' are in fact blind men, also appealing to the child for assistance. Not only do the men to the left of the image have the aforementioned closed, downwards facing eyes, but the man sitting on the bench holds a t-bar style crutch (used similarly to a modern guide cane), which appears to have been accidentally excluded by the addition of colour to the image.

British Library Royal 10 E IV, fol. 220v

Cripple Being Led to a Building.

This image of this selection appears to be a continuation of the second. It portrays the same young boy leading two figures towards a building (most likely a shrine where individuals with impairments can receive treatment). The first of the figures is a blind person, holding a shoulder-height staff in their left hand, whilst their right hand is placed on the boy's shoulder for support; the second is a male amputee (also depicted on the right-hand side of figure 2) who, missing his feet, relies on the use of a hand-trestle to drag himself along the floor. Not only does this image offer an insight into the various mobility aids available to people with disabilities, but it also demonstrates the willingness of the able-bodied to assist the members of their community who had bodily impairments.

Visible and Invisible Impairments in Images of Medieval Musicians

Contributed by Karen M. Cook

Introduction

In modern Western society, blindness is considered a disability—that is, a physical ailment that prohibits the afflicted person from fully participating in "normal," sighted society without special accommodations. Medieval societies, however, did not have such a word or concept. An issue such as blindness, for example, could be discussed from a medical perspective, especially with regard to treatment or cure; from a theological or philosophical perspective, as a sign of sin; or as a divine gift, such as prophecy or, especially relevant here, music.[1] Moreover, if a person with such a condition was able to engage with their broader societal contexts in productive ways, especially if said condition acted as "a diminution of one sense that redirects the body toward another ability," then that condition might not have been perceived as a disability at all.[2]

Quite a number of the most renowned medieval musicians had what modern society might consider to be disabilities. Yet descriptions of many of these musicians, by themselves and by others, in print and in image, reveal that their individual ailments were typically presented not as something that they needed to overcome but as something that might have enhanced, or at the very least did not disrupt, their abilities as composers, teachers, and scribes.

Such musicians include Francesco "Il Cieco" da Firenze (c. 1325–Sept. 2, 1397; better known today as Francesco Landini) and Conrad Paumann (c. 1410–Jan. 24, 1473), who were both blind. Antonio "Zachara" da Teramo (c. 1350/60–after May 19, 1413) had several physical ailments, including the loss of several fingers and toes, stunted height, a possible club foot, and a self-described itchy skin condition. Hildegard of Bingen (1098–Sept. 17, 1179) explained her lifelong spells of illness as holy visions, which some have later interpreted to be chronic migraines. And the monk Notker (ca. 840–April 6, 912) was called "Balbulus," or "the Stammerer," due to his difficulties speaking.

Bibliography

Cuthbert, Michael Scott. "Difference, Disability, and Composition in the Late Middle Ages: Of Antonio 'Zachara' da Teramo and Francesco 'Il Cieco' da Firenze." *The Oxford Handbook of Music and Disability Studies,* edited by Blake Howe et al. Oxford University Press, 2015, pp. 517–28.

Foxhall, Katherine. "Making Modern Migraine Medieval: Men of Science, Hildegard of Bingen and the Life of a Retrospective Diagnosis." *Medical History,* vol. 58, no. 3, July 2014, pp. 354–74. doi: 10.1017/mdh.2014.28.

Gallo, F. Alberto, ed. *Il Codice Squarcialupi: Ms. Mediceo Palatino 87,* Biblioteca medicea laurenziana di Firenze. Libreria musicale italiana, 1992.

Hsy, Jonathan. "Blindness," *Medieval Disability Glossary.* 7 Oct. 2012, http://www.medievaldisabilityglossary.wikispaces.com/Blindness.

Lerner, Neil, and Joseph Straus. *Sounding Off: Theorizing Disability in Music.* Routledge, 2006.

Metzler, Irina. *Disability in Medieval Europe: Thinking about Physical Impairment in the High Middle Ages, c.1100–c.1400.* Routledge, 2006.

Rankin, Susan. "The Earliest Sources of Notker's Sequences: St Gallen, Vadiana 317, and Paris, Bibliothèque Nationale Lat. 10587." *Early Music History*, vol. 10, 1991, pp. 201–33.

Singer, Julie. "Playing by Ear: Compensation, Reclamation, and Prosthesis in Fourteenth-Century Song." *Disability in the Middle Ages: Reconsiderations and Reverberations*, edited by Joshua R. Eyler, Ashgate, 2013, pp. 39–52.

Straus, Joseph N. *Extraordinary Measures: Disability in Music.* Oxford University Press, 2011.

Téllez Vargas, Alejandro Alberto. *Disability and Music Performance. Interdisciplinary Disability Studies.* Routledge, 2018.

Wheatley, Edward. *Stumbling Blocks Before the Blind.* University of Michigan Press, 2010.

Francesco "Il Cieco" da Firenze, alias Landini

Illustration from the Squarcialupi Codex (Florence, Biblioteca Medicea-Laurenziana, MS Mediceo Palatino 97).

Tomb in the interior of the Basilica of San Lorenzo in Florence; photograph taken by Sailko.

Francesco was born in Florence, the son of a well-known painter. He became blind in his early childhood due to smallpox, and as a result turned to music while quite young. Not only did he become well known as an exceptional organ player, improviser, and composer, he also built and tuned organs, sang, and invented other new instruments. He was also renowned for his expertise in other humanities, in particular poetry, and wrote a lengthy poem in praise of the logic of William of Ockham. Two images of Francesco remain. One is his tombstone, surviving in the Basilica of San Lorenzo in Florence; the other is one of the numerous detailed illuminations from the Squarcialupi Codex (Florence, Biblioteca Medicea-Laurenziana, Palatino 87). In both images, Francesco is depicted with the most obvious symbol of his musical career: his portative organ. In the Squarcialupi illumination, he is also wearing a laurel wreath, signifying his prestige as a poet (Cuthbert, 518). Francesco is also clearly depicted as blind in both images. His is the only illumination in the Squarcialupi codex in which the face is turned to one side, leaving only one (closed) eye visible. On his tombstone, Francesco is shown face-on, but his eyes have been hollowed out, creating the impression of a cavernous, unfocused gaze.

Conrad Paumann
Epitaph in the Frauenkirche in Munich, Germany.

Unlike Francesco, later musician Conrad Paumann was born blind. We know little about his early years, but by the time he was a teenager he was already being sponsored as a talented musician; by his mid-thirties, Paumann was considered to be the best organist in all of Germany. He visited many nobles and dignitaries throughout Western Europe, reports of which describe his abilities as worthy of marvel. His epitaph in the Frauenkirche in Munich shows him surrounded by a lute, harp, recorder, and fiddle, but like Francesco, he too is playing the portative organ, and his eyes are closed. As Julie Singer points out, Francesco is thus captured as his contemporaries understood him: a person who was blind, and whose blindness allowed him to excel in matters both intellectual and musical[3]; the same could also be said of the virtuoso organist Conrad Paumann.

Antonio "Zachara" da Teramo
Illustration from the Squarcialupi Codex.

Antonio da Teramo was often designated "Zachara" (Zacchara, Zacar, Zacara, Çacherias) in late medieval documents. The nickname, as Michael Scott Cuthbert points out, derives from the biblical Zacchaeus, who was too short to see Jesus and thus needed to climb a sycamore tree.[4] Antonio was also short, perhaps due to illness or a congenital issue; in a fifteenth-century necrology, he is described as being short-statured, with only ten total fingers and toes. He too is depicted in an illumination in the Squarcialupi Codex, and while it is impossible to determine from it whether he was short, he is clearly missing some of his fingers, and his left arm is in a sling. Moreover, it appears that his left foot is turned in toward his body, and that leg might be shorter than the other. Lastly, his face is unusually shaded, which Cuthbert suggests might be indicative of a condition such as lupus, which could also explain his loss of fingers and toes.[5] Yet despite his missing fingers, Antonio was a papal secretary, and extant examples of his handwriting show no discernible flaws. He was also a singer and composer for the Roman and Pisan popes and was held in highest regard by his contemporaries, being one of the most widely copied composers of his day. His illumination depicts him holding an open book, which, though blank, likely refers to his abilities as either a scribe or theorist/composer. While it cannot necessarily be said that, like Francesco or perhaps Paumann, his physical ailments caused him to excel in other complementary ways, they certainly did not impede him from his successes, nor does it seem that he was shunned in any way for them.

Hildegard of Bingen
Illustration from the Scivias in the Rupertsberg Manuscript.

With Hildegard of Bingen, the questions of disability, impairment, and representation are more blurred. In her various writings, Hildegard shares that even from her youth, she suffered periods of illness and interpreted them as divine punishment; at other times, she experienced moments of physical, mental, and emotional change or ecstasy as visions sent from God, which she was later encouraged to document in writing. Her current reputation as a migraine sufferer is due to early twentieth-century attempts to diagnose her retrospectively, but as Katherine Foxhall points out, modern scientific ideas of migraine have changed considerably in the last century. More importantly, though, a "purely" medical evaluation of Hildegard's descriptions does not take into account her own interpretations of her lived experiences, which were much less medical than they were theological. Still, if one were to propose Hildegard's visions *qua* visions, without any retrospective medical diagnosis, one might suggest that they, like Francesco's blindness, were a characteristic that diminished Hildegard's physical health while simultaneously strengthening her intellectual, musical, and theological prowess. As Hildegard's contemporary reputation was built in large part on the acceptance of the authenticity of her visions, they were certainly no detriment but instead one of her greatest assets. As such, they are depicted as gifts of the Holy Spirit, as in her portrait in the Rupertsberg Manuscript, where Hildegard's head is surrounded by tongues of flame reaching down from the heavens.

Notker "Balbulus" ("the Stammerer")
Illustration from a tenth-century manuscript.

The last example is the least like the others, for while it is a portrait of a person with a known disability (in the modern sense), that disability is not shown. There were several monks named Notker in and around the abbey of St. Gall, and in order to differentiate them, each had some sort of nickname Notker the musician was called "Balbulus," or "the Stammerer," and in his own writings he described himself as "stammering and toothless."[6] He worked as a scribe in the abbey but is best known to modern music scholars as a composer of sequences or hymns, setting new texts to longer existing melodies which quickly found themselves part of the local chant repertory. Due to his facility with language, he and his works were widely admired, and he won the favor, and the commission, of numerous noblemen, including the Emperor Charles the Bald. It was Notker's written texts, not his verbal prowess, that earned such esteem; his stammering was in no way prohibitive of his successes either within the monastic structure or secular interactions. But unlike the other images discussed thus far, Notker's portrait does not show any indication of his speech impediment. Far from this being an indication that his stammer was a source of shame or something that could be idealized via erasure upon his death (as many did upon Stephen Hawking's death by portraying him as physically whole, walking away from his wheelchair), a much more likely interpretation is that a stammer is an invisible disability, difficult to portray through a visual medium. Notker is shown slumped at his writing desk, holding what might be a scroll in his right hand; he is thus strongly associated with the written word, his personal forte, in a manner similar to Francesco or Paumann being shown playing their portative organs, Hildegard dictating her visions, or Antonio holding an open book.

Conclusion

.

These images show us, quite clearly, that the various ailments that these musicians had were considered to be fundamental to their identities; they were neither erased nor corrected, but were deliberately included, whether in "lifelike" or stylized fashion. Moreover, some of these images suggest that these musicians reached the pinnacle of their expertise precisely because of their disability. Francesco and Conrad Paumann focused their attentions on music and the liberal arts due to their lack of sight; Hildegard's visions were considered authentic revelations from God by the Pope, thus cementing her reputation as a scholar, theologian, and musician; and Notker's stammer might have focused his attention on the written, rather than the spoken word. Antonio might likely have already been highly trained as a scribe before he lost some of his fingers, but he maintained positions of prestige in papal circles for years despite his other physical ailments. Such images thus reinforce that, to the contemporaries of these medieval musicians, none of them had disabilities by modern standards, but rather their physical characteristics might instead have redirected them toward something in which they could excel.

Endnotes

1   Jonathan Hsy, "Blindness," *Medieval Disability Glossary*, 7 Oct. 2012, http://www.medievaldisabilityglossary.wikispaces.com/Blindness.

2   Julie Singer, "Playing by Ear: Compensation, Reclamation, and Prosthesis in Fourteenth-Century Song," *Disability in the Middle Ages: Reconsiderations and Reverberations*, ed. Joshua R. Eyler (Ashgate, 2013), p. 47.

3   Ibid.

4   Luke 19:2–4.

5   Michael Scott Cuthbert, "Difference, Disability, and Composition in the Late Middle Ages: Of Antonio 'Zachara' da Teramo and Francesco 'Il Cieco' da Firenze." *The Oxford Handbook of Music and Disability Studies*, eds. Blake Howe et al. (Oxford University Press, 2015), p. 523. This retrospective diagnosis is not widely known or accepted, and is mentioned here as one scholar's suggestion only in order to bring attention to the painter's rendition of Antonio's complexion.

6   Susan Rankin, "The Earliest Sources of Notker's Sequences: St Gallen, Vadiana 317, and Paris, Bibliothèque Nationale Lat. 10587," *Early Music History*, vol. 10, 1991, p. 218.

Thematic Table of Contents

Contributors

Danielle Allor is a PhD candidate in the Department of English at Rutgers, The State University of New Jersey. Her work focuses on vegetal life and late medieval literature, arguing that late medieval authors imported knowledge-organizing and classifying strategies from natural philosophy to bolster claims to religious authenticity and literary authority. Her dissertation, "Trees of Thought: Arboreal Matter and Metaphor in Late Medieval England," examines trees as material and figural classification systems in the work of William Langland, Geoffrey Chaucer, John Lydgate, and John Skelton.

Lucy Barnhouse is a Visiting Assistant Professor of History at Wartburg College. Her research focuses on the intersections between legal, religious, and medical history. Her prospective monograph, *Houses of God, Places for the Sick*, examines the place of hospitals in the religious and social networks of late medieval cities. Her publications include a study of a medical miscellany used in a hospital managed by religious women, and an article on leprosy in the Rhineland for *Leprosy and Identity in the Middle Ages: from England to the Mediterranean*. Her future research plans include a study of mobility and urban identities in late medieval Central Europe. She has been a podcaster with Footnoting History, on topics including women's history and medical history, since 2013.

Paul A. Broyles is a Lecturer in English at North Carolina State University, where he previously held a CLIR Postdoctoral Fellowship in Data Curation for Medieval Studies. His research concerns medieval romance, geographic imagination, and cultural identity, with broader interests in textual transmission and translation. He is active in the development of Digital Humanities projects, and serves as Technical Director of the Society for Early English and Norse Electronic Texts and Technical Editor of the *Piers Plowman Electronic Archive*.

Eliza Buhrer is a cultural historian, whose work explores intersections between the histories of medicine, law, and knowledge in premodern Europe. She recently began a new position as a Teaching Associate Professor at Colorado School of Mines, fulfilling a long-held dream of living in the mountains, and previously worked as a Visiting Assistant Professor of History at Loyola University New Orleans, and an Assistant Professor of History at Seton Hall University. She has published on intellectual disability in medieval law and culture and has forthcoming essays on how medieval jurists imagined monstrosity and how medieval society conceptualized learning difficulties. She is currently working on a book on the cultural history of attention and distraction.

M.W. Bychowski is the Anisfield-Wolf SAGES Fellow at Case Western Reserve University, holding a position as full-time faculty in English, and teaching seminars on gender, disability, feminism, racism, and queer Christianity. She received her Ph.D. in English Literature from the George Washington University in Washington, D.C. A few of her recent articles include "The Isle of Hermaphrodites: Disorienting the Place of Intersex in the Middle Ages" (*postmedieval* 2018), "Reconstructing the Pardoner: Transgender Skin Operations in Fragment VI" (Writing on

Skin in the Age of Chaucer, 2018), and "Mad for Margery: Disability and the Imago Dei in the Book of Margery Kempe" (*The Ashgate Research Companion to Medieval Disability Studies*, Routledge, forthcoming). She remains an ardent advocate for the Digital Humanities and public scholarship, maintaining an online center for the study of transgender and disability, medieval and post-medieval, www.ThingsTransform.com. Additionally, she serves on the executive board of the *Mental Health Network*, an advising think-tank for the national UCC church, as well as consults for local businesses, schools, and political groups on diversity and social justice. This work led her to serve at "the White House Forum on LGBTQ and Disability Issues" in 2016.

Karen M. Cook is associate professor of music history at The Hartt School at the University of Hartford. Her primary research is on late medieval music theory and notation, with her current work focusing on lesser-known or fragmentary treatises. She also maintains strong secondary interests in medievalism and in ludomusicology, with several publications focusing on the creative repurposing or reimagining of medieval music in video game soundtracks. Recent work appears in *Studies in Medievalism XXVII: Authenticity, Medievalism, Music*; *The Oxford Handbook of Medievalism in Music*; *Musica Disciplina*; *Plainsong & Medieval Music*; and *Oxford Bibliographies in Music*. She was a recipient of the inaugural ACLS Professional Development Grant, which she used toward her work on her forthcoming monograph on the development of rhythmic notation in the fourteenth and early fifteenth centuries.

Leigh Ann Craig is an associate professor of History and the Director of Undergraduate Studies in History at Virginia Commonwealth University. Her recent research has focused on loss of mind (including both physical illness and demonic affliction), disability, and community in Latin Christen-

dom, especially as it appears in later medieval miracle stories. Her publications include *Wandering Women and Holy Matrons: Women as Pilgrims in the Later Middle Ages* (Brill, 2009); "The Spirit of Madness: Doubt and the Miraculous Restoration of Sanity in the Miracles of Henry VI," *Journal of Medieval Religious Cultures* (2013); "The History of Madness and Mental Illness in the Middle Ages: Directions and Questions," *History Compass* (2014); and "Describing Death and Resurrection: Medicine and the Humors in Two Late Medieval Miracles," in *The Sacred and the Secular in Medieval Healing: Sites, Objects, and Texts* (Routledge, 2016).

Sarah Edwards Obenauf is the Public Services and Instruction Librarian at the New Mexico Institute for Mining and Technology. She earned her MA in Medieval History from the University of New Mexico and her MLIS from San Jose State University. As a historian of the Middle Ages, her research centers on analyzing medical pilgrimage through Digital Humanities. As a librarian, her focus is on teaching people how to find good, reliable information. In both of these capacities, she is a passionate supporter of increased and unrestricted access to information.

Will Eggers earned his Ph.D. from the University of Connecticut with his dissertation, "'Misticall Unions': Clandestine Communications from Tristan to Twelfth Night," which explores the tradition of lovers who have fashioned themselves as a conglomerate self that shares one mind and erases all distinctions between sender and receiver. He has found a home at the Loomis Chaffee School, having previously taught at Wesleyan University and the University of Hartford. His research interests range from medieval and early modern English literature to modern graphic novels.

Heide Estes is Professor of English at Monmouth University (New Jersey, USA) and founding director of Medieval Ecocriticisms.

491

She is the author of *Anglo-Saxon Literary Landscapes: Ecotheory and the Environmental Imagination* and co-editor with Haruko Momma of *Old English Across the Curriculum: Contexts and Pedagogies*, a special issue of Studies in Medieval and Renaissance Teaching. Her projects in process include the edited volume *Medieval Ecocriticisms: Animals, Landscapes, Objects, and the Nature of the Human* and the monograph *Gender, Disability and Jews in Old English Poetry: Intersections*.

Moira Fitzgibbons is Professor of English, and her teaching and research interests include medieval and modern pedagogies; disability studies; late medieval religious culture; and the interplay between verbal and visual rhetoric in a wide variety of texts, including graphic narratives. Teaching interdisciplinary First Year Seminars for the past 5 years has provided her with many valuable opportunities to explore these issues in collaboration with her students. Her research has appeared in such venues as *The Open Access Companion to the "Canterbury Tales"*; *Pedagogy*; *Studies in the Age of Chaucer*; *Medium Aevum*; and *The Ashgate Research Companion to Medieval Disability Studies* (Routledge, forthcoming).

Anne Galanaud graduated at Paris 4–Sorbonne University and earned her PhD in history at Franche-Comté University on the population of late medieval Dijon. She established a database that includes tax records from about 20,000 persons living between the mid-fourteenth century and the early sixteenth century, managed by an original program developed, with her contribution, by Henri Labesse (Paris–Sorbonne University). Her studies include an analysis of the socioeconomic and topographic characteristics of medieval Dijon winegrowers and an analysis of the fate of widows and orphans survivors to the Black Death in Dijon, deciphered from a so far untapped mid-fourteenth century source document. She studied, in collaboration with Pierre Galanaud, the cartography of medieval plagues and now focuses on their impact on fragile populations.

Pierre Galanaud is emeritus professor of immunology at Paris–Sud University. He graduated at Paris–Descartes University Medical School and performed post-doctoral studies at Tufts University, Boston. At Paris–Sud University, he was head of the Internal Medicine and clinical Immunology unit of Antoine Béclère hospital (*Assistance Publique Hôpitaux de Paris*) and director of the INSERM affiliated research laboratory *Cytokines and Immunoregulation*. His combined interests in the functional cartography of gene expression in the immune system and in the history of medicine led him to analyze, in collaboration with Anne Galanaud, medieval plagues by applying spatial analysis to the GIS based cartography of deaths (P. Galanaud, A. Galanaud, and P. Giraudoux, *Historical Epidemics Cartography Generated by Spatial Analysis: Mapping the Heterogeneity of Three Medieval "Plagues" in Dijon*, 2015). This collaboration is pursued for the impact of medieval epidemics on fragile populations.

Rachael Gillibrand is a PhD student in the Institute for Medieval Studies at the University of Leeds. Drawing upon her background in both history and art history, her research focuses upon physical impairment and the non-conformist body and between c. 1400 and c. 1600—particularly, the design, production and function of disability aids in the late medieval West. She is passionate about making her research accessible to a diverse audience and, as a result, she recently featured as a guest speaker on the KNFX radio show *Healthy Vision*, where she spoke about medieval attitudes towards blindness and the invention of spectacles.

Brandon W. Hawk is an assistant professor of English at Rhode Island College. He has published on early English literature, the history of the English language, biblical apocrypha, and medieval biblical commentaries, and serves as a member of the Editorial Board for the Sources of Anglo-Saxon Literary Culture project. His book *Preaching Apocrypha in Anglo-Saxon England* was published by the University of Toronto Press in 2018, and his full-length introduction, translation, and commentary for the apocryphal *Gospel of Pseudo-Matthew* was published by Cascade Books.

Ármann Jakobsson is Professor of Early Icelandic Literature at the University of Iceland and is currently involved with the "Disability Before Disability" research project that focuses on medieval and early modern attitudes towards disability. He is interested in categorisation in general and his done work on kingship, age, social classes and the supernatural. Among his books are *A Sense of Belonging: Morkinskinna and Icelandic Identity c. 1220*, The Viking Collection 22 (2014); *The Troll Inside You: Paranormal Activity in the Medieval North* (punctum books, 2017); and *The Routledge Research Companion to the Medieval Icelandic Sagas*, co-edited with Sverrir Jakobsson (2017).

Kolfinna Jónatansdóttir is a doctoral student in Icelandic literature at the University of Iceland and is interested in all aspects of medieval Icelandic culture and literature, its origins, development and reception. Her thesis is on Ragnarǫk, the end of the world in Old Norse mythology.

Anne M. Koenig is a cultural and medical historian specializing in late medieval Germany. Her primary research interests include madness and the spread of medical literacy and medical knowledge in popular culture. She has several forthcoming publications, including an essay "Magicking Madness: Secret Workings and Public Narratives of the Disordered Mind in Late Medieval Germany" in *The Sacred and the Sinister* coming out with Pennsylvania State University Press in 2019. She is currently a NEH Fellow at the Newberry Library in Chicago and was previously the Assistant Professor of History at the University of South Florida.

Cameron Hunt McNabb is an associate professor of English at Southeastern University. Her primary research interests include disability studies and early drama, and she has published in numerous journals, including *Early Theatre, Neophilologus, Studies in Philology*, and *Pedagogy*. Her chapter "Staging Disability in Medieval Drama" in forthcoming in the *Ashgate Research Companion to Medieval Disability Studies* (Routledge, forthcoming). She is a strong advocate for undergraduate research, and she and her students have contributed two entries to the *Medieval Disability Glossary*.

Kara Larson Maloney is an adjunct professor at Canisius College in Buffalo, NY. She earned her PhD from Binghamton University in 2015. Her research interests include the intersection of chivalry and identity in intratextual communities and how that creates identity in extratextual medieval communities. She focuses on King Arthur and medieval romance across the British Isles and France. Her essay on gendered readings of the textiles in *Sir Gawain and the Green Knight* will be published in *Medieval Clothing and Textiles* in 2019.

Frank Napolitano is an associate professor of English and coordinator of the Graduate Teaching Fellows Mentoring Program at Radford University in Virginia. His primary research interests include Middle English biblical drama, the history of rhetoric, disability studies, rhetoric and composition, and writing program administration. He has published in *Early Theatre* and *Studies in Philology* and is in the process of co-editing a collection of essays on the labor practices of writing program administrators.

Leah Pope Parker s an Assistant Professor of English at the University of Southern Mississippi. Her current book project, "Disability and the Afterlife in Old English Literature," explores how concepts of disability shaped both daily life and the eschatological imaginary in early medieval England. Her research engages with histories of the body and phenomenologies of religion, as well as using digital tools such as multispectral imaging to better understand medieval manuscripts. Her essays have recently appeared in the *Journal of English and Germanic Philology* and the volume *Monstrosity, Disability, and the Posthuman in the Medieval and Early Modern World*, edited by Richard H. Godden and Asa Simon Mittman. She also endeavors to share medieval disability studies with broader academic and public communities by tweeting as Medieval Disability, @MADisability.

Tory V. Pearman is Associate Professor of English at Miami University Hamilton. Her research primarily focuses on the intersections between disability and gender in medieval literature. She is the author of *Women and Disability in Medieval Literature* (Palgrave, 2010) and *Disability and Knighthood in Malory's Morte Darthur* (forthcoming, Routledge). She has contributed, with her students, to the *Medieval Disability Glossary* and is a cofounder of the Society for the Study of Disability in the Middle Ages.

Alicia Protze is a graduate of Fitchburg State University, where she majored in history. She continued her education at King's College, London, where she studied her master's in Arts and Cultural Management. She is currently enrolled at Fitchburg State University, where is is studying special education.

Alison Purnell is an independent scholar whose research interests focus on social reactions to mental impairments in the fourteenth and fifteenth centuries. She studied at the University of Toronto and the University of York and is an advocate for greater accessibility to historical materials.

Will Rogers is the Tommy and Mary Barham Endowed Professor of English at University of Louisiana Monroe. He is the series co-editor for *New Queer Medievalisms*, a book series published by Medieval Institute Publications. He has published on aging and disability, queer theory and medieval texts, and medieval mysticism. His monograph, "Staves and Stanzas: Writing Old Age and Impairment in Late Medieval England," is under contract with Arc Humanities Press.

Marit Ronen has recently received her PhD in History from the Hebrew University of Jerusalem. Her research interests include the study of marginalized and liminal groups in early Medieval Europe, including ethnicity, gender, and disability studies, and focuses on early medieval England. She has published on the agency of disabled people, on kingly impairment, and on religious constructions of disability. She is passionate about making Medieval Studies more accessible to the wider public, and has participated as an instructor in history workshops for high-school students.

Rose A. Sawyer is a PhD student in the Institute for Medieval Studies at the University of Leeds. Her research focuses upon changelings and child substitution discourse in the Middle Ages, as well as other aspects of the medieval imaginative landscape. In addition to her contribution to this volume, she has contributed "'That elfe and vile congion': Constructing the Body of the Child as a Site of Violence through Changeling Insults and the Child Substitution Motif" to the upcoming edited volume *Literary Cultures and Medieval/ Early Modern Childhoods*, edited by Naomi Miller and Diane Purkiss and published by Palgrave.

Kurt Schreyer teaches courses on Shakespeare and early English drama at the University of Missouri–St. Louis. His interests extend to a wide variety of genres and texts across the traditional medieval/Renaissance disciplinary divide, from Chaucer to Milton, and from epic and romance to devotional lyric. His book, *Shakespeare's Medieval Craft: Remnants of the Mysteries on the London Stage*, published by Cornell University Press, demonstrates the central importance of stage properties, technologies, and theatrical practices from pre-Reformation religious drama to Shakespeare's stagecraft.

Julie Singer is an associate professor of French at Washington University in St. Louis. A co-founder of the Society for the Study of Disability in the Middle Ages, she is the author of *Blindness and Therapy in Late Medieval French and Italian Poetry* (D.S. Brewer, 2011) and *Representing Mental Illness in Late Medieval France: Machines, Madness, Metaphor* (D.S. Brewer, 2018).

Jeffery G. Stoyanoff is an assistant professor of English at Spring Hill College in Mobile, Alabama. His teaching and research interests include Middle English poetry and medieval drama, particularly through the lens of Actor–Network Theory and Object-Oriented Ontology. His current book project, *Writing Networks: Performativity in Confessio Amantis*, stems from the nexus of these interets, interrogating the relationship between performance and performativity in the poem.

Kisha G. Tracy is an associate professor of English Studies and Coordinator of the Center for Teaching and Learning at Fitchburg State University in Massachusetts. Her main research interests include medieval memory and confession, medieval disability, and higher education pedagogy. She is the author of *Memory and Confession in Middle English Literature*, which is available through Palgrave.

Maura Bailey, Autumn Battista, Ashley Corliss, Eammon Gosselin, Rebecca Laughlin, Sara Moller, Shayne Simahk, Taylor Specker, Alyssa Stanton, and **Kellyn Welch** are Fitchburg State University students.

Made in USA - Kendallville, IN
22026_9781950192731
01.12.2023 1339